A HISTORY OF CHINA'S FINANCIAL THOUGHT

VOLUME 1

A HISTORY OF CHINA'S FINANCIAL THOUGHT

VOLUME 1

Yao Sui
Central University of Finance and Economics, China

Translated by

Wang Yong
University of Shanghai for Science and Technology, China

Wu Zhongxiu
Hanshan Normal University, China

World Scientific

NEW JERSEY · LONDON · SINGAPORE · BEIJING · SHANGHAI · HONG KONG · TAIPEI · CHENNAI · TOKYO

Published by

World Scientific Publishing Co. Pte. Ltd.
5 Toh Tuck Link, Singapore 596224
USA office: 27 Warren Street, Suite 401-402, Hackensack, NJ 07601
UK office: 57 Shelton Street, Covent Garden, London WC2H 9HE

Library of Congress Cataloging-in-Publication Data
Names: Yao, Sui, author. | Wang, Yong, translator. | Wu, Zhongxiu, translator.
Title: A history of China's financial thought / Yao Sui, Central University of Finance and Economics,
    China ; translated by Wang Yong, University of Shanghai for Science and Technology, China,
    Wu Zhongxiu, Hanshan Normal University, China.
Description: Hackensack : World Scientific, 2023. | Includes bibliographical references. |
    Contents: v. 1. -- v. 2.
Identifiers: LCCN 2020040399 | ISBN 9789811223600 (v. 1 ; hardcover) |
    ISBN 9789811223617 (v. 2 ; hardcover) | ISBN 9789811216800 (hardcover) |
    ISBN 9789811220005 (ebook) | ISBN 9789811220012 (ebook other)
Subjects: LCSH: Finance--China--History. | Money--China--History.
Classification: LCC HG187.C6 Y36413 2023 | DDC 332.0951--dc23
LC record available at https://lccn.loc.gov/2020040399

British Library Cataloguing-in-Publication Data
A catalogue record for this book is available from the British Library.

This book is published with the financial support of Chinese Fund for the Humanities and Social Sciences.

《中国金融思想史》
Originally published in Chinese by The Shanghai Jiao Tong University Press
Copyright © The Shanghai Jiao Tong University Press 2015

Translated by Wang Yong and Wu Zhongxiu

A HISTORY OF CHINA'S FINANCIAL THOUGHT

Copyright © 2023 by World Scientific Publishing Co. Pte. Ltd.

All rights reserved. This book, or parts thereof, may not be reproduced in any form or by any means, electronic or mechanical, including photocopying, recording or any information storage and retrieval system now known or to be invented, without written permission from the publisher.

For photocopying of material in this volume, please pay a copying fee through the Copyright Clearance Center, Inc., 222 Rosewood Drive, Danvers, MA 01923, USA. In this case permission to photocopy is not required from the publisher.

For any available supplementary material, please visit
https://www.worldscientific.com/worldscibooks/10.1142/11730#t=suppl

Desk Editors: Balamurugan Rajendran/Nimal Koliyat/Nicole Ong

Typeset by Stallion Press
Email: enquiries@stallionpress.com

Printed in Singapore

Preface

At the end of the 1980s and the beginning of the 1990s, I wrote an outline of *A History of China's Financial Thought*. At that time, I felt that China, a great country with 5,000 years of civilization, should have its own history of financial thought in addition to its history of economic thought and history of monetary thought (theories). As a teacher in the financial field, I had the responsibility and obligation to shoulder this task. So I made up my mind to use my spare time to draft such a book. After four or five years' endeavor, I finished the first draft and had it published by the China Financial Publishing House in October 1994. After the publication, I felt rather happy, because the book was sold out within a year, which was a good indication of the need for such a book. In the second year, the book was awarded the first prize among the fields of philosophy and social sciences in Beijing, because it filled an academic gap. However, I felt uneasy because my academic accumulation was shallow. Some of the financial thought was not explored in the social environment of its emergence and there wasn't any comparative analysis either. There were some things unsaid, some things unclearly expressed, some things too demanding of the ancient scholars and some things far-fetched in my writing. In addition, there were quite a few wrongly used or inappropriately omitted words, some of which were key words. As a result, readers might have found it hard to comprehend or would easily have misunderstood the text, which could lead to confusion or cause trouble. Moreover, in the postscript to the first edition, I mentioned that I had planned to write about the time before the founding of the People's Republic of China (PRC). But that edition stopped at the May Fourth Movement. My promise to the readers is a debt to be paid off as quickly as possible. During the past 16 years, though I have been quite busy making preparations and amendments, my diligence has not been enough for the task ahead. In this revision of and addition to the first edition, I implemented the following ideas.

First, for each historical period, I have presented the most advanced or representative ideas of the time. I have not made a general introduction. Instead, I have combined key points and less important points to introduce to the readers a more comprehensive picture. For example, during the Wei, Jin and the Northern and Southern Dynasties, the currency minting ideas of the Northern Dynasties were not advanced at all, but they were characteristic of the time and indicative of the unstoppable quality of the trend. Although there were twists and turns in the process, it was impossible to resist the landslide trend forward. Without an introduction, no one would be able to reflect on that historical development. The dispute over money shortage beginning in the Tang and Song Dynasties was related to monetary policy. I had bookishly thought that such a dispute was not academic or theoretical, and a description of such a phenomenon was a profane act. However, ten years of administrative experience changed my naive ideas. I came to realize that while it is important to have pure theoretical or academic enquiry, policy and management thought are of equal importance. On the one hand, Chinese people have never stopped their exploration of problems in the economic and financial fields. Otherwise, the flourishing time of the Han and Tang Dynasties could never have existed, and there would never have been paper money in the Song Dynasty, which circulated in the whole country in the Yuan and Ming Dynasties and even in foreign countries, lasting for five to six hundred years. How can we turn a blind eye to these and think nothing of our forefathers' contributions? Talking always of Western financial thought is lamentably like forgetting our ancestors. On the other hand, Western countries and China have their respective advantages. In the past one hundred and fifty to sixty years, the Western countries became stronger, while China fell behind. That is also true as far as economic thought is concerned. How should we sum up the lessons from our experience? Only when we can correctly treat our history and the present can we have a better understanding of the future and the world, especially in our dealing with the relationship between the East and the West as well as that between the North and the South.

Second, instead of being simplistic and crude, or being subjective, we should study the background and the unique environment of the financial thought carefully and intensively. I was impressed by the way Chohachi Itano, a Japanese scholar, studied the economic thought of Sima Qian. He analyzed Sima Qian against the background of the Yellow Emperor and Zhuang Zi, maintaining that Sima respected nature but supported some decisive measures to retain the dignity of the Han government, because he was a royal historian. That analysis was simply convincing. In my writing, I often wanted to challenge myself and tried to get rid of the simplistic way of thinking. I was determined to learn from masters in this field and followed all convincing suggestions. Unfortunately, I was often beset by my stupidity and ignorance.

Third, regarding citations, in the first edition I tried to be concise in my quotations and avoided, where possible, longer ones. Now, I have changed my ideas and think that this book is not only for myself but also for other people. It is to serve the needs of the readers and offer them a chance to make independent judgment and deeper enquiries. So there is indeed no need to impose my views on other people. Without much adjustment to the overall structure, I have tried my best to cite more quotations and have added my understanding and interpretation when the need arose. The effect of doing this shall be determined by the readers.

Fourth, the thirty years from the May Fourth Movement to the founding of the PRC, though seemingly short, was a period of great change. In order to strive for national independence and prosperity, there had been attempts to save the country by education, science and industry. With many active minds, there had also been different strategies and methods emerging, such as the clash between Marxist and non-Marxist beliefs, the conflicts between old and new ways of thinking, and the collision between internal and external forces. Such a scene was magnificent and unprecedented. As far as financial writings were concerned, research papers not included, monographs, collections of published articles, textbooks and popular writings were already voluminous. According to Hu Jichuang's *A Sketchy History of China's Contemporary Economic*

Thought published in 1982, there were already 60 monographs, textbooks and collected writings. 10 years later, in the financial part of the general bibliography in the Beijing Library of the Republic of China, it was roughly estimated that there were at least 200 similar items. If books related to the reform of currency were also included, there would be more than 300 of them. In the parts I want to supplement, I could only add those representative and influential people. No matter whether they were famous prime ministers, financiers, thinkers, writers, scientists or industrialists, they must have an innovative understanding of finance, a superior consciousness and a spirit of the time. Their pedigrees or ranks would not count. Their viewpoints had to influence policy decisions or the thinking of one or several generations of people. In addition, I also paid my tribute to those people whose deeds were grand and spectacular. Among the four representative figures, two of them had come back from their study in the USA. Chen Guangfu was a representative of the national bankers in the contemporary Chinese financial field. Ma Yinchu was a renowned economist and patriot, known to be tough as nails. Zhang Naiqi was a self-taught banker and financier, one of the Seven Gentlemen in the Anti-Japanese Salvation Movement, and a firm ally of the Communist Party of China. The last one was one of the founding members of the CPC and the one of the first to spread Marxism in China. These four people were basically positively viewed and so far I think no one has outdone them. It also seemed unnecessary to pick out one or two scholars to critique, at least not for the time being. The validity of this pioneering effort still needs to be tested over time. Besides, their financial thought was only introduced vaguely and the comments were also very brief, to be elaborated on in the future.

Fifth, it is challenging to complete the task of combing through the long history of financial thought of at least 2,500 years, during which the Chinese currency evolved. In ancient China, there was officially run credit in addition to usury. Besides, there were such ways of exchange as *bianhuan* and *feiqian*, for the purpose of avoiding hardship and the risk of long-distance transportation. As a matter of fact, there were different methods to avoid risks and the money shortage. The local restrictions on the cross-border circulation of currency exacerbated the shortage of money, during which *feiqian* emerged. It still needs to be clarified whether the development of credit catered to the need of money shortage or if something else played a decisive role in the process. The learning from this was that as long as credibility and other technical conditions were present, even if the transactions were carried out in different places and at different times, and the transactions were not in a cash-on-delivery mode, *feiqian* and paper notes would surely emerge, taking the place of coins and functioning as the media of exchange. The key point here was that the credibility of the issuers of these credit instruments should be unquestionable. Otherwise, cash would be required and they could not be used as the substitutes. As a result, it might be safe to say that China's commodity economy was unusual in some regions, such as large cities, political and economic centers, and key waterways and frontier places. Although the whole economy was still a small agricultural economy that was only self-sufficient but not very developed, in these regions, the commodity economy and currency economy were extremely active and developed rather quickly. The advanced development of credit, the vast territory of China, the needs of the border war, the supply of food and fodder, the government procurement and the concentration of taxes all needed corresponding solutions which were suitable for the national conditions of China. If we are oblivious to the achievements of our forefathers, how can we talk about our Chinese characteristics? How can we make other people understand the history of China's financial thought with our vague narration? For the convenience of writing, in this book I used currency to refer to cashable money and paper notes to refer to uncashable money. But both these kinds of moneys were different from the kind of currency issued by Western banks or Chinese banks in later years. There were also differences between the face value and the market value of the currency. Inevitably, there would also be people who manipulated the market and engaged in speculation and profit-seeking activities. In my opinion, we might conclude that the stock market in ancient China was thus born. Besides, because of the prominent feature of the Chinese government-run credit, something similar to trust institutions seemed to have also emerged, though insurance institutions had never appeared. It still needs to be clarified whether that had anything to do with the officially run feature of credit. I think this is probably due to the difference between Chinese culture and Western culture, to which we must pay enough attention. On account of these reasons,

I am deeply aware of my lack of learning, inability to conduct a comparative study and the superficiality of my grasp of China's history of financial system and history of thought, not to mention my ignorance of related things abroad. But I also firmly believe that as long as researchers, me included, start to do research in this field, there would be no need to worry about future success. That day will surely come.

With a somewhat reasonable knowledge structure, I could only turn for help to my predecessors, colleagues and students. I sincerely appreciate the time I am living in. Before the end of the Cultural Revolution, my courage and determination had been tempered, so I am not afraid of hardships and difficulties. Since the Cultural Revolution, we have been living in an era of emancipating the mind. This extremely active atmosphere brought about fruitful and flourishing academic outcomes. Classical literature, which used to be difficult to get, is now easily at hand. Chronicles, biographies, commentary upon people and various other research achievements keep coming out, to the extent that one cannot finish reading them all. The convenience resulting from the compilation of ancient literature made me strive all the more, being afraid that I am not diligent enough. The publication of *Quan Song Wen*, *Quan Yuan Wen*, *Xu Zizhi Tongjian Changbian*, *A Collection of the Writings of Kang Youwei* and *Complete Works of Ma Yinchu* came about so successively that my eyes seemed fully occupied. The *Selected Literature on the History of China's Economic Thought*, compiled by Wu Baosan, presented the literature from the pre-Qin period to the Ming and Qing Dynasties, benefiting researchers in this field and contributing immensely to the study of the history of China's economic thought. The collation and publication of various collections of writings provided firsthand information for research and made it convenient to carry out objective research from a historical materialistic perspective, thus getting rid of the possibility of being wrongly informed or doing ineffective study. We should not treat the ancient scholars as we wish and pay no respect to their thought. We should also not regard history as a little doll to be dressed up any way we like. Instead, we should adopt an attitude of historical materialism and carry out our research without any bias. For that reason, I have revised many problematic points, which were mostly too demanding of the ancient scholars or too imprecise about the general background of the introduction. In general, my basic viewpoints remain unchanged, which is also one of the reasons why there is not much comment in the newly added chapter.

Speaking of *China's Financial History* and the revision and supplementation of this book, I should first of all thank the related leaders and members of the Ministry of Education for their understanding and support. At the beginning of 2003, when a leader of the Ministry of Education talked to me, I submitted my request for my withdrawal from the administrative post to concentrate on teaching and research. With my requirements satisfied, I could only make good use of the time and do my best to repay such good will.

I also want to thank Shanghai Jiao Tong University Press. The press presented me with the chance to revise and supplement the original work and publish this book. At the time of the compilation of *China's Financial History*, Feng Qin, the editor, telephoned to inform me of their intention to republish *A History of China's Financial Thought*, for which I was very grateful. I had mixed feelings because I intended to make revisions but could not start the work at that time. Mr. Feng, the editor, was very tolerant and assured me that there was no hurry. Disappointingly, I dragged on until it was very late to submit my final version of the book. After a thorough reading, I still found many unsatisfactory points, for which I felt very apologetic to the press and the enthusiastic readers. On reconsidering, I realized that my limited scholarship could not be improved within a short time. So I could not keep putting off the publication of the book.

I want to add that I must thank the Central University of Finance and Economics, of which I have been a member, and to be more specific, the School of Finance I am teaching in. Since I came back in 2003, I have not been assigned any specific tasks except the tutoring of my graduate students. I have been offered a very comfortable, quiet and relaxed environment in which I could concentrate on my research. I would like to take this opportunity to express my thanks to the young teachers in the school. They shouldered the heavy task of teaching, scientific research and all kinds of pressure from their families, leaving me a quiet and undisturbed environment. It is only natural that I should say a sincere "thank you" to them.

In the course of writing, my students and my family members offered me help and support from different angles, which encouraged me substantially and could only be repaid by my intensified efforts.

On the publication of this revised edition, I want to say that I am not afraid of being laughed at. My intention is to be a stepping stone for others, so that we can all accumulate experience from such an endeavor. Consequently, I'm looking forward to suggestions from the readers, especially specialists in this field.

Yao Sui
July, 2010, revised in October, 2010

About the Author

Yao Sui is a Professor at the School of Finance of the Central University of Finance and Economics in Beijing and served as the Vice-President of the university from 1996 to 2003. As a PhD advisor, he used to teach courses such as "Money and Banking" and "An Introduction to Finance." His past Chinese publications include titles such as *Money and Banking* and *A History of China's Financial Thought*.

About the Translators

Wang Yong is a Professor of Linguistics at the University of Shanghai for Science and Technology (USST). He has published nearly 20 translations and has more than 20 years of experience in teaching translation. As Director of the Master of Translation and Interpreting (MTI) Center of USST, Wang is also responsible for the translator training program in the university.

Wu Zhongxiu, an avid reader of history and philosophy and English teacher from Hanshan Normal University of South China, has translated and published over a dozen books, ranging from financial works, company management manuals and biographies to popular science books.

Contents

Preface		v
About the Author		xiii
About the Translators		xv
Chapter 1	Financial Thought in the Pre-Qin Period	1
	1. Introduction	1
	2. Monetary theory in the pre-Qin period	3
	2.1. The mutual complementary theory of Shan Qi	3
	2.2. "Currency and grain are mutually representative" as discussed in Mozi	9
	2.3. "The appearance of gold means the disappearance of grain" in *The Book of Lord Shang*	13
	3. Credit theory in the pre-Qin period	16
	3.1. The state-run credit idea of *The Rites of Zhou*	16
	3.2. Usury as elaborated in Mencius	22
	4. The theory of money and credit in *Guanzi*	25
	4.1. Discussion of money and credit in other chapters than the chapter of "On the Degree of Seriousness of Various Issues"	26
	4.2. The section "On the Degree of Seriousness of Various Issues" and its theoretical elaboration	33

	4.3. The discussion of currency in "On the Degrees of the Seriousness of Things"	47
	4.4. The discussion of monetary policy in "On the Degrees of the Seriousness of Things"	60
	4.5. The discussion of credit policies in "On the Degrees of the Seriousness of Things"	65
Chapter 2	Financial Thought in the Western and the Eastern Han Dynasties	73
	1. The currency and credit theory at the beginning of the Western Han Dynasty	76
	1.1. Jia Yi's theory about the monopoly of the right of mintage	76
	1.2. Chao Cuo on "devaluing gold and jades" and "interest of 100%"	87
	2. The monetary and credit theory of Sima Qian	92
	2.1. On the origin of money	97
	2.2. On the circulation of currency and the price of commodities	99
	2.3. On credit	103
	3. The debate over mintage in the meeting about salt and iron	106
	3.1. Sang Hongyang and the meeting on salt and iron	106
	3.2. The debate on the origin of currency	109
	3.3. The debate on the right of mintage	112
	4. The currency and credit theory in late Western Han Dynasty	115
	4.1. Gong Yu's theory of currency disposal	115
	4.2. The interest theory of Wang Mang	120
	5. The theory of monetary policy of the Eastern Han Dynasty	125
	5.1. Zhang Lin on "the banning of currency"	125
	5.2. Liu Tao on "food first, commodities second"	127
	5.3. Xun Yue on "the appropriateness of the Wuzhu coins"	130

	6. Anti-usury theory in the Eastern Han Dynasty	134
	6.1. Huan Tan on "the suppression of usury"	134
	6.2. Taipingjing on anti-usury	138

Chapter 3   Financial Thought in Wei, Jin, Northern and Southern Dynasties   145

1. Introduction   145
2. The "Discussion of the God of Money" by Lu Bao   146
   - 2.1. The commodity fetishism in the "Discussion of the God of Money"   146
   - 2.2. Historical position of the "Discussion of the God of Money"   153
3. Kong Linzhi's refutation of "Abolishing Coins to Use Grain and Silk as Currency"   156
   - 3.1. Huan Xuan's proposal of "Abolishing Coins to Use Grain and Silk as Currency"   156
   - 3.2. Kong Linzhi's theory against "the abolition of metal currency to use grain and silk"   158
   - 3.3. Zhou Lang and Shen Yue on "the abolition of metal currency"   164
4. The debate over the shortage of currency in the Southern Dynasties   169
   - 4.1. The controversy over "one big coin equals two small ones" by He Shangzhi and Shen Yanzhi   169
   - 4.2. The dispute over the right of minting by Shen Qingzhi and Yan Jun   174
   - 4.3. Kong Yi's theory of "grudging neither the laborers nor the copper"   180
5. The dispute over minting currency in the Northern Dynasties   185
   - 5.1. Yuan Cheng on the use of coins   185
   - 5.2. Gao Qianzhi's plea for the minting of sanzhu coins   188
   - 5.3. Gao Gongzhi's memorial for the casting of wuzhu coins   191

Chapter 4	Financial Thought in the Tang and the Five Dynasties	193
	1. Theory of copper Ban by Liu Zhi	194
	2. On the evil of government loans by Chu Suiliang and Cui Mian	203
	2.1. Principal of government loan	203
	2.2. Chu Suiliang on appointing officials by turning over money	208
	2.3. Cui Mian on government loans harming the people	209
	3. Theory of banning the practice of storing away coin by Emperor Xianzong of the Tang Dynasty	210
	3.1. Emperor Xianzong of the Tang Dynasty on theory of banning the practice of storing away coin	210
	3.2. Implementation of ban on storing money	213
	4. Theory of government-run exchange by three persons including Wang Shao	214
	4.1. Remittance business — Bianhuan (convenience exchange)	214
	4.2. Wang Shao, Lu Tan and Wang Bo on government-run remittance	218
	5. Theory of money shortage in the late Tang Dynasty	221
	5.1. Lu Zhi on "expanding produces according to local circumstance"	223
	5.2. Bai Juyi on "prohibiting melting copper coins to make vessels"	228
	5.3. Han Yu's four measures on remedying ills	231
	5.4. Yuan Zhen on submitting copper vessels as rents and taxes upon conversion	233
	5.5. Yang Yuling on low commodity price and high coin price	237
Chapter 5	Financial Thought of the Northern and Southern Song Dynasties	241
	1. Introduction	241

2. The currency theory of Shen Kuo 243
   2.1. On the circulation of currency 243
   2.2. On the standard of precious metals 245
   2.3. On paper notes as currency 247
   2.4. On the money shortage 251
3. Zhang Fangping's monetary theories 254
   3.1. About the channels of money circulation 255
   3.2. About the money shortage in the Song Dynasty 259
   3.3. About the monopoly of distribution rights 262
4. The monetary theories of Li Gou, Ouyang Xiu
   and Su Zhe 265
   4.1. Li Gou's view on silver and gold as currency 265
   4.2. Su Shi and Su Xun's views on paper
        currency and money shortage 267
   4.3. Ouyang Xiu's view on the prohibition of
        the iron coins 270
5. Zhou Xingji's banknote issuance preparation theory 273
   5.1. The theory of currency deficiency 274
   5.2. Currency theory of lightness and heaviness 276
   5.3. The devaluation theory of currency 278
   5.4. Banknote issuance preparation theory 282
6. Ye Shi's theory of paper notes 284
   6.1. On commodities and currency 284
   6.2. On copper coins as the best currency 286
   6.3. On the expelling of coins by paper money 289
   6.4. Other drawbacks of currency circulation 291
7. Debates over the government-run lending 294
   7.1. Wang Anshi and Xining's new policies 294
   7.2. Government-run lending — Green Shoots
        Law and Market Trade Law 297
   7.3. The dispute over interest 303
   7.4. The dispute between the scattered and the
        suppressed 306
   7.5. The dispute between the green shoots and
        Changping 308

	8. Monetary theories during the early Southern Song Dynasty	312
	8.1. A discussion of *Guanzi* in the sixth year of Shaoxing	313
	8.2. Zhao Kai and Wang Zhiwang on the management of currency	316
	8.3. Theories on paper money during the reign of Emperor Xiaozong	320
	9. Monetary theories after the reign of Emperor Xiaozong of the Southern Song Dynasty	328
	9.1. Yang Wanli's monetary theory	328
	9.2. Father and Son of the Yuan family on currency	331
	9.3. Wei Jing's comment on the local conditions	337
	9.4. Wu Qian's discussion on paper money as the lifeblood of the country	339
	9.5. Chen Qiqing's theory of copper money	340
	9.6. Xu Heng on the theory of money exchange	341
	10. The credit theory of Yuan Cai	343
	10.1. On ethical lending	344
	10.2. On the operation of loans	347
	10.3. On the management of loans	350
Chapter 6	Financial Thought of the Yuan and Ming Dynasties	353
	1. Introduction	353
	2. Wang Yun on Zhongtong paper money	358
	2.1. On the experience of Zhongtong paper money issuance	359
	2.2. On lessons learned from the failure of the Zhongtong paper money issuance	362
	2.3. On promotion of Zhongtong paper money	368
	2.4. Discussions of monetary reform by Lu Shirong	374
	3. Zheng Jiefu's theory of coins supplementing paper money	377
	3.1. Analysis and comparison of coins and paper money	378

3.2. On paper money circulation law and metal coin circulation law	382
3.3. The checks and balance theory of the reserve and paper money	385
4. Hu Zhiyu on paper money circulation	391
4.1. On the checks and balance between the parent and offspring of paper money and coins	391
4.2. On incompatibility of paper money and coin	397
4.3. On paper money	400
Annex: Paper money circulation regulations authored by Ye Li	408
5. Wang Yi's theory of firm coin and weak paper money	414
5.1. On the nature of the concept of money	415
5.2. On firmness of money	416
5.3. On monetary reform	418
6. Pool and ditch theory of paper money by Ye Ziqi	423
6.1. On the scrapping of Yuan Dynasty paper money	424
6.2. On change of paper money	426
6.3. On the law of paper money circulation	430
7. Monetary theory of Liu Dingzhi	432
7.1. On monetary consciousness	433
7.2. On circulation of coins	436
7.3. On paper money circulation	438
8. Qiu Jun's theory of monetary metal	445
8.1. Labor theory of value	445
8.2. Theory of the origin of money	448
8.3. On monopoly issuance by the state	449
8.4. On monetary system reform	452
9. Anti-usury theories of Lv Kun and Song Yingxing	457
9.1. Lv Kun on usury killing people	457
9.2. Song Yingxing on usury brooding upheaval	459
9.3. Ai Nanying on usury — pawn shops	462

Chapter 7	Financial Thought Around the Period of the Sino-British Opium War	465
	1. Introduction	465
	2. Debate on silver shortage before and after the Sino-British Opium War	468
	2.1. Wei Yuan and Lin Zexu on imitation minting of silver coins	468
	Annex: Wei Yuan on foreign financial theory	484
	2.2. Theory of focusing on the fundamental and suppressing the incidental by Xu Zi and Zun Dingchen	485
	2.3. Theory of valuing coin over silver by Bao Shichen	493
	3. Nominal theory of money of Wang Liu	502
	3.1. On monetary reform	503
	3.2. Precondition for nominal theory of money	506
	3.3. The complete form of China's traditional nominal theory of money	510
	4. Theory of metal money by the Xu brothers	517
	4.1. "On paper money and coin" by Xu Mei	517
	4.2. Theory of metal money by Xu Mei	523
	4.3. Criticism on Wang Liu's monetary theory	530
	5. Theory of "maneuvering the intangible by mobilizing the tangible" of Wang Maoyin	537
	5.1. On monetary system reform	537
	5.2. On the tangible and the intangible	543
	5.3. On credit	562
	5.4. On loan shops	571

Chapter 1

Financial Thought in the Pre-Qin Period

1. Introduction

The birth of China's financial thought should be traced back to the emergence of Chinese currency and credit.

Currency originated from the end of the primitive society. In the Xia and Shang Dynasties, the currencies used were mainly seashells. During the Shang Dynasty, among the inscriptions on bones and tortoise shells, the Chinese words relating to the production and exchange of commodities were all connected with the Chinese word *bei*, which means "shell." As a reflection of the close ties between human beings, commodities, as well as currency, showed not only human being's pursuit and worship of currency but also the emergence of currency-related thought in people's minds.[1] During the Shang and Zhou Dynasties, coin money came into being, though until the early years of the Spring and Autumn Period, barter economy still existed in abundance. In non-governmental activities, people used commodity money such as millet and cloth, while among vassal states and in the large-volume domestic transactions, gold was used. Consequently, gold, millet and cloth were all money commodities. In the middle of the Spring and Autumn Period, when gold became the

---

[1] Cf. Xiao Qing, *A History of Ancient China's Monetary Thought,* People's Publishing House, 1987, p. 11.

main currency, cloth became complementary. At the end of the Spring and Autumn Period, coin money began to circulate in the country.[2] With different socio-economic environments and different socio-economic backgrounds, coastal and inland areas had different types of coin money. In agricultural areas, there was cloth currency. In hunting and fishing areas, there was knife-shaped currency. In cotton-producing areas, there was ring-shaped currency. In the state of Chu, there were *Yingyuan* and ant-nose-shaped coins. In the Late Warring States Period, with the ending of separation and division, currency in the northern part of China gradually became of the same round shape. However, metal currency and commodity currency, as well as currency swap and barter, coexisted all along in the long feudal society. Traditional concepts and theories of Chinese currency, such as the Mutual Complementary Theory and Theory of Lightness and Weightiness, began to emerge, while ancient monetary thought, such as Theory of Monetary Origin, Theory of Metallic Money and Monetary Nominalism, also started to take root.

Likewise, credit also originated in the last stage of the primitive society. With the emergence of private ownership, the differentiation between the rich and the poor would naturally result in lending practices. Born before the emergence of money, credit took the form of physical credit and monetary credit, without necessarily the need for interest. But money and interest could promote the development of credit. Finally, lending with interest took the place of interest-free lending and became the primary form of credit. In the Spring and Autumn Period and the Warring States Period, lending activities were quite common social practice, as recorded in *Commentary on Spring and Autumn Annals*, Guo Yu, and *Stratagems of the Warring States*.[3] During the Warring States Period, there were not only professional usurers called loaners or moneylenders but also part-timers who were wealthy merchants. The borrowing took the form of credit or commodity, and the universally adopted written form of credit demonstrated the development of the credit system. Private lending

---

[2] Cf. Wu Baosan, *An Analysis of the Financial Thought of Guanzi*, China Social Sciences Press, 1989, p. 106.

[3] Cf. Peng Xinwei, *A History of Chinese Currency*, Shanghai People's Publishing House, 1965, pp. 103–108.

was to be seen everywhere and met with no solemn accusations or strong opposition, which was in contrast to the fierce objection and severe legislation in foreign countries at the time. Thus, we can see the uniqueness of ancient Chinese credit thought, which might serve as proof of China leading the world in quite an extraordinary way in the development of its commodities and currency.

According to Li Xueqin, a contemporary historian, the ideological trend of this period should be as follows: From the Xia and Shang Dynasties to the Western Zhou Dynasty, the prevailing trend was respect for ancestors and the valuation of virtue. Nevertheless, after the middle stage of the Spring and Autumn Period, the emerging new ideas and concepts were a breath of fresh air. In the Spring and Autumn Period and the Warring States Period, the common trend of intellectual development was a combination of idealization and materialization, both of which were in agreement and worked in coordination, demonstrating a new spirit from which financial thought was not exempt.[4]

2. Monetary theory in the pre-Qin period

2.1. *The mutual complementary theory of Shan Qi*

Living in the late years of the Spring and Autumn Period, Shan Qi was the great-grandson of Duke Jing of Shan and was called Duke Mu of Shan in history. As a member of a family assisting the governmental affairs for generations, he was a minister (554–476 B.C.) of the Zhou Dynasty. Legend had it that in 524 B.C., while King Jing ruled, he opposed the minting of large coins and put forward the Theory of Mutual Complementarity. His argumentation was recorded in the second part of "Discourses of Zhou" in *Discourses of the States*. Because *Commentary on Spring and Autumn Annals* didn't keep any record of his remarks, or as a result of the absence of the word *qian* in the Spring and Autumn Annals, academics have varied ideas. In fact, the so-called "big money" should be *Kongshoubu*, the spade-shaped copper coins originating from farm-tool-shaped money.

---

[4]*Pre-Qin in the Words of Li Xueqin*, Shanghai Scientific and Technological Literature Press, 2009, pp. 277–278.

According to the second part of "Discourses of Zhou" in *Discourses of the States*, in 524 B.C., when King Jing of the Zhou Dynasty planned to mint large coins, Shan Qi, his counsel, opposed the move. "That is impractical. In ancient times, when there were natural disasters, the government would take the coins into consideration and weigh the pros and cons, in the hope of helping the needy people. If people are troubled by the lightness of coins, the government would mint heavy coins as a complement, and thus the heavy coins could circulate together with the light ones. If they are burdened with the heavy ones, the government would mint light ones for the circulation, without the need to abolish the use of light ones; thus the light ones and the heavy ones could both circulate, to the benefit of the people. Now your majesty plans to supplant the light ones with heavy ones, which would result in the loss of people's capital and end in their poverty. The poverty would naturally lead to the scarcity of your majesty's possessions, which in turn would result in your exploitation of the people. If people cannot afford to do that, they would think of leaving, which shows that we are forcing people to do that. A country should have precautions against disasters as well as emergency reliefs in case of these things, which in themselves do not contradict with each other. If it's possible for us to get prepared before a disaster but we fail to do so, then we are being negligent. If measures are taken before the due time, then we are courting disaster. Our Zhou state is already a weak one, but heaven has been unfavorable to us. Isn't it ill-advised to disperse the people to double the effect of the disaster? It is better to live with the people, but we disperse them; it is better to prepare in advance for emergencies, but we are anticipating them. Under such circumstances, how could your Majesty govern the country? Without the way of governing, how can your majesty enforce your orders? The disobeying of the orders would lead to trouble to your majesty. As a result, sages would uphold the virtue of the people to eliminate disobedience …. If your Majesty impoverishes the people to enrich yourself, that is like blocking the mouth of the river to make ponds, which would result in the drying up of the river. If the people of our state immigrate to other places and leave us in poverty, then when disasters come we wouldn't be prepared for that. How would you deal with that? In our preparation for the worst, our officials have been quite negligent. Now you are planning to rob the people of their belongings and worsen the disasters, which is no other than making them suffer from this. I hope your Majesty could think thrice before taking action." Despite his imploration, the king carried out his plan of casting the big coins.

Roughly, the above quotation elaborated on the theory of currency from three aspects, namely, the functions of currency, the representative of social wealth and the Theory of Mutual Complementarity.

The functions of currency: This is reflected from Shan Qi's opposition to casting the big money, as well as the king's "take the coins into consideration and weigh the pros and cons, in the hope of helping the needy people" in the time "when there were natural disasters." To take into consideration means to think about the currency. The whole sentence means that they were thinking about their possession in preparation for the help of the needy. From this, we can see that the so-called "taking into consideration and weighing" is a calculation of the reservation of their currency, and a judgment of the appropriateness of the currency in the market,[5] which is indeed the function of yardstick of the currency. On the contrary, "in preparation for the help of the needy" refers to the function of currency as the medium of circulation and payment.

Money as the general representative of social wealth: Shan Qi laid emphasis on the use of currency for the relief of the victims of the disasters. His understanding of the causal–effect relationship between the abolishing of light coins and the poverty of the people indicates to us his reflections on the relation between capital and currency: With currency, you have capital, while the abolishment of currency is the same as losing or robbing the people of their belongings. So currency is the general representative of capital, that is, the general representative of social wealth. Its existence determines the richness of every currency holder in the society, thus determining his/her dominance of social wealth, which, in turn, will shed influence on the normal process of social production and life, even on the safety of a nation. "Now you are planning to rob the people of their belongings and worsen the disasters, which is no other than make them suffer from this." There is no mistake that the sentence should be interpreted thus. From this, we can also say that currency swap had seen fairly

---

[5]Dong Lizhang, *Analysis and Interpretation of Discourses of the States*, Jinan University Press, 1993, pp. 122–127.

rapid development in the late years of the Spring and Autumn Period, or at least we can say that currency had been playing an important role in the political and economic life and had become indispensable. They were since planning to cast heavy coins to take the place of light ones, which is the same as robbing the people of their belongings to enrich the emperor's treasury. That is just like blocking the mouth of the river to form small ponds. If the treasury of a state is exhausted, and the common people flee from their native land, disasters would come, and the reserves for relief from bad fortune would be lost. Talking of this, Shan Qi couldn't help but lament, "My lord, how would you cope with this?" He further deduced that with the common people in poverty, the government would also lack financial resources, which naturally would result in their intensification of the exploitation. The common people, on the contrary, under such a heavy burden, would naturally leave their homeland for a better place. That insight is good for protecting the interests of urban residents and businessmen, and thus conducive to market stability and social harmony.

The Theory of Mutual Complementarity: According to Shan Qi, "If the people are worried about the lightness of coins, then we can complement with the issuing of heavy coins. Thus they can complement each other, and the people would be happy about this. If they are not satisfied with the existence of too many heavy coins, we can complement with the issuing of light coins, without the abolishment of heavy coins. As a result, the two could complement each and the people would benefit." That is to say, if the common people have a grudge against the lightness of the coins in circulation for their inconvenience and influence on trading, the government should mint heavier coins for the better circulation of goods. In this case, the heavier coins would complement the light ones. The common people would benefit from this, thus guaranteeing a smooth and convenient life and production, conducive to a harmonious and stable society. On the contrary, if the common people are burdened with the heaviness of the coins in circulation, the government should mint lighter coins while, at the same time, keeping the heavy coins in circulation. In this way, there would be a proper balance between the light and heavy coins in circulation, thus ensuring a normal circulation and a safe realization of the interests of all walks of life. In today's words, there are four meanings to this sentence: First, the amount of metal in the coins of circulation, that is, the size of the unit currency, must meet the objective need of commodity circulation and be in good proportion to the volume of the commodity. Second, if the unit of currency in circulation is too small to have enough capacity for commodity transaction, then the government should not hesitate to adjust the weight of the unit of currency, minting heavier coins. That is, the unit of currency in circulation should be in accordance with the commodity exchange, for the purpose of making commodity exchange a convenient practice. Third, regardless of whether the government mints heavy or light coins to complement the existing currency, the original ones shouldn't be abolished. The reason is that "The abolishing of the light coins for the minting of heavy ones will result in the common people's loss of their belongings and falling into poverty." Fourth, with the two kinds of currency in circulation, the government could use one unit of heavy coin as a criterion of price to calculate how many light coins it is equal to, which is called "heavy coins in proportion to the light ones." On the contrary, using one unit of light coin as the criterion of price to calculate how many heavy coins equal light ones is called "light coins in proportion to the heavy ones." Either way, there is the need for a reasonable and well-balanced proportion between the two. The government can never do as it pleases or change it at will. Neither will the relation between light and heavy coins be that of dominance and complementarity. Some people, holding the opinion that one is full-bodied money and the other not full-bodied money, maintain that Shan Qi is against inflation and that his writing is the very beginning of Chinese thought against inflation. As a matter of fact, if we don't take things for granted and overstate or understate the opinion, we may not arrive at the conclusion of its relatedness to inflation, which is both hasty and irresponsible. To sum up, the currency in circulation should suit the need of commodity exchange, and the ratio between different kinds of currency should be appropriate. From this we can see that the circulation of currency should serve the circulation of commodities and is governed by the latter, which, as the main body of Shan Qi's theory, is truly insightful indeed.

In addition, he also thought that it was vital to take time to adjust the content of metals in the currency. Doing it earlier or later would not be appropriate, because "if it's better to get prepared but we are not, that would be sluggish; if it's all right to remedy after the event but we do it early, that would be like courting disaster," which is not a good practice. His viewpoint is quite clear: The adjustment of the metal content of the unit of currency must take the situation into consideration, so as to adapt to the change of commodity exchange appropriately. Acting blindly or passively would not benefit the circulation of commodities. This progressive understanding is a further elaboration on the previous one, which also becomes a powerful theoretical weapon in the limitation of the king's excessive minting of currency.

Shan Qi was the first to put forward the Theory of Mutual Complementarity. This theory refers to the ratio between two different coins, which are of the same metal. This notion has been frequently cited by scholars of later generations, but its meaning has undergone changes together with the change of the monetary system. It can refer to the ratio between different coins of the same material, the ratio between coins of different materials, the ratio between coin and paper money, or that between different types of paper money. Before the monetary theories of Western capitalists were introduced into China, this theory had been one of the key notions of traditional Chinese monetary thought.

As to the understanding of his theory, there had been quite diverse interpretations throughout Chinese ancient history of financial thought, just like the different interpretations of Confucius and his doctrines. Originally, the Theory of Mutual Complementarity referred to the relationship between coins of different weights, but later the theory evolved into that of abstractness and truthfulness. As was pointed out by Sang Hongyang in the second chapter of *Debates on Salt and Iron*, "Swapping the lightness for the important item, exchange abstractness with truthfulness." The so-called "truthfulness" refers to things useful. Because they are purchased by the "abstractness" of money, they are naturally the commodities of the present days. In the Tang Dynasty, when Diwu Qi proposed the minting of Qianyuan Zhongbao, a kind of currency, he used the Mutual Complementarity Theory as his theoretical basis, in which the abstract "son" refers to the deficient coin, while the truthful "mother" refers to the full-bodied money, and thus the relationship becomes that of full-bodied versus deficient money.[6]

---

[6]Tang Renwu, *A Study of the Economic Thought in the Tang Dynasty*, Beijing Normal University Press, 1996, pp. 171–172.

This theory began to touch upon the relationship between the circulation of commodity and that of currency, and quite correctly expressed the basic understanding that the circulation of currency must be in accordance with that of commodity. Instead of being directed by the government or the emperor, the issuance of currency must be guided by sound principles and the demand of commodity circulation. That is, this theory maintains that the subjective mastery of currency must reflect the objective need of commodities; otherwise, there will be disasters. This preliminary understanding left much room for later-comers to elaborate on and there were quite a few theories deriving from it.

The Theory of Lightness and Heaviness was further discussed in *Guanzi*, thus making it possible to develop traditional cybernetics. It is the theoretical basis for the circulation of currency, thus becoming the earliest management thought with the most distinctive features.

2.2. "Currency and grain are mutually representative" as discussed in Mozi

Mozi (c. 480–389 or 390 B.C.), also known as Modi, was a native of the state of Lu (or the state of Song). He used to be a handicraftsman, and served as a senior official in the state of Song. He journeyed around the states of Qi, Wei, Song, Yue and Wei, being good at argumentation and persuasion and taking up the arduous job of saving the decaying world. With disciples following, he developed his teachings into an independent school of thought, which was as famous and prominent as Confucianism at the time. He was a renowned ancient thinker. "As long as it's advantageous to the world, I will do it even if I am worn out and exhausted." He was the first fighter in the sense of equality and fraternity and an outstanding scientist. He maintained that "the strong should not oppress the weak and the rich should not bully the poor." According to Han Yu of the Tang Dynasty, "Confucius and Mozi learned from each other, without which they wouldn't be Confucius and Mozi." In Liang Qichao's opinion, the doctrine of Mozi has been deeply rooted in the Chinese national features. "The only solution for today's dilemma is to put the doctrine of Mozi into practice." Lu Xun thought of Mozi as "the backbone of China." Mao Zedong, Chairman of the new republic, thought of Mozi as "a laborer and a wiser sage than Confucius." Mozi believed in respecting the virtuous, identifying with the superior universal love, economizing expenditures and simplicity in funerals, but he was against music, fatalism and Confucianism, as well as aggressive warfare. He held the will of heaven in esteem and had an understanding of ghosts. His doctrine of "universal love and mutually beneficial" has been deeply rooted in the Chinese national spirit and his managerial thought of enhancing agricultural production and economizing expenses is relevant even in today's world. *Mozi*, though with only 53 extant articles, is a collection of the writings of the school of Mohism, and the Canon of Mozi, one of the 53 articles, preserved his monetary viewpoint.

In a modern scientific sense, The Canon of Mozi, also known as The Defense of Mozi, is mainly about epistemology, logic, economics, natural science and argumentation with contemporary critics. Divided into the Canon (I), the Canon (II), Exposition of the Canon (I) and Exposition of the Canon (II), the Canon of Mozi is a self-explanatory whole. Section 30 of the Canon (II) goes like this: "We cannot say that what we buy is absolutely expensive, because the price may go up and down." That is to say, when we buy something, there is no need for the distinction between expensiveness and cheapness, because the commodity and its price determine each other. While a certain amount of money is the price of a certain amount of commodity, we can also say that the price of the currency could be seen as the purchasing power or the exchange value of the currency. So in his opinion, when the price is high, the currency value is low. That is to say, the purchasing power and exchange value of the currency are low. On the contrary, if the price is low, then the currency value and the exchange value would be high. Thus, a conclusion could be reached that there is no need for the distinction between expensiveness and cheapness. This understanding is confirmed in Exposition of the Canon (II), which points out, "Buying: The value of the coin decides the price of the grains and the price of the grains decides the value of the coin. If we do not think highly of the value of the coin, no matter how high the price of the grains is, we would not deem it expensive; if we think highly of the value of the coin, no matter how cheap the price of the grains is, we would deem it expensive. Actually the value of the royal coin does not change; what changes is the price of the grains. If the price of the grains keeps changing each year, the value of the coin is likely to change, leading finally to the selling of one's sons and daughters." In other words, the coin and the grains are mutually priced. If the purchasing power of the coin is low, then the high price of the commodity doesn't necessarily mean it's expensive. Vice versa, if the purchasing power of the coin is high, then a low price of the commodity doesn't necessarily mean that it is cheap. The coin minted under the king's rule doesn't change its face value, but the price of the grains is changing. The yearly changing of the price of the grains entails a yearly change in the purchasing power of the coin, just like the child being sold, though things are not supposed to be like this. These sentences show us the monetary viewpoints of Mohism. In today's words, it is as follows:

First, currency is a kind of commodity. From their talk of commodity and currency being the prices of each other, we can infer that the later Mohists were already aware that commodity and currency are in a relation of exchange, just like the swapping of simple forms of value, as in the form of X amount of A equals Y amount of currency, or Y amount of currency equals X amount of A. At that time, the equivalents hadn't been fixed to a certain commodity and hadn't been exclusively monopolized by a certain commodity. As a result, the coins issued by his majesty were considered common commodity. That is, the currency was seen as having no special significance. Nevertheless, this is an insightful observation. As was pointed out by Karl Marx, "That money is a commodity is therefore a new discovery only for those who, when they analyze it, start from its fully developed shape."[7] This insight of Mozi, in ancient China of about 2,500 years ago, touching upon the principle of exchange at equal value in commodity exchange, was no doubt an important discovery.

Second, in the exchange of commodity with currency, there is a negative correlation between the ratios of exchange. The rise of one side's exchange value means the decrease of the other side's exchange value, and vice versa. From this, we can say that the Mohists were already clear that the price of the commodities was not solely determined by the commodity itself and was also under the influence of currency. That was an innovation. In other words, the value of the coins and the price of the grains

---

[7] *Complete Works of Karl Marx and Friedrich Engels*, vol. 23, People's Press, 1965, p. 108.

influence and control each other. If the value of the coins was cheap, the price of the grains would be high, and vice versa. With the value of the coins in a stable state, the change of situation due to the climate change would lead to the change of supply and demand. Inevitably, the change would be reflected by the price change of the grains. Only when the buyers and the sellers both agree would the bargain become successful.

Third, the form of currency was identified with the simple and random value of form. As a universal equivalent, the currency, a commodity, has special social attributes, which any other commodity wouldn't possess. In the book of Mozi, currency was repeatedly mentioned. For example, "The rulers will be supplied with furs, cloth and silk in maintaining friendly relationship with the feudal lords of neighboring states." "Here is fourteen pounds of gold for the master to use." In these instances, currency was by no means an ordinary commodity. Instead, it is a special commodity with unique social attributes. But in the sentence, "The value of the coin decides the price of the grains and the price of the grains decides the value of the coin," the social attribute of the coin was negated. As a result, the universal equivalent feature of the coin also disappears, to the surprise of the Mohists. That may be an indication of the characteristics of the time. While metal coins had gained much popularity and development in circulation, bartering was still the main form of exchange in social and economic activities, and the majority of exchange between small producers was still in the form of bartering.

Fourth, the Mohists didn't reveal the internal cause for the change of the commodity price. That is, they didn't know the inner reason for the change of the commodity in terms of value analysis. They analyzed the price fluctuation from two aspects, of commodity and currency, and pointed out that if the price was high, then the purchasing power of the currency was low, and vice versa. As a result, a low price doesn't mean it is cheap. They further pointed out that if the purchasing power of the legal tender remains unchanged, the fluctuation of price illustrated that the grains in the market exceed the demand or fall short of the demand, leading to the change of price in the market, which would reflect the change in the exchange rate between commodity and currency. What the Mohists did not touch upon are deeply rooted substantive issues, such as what the causes for the change are, which were the main causes and subordinate causes, which were of the commodity itself and which were of the currency. They were blinded by the superficial change of prices, and reached the conclusion of "in the buying, there is nothing like being expensive," thus falling into the cyclical mess of agnosticism.

To sum up, the commodity nature of the currency of the Mohists is of universal significance. In Western countries, such an understanding was not put forward until the later decades of the 17th century. At that time, those acting as the currency, whether they were minted coins or gold and silver, were considered "no less a commodity than wine, oil, tobacco, cloth, or stuffs." Karl Marx affirmed this discovery, saying, "this step marks only the infancy of the analysis."[8] This understanding of the Mohist school of thought is more than two thousand years before the Western countries, making China a forerunner in the analysis of the currency.

2.3. "The appearance of gold means the disappearance of grain" in *The Book of Lord Shang*

With former names like Wei Yang or Gongsun Yang, Shang Yang (c. 390–338 B.C.) was a native of the state of Wei in the middle period of the Warring States Period. Because of his successful reorganization of the state of Qin, the duke of Hui gave the 15 cities of Shang to him, and thus he was named Shang Yang in history. In his early years, he used to serve as the retainer of Gongshu Cuo, the prime minister of the state of Wei. In the year 361 B.C., he went to the state of Qin, where he was deeply trusted by the duke of Xiao, and became an important official of the state. After the death of the duke of Xiao, he was killed. *The Book of Lord Shang*, though naming him as the author, was as a matter of fact a compilation of his school of thought by his disciples. In the Yiwenzhi of the *Book of Han*, there were 25 articles, but now we have only 24 extant. Because it is difficult to distinguish Shang Yang's writing from those of his disciples, we can only introduce and discuss the main doctrines of his school of thought.

---

[8]*Complete Works of Karl Marx and Friedrich Engels*, vol. 23, People's Press, 1965, pp. 108–110.

Shang Yang's economic theory placed an overwhelming emphasis on the military and agriculture, with the aim of making the state rich and the military forces efficient. His economic policies laid emphasis on agriculture, downgraded commerce and forbid non-essential activities. Consequently, he advocated the fostering of small-scale peasant economy and encouraged the development of production via the family way, which inevitably stressed the production in social reproduction, particularly the development of the plowing and weaving industries. He paid attention to the distribution, with special emphasis on the regulative influence of taxes on the distribution and redistribution of products. He cared less for business and commerce activities, and acknowledged grudgingly the effect of exchange and circulation in social reproduction, which was in sharp contrast to Mo Zi and Mencius.

A passage in *The Elimination of Strength* touched upon the relationship between grains and gold, mainly with two meanings. One is the contradiction between grains and gold, which, in essence, is the contradiction between agricultural products and currency. They are in a relation of one's waning as a result of the other's waxing, similar to the view expressed in "*Guanzi*." Second, he made clear the different functions of gold and grain in the variation of national strength. While the role of grain is positive and beneficial, the role of gold, in contrast, seemed negative and passive. The overemphasis on gold would even lead to trouble. That is, if the government pays attention only to the gold reserve, if stressed overtly, the reserve of gold and grain would both decrease, causing the national strength to deteriorate. On the contrary, if the government focuses only on the production of grains, the reserve of gold and grains would increase, and the national strength would increase. (The appearance of gold means the disappearance of grain, and the appearance of grain means the disappearance of gold ... For every ounce of gold appearing within its borders, 12 piculs of grain will disappear abroad, but for every twelve piculs of grain appearing within its borders, one ounce of gold will disappear abroad. If a country favors the appearance of gold within its borders, then gold and grain will both disappear, granary and treasury will both be empty and the state will be weak. But if a country favors the appearance of grain within its borders, then gold and grain will both appear, granary and treasury will both be filled and the state will be strong.)

The sentence "gold and grain will both disappear, granary and treasury will both be empty" means that if a country favors gold over grain, it would not stress the production of grain, which would result in a shortage of grain. If a country exports the insufficient grain for gold, in the end the country would have to use its reserve of gold to import grain to satisfy the need for consumption. In the end, both gold and grain would disappear and the national strength would diminish. By contrast, if a country pays due attention to grain reserve and spares no effort in its agricultural development, the grain reserve would increase substantially, which would not only meet the demand of domestic consumption and reserve but also be plentiful enough for exporting in exchange for gold. In this way, the reserve of gold and grain would both increase, and the nation will become prosperous.

The writer of *The Book of Lord Shang* held that the reserve of gold and grain was the criterion by which to judge a country's prosperity. He put grain before gold in importance and maintained that the former determined the latter instead of vice versa. That is, the possession of grain entailed the possession of gold, and the more grain in a country's reserve, the more gold a country would have. By contrast, the possession of gold did not necessarily entail the possession of grain. In the case of more gold and less grain, the reserve of gold would still decrease. According to such a way of reasoning, in order to achieve a country's prosperity, everyone must go all out to increase the grain reserve. If the grain reserve is insufficient, sooner or later there would be a crisis of the shortage of grain and gold even though there had been a large reserve of gold until then. To increase the reserve of grain, we must enhance agricultural development, for the purpose that "gold and grain will both appear, so granary and treasury will both be filled." From this understanding, we can see that, in terms of the relation between commodity and currency, in terms of the production and exchange of products and the circulation of currency, the commodity plays an active role, while the currency is passive. This kind of relation is both universal and correct. On the contrary, under the conditions of small commodity production, although currency exchange had emerged, it still had not played a leading role in the social and economic life. Production for the purpose of exchange was still in a secondary or subordinate position. At that time, the majority of the production was in the mode of self-sufficiency, with men and women working in cooperation. Products for sale in the market were only a minor share of the production and the buyers were mostly aristocracy. The foreign trade involved was mainly with other vassal states. This backward situation was particularly evident in the rural areas, while in the state of Qin, which had a weak economic basis and slow economic development, it was even worse. The author acknowledged the use value of gold and grain, but grain could also satisfy one's hunger and sustain life, which cannot be replaced by gold. While gold is gorgeous, admirable and can bring wealth and rank to people, in an age of starvation, poverty, and famine and chaos, grain is not only a prerequisite to man's survival but also a guarantee of victory in warfare. This is particularly evident in natural economic conditions and should never be overlooked.

In 68 B.C., Chao Cuo put forward the proposal that "grains should be valued while gold and jade should be despised," because in his opinion, "pearl, jade, gold and silver are not edible in time of hunger, nor are they wearable in time of cold," and thus not life necessities for human beings. His argument was the same as the writer of *The Book of Lord Shang*, though their conclusions differed. Chao Cuo arrived at the conclusion of the monetary view of nominalism, while *The Book of Lord Shang* got the conclusion of agriculture as the basis, considering that the root of ruling a country is "let the people focus on agricultural development."

3. Credit theory in the pre-Qin period

3.1. *The state-run credit idea of The Rites of Zhou*

The Rites of Zhou, originally known as *Officers of Zhou*, was also named *Cannon of Officers of Zhou*. Tradition has it that the Duke of Zhou authored this classic, but modern scholars hold that it was composed in the Warring States Period. As one of the 13 Chinese classics, with a total of over 45,000 Chinese characters and involving more than 360 names of officials, it is one of the most difficult and most challenging canons of China. The book includes six chapters, Offices of the Heaven, Offices of Earth, Offices of Spring, Offices of Summer, Offices of Autumn and Offices of Winter. The book integrated the thoughts of Confucianism,

Legalism, the yin–yang school and five elements in its discussion of governing the country, financing and official governance. In terms of financing, the book stressed the serving of the central government and laid emphasis on the central government's control and possession of economic resources, labor force and social wealth, as well as the intervention of economic activities. The theory of governing a country focuses on ten points, among which nine posts, nine ranks, nine taxes and nine expenditures are related to financing. The Ministry of Official Personal Affairs corresponds to the Offices of the Heaven, the Ministry of Revenue corresponds to the Offices of the Earth, the Ministry of Rites corresponds to the Offices of Spring, the Ministry of War corresponds to the Offices of Summer, the Ministry of Penalty corresponds to the Offices of Autumn and the Ministry of Works corresponds to the Offices of Winter. Under the emperor, there was the prime minister, who was the head of the ministers of Heaven, Earth, Spring, Summer, Autumn and Winter. Under the six ministers there were 360 under-officials. This was a tightly woven and well-organized structure. In the West Han Dynasty, Liu Xin added the *Record of Trades* to supplement the missing Offices of Winter. When Wang Mang instituted reform in the name of the ancient masters, he changed the name from *Officers of Zhou* to *The Rites of Zhou*. The *Officers of Zhou* was an extension based on the rites of the pre-Qin period. That is, it was a kind of design with an ideal model. So it wasn't a description of reality, but an idealized version of reality (Yang Xiangkui).[9] As an ideal political system, it attracted the admiration and pursuit of later generations. Wang Mang usurped the throne of the Western Han Dynasty. Yuwen Zhou and Wang Anshi reformed the government. They all used *The Rites of Zhou* as the blueprint and tried to put it into practice, though their efforts were in vain.

Wang Mang's viewpoints on state-run credit could be seen in the section of Quanfu in the part of Diguan in the *Rites of Zhou*. The main idea of this passage was as follows.

First, it was about the practice of "buying on credit." "Buying on credit" refers to the practice of an individual person's buying and a country's selling of goods on credit. It was different from loaning, which

---

[9]From Peng Lin's Preface to *An Analysis of the Main idea and Time of Composition of The Rites of Zhou*, China Social Sciences Press, 1991, p. 5.

usually charges the borrower interest. "Buying on credit" was normally free of interest, but loaning must involve interest. During the appointed time, the person "buying on credit" needn't pay any interest, and only those who are overdue should pay the interest. Buying on credit was restricted to two things: one was the sacrifice and the other was the utensils used in the funeral process. In these cases, if people couldn't afford to pay, they could turn to Quanfu for help and get permission to buy on credit, which is also an obligation of Quanfu. The time limit for buying on credit was 10 days for sacrifice and 3 months for the funeral services.

Second, it was about the practice of "borrowing." According to Quanfu, "those people intending to borrow money shall be interrogated by Quanfu and related officials before getting the loan, the interest of which would be in accordance with the prevalent interest at the time." In today's words, people intending to borrow money refers to the businessmen who want to borrow money. They had to be questioned by Quanfu and the related officials about the sum of the borrowing and the expected interest. The businessmen would pay the interest of the borrowed sum according to the prevalent rate in the region. This kind of interest collection was rather popular in the Warring States Period and it contributed to a large share of the income of the Quanfu.[10] Pondering over the interrogation procedure of the process, one may find that it was not so easy to borrow money. Otherwise, there wouldn't be the need for them to collaborate in their checking of the procedure. Possibly, they would make sure the borrower, the mortgage and the ability to pay off the loan in time were arranged well. So the Quanfu and the related officials would "clarify these details before granting the loans." That is, they would inspect the mortgage to get a clear picture of its worth or inquire into the borrower's personality and characters to see their credit status, in the hope of deciding whether the loan could be returned in full as promised. They were also likely to investigate the borrower's production and management to see if they were idle or lazy, for the purpose of finding out whether they were able to pay the principal and the interest on time. Only after a careful check would they make the decision about the loan, both in terms of its

---

[10]Peng Lin, *An Analysis of the Main idea and Time of Composition of The Rites of Zhou*, China Social Sciences Press, 1991, p. 171.

sum and the loan time. If they thought the applicant was trustworthy, diligent and hardworking, they would permit the loan, otherwise they would terminate it. The interest would be in accordance with the rate of the land tax. According to Zaishi, the rate of land tax for farmland would be in five grades, 1/20th, 1/10th, 3/20th, 2/10th and 5/20th, so the interest rate would follow suit. While borrowing money (buying on credit is no exception), the two parties would sign a written contract, so that when disputes arose, they could use the contract as a basis for judgment. Without a written contract, it would not be possible even to buy on credit. Even if such a practice did occur, and if there was any dispute, the written contract "should be the determining factor in deciding whether the loan had been paid off, whether the payment was in full, whether it was a case of false loan, and whether it was true that the loan had been paid but the lender still wanted more money." Without such a written agreement, the related governmental officials wouldn't be able to accept and determine a case, and the lawful rights and interests would not be upheld and protected.

These original conceptions should have a place in Chinese and even world history of monetary and credit thought, because this is the earliest government-run credit practice. According to the writer of the *Rites of Zhou*, as a subordinate body of Diguan, Quanfu was an agency exclusively concerned with official credit management, with 128 functionaries, including 4 *shangshi*, 8 *zhongshi*, 16 *xiashi*, 4 *fu*, 8 *shi* and 80 *tu*. That was a huge organization with a complex structure and miscellaneous business. The credit business was one of the "businesses of the royal government." In the ancient world, it was quite a unique practice that the rulers took part in such activities as the operator of credit activities. That is the first point to be noted.

Second, the officials would determine the interests of the loan according to its purpose. It was said that the kind of buying for the purpose of sacrifice and funereal would bear no interest if returned as promised. The governmental support for this non-productive credit showed that such borrowers were by no means ordinary people. As pointed out by Karl Marx, the borrowers were "first of all, the extravagant members of the upper classes."[11] Those not so wealthy or the declining aristocrats wanted to

---

[11] *Complete Works of Karl Marx and Friedrich Engels,* vol. 25, p. 672.

maintain their dignity and stress the "ritual"; meanwhile, they were impecunious and in need of support from local officials, who, for the stability of the rule, were more than willing to lend a helping hand. Therefore, this was a kind of favored credit especially designed for the aristocrats. Since it was not productive credit, it naturally would not result in the creation of wealth and the addition of revenue. As a result, it would not bear any interest. Any interest would inevitably lead to the aggravation of the borrowers' financial burden and the instability of the ruling. Probably out of such a consideration, the interest-free credit practice would suffice to demonstrate the merit of the thought of the author of *The Rites of Zhou*. The loans granted to the producers and business dealers would bear interest, because a majority of these borrowers were small producers, "who possess their own conditions of labor — this includes the artisan, but mainly the peasant."[12] At that time, the borrowers included artisans of agriculture, industry, commerce, fishery and hunting, a majority of whom were in the field of agriculture. As the profit margin of each industry differs, the interest rates would also vary. "Suppose the native produce of a country is silk wadding, then the interest could be paid in silk wadding. If the native produce of another country is fine ko-hemp cloth, then the interest would be paid in ko-hemp cloth." The industry of the borrower should determine the way of repaying the loan and the interest rates. "That was because the interest rates of different industries should not be the same and should be in accordance with common practice. Roughly, there are five categories, 1/20th, 1/10th, 3/20th, 2/10th, and 5/20th. With these categories as limits, no one should exceed the limit." With a five-scale distinction in the management of interests, that was indeed an advanced and reasonable arrangement.

Third, the development of official credit was a restriction on usury, the distinctive feature of which is the higher-than-standard interest rate. Consequently, the usurer "knows no other barrier but the capacity of those who need money to pay or to resist."[13] Interest rates vary substantially in different periods of different countries. In ancient China, usury was rampant. In the chapter titled On Governing a State in *Guanzi*, we have such

---

[12]*Ibid.*
[13]*Complete Works of Karl Marx and Friedrich Engels*, vol. 25, p. 677.

a sentence: "The farmers have to pay taxes collected by the state with borrowed money at an interest rate of one hundred percent." Some even charged an extreme interest rate of one thousand percent. For example, Lord Mengchang, the aristocratic official and landlord, was one of those good at doing this. "At that time Lord Mengchang was prime minister of the state of Qi, with a fief of ten thousand households at Xue. Feng Xuan, one of his protégés, upon his arrival in Xue, summoned all Lord Mengchang's debtors who owed interest amounting to a hundred thousand coins."[14] With three thousand protégés, his income was not enough to cover his expenditure, so he used to lend money in Xue. With the interest amounting to a hundred thousand coins, one can well imagine how ruthless the exploitation was. There were also rich businessmen with a sideline in usury, whose lending added up to a thousand *guan*, "as rich as those families with a thousand chariots." The Bing family of Cao made tens of thousands by smelting iron. "They engaged in usury as well as trade in all the provinces and principalities."[15] Usury would deprive the laborers of all their surplus labor and part of their necessary labor. "Usury thus exerts, on the one hand, an undermining and destructive influence on ancient and feudal wealth and ancient and feudal property."[16] On the other hand, it weakened and destroyed the production of small-scale peasant economy. To sum up, it shattered all forms of the production in which the producers were the owners of their own means of production. It constituted not only a menace to but also destruction of the society of the Warring States Period and beyond, as well as the booming and developing later society. In the eyes of the newborn sovereignty and those far-sighted scheming men, the variable options were either blocking or guiding. The former was often carried out by the governments in the form of strict resistance, oppression and prohibition from the point view of theory, policy and lawmaking, which used to be the practice of ancient Hebrews and Indians, as well as in Greece and Rome. The latter practice, in the way of guiding, was often carried out in the form of official credit, in the hope of restraining the rampant usury among the people. Giving the producers

---

[14] Biography of Lord Mengchang in *Records of the Grand Historian*.
[15] Biographies of Merchants in *Records of the Grand Historian*.
[16] *Complete Works of Karl Marx and Friedrich Engels*, vol. 25, p. 674.

a chance to catch up, this would ensure that they maintain their life necessities and the basic conditions of production, without the danger of miserable deaths, thus safeguarding the long-term interests of the ancient government. The writer of *The Rites of Zhou* offered such an excellent remedy, which was quite often employed by rulers of ancient China. In the second year of the Xin Dynasty, Wang Mang carried out the policy of five averaging and six offices, in an effort to restrain the overexploitation of peasants by wealthy traders, restrict the rampant usury practice and protect the fundamental interests of the country. For that purpose, the government set up agencies in Chang'an, Luoyang, Handan, Linzi (modern Zibo, Shandong), Wancheng (modern Nanyang, Henan) and Chengdu to regulate the market. If some people needed money for sacrifice or funereal, they could borrow from the government without paying any interest. People who need money for their production or management could borrow money at a low interest rate (10% of their total profit). In the Northern Song Dynasty, Wang Anshi implemented the Xining new policy. According to his regulations on trading in the city, urban businessmen could borrow money from the government or sell their products to the government on credit, at a half-year interest of 10% or a yearly interest of 20%. Those overdue would be further charged with a 2% of fine, for the purpose of animating the market and cracking down on the exploitation of the wealthy traders and usurers.

Fourth, the interest revenue became an organic component of the government revenue. The normal expenditure could be drawn from Quanfu, and, at the end of the year, the surplus revenue would be handed to an even higher agency. It is indeed a quite valuable insight in the history of world finance that the interest revenue should be considered an important part of a nation's financial revenue.

3.2. Usury as elaborated in Mencius

Mencius (372–289 B.C.), also known by his birth name Meng Ke, was a native of the state of Zou in the middle of the Warring States Period. Supposedly, he was a pupil of Confucius's grandson, Zisi. He traveled across the states of Wei, Qi, Song, Teng and more to offer advice to the rulers. During the reign of Xuan of the state of Qi, he was a minister.

A collection of the writings of Mencius and his disciples, *Mencius*, included seven chapters, each divided into two halves.

Extremely indignant over usury exploitation, Mencius openly condemned the rulers: "When the parents of the people cause the people to wear looks of distress, and after a whole year's toil, yet not to be able to nourish their parents, so that they proceed to borrowing to increase their means, till the old people and children are found lying in the ditches. Where, in such a case, is his parental relation to the people?" According to his analysis, the direct reason for usury was the continued toil and the inability to support parents, and the indirect reason was that a brutal monarch is even worse than a tiger, leading to people's looks of distress. The heavy tax burden threatened the survival of laborers and made them unable to raise their families. That is an important social and economic reason for the emergence and existence of usury. The consequences were that old people and children were found dying in the ditches and wilderness, thus offering a glimpse of the cruelty of the exploitation of usury. Based on his doctrine of people-centeredness, he maintained that the guiding principle of governing a country should be to bring happiness to the people, to love, nourish, benefit, treasure, cherish, care for and educate the people, and oppose the practice of oppressive governing, let alone trapping the people with usury and leading to the devastating ravage and relentless exploitation.

Meanwhile, Feng Xuan, a hanger-on of Lord Mengchang in the state of Qi, exempted the debt in the Lord's fief of Xue. While collecting debts, Feng acquitted those debts that were beyond the means of the bearers. When he was questioned by Lord Mengchang for the reason for doing so, Feng replied that those debts that were beyond the means of their bearers would become an even heavier burden to the debtors, possibly resulting in their running away without paying off any of the debt, which was of no advantage to the Lord's ruling of the fief of Xue. From this, we can see that at that time, for the purpose of life necessities, quite a few small producers were forced to borrow money and the heavy burden of interests compelled them to leave their hometown, resulting in social unrest.

According to *Records of the Warring States Period*, in 294 or 300 B.C., "Lord Mengchang put up a notice looking for an accountant. And he asked his hangers-on, 'Who is familiar with accounting and able to collect money from my debtors in Xue for me?' Feng Xuan wrote his name on the notification and said, 'I can do that.' ... Then he prepared his carriage, took his luggage and all the bills and said good-bye to the Lord. He asked, 'After I collect the debts, shall I buy anything for you before I come back?' Lord Mengchang said, 'You can buy something I don't have at home.' Feng Xuan drove to Xue and asked the officers in charge to summon all debtors owing money to the Lord to come to him to check their bills. After all the bills were checked, Feng Xuan stood up and issued a false order to exempt all the debts on behalf of the lord. Subsequently, he burned all the bills. All the people there jubilantly and loudly expressed their thanks to the Lord. Then Feng Xuan drove directly back to Qi and went to see the Lord in the morning ... and said, 'You told me to buy something you don't have at home. I think your buildings are full of treasures, all the stalls are crowded with dogs and horses, and you also have many beautiful women. So I believe that the thing you don't have here is righteousness. So I bought righteousness for you without asking for your permission.'" As far as the story goes, in the *Grand Scribe's Records*, Sima Qian's record was quite different from the previous one. According to Sima Qian, Lord Mengchang served as the prime minister of the state of Qi and got a fief of 10,000 households in Xue. With 3,000 hangers-on, Lord Mengchang was unable to cover the expenditure, so he used to lend money for interest in Xue. At the end of the year, Feng Xuan went to Xue to collect his money. "Upon his arrival in Xue, he summoned all the debtors who owed interest amounting to a 100,000 coins. He prepared wine in abundance and fat oxen and invited them all to come whether they could discharge their debts or not, bringing with them records of their loans. On the appointed day, he had oxen slaughtered and brought out the wine, and while they drank he checked their documents. He agreed to a date with those who were able to pay and burned the receipts of others who were too poor to pay their debts." When he was reprimanded by the Lord, he answered, "If I hadn't prepared plenty of oxen and wine, not all of them would have come and I shouldn't have known who had money and who hadn't. I set a time limit for those in a position to pay. As for those who have no money, even if I were to wait around for ten years the interest would simply accumulate until in desperation they ran away. In the event of that, apart from receiving no payment, you would win the reputation of a miser with no regard for the people, while they would be guilty of absconding. This is no way to improve the people's morale and increase your reputation. Burning those useless deeds and not attempting to dun the destitute will endear you to the people of Xue and spread your fame. Why do you doubt this?" Lord Mengchang was grateful for this and clapped his hands to express his gratitude. The record of Sima Qian distinguished those who could pay the interest from those who couldn't, as well as those who could pay the interest within a short time and those who would never be able to pay the interest. This kind of specific description was more reasonable, more convincing and closer to historic facts, while the record in the *Records of the Warring States Period* was sketchier.

4. The theory of money and credit in *Guanzi*

Guanzi (710–645 B.C.), also known as Guan Yiwu or Guan Zhong, was born in Ying Shang (in modern Anhui Province). He used to be a merchant in his youth; in 685 B.C., when Duke Huan became the ruler, he was appointed prime minister of the state of Qi. According to Sima Qian, "In his conduct of governmental affairs, he was good at turning from bad luck to good fortune and from losing to wining. With due consideration of the priorities, he was always careful in the decision making process." With his assistance, Duke Huan of the state of Qi carried out a reform to "increase the accumulation of wealth, enrich the country, and build up its military power" inside the state, externally "honor the king and drive off the barbarians," and finally "arranged nine meetings for the sovereigns of all the feudatories of his time and brought the whole world to good order." With the State of Qi becoming the first state of the five hegemons of the Spring and Autumn Period, Guan Zhong also became known as a distinguished statesman and left a deep impression on later generations. Over a hundred years later, Confucius, the great thinker, sighed in admiration, "If there were no Guan Zhong, we would likely be wearing our hair loose and folding our robes to the left like barbarians." The *Guanzi* as we see it today was supposed to contain 86 essays, 76 of which are extant, and 10 are only titles. It wasn't written by only one person, nor was it composed at one time. In the name of Guanzi, the book included words and deeds of Guan Zhong and the thought and views of the Guanzi School and other schools. The chapter of Art and Literature of *Hanshu* was classified under the category of Taoism because the Taoist doctrine dominated the writings of this book, though, as a matter of fact, it was mainly about the political and economic thought of the legalists. It may be safely assumed that *Guanzi*, based on the teachings of the late Guan Zhong, was elaborated on by that school in the state of Qi during the Warring States Period, and was finalized by Liu Xiang in the Western Han Dynasty. Inevitably, it was hard to avoid the combination of other writings of this school in the Qin and Han Dynasties. In this section, our discussion will mainly focus on the section "On the Degree of Seriousness of Various Issues," with a little more reference to other sections, such as "On Governing the People," "On Establishing Right Polices," "On Consolidating the Authority of the Throne," "The Most Important Economic and Political Affairs," "On Examining a State from Eight Aspects," "The Small Historical Documents of the State of Qi," etc.

4.1. Discussion of money and credit in other chapters than the chapter of "On the Degree of Seriousness of Various Issues"

In the chapter "The Most Important Economic and Financial Affairs," the sixth section, with a focus on the discussion of intellectuals, farmers, craftsmen and merchants, the author dealt with the topic of governing a country, centering on the discussion of markets and land tax. It involved the regulatory force of currency, and the standard of value of currency in the regulation of production and consumption. Four aspects can be inferred from the original passage:

First of all, it was about currency's function of the measurement of value. In the sentence "Gold is the measure for calculating expenditure," we may find that he was talking about the measurement of value in the expenditure by means of gold. Though he didn't make any clear elaboration on the gold's measurement of value, he was of the opinion that currency, as the embodiment and symbol of expenditure, was the tool of expense accounting, and could be used to calculate the spending and final balance. That is to say, the writer of "The Most Important Economic and Financial Affairs"

Financial Thought in the Pre-Qin Period   27

had grasped the essence of the first function of currency and realized the basic function of money, which was to be commended and affirmed.

Second, the passage involved the currency's regulation of production, circulation, distribution and consumption. According to the author, once there was a clear understanding of the currency's function of being the measurement of values, there would inevitably be an understanding of luxury and thrift, which would lead to an understanding of such issues as the following socio-economic effects and the application of currency in the adjustment of various financial revenues and expenditures. ("Knowing the function of gold, we can master the difference between extravagance and frugality. If the difference between extravagance and frugality is mastered, hundreds of expenditure can be well regulated.") The reason is that both extravagance and frugality would influence the price, and thus indirectly influence the development of production and circulation. Specifically, frugality would lead to the drop of gold prices, the depression of businesses, the declining of production and the shrinking of circulation. On the contrary, extravagance would result in the increase of gold prices, the falling of prices and a waste of resources. The reason for the delayed discovery of the shortage of the resources was that there was an ignorance of the necessity to control the total social supply of the resources. On the contrary, after all the things had been done, if an abundance of the resources was identified, then it was due to a lack of knowledge of how to regulate the total social demand and the purchasing power of the people. It would be no good to have no sense of anticipation of the future supply or demand. So, to have the initiative in this situation meant to abide by the laws. ("If frugality is in vogue, gold must be cheap. If gold is cheap, the undertaking commodities cannot be accomplished, so that it will cause damage to the undertakings. If extravagance is in vogue, gold must be expensive. If gold is expensive, other commodities must be cheap, so that it will cause damage to the commodities. If one cannot realize that commodities prepared are insufficient until everything stored has been used up, that is caused by not knowing anything about computation. If one cannot realize that the commodities prepared are overly abundant until the undertakings are finished, that is caused by not knowing anything about regulation. Not knowing anything about computation or regulation is wrong. There is a right way to realize that.") To sum up, both computation and regulation were the effect of the function of currency, which was no other than an elaboration of the measure of value of currency. At the same time, it was also related to the function as the medium of circulation, payment and international currency. That analysis, though rather superficial, was quite pioneering. Moreover, it was a discussion of demand and supply from a macroeconomic perspective, which makes it even more praiseworthy.

Third, it was a discussion of the underlying reasons for the gold's varying price in accordance with the frugal or extravagant practice of the society. If frugality prevailed, the monetary expenditure would drop sharply and the need for gold in circulation would also decrease considerably, which would result in the drop of gold price. This in turn, meant that the purchasing power of currency would diminish and the prices of commodities would rise. Conversely, extravagance could lead to a sudden increase in the spending of gold. The drastic increase in the demand for gold in circulation would inevitably lead to the rise of its price and the purchasing power of currencies. As a result, the prices of commodities would naturally fall. The author of "The Most Important Economic and Financial Affairs", in his discussion on the influence of the increase and decrease of the currencies in circulation on the prices of the commodities, as well as on the variations in the demand and supply of production and circulation, gave us his explanation of the changing relationship between commodities and currencies. We can also see that the writer was ignorant of the theory of value. Not knowing that commodities and currencies both have a certain amount of value, he was also blind to the function of currency as a means of storage, which would spontaneously adjust the currency in circulation and keep its value stable.

Fourth, it was important to keep in mind the function of computation and regulation of currency in the national economy. "Not knowing anything about computation or regulation is wrong. There is a right way to realize that." In other words, it was not possible to be classified as well versed in the governance of a country if the ruler didn't know how to use currency either in the computation or in the regulation and control of the total social supply and demand, which would bring about a state of balance, in the case of which, the government would have neither deficiency ("not knowing anything about computation") nor abundance ("not knowing anything about regulation"). Both "damage to the undertakings" (hindering the development of production and the expansion of circulation) and "damage to the commodities" (waste of resources and expenditure) were not applicable practice. Meanwhile, abiding by certain laws would ensure that neither damage was done. The law here is the control of the total social demand, making it equivalent to the total supply of commodities. The control was in the way of economic means instead of administrative measures. That is, the government would resort to monetary policies for that purpose. The author intended to make the feudal rulers understand and grasp this principle, thus making sure that the consumption would be neither too ahead of time nor lagging behind. An avoidance of damaging both the undertakings and the commodities would safeguard the smooth development of the process from production to circulation, distribution and consumption. It was quite clear that the author had realized, or at least was aware, that price had a stimulating and restricting function on production and circulation. Meanwhile, he was trying to have a clear understanding of this principle to help the ancient country intervene and manage economy, as well as adjust and control production and circulation. This also shows that the writer already had some insight into the regulation of production by the law of value. Though from today's perspective this understanding might seem superficial or simple, and some points were even faulty, these findings of over 2,000 years ago are to be deeply admired and are of quite a referential significance today.

The section of "On Consolidating the Authority of the Throne" held that currency and grain were in a relationship of competition ("There usually is a competition for importance between treasure and grain."). That is, in social life, the commodity economy as represented by currency and the natural economy marked by grain were in a relationship of competition. With a developed commodity economy, the role of currency would naturally become prominent. As a result, "the markets are overly supplied, and people wouldn't have enough utensils for everyday life." On the contrary, a developed natural economy would focus on the development of agriculture. Consequently, grains were more important than currency. And "the markets are not overly supplied, and people would have enough utensils for everyday life." With the natural economy well developed, there would be no need for shops and stores because every household had adequate supplies and people lived in contentment. Though they didn't go to the market place to shop, the government of the country could still reach a high level. On the contrary, "if a state does not have plenty of seasonable products produced at home, it still can be considered as poor even though it might have a lot of gold and jade." The so-called seasonable products referred to the agricultural products to be harvested in accordance with seasonal changes, such as mulberry, hemp, corn and domestic animals. According to the writer of "On Consolidating the Authority of the Throne," only agricultural products could be seen as social wealth and only the increase in agricultural products could be considered as becoming wealthy. Gold and jade amounted to nothing at all. In this case, if the ruler of a country focused exclusively on the attainment of currency and prioritized currency over the increase in agricultural products, or "If the sovereign favors merchants and peddlers but is not concerned with farming," consequently, "the common people will drag ignoble existences and no longer be concerned with storing grain" and "the granaries will be empty." That was the reflection of the objective reality of the natural economy at that time. Though it was a little bit like "The appearance of gold means the disappearance of grain" in The *Book of Lord Shang*, in their elaboration of the monetary theory, the two were considerably different.

The author of *Guanzi* was already keenly aware that, after reaching into economic sphere, the strength of currency was also trying to penetrate into political area. If the viewpoint of valuing possessions and commodities became prevalent, ranks and salaries would become trendy in the social underclass ("if the remark on gold, jade, and other treasures is prevailing, ranks and salaries will be conferred on unworthy people"). On the contrary, if the ruler of a country chased only gold, jade and other treasures, and allowed the businessmen to take charge of the governmental affairs, then treasure and wealth would be controlled by the upper class of society. Consequently, "it will be impossible for the common people to defend the state fiercely when it is in danger, nor will it be possible for soldiers and sensible people to devote their lives for the sake of maintaining integrity." Those wealthy businessmen, who had been powerless and without any necessary qualities or ambitions, could buy their way into the ranks and thus enjoy the corresponding reward. As a result, the authority and decrees of the rulers would be subjected to contempt and the rule of law would be abandoned. ("When wealthy people with huge amounts of gold, jade and other properties and rich merchants are conferred with ranks and salaries, without any care of how outstanding their aspirations and performance are, then orders issued by the sovereign will not be paid much attention to. Moreover, the law system will be destroyed.") That would even endanger the stability of the regime. This kind of practice should never be encouraged. Otherwise, the political agenda of enriching the country and strengthening its military forces would become empty talk. As was emphasized by the author of *Guanzi*, the government forbade the merchants and craftsmen from wearing mink coats and asked them to stay away from politics and never participate in governmental affairs. That was no other than the realization of this viewpoint in the government policy.

The author of *Guanzi* discussed the principles of "governing the country" and "measuring the expenses" from a macro perspective. "One *yi* of gold is the expense of one night for one hundred chariots. If there is no gold, a kind of thin silk of high quality can be used as its replacement, and thirty-three *zhi* of thin silk can be equivalent to one *yi* of gold. If there is no thin silk, cotton fabric can be used as the substitute, and one hundred *pi* of fine cotton fabric can be converted into one *yi* of gold. One *yi* of gold is enough for providing enough food for the soldiers and enough fodder for the army horses for one night. Thus, one *dou* of grain is paid as the tax for a piece of field about six *bu*. That is the average amount of tax collected at a time when the harvest is normal." From this quotation, we can infer that one *yi* of gold was enough for the expense of one night for 100 chariots. Without gold, thin silk could be used as its substitute, in which case 33 *zhi* of silk equaled one *yi* of gold. Without thin silk, cotton fabric could take its place, and 100 *pi* of cotton fabric equaled one *yi* of gold. That is, the exchange rate of gold and thin silk is 1:6.73. In his discussion, the author said that "without gold, thin silk could be used" and "without thin silk, cotton fabric could be the replacement," instead of using different kinds of currency. It was quite obvious that at that time, in addition to gold, thin silk and cotton fabric, and also material currency, were used as universal equivalents.

The section of "The Questions" included some remarks on usury. "The Questions" was the outline of an investigation into ancient society, covering diverse socio-economic aspects, such as land system, farming, civil affairs, bureaucracy, prison, population, military affairs, social wealth, and borrowing or lending money. The specific questions go like this: "How many families need to borrow from others for survival in each *yi*?" "How many families are lending grain to others and therefore are bondholders themselves?" "How many people are dependent on borrowing from officials for survival?" It seemed that the writer was only outlining the basic contents in preparation for the social investigation, so he didn't give any further elaboration on or answer to these questions. But these questions were definitely hot issues of the time and needed much effort to answer. The subjects to be investigated were, without any doubt, small producers, declining aristocrats and in particular peasants, who were deep in debt, at the bottom of the society and at the forefront of agriculture, though they were the basis for a rich nation and a strong military force. It is not known to us whether the investigation was similar to that of Feng Xuan as far as the motivation was concerned. But from the fact that the author intended to investigate peasants, we can catch a glimpse of his people-oriented approach. At the same time, we can also see that, with the development of the relationship between commodities and currency, the age-old usury was also developing and was devouring all the surplus products of the small producers, leaving them with only basic life necessities. "Wherever the laborer is the owner, whether actual or nominal, of his conditions of labor and his product, he stands as a producer in relation to the money-lender's capital, which confronts him as usurer's capital."[17] The author of "The Questions" discovered the destructive threat the peasants were facing under the new system of landlord's ownership of land, as well as the necessity of defending this system through the suppressing of usury activities. Just like the official credit system in *The Rites of Zhou* and Feng Xuan's remitting of debts on behalf of Lord Mengchang, the author in the third section of "On the Degree of

---

[17]*Complete Works of Karl Marx and Frederick Engels*, vol. 25, p. 673.

Seriousness of Various Issues" pointed out that Lord Huan of Qi granted beautiful brocade to the usurers in exchange for their remitting of poor people's interests of the debt. Thus, we can see that giving small producers the essential life necessities, advantageous to the country's development and the consolidation of the regime, was in urgent need and was the common view of outstanding statesmen of the landlord class.

4.2. The section "On the Degree of Seriousness of Various Issues" and its theoretical elaboration

Researchers in modern times have quite different opinions of the circulation age of the section "On the Degree of Seriousness of Various Issues." One opinion holds that it was written in the Warring States Period. The other opinion thinks that it was written in the Western Han Dynasty. The author of this book is in favor of the first idea.

The main idea and the core of "On the Degree of Seriousness of Various Issues" is as follows. With the section "The Savings Policy of the State" as the key link, the article "On the Degree of Seriousness of Various Issues" had rich content and covered a wide range of topics, including productive industries such as agriculture and handicraft, financial and economic industries as state reserve, currency circulation, market price, fiscal revenue and tax, credit and relief and domestic and foreign trade. It involved the government's direct and indirect organization and management of all the productive economic activities. The main idea of this section, among other things, was the managing and administration of the country for the purpose of becoming a rich nation and obtaining a dominant position in the world. The articles of this section were mutually illustrative and were the further elaboration of the political and economic thought of the Legalists of the State of Qi as expressed in *Jingyan*. For example, the section "On Governing the People" said that "Whoever has the authority over some land and governs the people should pay attention to opportunities provided by the four seasons to have all farm work done on time to make sure that enough grain can be stored. If a state is wealthy, people will be drawn there from remote areas; if the lands are cultivated, people will settle down there." That is to say, rulers with the ownership of some land should make efforts to do a good job in agricultural affairs so that there could be an ample reserve of grains. The wealthier a country became, the more people would come to settle in it. The more developed a nation's land was, the more people would tend to stay. The section "On Consolidating the Authority of the Throne" stated, "There usually is a competition for labor between commerce and farming; there usually is a competition for goods between the families and government; there usually is a competition for importance between treasure and grain; and there usually is a competition for power between the local and the central governments." In other words, farming and commerce competed for labor force, families and the national treasury competed for goods, treasure and grain competed for importance, and the local and central governments competed for power. The section of "The Most Important Economic and Political Affairs" pointed out that "Land is the root of all policies of a government. Court is the reflection of the rules of propriety. Market is the standard for checking the demand and supply of commodities. Gold is the measure for calculating expenditure. And territories of feudatories and the one thousand charities each of them own are their armament systems. The reason for these five aspects is recognizable, and there are right ways to realize them too." The author was saying that land was the basis of a government, court was a reflection of the order of hierarchy, market was the standard for the measurement of prices, gold is the way of judgment of the wealth and military forces are the regular employment of vassal states. Grasping the tenet of these five principles, people could have laws to abide by in their conduct of affairs. These thoughts were comprehensively and extensively elaborated on in this section and some of them were even repeatedly and fully emphasized. The theory of "On the Degree of Seriousness of Various Issues" was the ruling art of ancient kings, and centralized countries would "govern the world with the right economic policies established according to the degree of seriousness of various issues." The author pointed out that "Since Fu Xi was in power, no sovereign could manage to unify the world without making the right economic policies to regulate prices according to the degree of seriousness of various issues." From the time of Fu Xi, an ancient ruler, since the state had been governed with full consideration of the degree of seriousness of various matters, what was the point of putting the degree of seriousness of various matters into the governing practice? From a national point of view, the first aim of doing this was to prevent too much disparity between the rich and the poor, and stop the local separatist forces as well as the wealthy and the powerful from unifying and swelling, thus freeing the central government from their threats. The second aim was to increase the revenue of the central government and the economic strength of the country to serve the purpose of obtaining a dominant position in the world. As was said in the section "Number Ding on the Degree of Seriousness of Various Issues," "A sovereign who is clever at governing his state will take firm control over the properties by regulating the prices of things and issuing policies with greater or less urgency according to the actual situation, so that he can gain one hundred shares back with only one share of capital invested. Accordingly, the income of his state will be inexhaustible like water of the Yellow River and the sea even though he does not levy any taxes on his people. That is the so-called taking control over the whole world by mastering the properties and manipulating them correctly." From this, we can see that a good ruler of the country should bring the nation's finance into good order and use prices and policies to regulate the relationship between the wealth and the people, because the former served the latter, which was the ultimate purpose. As a result, the implementation of the former needn't be everlasting, but should be under good control and on the watch of the rulers. The author maintained that ancient kings "would take firm control over the food supply of their states and block off the paths for seeking profits among their people. Thus, it is dependent upon the sovereign exclusively to make a decision on whether to render the people something or to deprive them of something, whether to impoverish them or to enrich them." From an economic perspective, the central government should be in an absolute position of dominance, so that the common people would love the king as if he were the sun and the moon, and treat him as if he were their parent. Consequently, the centralized control and monopoly of finance would be ensured. Because of this, "When the sovereign takes control of the power over the wealth of the state exclusively, the state is invincible. When the power over the wealth of the state is shared between two departments, the army of the state can still manage not to be defeated by other states. When the power over the wealth of the state is shared among three departments, its troops cannot be dispatched for any military action. When the power over the wealth of the state is shared among four departments, the state will definitely be ruined" (*The Saving Policy of the State*). Put differently, a country with a concentration of wealth was unbeatable, a country with the wealth divided into two parts would have only one half of its military strength, a country with the wealth divided into three parts wouldn't be able to maintain its regular military forces and a country with the wealth divided into four parts was doomed to be conquered. That was quite different from the viewpoint expressed in *The Book of Lord Shang*. Shang Yang maintained that the means whereby a country is made prosperous are agriculture and war, while the author of "On the Degree of Seriousness of Various Issues" was of the opinion that the king should be the exclusive controller of the wealth. Shang Yang was in favor of "agriculture and war," while the author of *Guanzi* was of the opinion that "those who handle the financing of their states carefully and attach importance both to farming and to commerce and crafts industry can enrich their states" ("On Handling Government Affairs According to the Thought of the Five Main Elements"). He was saying that as long as the financial budget and final accounts were well considered, the agriculture was stressed upon, and the commerce and industry were consolidated, the country would surely become prosperous. Meanwhile, the author of Guanzi was also against the employment of administrative means. Instead, he was in favor of "sponsoring various state expenditures without collecting money or levying taxes directly upon the people." The country would take over the management of commerce and loans and monopolize the right of the coinage of currency, thus controlling the circulation of commodities, the revenue of which would be a substitute for the direct taxation on the people. In that case, "they would do it apparently as they rendered benefits to their people." "Thus, whoever is able to work will not manage to dodge the taxes." "The people cannot manage to dodge it even though you are going to take a profit of one hundred times over." The accumulation of wealth was done in such a delicate way that people who were able to work would not dodge the taxes. Though not forceful, this practice "would make people cover up the true situation of the population." As a result, the government revenue increased, but the productive forces weren't in any way damaged. They emphasized the government's direct participation in and firm control of economic activities, in an effort to control all the economic activities of the country, thus "controlling and administering the common people by managing the national macro-economy." It was the author's firm belief that as long as the natural resources and wealth were under government monopoly and the life necessities of the people were under government control, the rulers could keep the wealth of the people in their firm control.

The theory of "On the Degree of Seriousness of Various Issues" was the conceptual knowledge of ancient countries for the control of currency circulation and credit activities. It combined the nature of money capital and interest-bearing capital, as well as the compulsive nature of super-economy of the government. At that time, natural economy was in a dominant position and commodity economy was in a complementary position. The mentality of using currency to control the circulation so as to get the maximum advantage was reflective of the strength of the merchants who were rising on the social ladder. These persons "would investigate the demand, supply and price of things, trade things they possess for commodities demanded on the markets. Hence, precious furs and feathers produced at other places are supplied at the local market, and the state will no longer be short of bamboo arrows. Moreover, there are some stranger, precious goods transported here from time to time too" (*The Small Historical Document of the State of Qi*). "Merchants do not care about where they are staying. Nor do they care about which sovereign they are serving. When they sell something out, they do that for the sake of profits; when they buy something in, they do not want to keep it for themselves. They can use the resources of the mountain and forest areas to make profits. And thus the amount of tax collected from the markets can be doubled" (*On Extravagance*). Just like the exploitation of the resources of the mountain and forest areas, with merchants coming, the taxes from such transactions more than doubled. With such a quick pace of development, a new layer of the social spectrum came into being rapidly. In "Number Jia on the Degree of Seriousness of Various Issues," we have a brief introduction to such people: "So, high-ranking officials, people with fiefs, wealthy merchants, people with private store of grain and savings in terms of money, those who have earned profits and kept them and those who have cornered assets are all wealthy people of our state." As the ascending thinkers and statesmen of the landlord class, with their vision and political aspiration, they would never permit other people to rob them of their possessions and weaken their political influence. They were quite alert to the possibility that "High salaries are no longer inviting enough to attract the wealthy people and penalties are no longer formidable enough to threaten the poor. If the law is not complied with and the orders cannot be carried out, the common people cannot be well administrated while the gap between the rich and the poor is extremely large" (*The Savings Policy of the State*). Thus, they were supportive of the practice that "the nation will have some savings and the common people will have some surplus of grain" (*On Prohibitions and Storage*). They thought that "a sovereign good at governing the state should enrich his people first, and then he can manage to administer them and put them in order" (*On Governing a State*). About the government of the country, they put forward the assertion that "whoever expresses opinions but does not know anything about the degree of seriousness of the issues can be said to be talking nonsense" (*The Best Economic Policies for the Mountainous States*). Thus, we can see that they were ambitious and wise, as well as fanatical and naive.

Then, what was this theory really about? How should we understand and perceive it?

To put it briefly, the theory of "On the Degree of Seriousness of Various Issues" was a theory of the ancient Chinese ruler's administration of the country as propagated in *Guanzi*. It consisted of methods, measures and different means of administration, constituting the basis of ancient China's economic thought, and naturally, the basis of ancient China's financial thought.

The emergence of this theory was based on the following guiding thought. First of all, it was based on the human-oriented thought. *Guanzi* put forward clearly that a central tenet was the thought of human-centeredness. In "The Ideas of Establishing One of the Most Powerful States," there was such a sentence: "A sovereign who is going to establish one of the most powerful states or even to unify the world should start with regarding the people as the roots for his regime." To Lord Huan of Qi, who wanted to become an influential leader, it was only natural that "The people of the state of Qi should be the root of establishing a most powerful state in the world" (*On Establishing One of the Most Powerful States*). At that time, the people referred to "four kinds of people, intellectuals, farmers, handworkers, and businessmen, who are very crucial to the state" (*The Small Historical Document of the State of Qi*). Because of that, politically, policies must be "in accordance with the will of the people." That is, rulers should "be kind to the people," "reduce penalties" and "relieve forced labor and respect the common people." Economically, rulers should "enrich the people." "When agricultural taxes are collected according to the conditions of the fields, farmers will not move to any other area." Rulers should also "collect few things from the people," and when they do collect from the people, "it should be done properly." "People should live in separate places according to their profession." He was against the way that "the sovereign spends money endlessly, so the common people will have to work hard endlessly" (*On Examining a State from Eight Aspects*). His economic thought of enriching and benefiting the people was in total accordance with his political idea of "being kind to people."

The second basis was his profound and comprehensive understanding of the market. *Guanzi* didn't give a definite explanation of the market, but his elaboration of the functions of the market was quite amazing indeed. In his opinion, the market was a galaxy of all the commodities of the world and tens of thousands of people would profit from the transactions. "Markets are distributing centers of commodities produced all over the world, and tens of thousands of people are exchanging their products and doing business there" (*The Questions*). (The markets could judge the various demand for commodities. With goods at low prices and merchants earning little, all the businesses would try their best for profit, and thus the miscellaneous demands could be satisfied.) ("Market is the standard for checking the demand and supply of commodities. Hence, if all kinds of commodities are cheap, huge profits cannot be obtained by merchants. If huge profits cannot be obtained, all government projects can be put in order. If all government projects can be put in order, all kinds of needs of the state can be met moderately." — *The Most Important Economic and Political Affairs*) On the contrary, markets were also directory, persuasive and encouraging. They would guide the development of agriculture and at the same time promote the development of industry and commerce. ("Markets are set up to encourage consumption. And when consumption is encouraged, the state will be well developed. When all farm work is well done, commerce and handicraft industry will be encouraged." — *On*

Extravagance) So in the section "The Most Important Economic and Political Affairs," the author further pointed out that "Every *Ju* should have a market. Otherwise, if there is no market, the common people living there will be short of commodities." Without such mutual exchange of commodities, a shortage of commodities would arise.

Third, it was based on the author's understanding of people's mentality of the pursuit of wealth. *Guanzi* acknowledged that this mentality could be put to use in the administration of the country. As was stated in "The Savings Policy of the State," "according to the nature of human beings, they all trust their parents and will die for the sake of wealth. In this respect, people all over the world are the same. The common people will be happy when benefits are bestowed upon them and they will be angry if they are deprived of their wealth. That is the natural character of human beings. Ancient kings knew this so that they would do it apparently as they rendered benefits to their people; conversely, the former would do it secretly and unwittingly when they deprived the latter of things. Thus, the common people would feel close to their sovereign." The sovereign, well aware of the common people's mentality, should use it consciously in his governing of the country and administration of the economic affairs. When designing economic policies and regulations, those that were advantageous to the common people should be done openly, while those disadvantageous should be done secretly, and done in a manner acceptable to the common people. "If the sovereign sets up the statistics system in the state, he can control the wealth of his people like guiding a horse by simply pulling the rein" (*On Making Statistics and Keeping a Financial Balance of the Mountainous States*). Different from Western classical economic theory, the relationship here was not a naked relationship of interest or pure money relations, but a more harmonious, warm and veiled one.

Fourth, the author's understanding of the statecraft was much profound and mature. In the chapter "On Governing a State," the author proposed that "Regarding the government of a State, the most important thing is to enrich the common people." To enrich the common people, the first priority was to take the right attitude toward agriculture. The sovereign should ensure the welfare of the farmers and guarantee their seasonal agricultural activities. The expenses of production of the farmers should be taken into full consideration to make sure that they wouldn't be exploited by the usury of wealthy merchants. Thus, the farmers could have ample store of grain at home and the wealth of the country would be left to the common people. Guanzi was in favor of the following practice: "The common people can be well administered with suitable policies along with reasonable penalties. If this is the case, the common people will be led to concentrate themselves on food, clothes, and other benefits." Meanwhile, the author didn't reject propriety and righteousness and tried to bring a balance to the two. Consequently, "When gentlemen comply with the rules of propriety, the sovereign will be powerful and the common people will be obedient. When petty men are engaged in farming assiduously, there will be enough wealth and all kinds of supplies. If all these four conditions are met — the sovereign is powerful, the common people are obedient, and there is enough wealth and all kinds of supplies, it will not be difficult for the sovereign to unify the world and become the Son of Heaven in a short time" ("Of Sovereigns and Court Officials — II"). So the author's idea was different from the Confucianists and the Legalists, whose opinions were quite partial and bigoted.

The fifth point was the dominating idea of achieving unification and becoming the king of the world. "Therefore, unifying the whole world should be considered as the most virtuous contribution of ancient kings, because nothing else could provide more benefits to people of the world" (The Ideas of Establishing One of the Most Powerful States). The unification of the world by ancient kings was a most virtuous achievement and benefited, as was said by the common people, all things on earth.

According to "The Savings Policy of the State," "regarding governing the state, if the sovereign does not know the degrees of seriousness of things, he cannot manage to control and administer the common people by managing the national macro-economy. If he does not know how to regulate profits among his people, the state can never be regarded as in great order." Then what are "the degrees of seriousness of things"? As a matter of fact, "the degrees of seriousness of things" referred to the various prices of commodities and the corresponding purchasing power of the currency, the kernel of which is currency. Because of this, in *The Grand Scribe's Records*, it was said that "the degrees of seriousness of things refer to the money." So a good understanding of the degrees of seriousness of things could be used to mean that the country as a whole could control the total supply of money to regulate the prices at the market so as to realize the balance between demand and supply. The basic part of the degrees of seriousness of things was about the lightness or heaviness of money. That is to say, the purchasing power of currency could be controlled by officials. The government could regulate the commodities on the market by the injection or withdrawal of currency so as to maximize the revenue in the way of destroying monopoly and the accumulation of wealth. As was pointed out in the chapter of "The Savings Policy of the State," without mastery of such a skill, the rulers wouldn't be able to employ economic and monetary policies to control the common people. The country also needed to take financial measures to govern the profit-motivated business activities and illegal practice, in an effort to limit the disparity between the rich and the poor, help the needy, enhance the social cohesion, strengthen the national power and finally reach a state of great order.

It may be safe to say that the theory of the degrees of seriousness of things had a direct relationship with the thought of Guan Zhong. Or maybe, we can say bluntly that it was his posthumous doctrine. In Sima Qian's *Historical Records*, he mentioned more than once the question of the degrees of seriousness of things. For example, in the biographies of Guanzi and Yanzi, he mentioned that Guan Zhong, the prime minister of the state of Qi, was helping the administration of the country. "In his conduct of the government, he emphasized the consideration of the degrees of seriousness of things and was cautious in weighing the related matters." He also talked approvingly of such a topic in other parts, such as *Pingzhun Book* and *The Moneymakers*. In the over two thousand years of ancient Chinese society, whenever monetary issues were discussed, the theory of the degrees of seriousness would also be mentioned, though in a minor way of talking about the weight of coins. So it was quite different from the way in *Guanzi*, which used it as a complete theoretical framework and a systematic general plan for a rich country and a strong military force. This ancient theory of macro-regulation of China, as mentioned by Hu Jiacong, was a self-contained theoretical framework. The financial thought of this theory, "like a red line running through these articles, uses the law of value for macro-regulation in the field of commodity circulation." The emergence of these theorists represented "a school of theorists focusing on financial affairs among the contending schools of thought" and "they should be called the school of the degrees of seriousness of things indeed."[18] After that, this theory was debased to be a very simple term, no longer able to play a regulatory role in the market. In particular, some of the later kings only wanted to have a one-sided misinterpretation of the theory for the purpose of accumulating wealth or saving them from the doom or destruction. These last-minute attempts of application would never turn the theory of the degrees of seriousness of things into a ready-made panacea.

In the long-term practice of commodity exchange, these thinkers observed the economic activities of the market. Though without the guidance of the theory of labor value, it was impossible for them to have a rational and systematic understanding of the law of value, and they had quite an elementary grasp of the change of nature and human beings in terms of the degrees of the seriousness of things in the process of commodity exchange. As was pointed out in "The Savings Policy of the State," "sometimes the yearly harvest is good, but other times it is bad, so that the price of grain can be either low or high correspondingly. Some edicts are urgent but other are not, so that things can be either expensive or cheap." "When goods are dumped, their prices will fall. When goods are hoarded, their prices will go up." In the section of "On taking Suitable Economic Measures by Examining the Situation," the author maintained that "when commodities are hoarded, their prices will go up. When goods are distributed, their prices will come down." This was the first level of the theory of the degrees of the seriousness of things. In the process of the change of the degrees of the seriousness, grains and commodities were in an opposite position and changed reversely. As a result, it was said that "when the value of the currency goes up, the prices of tens of thousands of other items will come down. When the value of currency comes down, prices of tens of thousands of other things will increase." "When the price of grain is high, that of gold will be low. And when the price of grain is low, that of gold will be high. These two factors can never be in accordance with each other." Meanwhile, because at that time grains were the determining factor of human life and also a commodity money used as the universal

---

[18]Hu Jiacong, *A New Probe of Guanzi*, China Social Sciences Press, 2003, p. 163.

equivalent, there was also the concept that "when the price of grain is high, prices of tens of thousands of other things will be low. And when the price of grain is low, prices of tens of thousands of other things will be high."

The operational principle of the theory of the degrees of the seriousness of things was that "there is no fixed way to regulate the prices and distribution of items according to the degree of seriousness of various issues." That is to say, there wasn't any fixed pattern for the operation of the theory. "You can only use the right method to react to the situation when something happens, and make good use of the information you collect. Hence, if a sovereign is not able to draw the wealth of the whole world to himself or win over people all over the world, he will not be able to maintain his state" (Number Jia on the Degree of Seriousness of Various Issues). The notion of "there is no fixed way" originated from the saying that "regarding the guidelines on the economic policy of a state, the most important thing is to establish suitable policies according to the actual situation," which was the persistent theme of *Guanzi*. According to the author, ancient rulers, such as the Yellow King, Yu Shun, Xia Hou, Yin Ren and Zhou Ren, adopted different means to administer the country. Their styles of production varied a lot, but they all boosted the production. So, "these five sovereigns had all focused on the same purpose even though they had taken various respective measures." The author of *Guanzi* was of the opinion that the measures taken by the five sovereigns were all applicable, but shouldn't be employed in all. So he said, "We should adopt all the strong points of the policies taken by these five sovereigns, but do not copy any one among them automatically in disregard of the specific conditions." That is, "they will make investigations into situations to avoid troubles. Adhere to fixed principles but also reform things which became unsuitable due to the situation at the time. They will take action at the right time, but will not take action when the right time passes by. Nevertheless, policies of sovereigns who will unify the world in the future cannot be made in advance. These are the guidelines of the five above-mentioned sovereigns." The theory of the degrees of the seriousness of things operated permanently without any stop. As long as there were economic activities, it would never cease to function. In times of hardship, this theory could be put into use to regulate the reserve of grains for future use. When the nation was in peril, the ruler could use this theory for the purpose of controlling important materials in the preparation for war. After the unification of the country, it could be put into use to reward the benevolent and righteous people, and make the common people advocate propriety and maintain the social order, thus bringing the whole nation into great order. As was pointed out in "On Taking Suitable Economic Measures by Examining the Situation," "it is somewhat the same as the four seasons taking turns to return again and again. There will be no end at all. When the state encounters some problems, the expenditure of the government can be met by regulating the price of grain. Thus, a money surplus can be accumulated and then used to reward people who contributed to the state. If all other states of the world submit to your authority and you can maintain the power of the whole world, then you can enrich the honest, kind and righteous people, so the common people will adhere to the important rules of propriety and not commit misconduct any more. Regulating prices and supply according to the degree of seriousness of various issues is so important that it can be utilized to launch attacks against other states if they are disobedient. It can also be relied on to popularize the principles of benevolence and righteousness if the sovereigns of all other states submit to your authority."

With an understanding of the basic concepts and characteristics of the theory of the degrees of the seriousness of things, the author of *Guanzi* began the application in the administration of the country and the management of financial affairs to lay a solid foundation and increase the national reserve, for the purpose of bringing peace to the whole world.

In the section "The Savings Policy of the State," there was an excellent elaboration. "The greatest benefit provided by evaluating and acting according to the degrees of seriousness of the situation is to purchase and accumulate things at prices that are a bit higher compared with the market prices when things are cheap, and then dump them at prices when things are expensive. Lack of plethora of goods is ever changing, so that suitable measures should be taken to regulate the prices to balance supply and demand. Otherwise, if the balance is destroyed, the prices of some things in shortage will be driven up. A sovereign who realizes that will take measures to adjust supply and demand to maintain balance." That is because either the government or the rich businessmen would play a decisive role in the fluctuation of the prices and the variation of the relationship between supply and demand. As was discussed in this section, only the government, on behalf of the whole country, should apply the theory of the degrees of the seriousness of things in the market and gain the most advantage. That is, "to make sure that a city of ten thousand families will store ten thousand *zhong* of grain and one thousand *ji* of money .... Thus, both the spring ploughing and summer weeding can all be facilitated. And tools such as ploughs, ploughshares and other things like seeds, foodstuffs are all supported by the state, so that even the influential merchants and powerful families who have cornered things on purpose will not have any opportunity to take huge advantage of the common people. Why? The sovereign knows how to focus on farming and to take cautious action to facilitate it. In order to acquire silk and other clothing, loans can be rendered to the common people during the spring season and then ask them to pay back in terms of fabric. And in order to collect grain harvested during the autumn season, loans can be rendered to the common people during the summer season and then ask them to pay back in terms of grain. Thus, farm work will not be missed and the wealth of the state will not be lost." Here, the author drew up a blueprint according to which the government could put the theory of the degrees of the seriousness of things into practice, buy at low prices and sell at high prices, taking advantage of the ups and downs of the prices in the market, in the hope of increasing or decreasing the national reserve, stabilizing the prices of the commodities and the relationship between supply and demand.

The theory of the degrees of the seriousness of things maintained that the stability of the prices in the market was only temporary, while its changing was everlasting. As a result, the artificial adherence to a fixed price was disadvantageous to both circulation and production. We can catch a glimpse of this from a conversation in "Number Yi on the Degrees of Seriousness of Various Issues." "Duke Huan asked Guan Zhong, 'Is there a fixed method for balancing demand and supply?' Guan Zhong replied, 'No, there is no fixed method to balance demand and supply. Balancing demand and supply means regulating the prices of things to make them high or low according to the situation of the market. However, the prices of various things should not and cannot be kept fixed at all.' Duke Huan asked, 'The amounts of both the demand and the supply of things should not be made fixed at any rate?' Guan Zhong replied, 'No. they should not be made fixed. If they are fixed, the distribution of goods will become stagnant. When the market is stagnant, it will be changeless. When the market is changeless, the prices of things will be steadfast. When the prices of things are steadfast, tens of thousands of things cannot be used effectively.'" This conversation was suggestive of two mentalities. As the ruler of the country, Duke Huan wanted to have fixed and permanent prices in the market. On the contrary, Guan Zhong, with much insight into the functioning of the market, was in favor of respecting and following the objective laws of the market and tried to apply these laws to his advantage. While answering Duke Huan's series of questions, Guan Zhong proposed the new concept of "prices were never permanent. They were either high or low." The so-called "balancing" of Duke Huan meant "to regulate." Guan Zhong's idea of "there is no fixed method" meant that there could be no artificial regulation of the prices, which would mean that the prices couldn't reflect correctly and in a timely manner the supply and demand of the market. Consequently, the ruler could not make use of the theory of the degrees of the seriousness of things to make profits, and the prices of different kinds of commodities could not be controlled and made use of. As was stated in the section "On Taking Suitable Economic Measures by Examining the Situation," "if prices are higher in our state, goods will accumulate here. If prices are lower in our state, goods will flow out to other areas." For those commodities which accumulate because of higher price or which would flow out as a result of low price, we need to take immediate measures to acquire and accumulate them so that we could take possession of the wealth and commodities of the world.

4.3. *The discussion of currency in "On the Degrees of the Seriousness of Things"*

The author of the articles on the theory of the degrees of the seriousness of things laid special emphasis on the understanding of the function of the medium of circulation. The author very simply put currency to be the equivalent of the medium of circulation and treated them equally. "Lives of the common people are dependent upon gold and money to trade in the commodities they need" (*The Savings Policy of the State*). "The lives of the common people are dependent upon grain produced by all kinds of crops, and gold and money are the media of circulation" (*Number Yi on the Degree of Seriousness of Various Issues*). At the same time, currency also functioned as a channel of circulation. "Money is the means for trade" (*On Taking Suitable Economic Measures by Examining the Situation*). From this, we can see that at that time the circulation of commodities had reached a considerable scale. Without money, commodity transaction would become impossible. During the Spring and Autumn Period and the Warring States Period, natural economy played a dominant role. So the concept of currency as a universal commodity was an insight with some foresight, though its importance was underestimated and underappreciated by us. That was the first time in China that currency was considered to be the means of exchange or the channel of circulation. Ever since then, the connotations of currency have undergone quite a lot of changes and seen additions and omissions, but its basic meaning was still the currency in circulation, and other meanings like the currency itself, its substitutes and its symbolic meanings were of no significant importance. Similarly, without this means of trade, ancient countries could never control and manage the exchange of commodities, which would result in damage to the economic order and people's life. This had been illustrated by the free casting of currency throughout history, as was pointed out in "Number Yi on the Degree of Seriousness of Various Issues," which stated that "Sovereigns in ancient times were good at manipulating the price and supply of grain by taking firm control over their currencies, so that the strength of the common people could be well used by them." Because the sovereign took control of the power over the wealth of the state exclusively, the wealth of the state was concentrated to a maximum extent.

The articles on the theory of the degrees of the seriousness of things also touched upon other functions of currency. For example, about the function of currency as the measure of value, in "The Flexible Economic Policies Taken by the Mountainous States," it was said that "one *jin* of gold is about the equivalent of eight *dan* of grain." In "Number Jia on the Degree of Seriousness of Various Issues," it was stated that "when the price of grain is high, that of gold will be low. And when the price of grain is low, that of gold will be high. These two factors can never be in accord with each other." These were not exclusively on the measure of value, so we cannot say that the author had quite a clear understanding of the function of the measure of value. But judging from the manifestations of price, we can see that gold was considered to be the measure of value and the yardstick for value appraisal and its exchange value was inversely proportional to the price of grains, or more broadly, inversely proportional to the prices of all commodities. As to the function of the means of storage, in "The Savings Policy of the State," it was said, "Make sure that a city of ten thousand families will store ten thousand *zhong* of grain and one thousand *ji* of money and that a city of one thousand families will store one thousand *zhong* of grain and one hundred *ji* of money." In "The Flexible Economic Policies Taken by the Mountainous States," the author pointed out that "For a state with ten thousand chariots, the total amount of treasure saved by the state should be a value no less than ten thousand *jin* of gold. For a state with one thousand chariots, the total amount of treasure saved should be a value no less than one thousand *jin* of gold. For a state with one hundred chariots, the total amount of treasure saved by the nation should value no less than one hundred *jin* of gold." Actually, this suggested that the author was well aware that currency, as the general representative of social wealth, was conserved and accumulated, just like the treatment of grains. So it was quite different from the proposition that "The appearance of gold means the disappearance of grain, and the appearance of grain means the disappearance of gold," as was proposed in *The Book of Lord Shang*. As to the function of the medium of payment, the author mentioned borrowing, salary, bonus, relief and taxes in different forms of currency. For example, in "On Monopolizing the Salt and Iron Industry," the author mentioned, "suppose that thirty *qian* are collected on each person monthly." In the section "The Best Economic Policies for the Mountainous States," it was stated, "Disburse salaries to intellectuals in terms of money. Collect taxes from fiefs conferred upon the high-ranking officials in terms of money. Pay the people who work for the government and pay for horses purchased by the state in terms of money." In the section "On Making Statistics and Keeping a Financial Balance of the Mountainous States," the author stated that "all money borrowed from the wealthy people can be repaid in grain." As far as the function of international currency was concerned, during the Warring States Period, monetary transfer and payment were involved between the royal kingdom and the vassal states, between the vassal states, and between the State of Qi and its neighboring States. In the section "Number Yi on the Degree of Seriousness of Various Issues," it was stated that "People of adjacent states who came to live in our state will consume our grain, use our money and pay in terms of gold." In the section "Number Wu on the Degree of Seriousness of Various Issues," the author cited an example. "Guanzi told merchants of Lu and Liang, "If you can purchase one thousand *pi* of Di for me, you will be rewarded with three hundred *jin* of gold; if you can purchase ten thousand *pi* of Di, you will be rewarded with three thousand *jin* of gold."

About the origin of currency, the author of *Guanzi* maintained that there were three different explanations. The first was based on the relief of the common people from calamities by such sage sovereigns as Tang and Yu. The second explanation held that pearl, jade and gold were all imported from far away. The long-distance journey of transportation and the difficulty of purchasing made them valuable currency. The third explanation involved tools of production. Under the condition of agriculture-based economy, tools of production emerged and evolved gradually into currency. In what follows, the minting of currency by sage sovereigns for the salvation of the disaster-stricken people will be introduced. In the section "The Flexible Economic Policies Taken by the Mountainous States," it was stated that "During the time when Tang was in power, there was a severe drought that lasted for seven years. During the time while Yu was in power, catastrophes caused by floods lasted for five years. At that time, the common people did not have anything to eat so they were forced to sell their children for survival. Tang minted money with the metal produced by Mount Zhuang to ransom children sold by their parents, because they did not have enough food to support them. Yu minted money with the metal produced from Mount Li to ransom children sold by their parents, because they did not have enough food to support them." Compared with other theories on the origin of currency, this was the clearest explanation. The duration of the drought and flood in this explanation was different from other people's versions, such as that of Zhuang Zi, which was probably due to the differences in the legends or the variations in the process of retelling these legends. What was noteworthy was that only in these sections was common people's selling of their children linked with the minting of the money, for the purpose of demonstrating that the minting of money was the achievement of sage sovereigns to be retold by later generations and remembered throughout the ages.

There was also an analysis of the origin of the currency in these articles on the theory of the degrees of the seriousness of things. As was pointed out in "The Savings Policy of the State," "Jade is produced in Yu Shi. Gold is produced in areas along the Ru River and the Han River. And pearls are produced in Chi Ye. The provenances of these treasures are seven thousand eight hundred *li* away from the capital of the Zhou Dynasty in all four points of the compass. Paths to these places are often blocked by mountains and waters. Therefore, they cannot be reached with carts and boats. Since the provenances of these things were so far away and the transport was so difficult, ancient kings had made good use of their value, so that they appointed pearls and jade as first-rate currency, appointed gold to be secondary and coins to be third grade." These insights are in accordance with Karl Marx's observation. "The money-form attaches itself either to the most important articles of exchange from outside, and these in fact are primitive and natural forms in which the exchange-value of home products finds expression; or else it attaches itself to the object of utility that forms, like cattle, the chief portion of indigenous alienable wealth."[19] So does this mean that the author had come to understand that money was the final realization of value and a crystallization with its intrinsic value? The answer to this question is negative. The author thought that the reasons why "ancient kings used to make good use of their value" were as follows: "the provenances of these things were so far away and the transport was so difficult," "when supply is not enough to meet demand, prices of things will be high" and "at times when edicts of great urgency are issued, the price of gold will go up. At times when orders of less urgency are issued, the price of gold will come down." We cannot deny the influence of supply–demand relationship on the prices of the commodities, but its role was never decisive. The author, on the contrary, held that the supply–demand relationship was the only determining factor, which was at variance with the value theory of labor of Karl Marx.

---

[19]*Complete Works of Karl Marx and Frederick Engels*, vol. 23, p. 107.

The third explanation involved that evolution of tools of production. As was stated in "On Extravagance," "common people died as a result of being faithful, while the dukes died as a result of keeping a reserve of money." "All sovereigns of the other states have saved some money. How much do you think they have saved? And the answer is: Money is such a thing that can be used to mark the prices of goods. And the prices of goods are decided according to the importance attached to them." From the different pursuits of common people and the sovereigns of the other states, we can learn something about the origin of money. What the common people adhered to was their trustworthiness, while sovereigns of the other states cared constantly for money. So what was the matter with their money? One answer went like this: Currency was related to the cultivation of grains. For the farmers, food was the first necessity of life, which led to special attention being paid to agriculture. Consequently, farm tools, which enjoyed considerable popularity, became prevalent and finally were used as the medium for transactions, with the original productive function only in name. This explanation was not only in accordance with modern monetary theory but also agreed with the ancient evolution of Chinese money, thus validating the correctness of modern monetary theory. Together with the explanation of importation from afar, this illustration of the development of jades, pearls, gold and currency was rather comprehensive. It demonstrated to us that the author was making generalizations on the basis of reality, taking the development history of currency into full consideration, and finally arriving at a thorough, scientific, as well as accurate conclusion, which conformed to a contemporary materialist conception of history.

The author of these articles held that, as far as money was concerned, "people cannot keep themselves warm by simply holding them in the hands; nor can they quench their hunger by eating them." This is no different from the opinion of Chao Cuo that money "could be neither edible while hungry nor wearable while cold," though their understanding of the use of currency was at variance. Chao Cuo was of the opinion that "jades and golds should be devalued," while the author here was a strong advocate of the practice that kings "used them to keep control over the wealth of their states, to manage the common people and to put the world in order" (*The Savings Policy of the State*).

The monetary system had three kinds of currency. The author mentioned that "they appointed pearls and jade as first-rate currency, appointed gold to be secondary and coins to be third grade," meaning that there was a three-level distinction. In ancient China, there had always been references to three kinds of currency, but later observers used such expressions to refer to gold, silver and copper currency. In some other articles of this category, the three kinds of currency became two: "Grant gold to the wealthy big families and lend money to the small and less wealthy ones" (*On Making Statistics and Keeping a Financial Balance of the Mountainous States*). "Gold and money are things cherished by all" (*Number Wu on the Degree of Seriousness of Various Issues*). "Lives of the common people are dependent upon gold and money to trade in the commodities they need" (*The Savings Policy of the State*). Wealthy, big families used gold, while small and less wealthy ones used money. That is, gold was used by the upper class and big families for the purpose of large payment, valuation and wealth transference. Then how did the two adjust in proportion to each other? As was pointed out in *On Administering Financial Transactions According to the Geographical Conditions*, "At times when edicts of great urgency are issued, the price of gold will go up. At time when orders of less urgency are issued, the price of gold will come down. Ancient kings used to take into serious consideration the extent of urgency of orders they were about to issue to regulate the price of gold and therefore to control the prices of jade, pearls and coins. King Wen and King Wu were paragons of this kind." That was an important reason for King Wen and King Wu of the Zhou Dynasty to become the kings of the world. As to the minting of the money, without any mention of that carried out by the dukes, officials and the common people, it was pointed out in *Guanzi* that "with the money minted and put into circulation under the supervision of the sovereign, common people can make deals with each other." "According to the amount of money coined for circulation, everyone would have hundreds or even thousands of *qian*" (*The Savings Policy of the State*). The two quotations referred to the same thing: With the money minted under the supervision of the ruler, common people could carry out transactions for their non-governmental exchange.

Guanzi didn't give any specific elaboration on the introduction into circulation and withdrawal of currency. Based on the relevant discussion, we may sum up the following points: the circulation and withdrawal of gold were related to the inter-state payments. "Travellers and merchants ... pay in terms of gold" (*Number Yi on the Degree of Seriousness of Various Issues*). In terms of the rewarding of the victorious army, "Whoever can break the enemy front will be rewarded with one hundred *jin* of gold" (*ibid.*). In terms of expenditure, "after rewards were conferred that morning, forty-two thousand *jin* of gold was gone" (*ibid.*). The circulation and withdrawal of money were related to the following aspects. One was the government purchasing, which mainly involved the purchasing of grains, though other commodities were also included. As told in "The Best Economic Policies for the Mountainous States," "At times when the harvest of the year is good ... you can ask the people to repay the amount of money they borrowed in grain. Thus, grain produced by the state will belong to you and money will go to the common people." In "On Making Statistics and Keeping a Financial Balance of the Mountainous States," the author stated, "It is time to purchase other goods with cash. After that, most of the money will be controlled by the people and tens of thousands of goods will be collected by the government." The second aspect was related to the granting of loans. As was mentioned in "The Savings Policy of the State," "The sovereign knows how to focus on farming and to take cautious action to facilitate it. In order to acquire silk and other clothing, loans can be rendered to the common people during the spring season and then ask them to pay back in terms of fabric. And in order to collect grain harvested during the autumn season, loans can be rendered to the common people during the summer season and then ask them to pay back in terms of grain." The third use of money was in the field of foreign trade. As was explained in "Number Wu on the Degree of Seriousness of Various Issues," "Bo Gong, the left Minister of War was ordered to lead the recruits to mint money in Mountain Zhuang. Wang Yi, the *Zhong Da Fu* (*Zhong Da Fu* is a title of court officials with secondary ranks) was ordered to carry twenty million *qian* to Chu to purchase deer." These three ways of putting money into circulation and the three ways for circulation of gold made up the six channels for currency circulation.

The withdrawal of currency included the return of gold and money to the storehouse of the government. First, let's look at the withdrawal of gold. In "Number Yi on the Degree of Seriousness of Various Issues,"

"Guanzi went to the palace to set forth his proposal to Duan Huan, and he said, 'The sum of rentals collected by the state this year is forty-two thousand *jin* of god.'" Here, he was referring to the rental revenue, which belonged to the first category. The second category was the offerings at the court. In "Number Jia on the Degree of Seriousness of Various Issues," "Guanzi replied, 'Please issue an order to make clear that not only all kinds of gift money should be presented in terms of gold, but also taxes should be paid with gold.'" The third category involved inter-state purchasing and payment. Also in "Number Jia on the Degree of Seriousness of Various Issues," "Guanzi replied, 'Then please issue an order to ask people to sell salt in Liang, Zhao, Song, Wei and Pu Yang. People living in these areas are all dependent upon salt imported from other states.' Duke Huan said, 'Good.' He then ordered the salt to be sold to those areas and therefore gained more than eleven thousand *jin* of gold." In terms of the withdrawal of money, it mainly involved the governmental selling of different commodities to wealthy people and usurers for the adjustment of prices. In "On Making Statistics and Keeping a Financial Balance of the Mountainous States," it was said, "most of the money will be controlled by the people, tens of thousands of goods will be collected by the government, and prices of these goods will go up ten times. The government can dump them at the market prices till their prices return back to the previously normal level." "Then notify the wealthy people and usurers as follows: 'The sovereign is going to make a journey, and you people should all lend a certain amount of money to sponsor this trip.'"

To sum up, the channels for currency circulation mentioned in *Guanzi* included the purchasing of agricultural products and other commodities, loans, rewards, inter-state payment and other fiscal expenditure. The channels for currency withdrawal included rental revenue, court offerings, donations and revenue from inter-state business. Thus, the main channels for currency circulation and withdrawal were already roughly in shape, which was quite significant.

There was a relationship between currency and grains and other commodities. In "Ways of Keeping Financial Balance," it was stated, "Set down standards for prices of fabric and other goods and make prices of other goods fixed relatively according to their value. Only the price of grain should be regulated separately." In consequence, the prices of fabric produced by women workers and the utensils produced by other tradesmen were in a relationship of inverse proportional change with the purchasing power of the currency. That is, if the purchasing power of the currency was high, the prices of the commodities would be low. If the purchasing power of the currency was low, the prices of the commodities would be high. It was just like what was said in "The Best Economic Policies for the Mountainous States," "When the value of the currency goes up, prices of tens of thousands of other items will come down. When the value of the currency goes down, prices of tens of thousands of other items will go up." That was the first point. The second point was that the so-called "tens of thousands of other items" referred only to commodities such as fabrics and utensils, with the exception of grains. That is to say, "When the price of grain is high, prices of tens of thousands of other things will be low. And when the price of grain is low, prices of tens of thousands of other things will be high." "Only the price of grain should be regulated separately" (*Ways of Keeping Financial Balance*). The reason for the price of grain being regulated separately was that grain enjoyed a unique position in ancient society. Agriculture was the lifeline of a country, while grain was the center of agriculture. As was stated in "The Best Economic Policies for the Mountainous States," "A sovereign can maintain the throne by maintaining the grain produced in his state." From this, we can see the vital importance of grain. It was related to the destiny of a state and the control of the state over the common people. Consequently, "the lives of the common people are dependent upon grain produced by all kinds of crops and also depend on gold and money to trade in the commodities they need." So, a sovereign who is good at governing his state will take control of gold and money to operate the distribution of food supply among his people, so that all of the people will devote their strength to serving him in return. In other words, "If the sovereign can take firm control of grain, currency and gold and keep a balance between these three, the whole world will be kept in order" (*The Best Economic Policies for the Mountainous States*). Under natural economic conditions, especially in the vast countryside of China, a majority of the common people were farmers, who lived basically in a self-sufficient way. The grain, after all, was different from currency and was not comparable to the latter, because grain was not only the life necessity for people to survive but also could be used by the farmers for reproduction. Grains were need to ensure the basic food necessity and the necessary seeds for the future. With the two kinds of grain in ample supply, the simple agricultural reproduction could become possible, let alone the extended reproduction to enrich the country and strengthen the military forces. Judging only from this point of view, in the ancient society dominated by the natural economy, the currency was indeed less important than grain. At that time, agriculture relied mainly on the weather and manual labor, with households as the basic unit of production. If a small famine lasted three years in a row, it could be regarded as a severe famine. As a result, it was of special significance for the rulers to stress the importance of grain. Grains were without question an important reserve both for the common family and for the state. Theorists emphasized that a country should "have savings enough to support the nation for ten years" (*The Savings Policy of the State*). On the contrary, grains would easily rot and were difficult to transport. Under special conditions, the price of grains would indeed rise or fall independent of other factors, leading to a dispute over the relative importance of grain and currency. As was pointed out by Liang Qichao, "Grain has two features: one is the feature of the common commodity and the other is the feature of currency." "Grain is like today's coins, while metal currency is like today's paper notes."[20] From this, we can infer that he misunderstood the author's original meaning of currency and grains and confused the function of currency as the subsistence of value with paper notes as the symbol of value. According to Ma Feibai, "under certain conditions, the value of the currency, whether high or low, was determined by other factors. On the other hand, the value of the grain, whether high or low, was in an active position."[21] This view was also in variance with the author's original meaning. We mentioned earlier that "taking control of gold and money to operate the distribution of food supply among the people" was important and "Sovereigns in ancient times were good at manipulating the price and supply of grain by taking firm control over their currencies, so that the strength of the common people could be well

---

[20] Biography of Guanzi in *Collected Works of Yinbingshi*, vol. 28, pp. 59, 61.
[21] *A New Interpretation of "on the Degree of Seriousness of Various Issues" in Guanzi*, p. 169.

used by them." So we can see clearly that in its relationship with grain, currency was active and positive instead of being passive and negative. On the contrary, as to a country's practice of "trading grain for cash" or "salaries being paid in terms of money instead of grain," there wasn't much difference, because they were different ways of maximizing the revenue on different occasions or times. Throughout this process, the function of being the measure of value had always played a significant role. Based on these facts, it may be safe to assume that the author, on other occasions, might have maintained that the function of being the measure of value had been a passive one, but absolutely not here. Indeed, in ancient society, the commodity–money relationship was always in a passive and subordinate position, because in natural economy, it was quite common to exchange one commodity for another. So it was quite understandable that the author held the opinion that the price of grains should rise or fall independently. That is, "grain should be of first importance among the tens of thousands of things of the world" (*The Savings Policy of the State*). It was even possible that the grain was expensive while other commodities were cheap, or vice versa, with the grain and other commodities in a relationship of inverse proportional change.

As per the author's understanding of the price of currency at that time, there was no distinction between value and exchange value. People's understanding of the variation of the prices was that it was a result of the law of supply and demand, instead of the law of value. As was told in "The Savings Policy of a State," "When things are over supplied, their prices will be low. When supply cannot meet demand, prices of goods will be high. When goods are dumped, their prices will fall. When goods are hoarded, their prices will go up. A sovereign who realizes that will take control over the circulation of grain and other goods of the state." In "Number Jia on the Degree of Seriousness of Various Issues," it was stated that "if you are able to restrain the expansion of their wealth with the influence of national assets, prices of things will go up. If you do not take action to control their wealth, prices will come down. If you are able to take control over their wealth, prices will go up. If you do not take action to control their wealth, prices will come down." In "On Taking Suitable Economic Measures by Examining the Situation," it was said, "when commodities are hoarded, their prices will go up. When goods are dumped, their prices will come down. When goods are distributed, there will be plenty circulating on the market." To sum up, a thing is valued in proportion to its rarity.

Judging from the outward appearance, it was very easy to notice the opposition between the value of the currency and the prices of other commodities, such as the grain, as well as the opposition between the purchasing power of the currency and the prices of commodities. But why was it so? According to the author of *Guanzi*, the value of the currency was determined by whether it was in circulation or under the control of the government. Too much currency in circulation would lead to the decrease of its value and too much currency under the control of the government would mean the increase of value. When the government purchased grains or other commodities, more currency would surely be put into circulation, and thus the government would have a reserve of grains and much currency would be in circulation, and vice versa. Consequently, as was pointed out in "The Best Economic Policies for the Mountainous States," "grain will be controlled by the state and money is circulating among people all over the state. The price of grain will go up ten times due to the enforcement of this policy." Without touching upon the value of the currency itself, here the author maintained that the rise and fall of the market prices were closely related to the currency in circulation, and the prices of the commodities were proportional to the purchasing power of the currency and were reversely proportional to the amount of currency in circulation. As was pointed out in "On Making Statistics and Keeping a Financial Balance of the Mountainous States," "nine-tenths of the money will be controlled by the state and only one-tenth is in the hands of the people. So the value of money will go up and the price of tens of thousands of goods will come down. Therefore, it is time to purchase other goods with cash. After that, most of the money will be controlled by the people, tens of thousands of goods will be collected by the government, and prices of these goods will go up ten times." The dramatic increase or sharp drop in the prices of the commodities was related to the changes in the market's money and commodity supply. Therefore, the factors causing changes in prices included not only the changes of the amount of money in circulation but also the changes of the amount of commodities in circulation. It was determined by the supply and demand in the market and manifested itself in the form of currency. There was no need to discuss the value of the currency, nor was it necessary to elaborate on the function of the measure of value. From this, we can see that the author's theory of value, different from Western quantity theory of money, was a theory of supply and demand under specific currency and circulation conditions, which we might as well call the value theory of supply and demand.

4.4. The discussion of monetary policy in "On the Degrees of the Seriousness of Things"

The monetary policy as discussed in these chapters was adopted in ancient China when the government was becoming more centralized in its concentration of state power. The central government took control of the amount of currency in circulation and adjusted the supply of currency to regulate the economic interests of different social strata to influence their socio-economic position, for the purpose of "sponsoring various state expenditures without collecting money or levying taxes directly upon the people," satisfying the financial demand of the country, and thus consolidating the central government. To achieve this goal, the first priority was to monopolize the right to issue money and control the amount of currency in circulation, through which grain and other commodities could also be controlled by the government.

For a country to make use of the monetary levers, the starting point and a basic prerequisite is that the country should monopolize the minting and issuing of currency. As was stated in "The Best Economic Policies for the Mountainous States," "There are mountains in our state and these mountains have metal mines, so you can use the metal produced in our state to mint money." In "The Savings Policy of the State," it was stated that "according to the amount of money coined for circulation, everyone would have hundreds or even thousands of *qian*." Drawn from historical lessons, that was an important and canonical teaching to be remembered by later generations. Besides, it was also an important measure against segregation and private casting of money. Normally, a country would mint and circulate according to the per capita money quota, which was supposed to meet the demand of circulation. When common people felt the inadequacy, it must be the result of the hoarding by the wealthy families.

If no effective measures were taken to regulate the imbalance and stop the continuous minting of the currency, the country wouldn't be properly governed even though much stress was laid upon agriculture.

The government must use the currency to interfere with the social, political and economic life and organize the circulation of commodities. With the common people producing grains, the government was in charge of issuing the money. A sovereign good at governing a country should control its currency to control the grain. For that purpose, the government should "calculate the wealth of the state." According to the author, the way of calculating the wealth of the state is to make clear how much cultivated land each unit of six square *li* had, and conduct investigations to gain information about the quality of the fields, the total output of these fields, the price of grain produced there, the price of the grain in general and how much money is needed to purchase the grain. Accordingly, the total amount of currency needed nationally could also be known in this way. In addition, the national demand for grains under such diverse conditions as famine or harvest, emergent situations or peaceful times, as well as the money needed to purchase the grain, could also be calculated. The monetary funds needed in different localities must be in accordance with the fertility of the fields and the production of the grains. The amount of currency for each household should also be in proportion to the population and wealth of the family. If the government regulation wasn't done in time, the wealthy and powerful families would take advantage of the situation. In consequence, as was mentioned in "On Making Statistics and Keeping a Financial Balance of the Mountainous States," "If the measures on statistics are not kept secretly, authority over the throne will be controlled in the hands of the sovereign's inferiors."

Currency was indispensable in all expenditures of a country. As was said in "The Best Economic Policies for the Mountainous States," "Disburse salaries to intellectuals in terms of money. Collect taxes from fiefs conferred upon the high-ranking officials in terms of money. Pay the people who work for the government and pay for horses purchased by the state in terms of money." The significance of doing this is that, with the government putting money in circulation, the grains in circulation would be controlled by the government, and all the money would circulate among the common people. According to the theory "when goods are dumped, their prices will fall. When goods are hoarded, their prices will go up," the price of grain could become ten or even dozens of times higher than the normal price due to shortage. With the price of the grain rising, the price of other commodities would fall roughly by twenty percent. Throughout this process, being the biggest beneficiaries, the farmers would be encouraged to be more productive in their farming, thus strengthening the foundation of agriculture. That was the result of the government's adjustment of its monetary policy. The author laid much stress on the sovereign's application of the monetary policy in the adjustment of socio-economic life, production, circulation, distribution and consumption, especially the adjustment of the economic interests of different social strata. As was stated in "The Savings Policy of the State," "if the sovereign cannot manage to dispense money and grain garnered by redistributing wealth and rearranging work reasonably among his people to support those who are short of means, people all over the state will enthrall each other even though he might focus on farming and urging the people to work hard to cultivate their fields, and even though he might mint money endlessly. Could the state really be put in order this way?" What an ingenious and insightful observation that was!

After controlling the grains, the government could control other goods and materials by way of the grains. Take the fabrics produced by female workers as example. If they can meet the needs of the state, agreements would be made with the procurers to purchase these fabrics under contract. While purchasing, the government needn't raise money, but only needs to pay them in grain according to the value of the time. Other commodities could also follow this pattern. The grains under government control were usually stored by the local governments. After signing the agreement of purchasing, they could issue a notice informing the public that on a certain day those who signed agreements with the government should settle their business in nearby places. Within one day, the transaction would be over, including the employment of shipping personnel and the transportation of grains.

As far as the foreign trade was concerned, currency was a magical tool to vanquish the enemy states. The government could buy the goods and materials of other states and increase its national reserve to weaken the opponents' economic strength, thus conquering them without any need for war. For example, people of the state of Qi carried twenty million *qian* to the state of Chu to purchase deer. As a result, the people of Chu gave up farming to hunt deer. After a while, the people of Qi hoarded five times more grain, and the State of Chu saved five times more money. At that time, the state of Qi could "ask people to close all tollgates and stop doing any business with the state of Chu." Lacking a reserve, the price of grain would rise sharply in the state of Chu, just in time for the state of Qi to transport its reserve of grain to the frontiers between the two states. In this magic way, "four tenths of the people of Chu submitted to the authority of the sovereign of Qi, and three years later, the sovereign of Chu came over to Qi and pledged allegiance" (*Number Wu on the Degree of Seriousness of Various Issues*). The moral of this legendary story was that by making full use of the mentality of greediness and waging an economic war against a neighboring state, it was very easy to conquer another state without any need for military forces.

The way of adjusting the value of currency was as follows. The author of *Guanzi* talked repeatedly of a principle "to regulate the price of gold and therefore to control the prices of jade, pearls, and coins" (*On Administering Financial Transactions According to the Geographical Conditions, On Taking Suitable Economic Measures by Examining the Situation*). Regulating the price of gold as a means "to control the prices of jade, pearls and coins" was the ultimate purpose. The way of "regulating the price of gold" was to do it according to the urgency of the edicts. As was pointed out in *On Administering Financial Transactions According to the Geographical Conditions*, "At times when edicts of great urgency are issued, the price of gold will go up. At times when orders of less urgency are issued, the price of gold will come down." The government regulated the price of gold through administrative means to control indirectly the prices of jade, pearls and coins. Based on the law of supply and demand, the government could determine the value of currency or even decrease the currency in circulation to elevate its value. The government could also require all the taxpayers to pay in gold, leading to a rise in the price of gold due to the increase in the demand, and thus "the price of gold will go up four times" (*On Taking Suitable Economic Measures by Examining the Situation*). Similarly, the government could also force the usurers and the wealthy families to lend money to it to increase the national reserve and raise the price of commodities. It could also issue an order to make clear that gift money and taxes should be paid with gold, which would result in an increase of the price of gold to one hundred times the original. On the contrary, the government could also set aside some funds for loans to the public at some local authorities, because loans to the farms were equivalent to the currency put into circulation. After the harvest of the following year, the price of the grain would fall considerably. So the local authorities could ask the farmers to return seven-tenths of the loan in grain. In this way, a large amount of grain would be under government control and the price of grain would rise and the price of gold would fall.

In ancient China, while the monetary thought came into being, the author of these articles on the Degrees of the Seriousness of Things summed up the thought of previous thinkers and put forward an ingenious proposition. Creatively elaborating on the function of currency as the medium of circulation, he ventured the opinion that the government could adjust the demand and supply through the manipulation of the currency in circulation, for the purpose of stabilizing the prices of commodities, increasing the national reserve and cracking down on the illegal practice of wealthy traders. Unique in ancient Chinese society, this penetrating insight should be held in veneration in the world history of monetary thought. On the contrary, in ancient China, which was dominated by natural economy, currency had a limited sphere of usage, and the grain for commercial transactions took up a very small percentage of the total agricultural output. The concept of three kinds of currency, namely, pearl, gold and jade, reflected the underdevelopment of monetary economy, and that grain didn't break away from the special function of being the universal equivalent. The author of the articles on the Degrees of the Seriousness of Things tried to make use of the currency for the purpose of "taking firm control over their currencies, so that the strength of the common people could be well used by them." It might be possible to purchase commodities and gain control over civil affairs through the use of money, but it would be futile and unrealistic to harbor the thought of conquering the whole world. In the process of argumentation, to set people thinking, the author exaggerated the function of currency to an extreme extent, which only undermined the scientific significance of the theoretical reasoning.

For those of us living in the contemporary world, that was of much reference value indeed.

4.5. The discussion of credit policies in "On the Degrees of the Seriousness of Things"

Credit activities were described as *dai* in the chapters on the Degrees of the Seriousness of Things and credit policies were considered by the author to be ways "to regulate profits among his people." As long as "farm work will not be missed," "the wealth of the state will not be lost" (*The Savings Policy of the State*). How can that aim be achieved? In terms of the domestic affairs, "both the spring ploughing and summer weeding can all be facilitated. And tools such as ploughs, ploughshares and other things like seeds, food stuffs are all supported by the state, so that even the influential merchants and powerful families who have cornered things on purpose will not have any opportunity to take huge advantage of the common people" (*The Savings Policy of the State*). For that purpose, the state would grant loans to poor farmers to relieve them of their burdens. As a result, "people all over the world will be drawn to our state like water flowing down to low-lying areas." Suppose there was one chief official in each *zhou* of the state, each county would have five cellars' store of grain; for those people who didn't have enough money to pay their taxes, long-term loans were granted, for those people who were not able to afford burials for their deceased family members, some money would also be lent, and then "hungry people are supported with food, cold ones are supported with clothes, and the dead can be buried" (*Number Jia on the Degree of Seriousness of Various Issues*). In addition, the sovereign knows how to focus on farming and take cautious action to facilitate it. With the common people allowed to possess land, the basic condition for simple reproduction, the interests of the nation would never be badly influenced at all. On the contrary, if merciless usurers and unscrupulous merchants ran rampant throughout the country and exploited the common people, then "there seemed to be five sovereigns within one country." So it was quite impossible that "the state is not poor and the military strength is not weak."

The development and exploitation of usury occurred as follows. According to the fourth section of "On the Degree of the Seriousness of

Things," there were four categories of usury, which differed from one another in terms of the total sum, the interest and the number of borrowers. For example, in the western part of the country, "the wealthier usurers normally hoard about one thousand *zhong* of grain, the less wealthy ones normally hoard about six to seven hundred," the interest rate was "one hundred percent" and "there were more than nine hundred families living in debt." In the southern part of the country, "the wealthier usurers normally lend tens of millions of *qian* and the less wealthy ones normally lend about six to seven million *qian*." They would demand an interest rate of fifty percent, and there were "more than eight hundred families living in debt." In the eastern part of the country, "the wealthier ones among the usurers hoard about five thousand *zhong* of grain and the less wealthy ones hoard about three thousand *zhong*." They would demand an interest rate of fifty percent, and there were "about eight hundred to nine hundred families living in debt." In the northern part of the country, "the wealthier usurers would lend about tens of millions of *qian* and the less wealthy ones normally lend about six to seven million *qian*." They would usually demand an interest rate of twenty percent, and "there were about nine hundred families living in debt." To sum up, "the total sum of money lent out by the usurers was about 30 million *qian*, the total amount of grain lent out was about 30 million *zhong*, and there were about 30,000 families living in debt." The interest rates ranged from 100% to 50%, with the lowest being twenty percent. So the author pointed out rather poignantly, "How is it that the state is not poor and the military strength is not weak?" These figures also demonstrated how rampant the usurers were and how relentless the exploitation was.

Taking the country's fundamental interests into consideration, the author regarded the credit activities to be an important way for the government to intervene in social and economic life, and proposed that private lending be replaced by national credit. The government would have two ways: one was coercion and the other was encouragement. On the one hand, "by taking measures," that is, by means of administrative methods, the government would issue an order to ask all the people who are going to present gifts to the ruler to present them only in terms of silk fabrics with beautiful patterns. So these usurers would have to buy such fabrics. With the earnings from this business, the farmers would be able to pay off their debts. Moved by such action, they would surely produce fabrics at full capacity. Meanwhile, the wealthy families would vie to purchase such products, and the price of these fabrics would rise 10 times. Then, the sovereign could announce to the usurers that the government would pay off the farmers' debt with the earnings from these beautiful patterns, since each of them was worth 10,000 *qian*. In this way, the debtors would be free from their debts. By means of its power, the government could use supra-economic measures to raise funds for the purpose of paying the debts of the poor families. On the other hand, the government would employ wise schemes to require local officials to honor those usurers by "whitewashing their doors and heightening the memorial archways of their lanes," "presenting them with round flat pieces of jade and appointing them to certain honorary position" and extolling them as the "parents of the common people." This was intended to impel and commend the usurers, in order to make them lenient and abandon their claim to the rights of the creditors. Overawed by the sovereign and the imperial power, the usurers would bend down to kowtow, and "tore their bonds, destroyed the contracts signed with the obligors, and dispersed their store of grain and properties to help the poor and the sick" (*Number Ding on the Degree of Seriousness of Various Issues*). These dream-like fanciful ideas seem naive and ridiculous, but they were indeed part of our ancient Chinese financial thought. To us, their ingenuity lay in their combination of spirit and substance, as well as their unity of administrative means and economic means.

As for different forms of governmental credit activities, the author mainly mentioned two. One was real credit. The farming tools needed, "such as ploughshares and other things like seeds, foodstuffs are all supported by the state" (*The Savings Policy of the State*). Loans rendered to the common people during the spring season could be paid back in terms of fabric and loans rendered during the summer season could be paid back in terms of grain collected during the autumn season. Farmers without seeds could get newly harvested grain from the government for planting and stale grain for food. In addition, they could also get loans in cash. As a matter of fact, currency and objects were interchangeable. As was mentioned in "On Keeping Financial Balance," "Issue an order to people with one hundred mu of land as follows: 'Plough your fields and plant the crops during the next twenty-five days. And you can get a loan from the state.'

When the autumn season comes and the harvest is good, the state grain price will reduce by a half. And then they tell the farmers: 'People who have borrowed money from the state can return it to the government in the form of grain.' Thus, the sovereign can keep one half of the grain produced in the state. And then the price of grain will be increased ten times higher. After that, another order is issued to officials at different levels to ask them to present all kinds of utensils to the central government as follows: 'Our state is short of cash, so that you can trade grain for cash.' Thus, an interest rate of ninety percent can be gained for the store of grain by the state. They purchase grain at a low price and sell it out at a much higher one, so, all utensils of the state can be sponsored this way and they do not need to count on the common people anymore." That whimsical idea by *Guanzi* was a way of keeping financial balance. Combining this with what was said in "The Best Economic Policies for the Mountainous States," we can say, "calculating the grain in terms of gold" is important while granting loans and "calculating the gold to be returned in terms of grain" while paying off the loans. What the government did could thus serve two purposes. On the one hand, free from the threats of the wealthy families and usurers, famers' life would be properly maintained and production could carry on, without the possible danger of not surviving or becoming homeless. On the other hand, the government could take advantage of the exchange between grain and gold, preventing the wealthy people and usurers from speculating, hoarding and causing trouble in the market to scramble for profit. In this way, the government could firmly control the regulation of the prices of commodities, and the reserve of grains and other materials, thus having the initiative in the aspects of finance, material and human resources.

Then, did the national credit bear interest? If the answer is yes, what were the interests? Like what was said in The *Rites of Zhou,* was it interest-free or of low interest? The answer was negative. The government's substantial revenue from the wide gap between loans and its repayment was astonishing. This indicates to us that the government's opposition to usury was toward those who operated privately, not what was carried out by the government. From the perspective of a united central authority, the government was forbidding private acquisition and exorbitant usury, trying to maintain the concentration of financial resources and oppose the segregation, for the aim of enriching the country and strengthening the military forces.

From what was said in "On Making Statistics and Keeping a Financial Balance of the Mountainous States," we can see how the central government employed the credit lever to accumulate wealth and undermine private economic strength. After certain investigation and planning, the government would set up a public fund, "issue some money" or put a certain amount of money into circulation. For those farmers whose grain output exceeded the estimated quantity, the government should grant loans in an active way, and adhere to the principle of "more loans to the bigger families and less loans to the smaller families." For those farmers living in mountainous areas with a moderate possession of land, who were in shortage of grain, the loans granted would only be enough for them to sustain a minimum life condition, without the danger of becoming homeless. Should the harvest of the next year be good, rich farmers should repay seven-tenths of the loan in grain and the rest in cash. Then, the price of the grain would go up and the value of the currency will depreciate. Thus, the government would control the surplus grain of the best fields. Since the grain surplus of the secondary fields was inadequate to complement the deficiency of the mountainous fields, the price of the grain would be driven up 10 times higher. Regarding fabrics produced by female workers, if they can meet the needs of the state, the government would reach agreements with the producers to purchase their products under contract. It would be specified in the contract that the price of the fabrics should be in accordance with the price of the local region and should be paid in terms of grain instead of cash. This would not only satisfy the national demand for fabrics but also bring down the price of the grain to a normal level. Meanwhile, the government could still raise money to grant loans and purchase grains to increase its reserve, for the purpose of driving up its price ten times. At that time, the government could take advantage of administrative means to borrow money from the usurers and wealthy families. They would be notified that the sovereign was going to make a journey and they were supposed to lend a certain amount of money to sponsor the trip. Also, the neighboring counties would receive an order telling them that they should hoard grains, families with surplus reserve should not trade grains without permission and that if the sovereign's stocks run out before the end of the trip, he would borrow some grain and fodder to support his followers and feed his horses. Consequently, the price of grain of the counties near the capital will go up ten times again. Then, the government could issue an order to pay off the debt to those wealthy families in terms of the price of the grain. The order would tell them that all money borrowed from them can be repaid in grain. Thus, the price of grain would depreciate and the value of currency would go up. If this practice was carried out throughout the whole country, "the price of grain can go up ten times higher." Then, "order the people to return the amount they borrowed in grain. Thus, nine-tenths of the money will be controlled by the state and only one tenth is in the hands of the people. So the value of money will go up and the price of thousands of goods will come down." So, "it is time to purchase other goods with cash." Thus, "the financial statistics of a state should be well planned before commodities are produced and these commodities can be controlled after they are finished. The state should issue orders to purchase or dump goods at the right time. It is no longer necessary to collect money from the common people." That was the financial blueprint of the *Chapters on the Degrees of the Seriousness of Things*.

In its employment of credit means, if the government forces the usurers to lend money to the country, that would be the same as the issuance of a commendatory to them. During the third year of the reign of the Emperor *Jing* of the Han Dynasty, the feudal lords in Chang'an tried to borrow money from the usurers, but were disgracefully turned down because the situation wasn't certain at all. During the third year of the reign of Emperor Wu of the Han Dynasty, the government issued an accusation order for tax evasion, which resulted in the bankruptcy of most middle-income merchants. That was the outcome of a combination of administrative and economic means, which was especially necessary when the commodity economy was at an underdeveloped stage. But it was quite doubtful indeed that the author of these articles should have such high expectations and two different purposes toward the influence of government credit measures on the national economy. Presumably, "the sovereign benefiting from it" was out of question, but that "the prices of goods can be regulated" could be equivalent to the common people becoming destitute. It was quite imaginable that, faced with the aggressive merging of usurers with private funding, the ruler of the country would never yield and let them gain the advantage. As long as they were in a dominating position, they would rise to oppose the usurers' practice, an example of which was the salt and iron policy of the Western Han Dynasty. Put forward more than 2,000 years ago, this theory on the Degrees of the Seriousness of Things proposed distinctively that the laws of the market economy should be examined and followed, the government should take time to adjust its policy to meet the change in supply and demand, and that in the management of its national economy, currency, credit, as well as price levers should all be taken into consideration. However inexperienced, crude and unscientific these propositions were, they were also amazing and encouraging. They are to be acclaimed and admired by all of us.

Chapter 2

Financial Thought in the Western and the Eastern Han Dynasties

William Georg Friedrich Roscher, a German scholar, maintained in his *Grundriss zu Vorlesungen über die Staatswirtschaft nach geschichtlicher Methode* that "The privilege of minting coins enjoys a parallel history of development with the state power."[1] Moreover, the two are of a relationship of interaction and reciprocal causation. Mutually conditional, they complement each other. During the Qin and Han Dynasties, the currency issue always revolved around the conflict between the central government and the opposing centrifugal forces, or to put it more specifically, the struggle between the vassal kings and tyrannical tycoons in the monetary system. That was also reflected in the monetary thought.

With the Han nationality playing a dominant role in the multiracial country, the empires of Qin and Han started the centralized landlord-class economy in China, which lasted over 2,000 years. Emperor Yingzheng of the Qin Empire put forward the criteria. "The currency is divided into three grades: measured by *yi*, gold is the first grade; with a mark of 'Ban Liang', and weighing as the mark indicates, copper coins are the third grade." In between the two was Bu. In Chinese history, that was the first time to have a three-grade currency of gold, copper coin and Bu, thus abolishing the use of commodity money. (Jades, Beads, turtle

---

[1]*Grundriss zu Vorlesungen über die Staatswirtschaft nach geschichtlicher Methode*, Commercial Press, 1982, p. 107.

shells, silver and tin were all utensils or treasures, thus shouldn't be considered as money.) Gold was money by weight and copper coins were for measurement. After that, except in the early years of the Western Han Dynasty, all the following dynasties forbade the illegal minting of money with severe criminal penalties and the coinage of money was under the exclusive control of the central government. When the empire of the Qin came into being, the concept of centralized control of the finance was already in the formative stage. Thinkers like Han Fei maintained that the finance "should be controlled by the lord of men and should not be in any way controlled by the ministers." In terms of the minting of coins, this right should never be transferred to the lower level, otherwise it would mean the loss of "virtue" and "profit." The government of the Western Han Dynasty carried on such a monetary policy. During the 60–70 years after the founding of the empire, with the carrying out of a laissez-faire policy (except that Liu Bang, Emperor Gaozu, restrained the development of commerce) to recuperate and build up the economy, the coins in circulation were "more than ever before and much lighter," leading to the rocketing prices of commodities, thus threatening the development of the economy. In the early years of the Western Han Dynasty, not only were there many copper coins minted by the government but there was also much remolding of different types of coins. Occasionally, the minting of coins was an ad hoc policy for certain periods, for example, to restrain the development of commerce or to devalue the money in circulation to relieve the government's difficulties. That was most manifest during the reign of Emperor Wu, because at that time the ruler was starting to implement the policy of strengthening the unification of the country; meanwhile, the emperor was deeply troubled by the lack of financial resources. At that time, the government was faced with the difficult task of maintaining a good relationship with neighboring countries, developing domestic economy and meeting the various demands of financial expenditure. Though such measures as increasing tax, monopolized operation and the newly levied tax on businessmen were taken, the massive financial expenditure was beyond the means of the government, and the development of commodity economy was suppressed. At the time, there were *sanzhu* coin, *banliang* coin, *sanfen* coin, *wuzhu* coin, *guanchize* coin, etc. Under the influence of market forces, these coins gradually got unified and the *wuzhu* coins became the dominant one. As to the minting and issuing of currency, there were nine trials of strength between the central government and the local despots between 193 B.C. and 113 B.C., after which Emperor Wu ordered the abolishing of different types of copper coins, to the exclusion of *wuzhu coins*, which were in circulation in the whole country, thus entering the stage of a highly centralized monopoly of the minting and issuing of currency. According to "Treatise on Food and Money" in *The Book of Han*, from 118 B.C. to 1–5 A.D., the coins minted amounted to 280 trillion. In spite of this, other forms of currency, such as cloth, silk and millet, were also used as the medium of exchange. In particular, during the Warring States Period, these kinds of currency even took the place of cooper coins. In the Eastern Han Dynasty, silk even fulfilled the function of copper currency.

Meanwhile, usury had become an important trade. In the city of Chang'an, there were places exclusively for such practice, which, for the most part, were privately done or between the government and the private businesses. There were no private fiduciary institutions or any official standards of interests. In the Han Dynasty, the so-called debit and credit were in fact a kind of relief. Emperor Wu granted loans to those who couldn't make a living, such as widows, widowers, the handicapped and the sick. At one time, Emperor Yuan also announced that all the debts of the poor families in the country should be written off. Wang Mang, founder of the Xin Dynasty, "ordered his officials to buy in at a lower price and sell at a higher price. The monthly interest for the loan to the common people was 3%."[2] "For those who wanted to sacrifice or conduct funereal but couldn't afford it, the officials would lend them the taxes collected from commercial organizations and handicraftsmen. Within ten days of the sacrifice and three months of the funeral, the lending would be interest-free." For those people who could not run any business, the government would grant them loans. "After deducting the original capital, the interest would be based on the revenue from the business, the maximum of which would be 10%."[3] Successive dynasties would follow such practice, which gradually became a unique feature of Chinese monetary and

---

[2]Biography of Wang Mang in *The Book of Han*.
[3]Treatise on Food and Money in *The Book of Han*.

financial history. About the issue of usury, there were supporters like Sima Qian and opponents such as Chao Cuo, whose viewpoints were contradictory and insights divergent.

1. The currency and credit theory at the beginning of the Western Han Dynasty

1.1. *Jia Yi's theory about the monopoly of the right of mintage*

Born in Luoyang, Henan Province, Jia Yi (200–168 B.C.) was an outstanding statesman, thinker and literary man of the Han Dynasty. Lu Xun spoke highly of him: "He allowed the future generations, and generations after generations to benefit from his contributions" (*A Sketchy History of the Literature of Han Dynasty*). Jia Yi made significant contributions to and exerted enormous influence on the continuation and development of traditional Chinese culture and thought. At age 22, he served as a scholar of the Classics and the Grand Master of the Palace during the reign of Emperor Wen, and wrote his essay "Disquisition Finding Fault with Qin Dynasty." In the next year, he advocated strongly the revolutionary changes of the laws of the Qin Dynasty to better fulfill the needs of the Han government, and the constitution of system and confirmation of official positions. He also urged to promote the rite and music system, to consolidate the monarchical power and to send the vassals to govern the counties. These proposals met with jealousy, objections and slander from the senior members of the government, such as Zhou Bo, Guan Ying, Zhang Xiangru and Feng Jing. Jia Yi was then demoted to Grand Tutor to the prince of Changsha. At age 28, he was appointed to be the Grand Tutor to Prince Huai of Liang, the younger son of Emperor Wen. During this period, Jia Yi submitted memorials to the throne to elaborate on political affairs quite often and wrote his *Essay on Public Security*. At age 33, because Prince Huai of Lian died after falling off a horse, Jia Yi blamed himself for neglect of duty and died of sorrow a little more than one year later. His essay "Disquisition Finding Fault with Qin Dynasty" enjoyed great popularity and is read even today. His writings were compiled in *Collections of Jia Yi's Writings*.

Jia Yi advocated the combination of Confucianism and Legalism and the integration of virtue and punishment in the government of a country.

He described the concept of governing a state with a metaphor, "To rule with benevolence, righteousness and generosity is like to rule with a sharp knife; to rule with authority, power and laws is like to rule with an axe." On carrying out policies, he maintained that "people of virtue do politics," and claimed that "the whole country cannot be run by one family but rather by people of virtue," and "only people of virtue can run it." In terms of economic theory, he carried on the thought of Legalism and urged the government to crack down on strange and valueless businesses, as well as merchants and idle fellows. He proposed to "urge the citizens to return to farming, and to perform their duties." He maintained that the government should run the business, control the market and restrict the expansion of industry and commerce. In conclusion, on the failure of the Qin Dynasty, he criticized that they "abandoned the Confucianism but built private power, burned the official documents and practiced harsh set of punishment, and pursued cunning strategies and abused power but dismissed benevolence and righteousness." The Han government concluded that one among the lessons learned from the failure of the Qin's political system is that it "changed the emperor's ruling system" and "abandoned the feudal system of government," "with few holders of the same family name," after which the dynasty failed because of its solitude and helplessness. So the Han government "divided its lands" and made generous offers to Liu's family, and thus the centralized authority of government was changed into decentralization. To prohibit the Qin's harsh policies, guided by the thought of Huang Di and Lao Tze, the Han government advocated recuperating and rebuilding of the nation as well as the freedom for the citizen's activities in terms of its economic policies. As to the thought and policy on currency, the Han government changed the centralized official mintage to free mintage, and reformed the Qin's "weight as it reads" policy to a devaluation policy. Liu Bang, the Gaozu emperor of the Han Dynasty, was the first to promote the policy of free mintage by citizens, namely, "to demand citizens to mint light-weighted coins"; however, under this policy, coins of poor quality overflowed, opportunistic investments and deliberate stockpile for exorbitant profits flooded, and currency value and commodity price fluctuated, resulting in the unreasonable and ceaseless price inflation and a written record of "ten thousand coppers for only fifty kilograms of rice, and fifty kilograms of gold for only a horse."

In 199 B.C., the eighth year of the reign of Emperor Liu Bang, the government decreed a ban on private mintage to prohibit citizen from minting secretly; at the same time, it issued a decree of restraining commerce, aiming its spear at rich merchants. However, this policy could only be carried out in 15 counties within the direct control of Liu Bang's government. For the rest, more than 30 counties in the hands of different vassals, they were beyond the decree's grasp; since these counties had been under the control of Liu Bang's relatives, these vassals or people that lived on rents of the offered lands started their own groups of officers to manage food and salt trades so as to gain profits from demanding taxes. Liu Bang relied on these vassals as his arms and legs, thus he could only put up with their departments. The ban he decreed was just a piece of paper and existed in name only. In July of 186 B.C., the government started the mintage of coins of 25g (eight *zhu*), and it seemed that the government would decree a ban on private mintage. During the period of confrontation with the vassals and groups that had rendered outstanding services to the former government, the government consolidated its centralized economic policy through producing heavier copper coins. In 192 B.C., the minister reported the crimes of prosecutors and three chief executives, among whom someone had been accused of "private mintage of counterfeit money." Thus, we know that "private mintage" was forbidden at the time. Liu Heng, Emperor Wen of the Han Dynasty, was weak and was forced to yield to the vassals and groups who had rendered great services to the government. In May of 175 B.C., the government abandoned "ban on private mintage"; instead they reformed copper coins of 25g (eight *zhu*) and it became lighter (four *zhu*). Meanwhile, they revived the policy of "allowing citizens to mint freely," which corresponded to the policy of recuperating and rebuilding. On economic policy, Liu Heng's government yielded to the vassals and bestowed the right to mint on close vassals and favorite officers. Liu Bi, Prince Wu and the nephew of Liu Bang, minted money in Tongshan of Yuzhang County and called for numerous fugitives to take part in the activity. Thus, work force and financial resources converged to Liu Bi's department, which bred the intention to separate the country and the relatively illegal activities. Moreover, this drew widespread criticism from opponents, who argued from their different points of views and for their own profits; thus, it brought up the first argument about the right of mintage in Chinese history.

In his memorial to the throne about the minting of currency, Jia Yi put forward his viewpoint of government monopoly of the materials for minting currency and control of the issuance of currency. He was of the opinion of the need for a benevolent government and in favor of the economic thought of considering the degree of seriousness of things, in the hope of bringing a compromise between the rule of benevolence and the rule of force, the ritual and the law, as well as moral activities and profiteering activities. Fiercely attacking the thought of non-action, he suggested quite a number of countermeasures to deal with the problems of following the beaten track and doing nothing. According to this understanding, in economic activities, engaging in trade, minting currency and mining for copper led to the loss of labor force and the deterioration of the economy. "It is thirty years since the founding of the Han Empire, but the people are living a miserable life, without much to support themselves. Isn't the majesty aware of this? In the years of less-harvest, the rich were not able to grant loans because they were also in need, while the poor were starving. When there was famine, now and then would be heard the practice of selling official posts for a consideration, and selling one's own child to make a living ... It was indeed quite ridiculous that people in the country would be without any storage of the necessities for life." On the one hand, the nouveau riche and the corrupt officials colluded in doing evil things and raced to be extravagant and wasteful, disturbing social security and the rule of law. On the other hand, the stronger of the separatist regimes in local areas would tend to rebel soon. According to Jia Yi, the government should employ both gentle and stern measures and abolish punishment with punishment. There were four disadvantages to the private minting of currency:

The first disadvantage was the possibility of enticing the people to commit crimes. Since the government allowed the people to hire staff and lease mines to smelt copper for the minting of currency, according to Jia Yi, it would be futile to brand the face of criminals if offenders acted against the law requiring them to use only copper and tin and instead adulterated with the addition of lead and iron because "branding the face would never prevent offenders from committing their crimes because of the substantial profit gained." The purpose of private minting was the profit, but without fake adulteration it was impossible to make profits. The adulteration might not be too much, but the profits were huge. The common people minted coins privately, and there were hundreds of offenders even in one county. With those tortured by officials and those suspects at large counted together, there were indeed too many to count. That was the result of the local authorities, who "set up a most enticing trap to lure the common people."

The second disadvantage was the damage to the authority of the government decrees, which would threaten the stability of the centralized government. The private minting would encourage other unlawful activities and cause damage to the country. According to Jia Yi, in the days when private minting was prohibited, there had been too many common people committing capital offenses to be dealt with by the government. Now, with private minting allowed by the government, those offenders whose faces should be branded were equally too numerous to deal with. "Though the punishment of branding offender' face was imposed on a daily basis, it was futile to stop such crimes." Consequently, it would be even harder to maintain the proper functioning of government decrees. On the contrary, those law-abiding people would be enticed to do the wrong things, the prudent people would be punished by law for their indiscreet actions and the enforcement of the law would be very much improper. Under such circumstances, how could the laws and regulations of the country be held in esteem? The government felt deeply concerned about this situation, and officials of all ranks maintained that such things should be strictly prohibited. If the government couldn't take effective measures, the damage caused would be even more severe. "Now with a prohibition on the private minting of currency, money would surely increase in value, leading to more profits in the illegal minting, which would result in the large scale burgeoning of illegal coinage of currency. Even with capital punishment, the government would be able to put an end to this." "With such regulations in effect, what could your majesty rely on?" How could the government consolidate its rule of the country?

These two points were a political analysis of the damage of private minting of currency, which was neither good for the common people's living nor advantageous to the stability of the central government, thus departing considerably from the policy of recuperation.

The third disadvantage was that "the lawful currency would stand firm" and "the circulation of currency would be in a mess." According to Jia Yi, "the currency common people used varied from county to county. Some places used light ones while other places used heavy ones. With no lawfully accepted money in circulation, the officials would hasten to standardize the criteria, which was labor-consuming and beyond their power. If they don't do anything, the market places would be filled with different kinds of currency, resulting in a messy state of affairs. Without the proper way of dealing with such chaotic situation, no place could be governed harmoniously!" This laid the foundation for the minting and circulating of wuzhu coins during the reign of Emperor Wu of the Han Dynasty.

The fourth disadvantage was that with common people abandoning farming to mint currency, agricultural activities were also interrupted and the social atmosphere became increasingly degenerate. With much profit from the private minting, common people would give up their agricultural practice to engage in copper smelting and currency minting, which was naturally harmful to the economic recovery and development of the country.

These latter two points were the economic disadvantages of private minting of currency. With the market in disorder, the economic exchange between different areas and the recovery of agriculture would be hindered, which, in turn, would endanger the unification of the country and the development of the national economy, thus fostering the tendency of segregation and threatening the stability of the central government and the lasting peace of the nation.

On the idea of the national monopoly of minting, according to Jia Yi, it would never be practical to rely solely on the government's authority to prohibit the private minting of currency. It was essential to locate the source of the problem. Naturally, the sources of minting currency were the copper and copper mines involved in the process. Once common people were in possession of the copper, a basic material for the minting of currency, it would be very difficult for the government to put an end to the private minting, which was a source of much trouble. On the contrary, if the government carried out a copper prohibition policy in the country, and "let no copper circulate in the nation," then "all the calamities would be dispensed with, and seven blessings would ensue." "What are the seven blessings?" With the government controlling the copper of the country, common people wouldn't be able to mint money privately, and thus would not be able to turn to crime. That was the first blessing. Second, with less privately minted money in circulation, there would be less counterfeit currency in the market, and common people wouldn't need to pay much attention to authenticity of the currency. Third, those who used to smelt copper and mint money privately would take up agricultural work again. Fourth, after the country took control of the copper, the ruler could take advantage of the deposit to adjust the circulation of money in the market, and thus the prices of the products would become stable. Fifth, the government could use the copper to make weapons or grant awards to the barons or ministers according to their ranks. Sixth, the government could make use of the monetary means to adjust and control the transactions and demand and supply in the market for the purpose of high earnings for the government and low income for the businessmen. Seventh, after controlling the copper, the government could compete with Xiongnu, a confederation of nomadic peoples, in the field of military and national strength, in the hope of getting the support of the common people. As a natural result, the Xiongnu Empire would collapse without even a fight, and the people under their rule would surely come over and pledge allegiance to the central government.

In the section on current affairs in the chapter on minting currency in *The New Writings*, Jia Yi rebuked the illegal activities: "The law has stipulated that people in our country have the right to mint money and those who dare to adulterate lead or iron to make the money impure would be tattooed on the faces. But as far as the minting was concerned, the only way to make profit was to mingle lead, iron, or other impure substances during the process. On the other hand, such attempts were usually easily finished with much profit." In consequence, common people would give up their agricultural endeavor to mint money, and the number of people committing the crime of adulteration and being punished with tattoos on the faces would increase daily. The common people would look down upon each other. With these three illegal activities in vogue, people began to take up copper mining and smelting and casting money privately. "In consequence to the mounting number of counterfeit money, the authenticate currency became less and less. The kind people would be frightened by such practice and would in turn do evil things, thus end up in jail. With the punishment of face-tattooing accumulating, there were almost daily conflicts between government officials and common people. That was rather detestable both in the short term and in the long term. So how can we deal with that?" The so-called law of bad money driving out good in contemporary society was expressed explicitly by Jia Yi. His thought, originating from the monetary and economic life of over 2,000 years ago, was against the private minting of currencies. That was indeed the outward manifestation of ancient Chinese sages.

With his great political ambition and unique strategic vision, Jia Yi, a wizard of the landlord intellectuals, wrote the first monetary thesis in China, or possibly the world. Under the influence of Guanzi's theory on the degree of seriousness of things, he grasped keenly the issue of the national monopoly over the minting of currency, which was closely related to money circulation and national policy. Standing at the forefront of his time, he played an eminent role with his outstanding talents. First of all, he realized the necessity for currency nationalization. While the country was carrying out a policy of strong central government and weak local government, combining the practice of ceding territory and increasing the territory of some vassal states, he put forward the suggestion that it was harmful to abolish the decree on the prohibition of private minting of currency, for the purpose of a central control of the minting, which, in turn, would sustain and strengthen the economic foundation of the central government and weaken the financial resources of the local separatist forces of some regions. At that time, the greatest beneficiaries were the vassal states, bureaucracies and the wealthy traders. Among the representatives was Liu Bi, the Prince of Wu, whose fief included three commanderies and 53 cities, and who had enjoyed the privilege of minting money the longest time, thus becoming the most powerful in the country. Making good use of the copper mountain in the province of Yuzhang, he minted money and accumulated wealth to strengthen his troops and amass food and fodder, becoming almost as rich as a king. In his declaration to the vassals, he claimed that "my wealth can be found in every corner of the country, not necessarily in the state of Wu. Therefore, even though the dukes spent money like water, there was no need to worry about its exhaustion." That was not only a display of wealth but also a kind of instigation, which, consequently, led to the outburst of the Rebellion of the Seven States. Outwardly, Jia Yi's suggestion was to take a drastic measure to appease the current situation, but in fact he was planning a destructive blow to the separatist regime. Second, he was well aware of the subjectivity of the currency circulation. From his unwillingness to employ administrative means to abolish the private minting of money, it was clear that he was very conscious that currency circulation was not to be dictated by the king or the decree of the government. It was true that at that time, the practice of forbidding private minting by controlling copper was equally difficult, but that was indeed an insight into him. The economic way of solving such a problem was rather remarkable and well worth a second look. Third, he was the first to put forward the notion of flat money. For the proper circulation of currency, the prerequisite was that the country should mint its currency according to national standard of form, purity and weight. The private minting of currency, on the contrary, would adulterate for profit and lower the standard, leading to currency disorder and becoming a man-made obstacle for the exchange of commodities. In addition, he also examined the cost of coinage and considered the difference in the cost of private and official coinage a reason for the abolition of private casting. As an insight of over 2,000 years ago, it was quite remarkable and profound indeed, and it served as a theoretical forerunner for the emergence of *Wuzhu* coins during the reign of Emperor Wu of the Han Dynasty. Fourth, he was the first to extend the notion of the degree of seriousness of things, especially that of monetary issues, to the sphere of circulation of the commodities and currency, and thus became known as the originator of the notion in the Han Dynasty. The fourth point of his "Seven Blessings" suggested that the government could adjust the price of commodities by way of collecting or dispersing currency. That is, the government could increase or decrease the supply of currency to change the purchasing power and adjust the prices of commodities, for the purpose of stabilizing the market and cracking down on those ill-intentioned businessmen and merchants. That would increase state revenue and strengthen the nation, so that the Hun power would be under control.

From this, we can see that Jia Yi was a forerunner in the employment of the theory of the degree of seriousness of things of *Guanzi*.

Meanwhile, Jia Shan, a native of Yingchuan, also shared Jia Yi's opinion that the government should monopolize the minting of currency. When Emperor Wen of the Han Dynasty abolished the decree on the prohibition of private minting, Jia Shan said, "Money, though useless, could be used to exchange fortunes. Fortunes, on the other hand, should be handled by the king. Letting common people coin money was like sharing the control of fortunes with the king, which would never last long." What he said had two meanings. First of all, money was essentially something useless, but could be used to exchange fortunes. That is to say, currency had its exchange value, but didn't have any use value, so it wasn't a commodity. The rulers' monopoly of the right to mint and issue money was identical to their control of the national wealth to increase the fiscal revenue. The usefulness of money lay in the fact that it stood for wealth and the king used money to collect the wealth of the nation. That was the nominalistic view on money. Second, he emphasized the state monopoly of the minting of currency, considering it essential to the continuity and stability of the central government. As was pointed out by Karl Marx, "Currency empowers all power." After the establishment of a monetary economy, it became an irresistible force with the power to break away from all restrictions. In the early stage of a monetary economy, this force seems most formidable. As a result, coinage of currency must be under the firm control of the government, and the rulers should keep the financial power in hand. There was no possibility of surrendering the power to others, which would be harmful to the country. Friedrich Engels pointed out in *Outlines of a Critique of Political Economy,* "the most important article — money — requires a monopoly most of all."[4] Similarly, with the development of China's monetary economy in the Warring States Period and the Qin and Han Dynasties, and the political unification in the country, the early sages were already aware of the vital importance of the standardizing of the currency in a unified country. According to Jia Shan, abolishing the prohibition and allowing the private minting of currency were equivalent to letting the king and the common

---

[4]*Complete Works of Karl Marx and Friedrich Engels,* vol. 1, p. 623.

people share the ruling of a country, which should never last long, for it was most dangerous and should be dealt with as soon as possible. This kind of thought was somewhat similar to that of Han Fei, who stated that "All their doings as such should be based on the initiative of the lord of men and should not be started by the ministers at their pleasure." According to Han Fei, there were five cases under which the ministers should not deceive the king, and one of them was that "when they control public resources and revenues, the king loses his advantages." Should the minting of currency be controlled by people other than the ruler, the king would lose even more of his "advantages." If the central government wanted to strengthen the centralization of power, the minting of currency should only be under the control of the central government. Otherwise, it would be like the case where "supposing the tiger casts aside its claws and fangs and lets the dog use them, the tiger would in turn be subjected by the dog." The idea of both Jia Shan and Jia Yi could be both traced back to Han Fei's theory of the monopoly of power.

Emperor Wen of the Han Dynasty, however, didn't act on their advice. What the emperor embraced was the notion of "not taking advantage for oneself" and "the world is for all," which was embellished with Huang–Lao thought. As a matter of fact, Emperor Wen expanded the power of the local separatist regimes and limited that of the monarch. Located in the southeastern part of the country, the state of Wu covered three commanderies and 53 cities. Relying on the copper-rich mountain in Zhang commandery (called Danyang commandery), for thirty years Liu Bi's men minted money, accumulated wealth, produced weaponry, hoarded food and fodder and recruited the outlaws from around the country. Later, Emperor Wen granted the copper-rich mountain in Yandao (now Xingyang of Sichuan Province) to his minion Deng Tong as a reward, which put the court in as dangerous a situation as "sleeping on a pile of wood beneath which was an approaching fire drawing near." The money minted by the people of Liu Bi, the Prince of Wu, and Deng Tong was circulating throughout the country, making Deng Tong richer than the average vassal. The response of Emperor Wen, on the contrary, was rather lacking. He established the legal currency system and produced standardized money to check the weight of the money from private minting. He arranged for the local officials to check up on the minted money in circulation and carried out a tight monetary policy.[5] As the remedy to the aforementioned problems, these measures were not only ineffective but also conducive to the growth of the local separatist regimes, stirring up their ambition and conviction about their ability to rebel against the monarch. Deng Tong was not removed from his official position until Emperor Jing ascended the throne. In 154 B.C., with the aim of ridding the king of the evil ministers around him, the Rebellion of the Seven States broke out, involving Liu Bi, Prince of Wu, Liu Wu, Prince of Chu, Liu Sui, Prince of Zha, Liu Xiongqu, Prince of Jiaodong, Liu Yin, Prince of Jiaoxi, Liu Piguang, Prince of Jinan, and Liu Xian, Prince of Zichuan. After suppressing the rebellion, Emperor Jing enacted a law prohibiting the circulation of privately minted money and fake gold and the private minting of currency, bringing about a complete change of Emperor Wen's laissez-faire policy. He nationalized the right to mint money, which used to be forsaken, and prohibited strictly the private minting of currency. That practice was carried on without any change until the modern times. From this, we can also see that the profound ideas of Jia Yi and Jia Shan were beyond reproach of common people. Emperor Wu of the Han Dynasty put their ideas into practice and made important theoretical preparations for the standardization of the minted currency.

1.2. Chao Cuo on "devaluing gold and jades" and "interest of 100%"

Chao Cuo (200–154 B.C.), a native of Yingchuan, was an outstanding political theorist and a distinguished lecturer of *Book of Documents* in the early years of the Western Han Dynasty. He was a renowned currency nominalist. The emergence of Chinese nominalism was a little bit more than 100 years after Aristotle (384–322 B.C.) in ancient Greece, but it was more profound and clearer than the philosophy of Aristotle. On the contrary, it was 300 to 400 years earlier than that of ancient Rome.

In 168 B.C., in his famous article "Suggestion on Expensive Millet," Chao Cuo developed the notion of "stressing on agriculture and restraining

---

[5]Zhang Nan, *A Historical Analysis of the Currency in the Qin and Han Dynasties*, Guangxi People's Publishing House, 1991, pp. 33–35.

commerce" and "cherishing the grain while devaluing treasure," because he thought that pearl, jade, gold and silver were not all currency, but currency must be gold and silver. The so-called "cherishing the grain while devaluing treasure" meant that a wise king should lay emphasis on grain production and look down upon treasures, which were neither edible when hungry nor wearable in times of cold. It was because of the king's employment of the treasures that they were valued by the common people. This seemed to negate the use value of the treasures, considering them of no value for use and not able to satisfy people's need. In fact, his original meaning was that treasures were not the basic life necessities, unlike millets or cottons, which could protect the people from hunger and cold. So they were rather useless. Thus, we can see that his criteria for the usefulness of things lay in such small spheres as fighting against cold and hunger. The so-called "useless things" of Jia Shan, and the things that were mentioned in the chapter of "The Savings Policy of the State" of *Guanzi* in the following way, "People cannot keep themselves warm by simply holding them in the hands; nor can they quench their hunger by eating them," were all restricted by such a narrow sense of description.

In today's words, since pearl, jade, gold and silver were useless, the reason for people's valuing them was the king's employment of these things. Since their value derived from the king and wasn't related to their own use or use value, if the king stopped employing them, they would become valueless. The king's treasuring of these things seemed to be determined by his personal taste instead of their own value. Just as pointed out by Karl Marx, "Gold and silver are acceptable by law only because they are acceptable in practice .... Law is only the official recognition of fact."[6]

The root for this kind of thought was that the core of Chao Cuo's economic thought was "emphasizing agriculture and treasuring grains." He laid special emphasis on the unique position and significant role of agriculture in the maintenance and strengthening of the feudal regime. Of fundamental importance to the ruling of a country, grain production was of the paramount value. The reason was that "it was human nature that one would become hungry without eating and become cold without adequate clothing."

---

[6]*Complete Works of Karl Marx and Friedrich Engels*, vol. 4, p. 124.

"Tortured by hunger and cold, people would never care much about shame." "When people became poor, they would do evil and wicked things." In these cases, the loving mother couldn't take good care of her child and the king couldn't protect his people. With the country and all the families under the threat of cold and hunger, neither common family nor the whole country could survive any longer. On the contrary, instead of planting and weaving in person, those enlightened kings would give common people the chance to "become rich" and develop agriculture, for the purpose of ensuring the supply of grain and cotton, and thus the common people would get rid of cold and hunger. Contrarily, people would commit all sorts of crimes even if there were high walls and deep moats and strict laws. Only when "common people were fairly settled in farming and sericulture" would they have ample food and clothing, their minds become restful and the political power become consolidated. No matter what his subjective thinking was, we can see that was a reflection of the agriculture-oriented thought in a society of mostly natural economy, and it was the representative idea of the thought of the Physiocrats in the Western Han Dynasty of China.

Chao Cuo also analyzed the reason why people treasured pearl, jade, gold and silver. In his opinion, it was mainly because they were, though taking up little space, of high value, easy to preserve and carry about. In possession of them, the owners could travel around the world without the anxiety of cold and hunger. Therefore, it was obvious that Chao Cuo was well aware of the property of these things as the ideal candidate for currency.

Chao Cuo was conscious of the universal equivalent property of currency. Currency in hand was equivalent to possessing any other commodity. Consequently, with pearl, jade, gold or silver, one could travel around the country without the need to worry about cold and hunger. With the temptation of currency, ministers would be enticed into betraying their king. In today's words, currency has the same use value to all the commodity owners. In addition, he set the general purpose use value of currency against the specific purpose use value, and made a contrast between the special commodity, which was used as universal equivalent, and all other commodities, arriving at biased, simplistic and partial conclusions.

He overemphasized the negative influence of currency, but did not fully affirm its positive role. As a result, his understanding of the role of currency was one-sided. He believed that money would lead to disorder in the relations between the king and his ministers, result in common people becoming homeless and profit seeking. With much labor force in exile, the social order would become restless, and common people would never live in peace. In short, from the economic base to the superstructure, from common people to the king and the ministers, money would make all people "become profit-oriented like water flowing down, without any exception." That was dangerous indeed. So the only way out was "cherishing the grain while devaluing treasure," which would "persuade the farmers to return to the most basic agricultural activities." In this way, the vagrant people would take up farming again and settle down. From this we can see that in the early years of the Western Han Dynasty, commodity economy had occupied an important and unneglectable position in the socio-economic life. Unwilling to remain out of the limelight, it was challenging the natural economy. Both Chao Cuo and Sima Qian were aware of this development. The difference was that Sima Qian, the historian, gave a true account of the fact, while Chao Cuo, a politician, starting from the need to maintain the rule of the landlord class, made every effort possible to vilify and weaken the threat and destruction of monetary economy to natural economy. As the basis for regulation formation, the theoretical position of Chao Cuo was meaningful, though historically it was rather conservative an understanding.

Under natural economic conditions, the economic bases of small-scale producers and cultivators were very fragile. Because of the shortage of funds and the limited means of production and labor forces, the maintenance or loss of the means of production on the part of small producers depends on 1,000 contingencies, and every one of these contingencies or losses signifies impoverishment and becomes a crevice into which a parasitic usurer may creep. The mere death of his cow may render the small peasant incapable of renewing his reproduction on its former scale. He then falls into the clutches of the usurer, and once in the usurer's power he can never extricate himself. According to the study of Meng Wentong, in the Western Han Dynasty, the monetary taxes were much heavier than farm rents.[7] For the large number of small farmers, it was difficult to raise

---

[7]Meng Wentong, *A Screening of Ancient History*, Bashu Publishing House, 1999, p. 305.

money to pay taxes. In cases of natural disasters or when they had no ready money, the farmers would only turn to usury. Falling into the hands of usurers, it was inevitable that "they had to sell farms and even children," and finally lived in exile. This kind of environment was highly conducive to the emergence of usury, thus giving birth to a pack of professional usurers and various wealthy non-professionals, some of whom were officials at all levels. As a visionary, aggressive and ambitious politician of the landlord class, Chao Cuo, based on the long-term interest of his class, felt uneasy about the rapid development of commercial capital and moneylender's capital. "Nowadays though the law belittles merchants, merchants have become wealthy; though the law esteems farmers, farmers have become poor." Judged from an agriculture-oriented approach, that was something to be exposed and reprimanded.

He analyzed the socio-economic reasons for which famers fell victim to the usury and became helpless. According to Chao Cuo, the first reason was that with limited income, farmers were overburdened. A peasant family of five members with 100 acres of land would have a yearly harvest of 100 *dan*. As was recorded in "Treatise on Food and Money" in the *Book of Han*, a *dan* of grain was equivalent to the amount of food consumed by one peasant in 20 days. So 100 *dan* was enough for the consumption of 5.5 persons in a year. Coupled with other consumptions like welcoming visitors and seeing them off, offering sacrifices to the deceased, visiting the sick, supporting the old and raising the young, there could hardly be any balance of the grain, and in the worst cases the farmers would be burdened with debt. The second reason was the heavy taxes. Every year farmers had to cut down firewood and go on public errands for government officials. In addition, local authorities would impose excessive taxation under various pretexts, without any fixed patterns, so nobody was able to plan ahead to make arrangements. The third reason was the flood and drought disasters. At that time, farmers relied heavily on the weather for a good harvest, so they all longed for favorable agricultural conditions. Therefore, once it was time for them to pay the taxes, they had to sell at half prices if they had anything for sale. If they didn't have things for sale, they had to borrow money at "double interest rates." Consequently, things like selling one's fields, houses and even children to pay off debts became frequent occurrences. As a matter of fact, the root for the first and the third reasons was the low productivity at the time, which made it difficult for the farmers to fend off any unexpected assaults, whether from a capital perspective or from a technical perspective. The root for the second reason, on the contrary, was the brutal exploitation of the government. According to Chao Cuo, the existing laws despised businessmen and esteemed farmers, but businessmen were already rich and farmers were poor. What the world valued was just what the king despised, and what the government officials looked down upon was what the existing law esteemed. Chao Cuo thus came to the conclusion that stressing agriculture and valuing grains meant not only a political blow to the local separatist regime but also the implementation of emphasizing agriculture and suppressing commerce in the field of economy. Because of this, the vassals of the country, with Liu Bi, the Prince of Wu, as the representative, became his sworn enemies, and were more than happy to have him killed. Chao Cuo commented realistically and critically on the socio-economic phenomena of the time, though his procedures and means of doing this need further discussion.

The interest rate of usury in ancient China was much higher than those of foreign countries. So it was very difficult for small producers to shake off the bonds of usury once they were in debt. Chao Cuo described accurately how the capital of usury ruthlessly exploited the farmers, how they were forced to go into exile and ended with broken families and dead family members. *The Nine Chapters on the Mathematical Art*, a world famous mathematic masterpiece written in the Han Dynasty, also covered the interest rate of usury, which was a yearly interest of 36%, roughly 3–6 times the prevalent interest rate of the time and higher than the highest legal Roman interest rate (the prevailing interest rate of the time was 6%, 8% when the money was tight and 12% in times of much risk). This is not only about the author's prolonged anxieties over the consolidation of the newly born agriculture-oriented imperial regime of the Liu family but also a ruthless whipping of the exploitation by loan sharks.

2. The monetary and credit theory of Sima Qian

Courtesy name Zichang, Sima Qian (145 or 135 B.C.–?), a native of Xiayang, was the son of Sima Tan, the grand historian of the Western Han

Dynasty. In 108 B.C., he assumed his father's position. In 104 B.C., he was in charge of the reform of the calendar and started writing *Records of the Grand Historian*. In 99 B.C., he offended Emperor Wu because of his defense of Li Ling, who was defeated and taken captive. For finishing his *Records of the Grand Historian*, "he endured extreme penalty without any resentment." In 96 B.C., on his release from prison, he became head of the secretariat, and "lived with forbearance and in neglect of all the hardships." In about 92 B.C., he finished the writing of his masterpiece *Records of the Grand Historian*.

In the field of economic thought, he was able to "expound his own opinions." With his distinctive opinions, he was not only in sharp contrast with the theory on the Degree of Seriousness of Various Issues but also unique in ancient China. His economic thought was mainly reflected in his *Equalization, Biographies of Usurers* and in his random comments on some of the historical figures and events. It is very likely that his economic thought is seen as the representative of liberalist forces and opponents of the theory on the Degree of Seriousness of Various Issues. As a matter of fact, in the beginning of the Han Dynasty, the method of ruling the country was a combination of kingcraft and force. As was pointed out in an imperial edict in the second part of Annals of Emperor Gaozu in *The Book of Han*, "It was said that King Wen of Zhou dynasty was the most outstanding in terms of the ruling with kingcraft, and the Duke Huan of Qi state was the top one in terms of ruling with force. Both of them got the help of the sages to become renowned rulers." After six generations, his successor to the throne, Emperor Xuan of Han, also adhered to this creed, which was manifest in his denouncement of the crown prince, later Emperor Yuan of Han. "Since the beginning of our Han Dynasty, our ruling has been a combination of kingcraft and force. Why did you rely only on virtues? Are you planning to carry out the policy of the Zhou Dynasty? Besides, the scholars of shallow learning of Confucianism were not up to date in their thinking, admiring everything ancient and belittling present-day ways of doing things, which would lead to a confusion of concept and entity. Without a clear understanding of what is most essential, how could such a person be counted on?" The combination of kingcraft and force was a tradition adhered to by the founding rulers of the Western Han Dynasty, though their manners and emphasis of doing this varied in accordance with the time. For this reason, during the reign of Emperor Gaozu of Han, businessmen were suppressed and humiliated, while during the reign of Emperor Wu, they were promoted. These different ways were for the same effect, for the control of the power of the merchants. That is, by using the wisdom and financial resources of the merchants, it was intended to control the field of circulation. Under such a historical environment, as the historiographer in the time of Emperor Wu, Sima Qian held an economic outlook like that of Guanzi, considering the Theory on the Degree of Seriousness of Various Issues the best economic policy, while at the same time imposing no restrictions on common people's profit-making activities. He wrote biographies for those businessmen and deemed them vassal-like, though they held no official titles. In his opinion, with ample supply of goods and clothing, those merchants should be well informed about etiquette. The theoretical basis of his economic view was the "cause" as mentioned by Lao Tze and Zhuangzi, which required the satisfaction of men's interests in profits. That was determined by human nature. The Theory on the Degree of Seriousness of Various Issues followed human nature and specified measures, methods and policies for the accumulation of wealth into the hands of the king, while at the same time restricting the development of local powers and wealthy people. Sima Qian's idea that no restriction should be imposed on private profit-making activities, on the contrary, was different from the view expressed in Guanzi. Therefore, we might put it in the following way: *Guanzi* crystallized the inaction theory of Lao Tze and Zhuangzi economically and Han Fei did that politically. For those who sought profit and feared harm, the ruler should encourage the pursuit of profit and punish the fear of harm, so that they could fight for the king. That was the way of following nature and the way of inaction, the purpose of which was to maintain the autocracy of the Qin and Han Dynasties.

Moreover, Jia Yi carried on the Theory on the Degree of Seriousness of Various Issues of *Guanzi*, and Chao Cuo's opinion was the same as the legalist thought of Han Fei. In his support of the Theory on the Degree of Seriousness, Jia Yi pointed out, "*Guanzi* said, 'etiquette, righteousness, uprightness, and the sense of honor were the four reins of a country. If the four reins are not stretched open correctly, the state will be ruined.' Should *Guanzi* be an ignorant person, there was nothing to say about it. But if he had the slightest pretention to the governing of a country, he should be bitterly disappointed. The Qin Dynasty abandoned the four reins and the relations between the monarch and the ministers were chaotic. As a result, family members were not in harmony, evil people rebelled everywhere, and common people were also rising against the ruling classes." So his idea was that equal emphasis should be laid on etiquette, righteousness, uprightness and the sense of honor, on the one hand, and the Theory on the Degree of Seriousness of things, on the other hand. The position, quotations and conclusions of Sima Qian were almost the same as that of Jia Yi. The only difference between the two was in the policy related to merchants. Jia Yi's suppression of commerce did not interfere with the national economy, and the purpose was to control the whole country to carry out policies according to the degree of seriousness of things, so that the national economy would be in total control of the king. Therefore, his opinion on the control of the economy was at variance with that of Sima Qian. Confucians like Jia Yi and Chao Cuo all participated in the political struggle of the early Han Dynasty, and the hard reality made them aware of the importance of the policy and method of ruling with force, which was the only way to ensure development. The proper implementation of policies like the Theory on the Degree of Seriousness of things, the policy of *pingzhun* and the monopoly of salt and iron would not only lessen directly the burden of common people but also enrich the national treasury. That would not only do little damage to the agrarian relations in the countryside but also promote the concentration of national strength. As a result of this thinking, they wouldn't advocate Lao Tze's notion of small country with little population, which was preached by the renowned local Confucians during the conference on salt and iron.

Further, there were similarities and differences between Sima Qian's economic views and those of the ministers, virtuous people and the literati. He and the ministers shared the same opinion on the recognition of the importance of commerce and the proper functioning of different social classes, considering these things important for the normal circulation of commodities, the enrichment of the socio-economic life and the harmonious living of common people. So they thought it necessary to have the policy of *pingzhun*, the monopoly of salt and iron, and the practice of *junshu*. As far as the economy and the related policies were concerned, with the same stance, they worshiped Guanzi, taking him as a politician free from the bond of the ritual system, and formulated the policies in accordance with what the *Guanzi* prescribed. On the contrary, Sima Qian esteemed Guanzi for his recognition of the difference between becoming rich and becoming civilized, and he rejected the systems from the Warring States Period to the Qin Dynasty, while the ministers honored Guanzi through the words of the people in the Warring States Period and the Qin Dynasty. In the field of ways on the degree of the seriousness of things, Sima Qian was emphasizing the following of the order, while the ministers were stressing the controlling aspect. As to the monopoly of salt and iron, we may say that his opinion was in between that of the ministers and the literati, which was something special about Sima Qian. The school of literati was of the opinion that the monopoly of salt, iron and wine, as well as the practice of *junshu*, should all be abolished, and the industry and commerce should be suppressed, using rituals as a defense against the desires of common people. The school of the virtuous people respected Guanzi from the perspectives of the equal importance of riches and rituals. Viewing Guanzi as a sage, like Sima Qian, they came to an understanding of the Theory on the Degree of the Seriousness of Things from the perspective of following the order. In the Han Dynasty, though the government boasted a combination of kingcraft and force in their ruling, in effect the main option probably tended to be ruling by force. So in the field of economic policy, ruling by force stressed the implementation of the Theory on the Degree of the Seriousness of Things, which was a prime force for strengthening the country's centralized power. Based on his dual position of historian and politician, Sima Qian approved the practice of controlling the currency system and the monopoly of salt and iron. He proposed three ways of becoming rich: the way of agriculture, the way of industry and commerce, and the way of cunning techniques or even unlawful practice, "with the first way of the top choice, the second way secondary, and the third way the lowest." Accordingly, he put forward different measures to deal with them. The first way should be guided, the second way should be regulated and the third way should be cracked down upon. The latter two approaches were not of Sima Qian's inclination, because in the *Biographies of Usurers*, we have the following explanation of the ways of coping with these: "the best way was to act in accordance with the natural tendency, next to that was to guide with gain, next to that was to educate, next to that was to regulate, and the last was to contend with the practice."

2.1. On the origin of money

Talking about the origin of money in *Equalization*, Sima Qian maintained that currency was the inevitable outcome of the exchange of commodities and its development. His viewpoints were threefold:

- First, currency was the unavoidable outcome of the development of commodities exchange. In his opinion, "with the start of the exchange of products among agriculture, industry and commerce, currencies of all kinds came into being." He connected the emergence of currency with the social division of labor and the exchange of commodities, which indicated that he was quite aware of the fact that currency was not the outcome of the subjective will of human beings, nor the invention of wise kings to save the common people from natural disasters. Though he answered the question relating to the emergence of currency, he did not give any answer for the reasons for its emergence and what on earth currency was. More than 2,000 years ago, it was indeed a great insight for Sima Qian to put forward the original idea that the social division of labor and the development of commodity exchange would surely lead to the emergence of currency, which was in contrast to the traditional view that the judicious kings of early dynasties invented currency. His unique thinking and sharp vision were both very touching. That was probably due to the "acting in accordance" way of understanding things of Sima Qian and his father. The notion of "acting in accordance" was synonymous with the inaction of *Lao Tze*, and the understanding of the word in terms of *yin* in *Zhuangzi*, the *Spring and Autumn Annals of the Lv Clan* and the *Huainanzi*. His "acting in accordance" was complying with nature and following the natural order, rejecting any non-natural and non-heavenly human acts and selfishness. It was a state of inaction of Lao Tze, both complying and taking advantage. It was intended to deal with the object of complying and dealing with these things, for the purpose of understanding the objective economic activities. That was a conclusion drawn from human economic activities. For a long time in ancient China, there was no echo to such an understanding, without any similar thinking. It was only after 1,000 years in the Northern Song Dynasty that Li Gou put forward something new on the basis of Sima Qian's opinion.

- Second, it was about the time of the emergence of currency. Sima Qian maintained that there was already money in circulation before the time of Gaoshen, one of the Five Emperors of the Three Sovereigns and Five Emperors of Chinese mythology. However, without any written records, there is no way to look into this matter. Gaoshen, also known as Emperor Ku, was the ancestor of Emperor Yao, a legendary Chinese ruler of ancient times. Compared with the time of Yu the Great, the time of emergence of currency mentioned in "On the Degree of Seriousness of Things," this was far earlier. He also believed that there were three types of metal currency in the Yu and Xia Dynasties: gold, silver and copper. As far as currency was concerned, there was also a difference between metal currency, like *qian*, *bu* and *dao*, and commodity money, like turtle shells and seashells. Although the use of turtle shells as money in the Han Dynasty is still to be verified by archeological excavation, most people believe that was true, to which we should pay attention.
- Third, it was about the unification of the forms of currency. Sima Qian believed that in the Yu and Xia Dynasties there were gold, silver and copper coins, and there was a difference between metal currency like qian, bu and dao and commodity money like turtle shells and seashells. At the time of the Qin Dynasty, the country's currency was unified to three types. Gold was measured in terms of *yi* (a *yi* is equal to 20 *liang*), and it was called the first-rate coin. Copper coins with carvings, weighting half a *liang*, the same as the meaning of the carved word, were called third-rate coins. The original text might have some lost sections. The supposed second-rate coins, called *bu* coins, were measured by *bu*. At that time, pearl, jade, turtle shell, silver, tin and the like were no longer used as currency to perform the function of general equivalents. However, the value of currencies often changed in different periods. The immaturity of political and economic conditions led to the inconsistency of the currency forms and the non-metallic nature of

currencies in the Warring States Period. With the establishment of the Qin Dynasty, the state centralized the control of the right to mint and issue money. With a unified monetary system, the form of money was also unified, and the choice of material for the minting of coins was also concentrated on metals. Because of the level of productivity development, at that time the commodity exchange and currency relations were not advanced, and the volume of transaction was also not large. With a large value, gold, measured in terms of *yi*, was not suitable for the daily needs of small-sum private transactions. As a result, copper, which was of lower value, was chosen as the material for the minting of currency. As was pointed out by Karl Marx, "In proportion as exchange bursts its local bonds, and the value of commodities more and more expands into an embodiment of human labour in the abstract, in the same proportion the character of money attaches itself to commodities that are by Nature fitted to perform the social function of a universal equivalent. Those commodities are the precious metals."[8]

2.2. On the circulation of currency and the price of commodities

On the relationship between currency and the price of commodities, in *Equalization*, Sima Qian made the following observation: "Since the Jianyuan years of Emperor Wu, due to the lack of financial resources, county officials would often mint currency at places near copper mines, and people would also mint coins secretly, to the extent that such cases were too numerous to mention. With more coins in circulation, the purchasing power of currency decreased; with fewer commodities in the market, their prices would increase." As far as currency was concerned, the reason behind this was that there was a discrepancy between the nominal value and the real value of currency. So the currency in circulation was only symbols of value or representatives of metal currency, not full-valued coins, so they wouldn't adjust the amount of money in circulation automatically. Moreover, the currency that was minted secretly by common people or skillfully cast by the government would often become

---

[8]*Complete Works of Karl Marx and Friedrich Engels*, vol. 23, p. 107.

lighter and thinner after repeated polishing, finally far below four *zhu* in weight. This kind of bad currency would flood into the circulation domain. The lower their currency value, the lower their purchasing power, and the higher the prices of the commodities. Voicing his opinion through the mouth of officials, he was quite aware that under conditions of unchanged quantity of commodities and the devaluation of currency, the real value of coins would change inversely with the nominal value of the money and the price of the goods. This was in line with the law of exchange of commodities with currency and the actual situation at that time. But according to Ru Chun's annotation, "They focused on nothing but the minting of currency." That was a one-sided criticism of common people's obsession with the minting of coins, at the price of the neglect of normal agricultural production, which was very different from what Sima Qian intended. On the basis of this, he advocated the banning of private minting, the production of leather coins and the implementation of currency devaluation. He was even in favor of Emperor Wu's move to collectively cast the new sanguan coins and the establishment of a unified *wuzhu* coin system. That was a pretty clear indication that Sima Qian was realistic and wouldn't tolerate the threat to people's interests.

Sima Qian discussed the role of currency circulation in his "Author's Preface" to the *Records of the Grand Historian*: "The Circulation of currency was for the link-up of agriculture and commerce, the extreme case of which would resort to tricky measures to make profit. The pursuit of profit would lead to attending to the trivialities and neglecting the fundamentals." Here, Sima Qian fully affirmed the role of currency in the circulation of commodities. It was precisely the active role of money that linked agriculture, industry and commerce, and promoted the development of agricultural production as well as the expansion of businesses, thus enhancing and stimulating the socio-economic prosperity and stability. He praised very affirmatively the prosperity brought about by the development of commerce and the chasing of wealth by different classes. In the section of *"The Money-makers,"* he made the following classic summary: "They simply acted intelligently and kept up with the times. They made their fortunes in trade and handicrafts but preserved them through agriculture, seized their wealth in war but retained it by peaceful means. There was method in their rise to fortune which is worth studying.

Countless other cases might be cited of men who made money by working hard at farming, cattle-breeding, handicrafts, lumbering or trade, the greatest of them dominating provinces, the next counties, and the lesser ones villages .... From this we can see that there is no fixed road to wealth, and goods do not stay with the same master forever. Wealth flow to those with ability as the spokes of a wheel converge upon the axle, but it slips like a smashed tile through the hands of incompetent men. A family with a thousand pieces of gold is comparable to the lord of a city; a man with millions can live like a king. Not for nothing are such men called 'nobles without fiefs'." According to his summary, in ancient society, the most reliable method of investment was to make money through the management of businesses and then buy lands. A subtle variation of this technique was to unscrupulously seize up land and then protect the acquisition by legal means.

That technique is worth analyzing. People engaged in farming, animal husbandry, handicrafts, hunting and commerce enjoyed varied earnings, with the biggest exceeding that of a province, the middle one a county, and the smaller one a town. Things like that are too numerous to mention. After years of recuperation and rest and a government of non-interference, the Han Dynasty presumably saw the recovery of the economy and the booming and prosperous development of the commodity economy. So Sima Qian's conclusion was that there was no fixed road to wealth and riches didn't have fixed owners. Competent men could accumulate wealth by different means and the fortunes of those incompetent men would fall apart and disappear. A family with 1,000 pieces of gold was comparable to the lord of a city; a man with hundreds of millions can live extravagantly like a king or the so-called nobles without fiefs. His comment was absolutely positive, without any condemnation or derogation. Similarly, "if a poor man wants to become rich, it is better to be an artisan than a farmer, better to be a merchant than an artisan, better to be a vendor than work at embroidery. In other words, trade and handicrafts are the best way for a poor man to make money." Without the need to learn from others, it was human nature to hanker after wealth and seek profit. The war heroes who braved the dangers courageously were motivated by major awards. The youngsters in the neighborhood, who dug tombs, minted coins privately, killed people and did evil things, "were all for the purpose of money." Practitioners in the field of agriculture, industry and commerce accumulated wealth for the purpose of making themselves even richer. People were making every effort to make money and would never leave the chance to others. This was an embodiment of "following the natural order," objectively reflecting the development of the times and the social reality. "When all work willingly at their trades, just as water flows ceaselessly downhill day and night, things will appear unsought and people will produce them without being asked. For clearly this accords with the Way and is in keeping with nature." In the view of Sima Qian, this was the normal result of human nature and was in accordance with the laws of socio-economic development, which could be verified. At the same time, he was also clear that money aroused people's worship and pursuit. For this, he had the following objective observation: "How quickly the whole world races after gain; how madly the whole world chases after gain." "A man with a thousand pieces of gold will not die in the market place." In "Mencius and Xun Qing," "Alas, going all out for profit often leads to dissatisfaction.... The evil consequences of seeking profit are the same for a common citizen or an emperor." According to his description, the supremely honorable were as common and vulgar as the civilians, and even more hypocritical and shameless. As mentioned above, Sima Qian recorded human nature as the driving force for the development of social production and economy. He turned his focus from God to human beings and society, which was liberation of the theology at that time and also a leap forward in the concept of heroism. However, Sima Qian didn't know why human beings were the real motive and reason for the historical development. He was also not aware of the contradiction between productive forces and relations of production, and the contradiction between the economic foundation and the superstructure. These insights were the spiritual discoveries of later generations, and were far more admirable. That was simply a vivid description and a useful generalization of the human mentality in the context of commodity–money relations.

Currency led to a series of emerging social crises, such as opportunism in the sphere of circulation, fraud, infighting, commercial malformation and serious challenges to agriculture. Though he provided a description of this monetary economy as a social phenomenon, Sima Qian was unable to truly understand it and failed to put forward tangible improvements and solutions. After all, he was a historian and a thinker, not an economist. So it was not possible to put him in the same category as Jia Yi, Chao Cuo and Sang Hongyang, nor do we need to attempt such a thing.

2.3. *On credit*

Sima Qian listed three ways of becoming rich. The best kind of wealth came from farming, the next best from trade and handicrafts and the worst from evil practices. The best kind relied on the management of land, livestock, forests, orchards and ponds. The next best involved trade, industry and usury. The worst kind of wealth was from illegal activities. He put usurers on par with industrialists and wrote biographies for them. He described the profit-seeking activities of usurers in a compassionate manner, which reflected his dissatisfaction with Emperor Wu's policy against merchants.

According to "The Money-makers," "When Wu, Chu and the five other states revolted, the nobles in Chang'an joined the imperial army and tried to raise money for the expedition. However, because their principalities lay east of the Pass and the outcome of the fighting there was uncertain, most of the money-lenders refused to make loans. Only the Wuyan family lent them 1,000 pieces of gold at an interest of 1,000%. When three months later the rebellion was crushed, Wuyan received a tenfold return of interest, becoming one of the richest men in central Shaanxi area." The practitioner of usury was called a specialist in his profession. That was clear indication of the pervasiveness of such a trade. It was no longer the sideline business of certain professions, nor was it a kind of random socio-economic activity. It was already a profession majoring in the management of loans. The Wuyan family, on the contrary, was the most outstanding, most clever and most profit seeking. They were positively described by Sima Qian, and were put in the category of Fan Li, Ji Ran, Duanmu Ci and the Zhuo family in Shu. Their activities were portrayed as "neither harmful to the government, nor interfering with the life of the common people." Their profit seeking was "on the basis of good timing," so it was good example for later "sages" to follow, not to be criticized and opposed. Sima Qian regarded moneylending as a legitimate business. He believed that it was natural to accumulate wealth in the process of circulation and make profits for the purpose of becoming rich. In his description of the usury activities, he did not use any derogatory or negative words, constituting a stark contrast with the protests of Chao Cuo. He was the first person in China to openly recognize the legitimacy of usury, which was 1,700 or 1,800 years before that in Europe.

In "The Money-makers," Sima Qian used the expression "nobles without fiefs" to describe those people who earned much but hadn't any official titles. The land tax and other levies of the feudal lords and nobles were roughly 200 coins per household. With a fief of 1,000 families, the annual income would be approximately 200,000 coins. The annual net profit of 100,000 coins of the common people in the professions of agriculture, industry and commerce was 2,000 coins, so a fief of 1,000,000 families would get a yearly net income of 2,000,000 coins. That was an income based on the 20% rate of profit, which was the same as the 20% profit rate of Gong Yu and that of Sima Qian's recording. Different from interest rate, that was possibly the general rate of profit or the minimum rate of profit at the time. In ancient China where it was quite impossible to have an average profit rate, this interest rate was based on the thorough investigation of Sima Qian and was universally acknowledged. Businesses with such a profit rate would be counted as qualified or desirable, while businesses without such a profit rate wouldn't survive. As was pointed out by Sima Qian, "all the miscellaneous trades which don't have a profit rate of 20% were not earning money." Analyzing the role of profit rate in the history of capitalism, Marx once quoted a mid-19th century English critic, "Capital .... A certain 10% will ensure its employment anywhere; 20% certain will produce eagerness."[9] That was identical with the lowest profit rate in ancient Chinese society discovered by Sima Qian. It might need further investigation to arrive at a definite conclusion as to whether the sameness was purely a simple coincidence or had some universal significance.

Sima Qian also believed that the usury practice would enable the cruel-hearted usurers to get an interest of 30% and even-handed usurers to get an interest of 20%, with which their income would be comparable

---

[9] *Complete Works of Karl Marx and Frederick Engels*, vol. 23, p. 829.

to that of feudal lords and nobles with a fief of 1,000 families. That was the general situation. In other industries, without a profit of 20%, the business would not be able to carry on. Sima Qian did not explicitly distinguish between interest rate and profit rate. He put usurers in the ranks of other business practitioners and confused interest rate with profit rate, which was a clear indication that under that historical condition, the emergence of interest rate was before that of the profit rate. Consequently, the interest rate determined the profit rate, not the other way round. This phenomenon was quite normal at the time and was accurately and objectively portrayed by Sima Qian. In addition, although Sima Qian believed that an interest rate of 20% was normal, he did not rule out the possibility of higher interest rates or the possibility of the ruthless exploitation of usury. Therefore, above the 20% interest rate, there might be an interest of 30%, or even 1,000%. He thought that was because "the rich would achieve success with original ideas." As was pointed out by Frederick Engels, "After commodities had begun to sell for money, loans and advances in money came also, and with them interest and usury."[10] There were no restrictions on the interest rates of usury capital, the minimum of which was the rate of land rent, that is, the rent you receive from investing your capital in land, which was risk free. The usury was different. If the interest rate of usury was not allowed to exceed that of the lowest profit rate, the owners of monetary capital would invest in land rather than take the risk of usury. Sima Qian adopted an objective attitude here and did not voice any criticism or opposition. As an ancient historian, he was overshadowed by the limitations of the times and his class. Therefore, it was not surprising that he could not distinguish between the interest rate and the profit rate.

Sima Qian's contribution also lay in his special efforts to have the two sections of "The Money-makers" and "Equalization" in his *Records of the Grand Historian*. "The Money-makers" was a collection of the achievements of the famous merchants and their time, from the Spring and Autumn Period and the Warring States Period to the time of the Emperor Wu of the Han Dynasty, providing valuable historical data for research into the currency, credit systems and theories during this period.

---

[10]*Selected Works of Karl Marx and Frederick Engels*, vol. 4, p. 163.

Equalization recorded the development of the currency and credit system from the early years of the Han Dynasty to the reign of Emperor Wu, offering a systematic and rich historical source for studying the currency and credit history of the Western Han Dynasty. Though incomplete and inadequate, it set a precedent for later-generation historians, and its pioneering quality shouldn't be obliterated or underestimated. It was precisely because of his endeavor that history writers of the later generations have continued this style and attached importance to the recording of such content, which even developed into a special kind of history. He made it convenient for later-comers to investigate the history of finance, including the history of currency and credit thought, which is to be remembered. Well worth our cherishing, his great achievements in the field of history not only benefit us all but will also benefit future generations.

3. The debate over mintage in the meeting about salt and iron

3.1. *Sang Hongyang and the meeting on salt and iron*

Sang Hongyang (153–80 B.C.) was born in Luoyang to a family of merchants. In 120 B.C., he was invited to become an Attendant because "he was good at analyzing the profit-seeking activities and carrying out thorough investigation," and "also good at calculating." In the 29 years since 115 B.C., he served successively as an official of the Ministry of Agriculture, Commandant in Charge of millet and Minister of Finance. For quite a long time, he was responsible for the financial affairs of the nation, and became known as "one of the officials contributing to the enrichment of the country" of Emperor Wu of Han. His opinion was that "the way of becoming rich lies in planning instead of laboring, and the way of making profits is to achieve an advantageous position instead of ploughing." He took part in and firmly carried out policies like property tax and related punishments, and suggested the regulation of currency system, the centralized control of mintage and the standardization of currency. He implemented the renting of public fields and the stationing of troops in frontier areas for agricultural as well as military purposes. He devised and revised the policy of average transportation, and rearranged and improved the state running of salt and iron. He also put forward the practice of *pingzhun* and the monopoly of wine. These important financial and economic policies resulted in the "bankruptcy of many more-than-average merchant families," the deterioration of the country's industry and commerce, and worsening of the poverty of the common people. They was a heavy attack on the merchants, businessmen and the despotic forces, thus alleviating the domestic class contradictions. With increased fiscal revenue, the government could have more money for the war against Xiongnu and reverse the financial difficulties of the state, for the purpose of consolidating the rule of the country, thus contributing immensely to the political and military achievements of Emperor Wu.

In 89 B.C., Sang Hongyang submitted a memorial to the king, suggesting the stationing of army forces in Luntai to open up wasteland and grow grain there. Emperor Wu sent out an imperial decree, declaring that doing this "would increase the burden of the people, so it's a disadvantageous move." "The priority now is to forbid the harsh and ruthless actions, stop the collection of unauthorized taxes, promote the development of agriculture, which is of fundamental importance, raise horses and lessen the burden of conscript labor and taxes. These measures will supply the deficiency and make up for the armaments and military provisions." This was an indication that Emperor Wu "wouldn't resort to military forces again" and would take defense over offense in foreign relations and recuperate the nation to enrich its people, a determined shift of strategy. Sang Hongyang didn't approve of such practices at all. In 87 B.C., he became the imperial censor, and was ordered by the king to be a regent to his crown prince, together with Huo Guang, the grand general, Jin Ridi, the *cheji* general, Shangguan Jie, the *zuo* general, and Tian Tianqiu, the prime minister. In 81 B.C., with the proposition of Du Yannian, the official in charge of admonition and arbitration, Huo Guang, the great minister of war and the grand general, convened the meeting on salt and iron. In September 80 B.C., during the "Mutiny of the Prince of Yan," in which the royal family members contended for the throne, he was put to death by Huo Guang.

The meeting on salt and iron was the second major discussion of the mintage in Chinese history. The representatives of the Han government were headed by Sang Hongyang, the imperial censor. The non-government representatives included the so-called virtuous people (Confucians with scholarly honor but no official titles) and the literati (renowned local Confucians), roughly about sixty of them. Although Huo Guang wasn't present, without his support the meeting could never be held. He wanted to take advantage of the opinion of the above-mentioned people to deal Sang Hongyang a heavy political blow so as to rule out the obstacles to the implementation of the Luntai edict. Therefore, Huo Guang was often hostile to the complete negation of Emperor Wu's policies in his earlier ruling and the deliberate distortion of the Luntai edict by the above-mentioned people. He refused to accept their suggestions for the abolition of the state running of salt and iron and the adoption of a benevolent and converting policy concerning the *xiongnu* people. Later, the government announced the abolition of the county-level wine monopoly and the five officials governing iron trade inside the Hangu Pass, which was of no consequence in the overall national policy. On the surface, this struggle was a fierce debate between Sang Hongyang and the so-called virtuous people and the literati, centering on the topic of "the sufferings of the people should be the central point of education." But the essence was "the struggle between two groups of politicians with Huo Guang and Sang Hongyang as leaders, respectively, in the central government of the Han Dynasty, centering on whether or not to implement the *Luntai* edict. With this struggle, Huo Guang won a massive victory both politically and ideologically and paved the way for the implementation of the rehabilitating policy of 'forbidding the harsh and ruthless actions, stopping the collection of unauthorized taxes, and promoting the development of agriculture, which is of fundamental importance', as was prescribed in the *Luntai* edict." In terms of the mintage of currency, it was another major debate since the debate in the early Western Han Dynasty. After this struggle, the notion of centralized coinage became the dominant idea within the ruling group. During the reign of Emperor Xuan, Huan Kuan of Runan, based on the minutes of the meeting on salt and iron and the recollections of Confucian scholars, edited *The Discourses on Salt and Iron* (sixty articles in 10 volumes) after his own deduction and elaboration. Though clearly in the position of the so-called virtuous people (Confucians with scholarly honor but no official titles) and the literati, the author described the viewpoints of both sides of the debate rather objectively and completely.

The book was also a precious historical record of the political, economic, military and ideological aspects in the middle part of the Western Han Dynasty. There were two subjects that were related to the debate on currency. One was the origin of money and the other was the right of mintage, which shall be dealt with in the following part.

3.2. The debate on the origin of currency

Sang Hongyang stressed that currency would change together with the change of time. According to his understanding, "administration must adjust itself to society, and currency changes with the time. The emperors of the Xia Dynasty used black cowries, and those of the Zhou purple stones, while later generations at times circulated metal currency and knife money. Anything overripe tends to decay, as end and beginning alternate in cycles. Now, if the hills and marshes are not state-controlled, they will yield profit to both Prince and Minister. If there be no interdiction on coinage, the counterfeit will circulate with the genuine" ("Discordant Currencies"). Compared with the then-prevalent idea that gold, silver and copper were the three main currencies since the Xia Dynasty, this understanding was in accordance with the historical development of Chinese currency, and thus deserved our attention. The "counterfeit" of Sang Hongyang referred to the low-quality money minted privately by the people, while the "genuine" referred to the officially coined full-bodied money. He was convinced that if the private minting of currency wasn't prohibited, then privately minted currency would circulate together with the officially casted money in the market. As was pointed out by Jia Yi, "The lawful currency wouldn't stand" and "with the counterfeit money in circulation, the market would be in disorder."

The so-called virtuous people and the literati, on the contrary, were a group of advocates of restoring what was ancient. They blindly esteemed the past over the present and held that "in ancient times virtue was valued while profit was looked down, and righteous acts were honored while wealth was despised." They longed for the ancient practice of "bartering cloth for silk," the kind of primitive bartering life, and defamed the reform of currency as going from bad to worse. They complained that since the beginning of the exchange of money, the currency had undergone quite a

110   A History of China's Financial Thought: Volume 1

few changes, and folk customs had fostered a trend of falsification. In the early Han Dynasty, the government started the accumulation of wealth without getting rid of the malpractice of former days, and the reform of the currency system meant forcing businessmen to take up agricultural work. That was "to stop cooking by way of frying, and prevent the boiling of water by fire," the result of which would be contrary to the expectation. As a matter of fact, the trend of currency reform was always a process of becoming better, in a certain way developing together with the economic development. Reform entails successes and failures. But if the general trend of development was negated because of occasional failures, that way of doing things was utterly the reflection of wishful thinking, like a mad dog barking at the sun. Unhappy about the currency relations and the reform of the currency system, the so-called virtuous people and the literati were nostalgic for the bartering practice of former days. That was a demonstration of their attempt to say no to the development of the currency relations, which was a fundamental mistake as far as their stance was concerned.

They also accused the Han government of carrying on the old ways of ruling of the Qin Dynasty without any change and focusing on the accumulation of wealth without any reform of the currency in circulation. According to them, the intensification of the exploitation of the people through currency depreciation wouldn't persuade the people to take up agricultural work again, but add fuel to the fire. In the eighty years from 113 B.C. to 193 B.C., the laws on currency underwent nine revisions. Consequently, "there was more and more money in circulation, though with less and less purchasing power, and there were less and less commodities in the market, with the prices becoming more expensive." In the words of Emperor Wu and his officials, the reform of the currency system was to "mint new money to complement the shortage of the national reserve and wipe out the businessmen who was also acquiring land." To enrich the state finances, Emperor Wu carried out the policy of currency depreciation in 119 B.C. and issued white gold coins (made of silver and tin, with values of 3,000 and 500, respectively) and *sanzhu* coins (with the value of 300). In the following year, the government cast *wuzhu* coin for circulation because *sanzhu* coins were too light for convenient circulation. In 115 B.C., the capital of the country saw the emergence of *chize* coins, with one worth one hundred *wuzhu* coins, so it was still a way of deprecation. In the five years since the casting of white gold coins and *wuzhu* coins, hundreds of thousands of people were executed as a result of private minting of currencies, hundreds of thousands of people surrendered to the government and numerous people were murdered secretly. With even more people who did not surrender themselves, almost all the people of the country were somewhat involved in private minting, to the extent that "officials couldn't punish them all." On the contrary, in order to combat unscrupulous mergers and acquisitions, the government targeted not only large merchants but also officials and bureaucrats of all levels who also went into business because this wealthy social stratum was influential and they overtly agreed to, but covertly opposed, the government orders. With the ability to play against the monarchy, they were a centrifugal force, which was not conducive to the construction and consolidation of a centralized government. Since the government minted the "moderate weight" and full-bodied *wuzhu* coins, for decades there had been a stable circulation of currency. Every year, the central government employed 100,000 people in copper mining and money mintage, accumulating a total of 2.8 million *wuzhu* coins in the late Han Dynasty. In the more than 700 years from the Han Dynasty to the Sui Dynasty, *wuzhu* coins were always in circulation, thus becoming one of the most successfully minted coins in Chinese history. Regardless of the basic facts, however, the so-called virtuous people and the literati tended to attack the reform of the minting system to coin the *wuzhu* coins, which was approved of by people of the time and applauded by later generations. Adopting the tricks of substituting one thing for another and confusing right and wrong, they shifted the blame of the undervaluation of privately minted coins on *wuzhu* coins, and clamored insolently for the practice of "doing a disservice." Rather than venting their dissatisfaction with the currency reform, it would be better to say that they were expressing their hatred against Emperor Wu, who was strengthening the centralized power. Rather than longing for the full-bodied coins, they were expecting the chaotic condition of both authentic and counterfeit money in circulation. It was no wonder that Huo Guang took advantage of their voice to debunk Sang Hongyang, his opponent, but turned a deaf ear to their advice as far as economic matters were concerned.

3.3. The debate on the right of mintage

During the reign of Emperor Wu, Sang Hongyang and others proposed a currency reform and the minting of *shanglin* coin. A step further than the ideas of Jia Yi and Jia Shan, their proposition was that the government should not only monopolize copper, the material of minting currency, but also have a centralized minting of coins. The government should control not only the design of currency but also the concrete action of putting the design into practice. Until then, the right of mintage had been under the control of the government, and the currency system of ancient China entered the period of *wuzhu* coins, a new period in history. The distinguishing feature of this period was that the minting of coins was nationally standardized, which was a major victory of the policy of centralized state-run minting over that of decentralized private minting. In this regard, Sang Hongyang's attitude was in sharp contrast to that of the so-called virtuous people and the literati.

Sang Hongyang laid special emphasis on the state monopoly of the right of mintage and the necessity of a centralized minting of currency. "In the time of the Emperor Wen, the people were permitted to cast money, smelt iron, and evaporate salt. But the Prince of Wu monopolized the sea and marshes, and the family of Deng Tong monopolized the Western Mountain, whereupon all the rogues from east of the mountains congregated in the dukedom of Wu, and Qin, Yong, Han and Shu were brought to depend upon the Deng clan. The coins of Wu and Deng overspread the Empire. For this reason, the laws against coinage were promulgated. With these, dishonesty will cease, and with the occasion for dishonesty removed, the people will no longer hope for wrongful gain. Each will devote himself to his proper task. If this is not a return to fundamental principles, what is it?" ("Discordant Currencies"). He also criticized the policy of liberal and free minting of coins during the reign of Emperor Wen, considering it a reason for the mixed circulation of authentic and fake coins and the disorder in the market. In his opinion, that wasn't helpful for the consolidation of the centralized government, but advantageous for mergers and acquisitions of the local forces. As was pointed out by the Lord Grand Secretary in "Discordant Currencies," "When people are too wealthy they cannot be controlled through salaries.

When people are too powerful, it will be difficult to impose penalties upon them. These inequalities cannot be removed except by relieving congestion and evening profit." That was in the same vein as the thought expressed in "The Savings Policy of the State" in *Guanzi*. "If the officials and the rich vie with one another in extravagance, the lower classes will devote themselves to gain, and thus the two will undermine one another." Each vassal state dominated a place and stood up as an equal to the central government. Possessing wealth "exceeding that of the king," they were in no hurry to meet the national urgency, but threatened to subvert the central government. The private minting of currency was not conducive to the stabilizing of the value of the currency, the reassuring of the public and the development of production. Private casting was indeed lucrative. As a result, people would be induced to abandon farming and start the casting of coins, which, though illegal, was too difficult to prohibit. The incommensurability of the circulation of money and commodities in the society was for no other reason than the result of the hoarding of rich businessmen. The significance of banning the private minting of coins lay in the fact that a unified currency system and the centralized minting of coins would guarantee the production of legal and full-bodied *wuzhu* coins, which meant that common people would concentrate on their agricultural activities, without any possibility of abandoning agriculture for the purpose of private minting, and so the foundation of agriculture wouldn't be threatened.

With a unified currency system, the public would no longer felt doubtful about the authenticity of the coins, so that the credibility of the *wuzhu* coins would naturally be guaranteed. The stability of the currency system would ensure that production and circulation would smoothly go on. In this process, Jia Yi was the first to propose the concept of "legal money," and Sang Hongyang then proposed the concept of unity. That was an important precondition for the establishment of a unified currency system of the Han Dynasty of the Liu clan and made an outstanding contribution to ancient China's theory about the right of mintage.

The so-called virtuous people and the literati bitterly criticized Emperor Wu's abolition of the rights of vassal states to mint coins and his setting up of a unified *wuzhu* system. About the *shanglin* coins, their first criticism was that the state-minted coins had a few disadvantages, which they exaggerated and maliciously slandered. For example, "officials and craftsmen would use inferior materials for profit, and some coins are not so standard, so that the coins minted are varied in weight and shape." Generally speaking, the *shanglin wuzhu* coin was arguably one of the best coins in ancient Chinese history. Otherwise, it would not be so popular in China for such a long time. Today, archeological excavations also confirmed this point. Together with the *kaiyuan tongbao* coin of the Tang Dynasty, it became one of the most representative historical artifacts of the Han and Tang Dynasties, which was also proof of its success. On the pretext of the farmers' unfamiliarity with the new coins and the reason mentioned above, the second criticism was that "farmers suspect the new issue but trust the former coins, not knowing the false from the true." Third, in the exchange of old coins and newly minted coins, merchants would seek profit in the way of an unequal exchange. "The dealers and shopkeepers for the bad barter the good; and with a half, exchange for double. Thus in case he buys, the farmer loses value; if he sells, he violates his conscience." The fourth point was that the old coins were still in circulation. Although the government had issued an ordinance that "private minting of coins was a crime to be punished with death penalty," fake coins were "as many as before," not to be stopped by such a prohibition. The fifth problem was that with goods in an unsalable state, people were suffering. Merchants would not sell their goods unless they could get authentic coins, while those buyers could not buy anything even though they possessed money. Consequently, goods were unsalable and coins were in the hands of their possessors. In short, in the eyes of the so-called virtuous people and the literati, it was no good prohibiting the private minting of coins and centralizing the right of mintage. A better option would be "not to shut down on the privately made coinage." In effect, their idea was that the monopoly of the mintage of the central government should end and that common people should be permitted to mine for copper and mint coins, which was a manifestation of the laissez-faire policy in the field of currency. That claim represented the interests of small and medium landowners and merchants, reflecting the conflict of interest between the central government and local separatists.

4. The currency and credit theory in late Western Han Dynasty

4.1. *Gong Yu's theory of currency disposal*

After the death of Sang Hongyang, the laissez-faire economic thought gained opportunities for publicity and practice in the country. Coupled with the moderate policies of Emperor Zhao and Emperor Xuan, agriculture saw considerable development and people's lives improved to some extent. At the same time, the centralized power of the government was severely challenged, and the power of rich businessmen rose. They collaborated with merchants, landlords and bureaucrats to promote the intense concentration of land and the bankruptcy of small farmers. Under double pressure, the central government of the Liu regime was severely threatened. In 81 B.C., the so-called virtuous people and the literati voiced their attachment to ancient things and their longing for the practice of "exchanging that which he had for that which he lacked and substituting one's cloth for silk." Liu Shi, Emperor Yuan, was softhearted and fond of Confucianism. In order to achieve the ideal politics he pursued, he assigned a large number of Confucian scholars to various posts, among whom was Gong Yu. He publicly proposed the returning to the ancients and the abolition of currency, in an attempt to pull the wheel of history back to a primitive society, where there were neither commodities nor currency, and "all the people were farmers." Though very ridiculous, superficial and in effect not practicable, he elaborated on his proposition theoretically. Gong Yu was the first currency oppositionist in China who made public his viewpoints and he was venerated by the later currency oppositionists, most of whom didn't go beyond his theory at all.

Gong Yu (124–44 B.C.), courtesy name Shaoweng, was a native of Langye. During the reign of Emperor Xuan, he was drafted to be a learned scholar because of his thorough understanding of the classics and his exemplary conduct, which was the beginning of his various positions and posts. Serving as the imperial censor, he made a few remarks on the successes and failures of the government. Economically, he advocated thrift and the saving of government expenses to lessen the burden of the people. The abolition of currency was one of his concrete measures.

He advocated the ban of coins, the restoration of ancient ways and the use of material currency, such as cloth and grain. His opinion was that "the profit of industry and commerce led to people's infatuation with money." That is to say, commercial capital and other monetary forces permeated all spheres of society, to the extent that agricultural production was severely interfered with. As a result, commerce boomed, while agriculture declined and illegal activities as well as wrongdoers were too many to control, "the origin of which was nothing more than money." Currency became the number one reason for all the "evil" things of the world. Because the power given by society to currency had become the private power of individual persons, "The ancients therefore denounced money as subversive of the economic and moral order of things."[11] So the use of currency must be abolished. "Officials in charge of the mining of jades, gold and silver and the minting of coins should be done with. These things should not be used as money any more, and there should be no transactions of such things in the marketplace." In cases of inevitable value transference, such as the paying of taxes of the common people and the salary and rewards to the officials, "they shall be paid in cloth or grain." Other transactions would only take the form of bartering. "With people returning to agriculture, it would be easy to carry out the ancient ways of life." That would just be like the kind of ancient life described in the second part of *Lao Tze*, "a small state with few people may return to the age of recording by tying knots. A neighboring state may be within sight, with cocks' crow and dogs' bark within hearing, but people will not visit each other."

However, he wasn't aware that currency, the emergence and disappearance of which was not subject to anyone's will or preference, was an inevitable outcome of the development of commodity production and exchange. The only way to eliminate currency was to do away with commodity production and exchange, which was the inseparable socio-economic condition for the existence of currency. Any propositional disregard of such a fact was but wishful thinking. That was the first point to be noted. Second, pearls, jades, gold, silver and coins were currencies, but cloth and grains were also used as currency in history. The cloth and grains as mentioned by Gong Yu also functioned as general equivalents.

---

[11]*Complete Works of Karl Marx and Friedrich Engels*, vol. 23, p. 152.

What he wanted to do away with was only metal coins. He couldn't eliminate all the commodity currency. Consequently, the currency of his choice didn't include cloth or grains. As a matter of fact, it was impossible to return to a primitive society in which, as he imagined, there was neither currency, nor buying or selling, nor a market. It seems that his understanding of the emergence, status, role and significance of currency was less profound and accurate than that of Sima Qian, who was of the opinion that "the function of currency was to bridge agriculture and commerce, but the extreme case of using currency was the playing of tricks for the purpose of benefit, which was attending to trifles to the neglect of essentials." It was too pedantic and decadent of him not to understand or recognize such an idea. The long history of currency meant that an individual person's preference would never determine its existence, nor could his restoration of the ancient ways put an end to its circulation. While he blindly longed for things ancient and worshipped the ancient way of government, in an attempt to pull the historical wheel backwards, he never expected that currency also had the features of commodity and there was the form of currency. The third point was that currency was never the root of all evils. Because currency functioned as the general equivalent, in a society where the means of production was privately owned, it was used as the tool for the calculation of social labor. As a general representation of social wealth, currency became a target for people to pursue together, and it was also a form of existence for commercial and usury capital. Although it deepened or expanded the basic contradictions in a society, it was by no means the root of social conflicts, nor was it the root of the gap between the rich and the poor, or the underlying reason for social turmoil and the change of dynasties. Therefore, even if currency was abolished, these social conflicts would still exist, though in different ways and employing different tools.

Gong Yu was madly obsessed with the thought of restoring the ancient customs. He disliked all the socio-economic activities associated with commodities and currencies and always found fault with the existence of currencies. There were about five reasons. The first one was that "700,000 people were in constant hunger." According to his understanding, "in ancient times, people didn't use gold as currency, and they focused only on the development of agriculture. So should anyone not cultivate his land, someone else would suffer from hunger." Now that the government intended to mint coins, "they had to mine for copper and iron," for which the government had to assign more than 100,000 bureaucracies and handicraftsmen. Measured by a medium productivity of labor, one laborer could produce grains for seven people. Therefore, if 100,000 laborers stopped producing grains, 700,000 people would starve. The second reason was "the danger of droughts and floods." Mining for copper meant the digging up of mountains. "Digging down hundreds of meters would imbalance the *yin* and *yang* nearby, leading to 'emptiness of land reserve and the inability to form clouds.'" At the same time, "there wasn't any restrictions on the cutting down of forests." These were indeed reasons for the occurrence of droughts and floods. The third reason was that more people would be punished by the law. He disclosed that "in the more than seventy years since the emergence of *wuzhu* coins, more and more people was punished for their private minting of coins." This way of expression was exactly the same as that of the so-called virtuous people and the literati during the meeting on salt and iron. The fourth reason was the endless desire of people to make money. He blamed the rich because "they were still displeased though they had accumulated much money." With a huge gap between the rich and the poor, there were all kinds of social conflicts. The fifth reason was that "mixed popular feelings caused some people to become thieves." There was a marked discrepancy between the economic burdens of merchants and farmers. Merchants "had good food and clothing and enjoyed a yearly interest rate of 20% for their lending to others, but they didn't need to pay any rents or taxes." There was no need to mention the toil and suffering of farmers. The heavy burden of rents and taxes itself was already rather disappointing. "After the payment of land rent came the tax of harvest and the extortions from officials of all levels were too numerous to mention." As a result "the profit of industry and commerce led to people's infatuation with money" and "people would attend to the superficial and neglect the essentials, with only less than a half of the farmers engaged in agricultural activities." Even when they were given some lands, the farmers would sell the land at low prices to go into business. The hard-working peasants, on the contrary, had to rebel against the government and "became thieves," leading thus to social unrest and constituting a direct threat to the regime.

The above-cited reasons were not adequate and his viewpoints were hardly justifiable. An analysis of three of them would suffice to dispute his position.

First of all, it is a fact that mining for copper and the minting of coins would compete for labor forces with agricultural production. At a certain point in history, under the fixed conditions of the labor force, the demand for the labor forces in the two industries of mining and farming was mutually restricting. But a precondition for the separation of the handicraft industry from agriculture and its development brought the development of agriculture to a considerable level. In the Western Han Dynasty, agriculture saw a fairly high level of development. Arable land expanded, iron utensils and cattle were extensively used, the irrigation system greatly increased the output of agriculture and the new way of farming "was labor-saving but more rewarding in terms of harvest." Despite the unbalanced economic structure and the weakening of agriculture causing serious trouble, there would never be the phenomenon of "should anyone not cultivate his land, someone else would suffer from hunger." The prosperity of handicrafts and commerce was sound proof that the alarmist words of Gong Yu were one-sided empty talk.

Second, it is a fact that the mining of copper would lead to the indiscriminate destruction of forests, damage to ecological balance as well as floods and droughts. But it is purely superstitious to find his theoretical basis from *yin–yang* and *wuxing* theory and to talk about the "imbalance of the *yin* and *yang*." In an attempt to advocate "focusing on agriculture" and oppose mining for copper as well as minting coins, this way of doing things would mean that even agriculture, which he stressed to no less extent, would go back to the stage of picking, a period even before the slash-and-burn cultivation. It may be safe to assume that notions like his were one of the main reasons for the slow development of mining and smelting and other sciences and technologies in ancient China.

Third, it is a prejudice of confusing cause and effect to say that the root for attending to the superficial and neglecting the essentials was money. That is the best excuse for the people in power. According to his understanding, the abolition of currency would mean the disappearance of evil things, the elimination of the gap between the rich and the poor, the eradication of sharp social conflicts and struggles, as well as greed and plundering. Wasn't that absurd and ridiculous?

At that time, Gong Yu represented the interests of the small and medium landowners in the community, who were in control of the millets and silk but did not have or lacked cash. In the process of exchanging grain and silk for money, they were subject to the exploitation of the businessmen. Based on their own interests, they advocated the abolition of currency. He tried to reverse the process of history, taking it as the most ideal, most exalted and most suitable mission of his life. Well versed in classics, he had little life experience. He wasn't aware that a monetary economy had developed and the power of merchants could not be ignored. Merchants played an important role in the development of social productivity and the prosperity of the economy. It must be fully affirmed that socio-economic life, business and currency were closely intertwined. Therefore, his proposal was opposed shortly after it was put forward, and was shelved on the grounds that "transactions need money, while cloth and silk could not be split to suit the need." Decades later, during the reign of Emperor Ai (ascended to the throne in 7 B.C.), an official sent in a memorial, saying that "the ancients used turtle shells as their currency, and today we used coins as their substitute, leading to the poverty of the people. It is advisable to change our currency." The proposal was almost identical to that of Gong Yu, and the only difference was that Gong Yu proposed to use cloth and grain as the substitute for coins, while the official suggested the use of turtle shells. During the 600 years from the Eastern Han Dynasty to the Wei, Jin and the Southern and Northern Dynasties, occasionally there were arguments for the abolition of currency. In particular, during the Wei, Jin and the Southern and Northern Dynasties, after causing a great clamor, this idea was even put into practice, causing the rise of commodity currency and a disorder of the monetary system.

4.2. *The interest theory of Wang Mang*

Wang Mang (45–23 B.C.), courtesy name Jujun, the nephew of Emperor Yuan's queen, was the founder of the Xin Dynasty. During the reigns of Emperor Cheng and Emperor Ping, he served successively as imperial attendant, one of the sub-commanders of the imperial guards, the Chamberlain for Attendants, the commander of the armed forces, etc. After the death of Emperor Cheng, he ascended to the throne with the title of "Acting Emperor" and changed the name of his dynasty to "Xin." After the peasant uprising overthrew the Xin Dynasty, he was killed by a businessman named Du Wu in Jiantai.

During his reign, he implemented a wide range of social reforms, including the *wangtian* system of land redistribution, monetary restructuring, the *liuguan* system and the prohibition of the sale of slaves. He cited from the classics to support his reform. "For each of his reform, he would always find proof in ancient writings." Under the banner of carrying out the ancient ways of doing things, he started his reforms. Relying on ancient books, such as *The Rites of Zhou* and *Yueyu*, along with the state monopoly on salt, iron and liquor implemented by Emperor Wu, as well as other old systems, he exercised overall control over business, industries and transportation. His intention was to curb the wealthy businessmen and crack down on usurers to increase national fiscal revenue. However, the law enforcers were often rich people or wealthy merchants who had the identity of officials. Taking advantage of the opportunity to hand down the government orders, they would carry out extortion and prey upon the common people. They colluded with county and province officials to create false accounting statements and engage in malpractices for the purpose of feathering their own nests. As a result, the government's finances were not improved, and the people were becoming increasingly impoverished. That was a heavy blow to many laborers, industrialists and businessmen included, to the extent that "what they earned from their laborious work wasn't enough to pay the taxes." "Subjected to the harassment by cunning placemen and tricky scoundrels, common people couldn't live a stable life." The *liuguan* policies as he implemented weren't a step-by-step implementation after comprehensive planning. Instead, they were announced one after another from the founding of the dynasty in 10 A.D. The government gradually exercised a monopoly over salt, iron, wine, profits from mining for copper and minting coins, as well as the yields from the management of famous mountains and big lakes. The government also had unified control over the policy of "Average Prices of the Five Cities and Buying on Credit and Loan." (The so-called "Average Prices of the Five Cities" referred to the establishment of the agencies in cities like Chang'an, Luoyang, Handan, Linzi, Wan and Chengdu, for the purpose of regulating the prices of these cities. The so-called "Buying on Credit and Loan" meant that there would be officially controlled sales on account, taxes included. The Liuguan meant that no privately owned business would be allowed in the business of liquor, salt, iron, etc., which was closely related to the theory on the degree of the seriousness of things.)

Among these policies, "Buying on Credit and Loan" meant that the government would engage directly in loan activities. Wang Mang intended to achieve the goal of "regulating the wealth of common people and suppressing the acquisition of land to benefit the public" by strictly implementing the loan policy. In order to combat the usury exploitation and land acquisitions of businessmen and landowners, he once gave an imperial edict: *"The Rites of Zhou* had descriptions of the practice of buying on credit and loan, while *Yueyu* had descriptions of average prices. So each practice had its origins. Now we are carrying out a similar practice to regulate the wealth of common people and suppress the acquisition of land." For that purpose, it was stipulated that a city's money house should help all those people who couldn't afford to sacrifice or arrange funereal services to pay their taxes later, without any charge of interest. For those who couldn't afford the expenses of sacrifice, the time limit was 10 days, while for those who were unable to afford the expenses of funerals, it was 3 months. It was not known how people with overdue taxes were dealt with. Those who are impoverished and unable to operate any business might borrow money from the government. As long as they were engaged in production or business activities, they should be granted loans. When repaying the loans, the interest should be no more than one tenth of the net profit after deducting food and clothing expenses.

As far as the buying on credit and loan was concerned, the credit and the loan were different. First of all, the targeted recipients were not the same. Those who couldn't afford the expenses of sacrifices or funerals shouldn't be associated with those who had no livelihood and were unable to run any business. Most of the recipients of the buying on credit policy were members of the landlord class going downhill, still in the ranks of the ruling class, while the targets of the buying on loan were small producers characterized by small businesses, such as peasants, small craftsmen or small business owners. Second, they were different in nature. Buying on credit was for the purpose of non-productive consumption, while buying on loan was for production, a kind of capital loans. The third difference lay in the use of the money. The former was for sacrifices and funerals, while the latter was for production and management. Fourth, the time limit was different. For the former, it varied from 10 days (in the case of sacrifices) to 3 months (in the case of funerals), while the latter was on a yearly basis, either shorter or longer than one year. The fifth difference was the interest rates. For the former, it was interest-free during the time limit, and for the latter, the interest was a monthly 3% or a yearly 10% according to the net income. With a yearly interest of 10% or 36%, the differential interest rate was an innovation in history. Compared with the Roman practice of the same period, the short-term interest rate was pretty high, but long-term interest rate was almost the same. Julius Caesar stipulated that the monthly interest rate should not exceed 1%, there should be no compound interest and the accumulated interest should not outnumber the capital. Loans were for productive purposes and would bring the borrowers profits, so it was only natural and reasonable for them to pay interests to lenders. As was recorded in "Treatise on Food and Money" in *History of the Former Han*, the yearly interest rate was not allowed to exceed 10%. According to biographies of Wang Mang, in 10 A.D., the yearly interest rate was 36%. So it was hard to tell which was true. Fortunately, that would not influence our analysis below.

There is an important sentence in "Treatise on Food and Money" in *The Book of Han*: "After deducting the original capital, the interest would be based on the revenue from the business." That is to say, the annual interest rate of no more than 10% was based on the net profit after deducting various expenses, instead of counting the total sales revenue. Irrespective of the amount of the loan, the interest was no more than 10% of the net profit after deducting the costs. Because of their ownership of the capital of the business, creditors enjoyed the share of the profits from the production and operation, with a minimum of 10%, without the possibility of 20% or 30%. Thus, we can see that Wang Mang's design of the interest-bearing program was rather advanced and scientific. There were the following reasons:

The first reason was that consciously or unconsciously, he was aware that interests came from profits. No matter how he felt then, in an objective sense, the formulation of this policy was based on a clear understanding of the clear distinction between costs and profits and that interests were only part of the net profits. Arrived at in 10 A.D., this understanding was insightful indeed. In Europe, "it was discovered (by Massie and after him by Hume) as late as the middle of the 18th century, that interest is but a portion of the gross profit, and that such a discovery was at all necessary."[12] In the backward kingdom of pre-capitalism, "interest comprises all the profit, and more than the profit, instead of merely expressing an aliquot part of the produced surplus-value, or profit, as it does in countries with a developed capitalist production."[13] Exhilaratingly, Wang Mang's understanding of the issue was an exception to this conclusion. Our ancestors were far ahead in the field of economics at the time, which was a clear demonstration that the currency and credit system had reached so advanced a level that the theoretical understanding was clearly extraordinary.

The second reason was the way interests were calculated. It was a completely new concept to calculate the taxes according to the net profits. It would be more obvious if we take his calculation of the taxes for other urban industries into consideration. Practitioners of all trades should pay the local governments taxes, whether they engage in hunting, fishing, livestock husbandry, or housewives taking part in silkworm raising, spinning, weaving and sewing, or they were artisans, doctors, wizards, fortune-tellers, hotel managers, businessmen or other professions. "After deducting the costs, the profits would be counted, with one-tenth of it as taxes." It served to show that Wang Mang had a very keen understanding of the concept of costs, so it was not surprising that when calculating the interests of loans costs would be taken into consideration.

Wang Mang enjoyed a noticeable status in China's history of financial thought. He claimed that he was copying the practice of *The Rites of Zhou*, but he was not a stickler and did not copy blindly. He had his own unique insights. Otherwise, this concept of interest-bearing, which was beyond *The Rites of Zhou*, would have never come into being. That was the first point. The second point was that in ancient

---

[12]*Complete Works of Karl Marx and Friedrich Engels*, vol. 25, pp. 422–423.
[13]*Complete Works of Karl Marx and Friedrich Engels*, vol. 25, p. 240.

China, particularly in the Western Han Dynasty, commodity economy had developed into a rather advanced level, so that the way of interest-bearing was adopted over 1,000 years earlier than in Europe. Although Wang Mang's understanding was extraordinary, it was never beyond the socio-economic environment in which he lived. It was likely that the thought originated from certain cities with mature commodity economies, especially big cities like Chang'an, the capital city, and the 5 major cities of Luoyang, Handan, Linzi, Wan and Chengdu. At the same time, this understanding would further promote the development and expansion of the commodity economy and the credit economy. The third point was that in an economic environment where currency systems changed frequently and the devaluation of currency often occurred, "farmers and businessmen were often out of job, food and life necessities were frequently scarce, and people were weeping in the street." In this case, the policy of "Average Prices of the Five Cities and Buying on Credit and Loan" could never play any positive role in the socio-economic field. "Subjected to the harassment by cunning placemen and tricky scoundrels, common people couldn't live a stable life." In consequence, the related theory of interest was nothing but a mere scrap of paper, without any practical significance.

5. The theory of monetary policy of the Eastern Han Dynasty

5.1. *Zhang Lin on "the banning of currency"*

Zhang Lin, the magistrate of Zhending during the reign of Emperor Zhang (76–78 A.D.) of the Eastern Han Dynasty, was appointed minister upon the recommendation of Dou Xian, the Queen's brother. In order to ease the financial shortage of the imperial court, he proposed that the government could collect cloth and silk as the substitute for rents, the profits from salt should belong to the government and the system of *junshu* should be restored. "Banning the use of currency" was also one of his propositions and was often adopted by the government. In the *Yuanhe* era (84–87 A.D.), the Grand Commandant Zheng Hong presented a memorial to the emperor, alleging that he was an appendage to Dou Xian, and thus unsuitable for his post. He was later convicted of taking bribes.

After the reform of Wang Mang, the monetary system of the Western Han Dynasty had been unstable and "people all found it inconvenient." At the beginning of the Eastern Han Dynasty, the economy was languishing and the prices of commodities were shooting up. In 40 A.D., Ma Yuan, prefecture chief of Longxi, submitted a memorial, saying, "The foundation of enriching a nation lies in the food and commodities. It is advisable that *wuzhu* coins should be minted as before." Liu Xiu, the Emperor Guangwu, accepted his advice and began to recast the *wuzhu* coins, which was greatly applauded. During the reign of Emperor Zhang, "the grains and silk were expensive. As a result, county officials all found their funds inadequate, for which the government also felt anxious. Then the minister Zhang Lin said, 'nowadays not only are grains expensive, but also all other commodities. That is due to the cheapness of our currency. Now our sovereign should send out an imperial decree, asking the public to turn in cloth and silk as rents. In their transactions at the market, cloth and silk should also be used. The use of coins should be banned, so that there would be less money in circulation and the prices of the commodities would fall.'" In the biography of Zhu Hui in *History of the Former Han*, there was the same recording: "The minister Zhang Lin Liyan said to the king, 'grains were expensive as a result of the cheapness of our currency. We should ban the use of coins and collect cloth and silk for rents and use these as the substitute for money throughout the country.'" Accordingly, the king summoned all the ministers to discuss the issue. Zhu Hui, a chief minister, said that "what Zhang Lin suggested was not practical. As a result, that practice was ended." In *Comprehensive Mirror in Aid of Governance*, it was recorded that the discussion took place after the king returned to the palace on November 7 in the year of 84.

From the above-cited recordings, we know that at that time Zhang Lin thought that all the commodities were expensive, grains and silk included, so he arrived at the conclusion that currency was cheap. That is, the expensiveness of commodities was due to the cheapness of the currency. To solve this problem, he proposed to "ban the use of money" or "to total eradicate the use of currency." In modern words, it means that a deflationary policy should be implemented to stop the increasing of money supply for the purpose of less money in circulation and the cheapness of commodities.

But he wasn't aware that collecting cloth and silk as rents meant that commodities would take the place of currency, which reduced the channels for the withdrawal of coins. If the main channels for the withdrawal of currency were closed and the channels for the supply of coins remained unchanged, the contradiction of there being too much money in circulation would become even worse. So the situation that all the commodities were expensive would never remedy, and would even deteriorate. That was the first point to be noted. Second, the intention of Zhang Lin was that some commodities would be used as the substitute for money. That is, though cloth and silk were used to pay the taxes, coins would still circulate in the market. That would interfere with the circulation of currency and lead to a chaotic result.

The memorial of Zhang Lin was approved by Emperor Zhang, but afterward other people mentioned his proposal again. "In the end, the king assented to such ideas." The adoption of such an ignorant and foolish proposal was nothing but a handful of salt added to the economic wound.

5.2. Liu Tao on "food first, commodities second"

Liu Tao (?–85), also known as Liu Wei, courtesy name Ziqi, was a native of Yingyin of Yingchuan. While studying at the Imperial College at a young age, he submitted a memorial to the king, denouncing Lian Ji for his grabbing of power. During his lifetime, he served successively as Imperial Clerk, head for the executive bureau, Mayor of the Capital City, Supervisory officer, etc. In 185, he presented a memorial to the king to elaborate on eight points of government and attributed the chaotic situation to the eunuchs. Later, he was falsely charged and taken into prison, where he died. His writings amounted to hundreds of thousands of Chinese characters, though they are already lost now.

In 157, due to successive years of war with the Qiang people, the government met with financial difficulties. Under the pretext that "thin and light money was the root of poverty," some scholars suggested the minting of larger coins. Liu Tao, a student of the Imperial College, opposed such a practice, saying, "I read reverently your majesty's edict on the minting of currency and the discussion of the seriousness of the matter …. Nowadays, what worries our king is not the supply of commodities, but the hunger of the people. The law of life is that food takes precedence over commodities ... according to my humble observation, in recent years, the crops have fallen victim to the locusts and the production was not sufficient for the public and private need. What consumes our attention is the daily food and life necessities. Does it have anything to do with the weight and shape of the coins? Even if the sand were turned into gold and the stone jades, with as wise a king as Fuxi, a famous sovereign, in as harmonious a society as the time of Yao and Shun, suppose the common people don't have enough for food and drink, it is still rather hard to have a stable and peaceful country. The reason is that people can live without commodities for a hundred years but can't go on with their life even if there is only one day's shortage of food, which is of paramount importance. Without any understanding of the fundamental importance of agriculture, the contenders delve mainly into the convenience of minting coins. Probably that was for the purpose of cheating at the disadvantage of the national treasury. With the national treasury under threat, there will be even more people joining for the profit therein, thus the emergence of the contention of minting coins. With 10,000 people minting coins and one person joining in to share, the outcome won't suffice. Even worse, now we have 1 person minting coins and 10,000 people joining to share. It is beyond the capacity of production even if we use *yin* and *yang* as charcoal, all the other things as copper, and people who do not need to eat was workers there. If your majesty wants to have rich people and a wealthy nation, the key is to stop corvee and prohibit robbery, so that common people could have enough good without much difficulty. Your majesty is very virtuous and worries about the hardship and sorrow of the people. But it was futile to save the people from dire conditions by minting larger coins to regulate the price of the commodities, just like putting fish into hot water and birds above burning wood. Water and wood are essential for the life of fish and birds, but the untimely use of them will lead to trouble. I do sincerely hope that your majesty would be lenient in the policy of the minting of coins and postpone the minting of larger coins."

Emperor Huan felt that Liu Tao was right, so he did not start the minting of larger coins. Liu Tao's opinion can roughly be reviewed as follows:

First of all, there was something similar to the opinion of Chao Cuo, who said that "pearl, jade, gold and silver were neither edible when hungry nor wearable in times of cold. The reason for their being valuable was that the king made use of them." The two opinions were almost the same, but on second thought, we may notice that the value as mentioned by Chao Cuo derived from the king's use. On the contrary, according to Liu Tao's understanding, currency itself was not enough for the peace of the country and the safety of its people. So the two opinions were not identical at all.

Second, Liu Tao's notion of comparing the importance of survival and the minting of currency was in effect the relationship between production and circulation, as well as the relation between politics, military affairs and economy. Undoubtedly, production determines the circulation, politics and military affairs were the manifestations of the economy, and warfare was the ultimate solution to political problems. However, circulation also influenced production, and in some cases or at some points it restricted production. Similarly, political and military actions also greatly influence economic activities. Liu Tao emphasized the catastrophic effects of social turmoil. Production was halted and people led miserable lives. The country had no peace, and all the families were in a chaotic state. Grains were the basic guarantee for the people's survival, and people could go on with their living even without any commodities. That was in the later years of the Eastern Han Dynasty, where money was indispensable in the socioeconomic life, but common people, surprisingly, could do without currency. This kind of paradoxical reality was the true reflection of the gap between the rich and the poor, between the well-developed and backward areas. The devaluation of the currency and inflation were aggravating this gap and putting the people in a miserable situation.

Third, what kind of coins should be minted? Should they be of the same weight? Fully valued or undervalued? Because there wasn't any detailed recording, we have no way of guessing. However, from Liu Tao's pretext that the coins were too light not to have larger coins, we may infer that what they wanted were definitely not full-valued larger coins. According to Liu Tao, years of plague of locusts destroyed the crops. In their spare time, housewives worried about whether they would have rice to cook or enough salt. So no one would care about the weight and thickness of coins. The emperor wanted to mint new coins to overcome the difficulties, which was like putting fish into hot water and birds above the burning wood. Water and wood were inseparable for the life of fish and birds, but if handled improperly, both fish and birds would die. So he asked the emperor to lessen the burden of taxes and put off the minting of new coins. This should be practical. At that time, the so-called "minting larger coins" must have been undervalued coins. Liu Tao used this method to eliminate the possibility of making money in a public or private way, so he should not have been rebuked as "knowing little but trying to make a fuss" (Peng Xinwei).

5.3. *Xun Yue on "the appropriateness of the Wuzhu coins"*

Xun Yue (148–209 A.D.), courtesy name Zhongyu, was a native of Yingyin of Yingchuan. Descendant of a Confucian family, he was a historian and political commentator in the late Eastern Han Dynasty. Fond of learning since childhood, he was able to explain the *Spring and Autumn Annals* when he was 12 years old. Quiet and good at writing, he was given a post by the General guarding the East. During the reign of Emperor Xian, he served as an imperial tutor, and later Custodian of the Private Library and Palace Attendant. His writings included *Annals of Han* and *Shenjian*.

Shenjian recorded the currency proposition of Xun Yue. The basic tone of the book was that "those who did the benevolent and righteous things would become king while those who acted against that would perish." The thread running through it was that "when the law and education prevail, the country would be harmonious; when the law and education fail, the country would be in disorder." Combining the principles of rites and legal penalty, the book laid special emphasis on education, and put "the prosperity of farming and sericulture for the better government of a country" of paramount importance among the "five kinds of political affairs." He had a keen understanding of the relationship between politics and economy and was of the opinion that "both good and evil were human nature" so law and education could help civilize the people. With its progressive outlook, the book criticized the prevalent theory of Confucianist divination and denounced the absurdity of immortality.

In the last years of the Eastern Han Dynasty, there were repeated mishaps caused either by eunuchs or relatives of a king or an emperor on the side of his mother. The country was in utter disorder, with the life in the royal palace in chaos, bureaucrats greedy for money, people miserable, peasants rising and feudal lords setting up separatists. According to the records in "Food and Commodities" in the *Book of Jin*, after the army of Dong Zhuo arrived in Chang'an, "after all the *wuzhu* coins were destroyed, smaller coins were minted. They collected all the bronze sculptures in Chang'an and Luoyang to use the material for coins. At that time, the new coins were not clearly distinguishable from one another, thus rather inconvenient ... the price of millet was 500,000 coins for one *hu*, and the price of bean and wheat was 200,000 coins for one *hu*. There was even the terrible practice of man-eating, with bones piled up and the stinks smelt on the road." In 189, Dong Zhuo dethroned Emperor Shao and Emperor Xian ascended the throne. In the second year, someone said that "the price of millet was tens of thousands of coins for one *dan*" or "the price of millet was hundreds of thousand coins a *hu*." After Cao Cao took control of the situation, he reorganized the currency system and began to reissue *wuzhu* coins, upon which disputes arose again. Some people thought that *wuzhu* coins were scattered everywhere, and the capital city was in short supply, so that most such coins accumulated in faraway places. The reissuing of *wuzhu* coins meant that using coins of not much value to buy useful material, which would result in the needy state of the capital and the abundance of *wuzhu* coins in faraway places. Other people argued that the reissuing of *wuzhi* coins was based on the condition that all the holdings of the common people should be collected by the government and the coins of faraway places should be collected and sent to the capital. There were also people supporting the "minting of *sizhu* coins" to devalue the *wuzhu* coins. There were even some people in favor of the abolition of currency and the practice of commodity exchange. Xun Yue voiced his opinion in a targeted manner with the following arguments (the sequence of the questions and answers were adjusted).

First of all, "it was appropriate to mint the *wuzhu* coins." In his opinion, "money is indeed very practical and people are willing to use it, so it is difficult to prohibit. It would be ill-advisable today to prevent people from using money at their will." "The urgency of officials was about the millet production. The prohibition on cattle and horses was that they may not go far beyond one hundred *li*. As to other things, people spend their money buying what they need. All the country was a big market. So what is the harm of doing that?" As to the shortage of coins in circulation, Xun Yue said, "With less money in circulation, people would feel at ease. If the circulating money isn't enough, the government could mint new coins to make up for the shortage." If a strict order was executed to accumulate the coins in the capital, "that would be difficult to implement and there will surely emerge some disobeying or deceitful people. There will also be many lawsuits and punishment. Consequently, the disputes over this issue shall be heard throughout the country. So that option isn't helpful in appeasing the war-torn people and bringing about a harmonious society." The time was already ripe to recover the use of wuzhu coins. "With the country in peace, it is a practical option."

Xun Yue was a firm supporter of the *wuzhu* coin system and had clear-cut viewpoints. In the fierce debate on the currency issue, he directly made open his understanding and maintained that *wuzhu* coins were appropriate. He dispelled the idea that *wuzhu* coins should be devalued to *sizhu* coins and the idea of discarding *wuzhu* coins. In today's words, the system of *wuzhu* coins was most appropriate.

Second, the role of currency was for convenient exchange and people were happy to use money in their life, so it would be difficult to prohibit the use of money. For that reason alone, it was clear that *wuzhu* coins were in line with the trend and the public opinion, so they were not to be stopped or abolished by human effort. According to his analysis, the urgent need of the government was grain, cattle and horses, which would be prohibited from being shipped to places over 100 *li* away. As to the circulation of other commodities, there was nothing to be noted, and with the help of the currency, it would circulate more smoothly. So what was the point of worrying? With money as the medium, commodities could travel around the country and various needs would be satisfied. People's lives would become diversified and the production of commodities would be enhanced. That was all that one could wish for, so what was the point of arguing or criticizing?

The advantages of coins were that they were convenient to use and that people were willing to use them. Now the government wanted to abolish the use of coins, which was probably hard to put into practice. Indeed, it would be such a nuisance to carry out a prohibition of coins, which were popular in society. The implied meaning here is that the exchange of commodities for commodities was very much inconvenient, leading to all kinds of shortage, inconvenience and endless trouble. He undoubtedly was a firm supporter of the *wuzhu* coins and an unyielding defender of the currency system. Complying with the trend and the public opinions, he was considering the long-term interests of the rulers and the fundamental interests of the whole society and the people, instead of thinking only of the present and only of the interests of the officials. The aforementioned idea of Zhang Lin, which was to ban the use of currency, seemed to be in the interest of the government. As a matter of fact, it was a move backwards, against the historical trend. So it had no future and was not applicable at all.

He not only theoretically demonstrated that currency was convenient, conducive to the revitalization of the economy and the enrichment of life, thus benefiting the economic exchange and the unity of the country, but also explained the Confucian standpoint of the public attitude, which meant that those supported by the public would win and those disfavored by the public would perish. His profound meaning would surely get the attention of the rulers who were planning to do something, and even treated with caution. From this point of view, Xun Yue was in favor of Cao Cao's restoration of the *wuzhu* coin system, no matter in which way he considered the issue.

The third point was about related specific issues. After the circulation of *wuzhu* coins, if there was a shortage of them in the market, how should the government deal with that? Xun Yue's answer was very simple. The government would mint new coins to make up for it. In addition, was it necessary to collect the *wuzhu* coins in the country and send them to the capital? He thought that it would be improper and difficult to collect the *wuzhu* coins first to send them to the capital and then restore the *wuzhu* coin system. In this process, there would surely be many fraudulent and treacherous things, which would lead to complicated lawsuits and severe penalties. Besides, discordant voices would be heard in the country. That would not be a good way to appease the war-torn people and bring about transparent governance. In other words, the currency issue would evolve into a socio-political issue, which in turn would affect the stability of society. So a wise ruler would never do things like that.

Finally, in today's words, since he opposed barter economy, adhered to the monetary system, and thought *wuzhu* coins were the most appropriate, did it mean that he was in favor of an immediate restoration of the old currency system? His answer was a negative one, because the restoration was based on the condition of a peaceful world, which was an environmental requirement to the socio-economic system. Instead of a chaotic situation of war, the condition was "a peaceful world in which to implement the policy." Otherwise, it would be difficult to sustain the system and the ending would be a sad one.

6. Anti-usury theory in the Eastern Han Dynasty

6.1. *Huan Tan on "the suppression of usury"*

Huan Tan (23 B.C.–50 A.D.), courtesy name Junshan, was a native of Xiang in the state of Pei in the Western Han Dynasty. A well-known scholar at the time, he was versatile and well versed in the five classics. "Adept at writing, he was especially fond of classic learning." Indulging in dance and music, he paid little attention to his appearance but liked to defame scholars of shallow learning, for which he was often marginalized. During the reign of Emperor Guangwu, he served as a supervisory officer. Politically, he was honest and loyal and opposed to malpractice through connections. Economically, he was against part-time jobs and laid emphasis on science and technology. He openly and fiercely voiced his opposition to the superstitious activities advocated by Emperor Guangwu, which almost led to his death. In the early years of the Eastern Han Dynasty, he finished his *New Discussions*, of 29 articles. Now we have an edited version of the *New Discussions* with 16 articles.

In the early years of the Eastern Han Dynasty, due to the long-term war, "people in the country died and roughly 20% of the population survived." Although the law prohibited "businessmen from taking up agricultural job" and "no part-time job was allowed," the fact was that landlords without city registration would do business as usual, and merchants, though with city registration, also owned lands. Huan Tan was against such things. He pointed out that this social phenomenon would weaken agriculture and affect grain production. In addition, the side effects of usury could not be underestimated. He submitted a memorial to Emperor

Guangwu, stating the current affairs and the measures to be taken.[14] Elaborating on usury, he put forward the following points. "The way of governing a country is to advocate agriculture while suppressing industry and commerce. So the previous emperor forbade people to take up part-time jobs and prohibited businessmen from becoming officials, for the purpose of stopping the acquisition of land and cultivating the sense of honor and shame. Nowadays, wealthy businessmen would often lend money to others, while members of the middle income families acted as guarantors. As diligent as servants, their income was comparable to that of the princes and nobles. As a result, other people were envious and wanted to follow suit for the purpose of gains without pains. Such people indulged in extravagant lavishness, to the enjoyment of their ears and eyes. Now your majesty could order the businessmen to report on the malpractice of others. If the money were ill-gotten, the one who reported on the case should be awarded with it. In this way, people would focus on their own occupation and dare not sell their products. With fewer transactions and less strength, they would concentrate on agricultural production. With much effort in agriculture, there would be more grains and the land would be made good use of." There were mainly four points.

First of all, the main lenders of usury were wealthy businessmen. "Nowadays wealthy businessmen would often lend money to others." The wealthy businessmen referred to the registered and unregistered landlords. The difference between the two, politically, was that the latter included powerful people of the upper class, represented by aristocracy and big bureaucrats, while the former was composed of powerful people of the lower class, represented by wealthy merchants, though they were not favored by the latter. Economically, the latter operated their businesses, while the former merged land and needed to bribe the latter in order to obtain the latter's political protection. Therefore, the combination of merchants, landlords and bureaucrats was even closer and more apparent in the Eastern Han Dynasty. Liu Xiu, Emperor Guangwu, was himself a wealthy businessman, and his founding fathers were mostly wealthy businessmen in Nanyang and Hebei. These merchant turned landlords were

---

[14]Biography of Huan Tan in Book 4 of *The Book of the Later Han*, pp. 956–958. Later citations will not be specified.

conferred dukedoms for their military achievements, and their fief, with tens of hundreds of tenants, covered an area of four to six counties. In general, the annual rent tax was nearly 80 million *hu*. In addition, they enjoyed various economic privileges. They would never crack down on businessmen. Instead, they would do their best to protect them. As a result, businessmen suffered little during the war years. During the early years of the Eastern Han Dynasty, businessmen were allowed to develop freely, which promoted the expansion of the merchant turned landlords. The usury activities were more common than in the Western Han Dynasty, with the wealthy merchants and the usurers in collusion, managing both commercial capital and usury. From the very beginning, these wealthy businessmen controlled and dominated the social and economic activities and the financial market of the Eastern Han Dynasty.

Second, with rampant usury activities, the exploitation was ruthless and the usurers were formidable. Although Huan Tan did not mention the interest rate of usury at that time, he described vividly the loan sharks' supreme arrogance and awe-inspiring reputation. "Members of the middle income families acted as guarantors and behaved as diligent as servants." Therefore, other people were envious and wanted to follow suit for the purpose of gain without pain. Such people indulged in extravagant lavishness, to the enjoyment of their ears and eyes. Their income of interest was comparable to that of the princes and nobles. The so-called income of these people was not the collection of rents. According to Li Xian's annotation, "The collection of rents referred to the income from the interest of the usury." The private collection of interests was considered the same as the collection of taxes by the government, from which we can catch a glimpse of the arrogance of the usurers. Because they had direct contact with the debtors, the way they treated the debtors was even harsher than the government's collection of taxes. So the members of the middle-income families followed their orders respectfully, like the accountants submitting their annual accounting report, for the purpose of carving up the interest.

Third, the usury activities were corrosive to the ancient society. Huan Tan believed that usury was not conducive to "stopping the acquisition of land and cultivating the sense of honor and shame," and fostered the extravagant social atmosphere. People were beginning to love leisure and hate labor, envying the practice of gain without pain. The harsh exploitation of usury led to the bankruptcy of many land-holding peasants and even small and medium landlords. Without land, they were reduced to the ranks of servants or vagrants. Faced with the fierce competition of land acquisition, some middle-class families became the dependents of wealthy merchants, in order to get out of the difficulties and avoid being ruined. During the reign of Emperor Ming of the Eastern Han Dynasty, when acquisition was the rage, politicians with achievements and relatives of the king on the side of his mother or wife were all taking away other people's land by force or trickery. By the time Emperor He ascended the throne, the number of vagrants was astounding. During the reigns of Emperor Huan and Emperor Ling, the acquisition of land had reached its zenith, and collapse was inevitable, which was what Huan Tan felt anxious and uneasy about.

Fourth, the suppression of usury would ensure the normal development of agriculture. Huan Tan maintained that "no part-time job was allowed," "prohibiting businessmen from becoming officials" and "businessmen reporting on the malpractice of others." The government should consider all the unlawful income as bribes and reward the whistle-blower. According to his understanding, this would suppress the accumulation of capital and restrict usury activities, thus making people concentrate on agriculture. However, he was too bookish and too naive. First of all, without any sense of law, how could the wealthy merchants "report on each other's malpractice?" Second, though his suggestion was too general to put into practice, it was not beyond remedy. As long as his thinking was correct, his proposition, after revision and improvement, could still be carried out. The vital point here was that he was aware of the object of the policy. When Liu Bang, Emperor Gaozu of Han, ordered that merchants shouldn't wear silk clothes or ride in the carriage and descendants of the registered businessmen should be officials, the main reason was that he himself wasn't a rich businessman. On the contrary, Liu Xiu, Emperor Guanggu of Han, was the offspring of a millet merchant. Around him were rich merchants and businessmen. So how could he tolerate the violation of the fundamental interests of these people and not turn down his suggestion?

Although the idea of "no part-time job was allowed" didn't come from Huan Tan, he put forward the dual purposes of such a regulation. The first purpose was to "prohibit businessmen from becoming officials" for the aim of "stopping the acquisition of land and cultivating the sense of honor and shame." On the basis of a clear distinction between merchants and officials, it seemed that such a practice would prevent the collusion of the two kinds of people and get rid of usury practice and exploitation. The second purpose was "to advocate agriculture while suppressing industry and commerce." It was acceptable to manage and develop one's own business so long as it was lawful. Businessmen could report on their peers' malpractice. This understanding had the significance of restoring agricultural production and ensuring the stability of people's life. Meanwhile, it would crack down on legal business activities because the government encouraged the practitioners to report on their peers' malpractice, which inevitably would affect the normal businesses. So it was quite negative and disadvantageous to the development of production as well as the prosperity of society and economy.

Unfortunately, "after the submission of the memorial, the king paid no attention to it." Neglected by Emperor Guanggu, Huan Tan could do nothing but leave it unsettled.

6.2. Taipingjing on anti-usury

Taipingjing (Scriptures of the Great Peace) was the writing of the upper-level Taoists in the early period of Taoism. Tradition has it that the book was a divinely bestowed gift to Yu Ji (or Gan Ji), a Taoist priest, in the name of *Taiping Qingling Shu*. Originally with 170 volumes in 10 parts, now we have 57 extant volumes in the name of *Taipingjing Hejiao*, edited by Wang Ming. The book was supposed to be written by Yu Ji, Gong Chong and other Taoist priests during the years between 107 and 144. The existing version is hardly free from the revision, addition and omission of later generations, but it is definitely not the combined efforts of patching together by a lot of people. Mainly in the form of questions and answers, the book had a rather consistent view and writing style. Much like the transcript of a certain priest's teaching, there weren't any self-designed questions. Part of the book had a sharp change of tone in its narration, which suggested the possibility of some other writer.[15] The contents of

---

[15] Ren Jiyu, the volume of Qin and Han Dynasties in *A History of Chinese Philosophy*, pp. 658–660.

the book were diversified, with both the essence of democracy and the dregs of fatalism. The core of the book was a divine theory and heaven was the supreme god in this system. The book held that man was a product of nature and should strive together with heaven and earth. As the product of human society, each family member had his or her role to play, such as father, mother or son. They should work together, love each other and jointly manage the family affairs. In each country, people lived according to their social position, such as the ruler, the minister or the governed and they should also work together, love each other and jointly manage the affairs of the country. If this was the case, a harmonious state of being would ensue, which was called *Taiping*. Emphasizing the idea of benevolence, love and the rule of king, the aim of the book was to uphold "the rule of the king to achieve harmony." The averageness of Taiping wasn't that everyone was equal, but that for everything in the world, there should be a proper way of dealing with it, everyone should strictly observe his or duty. Thus, there was the saying that "averageness means fairness," In the socio-economic aspect, wealth was a product of the harmony of *yin* and *yang*. Heaven and earth were benevolent to human beings and that benevolence was all over the world, freeing people from the calamities of poverty and misery. On the contrary, there could be much wealth in the world, like the existence of water, flowing ceaselessly and regularly. Often the humblest was in the lowest position, the rich people were mostly very modest and amiable and the oppressors wouldn't be blessed by the heaven. In most cases, families with many people, much material or many financial resources were in possession of large fortunes, but many of these families would become poor and meet with bad luck. What was the reason for that? According to God, heaven would never bless those disobedient and rebellious actions in the cases where some people took advantage of their wisdom to bully those who were not as intelligent as them, some people made use of their strength to threaten the weak, or young people acted against the wishes of the old. In the socio-ideological aspect, they attempted to eliminate social scourge through the use of the Taoist theory of theology, ease social conflicts and socio-economic crisis in order to maintain social order and stabilize the political power. At the end of the Eastern Han Dynasty, when the rebellion of the peasants was like ignited wood and there would be ceaseless warfare, *Taipingjing* advocated the integration of loyalty, friendship and kindness, and the unification of the ruler, the ministers and the governed to create a united nation. The "Triad-for-Harmony Tricks" was an utter erosion of the peasants' will to rebel for the consolidation of the decadent ruling regime. However, it had also something in the spirit of opposition to the accumulation of wealth of the ruling class and exploitation, in particular the high interest rate exploitation of usury, as well as denouncement of the usurers as being heartless rich.

In the section of "The Six Sins and Ten Punishments,"[16] which included "Questions of the Immortal" and "Answers of Taoist Master," it was said that human beings had six major sins, among which three were related to the interpersonal relationships and the relationship between human beings and society, and the other three were concerned with individuals. These six sins were not forgivable, and whoever committed one of them would have himself and his descendants punished. The condemnation of and accusation against the exploitation of usury can be analyzed from four aspects.

The first aspect was the rampancy of usury. For starters, interest rates were very high, and the income from interests was extremely large. The interest rates ranged from 100% to 400–500%. Such astonishing interest rates might be the general rates at the end of the Eastern Han Dynasty, which were much lower than the "1000% interest rate of Mrs. Wuyan in the Western Han Dynasty." However, the actions of Mrs. Wuyan were after all a unique move in a specific environment, or a risky choice of a person of insight. It could only be considered as a typical example of the astonishing exploitation of usury, instead of being treated as the usual practice. Even so, the interest rate in the Eastern Han Dynasty was much higher than the 20% legal interest rate in the West Han Dynasty. It reflected the sharpness of the class contradictions in the last years of the Eastern Han Dynasty and the brutal exploitation of the people by landlords and merchants. In addition, usurers had hundreds of millions in money but were not willing to help impoverished people, who were dying of hunger and cold. Such sins should not be tolerated. If they themselves were not punished, their descendants would pay a price for that. Heaven

---

[16]*A Comprehensive Proofreading of Taipingjing*, Zhonghua Book Company, 1960, pp. 24–257. Later citations will not be specified.

bestowed wealth to the rich, but the rich refused to aid the poor, resulting in their death of hunger and cold. Instead of being reasonable, the rich made fun of the poor and had a grudge against the heaven, the earth and other people. Consequently, all the gods would hate the rich. For those usurers, whoever could pay off the interests would get the loan. Otherwise, even though "poor people were begging," they would "scold them but would not lend them any money." After much humiliation, the poor would die of hunger or cold without getting any mercy. Instead, they would be laughed at. In addition, the rich would make use of the government and occupying poor people's property. As long as the accumulation of capital could be achieved, these people were capable of all the unscrupulous things and would resort to all the vile and nasty tricks.

The second aspect was about the root cause of the rampancy of usury. The theoretical basis of the authors was that "heaven only cherishes Tao, earth virtue, and the harmony in the middle benevolence." Wealth was the property of the heavens and the earth, and the wealthy shouldn't be allowed to take the wealth as their own. The authors publicly denounced the ancient emperors as ignorant fools and considered them far from being benevolent. These heartless rich were not aware of this and mistakenly believed that all the wealth of the world belonged to them alone. The authors of *Taipingjing* compared the usurers to "rats in the warehouse" and called them "ignorant villains." According to the authors, the usurers were like rats in the warehouse, which often enjoyed themselves alone and thought the warehouse belonged to no one else. As a matter of fact, the food in the warehouse wasn't exclusively for the rats, and the wealth of the rich was also not the possession of certain persons. The rich took possession of the public property but wouldn't let other people make use of it. In cases of lending, they demanded "a more than double return," extorting many more interests than the original capital.

The third aspect was about the consequences of usury. The authors of *Taipingjing* were very clear that with the disparity between the rich and the poor in society and the intensification of conflicts, the ruling regime was in danger. The first indication was that with the polarization of income, the disparity between the rich and the poor tended to deteriorate. "The rich accumulated millions of billions in wealth, and their treasures amounted to the billions. But they kept their possessions in secluded rooms, causing them to become filthy." The poor, on the contrary, without any means of living, were desperate. "Some of them don't have any planting in spring and so don't have any harvest in autumn." "Some others died of hunger or cold, only to be laughed at by the rich." Compared with the life of the rich, the poor suffered a miserable life, poles apart from that of the rich. The second indication was that social conflicts were intensifying and civilians were forced to resist the oppression. The authors of *Taipingjing* thought that the rich accumulated wealth but were stingy with their possessions and hid their wealth in caves. In the end, the country's financial resources were insufficient, the state treasury was empty and the society was in a state of unrest. The authors of *Taipingjing* maintained that wealth was the product of the harmony between heaven and earth. "The wealth was for the sake of the country, so there was no reason to abandon or dispose of wealth without any reason." "If wealth was disposed of without any reason and the country was left poor and without enough financial resources, that would lead to the poverty of the people. So the virtuous king would have not man options in his government." The helplessness of the virtuous king was caused by nothing more than the monopoly of wealth by the usurers, who were unwilling to lend a hand to the poor and afraid of being robbed of their possessions. They buried their wealth deep underground, leaving the common people unable to go on with their lives and the government hardly able to sustain their ruling of the country. Therefore, it was imperative to help the needy and the poor and oppose the deep burial of wealth. The authors then preached the transformation of the status of the ruler and the ruled. "The change from poverty to prosperity would eliminate the difference between the rich and the poor. Prosperity would lead to the possibility of becoming rulers or immortals, while poverty would result in the likelihood of becoming common people and even being imprisoned." That was a clear warning to the rulers and the heartless rich villains that if they offended heaven and earth and all the gods, they would surely have a bad ending.

The fourth aspect was the class limitations of the authors of *Taipingjing*. They were of the opinion that "all trades have profits" and "seeing people in need, it is not punishable to lend them money and ask for interests." What they opposed was the usury practice of the rich to exploit the poor instead of helping them. They didn't argue for the equal division of wealth and were not against the monopoly of wealth by the rich. In their opinion, as long as it was possible to prevent the excessive concentration of wealth, common people should "be content with their poverty," with no intention of seeking wealth and official position. That was in accordance with *Tao*. Striving to preach fatalism, the authors of *Taipingjing* didn't acknowledge that the wealth of the rich derived from the exploitation of the poor, and they stressed repeatedly that wealth was "the support of the land." The rich were lucky enough to "possess the promising land to enrich themselves," so that they could accumulate thousands of billions in wealth. The peasants' rebellion after brutal exploitation was attributed simply to retribution for the sins of the rich. They didn't think that usury was a means by which the rich make profits. Their opposition of usury was based on their disapproval of not helping the needy and they were not clear of the distinction between lending and aiding. Their opposition of usury and exposure and criticism of the exploitation by the rich were not from the position of the ruled classes, but from the reformist position of the ruling class. It was for the purpose of maintaining the long-term reign of the ruling class and easing the class and social conflicts that they rebuked the powerful landlords for their caring for the immediate interests and neglecting the long-range fundamental interests of the nation. They advocated the implementation of reforms, and believed that diverting wealth was better than accumulating. "The people of virtue know that giving would bring the poor happiness. That is benevolent." That kind of practice was advantageous to the rich themselves and to the ruler, because it would aid the king to "take care of the good people." Economically, as long as they did not love wealth as their life, disposing of deteriorated grain and taking back new grain in the way of lending out old would help people get high official positions and become rich, so all the gods would approve of them and heaven and earth would love them. However, that was but an impossible illusion, and shouldn't be considered of equal importance with the thought of "equal division" of the peasant uprising.

Chapter 3

Financial Thought in Wei, Jin, Northern and Southern Dynasties

1. Introduction

In the 360 years of the Wei, Jin, Southern and Northern Dynasties (220–580), the whole country was in a state of division, separation and war, except for the 20-year unification of the Western Jin Dynasty. With the development of natural economy, currency circulation was sharply reduced, and the status of metal currency also declined. The manor economy developed quickly and became a universal existence, thus currency was confined to a narrow sphere. Except in the years between 280 and 289, copper coins would never compete with commodity money. The disordered currency system and the low-quality coins further enlarged the circulation scope of commodity currency. In 221, Cao Pi abolished the use of *wuzhu* coins and began to use grains and silk as money. But an increasing amount of wet grains and thin silk was used as money, which couldn't be prohibited even by strict punishment. In the Southern Dynasties, the state of Eastern Wu minted big coins equivalent to 500 or even 1,000 coins. Shen Chong of Wuxing also minted small coins. But these coins could not meet the needs of agricultural restoration and development, and the money in circulation was scarce.

The usury saw some development in the Wei, Jin, Southern and Northern Dynasties. The earliest credit institutions in China appeared in temples and warehouses. The bureaucrats and the rich entrusted their possessions to the temples, and the monks there exploited the poor in the name of charity. The warehouses were originally used for living, storing goods and transaction, but now they were also places for usury practice. The official residences also lent money and oppressed the people. The forms of credit included commodity, money, goods in terms of money, prepaid service or buying on credit. The lending could be in the manner of public, official, temple or the combination of bureaucrats and religious forces. The interest rates were also varied, from more than double to ten times or even a hundred times more, and there was a written contract for the lending.

2. The "Discussion of the God of Money" by Lu Bao

2.1. *The commodity fetishism in the "Discussion of the God of Money"*

In the Western Jin Dynasty (265–306), there were two books titled *Discussion of the God of Money*. The first one was written by Cheng Gongsu, and the second one was by Lu Bao.

Cheng Gongsui (231–273), courtesy name Zi'an, was a native of Baima in Dongjun in the Western Jin Dynasty. He served as an assistant at the Palace Library and later as a communications secretary. He was good at *cifu*, a sentimental or descriptive literary form, but his collection of writings was already lost. In the Ming Dynasty, people compiled *A Collection of the Writings of Cheng Zi'an*. Now we have only 69 Chinese characters left of his *Discussion of the God of Money*, which was the same as the one written by Lu Bao, except for four sentences.

Lu Bao, courtesy name Yuandao, was a native of Nanyang (present-day Henan Province) in the Western Jin Dynasty. He was good at learning and very knowledgeable. After the Yuankang years (291–299) of Emperor Hui of the Western Jin Dynasty, the country was in great disorder and there was a trend of being greedy and extravagant. The officials were all miserly, and the rich and the powerful took bribes and bent the law. Lu Bao was cynical, so he lived incognito and never again became an official in his lifetime. "He wrote *Discussion of the God of Money* to satire the times"; "those like him transmitted article to other places.[1]" From this we can infer that this article was written in the years between 300 and 306. The article, though seemingly a discussion, was in fact not a treatise on money fetishism, but an economic essay in the form of questions and answers. It started in the history of China the satirical way of mocking money fetishism, in a fashion of combining criticism, irony and hyperbole. But this article did involve the functions of currency, the characteristics and scope of currency circulation, and the author's understanding, reflection and doubt of money fetishism and a series of social phenomena and problems. So, it is quite necessary to make an introduction here.

In this article, there were questions and answers of two fictional characters. One was a child with a family name of Sikong, and the other was Mr. Qi Wu. The former, who was very rich and looked down upon the poor, was the personified currency. The latter, penniless, was an old fellow under the constraint of the feudal code of ethics. From Sikong's point of view, the article touched upon the change in interpersonal relation, social position, ethical and moral ideas, and the way of ruling from four aspects: the origin of money, its function, power and fetishism. Although "with the change of time and circumstances, there were differences between ancient and present customs, a universal phenomenon is that the rich would live in glory while the poor would live in disgrace." So, people should live like the ancients, advocating rusticity and honesty. Otherwise, the result would be "a state of poverty and infamy," a kind of ridiculous and stupid action, which was mainly due to the "ignorance of both the ancient and the present practice." In this article, the author spoke highly of the clever use of money, as if money was a God. For this reason, Lu Bao deserved a place in the history of Chinese financial thought.

There were six main aspects in this article as follows.

First of all, money was the outcome of the subjective will of the earliest sages, whose shape was a realization of the concept of round heaven and square earth, an ancient notion of the universe. After Shennong-*shi*, "The Yellow Emperor, Yao and Shun taught people agriculture and the raising of silkworms, using coins and silk as the most fundamental." Under the direction of those "superior minds with sharper thinking," the

---

[1] Biography of Lu Bao in *The History of Jin*.

exchange of commodities was substituted by the exchange with currency. People began to mine copper and mint copper coins. Under the influence of the ancient notion of the universe, it was determined that coins should have a round outside and a square inside, which resembled the heaven and the earth, respectively. That was a great invention. The reason for money's being valued and being of magic force was that "money was indeed omnipotent." That was Lu Bao's explanation of the money worship and the reason why money was capable of everything. With the shape of heaven and the earth, it embodied the form of both heaven and earth and integrated their soul, thus becoming even powerful than heaven and earth. Money could "bring safety to those in danger, life to those dying. Man's life and fortune are both determined by money. How about heaven? Heaven has its limitations, but money has its advantages." He was the first to connect the shape of heaven and earth with money worship, which was a clear demonstration of his rich imagination and strong urge to uncover the mystery of money and money worship.

He also believed that the copper money was originally produced at the end of the Zhou Dynasty. During the reign of King Jing of Zhou, the government began to mint copper coins, using copper from the west. Copper mines scattered around the vassal states, from the eastern city of Changsha in Hunan to the Western city of Yuexi in Sichuan. As a mixture of various metals, copper coins are made of "gold as father, silver as mother, lead as the eldest son, and tin as the wife," making it convenient for fulfill the function of circulation.

The second point was about the function of money and its circulation features. The main characteristics of currency circulation were that "its accumulation was like a mountain and its movement was like a flowing river. It was sometimes in motion and sometimes motionless." It moved around rhythmically and regularly, functioning as the means of circulation, payment as well as storage. In fulfilling its role, copper money was not easy to wear out and could last a long time, which ensured the continuity of money circulation. This was conducive to market exchange. There was no need to worry about the difficulty in transaction caused by wear and tear, nor would things like the shortage of money interfere with the normal transaction of the market, which would result in the termination of commodity exchange. From the perspective of monetary development, this understanding was progressive, especially in the Western Jin Dynasty when natural economy had seen development.

Third, the function of currency had gone beyond the scope of commodity exchange, showing a magical and omnipotent force. The power of money was really magical and great. The most prominent feature was that it was easy to carry about, having the ability to get everything. The daily life of urban people couldn't function without money. With enough money, one could go anywhere. "No matter how far or remote it is, there is nowhere money can't reach." It conquered everything and was invincible. "With no wings, it could fly; with no feet, it could walk. It could make the grave people laugh and make man of few words talk." "Those with more money would be in the front, and those with less money would follow in the rear. Those in the front were the king and the superior, while those in the rear were subjects to the king or servants. The king and the superior were rich and have enough money to spend, while the subjects or servants were poor and in need." To sum up, "the loss of money would result in poverty and the gain of money would make one rich." Consequently, people liked money as if it was their brother, calling money "Brother Kongfang." Because of money, the rich young men in the capital city loathed to study or discuss questions and preferred to nap in the classroom. That was a lament over the uselessness of studying. It was money that determined the social status of the person, not the emperor, the sages, the riches, the law or destiny. As long as money was a blessing, there is no good or bad luck. To seek fortune, one needn't study and walk the path of officials, because all these things would come together with money. Lu Bao even cited the example of Emperor Gaozu of Han, and the story of Sima Xiangru and Zhuo Wenjun. The former wrote a letter of congratulations to his father-in-law and pleased him, thus marrying his daughter. The latter embarrassed his father-in-law after eloping with his daughter and got part of his possessions, thus getting rid of poverty. From these examples, it was quite clear that money could buy off all the dignitaries who occupied dominant positions. They were nothing but servants of money. They all had to pray at the feet of the currency for protection and assistance. So, it was clear that money was God, the "divine treasure" or "Godly thing," with "divine power" incomparable to heaven, earth, ghosts or even Gods.

Fourth, the divine power of money was manifest in that money was omnipotent. Money could move the Gods, and money can maneuver ghosts, let alone human beings. As a social force, the power of money was above everything else. "With no position, money was respectable; with no power, it was touted." Money was the power that dominated and governed everything. Everything, whether it was a commodity or not, must be tested by money and turned into something that money could purchase and possess. Money had the power to purchase, possess, change and manipulate everything. It could adjust the social relations in ancient China. In the face of money, fame and fortune would be cast into the shade. Instead of seeking fame, it was better to pursue money. "Position and rank were all determined by money." "Human life was decided by the fortune, but a person's wealth and rank were determined by his possessions." "Why do you read for the purpose of wealth and rank?" As long as there was money, good fortune should naturally follow. Even calamities would be turned into blessings. "Dangerous situations would become safe, and dying people would survive." Without money, you couldn't even move one step. "The honorable would become mean, and the living would be punished with death." The traditional blood and clan relationship became loose and weak, difficult to maintain. Before money, "people behaved as if they were brothers." Among relatives and friends, "Hold hands together and embracing each other, people were very intimate. Those with more money would be in the front, and those with less money would follow in the rear. Those in the front were the king and the superior, while those in the rear were subjects to the king or servants." Money would make the love between family members or loved ones even more intimate. It was flowing ceaselessly like the water of a spring. "Money is like a fountain. Though people use it every day, it will never exhaust. It will reach all the faraway or impenetrable places... Money is used to get what one wishes, with no restrictions." "The accumulation of money was like a mountain and the flowing of money like a stream. Sometimes it flows, while at other times it would remain motionless. There is some regulation as to its movement." He not only revealed the functions of money and the rules governing its circulation but also exaggerated its status and role. He believed that money "will reach all the faraway or impenetrable places" and money "is used to get what one wishes, with no restrictions." According to his understanding, at that time, the key to a family's prosperity was money. Otherwise, "even if one has some influential connections in the royal court, without money, it would be like wanting to go without feet or fly without wings." Even if you were as talented as Yan Hui or as handsome as Zizhang, there would still be no hope, just like a man without arms. As a result, "it's better to return home early to start the management of agricultural and business affairs, for the purpose of earning money. With all their efforts, gentlemen would have even better reputation." In the course of trading activities, currency could fully play its role and be useful. Therefore, "the marketplace will be convenient, without the worry of wear and tear. And there will be no shortage of any kind, so that the harmonious state will last and money will be treasured by people around the world." Scholars and wealthy people also didn't read books and focused their attention on making money. Money could enrich the poor, comfort the rich and make the timid brave. For this reason, it was said that without money, the ruler could neither recruit the talented people nor order the warriors to accomplish any tasks. That was what we called human beings dying in pursuit of wealth. The power of money could go beyond the heaven and the earth, reach the heavenly court and order about ghosts and Gods. Though with no position, it was respectable; with no power, it was pursued vigorously. It reached into the rich families and was earning the highest acclaim of the people. So it was said that "money could settle all the things, such as lawsuits, the help of the needy, and the hatred between different people. As the saying goes, 'though with no ears, money would be ordered about'. Wasn't that really true? And there was another saying, 'money could instigate the ghosts.' So it was even so with human beings." The description of the power of money by Lu Bao was also identical to what was said by William Shakespeare in *Timon of Athens*. Shakespeare wrote that gold "will make black white, foul fair, wrong right, base noble, old young, coward valiant." It "will knit and break religions, bless the accursed, make the hoar leprosy adored, place thieves and give them title, knee and approbation with senators on the bench: this is it that makes the wappen'd widow wed again."[2] The depiction of monetary power was so vivid and lifelike. As a result, Karl Marx praised Shakespeare, saying that

---

[2] Quoted from *Complete Works of Karl Marx and Friedrich Engels*, vol. 23, p. 152.

"Shakespeare excellently depicts the real nature of money"[3] and "his understanding is on the mark."[4] This comment also applies to the *Discussion of the God of Money* by Lu Bao. The difference between the two was that one was an essay and the other was the lines of a drama. One was written in the 4th century and the other was composed in the 16th century. One aimed at the copper coins minted from cheap metals, while the other was about gold, a precious metal. One was written in ancient China and the other in Britain when feudal society was disintegrating and capitalism was developing. Though the two were 1,200–1,300 years apart, the power of money as they described was the same, just like Karl Marx's opinion, "everything, commodity or not, is convertible into gold. Everything becomes saleable and buyable. The circulation becomes the great social retort into which everything is thrown, to come out again as a gold-crystal. Not even are the bones of saints, and still less are more delicate res sacrosanctae, extra commercium hominum able to withstand this alchemy .... Thus the ancients therefore denounced money as subversive of the economic and moral order of things."[5]

Fifth, currency changed people's moral concepts, ethical ideas and ideology. Bu Shang, a disciple of Confucius, held that "life and death, fame and wealth are all predestined." Sikong blatantly changed the sentence into "life and death were not predestined, and one's fame and wealth were determined by money." The former preached the theory of destiny, while the latter replaced the former with the omnipotence of money. This not only denied and challenged the traditional fatalistic view but also challenged all the old ideas and concepts. All the old ideas and concepts were to be tested before money. Since currency could change everything, it was fully qualified to challenge the traditional fatalistic view and subvert its existence. Wasn't that so? "Heaven has shortcomings while money had advantages. For the change of time and the birth of all the different things, heaven was better than money." But in human society, "to help the needy and the poor, money would function better than heaven." In the Spring and Autumn period, there were men who excelled in such aspects as being

---

[3]*Complete Works of Karl Marx and Friedrich Engels*, vol. 42, p. 152.
[4]*Complete Works of Karl Marx and Friedrich Engels*, Book one of vol. 46, p. 109.
[5]*Complete Works of Karl Marx and Friedrich Engels*, vol. 23, p. 152.

resourceful, brave or versatile, but they had to be good at ritual and music to be called perfect men, but with the possession of money nothing else would matter.

Sixth, the power of the money changed the king's way of ruling. "Without money the king could neither attract talents nor order talents about even if they come." Money could make the poor rich. The interpersonal relationship would change from being icy to being friendly and the timid people would become brave. As the saying goes, "without any background in the royal court, it is better to go home farming." Even if you had some background, without much money, it would still be like wanting to walk without feet or fly without wings. Even though you were handsome or talented, being empty-handed meant that you had no chance at all. It was better to go home early to manage business to make money by different means. Loving money like other people and buying up people around you, you would surely become reputable and powerful.

2.2. Historical position of the "Discussion of the God of Money"

The *Discussion of the God of Money* was the first monograph to discuss exclusively the fetishism of money in the history of China. After the establishment of the monetary economy in the Warring States period, the fetishism of money had been increasingly noticeable in people's social life and ideas. In "The Money-makers" of *Records of the Grand Historian*, there was a proverb illustrating this: "The son of a family with a thousand pieces of gold will not die in the market-place." Sima Qian also lamented that "a family with a thousand pieces of gold is comparable to the lord of a city; a man with millions can live like a king. There are indeed reasons for calling such men 'nobles without fiefs?'" In the Wei and Jin Dynasties, although the rise of the natural economy suppressed the monetary relations, in the big cities, the upper class of the ruling clique was worshipping and pursuing money as usual, or even more than before. During the Western Jin Dynasty, the fetishism of money became the paramount principle governing the behavior of people, especially the upper class of the ruling group. The greed, parsimony, extravagance and debauchery of the ruling class were as open as shameless.

The idea of monetary fetishism and the powerful status of money were most clear in the cities, especially among the ruling class in the metropolitan cities centering on the capital. The exposure and satire of the article targeted the king, the king's relatives, merchants, aristocracies, landlords, the gentry and the literati. Loving money more than their life, these people would trade anything for money, displaying their ugliest aspects. From this, we can see that in ancient China, the cities were the camps of the ruling class and the political and economic centers of a country. Inside the cities lived the elites of the ruling class and those literati, politicians, as well as businesspersons whose lives circled the ruling class. The cities were also the distribution centers for commerce and industry, and the places where commodity and currency economy was more developed. Commodity and currency relations developed even more quickly in this small world of the cities.

In ancient China, with power one could easily get money. With the development of monetary relations, with money one could also become powerful. Therefore, money and power were complementary. "After three years of clean service as the magistrate, you shall earn 100 thousand taels of silver," which was a clear demonstration that with power one could get money. Selling official posts or titles and redemption after paying fines were examples of money buying power. Lu's crude advocating of the idea that study was useless was unprecedented and had a negative effect on later generations. However, his satire of the dirty social practice was enlightening and shocking. Very forcefully, he removed the ethical veil of loyalty, filial piety, brotherly love, matrimonial love, family love and the relation of the king and his ministers, which used to be affectionate and pervasive. People of all persuasions, without any exception, loved nothing but money. The ties of kinship, already shocked and questioned, became those of less meaning. The paramount tie with and love of money was greatly enhanced. Money could help you get a title, respect, honor and all other things, which was true in a society where commodity economy was highly developed. As a result, "it has ... put an end to all feudal, patriarchal, idyllic relations. It has pitilessly torn asunder the motley feudal ties that bound man to his natural superiors, and has left remaining no other nexus between man and man than naked self-interest, than callous 'cash payment.'"[6] During the Wei, Jin, Southern and Northern Dynasties, the aristocrats were some hereditary nobles, who not only controlled the state apparatus from generation to generation but also had an insurmountable gap with the ordinary people. Such a situation would present itself in ancient China because there were changes to the regime controlling the nation, but it would never become a universal reality that one's money would determine his official title or honors. Lu praised the supernatural and unmatched power of money in a literary way. He was being deliberately partial and exaggerated the role and position of money currency in ancient China, but that would not influence our research interest in and admiration of this article.

The appreciation and citation of this article no doubt indicate its profundity. However, why could there be such a social phenomenon of money being omnipotent and paramount, and leading to everything else? Under the temptation of money, why would the mentality and conception of people undergo such a huge change as to reverse all the normal criteria and put everything under the test and validation of money? Commercial capital includes the circulating monetary capital and commodity capital. Merchants use currency to exchange currency and multiply currency for profit reciprocally, so a huge flow of currency would come into being. Within the scope of the exchange of goods, whoever owns money could dominate everything and possess everything, including land, the most basic means of production in ancient society. All these things were unbelievable, and it was hard to figure out the underlying reasons, because the mean or dirty practice in the monetary economy was previously either covered up or too familiar for people to pay any attention to. After Lu Bao made it known, money changed from the darling of all the people to something despicable. The "evil desire to seek fortune" became at once a source of trouble. Therefore, what was the real reason for such a tremendous change? He did not give any answer. However, he revealed the fanatical pursuit and unlimited worship of money by the upper-class people in ancient China that was more than a social phenomenon of monetary

---

[6]Selected Works of *Karl Marx and Fredrick Engels*, vol. 1, p. 253.

economy. He noticed the universal purchasing power of money, but he did not reveal the source of such power and the intrinsic link between commodity and the currency, or the labor theory of value. Meanwhile, he aroused the hatred of money and created a potential rebellion against currency. In the case of not being able to get rid of the relation between currency and commodities, it was one of the bad effects of this article to deny the necessity of its existence and its positive roles.

3. Kong Linzhi's refutation of "Abolishing Coins to Use Grain and Silk as Currency"

3.1. Huan Xuan's proposal of "Abolishing Coins to Use Grain and Silk as Currency"

In 208, after Cao Cao became the imperial chancellor of Emperor Xian of the Eastern Han Dynasty, he ordered the abolition of the smaller coins minted under the order of Dong Zhuo, for the purpose of resuming the circulation of *wuzhu* coins. However, at that time, it was quite popular to use grain and silk as money or exchange commodities with commodities. In 221, the government reordered the use of *wuzhu* coins. In October, grain became expensive, so *wuzhu* coins were abolished again, and grain and silk were used as currency. During the reign of Emperor Ming (227–238), after a long time of using grain and silk as money, there emerged more techniques of forgery. People "used wet grain for profit and made thinner silk to transact, which were not to be stopped even by severe punishment." In 227, the court held a meeting to discuss monetary problems. Officials like Sima Zhi unanimously held that "using metal coins would not only enrich the nation, but also cut down punishable offenses." Consequently, *wuzhu* coins were in circulation again. In the two hundred years after the Jin Dynasty, "no action of changing coins was taken."

In the period of the Sixteen Kingdoms, there were frequent wars and the nation was in chaos, with the commodity and currency relations deteriorating substantially. Every now and then, "coins would not circulate, but grain and silk would prevail." At the end of the Jin Dynasty, although "the central part was in disorder," the Hexi area, at the border frontier, was temporarily stable, and became a refuge for people of the central part. In 313, Zhang Gui, the prefectural governor of Liangzhou (now Wuwei county, Gansu Province) adopted the suggestion of Suo Fu, the military staff officer of prefecture chief. "The government decided to put coins in circulation. Metal coins became very popular, and people relied on its convenience." According to Suo Fu, "in ancient times people used gold, shells, and leather as money, whose consumption was very large consequently. During the two Han Dynasties, *wuzhu* coins were in easy circulation. During the *taishi* years of the Jin Dynasty, the area of Hexi was in an abandoned state, which resulted in the abolition of metal coins and the use of silk as money. Silk would easily become bad, which would make it difficult to transact. What was more, female workers would work even harder. So there were indeed too many disadvantages .... It is indeed time to re-use *wuzhu* coins to make it convenient." It was clear that Suo Fu had realized the three shortcomings of using grain and silk as currency: One was that since grain and silk played the role of means of circulation, there would be a large consumption of the two things. In the years of war when clothing and food were in great need, such a situation was unbearable. Second, using cloth as currency was even more disadvantageous than using grain, because much cloth would be in use. Besides, when necessary, cloth would have to be torn apart to satisfy the different needs. That would be a waste of the labor of women workers. Third, using grain and silk as currency would pose problems to the exchange of commodities. The author did not give any specific explanations for this. It might be safe to assume that the problems would concern the carrying, handling, storing, inventorying and even security. After the normalization of social, political and economic life as well as the exchange of goods, commodity currency would become troublesome and need to be dealt with.

In the Eastern Jin Dynasty, the government used the old currency of Eastern Wu and did not mint any coins, so there was a serious shortage of currency. To solve this problem, in 403, Huan Xuan, the supreme government official in charge of military affairs, who was also controlling the government, reintroduced the old proposal of abolishing metal currency to use grain and silk, which was naturally opposed by Kong Linzhi.

3.2. Kong Linzhi's theory against "the abolition of metal currency to use grain and silk"

Kong Linzhi (369–423), courtesy name Yanlin, was a native of Shanyin, Kuaiji (now Shaoxing, Zhejiang Province). Good at the classics and music, he did not manage any business because his family was poor. During the *yuanxing* years of Emperor An, Huan Xuan was dominating the national affairs, but Kong would not follow Huan Xuan's voice and opposed the use of grain as currency.

"While Huan Xuan was assisting the governing of the country, he proposed to abolish the use of metal currency in favor of grain and silk." Drawing upon the understanding of his predecessors, Kong summed up the historical experience of monetary circulation and voiced his own points of view, which included five aspects:

The first was about the function of currency as the means of circulation. Quoting from "Great Plan" of the *Book of Documents*, he held that among the eight important things governing a country, currency was second only to grain, which indicated the importance of currency circulation. It was vital to the governing of a country and played an important role. Although money was very important, common people did not make every effort to mint coins and the development of agriculture was not influenced at all. Therefore, there was no need to prohibit the use of metal currency. Now the peasants settled themselves in their farming and the handicraftsmen could work at ease. All the people were caring about their own business. No one was striving for money ceaselessly. Besides, the reason for the early kings' invention of such useless currency was that it communicated the transaction of useful things. With the advantage of reducing the wear and tear of goods and the trouble of transportation, metal currency took the place of turtle shells and was used ever since. Following the theory in *Guanzi* and that of Chao Cuo, Kong inherited the nominalistic idea of currency. As a result, he maintained that "early kings invented the useless money for the transaction of things useful" and that "the use in the transaction was of paramount importance."

Second, metals were the most suitable monetary material. Compared with turtle shells, grain and silk, metals had unparalleled superiority. According to his understanding, compared with turtle shells, for metal coins "there was neither the cost of damaging or destruction, nor the burden of transportation." Compared with grain and silk, the advantages were even more obvious. "Grain and silk were treasures of the world and were used for food and clothing. Now we use them as money, which will surely lead to much destruction. In business transactions, there will be more wear and tear, posing a big problem." It was found that "devious people even wet the grain and make thinner silk to make profit." "Even though there was severe punishment, it was hard to get rid of." This analysis of Kong was more profound and more comprehensive than that of Suo Fu.

As we know, the requirements for currency material include unitarity, homogeneity, separability and combinability. Currency should be small but of high value, not perishable, easy to carry and transport, and have no direct impact on production and consumption. In this regard, Kong's analysis was incomplete and not clear. He did not delve into the need of the five functions of currency on the grounds of value theory to elaborate on the physical properties of currency material. He emphasized the superiority of metal currency and exposed the disadvantages of commodity currency, which was far more systematic and profound than the opposition of his predecessors.

Kong's discussion of the usefulness and uselessness of currency was on the premise of the nominal theory of money. That is, he denied its use value but recognized its social property as a means of circulation. We should have a clear understanding of this issue. Should we reject it totally without any reservation? The answer is no. According to Karl Marx, "Useless as they are in the direct process of production, they are easily dispensed with as means of existence, as articles of consumption. For that reason any desired quantity of them may be absorbed by the social process of circulation without disturbing the processes of direct production and consumption. Their individual use-value does not come into conflict with their economic function."[7] On the choice of currency material, Kong realized that in contrast to grain and silk, metal currency was of little or even no value to human existence. Therefore, it was not

---

[7] *Complete Works of Karl Marx and Friedrich Engels*, vol. 13, p. 145.

surprising that he emphasized the usefulness of grain and silk and denied the usefulness of metal currency. However, we must point out that metals have some special features, which, though not shared by grain and silk, were essential to being currency material. Meanwhile, he denied the usefulness of metal currency material in human production and life, so he was not able to know the difference between copper, a cheap metal, and precious metals like gold and silver. During the long history of Chinese people's use of copper coins, copper also served as the raw material for production tools, household items, military equipment, decorations and religious artifacts. In the circulation of currency, copper was the main currency material for the minting of copper coins. Consequently, its economic function invariably conflicted with the function of being production tools, military weapons and household items. Besides, there was always a difference among the price of copper, the real value of copper coins and the nominal price of the coins. As a result, government or private institutions would often cast copper to make utensils or weapons, leading to the lack of currency in circulation and the retardation of the exchange. On the one hand, money shortage occurred from time to time, often bothering the government and the literati of the enlightened landlords. On the other hand, the old way of thinking would be mentioned again: "Early kings invented the useless money for the transaction of things useful." This conflict between practice and theory was adequate to reveal the deviation of this theory and thus led to long-term practical problems.

Third, the abolition of money would lead to many disadvantages. According to Kong, the reason for not using money was not money itself, but the long-lasting war since the end of the Han Dynasty. As a means of circulation, if money was banned, its functions would cease to work and its feature as a general representative of social wealth would not be reflected. If people were forbidden to use money to buy things, holders of copper coins would not be able to go on with their normal production and life. According to Kong's explanation, some families in the country were overflowing with the deposit of grain, while other families did not have much grain in reserve. The adjustment of such a discrepancy would only be possible with the help of money. Once metal currency was out of circulation, rich men in need of grain would starve and the common people would suffer economic loss. That was the first point. The second point was that people were long accustomed to the use of metal coins. A slight change would result in the worry or even panic of the people, which in turn would lead to the instability of the market and the disorder of social life. The third point was history had shown that such practice would not enjoy popular support. Emperor Cao Rui had been using grain as money for thirty years at that time. However, because of "the inconvenience to the people," ministers were debating and those able and talented in politics all agreed that metal coins should be restored. The unanimity of the ruling class and the common people in their opposition to the use of grain and silk as money was ample proof of the unpopularity of these things. That was the so-called "inconvenience to the people."

Fourth, the use of metal currency did not bring about any drawbacks. Kong elaborated on the role of money from the reverse side. As was pointed out by Sima Zhi, "the use of metal currency not only enriches our country but also reduces the punishable crimes." Metal currency was conducive to the normal process of social reproduction, which was an economic as well as a political issue. According to Kong, if common people were fully committed to casting money, such a practice would interfere with their own life businesses. Even the government would not be able to prohibit such things. If all the people focused on their own businesses and tried their best, would anyone of them care about money? That is to say, production (limited to agricultural production at the time) determined circulation and the existence and development of a society depended on the smooth progress of social reproduction. The size of the circulation, the amount of labor involved and the number of coins required for circulation must all be within the limits of social reproduction, particularly within the quantity and price range of the final products it provided. Otherwise, the prohibition of money would be reasonable. In his argumentation, there were exaggerated elements. For example, at that time civilians did not take part in the private minting of coins. The reason was that ancient China was, after all, mainly a natural economy. Except for the payment of government funds, in the areas where commodity economy developed rapidly, or the commercial and trade cities, most of the socio-economic structure was not aimed at the production of commodities or commodity circulation. In addition, at that time the money in circulation was mostly old coins. This might be due to the restriction to the scope of the circulation of currency or due to the private minting, which had not become a serious social problem. Otherwise, the minting of coins would always compete for labor forces with agricultural production. That was the first point. Second, the places where money was used were not poor, while the places where grain took the place of money were not rich. In other words, the richness of a region was not connected to the abolition of metal currency. Metal material was not the root of commodity production and exchange, but it was the hallmark of that development. Consequently, the richness of a place was not associated to the currency material of that place, but the kind of currency material chosen was a reflection of the level of productivity and the development of commodity production and exchange, of which Kong was well aware. Third, during the last years of the reign of Emperor Xiaowu of the Wei Dynasty, "with the country at peace and a good harvest in agriculture, people were enjoying a good life. Almost all the households had ample supply of grain and silk." That fact demonstrated clearly that "money would not interfere with the normal social, political and economic orders. In consequence, he concluded that the real reason for the discussion on the abolition of money was that "there were many wars and famines." The way out of this difficulty was not the abolition of money, but to change people's concepts and to get rid of the outdated idea which put money as the opposite of agriculture, and attributed the reason for the backwardness of agriculture, the shortage of food and clothing, and the poverty of the people to the use and circulation of metal currency. To develop agriculture, the only way was to strengthen education in agriculture and publicize the policy of developing agriculture. The government should educate the peasants in the understanding of the timing of the farming season, the settlement in their livelihoods and the promotion of jobless people taking up agricultural work. Even the merchants would stop their business to be peasants. In this way, the whole country would make concerted efforts in the development of agriculture, without any land left uncultivated. As long as such practice continued, all the food and clothing problems would be solved, and a peaceful and harmonious society would surely come. So the conclusion was that "in my humble opinion, the way to get out of difficulty has nothing to do with the abolition of metal money."

Fifth, it was the general trend and a kind of long-term policy that metal currency would take the place of commodity currency and coins would replace grain and silk. After a comparison of the positive and negative sides and a tracing of the history to the reality, Kong refuted the idea that the Wei Dynasty restored the use of metal currency to increase the nation's financial resources. He pointed out that at that time, many virtuous and talented people held official positions. They were assisting the emperor to draft polices for the benefit of the whole country. If the use of grain and silk was more convenient than that of coins, those wise celebrities would never quit the use of grain and silk, even if they were blinded by the immediate interests. He held a firm belief that the decision to restore the use of metal currency of the Wei Dynasty was a reforming move based on the long-term and fundamental interests of the country. This showed that he believed in "the permanent use of metal currency." His opinion was that it was the fundamental choice and the long-term trend that metal currency would supplant gain and silk.

According to Kong Linzhi, the replacement of coins by grain and silk was only a special social phenomenon under certain historical conditions. It was an expedient measure. It was by no means the long-term and final solution to the problem of the transaction and transfer of commodities. Metal coins had advantages that were incomparable to those of grain and silk, and metals, as the best currency material, "would be permanently used." That comment on metal currency was the highest and most unprecedented, though not scientific and accurate enough as well as a little biased. Amid the noise of abolishing the use of metal currency in favor of grain, in a period of difficult relation between commodities and currency, he held his own opinion against that of the majority and clearly put forward the idea that "money was more convenient than grain." His wisdom and firmness were beyond those of ordinary people. His resolution and realistic attitude should be of the first class in ancient China, especially in the Northern and Southern Dynasties. His full affirmation of the positive role of money was indicative of his firm belief, outstanding judgment, deep understanding of the circulation of currency and his active as well as progressive way of argumentation. Upon his insistence, "most officials in the court agreed with him, so the proposal of Huan Xuan was not put into practice."

3.3. *Zhou Lang and Shen Yue on "the abolition of metal currency"*

In 453, 50 years after Kong Linzhi's opposition to the abolition of money and the use of grain and silk, Zhou Lang proposed the practice of "stopping the use of metal currency to use grain and silk as the means of punishment and awarding." Later, when Shen Yu wrote the biography of Kong Linzhi, he preserved Kong's memorial to the throne on the advantages of currency, but denounced it as "seeing the minor points overlooking the fundamentals." Echoing the opinion of Zhou Lang, he put forward clearly the idea of "stopping the use of money."

Zhou Long (425–460), courtesy name Yili, was a native of Ancheng in the Song Dynasty of the Southern Dynasties. During the reign of Emperor Wen of the Song Dynasty, he served as an officer of Liu Yigong, the Prince of Jiangxia. During the reign of Emperor Xiaowu, he served successively at different posts. In 460, he was discharged from his post for disobeying the royal edict. On his way to Ningzhou (west of Qujing County, Yunnan Province) as a prisoner, he was put to death.

For a long time, the Eastern Jin Dynasty had not minted any coins, so there was a long-term shortage of currency. After the establishment of the Song Dynasty of the Liu clan in the Southern Dynasties, currency became even scarcer and the flow of commodities was blocked, restricting the recovery and development of production. In 421, it was suggested that the government should collect all the copper utensils of the common people to mint *wuzhu* coins. Fan Tai voiced his opposition to this, on which Emperor Wu made no comment. In 430, after Emperor Wen ordered the minting of *sizhu* coins, the tight circulation of coins was eased. In 447, Liu Yigong suggested the use of big coins, using one *wuzhu* coin to replace two less-heavy *sizhu* coins, but both public and private sectors felt its inconvenience. In 453, after Emperor Xiaowu ascended the throne, he asked the officials to offer their ideas. Zhou Lang put forward a memorial to talk about agricultural production, which involved monetary issues. According to his understanding, he made the following points:

First, attaching importance to agriculture meant that metal currency should be canceled. In his opinion, "as the root of a country, farming and sericulture were of paramount importance to the life of common people. With either one missing, etiquette would not prevail." It was considered an unquestionable orthodox idea in ancient China that farming was the basis of a country and the booming of farming and sericulture would lead to the prevailing of etiquette. Therefore, he believed that grain and silk were not compatible with money and the life of one aspect meant the death of the other aspect. Consequently, he put forward his suggestion firmly: "If the king considers it important, he should ban the use of metal currency and use grain and silk as the standard of punishment and reward."[8] He put agricultural production and the circulation of currency in complete opposition relations, believing that farming and sericulture were the lifelines of common people and the fundamental basis of a country. The prospering of farming and sericulture meant the prevailing of etiquette. As was pointed out in the section of "On Governing the People" in *Guanzi*, "if people have enough food supply stored in granaries, they will pay attention to etiquette; if people are not short of food and clothes, they will lay stress on the sense of honor and shame." However, in view of the shortage of storage and insufficient food and clothing, the author of *Guanzi* and Zhou Lang had different ideas. Zhou Lang considered money as the root of evil. Stressing agriculture meant the abolishing of the metal currency. After the abolition of the metal currency, the loss of labor in the agricultural sector could be prevented. In fact, the restoration and development of agricultural production and the circulation of metal currencies were not opposed to each other, but promoted each other. Kong's criticism showed that this theory was untenable. That was an inheritance of Gong Yu's idea and was only one aspect of the matter. The other aspect was that after the abolition of metal currency to use grain and silk as the standard of punishment and reward, the main body was the landlord class, because the labor

---

[8]Biography of Zhou Lang in *The Book of Song*, Book 7, pp. 2093–2094. The following citations will not be specified.

forces were guaranteed, and the object of the measure was the farmers. The landlord class was able to guarantee the development of agricultural production to enrich the country. Such a practice was the duplication of Chao Cuo's "idea of using grain as the standard of punishment and reward." This idea of agriculture as being of fundamental importance was most fully affirmed by Shang Yang in the Warring States period. But after a considerable development of the commodity and currency economy in the Han Dynasty, at a time when natural economy saw little development because of war, the resurfacing of such an outdated idea was but the rise of a conservative and backward idea.

Second, the government should establish a currency model of using commodity currency as the medium for large payments and metal currency for small payments. Zhou Lang feared that after he put forward the idea of "abolishing metal currency," common people would be too dumb to put his idea into practice and would only discuss the issue but do nothing. Because of this, he wanted to take a realistic approach. That is to say, the first step was to narrow the scope of circulation of metal currency, and use silk and rice for large payments. Should the amount exceed 1,000 coins, it would be paid in silk or rice. Should the amount of money be below 1,000 coins, it would be paid in metal currency. He also believed that in places north of the Huai River with the transactions above 10,000 *pi* of silk, there would be a market, and in places south of the Yangtze River, with the transactions above 1,000 *hu* of grain, there would be a market. He put it very lightly to prove the feasibility of this idea.

Third, the true meaning of Zhou Lang's "abolishing metal currency" was not to cancel the currency, but to change the currency material and narrow the scope of the circulation of metal currencies. On the basis of adhering to the idea of agriculture as the most fundamental, Zhou planned to put forward more flexible measures to meet the requirements of the socio-economic development, namely, using silk and rice for large-sum payments and money for small payments (within one thousand coins). Different from Gong Yu, Huan Xuan and later Shen Yue, he learned from the defects of grain and silk, which were pointed out cuttingly by Kong Linzhi. He remedied their shortcomings and did not deny the circulation of coins from a legislative perspective. In this way, not only was the need of circulation for currency satisfied, which would prevent the reemergence of the competition for labor forces between private minting and agricultural production, but also the inconvenience of the cutting of silk and the use of metal coins in large-sum payments. Using the whole *pi* of silk as currency to meet the need of large-sum payments was probably the prevailing practice in areas north of the Huai River and south of the Yangtze River at the time, which was formally put forward as a proposal by Zhou Lang after revision. Zhou Lang was the forerunner of the prevalent practice of "money and silk both in use" in the Tang Dynasty.

Shen Yue (441–513), courtesy name Xiuwen, was a native of Wukang, Wuxing in the Liang Dynasty of the Southern Dynasties. Being poor since childhood, he was studious and well-read. He was also good at writing articles, especially writing poetry, and created the *yongming*-style poetry. He served in the Song, Qi and Liang Dynasties. His writings included *The Book of Song*, *The Book of Jin*, etc. People of the Ming Dynasty edited for him *A Collection of the Writings of Shen Yinhou*.

Eighty years after Kong Linzhi's proposal of abolishing money to use grain and silk, Shen Yue wrote an appendix for the section of "Biography of Kong Linzhi" of *The Book of Song*, in which he voiced his sharp opposition to Kong. His main ideas included the following three points:

First, money was not important in social and economic life at all. He acknowledged that "what people stress was food and commodities, with the former of paramount importance and the latter for the circulation of money." Together with food, currency was one of the things "people stress."[9] Currency was for the purpose of circulation and food was for people to enjoy their living. However, in ancient times, the people were simple, honest and did not expect too much, so they were often easily satisfied. "With the labor of one man and the weaving of one woman, the food and clothing of a family would be enough. With the family as a unit of production, man ploughing and woman weaving, the family would be

---

[9]Biography of Kong Linzhi in *The Book of Song*, Book 5, pp. 1565–1566. The following citations will not be specified.

self-sufficient and all the need for production and life would be satisfied without resorting to others." Naturally, there was little contact between the family and the market. "So at that time, the role of currency was not important at all."

Second, currency circulation was already a major public hazard in society. In his opinion, "the function of money was not the re-emergence of the original intention." The so-called "original intention" was that "for the transaction of commodities, money was insufficient." If the function of money had extended from life necessities to non-necessities, and people were "buying precious things as well as unknown goods," we can say that there was not any change to the role of money at all. It only meant that the scope of influence was expanded from the minority to the majority of the commodities, from life necessities to luxuries and from a small scope to inter-state. Besides, merchants lived a luxurious and comfortable life, which was often envied by other people. As a result, an increasing number of people would abandon agriculture to take up businesses. "All around the country, people would abandon their agricultural practice." In addition, "when there is a harvest, all the families would have abundant rice; in times of hunger and famine, their preserve of grain would be reduced." The circulation of currency aggravated the disparity and polarization between the rich and the poor. For this reason, Shen Yue inherited the idea of abolishing money to use grain and silk and pushed such a concept to the limit. He denied the positive role of the metal currency and considered metal currency of no use at all. "Money was good neither for the salvation of hunger nor the appeasement of thirst." He would rest in ease only when money was completely denounced.

Third, the goal of "abolishing money" should be carried out gradually, not all at once, because the habits of common people were hard to change. In essence, the overall interests of the landlord class should not be interfered with. His goal of "abolishing money" was only the ultimate goal, before which there were still two more stages. The first stage was the elimination of commerce and the restoration of agriculture as the only economic activity. That was the "small country with a small population" mode of Lao Tze, in the case of which people would go back to the primitive society. The second stage aimed at the destruction of metal currency and the abolition of monetary laws, which would "be followed by later generations."

He was confident that it was a bold move to discard the use of money and had the intermediate goals to achieve this ultimate goal. So he felt complacent, saying, "Huan Xuan knew the beginning but not the end, while Kong Linzhi saw the minor points instead of the fundamentals." In his opinion, he was the only representative of the theory of "abolishing currency" in the history of China.

4. The debate over the shortage of currency in the Southern Dynasties

In the Southern Dynasties, there were several debates over such issues as the currency crisis, the instability of the value of currency and the overflow of privately minted currency. The three major debates in the Liu Song Dynasty included the controversy over "one big coin equals two small ones" by He Shangzhi and Shen Yanzhi, the dispute over the right of minting by Shen Qingzhi and Yan Jun, and Kong Ji's theory of neither caring for copper nor treasuring the labor. The following part is an introduction to these debates.

4.1. The controversy over "one big coin equals two small ones" by He Shangzhi and Shen Yanzhi

In 447, after the minting of *sizhu* coins, there was the malpractice of "private minting and devious people would cut old coins for copper." Liu Yigong, the prince of Jiangxia, proposed the practice of "one big coin equals two." That is, he wanted to adjust the rate of exchange for old coins and new coins to increase the nominal value of the old coins, thus preventing the deterioration of the monetary system. Shen Yanzhi, commandant of the central army, voiced his support of the suggestion.

Shen Yanzhi (397–449), courtesy name Taizhen, was a native of Wuquan, Wuxing in the Song Dynasty of the Southern Dynasties. Well versed in the study of *Lao Tze*, he became a *xiucai* after the recommendation of many people. After that, he served as the county magistrate of

Jiaxing. In his later years, he served such titles as the minister of the department of personnel. A modest man, he liked to find and use talented people.

His main points included three aspects:

First, the circulation of currency should be compatible with the need of commodity circulation. When the commodities in circulation increased, the currency in circulation should also increase, and vice versa. According to Shen, though there was the development of the East Jin Dynasty in southern China, the territory was still not so vast, the currency in circulation was still not widespread and the amount of currency in circulation was not big enough to cause much trouble. However, with the development of the territory, currency began to circulate in remote areas hitherto unknown, for which there was not a corresponding increase of the currency in circulation. The more urgent the need for the money in circulation, the more purchasing power the currency would have and the less able poor people would become to pay for their needs. Though hardworking, they could not feed their families. The reason was that money became more valuable and commodities cheaper. Without any change in the taxes, the burden on the people was aggravated and they had to sell even more agricultural products to get the money to pay the taxes, which imperceptibly exacerbated the poverty of the laborers. If the government did nothing to reform the monetary system, social evils would become even worse. Therefore, the reform of the currency system was imperative. His argument was undoubtedly correct. The circulation of currency was for the circulation of commodities and was subject to the restriction of the latter. The scale of the commodity in circulation determined the scale of currency in circulation. His idea reflected the actual situation of the time and offered us the root cause of the problem.

The second aspect involved the reform of the currency system, "one big coin equals two small ones," to increase the national revenue and family income. The advantage of doing so was that the state did not need to have new laws, but "those skillful techniques would cease." Without the need to increase the cost of minting coins, the malpractice of cutting old coins for copper would disappear, thus bringing about a stable currency system, an increase of national revenue and "an imperishable treasure to be handed down to later generations." For ordinary families, because of the increased purchasing power, those with big coins would easily get "double the profit" of other families. Of course, this double benefit was not enjoyable for any family, but only for those rich princes, nobles and mighty families. The amount of money in the hands of common people was not enough for them to pay taxes and all kinds of extortions. Without surplus money, how could they profit from it? Therefore, Shen Yanzhi's defending of the reform of the currency system and offering of a theoretical basis for that were equivalent to publicly affirming the state's monetary policy, which pursued the appreciation of big coins and the depreciation of small coins to exploit the common people. This kind of temptation was huge and hard to resist both for the country and for the people. Therefore, it was favored by all.

Third, the above understanding was based on his apprehension of currency as the means of circulation, and he was using the nominalistic theory of currency to seek economic benefits for the rulers. He acknowledged and fully affirmed the function of currency as the means of circulation. "It is a good way of making profits and making the country rich. Though with a long history, it is still easy to put into use." However, he never touched upon the continuity and complexity of the circulation of currency and the function of currency as the medium of value. He only believed that the change of the exchange price between different coins could ensure the personal interests of the individuals and those of the country. This reform plan would never meet the cold reception or opposition of the ruling class. "The king followed the advice of Yanzhi and put it into practice. Nevertheless, a period of trial witnessed the inconvenience to both the public sectors and the private transactions, which led to the ending of so doing." From this, we can see that even the will of the rulers would have to give way if people departed from objective laws.

While the discussion was leaning favorably toward the idea of Liu Yigong, He Shangzhi[10] stood up to express his disapproval. He had three reasons:

---

[10]He Shangzhi (382–460), courtesy name Yande, was a native of Qianxian county, Lujiang. In the Song Dynasty of the Southern Dynasties, he lectured to the assembled disciples and started the so-called "Southern School." During the reign of Emperor Wen, he served as

First, the measure of value was the most basic monetary function. He clearly pointed out that since its emergence, the first and foremost function of currency was to reflect and measure the prices of commodities. Under the condition of the strongest natural economy, he vividly described the function of being the measure of value as the most fundamental, which indicated that in ancient China there was already a rather fixed understanding of such a function. No matter what changes occurred to the relation between commodity and currency, even if the relation was at low ebb, such an understanding would never falter. He even put forward a more profound understanding that trading activities were not dependent upon the currencies in circulation.

He also believed that the more currency there was, the higher the prices of commodities, and vice versa. Although there were differences in currency, that did not affect its function at all. Under the circumstance that the nominal value was at variance with the actual value of currency, it made sense to say that "less money meant that money was more valuable and more money meant that money was less valuable." However, how could the number of coins not affect the function of being the measure of value? Being the medium of exchange, that function was identical. Nevertheless, the function of being the measure of value could never be the same. He mistakenly confused the means of circulation with the measure of value. Before people came to understand the value theory of labor, his concept of value was only by intuition. With one old coin equivalent to two new coins, the nominal value of old coins was raised, leading to the "admiration of the nominal prices." The old *wuzhu* coins were bigger and heavier than the newly minted *sizhu* coins, but not to the extent that one *wuzhu* coin would be equivalent to two *sizhu* coins. The government forcibly stipulated that ratio, resulting in the nominal value exceeding the actual value. The kind of value as mentioned by He Shangzhi obviously referred to the weight of metal contained in the coins, not something else. Therefore, it was different from the labor value.

---

the Chief Imperial Secretary and would often criticize the king's faults frankly. During the reign of Emperor Xiaowu, he was also the Chief Imperial Secretary. Known for his good conduct, he was especially fond of learning and literature.

Second, the reform of monetary system should be in accordance with the national conditions and in line with the public opinion, with a unified and systematic plan. He put forward two principles. One was that "the reform should listen to the voice of the public." The other principle was "opposing the unsystematic practice." He wanted to set up a stable and unified monetary system, which would be readily accepted by the public. If the government deviated from such principles, the plan would never last. As a result, the existence of a sound monetary system was of great importance. He criticized Emperor Wu of the Han Dynasty, because the *chize*, *wuzhu* and the platinum coins were quickly abolished, and he denounced the monetary system of Wang Mang, which caused much inconvenience. The reason was that "things were done in a hurry" or that "the plan was not systematic." The currency system should not be inconvenient for people or difficult to comply with, nor should it be used to "deal with emergency," caring for the immediate rather than long-term interests. It was a historical choice to establish a unified and stable currency system. Although in ancient China the social, political and economic conditions were not ready yet, with the rise of the natural economy, especially within the voice of one old coin equivalent to two new coins, it was indeed very visionary for him to have such far-sighted understanding.

Third, he believed that "if the circulation of commodities was in a state of imbalance, common people would suffer from it … so that the rich would not be obscene and extravagant and the poor would not be too needy. Although this law had been long abolished, we should not put it immediately into effect. There should be some suitable occasions to carry it out roughly, like what we did now." That is to say, if the policy of "one big coin equals two small coins" was in practice, public sentiments would not support it, and the gap between the rich and the poor would widen, making the rich more rich and the poor poorer, which was contrary to the intention of equality between the rich and the poor. He was quite aware that the government intended to appreciate the old coins and depreciate the new coins, the purpose of which was a redistribution of national revenue. Consequently, the fortune of the holders of old coins would double, and the poor men without old coins would get either the depreciated new coins or the appreciated old coins. Using new coins as the standard for selling grain and silk would get 50% less earnings because of the deprecation. Using old coins as the standard would mean the payment of twice the original amount of new coins. In either case, the self-employed peasants would suffer huge economic losses, so this was clearly a biased monetary policy. It was contrary to "the systematic principle." According to He Shangzhi, "The form and size of coins vary a lot. If we refer directly to the big coins, nobody would be clear about our meaning. Take *sizhu* and *wuzhu* coins as example, the words printed on the coins were of a different writing style, not recognizable to ordinary people. Besides, the words were often dim and it was difficult to tell the numbers. In the private and public transactions there would surely be lawsuits, making this point the most hard to ascertain." In addition, the government "did not pay enough attention to supervision" and there was both neglect of duty and indulgence, leading to the daily increase of cutting old coins for copper. As long as the old decrees were strictly carried out and the government punished the offenders without leniency, common people would "fear the punishment and hope for awards," and the above-mentioned malpractice "would cease very quickly."

He Shangzhi's opinion was approved and supported by a few officials, such as Geng Bingzhi, the minister of the personnel department. However, the emperor eventually adopted the advice of Liu Yigong.

4.2. The dispute over the right of minting by Shen Qingzhi and Yan Jun

This was the third time in Chinese history that there was a dispute over the right of minting currency. It was triggered by Shen Qingzhi, who proposed to ease the control of private minting under specific restrictions.

Shen Qingzhi (386–465), courtesy name Hongxian, was a native of Wukang, Wuxing in the Song Dynasty of the Southern Dynasties. Though not literate, he was quite resourceful and good at using military forces. As a general of the Liu Song Dynasty, he scored military successes one after another and became the *Jianwei* general during the reign of Emperor Wen. During the reign of Emperor *Xiaowu*, he served as minister of infrastructure.

In 457,[11] the government minted *sizhu* coins, which were thin and small. There were illegal mintings here and there, and the cutting of old coins was frequent. With the coins becoming smaller and smaller and at variance with the official format, the prices of commodities went up a lot, resulting in the suffering of the common people. Even severe punishment would not put an end to this. Shen Qingzhi proposed the permission of private minting. According to his plan, "common people should be allowed to mint coins. The government would set up an agency for minting coins, where those in this business would join to live. The government should set the standards and clear away the impurities. With a uniform standard, new coins would be minted there. The illegal minting of new coins and cutting of old coins would be strictly prohibited."[12] Thus, it was clear that his permission of private minting was conditional. His idea was unrealistic, because those practitioners were overburdened by the tax of 30%. If the law was enforced strictly, there would be no profit in minting coins, so nobody would join in this business. On the contrary, if the people minting coins colluded with the government, and the government relaxed or stopped the supervision, there would inevitably be many offenders of the law to mint coins illegally. Consequently, the government would not achieve the aim of increasing its revenue.

Shen Qingzhi's free-casting policy was similar in form to the free casting of the modern monetary system. However, they were different in their ways of doing things, their effectiveness and their theoretical basis, thus we should not consider them the same. As far as the ways of doing things were concerned, the modern monetary system required that when citizens requested the government to mint standard coins, no taxes or fees would be collected. For those countries that charged fees for the minting, the amount was very small, never to be compared with the 30% tax. For example, Russia charged a tax of 2% and the Biyang government of China 6%. In terms of the purpose of doing such things, the free casting of modern times was to ensure the stability of the currency. Its intention was to prevent the fluctuation of the prices of currency materials and to ensure

---

[11] According to Ye Shichang, *A History of Chinese Currency Theories*, Book 1, p. 51.
[12] Biography of Yan Jun in *The Book of Song*, Book 7, pp. 1960–1962. The following citations will not be specified.

that the nominal value and the actual value of the coins were the same, and that the coins in circulation were in accordance with the objective need. In short, it was one of the factors influencing the stability of the currency system. In Shen's words, the purpose was that "in a few years both the public and the private sectors would have sufficient money. With the banning of copper, illegal activities and devious practice would end naturally. Besides, the banning of copper would result in the conversion of copper into utensils, which after the casting of coins were permitted would be used to make profit, thus becoming advantageous." His real intention was to increase the revenue of the government. What he said afterward was merely a kind of ornamental expression, which aggravated the already disorganized currency system. Finally, as far as the theoretical basis was concerned, he believed that Emperor Wen of the Han Dynasty did not adopt Jia Yi's suggestion of the monopoly of copper and the privilege of casting money. "As a result, there had been private minting of coins, which brought about a rich country." He mistakenly attributed the restoration and development of the productive forces, which were due to the policy of rest and recuperation, to the socio-economic effects of free minting of coins. He also treated minted coins and wealth equally, which was the same as the prevalent idea "that wealth consists in money, or and silver,"[13] though seven or eight hundred years earlier than that. He held the wrong belief that "the prohibition of coins would result in copper cast into devices, and the start of the minting of coins would lead to the transformation of devices into wealth." That is to say, money meant social wealth and if the government allowed free minting, both the private sectors and the public would benefit. In due course, "the warehouse is not full and the private sectors as well as the public were suffering," because the lack of currency was due to the prohibition. He believed that free casting would help reverse the ethos and stabilize the social order. "When copper was exhausted, there would be no dispute and the malpractice would stop." This was the typical view of metalists, which was the official version coined under the ruler's selfish desires. Even so, he still became a victim of injustice under the supreme tyrant of the time.

---

[13] Adam Smith, *An Inquiry into the Nature and Causes of the Wealth of Nations*, Book II, p. 1.

Among the opponents of Sheng Qingzhi's proposition of casting money to increase the financial revenue, Yan Jun was the most representative one. He had four reasons:

First, the currency reform must follow certain strategies and methods. He believed that the role of currency had always been the same. The weight of *wuzhu* for each coin was determined in the Western Han Dynasty and had not changed in the Wei and Jin Dynasties. That was because such a weight was most suitable for the need of commodity exchange at that time. Any change would lead to non-standard coins. Of course, with the passage of time, the accumulated disadvantages would also surface. There was naturally the need for reform. Nevertheless, "there should be some strategies for reform." In other words, the idea of reform should follow its natural course, so that the minting of coins should base on the *wuzhu* standard. Even the *sizhu* coins of the Liu Song Dynasty were full bodied, "fake coins would go together with the change," not to mention that the *sizhu* coins of later times were only nominal. Therefore, we may assume that Yan Jun thought that the reform proposal of Shen Qingzhi was not proper in tactics and methods. He affirmed Shen Qingzhi's overall plan but disapproved some points.

Second, the reform plan of Shen Qingzhi was doomed to trouble. According to Yan Jun, "If the privately minted coins are to circulate and the minting is not exclusively controlled by the government, there would be much profit involved. Consequently, it would become very difficult to prohibit the private minting of coins and other malpractice. *Wuzhu* coins and *banliang* coins would be exhausted within a year. Such a practice at a time of no abundance would be too bad. At present, the commodities were becoming less, but people did not complain. The reason was that at the early period of the prohibition, there was not a unified standard. That trouble would soon be over so there is no need for your Majesty to worry. However, the deficiency of the state revenue is indeed a big worry. Now we are allowing the circulation of lighter coins, but the government has no reason to increase the taxes. Although common people are prosperous, that would never ease the needy state of the government. The only way out is to be economical and thrifty. On the other hand, there is a limit to the number of coins in circulation, though the consumption is endless. With the malpractice of cutting coins comes to an end, the officials in charge of minting coins should start the mining for copper, eliminate the use of copper for the production of other utensils, and prescribe a standard for the coins. With the new coins coming out every now and then, that would not be useful to the country after a certain period of time." In other words, if Shen's plan was carried out without any reservation, the currency system would be in disorder and there would be a lack of coins. Instead of the government, the smaller coins were all privately minted. With much profit, people would be very much inclined to persist in their malpractice. With the government doing a poor job in the prohibition of private minting and cutting of coins, it was hard to maintain the national revenue and currency. Consequently, the standard coins were disappearing from circulation. That was the first point. The second point was that such practices were detrimental to the dignity of the authorities, since the new coins prohibited last spring now began to circulate as the standard coins, though "there is no need for your Majesty to worry." The third point was that such practice would not add to the financial revenue of the government. The most worrisome thing was the lack of financial resources. With the smaller and lighter coins in circulation, the government could not possibly increase the taxes on currency. "Although common people are prosperous, that would never ease the needy state of the government." According to his understanding, "the only way out is to be economical and thrifty."

Third, the shortage of currency was not a serious social problem. He believed that although fewer coins were being possessed, people did not complain. The solutions to the shortage of coins included the maintenance of public casting and the imposition of a prohibition of copper use. Without profit, "official order would not put the illegal practice into action." For quite a long time, there had not been any mining of copper. With the increasing consumption of smelting, the deposition of copper was decreasing gradually, and the prices of copper utensils were becoming increasingly higher. If a copper utensil was worth a thousand coins and using the same amount of copper to mint coins would only get 500 coins, it meant minting coins was profitless. As a result, even state laws could not force people to mint currency. This analysis was not only reasonable but also cut into the malpractice of the time. In the case of copper coins as the main currency, one of the main causes of copper shortage was that copper and precious metals played different roles in people's daily lives.

On the one hand, in addition to being the material for coins, gold and silver were less useful in social production and people's life. Therefore, their monetary role did not have much influence on production and life. Copper, on the other hand, was much different and closely related to the social production and life. When playing the role of monetary function, it was bound to have a violent collision with the functions in production and human life. In addition, due to the low value of copper and the restrictions on its mining and smelting, the concerns of Yan Jun were worth pondering.

The fourth point was his opposition to the minting of *erzhu* coins. Some people held that copper was rare and "intended to mint *erzhu* coins." Yan Jun was against such an idea, believing that this would result in the total destruction of ancient coins. In his opinion, the minting of *erzhu* coins would not only not solve the financial difficulties but would also lead to the "rampancy of tricky practice." Under the temptation of lucrative profits, all the ancient and standard coins would be destroyed, even though there were laws and regulations against such practices. That was the first reason. The second reason was that it would induce the devious people to commit crimes. With a limited profit from the minting of currency, it was hard to make a quick profit of one or two hundred million. Even if they could get such a profit, it would take them a year, which was too far away to ease their greed. The third reason was that the minting of *erzhu* coins would disrupt the market and widen the gap between the rich and the poor. Without any possibility of long-term interests, disasters would come one after another. In short, "without any profit, such practice would lead to many disadvantages. Doing such things is a mistake, and would be condemned by later generations."

In his argument against smaller coins and support for the wuzhu coins, Yan Jun seemed to show the kind of feeling that smaller coins were expelling big money. With smaller coins in circulation, the big coins would be withdrawn. As a result, "within a year, the big coins would disappear from circulation." That is, "the big coins were exhausted." Was this not a reflection of the phenomenon that we call bad money drives good money out of circulation? Or to be more specific, it may be safe to assume that he already knew something about such a monetary phenomenon, though he did not elaborate on it.

Liu Yigong, another opponent of the proposition of Shen Qingzhi, had five reasons: First, "the profits of forgery are from the fake coins." With the prohibition of fake coins, there would not be many people joining this practice. Second, the government was in possession of those coins that were in good shape. Their prices were much higher. "If people were forced to change for those coins, it would be like robbing." Third, compared with the 30% tax for minting coins by the government agency, private minting was free from such burden. "For the purpose of profit, people would go against the law." It was impossible to ban private minting of coins. Fourth, instead of "with the exhaustion of copper there would cease to be any malpractice," after the depletion of copper, "there would have been an accumulation of wrong doings." Fifth, "the recent trouble was characterized by an uneven form of currency and the illegal cutting of coins. There is no need for a strict prohibition of adulteration of lead or tin in the minting of copper coins." Such a remark was targeting the weakness of Shen Qingzhi's argument. At the same time, as was pointed out by him, putting the plan into practice would surely lead to what he expected.

After the two debates, the imperial government adopted the proposal of minting *erzhu* coins. In 465, the government finally minted the thin and small *erzhu* coins. The privately minted *erzhu* coins were even thinner and smaller. In the same year, Shen Qingzhi presented a memorial to the emperor, suggesting the permission for private minting of coins. It turned out that the anticipation of Yan Jun was completely correct. In 465, the government prohibited both the private and the public minting of coins and allowed only ancient currency to circulate, which put an end to this controversy over the right to mint coins.

4.3. Kong Yi's theory of "grudging neither the laborers nor the copper"

In 482, Kong Yi, a disengaged official, presented to the emperor a memorial suggesting the minting of coins and the averaging of commodities. He suggested that in the minting of coins, the government should grudge neither the laborers nor the copper used. At a time when currency was long in short supply, minted coins were less weighty than before and bad coins ran rampant, Liu Yu, Emperor Ming of the Liu Song Dynasty, allowed only ancient coins to circulate, leading to the scarcity and derogation of currency. In 479, after Xiao Daocheng ascended the throne and established the Southern Qi Dynasty, he abolished the ancient coins and cast new currency, seriously tightening the currency in circulation. In response to this, Kong Yi opposed clearly the implementation of the devaluation policy and made substantial contribution to monetary theory. His points included the following three aspects:

First, he stressed the importance of the circulation of the currency. The basis of his argument was that "grain and currency were naturally connected." That is to say, grain and currency were connected and influencing each other, which was an objective law. Broadly speaking, the circulation of commodities and currency was interdependent. To meet the need of the circulation of commodities, a certain amount of currency was indispensable.

In order to analyze the circulation of currency at that time, he pointed out, "When the civilians were hurt, they would abandon their hometown; when the agriculture was injured, the nation would become poor. Both being unreasonably expensive and being unreasonably cheap would do the same harm. We must be clear that the key for our country was that there was not enough currency in circulation. Things like repeated flooding or the cheapness of grain mattered not so much." He first analyzed the factors influencing the change of the grain price: grain and currency. Historically, Li Li had such an idea. "The expensiveness of grain would hurt common people and the cheapness of grain would hurt the peasants." The intention of that proposition was to state the negative influence of the variation of the grain price on farmers and the non-agricultural population. The non-agricultural population would flee hither and thither, while the damaged agriculture would lead to the poverty of the nation. As a result, the consequences were self-evident because there was always a damaged party. At the time, the region had suffered from repeated flooding for years, but the price of the grain was not high. "It was because there was less money in circulation instead of the grain being cheap." He also warned the authorities "this aspect should never be overlooked." That is to say, the government should understand very well the change of purchasing power, the commodity production and the price level in the market. His argument was that "the

Jin Dynasty did not mint coins. However, in the following years there were wars, repeated flood and fire. In consequence, the coins in circulation naturally became less and less." In addition, Emperor Wen of the Song Dynasty minted the *sizhu* coins and posed no restriction on the common people's practice of cutting old coins. "The negative influence of that malpractice continues to this day. It was indeed lamentable." That was really one disaster after another. The short supply of coins became even worse. On the contrary, if the national circulation of currency was in accordance with the circulation of commodities, "common people would be happy with their work, there would not be disputes, and the supply of food can clothing would be sufficient." In other words, "the implementation of the laws and regulations of the Han Dynasty would lead to national sufficiency and people's good life." If not, "money would be exhausted, leading to the unemployment and misery of different people." In his opinion, the circulation of currency had great influence on the country's political and economic life and people's family life. The good intention of Kong was to warn the authorities that with the development of the natural economy, the government should pay attention to the shortage of currency in circulation. In today's words, for a country, not only is production important but the circulation of currency is also equally important. The government should consider the issue of currency circulation to be of the equal importance as agricultural production. His understanding was indeed very profound and represented the highest level of his era.

Second, he analyzed the source of the disadvantages of coins. According to his understanding, "the disadvantage of minting coins was that there were repeated changes of the weight. The heavy coins were difficult to use." "The light coins were often easily forged illegally." The illegal minting of coins would lead to endless trouble, and no strict punishment could put an end to it. The authorities "don't care much about its consequences" because "they grudged the use of copper and the work of laborers." He attributed the reason behind that to the understanding that "money was useless and used for easy transaction. The government wanted coins to be light, numerous, as well as labor-saving and easily minted." Even the use of inferior materials would not cause any trouble.

Moreover, people's pursuit of profit was as natural as flowing water. "Now we have given them a source of profit, accompanied by severe punishment. It is like guiding them to the wrong way and putting them to death. Is this the right way of government?" Since the early years of the Han Dynasty, there had been light coins and many people forged coins for profit. It was not until the time of Emperor Wu of Han that the government started to punish such malpractice. Emperor Wen of Song began the minting of *sizhu* coins, but "his government did not prohibit the malpractice of common people, which resulted in great trouble. Was not that lamentable?" The unexpected thing was that "illegal minting led to much trouble." In consideration of the ruler's own interests, Kong Yi consciously or unconsciously disguised or avoided the main aspects of the problem. In the difficult period when the authorities were plagued by a financial crisis, they used the governmental minting of bad money to get out of the predicament and increase the national revenue. Unfortunately, illegal private casting was rampant, and bad money circulation lead to currency confusion, which was difficult to end. Proceeding from the standpoint of the rulers and alluding to the damage of a nominalistic view of currency, his criticism created immense difficulties for currency circulation and brought endless disasters to the country. Although his criticism was imperfect, incomplete and a little biased, he hit the nail on the head by saying that "the government was stingy with the use of copper and the work of laborers." That statement was clear and unambiguous, illustrating his scientificness and seriousness. It laid a solid foundation for the coinage policy that made full use of copper and the laborers, which implied the coinage of full-bodied coins. A powerful weapon against the devaluation of the currency, this theory was in line with the theoretical basis of free casting in the modern currency system. At the same time, it became the theoretical weapon of the anti-nominalistic viewers of later generations and later metalists often speak approvingly of it.

The third aspect was his adherence to the full-bodied minting of coins. He objected to the notion of nominalism, which held that "money was useless and used for easy transaction. The government wanted coins to be light, numerous, as well as labor-saving and easily minted." He maintained that the basic principle of coin casting was that "if we cannot get the middle state, we would have heavy rather than light coins."[14] That is, even if the weight of minted coins could not match the volume of commodities transaction, he would prefer heavy coins to light ones, which sufficed to show his metallic theory of money. He believed that in the 500 years from the reign of Emperor Wu of Han Dynasty to Emperor Wen of Song Dynasty, although there were changes to the social systems, *wuzhu* coins remained unchanged. The reason was that their weight and size were suitable for the need of commodities circulation. Moreover, in the minting process, the government grudged neither the copper used nor the labor of the laborers. In the 35 years between 430 and 465, "coins became even lighter and the minting was not refined. As a result, there were repeated illegal mintings of coins, which the government could never prohibit. That was due to the grudging of the copper and the labor." He advocated the minting of *wuzhu* coins to lessen the shortage of currency. The implementation should be in the following order: Copper-producing states and prefectures sent their copper to the bureau in charge of the minting of coins, where standard *wuzhu* coins were minted. Once the officially minted coins began to circulate in the market, the government should take strict measures to prohibit the circulation of non-standard coins. The officially minted non-standard coins should be taken back to be minted for the second time. Such practice would both "do away with the malpractice" and "be advantageous to the poor and honest people," so that "people would live and work in peace, there would not be disputes in the market, and people would not suffer from lack of food and clothing."

Though very refined, his proposition did not become reality. The reason was not only the sudden death of Emperor Gao but also the restrictions of the historical conditions at the time. The political and economic conditions for the unification of the currency system were not there. Besides, in the war-torn Southern and Northern Dynasties, it was never possible to discuss seriously the unification of the currency system. Everything was but a fantasy. The good prophecy or longing of ancient Chinese prophets of the future currency system was not gradually becoming reality until the Sui and Tang Dynasties.

---

[14]Chapter 3 of Qi in *Zizhi Tongjian*, Book 9, p. 4303, Zhonghua Book Company, 1956.

5. The dispute over minting currency in the Northern Dynasties

5.1. *Yuan Cheng on the use of coins*

During the early years of the Northern Wei Dynasty, people were mostly nomadic and the monetary economy was quite backward, so the transactions were by means of grain and cloth. After the reform of Emperor Xiaowen (471–499) of the Northern Wei Dynasty, the economy recovered and began to develop. In 495, the government minted the *taihe wuzhu* coins and forced the circulation of such coins, which were rejected by the common people. With grain and cloth playing a dominating role, *taihe wuzhu* coins circulated only in the capital and its vicinity. In other places, people used either ancient coins or grain and cloth. To unify the currency system, in 510, the government minted *yongping wuzhu* coins and banned the use of non-standard coins. Because of the difference in the currency in circulation, the merchants were unable to manage their businesses. As a result, the government permitted the use of *taihe wuzhu* coins, the newly minted coins and the ancient coins, prohibiting only the use of non-standard coins. However, there were not enough coins in circulation in Hebei, which resulted in the use of cloth as money. The government mined for copper in such places as Wangwu Mountain to mint coins. Since then, there was often illegal minting among the common people, and the coins became even thinner and smaller. In order to stabilize the prices of commodities, in 529 the government minted *yongan wuzhu* coins. The minting lasted four months, because the government wanted to control the coins in circulation. Meanwhile, the government dumped silk and cloth in the market at a price lower than the market price to recover coins, which only resulted in the prevalence of private minting. As a result, the chaotic monetary circulation further deteriorated.

In 516, in the capital city and other cities or towns, the money in circulation included newly minted coins and ancient coins, which led to the inconvenience of exchange and difficulty in trading. Yuan Cheng, the Chief Imperial Secretary, courtesy name Daozhen, was the son of Tuoba Yun and the great-grandson of Emperor Taiwu. His title of nobility was the Prince of Rencheng. Studious from an early age, he became the Great

General Who Assails the South and the prefectural governor of Liangzhou. During the reign of Emperor Xuanwu, he was the prefectural governor of Yangzhou. During the reign of Emperor Xiaoming, he was the Chief Imperial Secretary. Whenever there was disagreement, he would always give advice to the emperor; thus, all people respected him with awe. He died in office.

"The Treatise on Food and Money" in *The Book of Wei* recorded two memorials of Yuan Cheng to the throne, giving advice on the use of coins, which might be summed up as follows:

The first point was about the importance of monetary wealth. According to his understanding, "money was of fundamental importance for the emperor, by means of which he could gather together talents to fill up important positions, take care of the lives of the common people, follow the virtues of the heaven, as well as govern the whole country and rule the people." During the Xia and Yin Dynasties, the government divided the country's tributary copper into five grades, which was carried on by the Zhou Dynasty. Lv Shang, Duke Tai of Qi, set the standard for the nine states. "From then on, money began to circulate, and there was the standard of minting coins. Duke Huan of Qi followed that practice and became a dominant ruler. In the following Qin and Han Dynasties, there emerged differences in the weight of coins. The coins of Wu Bi and Deng Tong circulated in the whole country. In Henan, the coins were especially abundant … in my humble opinion, the *taihe* coins were the invention of Emperor Gaozu of Han, which later circulated together with wuzhu coins. These models were never to be changed." He further added, "After repeated deliberation, I think that the *taihe wuzhu* coins were the currency of our Wei Dynasty, immortal and imperishable." He maintained that in the beginning, there was but one kind of coin, which would be followed by the handicraftsmen of later generations to the far future. In addition, what mattered was not whether there was only one kind of coin, but how to make coins circulate. Like a spring, when the water flowed, it would flow around. Lessons from history should be remembered. King Jing of the Zhou Dynasty and Wang Mang of the Xin Dynasty repeatedly changed their currency systems, resulting in uneven currency specifications, the blockage of border trade and the slack circulation of commodities. The normal order of life and production was interfered with, let alone the recovery of production and the development of economy. It was empty talk indeed to unify currency and stabilize the prices of commodities for the harmony of the market.

The second point involved the drawbacks of a non-uniform currency. His analysis included two aspects. The first aspect was that the poor people were deeply troubled by the painful difficulties and the unavailability of education, which triggered repeated disputes and legal issues. Although the *taihe wuzhu* coins were conducive to the trading activities in the capital city of Luoyang, they were impractical in such areas as Xuzhou and Yangzhou. Due to the different produces and trading objects, what was practicable in one place would become impracticable in another place. In consequence, the poor people would feel greatly pained, and the benevolent rule of the government would fail. Second, the hard toil of textile work was wasted, without getting any help in withstanding hunger and cold. In 513, the government issued an official order to prohibit the circulation of two coins, which were already out of circulation, but allowed the circulation of other kinds of coins. According to his observation, the coins circulating in areas south of the Yellow River were permitted by early kings, the prohibition of which puzzled him. However, in areas north of the Yellow River, there were no newly minted *wuzhu* coins. Even if there were old coins, they were prohibited. As a result, people had to use thinner silk fabrics and substandard cloth in their transactions, and they were often forced to cut the fabrics and cloth into pieces for easy transaction. That was a waste of the women's labor, and would not be of any help in ridding them of hunger and cold. Indeed, the cutting of fabrics and cloth into pieces was no way of helping the people because such a practice blocked the circulation process. It seemed quite clear that Yuan Cheng realized that coins were convenient and the most suitable means of trading. From this, we can also see that the rulers of the nomadic race, while facing the cultural and economic achievements of the advanced areas, were not rejecting and denying, but recognizing and inheriting, and they had quite strong consensus. It was the good will of the time that there should be the smooth flow of commodities across the country and unblocked public and private transactions. Such a good will sufficed to show that the Chinese nation was developing irresistibly as a whole in the process of integration and unification.

The third point was about the specific plan of putting coins in circulation. The ancient coins were in circulation, and those who minted coins illegally were more severely punished than under normal circumstances. With war looming and the area around the Yangtze River in a state of separation, it was a better choice to leave the currency in the southeast area alone, because the condition for the unification of currency was still not favorable. In Yuan's opinion, the way of treating different coins in different areas of the Northern Wei Dynasty was to be adopted. The *taihe wuzhu* coins, the newly minted *wuzhu* coins and the ancient coins in good condition should all be allowed to circulate. The exchange ratio between different coins should be determined by the local price. The government should punish the users of the coins out of circulation and the illegally minted coins according to the law and prohibit the circulation of substandard coins. In areas south of the Yellow River, by convention, the use of coins would not be limited. Different coins from all around the country were allowed to circulate in the capital city together with *taihe wuzhu coins* and the newly minted *wuzhu* coins. It seemed that such a transitional solution in time of political instability was an expedient measure. In the long view, there was still the need for a unified way of commodity flow and monetary system, which was the thinking and ambition of those far-sighted politicians.

5.2. Gao Qianzhi's plea for the minting of sanzhu coins

Gao Qian (486–528), courtesy name Daorang, was a native of Tiao of Bohai. When quite young, he inherited the title of nobility and then was promoted to the honor of general of Extending Power. In 525, he became the magistrate of Heyin County. He presented a memorial to the throne to warn of the misbehavior of Qi Shu, a courtier, which aroused the jealousy of other minions of the king. Later, he was transferred to the position of *Guozi Boshi*, a professor at the national university. Offending Li Shengui, the minion of Empress Dowager Hu, he was forced to commit suicide by imperial order.

According to the biography of Gao Qianzhi in *The Book of Wei*, Wei Shu, in the year 528, there was a discussion of minting coins. Gao Qianzhi, the official in charge of the minting and the chief secretary, presented a memorial entitled "A Plea for the Minting of Sanzhu Coins," suggesting the minting of *sanzhu* coins to make up the financial deficit.

Speaking with certainty, Gao Qianzhi drew lessons from history to allude to the present. According to his understanding, "the emergence of currency was for the easy transaction of commodities, so there was naturally a difference in the weight of coins." At first, there seemed to be no fault in saying this. The emergence of currency was indeed for the convenience of transactions. Currency evolved in the process of continuous commodity exchange, from being accidental to being frequent. The ways of exchange also developed from being complex to being simple. In the process, metal currency became dominant and in the end, precious metals took the place of base ones. In consequence, the weight of currency varied in different times. The question was the variation in different dynasties, which was already touched upon by his predecessors. It was the choice of history, the choice of the history of the exchange of commodities, which was not subject to the will of sage rulers and wise prime ministers. Seeing only some outward appearances, Gao was making his points by using unsuccessful or even failed examples of history, and arrived at the conclusion that "the weight of currency varied in accordance with the time." Unexpectedly, this conclusion was not conditional and without any regard for the consequences. As a historical conclusion without firm basis, it would lead the theory of monetary policy down the evil path. People with ulterior motives might even use it to form a public opinion for their devaluation policy, since there seemed to be a historical precedent.

He quoted from the classics to illustrate his points as follows. He said, "In my humble opinion, food and commodities ranked the first among the eight important administrative affairs. The accumulation of wealth was so important that decrees and regulations all prescribed doing such things. Also due to this, the former emperors, making use of the abundance of heaven and earth and the richness of the country, all accumulated grain and currency. With a rich accumulation, common people would not suffer from the shortage, and the whole country would rest in peace …. With the rising up of salt and iron, coins underwent many changes. The whole country became even more prosperous. In foreign relations, the government was able to resist all the barbarian states, and there was no need to increase taxes domestically, which was a result of pursuing profits …. Nowadays, there was still the difficulty posed by invaders. The state and the whole country were in chaos. With people in difficulties, the country was also in need. The minting of smaller coins would enrich the country. What harm would that do to the government and the people? Besides, the size of coins does not determine the prosperity or failure of the government. What truly matters is the proper distribution of wealth. That was something carried out in ancient times and something to follow for our generation." This argument, though similar to the idea of Yuan Cheng, was in fact different. According to Yuan, "from what I know, commodities ranked the second in the eight administrative affairs. As was pointed out in *The Book of Changes*, 'The great virtue of heaven and earth is the ceaselessness of things. The great treasure of the sages is the noble position. What ensures the noble position is benevolence. What attracts people is wealth.' Wealth is what kings use to attract talents for the noble position, the people, and the governing of the country ... later, in the Qin and Han Dynasties, there were variations in the weight of coins ... because of the difference in profits, there was also change in the weight of coins. In my humble opinion, the *taihe* coins were the invention of Emperor Gaozu. Such coins circulated together with *wuzhu* coins and became the standard." The differences between the two views lay in their different ways of thinking. First, they had different starting points for their quotation of the classics. Yuan Cheng held that the emperors should rely on virtue for the maintenance of the monarchy and depend on wealth for the gathering of people. Consequently, wealth was fundamental in attracting talents, safeguarding the monarchy, nourishing the people, following the intention of heaven and governing the whole country. However, Gao Qianzhi did not elaborate on the importance of accumulation of wealth in the teachings of the deceased sages. He only talked about how early kings kept their revenue in good supply and freed the people of difficulties and how Emperor Wu calculated the profit. In consequence, the finishing points were also different. Gao aimed at the provision of a prerequisite for economic development. The first step was to put the money in circulation in good order. When conditions became favorable, the government would unify the currency system. Gao Qianzhi, on the contrary, held that to relieve people of their sufferings, the old *wuzhu* coins could also circulate in the market. Moreover, the minting of smaller coins would increase the national wealth, with no harm to the people and the governing of the country. In his opinion, the success or failure of the government was not dependent on the size of the coins, but on the proper distribution of wealth, which would do no harm to the politics and folklore. Ancient people had carried out such a practice, so today people should follow suit, which would benefit the whole nation. His real intention was to benefit the country indeed. He also compared his claim to "the fulfillment of Shan Qi's proposal." In fact, it was hard to tell whether his idea of *sanzhu* coins in circulation with *wuzhu* coins was the same as that of Shan Qi. It was equally hard to tell whether that practice would result in bad money driving out good. Therefore, we shall not offer any comment here.

The proposal of Gao won the graces of Emperor Xiaoming. However, before the imperial edict was given, Gao had been put to death. As a result, his plan failed to become reality.

5.3. *Gao Gongzhi's memorial for the casting of wuhzu coins*

Gao Gongzhi (489–530), courtesy name Daomu and popularly known by his courtesy name, was the younger brother of Gao Qianzhi. With his learning covering classics and history, his contacts were mostly celebrities. At a position to censor, he impeached with no exception the powerful. After his elder brother's death, he sought the protection of Yuan Ziyou, the Prince of Changle. After Ziyou became Emperor Xiaozhuang of the Northern Wei Dynasty, he was appointed to quite a few different posts. Being a straightforward man, he took part in the discussion of many confidential affairs. Whatever was beneficial to the people, he would always speak up without any constraints. He was killed by Er Zhushilong.

In 529, Gao presented a memorial to the throne. In view of the circulation of under-valued small and thin coins and the proliferation of private castings, he suggested the minting of *yongan wuzhu* coins to save the country from the current crisis. His article was recorded in the Biography of Gaochong in *The Book of Wei*.

For starters, he proposed that in the livelihoods of the common people, currency was of fundamental importance. The first priority of a benevolent administration was to reform the minting of coins to get rid of the current crisis. The aim of his reform was different from that of his elder brother Gao Qianzhi, but similar to that of Yuan Cheng.

The reason for currency being the source of a crisis was that in recent years, illegal private minting was rampant and those punished by the government were not individual cases at all. In the market, the price of a copper was 81 *wen* for one *jin*. The privately minted thin coins of one *jin* of copper would lead to a profit of 200 *wen*. At that time, the price of rice was nearly 1,000 *wen* for one *dou*. Enticed by the fat profit, common people rushed to join the private minting of coins. As a result, many offenders were severely punished. With so many illegal private mintings of coins, there were many lawbreakers. At that time, the coins were only *wuzhu* in name, but in effect they were even less than *erzhu*. They were so thin that the strings for cash would damage them and they would even float on the surface of water. According to Gao's analysis, that was due to the fault of the government. How could those engaged in private minting be accountable for that? For a long time, the government clung to the old system and implemented its law of prohibition ineffectively. Then he added, "In earlier times, Emperor Wen of Han, dissatisfied with the smallness of *wuzhu* coins, started the minting of *sizhu* coins. When Emperor Wu ascended the throne, he changed the *sanzhu* coins to *banliang* coins. These were both the replacement of the big and heavy with the small and light." The subtext of this remark seemed to find fault with the practice of replacement to put forward his own proposition, which, different from the way of his brother, was a way of using historical evidence for present-day thinking and decisions.

He maintained that the government should mint full-bodied coins, which would prevent the emergence of illegal private minting, for that would lead to no profit and have no exemplary effect. Moreover, the government was severely punishing such a practice. According to his opinion, only in this way "could currency and commodities circulate permanently and the public as well as the private transactions continue." Such an understanding was similar to Kong Ji's theory of caring neither for the laborers nor for the copper in the Southern Qi Dynasty, but lacked a kind of theoretical elaboration.

Later, Yang Kan, another senior official, also presented a memorial, begging the king to allow the minting of coins by both the government and the common people for the reason that people would enjoy doing that and do away with their malpractice. Emperor Xiaozhuang gave an imperial edict for the minting of *yongan wuzhu* coins, which were of the same form and weight as *yongping wuzhu* coins. He also allowed people to bring copper to the official furnace to mint money.

Chapter 4

Financial Thought in the Tang and the Five Dynasties

The commodity–money relationship recovered and gained some development during the Tang Dynasty. In the early Tang Dynasty, "coin and silk cloth were employed concurrently"; however, the primary money was metal money, with commodity money being complementary. Silver started to perform the monetary function by the late Tang Dynasty, which dealt a fatal blow to money in kind. The early Tang Dynasty broke ground and introduced the *Tongbao* (universally circulated treasure) monetary system. In 621, *Kaiyuan Tongbao*, also called *Kaitong Yuanbao*, was issued, which put an end to the five-*zhu* coin system which named the coin by the weight, and a history of almost a millennium of the *Tongbao* system was established. Coin shortage occurred in the middle of the Tang Dynasty, and dual taxation measures greatly spurred commercialization of the products of labor which also led to a surge in money demand: "the less the coins are held in the hands of the people, the lower the prices of silk and cloth become, the prefectures and counties prohibited the practice of transporting coins beyond their borders, commerce and business vanished."[1] The phenomenon of high coin price against low commodity price continued for a whopping 60 years, and the situation was not eradicated till the dual tax law was replaced by the system of land rents and

---

[1] *New History of Tang Dynasty — Annals of Economy*, Zhonghua Book Company, 1975.

labor service; it did not finally ease until the Huichang period (841–846) of Emperor Wuzong.

Credit businesses, including accepting deposit and money withdrawal, buying and selling gold and silver, exchange and remittance, appeared in cities in the Tang Dynasty. Institutions engaging in brand-new credit businesses included pawn shops which engaged in independent mortgage loan operations, safe shops which kept property on behalf of customers, accepting consigned property and customers withdrawing funds against credit vouchers. There were also gold and silver shops engaging in buying and selling gold and silver as well exchange thereof; such gold and silver shops united into gold and silver markets or gold and silver guilds. The government engaged in the lending business with public funds for interest, which became a model for usury practices. Interest rates on loans made by the government were higher than those of private loans. *Feiqian* (flying money) which was equivalent to drafts of the modern means of payments, also known as "*bianhuan*" (convenience exchange), came into existence before 811. Under this mechanism, businessmen in the imperial capital were only required to hand over their funds for goods to the associate firm stationed out by the firm from their home Dao (Dao was the administrative area of the Tang Dynasty, roughly equivalent to modern day province) and got a half of the certificate; such businessmen may collect their cash when they returned to their home Dao, when their half of the certificate was found matching the other half held by the firm. Activities including private debt increased, and lending for interest in the cities was more active. Loans made secured by real estate, land and property were called "*tielin*" or "*dianzhi*" (hypothecation). Loans were predominantly made in kind, while loans made in coins might be more likely in areas adjacent to temples. These constituted the earliest financial market of China.

1. Theory of copper Ban by Liu Zhi

Liu Zhi (?–756), courtesy name Zuoqing, was born in Pengcheng (present-day Xuzhou of Jiangsu Province). His works included *Governance Canon, Remarks on Stemming War*, etc.

In 734, in order to alleviate the government of the straitened situation of coin shortage and currency insufficiency, Zhang Jiuling, the newly appointed prime minister, submitted the Proposal of Lifting the Ban on Privately Minted Coins. Xuanzong of the Tang Dynasty ordered the officials to deliberate on the proposal. Pei Yaoqing, Li Linpu and others objected; they argued that "coins are currency, which enjoy the authority of the state, hence all dynasties banned it to eliminate vicious spreading."[2] Liu Zhi also submitted a memorial titled "On Petitioning for Banning Privately Minted Coins," and aired his own views. This was the historically reputed theory of copper ban. His theory of banning copper could be introduced through two aspects:

(1) Money was "an authority belonging to the supreme ruler." Liu Zhi inherited the nominal theory of money from Guan Zi–Qing Zhong (the light and the heavy), arguing that money had a long history; its function was to "even the light and the heavy," "weigh the fundamental and the incidental." That is, the functions thereof were to balance commodity price and regulate the relations between agriculture, industry and commerce. Money determined the success of a country, hence the supreme ruler must firmly grip the right of minting in hand. The so-called balance actually referred to regulating and evening commodity price, "making the violent fluctuation an irregular phenomenon." In today's words, the ruler must utilize money in regulating commodity price, render it an instrument for regulating the structure of national economy in the process of price fluctuation, that is, adjusting the ratio structure between agriculture, industry and commerce, and taking firm control of property, managing the livelihood of the people and pacifying the world. Hence, it could be seen that the endowment, deprivation, impoverishment and enrichment of the people by way of money employment lay in the hands of the supreme ruler, while the supreme ruler had absolute power to employ this means. All unspecified contents quoted from Guan Zi are from Guan Zi to Guo Xu (state reserve), unless otherwise specified; only minor changes are made in a few words. While the statement of "weighing the fundamental and the incidental" was indeed his innovation, it was unheard of in essays

---

[2]*Old History of Tang Dynasty* — Annals of Economy, Volume 6, Zhonghua Book Company, 1976, pp. 2097–2099. No more citations shall be provided for further quotes from this book hereinbelow.

by other people. As regards the situation of monetary systems, "The success of a country is indeed hinged on this matter"; in this way, the position and function of money in the political, economic life of a country were elevated to an inconceivable height.

(2) There were theories of "five don'ts" in lifting the ban. It concentrated the monetary views of Liu Zhi, and was most typical of his thought, of which, the first, second and fifth "don'ts" inherited and developed the monetary theory of Guan Zi–Qing Zhong, while the third and fourth "don'ts" inherited and developed the monetary theory of Jia Yi. A step-by-step introduction is given as follows.

The first "don't" was based on the ancient theory of three moneys; he pointed out that "the coin of today is the inferior coin of the ancient times, if your majesty leaves it to the people, then the superior will have no way to control the inferior, and the inferior has no way to serve the superior." If the people were allowed to engage in unrestrained minting, then the supreme ruler would have no way to regulate the people and the people have no way to serve the supreme ruler. The unsaid words were that the country would cease to be a country, and the ruler cease to be a ruler, and that would constitute a grand chaos! The fifth "don't" was an adaptation of the words from Guan Zi–Guo Xu, stating that "awards and exhortation do not work on the rich and arrogant, authority and prohibition do not work on the poor and upset; the reason laws do not work and the people do not follow the reason lies in irregularities between the rich and the poor."

"If the people are permitted to mint coins, then it would be absolutely impossible for the poor to do it. I fear that the poor will get poorer and have to sell their labor service to the rich, while the rich will take the opportunity to get more undisciplined." That is, awards would not work any exhortative effect if the people were too rich, while the poor and the starving were not deterred by punishment, hence it would be difficult for laws and decrees to be implemented; therefore, difficulty of governing the people arose from the inequalities between the rich and the poor. If the ban on private minting was lifted, it would widen the gap between the rich and the poor. Historically, Liu Bi, the prince of the princedom of Wu in the reign of Emperor Wendi of the West Han Dynasty was nothing more than a prince; however, his "wealth equaled that of the emperor." Zheng Tong was nothing but a minister but "his wealth equaled that of the prince."

These were all consequences of lifting the ban on minting. Therefore, if the ban on private minting was to be lifted, it would amount to "offering the people the economic right and relinquishing the right of control thereof." Jia Shan of the earlier period just went so far as to remark that "it is sharing the control with the supreme ruler," while Liu Zhi went one step further and pointed out that this move equaled the supreme ruler automatically relinquished power; from the perspective of financial right, it was the right to enrich the people and the country. Such a move meant the power to control the rich and the poor was entirely lost, relinquished and handed over to others. Under the new historical conditions, Liu Zhi's attitude toward safeguarding the centralized authority of the ruler was more definitive, and his stance firmer.

The second "don't" held that "those who are good at governing the state would observe the fluctuation of commodities and weight of coins (and make proper arrangements accordingly). If commodity price rises, then the coin is too light, and lightness of coin arises from oversupply thereof, while oversupply of coin shall be addressed by working out measures to shrink it; on the contrary undersupply would lead to high price of the coin (heaviness), which shall be remedied by working out measures to release more to make it light. The foundation of the light and the heavy is hinged on such, how come this be entrusted with others?" First, the supreme ruler must monitor the change in commodity prices and money. Under the commodity money conditions, the advancement of this view was of utmost importance, and it still does not lose its relevance today as an integrated indicator in evaluating the stability of the economic situation in a country. Commodity price level, currency value, that is, whether the purchasing power of money was stable, was not only an economic issue but also a social issue; it was an issue concerning not only the ruler but also the people. The second was that "commodity price rise entails coin price drop," which was from Guan Zi–Shan Zhi Shu: "prices of the myriad articles drop when coin price rises, whereas the fall of coin price leads to a rise of the prices of the myriad articles." Statements such as "less coins lead to price drop of the myriad articles" by Zhang Lin of the East Han Dynasty and "corn price drop is due to lack of coins" by Kong of the East Jin Dynasty were all discussions of the relation between money and commodity price. Liu Shangzhi of the Song Dynasty of the Northern and

Southern Dynasties touched upon the relation between the quantity of money, currency value and commodity price for the first time, saying, "the less the quantity, the higher the price the coin will be, the more the quantity the coin is, the higher the commodity price will be." Similarly, Liu Zhi proceeded first to determine the level of money value by measuring the level of commodity price, and further determined the quantity of money by measuring the level of commodity price; hence, he could correlate the quantity of money with money value. The money value reflected here was the first-tier relation, whereas the relation between the level of money value and the quantity of money was the second-tier relation. The quantity of money and money value were considered directly correlated," and the "low price of coin is due to oversupply of coins, and undersupply thereof would lead to high price of coins." This statement was already a huge leap from the theory advanced in Guan Zi–Qing Zhong and followers thereof. However, he still based his theory on the relation between money value and commodity price, failing to completely detach himself from the theoretical constraints of supply and demand theory of value put forward in Guan Zi–Qing Zhong. Different from the typical quantity theory of money, the theory had not been directly expressed as the quantity of money determining the value of money, and the value of money was reflected by commodity price. Liu Zhi's theoretical viewpoints were still in the inchoation phase of quantity theory of money.

He further modified the statement by Li Li that "too high corn price ails the people, and too low corn price ails the peasant" and proposed that "low commodity price harms the peasant, while low coin price harms the merchant." He modified half of the original meaning. The original high corn price harming the people was replaced with low coin price harming the merchant; the meaning of the whole sentence was also modified by taking the interests of both the peasant and the merchant into consideration from setting store by the peasant in the original statement, that is, low price of agricultural produce would harm the agriculture, money deflation would harm the commerce. The theory was no longer placing focus on slighting the commerce and suppressing the incidental; quite the contrary, the stance of safeguarding the interests of small- and intermediate-sized merchants stood out from the statement. The fact was that, in the money deflation process, the ones that sustained the heaviest losses were not the big merchants but the likes of land-owning peasants, small handicraftsmen, small vendors, etc.

Based on the foregoing two paragraphs, he put forward his specific measures on controlling and regulating money circulation quantity by the country. Oversupply of money required recalling in order to reduce the quantity of money in circulation, whereas undersupply of money led to increase in purchasing power of money, and more money should be released on the market to lower the purchasing power of money ("measures shall be worked out to reduce the amount of money in circulation when there is an oversupply; while undersupply of money leads to heaviness of money, measures shall be worked out to release more money to make it lighter"). This measure originated in the remark, "measures shall be made to recall coins when coin is light, and measures be made to release coins when coin is heavy."

The third was that it may not be considered that delegating minting right was "setting up a trap to lure the people in." The reason was that "coin minting would be profitless without adulterating lead and iron therein, while adulteration would debase the coin; such evil practice could not be stemmed without grave punishment applied thereon. Now that people would even risk capital punishment in pursuit of private minting, how could it be conceivable to lift the ban on minting by opening up the source while expecting the people to follow the law?" While private minting would not be profitable without adulteration, even banning would be of little avail in prohibiting people from conducting private minting when driven by interest. So how could it be reasonable to lift the ban on minting? It would be entirely impossible to require the people to abide by the law while lifting the ban on minting.

The fourth was that it was undeniable that minting would compel people to discard practicing agriculture. "While the people are permitted to engage in private minting, no one would engage in minting when there is little profit; throngs of people would desert their land and pursue minting when minting is profitable. When throngs of people deserted practicing agriculture, weeds would not be extirpated, and famine would ensue."

The third and fourth points had already been demonstrated by Jia Yi, and also been discussed by Cui Mian. Liu Zhi reiterated the theory under changed historical conditions in a clearer and more orderly manner.

In the eyes of Liu Zhi, the copper ban may have the practical effect of "obtaining four virtues in one measure." "If copper is distributed among the people, then private minting could not be effected due to absence of copper, then government minted coin would not deflate, no capital punishment would be committed by the people, and there would be an increase in coins, and the commerce would benefit therefrom. This is indeed a measure bringing about four virtues. I hope that your majesty would thoroughly examine the matter." This was originally proposed by Jia Yi; however, the proposal had never had a devoted follower like Liu Zhi. Besides, he did not simply repeat the words of his predecessor, instead, he made a penetrating exposition thereon against new historical conditions.

First, he correlated the purchasing power of money and the size of population for the first time, and argued that the quantity of money required for circulation must be inspected in connection with the size of population. Increase in purchasing power of money was due to the fact that "population grows while no new mint furnace is introduced"; this view was indeed novel. Shen Yanzhi of the Song of the Northern and Southern Dynasties put forward the view that "the wider the use is, the narrower and the more stretched the commodity will be." He discussed the effect of expanding circulation scale on the amount required for money circulation; however, he had not touched on the population factor. Marx said, "the quantity of means of circulation is determined by factors ... all of which are contingent on the metamorphosis proceeding in the world of commodities, which is in turn contingent on the general nature of the mode of production, the size of the population, the relation of town and countryside, the development of the means of transport, the more or less advanced division of labor, credit, etc."[3] According to the statistics in historical records, his theory was founded on solid ground. In the Wude period of Emperor Gaozu in the Tang Dynasty (618–626), there were two million odd households in China, while the number exceeded eight million when Liu Zhi turned in his memorial. The number of households surged almost four times over the period of a century; the population of the country in the year 705 stood at 37 million odd, by the year the

---

[3]*Complete Works of Karl Marx and Frederick Engels*, vol. 13, p. 95.

memorial was submitted, the number exceeded 45 million. The population grew by 22% over a period of 30 years.[4]

Although there was some growth in population, coin minting quantity did not increase accordingly, and hence the problem of "heaviness of money" occurred naturally. Liu Zhi made a correct theoretical exposition by combining a newly occurred situation in money circulation, introducing fresh content to monetary theory and making his own contribution to monetary theory.

Second, targeting the situation of heaviness of government-minted coins the purchasing power of which was equal to the price of copper and that heavy coins were destroyed and reminted into lighter coins, he pointed out that if the government relaxed the ban it would result in lighter coins entering the realm of circulation, while a stringent policy would lead to lighter coins being driven out of circulation and discarded: "government minted coins are heavy, the value thereof is roughly equal to that of the same amount of copper, hence pirate minters melt heavier coins and mint such into lighter ones. Lighter coins would be circulated under relaxed regulation, and cease to circulate under tighter regulation; if they do not circulate they would be discarded, this is the reason that there is a lack of coins. The reason that the use of minted coin does not suffice lies in the expensiveness of copper, while the expensiveness of copper lies in the fact that it is used by the multitudes."

Finally, the reason that the government could not recover production cost from the government-minted coin lay in the fact that copper was expensive. "And the reason of expensiveness of copper lies in the fact that it is used by the multitudes." The reason that it was used by the multitudes was because copper was a material used for making military instruments and articles for everyday use. However, copper was inferior to iron in making weapons, and inferior to lacquer in making articles for everyday use; hence, it "brings no harm in banning the use of copper." If nobody

---

[4]Liang Fangzhong, *Statistics of Households, Land, Land Rent of the Various Dynasties of China*, p. 69. The household number and population stood at 8,018,710 and 46,285,161, respectively, in the 22nd year in the Kaiyuan period of Emperor Xuanzong, and 6,156,141 and more than 37,140,000, respectively, in the first year in the Shenlong period of Emperor Zhongzong. Figures of the Wude period of Emperor Gaozu shall not be included here.

used copper, copper would naturally "get cheaper" and "copper for minting coin would be sufficient." It would definitely have the effect of "obtaining four virtues in one move": Copper would not get scattered among the people, and the people would have no way to engage in pirate minting, "government minted coins would not get destroyed," and the people would not violate the law arising from pirate minting, nor "commit crime punishable by death penalty." When government-minted coins were not destroyed, copper material could be concentrated for minting coins, and "then the number of coins will grow by the day"; when deflation was gradually easing, the industry and the commerce would gained some development, and profit could be obtained therefrom, that is, "the incidental could also benefit therefrom."

His copper ban program originated in the copper ban theory proposed by Jia Yi. While Jia Yi's copper ban theory had seven blessings, Liu Zhi's copper ban had four virtues. The purpose of Jia Yi's copper ban was to eradicate pirate minting, while that of Liu Zhi's was to lower copper price; besides, the items enumerated by Liu Zhi that copper was inferior to iron in making weapons and inferior to lacquer in making articles for everyday use were also facts. However, copper could not be done away with from the everyday life of the people, and the path to riches for the noble and the powerful could not be effected without copper; religious activities of the supreme ruler would be less possible without copper, and the everyday life of the people still could not entirely do away with copper. Under such circumstances, Liu Zhi remarked, "If the people are allowed to mint coins .... I fear that the poor will get poorer and have to sell their labor service to the rich, while the rich will take the opportunity to become more undisciplined." Because the vast majority of ministers considered "that it would bring about vice in allowing the people to mint coin, hence an edict was promulgated to ban bad money."[5] Hence, Zhang Jiuling's proposal of lifting the ban on minting coin was shelved. This move laid the economic foundation for the "*Kaiyuan* Boom" of Li Longji, Emperor Xuanzong of the Tang Dynasty. Banning private minting would work an irreplaceably important role in safeguarding the financial strength of the central ruling group, in stabilizing and developing national and even international trade.

---

[5]*History of the Yuan Dynasty — Biography of Economy*, vol. 5, p. 1385.

However, we must acknowledge that the younger brother of Emperor Xuanzong, Li Wei, prince of Xin'anjun, again brought up the issue to "relax regulation on private minting" on account of "insufficiency for national use." In *New History of Tang Dynasty — Annals of Economy*, the following remarks are entered: "most ministers were awed by the authority of younger brother of your majesty and dared not put up a debate, however Wei Boyang alone thought otherwise, he opposed even the proposal from Li Wei." It could be seen that even with a great multitude of benefits and most favorable conditions for implementation, it would still be possible for the copper ban to be shelved explicitly or implicitly in a centralized society where the power served the few against the backdrop of a slew of resistance and obstruction put up by the noble, the powerful and the wealthy, even if such a conception might be pretty good.

The copper ban proposal of Liu Zhi was much more brilliant than the measures of banning private minting for the purpose of eliminating forgery and sloppy production raised by Pei Yaoqing, Li Linpu, Xiao Jiong and others which focused on treating the symptom to the exclusion of the root cause. It took 70 years for the thought of Liu Zhi to be accepted by the authorities gradually and translated into a practical economic policy. After the copper ban edict was instituted, in 793, Zhang Pang argued in one memorial, "I hereby petition Your Majesty to implement former edicts, all trade of copper shall be banned except for minting mirror." Thereafter, the copper ban policy was followed by later dynasties. However, private minting and bad money had never been eradicated or disappeared.

2. On the evil of government loans by Chu Suiliang and Cui Mian

2.1. *Principal of government loan*

The principal of government loan referred to a regular economic measure conducted by the government of the Tang Dynasty; it was government-conducted usury capital. Profit obtained from such loans had been employed to subsidize monthly emoluments for government officials (including foodstuff, miscellaneous expenses, and servants) and shortfalls in government funds. The principal of government loan actually referred to the principal employed in making usury loans by the government. It introduced new channels to the national treasury revenue, and furnished guarantees for official emolument disbursement from the national treasury. Prior to 806, government loans had been under the direct control of the local repositories proper; such local repositories proper offered designated local businessmen a certain amount of capital, directing such to engage in consigned operations via business modes including trade and usury, and "sixty percent or seventy percent" profit obtained therefrom shall be turned over to the government repositories.

After 756, government loans developed into one of the main sources of government expenses disbursed from the national treasury. In 818, the Government Loan Repository was officially set up, and the government established a uniform operation agency thereafter, which not only brought under control the activities of usurers but also furnished a special backup fund guaranteeing the revenue of the national treasury.[6]

The Initial Years of Establishing Principal of Government Loan: According to historical records, as early as in the Sui and Tang Dynasties, the government regularly appropriated public funds and diverted such funds to commercial activity or the loan market for profit. In *New History of the Tang Dynasty — Annals of Economy*, the following remarks are entered: "in earlier years, officials in the imperial capital and officials from the various provinces all contributed to the principal of government loans, such was then offered to business activities for profit which would then subsidize public expenditure." The "earlier years" could be traced back to the times of the Wei, Qi and Zhou Dynasties of the Northern Dynasty.[7]

In 618, the government officially set aside principal for government loans. In *Evolution of Systems in the Tang Dynasty — The Variety of*

---

[6] Lv Simian conjectured in the Histories of the Sui, Tang and the Five Dynasties, "government loan conducted by the early Sui Dynasty must have originated in Zhou and Qi of the Northern Dynasty. It is suspected that in the Kingdom of Wei of the Three Kingdoms Period, such practice was not totally absent. While it was more prevalent in the Tang dynasty," Shanghai Chinese Classics Publishing House, 1984, p. 869.

[7] Ge Chengyong, *National Treasury System of the Tang Dynasty*, Sanqin Publishing House, 1990, pp. 136–137.

Principals from the Various Bureaus, the following remarks are found: "in December of 618, principal of government loan was appropriated, officials of the various prefectures shall be designated to supervise the matter, referred to as *Zhuoqian* officer (literally, officer responsible for capturing money), each bureau is staffed with nine persons, affiliated to the ministry of personnel. The principals allocated thereto were under fifty thousand *qian*, and such shall be offered to vendors for business, monthly interest was fixed at four thousand *qian*, and interest shall be handed to the government at the expiration of one year's term. The officers in charge shall be officially appointed at the expiration of the one-year term." As the national treasury was not yet well furnished at the time, emoluments of officials in the imperial capital depended exclusively on the performance of the principal of government loan. Such a principal should be allocated to the deputy officer and the protocol officer of the respective bureau to turn around in business and obtain profit therefrom, and proceeds obtained therefrom shall be distributed according to the size of staff. Hence, governments at all levels, from the central government to the local governments, engaged in operating principals of government loans. In 638, the establishment was abolished. However, it was reinstated in 641.

Purposes of Establishing Principal of Government Loan: Interest obtained therefrom was established as the source of government official emoluments as stated above. In addition to the various bureaus in the imperial capital, officials from the various peripheral provinces, prefectures, military garrisons and counties also engaged in the practice. In addition to setting up government loans to procure interest in support of expenditure on official emoluments, later "principal" had also been established for some special, regular expenses.

They came under a host of names, including the miscellaneous expenses of the various bureaus, awards to foreigners, banquet expenses granted by the emperor, fees for students in the imperial academy and what not — the use thereof ranged extensively. Expense of emoluments for the officials had always been a major expense item for the national treasury of ancient countries; a vast majority of them came from the interest obtained from government loans, that is, it originated in the income of profit resulting from government-conducted usury and commercial capital. Therefore, it had been discarded and reinstated multiple times in spite of opposition from some officials.

In order to provide for such a great variety of uses, such a grand scale and variegated expenses, the interest income resulting from the principal of government loans must have been quite substantial and guaranteed. It was either of substantial size of principal or of an exorbitant interest rate with an annual rate of 96% (monthly interest of 4,000 *qian* on the principal of 50,000 *qian*); in the Kaiyuan, Yongtai and Jianzhong periods (713–783), the monthly interest rate stood at 5–6%, annual interest at 60–72%, while around the year 718 the monthly interest rate was 7% and annual interest rate 84%. In the Changqing period (821–824) and Huichang period (841–846), monthly and annual rates were 4% and 48%, respectively. There had been a trend of diminishing rate. However, the total principal of government loan was far exceeding that of the previous period; hence, interest generated therefrom did not decrease but increased. For instance, in *Systems in the Tang Dynasty — Emoluments for the Ministers of Imperial Capital and Officials of the Localities*, the following remarks are entered: "when the principal of government loan was installed from the Wude period to the Zhenguan period, the principal allocated thereto was under fifty thousand qians, monthly interest generated therefrom with such being lent to vendors for business was four thousand *qian* and annual interest amounted to forty eight thousand *qian*; in the edict promulgated on December 9, 823, the principal granted to the various bureaus totaled 84,500 *guan* at forty percent interest rate, and annual proceeds amounted to 40,992 *guan*." According to statistics, government loan took up a substantial proportion in the national finances in the late Tang Dynasty. The amount equaled 1/3.6 of the dual taxes collected, while the principal of government loan for the various bureaus equaled one sixth of the nine million odd guan, the overall national dual taxes of the country, which had already been an item too big to be discarded.[8]

---

[8]Li Jinxiu, *Draft of Finances in the Tang Dynasty*, Second Half Volume, Beijing University Press, 2001, p. 1165.

Source of the Principal of Government Loan: Said principal came from taxes on the people, while moneylenders or businessmen paid the interest via "engaging in market trade" or lending such for interest. Therefore, the foregoing interest rate was both profit margin and interest rate; there was no difference between the two here. Regardless though, the government interest rate may be lower than non-governmental interest rate (which stood at 10% monthly); it was actually a standard interest rate publicly fixed for the usury industry by the feudal government in the capacity of the biggest lender, while the actual interest rate of usury was by no means limited by the standard fixed by the government. "The principal of government loan for the various bureaus shall be drawn by the various persons" and put such into operation on the market, the government exploited the moneylenders, while these rich people drawing the principal of government loan would further extort their respective borrowers on the back of government support, which made the life of the people insufferable. Of course, the possibility that the government furnished stores and vendors directly with the principal and made commercial profit could not be ruled out. In short, for the ordinary people, the interest rate was not low; quite the contrary, it was way too high.

Management of the Principal of Government Loan: The principal of government loan was the indirect government credit, that is, the government made loans to moneylenders, and the lenders then further lent such capital to the ordinary people. In order to accommodate to the characteristics of complicatedness in personnel and means of management, petty officials were appointed to handle the issue.

Such petty officials lent the principal of government loan to powerful and wealthy houses, mandating them to repay the capital and interest when terms expired; such persons and houses were called *Zhuoliqian* handlers (literally, profit or interest capturer, moneylender). Such specialized moneylenders were entitled to many privileges so long as they performed obligations of delivering specified interest on time as scheduled, while the petty officials could be promoted when they handed over 41,000 monthly interest, 50,000 a year without missing scheduled payment. Moneylenders were entitled to being exempted from labor service and reprieved from punishment (the prefecture and county would not dare punish them when they were found guilty). Wealthy houses mostly were willing to accept such assignments as they could lend money to businessmen and collect interest, or they could engage in business operation themselves with principal allocated from government loans. Such commercial capital and usury combined with the government backing featured extra economic exploitation, the ruthless extortion of which was conceivable.

Moneylenders were required to enter into warrantee when taking out principals from the government loans, and a security certificate was to be posted by a guarantor. In order to acquire the privileges of a moneylender, some people would willingly enter into a certificate of guarantee without actually taking out the principal, "so that the petty official in charge would exempt their labor service, and the pertinent authorities dare not punish them when they are found guilty."[9]

Strict regulations on management of the principal of government loan were enacted. If found to be in dereliction of duties by the competent officer, legal responsibilities thereof shall be investigated, principal shall be repaid thereby and punishment shall be administered thereon.

When the principal of government loan was allocated, there were quite some people submitting memorials and pinpointing flaws of the scheme. Even as early as in October of 594 of Emperor Wendi of the Sui Dynasty, Su Xiaoci, minister of the ministry of works, criticized government loans as "in exclusive pursuit of profit. Nothing is worse than it in disturbing the people and vitiate the customs."[10] The most representative remarks were none other than the theory of obtaining official appointment by turning over money by Chu Suiliang and the theory of harming the people advanced by Cui Mian. If Chu Suiliang dissected the evil of government loans from the perspective of politics, Cui Mian analyzed the evil from the perspective of economics.

2.2. Chu Suiliang on appointing officials by turning over money

Chu Suiliang (596–658), courtesy name Dengshan, was born in Qiantang (Hangzhou) or Yangzhuo (Yuxian county) of the Sui Dynasty.

---

[9]*Systems in the Tang Dynasty — The Variety of Principals from the Various Bureaus*, Volume 2, Zhonghua Book Company, 1955, p. 1677.
[10]*History of Sui Dynasty — Annals of Economy.*

In 638, Chu Suiliang, the then imperial admonishing officer, submitted a memorial forcefully arguing the future evils of practicing government loans, claiming that such a practice was no different from selling government offices in the Han Dynasty. It was literally following "the sale of government office in the Han Dynasty which has been ridiculed, now that this practice is embarked on, where is the difference."[11]

His argument was that official governance was the foundation of a country. However, a petty official in charge of moneylending could be entered into the rolls as a candidate for government position so long as he was good at conducting business and making money and was of solid financial means, with neither having his virtue and capacity inspected nor having his political attainment reviewed. This was one of the inconceivable consequences.

In conclusion, official governance was corrupted and the future of the country would be jeopardized. This was not only an economic issue but also a political problem. However, the political problem was induced by the economic problem: "granted that government loan shall be reinstated as it was by the various bureaus in the imperial capital, principal was furnished and petty officials were appointed to be in charge of loan making to provide for emoluments of officials." While the issue of emoluments for officials was solved, the ruinous cause undermining the foundation of the Tang Dynasty had been introduced.

2.3. Cui Mian on government loans harming the people

Cui Mian (673–739), courtesy name Shanchong, was born in Chang'an. He was a man of integrity and frankness.

In 718, in the memorial titled "Deliberation On Monthly Emoluments for Prefecture and County Chiefs," Cui Mian lashed out against the evils of government loans, arguing that such practices freed the rich from labor service while redoubling the harm on the poor and drove a multitude of poor families into bankruptcy.

---

[11]*Systems in the Tang Dynasty — Emoluments for Imperial and Non-Imperial Officials*, Second Volume, p. 1651. No more citations shall be provided for further quotes from this book hereinbelow.

"The rich are exempted from their labor services, while the poor bear the consequence of the evil." The first sentence said that the rich were entitled to privileges of being exempted from labor service, and the authorities did not impose punishment thereon even if they were found guilty. Some lawless rich would prefer to turn over the interest and take out a certificate to shield them from punishment for crimes, and some would go so far as to not take out the principal but simply enter into a virtual deed for protection rendered thereby.

Hence, *History as a Mirror for Governance* recorded the circumstances of 718: "at the beginning of the Tang Dynasty, official emoluments for the prefectures and counties had all derived from interest generated from the scheme of entrusting money at an interest with the wealthy houses; interest ran as high as approximating the principle, many houses went bankrupt." In the closing period of the Tang Dynasty, the amount of principal grew gradually, and monthly interest became a burdensome issue.

Based on facts examined, Cui Mian put forward his strategy that national revenue and expenditure must "all come from tax proper, and all new levies must be cancelled." "A tithe tax would suffice for the use of the government and the people." All revenue and expenditure should be disbursed from the tax proper.

3. Theory of banning the practice of storing away coin by Emperor Xianzong of the Tang Dynasty

3.1. *Emperor Xianzong of the Tang Dynasty on theory of banning the practice of storing away coin*

Emperor Xianzong (778–820) of the Tang Dynasty reigned in the period of 805–820. In June of 808, Emperor Xianzong planned to institute a ban on storing money, restricting the amount of cash stored away by the people. The reasons he presented were that "the proper law of money lies in circulation. If there is a surplus of money, commodity price would inevitably drop. Therefore those who store away money are taking advantage of others' perilous state, and those who hoard goods are debasing capital thereof. How could those who seek profit know the states livelihood? If such ill is not eliminated, the people would have no means to live on."[12] "These days cloth and silk prices drop, available cash dwindles, all these phenomena arise from stagnation of money circulation."[13]

Shortage of copper coin led to money appreciation and commodity price drop, deflation ensued and myriad industries suffered, which created difficulties for the production and life of the people; while houses of wealth and nobility stored away a tremendous amount of copper coins, engaged in commerce and finances concurrently, specialized in financial business, reaped substantial profit and amassed considerable amount of capital, their impact on money shortage could not to be ignored.

Safe shops: In the Tang Dynasty, there appeared a type of financial institution which took care of property for customers and had safes to lease to customers for a keeping fee. There were a great slew of businesses in the two markets of Chang'an, some depositing money as much as a hundred thousand guans. Vouchers or other evidence was to be presented when such a deposit was to be withdrawn; such a voucher must have been the premature form of checks. Money deposits had been very prevalent in business at the time. Such must be the rudimentary form of the bank. Internationally, the financial industry came into being around the turn of the sixth and seventh centuries; for instance, the house of Medici of Florence and the houses of Baldi and Peruzzi appeared six or seven hundred years after the appearance of safe shops in the Tang Dynasty.

There was also *Didian* (mansion shop) which engaged in concurrent financial businesses; in addition to engaging directly in business and intermediary business, it also engaged in buying, storing, allocating and exchanging which involved a huge amount of money. As "rarities from all corners of the world are shipped to the market," businessmen from the various places thronged the market. Most *Didian* engaged in wholesale business and some retail businesses; they handled huge volume of imports and exports with substantial sums of business turnover, amounting to tens of thousands.

---

[12]*Collection of Grand Edicts of the Tang Dynasty*, Xuelin Press, 1992, p. 536.
[13]*Systems in the Tang Dynasty*, vol. 89, Second Half, p. 1631.

The powerful and influential engaged in the financial industry, competing with the people for profit. Safe shops and *Didian* drew a great many nobles and bureaucrats into the business for its substantial profit.

They flocked to the business, set up financial institutions and competed with the people for interest, all of which prompted the government to step in to intervene and put a stop to the situation.

It could be seen that operating safe shops and *Didian* by the powerful and the influential was all the rage, which monopolized financial resources and posed a tremendous peril to the finances of the central government.

Restricting Private Hoarding of Cash: In order to safeguard the normal order for money circulation of the feudal country and ensure the requirements for production and normal development of agriculture, Emperor Xianzong decreed that "let the commerce and travelers know the bounds, agriculture gets settled, the measures are promulgated to save the time instead of seeking profit therefrom."[14] In June of the third year (818) in the Yuanhe period, he further promulgated that "the emperor hereby notify the country, there is a shortage of money, people who have hoarded money are mandated to bring their hoarding to market as they see fit, no more money hoarding is allowed."[15] The purpose of the edict was to turn around the situation of money shortage.

Theoretical outcome of banning on storing money: Though the purpose of the ban was to bring out the copper hoardings, if it was thoroughly implemented, it would be equivalent to inhibiting and strangling credit activities. Any credit organization would require a substantial amount of initial deposit fund (commerce was no exception; however, such amounts would not match up to the credit and no further elaboration shall be made in this text), and deposits should be coming in continuously, the cycling of which constituted the inexhaustible key source of funds. While the promulgation of the ban on storing money signaled that there was a limit established on the amount of initial deposit fund, and the source of deposit would also be narrowed down to a very limited range of amount, it was inevitable for the financial industry to contract. Even if the existing credit

---

[14]*Collection of Edicts of Tang Dynasty*, p. 536. No more citations shall be provided hereunder.
[15]*Old History of Tang Dynasty — Biographic Sketch of Xianzong Emperor*, vol. 2, pp. 425–526.

institutions continued in operation, they would be limited to a certain quota; that is, they may continue their business activity on the condition that they do not exceed the amount of the two items of capital fund aforesaid, and the precondition for the development of credit development was no longer in place. This was no different from cutting down the foundation and taking away the monetary capital fund accumulated and amassed, severing the foundation and source for the existence and development of the credit system. This measure would definitely meet with opposition and resistance from the wealthy and influential businessmen, especially those with the backing of nobles and bureaucrats, who would disregard the government decrees and have their own way; they would accumulate and amass monetary capital funds without much restraint, expand and develop credit institutions. On the contrary, the ordinary businessmen would deposit their monetary capital funds into financial institutions set up by and under the shelter of powerful officials and nobles in order to avoid exacting legal provisions, which would result in ballooning of the amount of deposit available over a short period, the credit industry gaining abnormal development and capital getting all the more concentrated under the man-made environment, and the situation of acquisition becoming further aggravated.

In consideration of the situation, Emperor Xianzong of the Tang Dynasty was forced to stringently reiterate the ban, mandating that the monetary capital fund must be disposed of within a specified period, and anyone violating the ban should be punished in accordance with the gravity of the circumstance and the gravest may be whipped to death.

3.2. *Implementation of ban on storing money*

The objective outcome of implementing the ban on storing money prepared conditions for the great development of the credit industry. After the promulgation of the edict, monetary capital funds of ordinary businessmen were invested into real estate in the cities for the sake of maintaining the current monetary value; properties of an entire lane or street were bought and large tracts of land were acquired in the countryside. While businessmen of solid means attached themselves to the imperial guard under the leadership of eunuchs, when funds were deposited in the name of government funds under their names, government edicts could do little to the situation. After the promulgation of the decree on restricting the storage of cash cited above, "accumulated money in both the imperial capital and the peripheral areas, the various military garrisons, amounted to over five hundred thousand guans. Hence, the people strove to purchase big mansions to turn over their cash, houses of solid means even purchased an entire lane for rent in order to maintain the monetary value of their hoardings. While businessmen of powerful background mostly attached their money to the imperial guard in the name of government fund, hence the prefectures and counties had no way to verify their estate, the edict ultimately failed."[16] Land acquisition was aggravated in the Tang Dynasty and developed into a serious social issue. New financial institutions and brand-new financial instruments were introduced, including safe shops, *Didian*, *Feiqian*, government loans, etc. The credit industry gained substantial development in the Tang Dynasty.

According to historical records, after the government relaxed the restriction on the amount of cash to be stored away and extended the term of regulation, the decree could still not be carried through. The ban was unfavorable to commodity circulation and the expansion and development of the credit system; it met with fierce resistance from powerful officials and nobles. Though the ban on storing money had been reinstated multiple times and forcefully reiterated, it ultimately failed to materialize.

The policy of banning the practice of storing away money continued to the Five Dynasties; it had been reimplemented, which spoke volumes of the appeal and market space thereof to the supreme ruler. The policy was brought back to life after 100 years.

4. Theory of government-run exchange by three persons including Wang Shao

4.1. *Remittance business — Bianhuan (convenience exchange)*

In order to adapt to the requirements of the development of domestic and overseas trade (tea, silk, chinaware, paper, etc.) of the Tang Dynasty,

---

[16]*Systems of Tang Dynasty — Money*, vol. 2, p. 1631.

remittance came into being, that is, *Feiqian*, *Bianhuan* and *Bianqian* (convenience money). The original intermediary of business transaction-money may be consigned to the safe shop for safekeeping, and businessmen may draw cash from said safe shop against the voucher or other evidence. This scheme furnished big merchants with a means of convenience and possibility; it freed them from employing cash in large-sum transactions where a slip of paper evidence with words inscribed thereon would suffice. Realization of transactions between different places would no longer require employing cash, and *Feiqian* would suffice.

After the implementation of the dual tax law, there appeared a serious shortage of money in circulation, and the various localities prohibited coins from being carried outside their borders, which further promoted the generation and development of Feiqian. According to *New History of Tang Dynasty — Economy Four*, in 794 Emperor Dezong decreed that forging and trading of copper vessels were allowed, the maximum weight of each vessel not exceeding one *jin* (half a kilogram) and the price thereof not exceeding one hundred and sixty *wen*; anyone melting copper coin into copper was to be punished with reference to pirate minting. However, copper coins held by the people dwindled, silk and cloth prices were kept very low, and the various prefectures and counties instituted measures prohibiting coins being carried out of their respective areas, and hence businessmen vanished. When the recommendation of lifting the ban on money circulation put forward by Li Ruoqi (west Zhejiang inspector) was approved, the number of businessmen from the imperial capital who went to various places for business was "beyond counting." In the 20th year of the Zhenyuan period, an edict provided that silk, cloth, miscellaneous articles and coins were allowed to be used concurrently; when Emperor Xianzong ascended the throne, he reinstated the ban on copper vessels on account of a shortage of coins. Against the backdrop of extreme currency shortage and dire chaos, *Feiqian* came into being. During the reign of Emperor Xuanzong (847–859), Zhao Lin, governor of Quzhou, noted in his diary, "a certain man conducted business outside his native place, and earned several hundred strings of coins, he was concerned about the difficulty of traveling. He turned the money over to the government remittance office, brought a voucher home. This was the so-called *Bianhuan*, and tucked it under his clothes' parcel." Now that there was government remittance, of course there would be private remittance, or the concurrent existence of government and private remittances. In *New History of Tang Dynasty — Economy Four* the following is entered, during the reign of Emperor Xianzong (806–820): "businessmen going to the imperial capital would consign their money to the *Jinzouyuan*, the various military garrisons, the envoys, wealthy houses, etc., and traveled afar without much burden of carriage, they would then draw the consigned money against matching of vouchers, this is called '*Feiqian*'." The *Jinzouyuan* mentioned herein is definitely a government-run remittance organization, whereas the military garrison and envoy might either be a government-run or private-run business, and the wealthy house was obviously a private remittance organization; however, due to limited historical records, conjecture is made herein only by comparing government- and private-run businesses.

Indeed, as remarked by Li Jiannong, tea was not produced in north China; however, the people there were fond of drinking tea, and hence people from north China went to the south to purchase tea and sell it back in the north. The inconvenience of carrying money brought into existence *Feiqian* for the occasion. *Systems of Tang Dynasty — Money* recorded that the edict promulgated in February 811 stated that "tea merchants remitted their funds in the government run or private run remittance businesses, such practice must be banned." Hence, it could be seen that the tea trade definitely had an unusual relation with *Feiqian*. Li Jiannong also remarked, "now that copper coins were prohibited from leaving the border, and the use of silver coin had not yet been universally accepted; if businessmen wanted to conduct business activity, there was no other means available to address the straitened situation than the employment of remittance via '*Feiqian*'. As the circulation of *Feiqian* had mostly been originally instituted by big merchants (especially tea merchants), it was not something originally installed by the government, as such had been detested by the government."[17]

Appearance of Feiqian: According to instructions recorded in the *Remittance*, the 10th volume of *Origins of Things*, *Bianhuan* originated

---

[17]*Draft of Ancient Chinese Economic History — Wei, Jin, Northern and Southern Dynasties*, Wuhan University Press, 2005, p. 236.

in Emperor Xianzong's time. There were records in *Old History of Tang Dynasty, Systems of Tang Dynasty — General Prologue to Salt and Iron Transportation*. At the latest by the first year of the Yuanhe period (806) in the reign of Emperor Xianzong, merchants in the imperial capital would consign their money to the *Jinzouyuan*, military garrison, envoy, or agency stationed in the imperial capital from the provinces where they came from or with a wealthy businessman in the capital, and take out one half of a certificate slip, with the other half being delivered to the corresponding institution and firm in the home province. The merchants would draw money against the counterpart of the certificates when they returned home. In the same year, the government banned the practice, and instituted the ban again in the sixth year (812) of the Yuanhe period. In 813, businessmen were ordered to conduct *Feiqian* business in the ministry of revenue, the department of expenditure and the department of salt and iron, and hundred *qian* were charged as the processing fee on every 1,000 *qian* consigned. No businessman came for the business, and the charge was dropped, and *Feiqian* was still free of charge. During the reign of Emperor Yizong (860–874), money consigned by businessmen from the areas of the Yangtze and Huaihe Rivers in the three pertinent departments was detained by the home prefecture, and no businessman dared to remit any money thereafter, which negatively affected the income of the three departments, and the central government decreed in 867 that no detention may be conducted. The practice continued till the South Song Dynasty, and it had been a pretty prevalent practice at that, after which it fell into disuse and was replaced by paper money.

Remittance business was profitable. In remittance business, the monetary funds to be processed in the remittance could be utilized by the handling party at no cost, and hence the government would forever attempt to monopolize the *Feiqian* business and pocket the profit generated therefrom exclusively. When the business was monopolized by the three departments, it had been under the exclusive control of the central government; in times of fiscal deficit and demand for tremendous military expense, the local governments were also lured by the profit and would detain the fund and refuse to honor the voucher, which led to "distrust of merchants, and the result was that the pertinent department could not continue the business."[18] Therefore, all evils of government-run remittance were exposed, making it impossible to win over the trust and support of businessmen, and *Feiqian* ultimately fell into disuse.

4.2. Wang Shao, Lu Tan and Wang Bo on government-run remittance

Military minister Wang Shao, deputy revenue minister Lu Tan and salt and iron envoy Wang Bo submitted a memorial on permitting businessmen to remit cash in the three pertinent departments in May of 812 as well as a memorial on lifting the hundred-*qian* charge on remittance submitted in July. While the former was recorded in *Old History of Tang Dynasty — Economy, Volume 1, Systems of Tang Dynasty — Money Division First Half*, the latter was recorded in *New History of Tang Dynasty — Economy Four*.

Reasons for conducting government-run remittance: The government attitude at the time toward *Feiqian* was prohibition instead of development. The imperial capital governor Pei Wu petitioned to refuse furnishing businessmen with *Feiqian*, search the market and institute a system of ten-person mutual collateral. The result was that every household stored away coins and commodity prices dropped. Hence, Wang Shao proposed to institute government-run remittance. The reason they advanced was that it may have driven coins back into circulation and relieved coin shortage. They argued that the government "more values ready cash, while lately the government spends particularly less; the reason for the situation is that businessmen are not allowed to conduct remittance, hence people would stash away their money, and commodity prices drop due to the fact that money has been usually stashed away."

Most people at that time cherished cash, which was particularly the case in the imperial capital. The government was keenly aware of the shortage of cash when it came to cash required in government spending, and the reason was that *Feiqian* was banned. The reason that money was retained in the cities via familiar businessmen or stored away in private houses was that they suspected that stealthy *Feiqian*

---

[18]*Systems of Tang Dynasty — Director of Finances*, vol. 2, p. 1018.

flow had never really stopped for a minute. The reason that *Feiqian* stayed in operation even after the ban was the stealthy scramble for coins between the central government and the local forces. It had been banned previously because the scheme was favorable to the local forces while detrimental to the three pertinent departments; however, after the ban, the circumstance was still not favorable to the three departments, while monetary circulation stagnation was aggravated. In order to ease the towering problem of currency shortage, the three departments attempted to lift the ban on the condition that all interests went to them. Therefore, they proposed that remittance must be monopolized by the state, "the businessmen are allowed to remit cash in the three departments, while the rest shall stay banned." The government attempted to induce private hoarding and cash back into the market and recirculate by conducting state monopoly on the remittance business, guiding the flow to the central government and bringing them under the centralized control by the state.

On the face of it, this proposal was made for the purpose of easing money shortages. They sometimes impugned that "money gets stashed away in houses and stagnates, therefore commodity price drops, the reason is that money has been mostly stashed away" or they would then impugn that "money of the various departments, envoys, etc., or money of businessmen is mostly retained in the cities, gets stashed away in private chambers and stops to be circulated in the market." Actually, all these imputations were false, and they were nothing but glossing over the situation. Only the opening remarks in the memorial hit the point in unequivocal words, "fund available for the government dwindles lately," and the fear that private remittance might reemerge after the proposal to monopolize remittance by the three departments was genuine; hence, it was specifically pointed out that "all else must be banned as usual." As regards the situation that many bureaus and various envoys retained a huge amount of cash in the cities via familiar businessmen, grasped the opportunity to collect more, hoarded cash in private chambers and retired such from circulation, the memorial requested "Stringent prohibition shall be applied hereafter." This was the essence of the issue: remittance monopoly and money should be concentrated in the hands of the central government, satisfying the requirements of the interests of supreme ruling groups, satisfying their requirements for remittance credit and cash. This was the national interest upon which no individual or even local government may encroach.

Hu Rulei noted that the purpose of the Tang Dynasty running remittance business was, in addition to resolving the coin shortage in the imperial capital, to relieve the difficulty of transporting taxes from the various provinces to the capital.[19] *Old History of Tang Dynasty — Biography of Geng Jingxiu* had the following entry: "tea tax and transaction tax revenue from Jiannan, Xichuan, Shannanxi used to be remitted via the circuit division of the department of finances, while monopoly sale tax could be remitted via summoning businessmen in the capital. However, the original arrangement has fallen into disuse in recent years, the variety of moneys and articles have been frequently retained by the prefectures." Hence, it could be seen that remittance had the advantage of being timely, convenient in guaranteeing the revenue of the central government and it could also eliminate the labor and difficulty in transporting currency. By the reign of Emperor Wenzong (827–835), money transfer had been shifted to cash transportation, but the shift had unexpectedly incurred retention thereof by the local governments and there appeared the issue of deferment in transferring such cash into the treasury. Similar situations occurred especially when local governments faced fiscal stretches.

However, matters went awry when the three departments monopolized the remittance business: "no businessman would conduct remittance business therewith." The reason was that "a charge of one hundred *wen* is imposed by the government on the remittance per *guan* processed, hence no one would proceed therewith."[20] The three departments imposed a 10% remittance charge, and businessmen considered such a charge too exorbitant. Hence, remittance business dwindled, and the government had to revert to the old practice established in 810, rolling back to "remittance at a ratio of a *guan* for a *guan*"; that is, businessmen were allowed to remit one *guan* for one *guan*, free of charge. Even after such a change, it was

---

[19]Hu Rulei, *Comparative Study of Social and Economic History of Sui, Tang and the Five Dynasties*, China Social Sciences Publishing House, 1996, pp. 173–197.

[20]*Ce Fu Yuan Gui — Statecraft — Money Three*, vol. 6, p. 6002.

still "the same situation where coin appreciates and cloth price drops." Undeniable facts furnished a forceful answer, the theory of remittance monopoly by the state advanced by Wang Shao did not work out and the argument that government-run remittance could ease money shortage did not work.

However, in the beginning of the 9th century, the government of the Tang Dynasty after all monopolized remittance and pioneered government-run remittance in the history of finances in the world. Equally, the position of the theory of government-run remittance advanced by Wang Shao should not be ignored. Exactly as Lv Simian, a famous Chinese historian, remarked in the commentary made in the *History of the Sui, Tang and the Five Dynasties*, "the arrangement could both put through exchange between the imperial capital and the peripheral areas via *Feiqian* and furnish businessmen with capital via remittance, it was actually the origin of the bank; if the interest thereof could be regulated, it would be more than simply ease the money shortage. However the government proceeded to put a check thereon and then would procure a tithe therefrom, it was truly much ado about nothing."

5. Theory of money shortage in the late Tang Dynasty

In *the History of the Sui and Tang Dynasties*, Cen Zhongmian noted, "in the beginning of the Tang Dynasty, the concern was too much private minting, while by the closing period of the Tang Dynasty, the concern was lack of money; the ill was attributable to the price ratio between copper and coin, the two could barely be evened." However, over a long period, people always used to connect money shortage with the dual tax law. *The New History of Tang Dynasty — Annals of Economy Two* recorded, "since dual tax law was instituted by Dezong emperor (780–805), the situation of rising coin price against falling commodity price came into being, the people considered it as a peril." Many scholars and wealth management experts also believed that the dual tax law was the cause of money shortage as it calculated taxes in money, and they opposed calculating taxes in money by the dual tax law and argued that tax should be paid in kind; Lu Zhi initiated the proposal, which was seconded by Qi Kang, Li Xiang, Han Yu and others.

The dual tax law was a means of taxation by denominating tax in money and converting commodity into money; it was the turning point of shifting the traditional taxation in kind to monetary taxation in ancient China finances. Because generally the products the ordinary houses employed in paying the dual taxes were articles, while tax was calculated in the amount of money converted from products to be turned over, on the condition that the amount of tax remained unchanged, the price level of the said products determined the amount of products to be turned over.

In the mid-Tang era, in the period from the An Shi Rebellion to institution of the dual tax law by Emperor Dezong, as the war disrupted production, there was a severe shortage of foods, commodity price surged and inflation ensued where commodity price rose and coin value dropped. In the Dali period of Emperor Daizong (766–779), as production had not yet been restored and commodity price had yet to stabilize, when he ascended the throne (780), he rolled out a tax system reform, changing from the original law of *"Zu Yong Diao"* (land rent, labor service and tax in kind) to a dual tax law "based on asset" which stipulated that house category should be classified according to production capacity and tax should be collected in two seasons, summer and autumn. After the initial implementation of the dual tax law, physical articles were converted into money in calculating tax, and the scheme played a positive role in restoring production, stabilizing society and the livelihood of the people, improving government finances and consolidating the regime. This scheme had been followed by rulers of later dynasties for its simplicity, universal acceptance and monetization and characteristics of tailoring the expenditure to revenue and in conformity with principles of finances; it became a pillar in the taxation systems of the later dynasties, and had a tremendous revelation effect and influence on financial policies over the eight hundred years which followed. "Thereafter the power of regulating price reverted to the government." However, after the Zhenyuan period (785–805), a long-term sluggish trend of coin value appreciation against commodity price drop ensued, the prices of corn and cloth were on sustained decrease and the burden on the ordinary tax payers became increasingly heavy: "after the dual tax law was implemented, commodity price rose and coin depreciated, hence silk cloth was converted to equivalent amount of money when taxes were to be paid. And then commodity price dropped, more tax in kind was required to be handed in, originally a bolt of silk cloth was worth thirty two hundred qian, and then the price dropped to sixteen hundred qian, the amount of tax in kind to be submitted redoubled, though the tax remained the same, the people got increasingly poor" (*New History of Tang Dynasty — Economy Tow*). The result was just as Lu Zhi said, "though the government did not increase taxes, the taxes delivered by the people had doubled." *New History of Tang Dynasty — Biography of Quan Deyu* recorded the following remarks: "taxes remained unchanged, however the people had turned in five times that of the original." Faced with the grave situation of commodity price drop against coin appreciation, issues including how to evaluate the dual tax law, the monetary situation of coin deflation, what strategy should be taken and how to address the relation between the dual tax law and money had become the focus of the government officials and the people for the 20-odd-year period after Lu Zhi advanced his proposal of "tailoring to the characteristics of local produces" from 794 to the year Emperor Muzong ascended the throne in 821. What the author introduced here are understanding of the policies regarding money shortage relating to money, causes and route of the solution thereof aired by his contemporaries. As regards Qi Kang's opposition to calculating tax in money and that tax should be delivered in kind, the author will not dwell further on the subject.

5.1. Lu Zhi on "expanding produces according to local circumstance"

Lu Zhi (754–805), courtesy name Jinyu, was born in Jiaxing of Suzhou (in present-day Zhejiang). He was a renowned statesman in the Tang Dynasty, and had insightful understanding in managing national economy. His works included the Hanyuan Collection and the annotated Collection of Works by Lu Zhi, which is currently available.

In 794, the then prime minister Lu Zhi submitted a memorial titled "Six Items on Averaging and Reducing Rents and Taxes to Solace the People to Emperor Dezong," of which the second item titled "Petition to Collect the Dual Taxes in Cloth and Silk without Converting to

Money" addressed issues of coin appreciation and coin shortage, airing his strategy of understanding and theoretical grounds, an excerpt of which is duplicated herein:

"The great authority of managing wealth is the economic right of the country, it must be kept in the hands of the government and may not be relegated to the underlings. Corn and cloth are what the people produce; coin and commodity are what the government regulates.... When had there been a time where private minting was prohibited and coin was established as the form of rents and taxes."[21]

"It is indeed appropriate to expand production according to the local circumstances, step up the ban on forging copper into vessel; if said schemes are properly implemented, then there will no more be coin shortage."[22]

Having recognized the two basic functions of money, price level of commodity and benchmark for transaction, Lu Zhi set special store by the fact that money could not be done away with in activities concerning regulating price level, market transaction, concentration and transfer of wealth, turnover and circulation of commodity; without money, the so-called high and low price would be out of balance, circulation of commodity and distribution of money would not be reasonable and it would be difficult to conduct transactions in accordance with the standard. Such issues concerned whether the function of money as a measure of value could be properly played or whether such a role could be adequately played. Similarly, enacting monetary laws meant that money should flow like a river issued from a gushing fountain while abiding by laws, regulations and rules, and laws of monetary circulation as well as relevant content respecting the monetary system must be included naturally. The price level of the commodity would not lose balance, and it would not be difficult for the people to grasp price standards in transactions and regulate the fluctuation of price, concentration and distribution of wealth, release and recall of money, and contracting or relaxing of monetary policy; in the process, money must be employed, monetary systems established and laws enacted. Hence, it could be seen that Lu Zhi inherited the theory of the light and the heavy, emphasized control of monetary systems and

---

[21] *Collected Works of Lu Zhi*, Volume 2, Zhonghua Book Company, 2006, pp. 736–737.
[22] *Ibid.*, p. 744.

regulation of monetary policy by the government. In his argument against converting taxes in kind into money in calculating taxes under the dual-tax law, he proposed that the power to regulate wealth was the financial right of governing the country, and as such must be placed in the hands of the country and may not be relegated to the people. The reason that ancient sages mined copper from mountains and valleys and minted into coins was that all benefits from mintage monopoly should be kept exclusively with the country and no interest from this area should be shared. What are the reasons for such an arrangement where the people were prohibited from minting coin while tax was calculated by converting articles into coin? Hence, the poor went bankrupt and raised loans from the rich and the rich amassed wealth and commodity, stealthily usurping the power to manipulate wealth and commodity as well as price fluctuation. The people were impoverished, national financial interest drained, and the ills of the society lay in these issues.

The underlying significance of Lu Zhi's question on why the people should turn in the product they actually produced lay in his effort to reduce the burden on the people and cutting taxes.

"If it is a lucky year of bumper harvest with little military activities, while the people are still constantly in want of use, what is the cause? As thing begets thing, expense arises from expansion, there is a limit to thing and no limit to the use thereof, how could it not be poor? If reduction and saving could be made in thing and use thereof, it would not only make cloth and silk tax possible but also make it possible to reduce tax. If things and the use thereof are let loose, not only the exacting tax would not suffice, but increasing tax would still fall short."

Lu Zhi was truly worthy of the title of the first Chinese to have advocated a tax cut policy. In the vast sea of natural economy in China's countryside, the dual tax law was implemented while no corresponding proportion of coins had been released on the market. How could the situation not draw suspicion and criticism? Besides, Lu Zhi had the backing of monetary theory and understanding.

The famous statements aired by Lu Zhi that "money shortage leads to commodity price drop" and "high commodity price results from oversupply of money" made him a typical representative of the quantity theory of money in ancient China. In his view, in today's terms, emoluments for officials and equipment for soldiers, though allocated in the form of cloth and corn, were purchased and allocated in accordance with the change of seasons; hence, money must be employed in the process as the standard for evaluating commodity price level. On what basis were they to be acquired and allocated? The answer was that the control of mintage should be in the hands of the country while no private minting was allowed; then commodity price drop would be attributable to a lack of money, a lack of money would lead to money price rise, and high money price should be addressed by additional minting and release of money into circulation, so that the purchasing power of money may be reduced. On the contrary, exorbitantly high commodity price resulted from expansion of money and oversupply of money in circulation would lead to coin price drop, that is, its purchasing power would drop, and the government should recall money and drive up the purchasing power of money. Therefore, in his eyes, the price level of commodity was determined by the amount of money available in circulation, whereas the amount of money was further determined by the regulation of government via release or recall thereof; that is, "commodity price level is hinged on the amount of money in circulation; whereas the amount of money is further hinged on the expansion or contraction of money by the government." Hence, it could be seen that Lu Zhi believed that the amount of money determined commodity price level; on the contrary, commodity price level could also be employed to reveal the amount of money in circulation. Therefore, commodity price was hinged on money, while money was regulated by the government; the government could decide whether to release or recall money according to the actual requirement for circulation and regulate the price level of money in circulation. It seemed that the quantity theory of money regarding ancient money was advanced inadvertently by Liu Zhi in his demonstration of the dual tax law within the framework of the national financial system; actually, he had pondered on the issue seriously, having inherited the theory of the light and the heavy proposed in *Guan Zi*, especially the value theory of supply and demand. He made the most clear and most complete exposition on the relation between money and commodity price. It was the result of careful investigation and profound deliberation, and also a crystallization of the understanding of the relation between money and price based on an understanding arrived at by the forerunners in this field. This theory was one thousand years ahead of the quantity theory of money systematically demonstrated by David Hume, the earliest quantity theory of money in the United Kingdom; of course, due to the difference in environment in which Liu Zhi lived, the depth of exposition differed somewhat.

Now that the country had the power to regulate the price level of money in circulation, on the historical conditions of the times, Lu Zhi believed that the amount of money in circulation should be increased by both expansion and reduction, that is, by expanding copper mining and strictly implementing laws prohibiting manufacturing of copper vessels. Besides, he believed that so long as proper measures of regulation and control were in place, there would be no occurrence of money shortage in circulation. That is, "It is indeed appropriate to expand production according to the local circumstance, step up the ban on forging copper into vessel; if said schemes are properly implemented, then there will no more be coin shortage." The problems were whether the government could increase minting and release money in accordance with actual requirements, whether the government could properly regulate and control the situation, whether proper measures could be introduced, and whether the quantity and opportunity were appropriate. Lu Zhi did not elaborate, and we are not at liberty to a make unjustified comment thereon.

At least the government at the time should have been well aware of the situation it was in, whether or not the government would place financial interests as the top priority and ensure the requirements for money in circulation, mint high-quality and quantitatively adequate money. If it could not make it, then money shortage definitely could not be eased. Similarly, whether the copper ban could be implemented from the top depended on whether the emperor, the powerful, decorated and reputed nobles and ministers could lead by example; otherwise it would be nothing but empty words, while alleviation and elimination could definitely not be effected. It remained equally unclear whether the net recalled money should be released on the market or stored away in the national treasury and sealed. A definitive answer could not even be made by Lu Zhi as the prime minister at that time, as the practicality and the thought or, in other word, the guidance thereof in practice would naturally arouse suspicion.

He also believed that the country could recall money by selling salt and absorb money by instituting a liquor monopoly sale; if increase or decrease of money was properly regulated, net recall could also be realized. So long as there was net recall, it would be possible for the government to increase money supply and bring down commodity price. If the expansion and contraction of money were both controlled and regulated by the government, what else remained unattainable? Whether the fear that money supply could not be guaranteed was due to ignorance of measures on regulating monetary circulation or other difficulties also remains unknown.

In the 12th year of the Zhenyuan period, Qi Kang from Henan (740–804) submitted a memorial of "engaging in minting to alleviate the national livelihood."

5.2. Bai Juyi on "prohibiting melting copper coins to make vessels"

Bai Juyi (773–846), courtesy name Letian, was born in Xinzheng of Henan. He was a renowned poet in ancient China. His works included the Collection of Works by Bai Juyi and the annotated Collection of Works by Bai Juyi, which is currently available.

The poems of Bai Juyi mostly reflected the suffering of the people, exposed the corruption of politics, and such motifs had been well known to the Chinese. In order to alleviate the people economically, he made an extensive exposition on the theory of the light and the heavy in *Guan Zi*, and put forward quite some original ideas of his own on money and loans. In 806, Bai Juyi wrote a strategy which was incorporated in *Strategies* (75 essays), in which there were proposals regarding money. His thought on monetary strategy of "regulating the prices of the myriad of commodities" was mainly reflected in the following two points: (1) "inhibiting game and idleness, urging practice of agriculture and weaving, deliberating rents and taxes by restoring rents and labor service, discarding money and employing corn and cloth"; (2) "regulating the prices of the myriad commodities, implementing the measure of contraction and expansion, requesting to ban the practice of destroying coin and forging such into vessel."[23]

---

[23] *Collection of Works by Bai Juyi*, Volume 4, Zhonghua Book Company, 1979, pp. 1311–1312.

The theory of state control of money by Bai Juyi was the starting point and precondition for his understanding and analysis of money. He believed that "there is no constancy in the providence, therefore there are inevitably lean years and bumper years; there is a limit to the bountifulness of the land, therefore it would be inevitable for things to expand and to contract. The sages were aware of the inevitability, therefore they devised articles including money, cloth, silk, and traded such articles as occasion arose, contracted and expanded as occasion arose. Hence they alleviated the lean years with savings from the bumper years, subsidizing the shortage with the surplus. Therefore the expenses of food and clothing, the growing of corn and production of cloth were regulated and evened out, which would more than suffice."[24] On the basis of the theory of state-controlled money, Bai Juyi argued that so long as the exchange of equivalents such as money, cloth and silk was conducted in proper time and in an appropriate manner, the lean years could be alleviated by the harvest from bumper years and the deficit be made up by the surplus, and expenses of food and clothes, production of corn and silk could be evened out by regulation.

The instrument employed for regulating the balance was money. What was implied in this statement was that, without money, there was no other means to realize such assistance and coordination; the theory of the light and the heavy by Guan Zi, the theory of regulating commodity price by Li Li and the stabilizing theory of Geng Shouchang emphasized by Bai Juyi were exactly the theoretical foundation and origin of his thought.

Regarding functions of money, Bai Juyi believed that the regulation and coordination of the relations between agriculture, industry and commerce as reflected by corn, silk, vessels and commodity must be effected by the supreme ruler via money. "The supreme ruler holds one and regulates the three, the three could definitely not be harmonized without the office of money." This involved both the reasonable arrangement of the industrial structure and the coordinated development between agriculture, industry and commerce, the city and the country; such grave issues concerning economic harmony, social tranquility and measures regarding money mattered significantly, tolerating no sloppy work. Money deflation harmed the people, and inflation harmed the peasant. In an answer

---

[24]*Ibid.*, pp. 1308–1309.

to strategy examinations administered by the ministry of rites in 800, he noted, "cloth and silk prices drop resulted from money circulation stagnation. If corn supply is ample for use, money is properly circulated, then prices of cloth and silk would be evened out."[25] So long as there is ample food supply, prices of cloth and silk would be balanced; the duties of the supreme ruler were to "even out the high and low prices, regulate price level, make the myriad articles circulate and all parties benefit. And then the ruler will not be want of use, and the people would live in peace and content." High corn price would harm the interests of industrial and commercial producers, whereas low corn price would harm the interests of the peasant. If the interests of the industry and commerce were harmed, the financial requirements of the country would not be satisfied; if the interests of the peasant were harmed, few would be content to engage wholeheartedly in agriculture.

Regarding measures of regulation to be employed by the government, Bai Juyi advanced the following three: (1) To release or recall money, corn price rise meant money price drop, and the government was required to dump corn to recall money from the market, and the government was required to release money to purchase corn and cloth when corn and cloth prices went down. It seemed that this theory had been mentioned by some people, whoever might it be, and they could not shake off the influence of the theory of the light and the heavy advanced in *Guan Zi*. The theory was significant as a concept; however, it would not be an easy matter when it comes to practical implementation. (2) Laws were stipulated on copper control by the country, prohibiting private hoarding of copper or forging of copper vessels, stating that copper may not be used anymore in making vessels, and therefore no more profit shall be obtained from destroying coins and forging such into vessels, and minted coins would no longer be destroyed. He believed that this was the key to regulating the price ratio between coin and commodity, and the key to regulating market price level and appropriateness of price structure accordingly. Because the government monopolized copper mining and coin minting, minting one wen coin would entail the cost of several wens, while private minting of copper vessels by melting coins would obtain the profit of several wens by

---

[25]*Ibid.*, vol. 3, pp. 999–1000.

destroying one coin. While there was a limit to minting by the government and there was none in the private destruction of coins, even though the government minted coins year by year, how could such effort offset the coins destroyed by the private individuals? This was exactly the situation "where the amount money of the country decreases while money price rises by the day"; it was the reason that the amount of money dwindled and the price thereof rose. (3) The amount of coins in the country was dwindling; they were either accumulated in the state treasury or stashed away in private chambers. He believed that if more coins were to be collected from the people, when coins were to be paid to the government repositories, prices of corn and cloth would trend still lower, agricultural production would suffer and the harm it would bring about 10 years thereafter would be far more serious than before. This should not be viewed as a measure to even out the high and low prices or regulate the light and the heavy. When coins exited circulation and entered the repositories of the government or private chambers, the amount of coins in circulation reduced and this stepped up pressure on deflation. The situation had occurred in both the Tang Dynasty and its preceding dynasty. However, on the one hand, wealth got concentrated with the powerful and in the government repositories and, on the other hand, there was a dire shortage of coin in circulation in a deflationary situation, which was a dilemma; it would be highly unlikely to make the ruler and the interest groups disgorge the netted wealth unless a harsh lesson or misery was administered thereon.

The foregoing thought must have been the fruition of the youthful wisdom and years of association with the people by Bai Juyi.

5.3. *Han Yu's four measures on remedying ills*

Han Yu (768–824), courtesy name Tuizhi, was born in Heyang of Henan. He broke away from the traditional ideas and proposed to equally emphasize agriculture, industry and commerce. His works included *Collection of Works by Han Yu*.

In February 812, Emperor Xianzong ordered the ministers to deliberate on "the situation of high coin price against low commodity price which incurred grave evils. Elaborate measures of change shall be solicited to bring convenience to the people. It is expected that money will be properly circulated, and the people do not suffer."[26] Han Yu submitted a memorial titled "Addressing High Coin Price and Low Commodity Price,"[27] in which he proposed four measures to remedy the money shortage.

The first was that "tribute in the form of local produce" and rents and tax in kind shall be practiced. He was of the same opinion as Bai Juyi, and held that "the people has no right to mint coins, and they are made to sell cloth, silk and corn to acquire coins in order to pay the government, hence commodity price drops while coin appreciates." He proposed that rents and taxes should be collected in cloth in places where cloth was produced and in silk in places where silk was produced; firewood was to be collected from the area within the perimeter of a 100 *li* (50 km) of the imperial capital, and corn from the perimeter of 300 *li* (150 km), with an option between firewood and corn to be shipped as tax via canals from the perimeter of 500 *li* (250 km). He believed that the benefit of implementing such measures was that "the people would be content with farming, coin price drops, prices of corn, cloth and silk rise," and the problem of rising coin price against dropping commodity price may be eased.

The second measure was "stopping the loophole, making it waterproof." Stopping the loophole and preventing money drain required instituting a ban on copper and coins. A copper ban involved banning the making of copper vessels, Buddhist images and Buddhist instruments; hoarding of copper in excess of several jin was prohibited, and capital punishment was imposed on anybody destroying coins and forging such into other articles. A coin ban meant that coins may not be carried over the boundary of the Wuling range, and anyone smuggling coin beyond the Wuling border and anybody engaging in contraband transactions was put to death. For areas south of the Wuling, silver may be employed in transaction and circulation; old coins in the Wuling area were allowed to be carried beyond the border. "If these measures are implemented, coin price would surely drop."

---

[26] *Old History of Tang Dynasty — Biographic Sketches of Xianzong Emperor*, vol. 2, p. 442.

[27] *Annotated Collection of Works by Han Yu*, Shanghai Chinese Classics Publishing House, 1986, pp. 595–596. No more citations shall be furnished herein.

The third measure was "to replace its denomination with bigger figure inscription, make one worth five, and employ the old and the new concurrently." Minting big denomination coins and circulating the old and the new side by side, he believed, would "bring in five with one minted, the cost of one thousand coins brings in five thousand coins, the government stands to gain more." This had been proved by history to be a self-deceptive depreciation policy, under the law of good money being driving out by bad money, and it could neither ease money shortage nor have the concurrent use of both the new and the old coins.

The fourth measure was "to alleviate its ills and brace up the law." Flaws in the new law must be cured in a timely manner so that it may be perfected and firmly established. Whenever a new law was freshly implemented, there would inevitably be a slew of imperfections. Now that the people were allowed to turn in local produce as rents and taxes, the prefectures and counties would be short of cash, while the prices of corn and cloth would not increase, and government finances would suffer from financial deficit and official emoluments might be reduced by one third. The prefectures and counties should then be allowed to mint new coins; when such newly minted coins, which should be denominated five times the value of the old ones, were distributed to the officials, "the situation of high coin price and low commodity price would be eliminated." What a miraculous and grossly impractical idea it was, which exposed Han Yu's ignorance of the history of money.

5.4. *Yuan Zhen on submitting copper vessels as rents and taxes upon conversion*

Yuan Zhen (779–831) was born in Henan. His works included *Collected Works of Yuan Zhen* and the annotated *Collection of Works by Yuan Zhen*, which is currently available.

Some of his essays discussing current political affairs involved monetary issues, especially issues of high coin price and coin minting. Examples of his essays are the *Memorial Deliberating Coin and Commodity* and the *Memorial on Deliberating Rents, Taxes and Coin Minting Proposed by the Ministry of Secretariat*.

In 820, when Emperor Muzong ascended the throne, it was the 40th anniversary of implementing the dual tax law, and he decreed that the ministers should deliberate on the situation: "the national expenditure does not allow tax cut, while maintaining the status quo would aggravate the current strained situation, these are all caused by high coin price and low commodity price, which leads to redoubled tax levy." Yuan Zhen and Yang Yuling had both submitted memorials to discuss the issue, laying bare their positions and attitudes. Yuan Zhen believed that "the lightness or the heaviness of coin does not lie in the inappropriateness of discussion, but in the failure of implementing the law."[28] In his opinion, the extreme poverty of the people did not lie in the stealthy increase of the various rents and taxes, but in gradual deprivation thereof. Now that there were uniform laws and standards regarding rents and taxes, if able officials of integrity were appointed, the people would be able to gain a reprieve and restore livelihood; however if greedy, foolish and stubborn officials were appointed, then both the country and the people would be at peril. This was plain evidence of appropriateness in official appointment. How could that result from stealthy increase of rents and taxes? He further demonstrated with instances that, if officials were properly appointed, the country could be well managed. How could that originate in a coin shortage or commodity price drop? Based thereon, he put forward a challenging proposal to Emperor Muzong who had freshly ascended the throne: Tributes from the various military governors and finances officials should be stopped, bribery and presents must be eliminated, luxury be restrained, disciplinary regulations be strengthened, punishment on graft and bribe taking be stepped up, provisions on examination and review be tightened, and screening of officials in charge of personnel management be prudentially conducted. "Since the beginning of the Yuanhe period, the edict of copper ban in government and private use was first implemented, and then there was the edict on concurrent circulation of coin, silk in transaction, and lately there was the limit on hoarded coins instituted. However, the effectiveness of the measures depended on whether such laws are strictly carried out." The key lay

---

[28]*Collected Works of Yuan Zhen*, Volume 1, Zhonghua Book Company, 1982, p. 396. No more citations shall be provided for further quotes from this book hereinbelow.

in whether the laws could be thoroughly implemented. This point was of the utmost importance, otherwise, even supremely perfect legal provisions would still be of no avail. Never had he heard of a single individual getting whipped, an official being demoted, a single informant being awarded or a hoard destroyed: "it is not that the law does not suit the times, but that implementation thereof does not get followed through." It was not because the law was unfit or outdated, but that it was not implemented or not thoroughly implemented; therefore, so long as "remedial measures of the ancients and the contemporary are adopted, edicts of award and punishment are thoroughly followed through .... What's the point of my usurping the views of the ancients and claiming such as a measure eliminating ills." It could not be denied that this change of point of view in examining solutions to the issue of coin shortage was indeed a fine cure against the then prevalent ills; it really required audacity, courage and a sense of responsibility. This understanding must be recognized. The question raised by Yuan Zhen seemed not directly related to the solution of coin shortage at first sight, but it was actually an attempt to strike at the root cause of the social evil, an attempt to try to rectify official governance from the very source of the evil and an attempt to cure the deeply entrenched ill of the late Tang Dynasty; this was exactly the key that other theorists failed to touch upon. This should have attracted adequate attention from and serious treatment by the people.

The key issue elaborated in the second memorial was coin minting. Yuan Zhen advanced his own understanding on the issue, opposing the planned measure submitted by the Ministry of Secretariat which planned to order the various Daos to collect copper vessels from the government, the people, the military governors, etc., and to have soldiers thereof mint coins.[29] That is, the various *Daos* should be allowed to mint coins on their own, the principal of the coins shall be disbursed from the fund allocated to the various *Daos* respectively and no commodity setoff of coins was to be allowed.

The minting should be stopped after one year. For prefectures where copper and lead were mined and places where coins could be minted on

---

[29]*Ibid.*, vol. 1, pp. 414–416. No more citations shall be provided for further quotes from this book hereinbelow.

a large scale, the cost of minting should be disbursed to the minting operator to replenish their principal. According to the rough estimation by Yuan Zhen, "there is no great amount of copper vessels scattered among the people, when such is handed in to the various envoys, there would naturally not be a great quantity. Building a furnace would require a great variety of instruments. When the furnace is discarded after the one-year term expires, all would be turned into waste." In short, such undertakings were actually schemes wherein the gains failed to recover the loss, which was a pure waste of both energy and money. That is, it would be an effort of wasting money and harassing the people. Originally, the amount of copper vessels held by the people was not great, and less would be concentrated to the government, while requiring a great variety of instruments to build furnaces for minting. Moreover, minting had to be stopped after the one-year operation, and all the stuff had to be discarded. Wouldn't all that be wasted effort? Having compared the investment and return, it was found far from profitable, and this was just one aspect of the issue. The other issue was that "soldiers are not used to be trained for this business, it would be rather difficult for them to mint coin." Because the armies had not received any special training in minting coins, they had not grasped the expertise on minting coins, and therefore it would surely be a difficult undertaking. The unspoken truth was that it remained uncertain whether it would be profitable or not, and this was rather unsettling. The third was that a certain fixed quota was set aside for minting coins from the fund allocated to the prefectures and counties, and hence minting would inevitably affect "a myriad of causes, and timely need might not be met." Many matters waiting to be handled in the localities would be delayed or postponed due to the fact that corresponding funds were not in place.

Yuan Zhen proposed that the people should be allowed to convert their copper vessels into tax payment, and such vessels should be purchased by the officials of finances. The copper vessels so purchased should be delivered to the nearest minting unit in each season of every year. In his opinion, there would be the benefit of both eliminating the need to build new furnaces and the guarantee of having well-trained craftsmen conducting the minting; when there was the guarantee of both expertise and capital, profits and advantages naturally ensued. Though it was but a "rough estimation" in monetary policy, it was conceivable that it could save expenses while guaranteeing quality and producing benefits, and it would naturally be profitable. It embodied his ideas of comparative cost and management thought. In his strategy proposals, he proceeded from reality, started from official governance, rectified government conduct, then devised specific design solutions, and raised the optimal solution by comparison, examination and investigation. With such a sense of responsibility and style of performance, he was more a trained and able management official than a poet, who well deserves our commendation and careful study.

5.5. *Yang Yuling on low commodity price and high coin price*

Yang Yuling (753–830) was born in Hongnong of Guozhou (in present-day Henan).

According to *New History of Tang Dynasty — Economy Two*, since the dual tax law was installed in the Jianzhong period of Emperor Dezong, the situation of rising coin price against falling commodity price seriously ailed the people; forty years later, the amount of coins which could have purchased two and a half bolts of cloth could purchase eight bolts of cloth, and the purchasing power increased about threefold. The rich merchants accumulated coins and property, and along with price fluctuations, they added fuel to the fire, engaging in speculative activities and profiteering therefrom. While the peasants were impoverishing, the merchants were gaining by the day; "the emperor was concerned about the situation where commodity price drops and coin price rises, the people suffer from the unavailability of coin, and the ministers are convened to deliberate reforming the evil, most proposed to reinstate the copper ban."[30] Most people requested that the implementation of the law on copper ban be strengthened; however, having analyzed the cause of coin shortage, Yang Yuling put forward his strategy.

The theoretical basis of Yang Yuling's strategy was as follows: (a) "The ruler produces coin to weigh the myriad articles, bridge the disparity between what the people have available and what they need through trade, set it in circulation without end, even out the price differences

---

[30]*New History of the Tang Dynasty — Economy Five*, vo, 5, pp. 1360–1361.

between articles, there is nothing special in this measure, only that it is exercised by the ruler. What is the rationale underlying such a phenomenon? Whatever the ruler values, the people would surely follow suit." The purpose of minting coins by the supreme rulers was to weigh the prices of commodities. If there were price differences between different articles, such differences must be kept under an acceptable level to accommodate trade, and all must depend on the regulation of price by the emperor. (b) Coins had the functions of "weighing the myriad articles, bridging the disparity between what the people have available and what they need through trade, setting it in circulation without end." That is, giving play to the functions of money as a measure of value and means of circulation was positively conducive to production, circulation and social life.

Yang Yuling analyzed the causes of coin shortage, concluding that there were at least seven points. His investigation and understanding must have been the most complete in the Tang Dynasty.

1. "In ancient times, power of the coin is held in the hands of the ruler, while it is nowadays sought from the people." In ancient times, coins were controlled by the ruler, whereas in Yang Yuling's time they were sought from the people, which implicitly referred to the rents and taxes, which shored up the need for coins.
2. "Coins used to be distributed among the people across the country, while nowadays they are hoarded in the government repositories." Coins used to be retained in circulation, going around, and flowing in all directions; however, they were since retired from circulation and stashed away in government repositories.
3. "Coins used to be extensively minted to satisfy the need for circulation, while nowadays furnaces had been shut down, hence they lost the function of satisfying the need for circulation." Extensive minting and releasing of coins used to be for the purpose of satisfying the need for circulation; however, many furnaces had been shut down, and coins had lost the function of satisfying the need for circulation.
4. "Coins used to be circulated in central China, now their use has been spread to the peripheral areas." They used to be circulated in central China alone, but since then their circulation had spread to the frontiers, which inevitably led to strained use thereof.

5. There was extensive "funeral use by the people." There were customs of burying coins with the deceased, which reduced the amount of coins in circulation.
6. There existed "hoarding by merchants for loan business." Merchants accumulated coins for the purpose of lending them out, which led to the diminishment of coins in circulation.
7. There was significant "loss arising from sinking ships." Wastage arising from sinking ships in water transportation similarly reduced the amount of coins available for circulation. In conclusion, while the need for coins in circulation surged and supply thereof lagged behind, "coin shortage" ensued.

Yang Yuling had some ideas addressing coin shortage. On the one hand, he proposed to reduce the need for money, stating that "the dual taxes, liquor, salt, tribute to the central government and money to be retained in the prefectures should all be paid in cloth, corn and silk, then the demand for coin by the people would not be so urgent." That is, if the dual tax payments, salt and liquor profits, tributes to the central government as well as money to be retained by the prefectures were all paid in cloth, corn and silk, then the demand for coins by the people would be easily satisfied, and the people would be relieved of certain taxation burdens. On the other hand, "the hoarding of the imperial chamber should be brought to the market, produce that does not sell shall be purchased, the number of copper mine minting furnaces shall be increased, a limit shall be placed on coin exporting, private hoarding shall be prohibited, then commodity prices will rise and coin price will drop." With the following measures implemented, commodity prices would rise and coin price would drop: taking out the hoardings from the imperial chamber to purchase produce that did not sell, opening up more furnaces to mint coins in copper mines, restricting coin export and prohibiting private hoarding.

Emperor Muzong adopted part of Yang Yuling's proposal, from 821, that is, the payment in cloth, silk, etc., for the dual tax and as tribute and money to be retained by the prefectures was accepted, while coins were still to be paid for liquor and salt profit. However, if the law could not be carried out thoroughly, the ban would not work. While expenses were cut, no new resources were opened up. What should have been reduced remained unreduced, and what should have been banned remained unbanned; it was natural that the coin shortage was not brought under effective control, and the phenomenon of high coin price against low commodity price continued as ever.

Chapter 5

Financial Thought of the Northern and Southern Song Dynasties

1. Introduction

Due to the revival of the ancient Chinese monetary economy after a long period of decline, the monetary economy in the Song Dynasty saw a period of comprehensive development. It created a new historical period in which copper coins were the mainstay and copper and silver coins were in parallel circulation. The main feature of this period was the complexity of currency: With money in great need, the circulation was suffocating. The names of different currencies were complex, and reforms of coins were frequent. First of all, copper coins were used primarily in name. As a matter of fact, iron coins, lead coins, tin coins, silver coins and paper notes were all simultaneously used. Coin sizes and values were different. There were fixed areas of money circulation, which were never to be transgressed. No currency could circulate freely all across the country. Though there were many coins in circulation, money shortage occurred frequently. Both the government officials and the common people were concerned about the outflow, destruction, private casting and storage of copper coins, as well as the decreasing minting of coins of the Southern Song Dynasty. Second, although the legal status of silver had not been established, silver was already circulating as a kind of currency and playing a corresponding role, which was one of the biggest achievements of the monetary economy and a symbol of the booming development of the monetary economy in the Song Dynasty. Third, paper notes emerged in this era. China was the first country in the world to use paper notes. The root cause of the emergence of paper notes was the development of commodity and currency economy, especially the development of commercial credit. The direct cause was the inconvenience of the iron currency circulating in the Sichuan area. The replacement of metal currency by paper notes was supposed to be progress in the history of currency development. But in the Song Dynasty, forced by the circumstances, the government, in particular that of the Southern Song Dynasty, repeatedly increased the circulation of paper notes. At the end of the Southern Song Dynasty, twenty strings of cash were only equivalent to one string during the reign of Emperor Xiaozong. With the dramatic increase of paper notes, the value of the currency plummeted. Both the king and the ministers voiced their opinions over this issue, which induced a unique theory on China's paper notes. Fourth, the separatist situation in the Song Dynasty made it inconvenient to have cross-regional trade. Cross-regional trade, especially trade between different currency areas, was difficult both in terms of transportation and in terms of currency exchange. At that time, there were frequent wars and calamities at the border, leading to a soaring need for military necessities. However, inconvenient transportation made it challenging to transport these military necessities. In the commercial field, the government adopted the policy of official monopoly. To ensure the profits of the monopolized goods, the government resorted to all sorts of credit notes or fiduciary money, raising the credit instruments to a very high level. In addition, there was even a market for the transaction of credit instruments, which symbolized the burgeoning of the traditional financial market of China.

The credit business in the Song Dynasty developed rather slowly. Compared with the practice of the Tang Dynasty, government lending was more institutionalized. During the reform of Wang Anshi, the government implemented the Law of Market Dealing and the Green Sprouts program for the purpose of suppressing usury, using the 40% interest rate of the Green Sprouts lending to take the place of the one hundred or even two or three hundred percent interest rate of usury. The interest rate of usury in the Song Dynasty saw a tendency of decline, from the original 100% to 60, 50 or even 30%, which was advantageous for economic development.

2. The currency theory of Shen Kuo

Shen Kuo (1031–1095), courtesy name Cunzhong, was a native of Qiantang of Hangzhou. Of his more than 40 publications, only six are extant, among which *Dream Pool Essays* is one.

Shen Kuo's monetary thought was mainly included in his *Countermeasure for the Shortage of Money* proposed in June 1077. In his argument, there were three kinds of unique monetary views:[1] the circulation speed of currency, precious metal as the legal currency and paper notes as currency. The following part is an introduction to these issues.

2.1. On the circulation of currency

This is the most brilliant and outstanding part of Shen Kuo's currency theory. He was of the opinion that "circulation is advantageous to currency." Suppose a family possessed 100,000 coins, the number would remain unchanged if the coins did not circulate. On the contrary, if these 100,000 coins were in circulation, they would move from one family to the next, to the last of 10 families. The function they would perform would also be greatly changed, becoming 10 times the original. The profit from this circulation would also become 10 times the original. If money is still moving from one family to another in a continuous cycle, the role of the currency is more than 100,000 and 1 million. It cannot be valued at all. We have reason to conclude that Shen Kuo had realized that the currency circulation speed (currency turnover) had a negative correlation with the amount of currency circulation over the same period; that is, the greater the number of currency turnovers, the smaller the amount of money required for circulation during the same period. The number of currency turnovers is inversely proportional to the amount of currency in circulation. Therefore, accelerating the number of currency turnovers can reduce the demand for currency in circulation. Thus, he believed that even the smallest towns at that time had a lot of Changping money. If they can return from a motionless state to circulation, there is just as much money

---

[1]Li Tao, *Xu Zizhi Tongjian Changbian*, Book 20, pp. 6928–6929, Zhonghua Book Company, 1986. Further quotations from this book will not be specified.

as 1,000 coins. "I do not know how much money to play, so why should we worry about deflation, financial tightness, and departmental barriers?" As it was, the government's storage of large amounts of money was an essential cause of the money shortage. As long as the government put money into circulation and participated in transactions, the elimination of money shortage would have occurred naturally.

Shen Kuo began to study the speed of money circulation from the storage methods of money, and thought that if Changping money does not move, how can it not cause a shortage of currency. Before he began to study the impact of currency storage on the circulation of money, there were many other people in the Tang Dynasty who did the same. Bai Juyi believed that "the shackles of the shackles are also the ones with the money." In order to solve the dilemma of money and the problems caused by the money shortage, Han Yu, Yuan Xiao and others all advocated the prohibition of collaring. Yang Yuling also believed that "the product of credit loans by merchants" was part of the cause of the money shortage. Behind their theory, it was implied that in China money can only work if it is circulated and traded. If it accumulates and hides, it is tantamount to saying that the currency is passing out of circulation. Therefore, in the third year (808), Tang Xian Zong Yuan of Xia said, "The law of *Quanhuo, Yiyi* is in circulation. If there is any money, the goods will be beneficial." In the 12th year (817), he also said, "If you see less money, you will be able to pass the flow." However, none of them went further and studied the relationship between deflation and currency turnover. In the Song Dynasty, Zhang Fangping began to touch upon the circulation of money, proposing "public and private flow, day and month." In the sixth year of Xining, 4 years earlier than Shen Kuo (1073), Zhang Fangping put forward in *On the exemption of money* that "Of all the things in the world, only money was minted by the government. In the previous days I got to know that the annual minting of money amounts to millions of *min*, but the different taxes of the country collected are roughly 50 million *min*. With the expenditures covered by such a circulation of money, the velocity of money circulation is indeed of great significance." Reading between the lines reveals that Chang already knew the inverse relationship between the velocity of money and currency circulation, and the value of central government-centric currency circulation, currency circulation channels and the influence of money on currency circulation at different levels of society. The understanding of the Tang Dynasty took a step forward, but it did not touch upon the relationship between the number of currency turnovers and the amount of currency in circulation. Coinage was not previously noticed, so it developed rapidly. Under the enormous pressure of the money shortage, the circulation of goods became the focus of attention for the ruling and opposition regimes. Zhang's arguments were enlightened by Shen Kuo from both direct and indirect perspectives. In addition, Shen Kuo's in-depth knowledge of the biological sciences, especially mathematics, was more conducive to his marvelous and extraordinary answers, and also earned him the reputation of a genius in world of financial thinking.

Shen Kuo was a leading figure in the study of the circulation of currency in ancient China and the world. In Europe, William Petty from the 17th century was the first to look into the speed of circulation of currency.[2] Later, John Locke's statement was clearer: "The very same Shilling may at one time pay Twenty Men in Twenty days, at another, rest in the same Hands One hundred days together."[3] As enlightening as Locke's statement was, Shen's exciting statement in the 11th century was of global significance.

2.2. On the standard of precious metals

Precious metal (gold) acted as a legitimate currency instead of copper to complete fiscal payments. Shen Kuo thought, "Ancient coins are things, gold, silver, pearls, jade, turtles, and shellfish are all but not dependent on money. This is a gold and silver coin that is expensive for everyone in the world. Poverty is low and the price is light." The defects of the contemporary currency system were becoming increasingly obvious, and they could not adapt to the contemporary conditions of currency circulation. For

---

[2] Citing the words of William Petty, Karl Marx spoke affirmatively of his pioneering work in the study of the speed of circulation of currency. Cf. *Complete Works of Karl Marx and Friedrich Engels*, vol. 23, Note 78 on p. 117.

[3] *Some Considerations on the consequences of the Lowering of Interest and the Raising of the Value of Money*, p. 21, Commercial Press, 1962.

example, "if the copper coins transferred can be changed to gold, gold can be invoked as a means of payment to play a role through monetary payment. If it is also the same, then the road to the current will be broad, and the profit of the money will be slightly different." The demand for copper coins would decrease.

Shen Kuo's claim of using gold as a currency had two meanings. The first was to establish the legal status of the precious metal in the form of legislation, rather than to solve the problem in actual economic life. Since the end of the Tang Dynasty and the early Song Dynasty, silver had begun to be used for bulk payment, such as public and private gifts, rewarding heroes and as the safest means of storage. It was also used in large-scale fiscal payments, such as increasing military grain reserves, helping victims and supplying side fees. These were all exercising the functions of payment means. The second was that the precious metal really assumed the full function of the currency, fulfilling the functions of value scale, payment means, storage means and world currency, and acting as a means of circulation to replace copper money by carrying out its functions. With the development of the relationship between commodity and currency, the social division of labor objectively required a precious metal with a larger unit value to serve as a medium of exchange. Shen Kuo seemed to have realized this, so he stated the following: "with gold and silver in the world, the instrument is not the right currency." At the same time, he believed that gold and silver could get rid of the predicament due to the fact that precious metals had not acted as currency. Therefore, he had to conform with the trend of commodity currency economic development and advocated replacing cheap metal currency with precious metal currency. We cannot but acknowledge his keen insight. Force, scientific innovation and bold prophecy were traits found in ancient China, but there were not enough such innovative people with a forward-thinking attitude and a spirit of advancement. We should be proud and spurred to greater heights.

However, when gold and silver were invoked as currency, copper coins were also in circulation. They jointly performed monetary functions. They were both legitimate forms of money, having parallel relations, and main and auxiliary relations. Shen Kuo did not explain this. In addition, since he knew that "the people are poor and the (gold and silver) are helpless as the widow," even the exercise of using gold and silver would have been examined by the ordinary people. If copper coins were really banned, it would have been difficult to implement in the whole society.

2.3. On paper notes as currency

Shen Kuo believed that "in the old days, when the rich prepared for being looted by robbers and other emergencies, they would resort to keeping salt and banknotes, while silver was looked down upon. Banknotes are with the millions of people. The law of the banknotes is easy, the people do not think that, they must sell the banknotes. If you want to go to the trade, you will be unable to pay for it. The court says that the banknote law can't be hard. If the people don't doubt the banknotes, then the banknotes can be coins, and the money can't be self-sufficient." Even if Shen Kuo discussed salt banknotes, at that time it was a type of marketable security that could be transferred and circulated. Salt banknotes were different from other banknotes, in their frequency of occurrence, distribution, application and scope of action; salt banknotes were also smaller. Salt banknotes were unique, but they represented money and acted as equivalents and played their part. He pointed out that when the price of salt banknotes was stable, the rich people were willing to save the salt banknotes rather than save the copper coins, "The banknotes are with the millions of people." But because of the repeated changes in the banknote method, credibility had been shaken. "If you have to sell (buy) the banknotes, you will have to sell it (the sale), so the banknotes will not be left without money." Along with his idea of reforming the central government's annual transfer of copper coins to the border areas, we can see that his attitude and understanding of the securities of the salt banknotes affirmed the advantages of their usage. The benefits of "banknotes" were that they were portable and easy to preserve, but the people were "unfavorable to silver." He also noted that the problem in the issuance of salt banknotes was not in blindly seeking complete blame or negating it, nor was it intentional partiality. He proposed that "banknotes can be coins." He could have referred to something other than currency. Under certain conditions, salt banknotes can act as money. Naturally, they cannot play the role of money. How do we understand the specific relationship between salt banknotes and money? Because Shen Kuo did not elaborate, we do not know what exactly he meant. However, he believed that in order to act in accordance with the banknote law and maintain the credibility of the salt banknotes, it was important to not shake its representativeness. The defeat of the salt banknote system was because "the banknotes are available easily, and the people are not convinced." Therefore, the salt banknote as the symbol of the currency had to gain the trust of the people. The condition for maintaining the salt banknote system was that "the banknote law cannot be strengthened. If the people are confident in the banknotes, the banknotes can be coins." It was equally a way to solve the money shortage. "Money does not benefit and scorn." As long as the banknote method remained the same, the value of the currency would be stable. If the people were confident in the banknote, the banknote could be a currency, and there would be no problems. It is clear that Shen Kuo did not oppose the circulation of banknotes, but there was a precondition for circulation. Otherwise, the people would lose their confidence and replace the currency in circulation, which would cause problems. Shen Kuo's analysis and understanding of this statement are positive, serious and responsible. It is also reasonable and correct and he should be honored for it.

According to the *"Zi Zhi Tong Jian Chang,"* in *Xi Ning* in February, when Shen Biao talked about the benefits of Shaanxi's salt–salt method, Shen Kuo once again comprehensively analyzed the ills of the salt banknotes at the time, mentioning the lack of banknotes, the issues in Tongshang County, the sale of official salt, business travel, etc., and suggested targeted rescue measures:

Limited amount of salt banknotes issued: Shen Kuo pointed out, "The salt has a recurring fee and there is no (extreme) art. That is the reason why this banknote is also light. In addition to practicality, it can benefit 200,000 baht, in case of water and fire loss." With no fee and costing no extra money, the price of the banknotes would naturally be low. Because the salt was of limited quantity, only 250,000 bags a year and the amount of money was more than 2.1 million, the salt banknotes were worth 3.5 million. The circulation of salt coins was restricted to 3.5 million *min* to ensure a balance between supply and demand, and the price of the banknote was stable.

Unify the two-way sale price: The price of salt on the East Road and West Road was different, and it was different every time. "The price of the salt in the West is low, and the salt is to be won, and the price of the salt is not enough. In order to benefit from the sale of the East, the West Salt flows on the East Road, while the East Salt is not sold, and the Guardian of the West cannot ban it." According to Shen Kuizhi, it would have been better to divide the sale price between the East Road and the West Road, and reduce the number of officers and men at the border by a few hundred. His suggestion would not only have saved expenses but also have saved the trouble of dividing the land for rule.

Unified banknotes: Shen Kuo proposed that in the past because of the "salt banknotes, the foreign ministers have often controlled profit and loss," and the institutions in the salting zone had the right to increase or decrease the salt banknotes, which was equivalent to controlling the paper banknotes. They disregarded the financial resources of the three principal divisions. As long as the banknotes were cheap, they had to be paid for. "There are hidden treasures in the capital, and the sale is over." The price of salt banknotes fell, the central government had no money and the salt banknote issuance exceeded the yearly amount. In the face of the passive situation of the right to issue money in the salting area, which was out of control, he said, "please ask the foreign company to pay for its cashier, and the banknotes belong to the third division." That is to say, the local salt-dissolving division should guard the cashier's position, and the power to make money and collect money should be returned to the crucial three divisions.

The same official price expanded the scope of commercial sales: In the fifth year (1072) of the Shenzong Xi Ning period, on the basis of the eighth year (1048) of the Fan Xiang Yu Renzong Qingli period, Banknote Law 2 was implemented in many areas of Jiexi West Road and East Road, causing Zhang Jingwen and other people to change their official sales. Eight years after Shenzong Xi Ning, in order to appease local interests, official sales became self-selling by the government, and they were arbitrarily brought down to a random price, making it difficult for marketers to maintain their business, and the phenomenon of salt banknotes stagnated. Shen said, "The sputum salt of the divisions is the same price, and there is no need to be low-priced and profitable. The sales of the older people are common, and the banknotes can be free of defects, while the stagnation of money is hidden in the people. By aligning the price of salt, avoiding price shock, the interests of merchants are damaged, which in turn affects the normality of salt purchase activities, and the normal order of social production and life. Maintain the reputation of salt banknotes and ensure that salt is sold well to achieve routine salt sales every year."

In addition, for the salt banknotes, Shen Kuo also suggested the following two recycling proposals: The first was to collect or recycle the banknotes: "the law has already existed, and the banknotes are hidden with the people, so there is no salt in the closed pool, so the salt is collected at the current price, and the money is more than 800,000 yuan in *Shaofu* (Royal private library), to collect the banknotes, and the public and private banknotes is known." The old banknotes hidden in the private sector would have been recovered at the current price, 30% would have been paid and 70% would have been paid for the extra banknotes to stop and tighten the circulation.

The second proposal was tantamount to plugging the loopholes and guaranteeing the revenue of the goods. Hebei's border millet cost 3 million baht in the country's southeast salt banknotes, and the levy of the goods per day was tens of thousands of dollars, with the income gap being larger. Shen Kuo thought that "its native to the law is porous, the province, the temple group have a division or borrow a salt banknote and Yin uses it for easy department stores. It is described as a self-employed price, and the people are willing to take all the benefits. Banknotes are light. As for the quality of salt, people do not have a dollar, and beat the hands to take the salt. In addition, four parties tried to raise funds for the people, accept the money of the foreign state, to the province to transfer the fee." That is, the government has many options; the province, the temple and other departments have colluded with businessmen, making it easy to make money. The market price of salt banknotes fluctuated, and it was also pledged against the levy of the land. If they could get much salt without using any cash, how would they resort to the use of salt banknotes? If the money to be handed in to the central government was done by the settlement of transferring, they would also save on freight costs, with only the disadvantage of influencing the central government's fiscal revenue. Shen Kuo believed that between the salt banknotes and money, even if this exchange method was changed, "the two laws want to be discrete, and the salt is expected to be sold, so that money is available. Adjusting its surplus, you can't control it (governance) too. Weigh the pros and cons, sell salt, hope that the salt of the people has a constant; use the money to adjust the truth of the salt banknotes, 'close the road of money, and sell it exclusively. Salt is a profiteer. I don't know if the salt is common, but for the old year's banknotes, the disadvantages of Shaanxi's estimation are reemerged in the east.'" It was suggested that these three holes must be blocked: "three holes are plugged, and goods are sold. The entry of Wan Hao, no more than the moon."

The circulation of paper money in the Song Dynasty was not only an inevitable outcome of the development of current circulation but also an inevitable result of the development of credit instruments. It evolved from the process of accessing the money for the credit currency, with the banknotes and even the salt banknotes (cash) being the circulation of the securities, becoming tokens. Money and paper money were related, but there is also a difference. How could one protect the legitimate credit instruments to ensure credibility, ensure the stability of the market and the stability of the currency? Shen Kuo began to conduct research. He seriously studied their relationship, difference and connection, their respective statuses and roles. Although not inconsistent with our requirements, Shen Kuo is the pioneer of research on paper money and related financial instruments in China and even the world. At that time, Shaanxi salt banknotes appeared to be "false banknotes" due to excessive issuance. The price of salt banknotes fell, credits were shaken and the ability to save was lost. Shen Kuo presided over the rectification of the salt banknote system, and maintained the value of the salt banknotes by purchasing old banknotes, adjusting salt prices and expanding the scope of profitable sales. It is obvious that Shen Kuo had solved the problem that "banknotes can be coins" using a combination of theory and practice, and had become a pioneer of the theories of banknotes and credit currency.

2.4. On the money shortage

In 1077, on the authority of the highest financial affairs of the country (generation), the three divisions (Caixiang), Shen Kuo answered the questions of Emperor Shenzong on why "the public and private coffers are all empty," the cause of the money shortage and the government's countermeasures. His remedy was his personal opinion. According to him, there were eight reasons for the shortage of currency, out of which five could be remedied, one did not have a sufficient remedy and two that could not be remedied. "Today's birth is the age of the Fan, the public and private use of the sun. With the cost of the sun, for the people of the age of Fan, the coin is insufficient, this is not strange; on the other hand, the damage from different circumstances would also lead to a big loss. This is an incompetent person. Copper has been prohibited, selling money for the benefit of the instrument is 10 times more expensive, and then the money is in the geometry of the person not the instrument. Chen said that copper cannot help. On different days, rich families prepare for the disaster, but the water and fire are defeated, but the salt banknotes are stored, but the Tibetan Mastiff is not good. Banknotes are with the millions of people. The number of banknotes is easy, the people are not convinced, and there are those who sell money. If you will be in the future, you will not be able to pay for it. Chen said that the banknote law must not be strong. If the people are confident in the banknotes, then the banknotes can be coins, and the money is not scornful. Ancient coins, gold, silver, beads, jade, turtles, shellfish are also not devoted to money. This is the most expensive gold and silver in the world, the only thing is not the currency, the people are poor and the instrument is widowed, so the price is light. If the loser is to lose money today, *Gao* will be assessed and will be as good as it is, then the road of the currency will be broad, and the profit of the money will be slightly divided. Money is great for the flow .... The four barbarian tribes on the borders are reliant on China's copper coins, and those who get out of the country are not jealous. The parliamentarian wants to smash the salt of Hebei. The salt is heavy and the salt is coming, and the money of China is in the north. The capitalist of the capital, he took the sheep and cattle in the clandestine market, but the department store is easy. Nearly old years .... All the people who are recruiting people are attracted to the capital ... and the cattle and sheep come to foreign countries, all of which are private money. In this approach, the money that vents China is in the north, and the age is not known. This is the practice of driving, private and easy do so, the first to be banned. This can save the five." The first two reasons for the shortage could not be remedied. The so-called irremediable factors referred to the product of the subjective will of non-state individuals, which could not be avoided, such as the increase in population and public and private expenses, that is, "the age of the country, the use of public and private (Up), so 'there is not enough money, this is not strange.' This has been discussed by Liu Ren in the Tang Dynasty." "The water and fire are defeated, and the defects of the wear and tear are unknown." The former increases the demand for money, while the latter reduces the money supply. This was accompanied by the "Rescuable Five," which referred to the remediable reasons. The first was to open a copper pan: "Selling money to the benefit of the device is 10 times" and "money is done." People spoke about the difference in the profitability of selling money. Among them, Shen Kuo stated that profitability was high. The second was that the banknote method was not robust and the credit was not good. The third was that gold and silver were not coins. The fourth was that the accumulation of coins hindered the circulation of money. The fifth was the outflow of coins to the north of the Great Wall. This was partly due to the official monopoly on salt, which resulted in the inflow of salt from other sources. Another reason was the selling of cattle from outside the country, which would also lead to the shortage of coins. In short, "all the tribes around depended upon China's copper coins, and the outflow of coins was immeasurable." Although some of Shen Kuo's predecessors had discussed this, they had different conclusions because of different points of view. For example, Zhang Fangping issued a monetary policy on the abolition of the copper band, while Shen Kuo made a foreign trade. So, one advocated forbidding money and the other advocated the prohibition of private and easy money. In the Hehuang area near the Xixia border in the northwest, hundreds of thousands of copper coins were transported from the capital every year, and 400,000 iron coins were cast in the area. As a consequence, the number of currencies in the three states of the Weihe River was excessive, and prices were rising. "When the mills fight for a hundred dollars, today it is four or five times, and this money is a disaster." Contrary to the situation in the Central Plains where "public and private coins were empty," Shen Kuo advocated "venting" the extra currency in this area, allowing the people to use iron money to trade with foreign monks, and the government only had to collect taxes from it. This was a good idea. One could buy back war horses and other useful materials, and increase the monetary income by tens of thousands of dollars a year. It could also save the cost of food and lower prices. At the same time, he also advocated that the central government replace the copper money that was shipped to the northwest with banknotes, and cast-iron money nearby. This would have cost the iron of the mountain, but would have alleviated the labor of transportation.

In short, in the face of deflation and financial urgency, Shen Kuo was not bound by the traditional currency theory and was not bound by the traditional increase or decrease of the money supply, that is, the constraints of the ready-made countermeasures such as casting, prohibiting copper and prohibiting private storage. He boldly proposed the rectification of the salt banknote system, the use of precious metals as currency, acceleration of the circulation of money and combining the policies of foreign trade, production, monopoly, price and taxation to comprehensively examine and control the economy. Therefore, his pecuniary credit thoughts are not only innovative and novel but also far-reaching and fully demonstrate the positive and bold explorative spirit of feudal social thinkers and scholars who made a difference, which is worthy of praise and study.

3. Zhang Fangping's monetary theories

Zhang Fangping was born in Yingtian in the Northern Song Dynasty.[4] His style name, also known as courtesy name, was An-dao. He was also known by the pseudonym of Lequan Jushi. He used to be an official during the reigns of Emperors Renzong, Yingzong and Shenzong. Zhang once served as an essential official in the court. He also worked in the Remonstrance Bureau and drafted decrees for the emperor.[5] He also served as an imperial minister, chancellor of the treasury, Hanlin academician and deputy prime minister. Aside from that, he once served as a county governor in Chuzhou,

---

[4]Yingtian, formerly recognized as Shangqiu, is a city in eastern Henan Province, central China. Shangqiu was the first capital of the Shang Dynasty and an ancient city with a rich history.

[5]The Remonstrance Bureau: It was an important government agency during the Song and Jurchen Jin Dynasties. Its main function was to scrutinize documents passing between the emperor and the central government.

Jiangning, Huazhou, Yizhou, Qinzhou and Yingtian. In 1079, he became *taizishaoshi* (the closest official to the emperor and the prince). His main works include *Lequan Set* and *Yutang Set*. His corrected work *Zhang Fangping Set* was also known throughout the world.

When he first entered into official life, he was an officer of the upper middle class. He often criticized the existing problems and submitted opinions to the emperor. He proposed solutions for political, economic and military crises resulting from official inaction, ineffective officers and soldiers as well as excessive government spending. As an officer with a strong sense of justice, he made efforts to seek remedies and hoped to inject new vitality into the court. His spirit was positive and consistent with the historical trend. During the enforcement of The New Policies in the Xining Period, as an important minister who had worked with three dynasties, he insisted on maintaining the old order and repeatedly made suggestions to oppose the appointment of Wang Anshi in the court. He claimed that if a new decree was implemented, it would surely lead to disasters like the sinking of ships and self-immolation. He wrote three memorials to the throne on exemption from service, offering taxation and relaxation of the controls on copper and coins. He described the important role of money in the ruler's power and carefully analyzed the causes of the money shortage that had already been discussed by former officers. On the basis of his predecessors' work and the new historical conditions, Zhang merely reinterpreted those circumstances and brought forward his views on them. His knowledge of money supply and repatriation channels was quite unique. He brought forward ideas that had never been suggested by anyone before and made new discoveries that deserve our attention. However, his arguments on the origin, essence and functional role of currency are nothing special. Therefore, there is no need for us to make further explanations here.

3.1. *About the channels of money circulation*

In order to demonstrate the reasons for the shortage of money, Zhang Fangping explained that the amount of currency in circulation should be determined by the difference between the amount of money put into and that recouped by the government, also known as government spending. If the government invested too little money and the ordinary people's economic conditions were not good, then how could there be enough money in the market? If the government did not invest enough money and people did not have enough money, how could they pay extraneous money other than normal taxations? This argument showed that if the withdrawal of money amounted to more than the invested money, there would be money shortage owing to monetary tightening. However, there would be a phenomenon known as currency expansion. Actually, there were no big differences in the investment and withdrawal of public and private money. The so-called issuance of money was referred to as money supply. The so-called accumulation of money was referred to as the withdrawal of money. The so-called rule was the law of money investment as well as withdrawal. In a nutshell, the laws of money delivery and withdrawal were not mysterious. "Because it was necessary to provide wages for the government officials as well as the civil and military authorities, to buy grain and cloths in the summer and autumn, and to ensure that the laws of the market were operating correctly, the money must be issued." There were three ways for the government to issue coins and invest money into the market: The first one was the use of money to maintain the authority of government, support the officials and pay for the expenses of the military forces, also known as "wage supply." For the second one, in order to increase government reserves, the money paid for the purchase of grains and fabrics could be referred to as "commodity delivery." (Grains included millet, rice, wheat, broomcorn millet, a grain named *ji* and a kind of bean named *shu*. Silk included damask silk, thin silk, yarn and silk yarn.) The third one could be regarded as the government's decision to increase material reserves, control mines and mineral products as well as purchase mining property products. The government paid money to cover the expense required by the mining areas, which could also be referred to as "commercial delivery." (The so-called products included gold, silver, copper, iron, plumbum, tea, salt, spice and alum.) It could be seen that there were mainly two types of money supply channels at that time, known as wage supply and commercial delivery. According to the types of peasants, commodity delivery could be divided into two kinds. When the currency was issued from the government to people, it would flow back to the government through certain channels. Under normal circumstances, there were two ways for the government to recoup money. The first one was known as "*Tianlu* positive tax," which was the main body of the state revenue. The second was tea, salt and liquor tax, which was also a component of the national fiscal revenue. With the reduction of land tax and the increase in fiscal expenditure, the state revenue had increased 3.6 times in 40 years. Similarly, the government-recouped funds mainly existed in the form of tax revenue which could also be termed fiscal withdrawal. Zhang Fangping believed that if a service offering money was included in the channel of currency repatriation, it would cause money shortage. Moreover, money could be seriously insufficient in the market. Obviously, the money withdrawal channels in the economic life of the Song Dynasty did not include "service offering money"[6] and "Green Sprouts money";[7] the former was monetary withdrawal, while the latter was credit recovery. These constituted the main channel for money circulation in the Song Dynasty.

Zhang Fangping described the budget centered on the feudal government for the purpose of guaranteeing normal operation of the central government and paying for bureaucrats and the army's salary, transportation, rewards, etc. In order to satisfy the ruling group's need for extravagant pleasures, money was allocated to royal family members and officials in exchange for the products produced by small producers in both urban and rural areas. The establishment of specific payments and numerous taxations (tea, salt and liquor) could be regarded as the two channels of money supply and withdrawal, which embodied the regime's tactics of extortion as well as the exploitation and plunder of civilians. Therefore, both currency supply and currency directly served the government and indirectly contributed to the production and livelihood of small producers. Since the circulation channels of money were shifted by the interests of the ruling group, they were arranged around various activities related to politics, military affairs, diplomacy and economy. However, if

---

[6]Service offering method: It was a method called the New Law set in the Song Dynasty. Based on the level of social status and economic situations, a family should offer certain services to the government.

[7]Green Sprouts money: Refers to the money involved in the Green Sprouts Program in the Song Dynasty. It was set and enforced by Wang Anshi.

the government issued fewer coins that only allowed people to pay for daily expenses, there would be insufficient money for them to pay for other expenses. Therefore, the amount of private currency depended on the government's policy on currency circulation. If the government restricted the issuance of coins, the amount of money circulating in the market will be insufficient. In addition to the payment of daily necessities, how could people have enough extra money? Excessive government storage will surely lead to money shortage.

Zhang Fangping conducted a preliminary analysis of the changes in economic life and agricultural production caused by the changes in the distribution of money based on different structures of residents of different levels and used a counterargument to clarify his point of view. Some people thought the exemption money was concentrated to the government, not for the purpose of gathering wealth but aimed at financing. The idea that the money raised would flow back to the people could not be agreed upon. Generally speaking, the recipients of raising money were peasants, and in most cases, the recipients of the so-called "service offering law" were unemployed people in the towns. Fund-raising could only be beneficial to the city regions, not to the countryside. The peasants were impoverished and had nothing to do. There was almost no difference in cities; however, things were just the reverse in the countryside and the life of farmers had been changed for the worse. The stern bureaucrats exploited normal people. Under such severe circumstances, peasants could only leave their homes. This was not conducive to the development of agriculture. Some people believed that those poor families below the fourth class only had small amounts of money to pay and it was not difficult for them at all. Zhang Fangping retorted that the poor people with a low social status lived in the remote and backward places and they rushed to the city in the twelfth lunar month. They had to go back and forth for dozens of miles to get fifty or seventy currency units and managed to buy some green onions, vegetables, salt and vinegar, which could provide for the whole family. However, they could barely save a penny in their daily lives. This remark was definitely not an exaggeration, and it was not deliberately fabricated to accuse political opponents. We can learn from his analysis of the currency circulation situation: "The disparity in currency distributions between urban and rural areas as well as the rich and the poor was quite extreme under the established currency circulation condition." We also realize the impact of unreasonable distributions on agricultural production as well as social and economic life. We not only recognize this point but should also conduct a specific analysis on it. From today's point of view, we can recognize that the different currency circulation channels and the residents' different levels of currency distribution had different impacts on the circulation of money. We should approve of his contributions to the monetary theories.

3.2. About the money shortage in the Song Dynasty

Zhang Fangping stood against the new law and believed that the implementation of the "Green Sprouts Program" and the "service offering method" had increased the demand for money. At the same time, the outflow and private sales of coins had reduced domestic currency circulation. The inevitable result of the positive and negative effects could only be the formation of a serious crisis of money shortage.

Regarding the positive, he took Yingtian Prefecture as an example to show that before the implementation of the new law, food and cloth could be used to pay the regular tax or other taxes, with only the housing tax to be paid with currency cash (the housing tax was about 5,000 $guan^8$). Based on the law, only the third-class families could have the honor to serve the government, so the officers in prefectures and counties were mostly employed. Most of their salary was paid in coins, and a small part of it was paid in grains and cloth. After the implementation of the two new laws, normal people had no other choice but to pay more than 75,300 *guan* in a service-offering fee twice a year. Families were suppressed and forced by the government and no one was spared from this duty. They had little extra cash in their hands. Moreover, those cruel and greedy bureaucrats frequently extorted the local people, hoping to get credit and profit from their actions. They frequently checked the fields and houses of the local people, and even the farm tools, cattle, crops, mulberry and jujube trees and various other seedlings were taken into consideration. Farmers were graded based on these inspections. This approach was also applied

---

[8]*Guan*: In ancient China, people used string to put coins together. "Guan" is a unit of measurement, which means a string of 1,000 coins.

to poor families. Farm tools, mills, shovels, axes, dogs and pigs were all valued. As a result, poor households were poorer owing to the lack of money. The evaluation of items and crops would cause at least a 1/10th loss to farmers. The cruel bureaucrats also forced local people to cut off their own seedlings, sell fields and houses, slaughter cattle and other livestock. When the conditions were poor, people's livelihoods were more seriously affected. This also intensified the contradictions between the supply and demand of the money, and therefore, the demand of money in circulation was greatly amplified.

Zhang Fangping believed that the reduction of the domestic currency circulation was caused by the loosening of the border ban and the allowance of selling and buying copper coins. First, after loosening the border ban, coins could flow to foreign nations. Since the implementation of The New Policies in 1074, by paying a certain amount of tax on certain pennies, the coins and armed forces were allowed to leave the border. The only places where the new decree had not been implemented were Guangzhou, Hangzhou and Mingzhou (a city named Ningbo). Only the regulations in those places were fairly strict; however, other places had long been under new regulations. At that time, the government did not impose any restrictions in Guangnan (Guangdong and Guangxi), Fujian, Zhejiang and Shandong. Items prohibited from being carried in the past could also be bought and sold privately and freely. Coins had always been valuable in ancient China. However, after the relaxation of certain restrictions, foreigners could easily use the precious Chinese coins. The copper ban had also been loosened at the same time, allowing private sectors to melt copper coins privately. The government had no idea of how to deal with this issue. In the old days, the management of overseas trade used to be very strict under the leadership of the ship management office. People who tried to carry money out of the country would be sentenced to death and a large amount of money was rewarded to hunt the criminals. However, after the establishment of The New Policies,[9] the restrictions were relaxed in Guangnan (Guangdong and Guangxi), Fujian, Zhejiang

---

[9]The New Policies: They were a series of reforms initiated by the Northern Song Dynasty reformer Wang Anshi when he served as minister under Emperor Shenzong from 1069 to 1076.

and other states. Foreigners could legally leave the country with Chinese coins. Surprisingly, the consequences of this situation were unforeseen. From a political and military perspective, the outflow of coins and troops had provided opportunities for foreign nations and might have triggered wars around the border areas. The outflow of coins in the Song Dynasty was much more severe than that in the Tang Dynasty. The problem of money outflow was extremely serious in the Lingnan region and other coastal areas. The ship management office was in the Guangdong, Fujian and Zhejiang Provinces during the Song Dynasty and numerous coins were taken to foreign nations from those regions. Then, the same situation also occurred in the northern part of China. At that time, the copper coins circulating in the Liao and Xia (the name of two dynasties in ancient China) from the Song Dynasty were exchanged with native products and iron coins. Therefore, Zhang Fangping sighed and said, "the foreigners were able to use China's precious coins."

Second, the sale of copper had also been legalized. Domestic copper coins could be melted by the common people. The quantity of copper coins was very limited, resulting in heavy losses in the economic field. The reckless melting of copper coins by people had always been a big problem in China. Before the implementation of the new regulations, the copper policy of the Song Dynasty had been very strict. However, people at home and abroad needed bronze in their daily lives. Therefore, they began to melt copper coins so as to cast bronze on their own. A massive quantity of copper coins was cast during the Shenzong Dynasty. Zhang Fangping believed that if copper coins could be legally melted by people, it would be impossible for the government to control the situation. Only by melting 10 copper coins could people get one *liang* (a unit of weight, equal to 50 grams) of copper, which could be used to make artifacts to obtain a five times greater profit. People were attracted by the huge profit and naturally followed suit. Every state placed a furnace to melt copper coins and the number of furnaces was increasing. This tiny profit would eventually lead to huge losses. Within a few years, China's copper coins would gradually decrease. After a period of time, the coins would flow into foreign nations, while the domestic coins were melted by the local people. This would undermine laws and regulations. The economic order and people's livelihood would be seriously affected. Although more coins were cast in the Northern Song Dynasty, the amount of coins was still insufficient. Copper coins and iron coins were both being used during the Northern Song Dynasty depending on various demands.

The government canceled the ban on money in order to maintain the majesty of the court and its monopoly on coins as well as to ensure normal and complete currency circulation in the Northern Song Dynasty, for which Zhang criticized the government. He believed this policy would further exacerbate the shortage of money and undermine social order. He recommended restrictions on the use of ancient Chinese coinage by foreign nations. In order to severely punish criminals who stole money and illegally smuggled money, strict legal measures were to be taken. From Zhang's point of view, these would have effectively prevented the crisis of money shortage.

With the development of commodity economy, the Northern Song Dynasty really took a big step and made great progress compared to the past. Both domestic and foreign trade had been expanded and flourished, and people were satisfied if they had enough money. A trade zone centered on the Northern Song Dynasty had been formed in East and South Asia. Therefore, the copper coins from the Northern Song Dynasty became the target in many countries. Such a trend could not be prevented by anyone or any administrative power; on the contrary, it vividly depicted the decay and shortcomings of the feudal forces. Owing to that, Zhang's pedantry and stubbornness were justified.

3.3. *About the monopoly of distribution rights*

Currency is an important symbol of the strength of a country and it is also a significant component of its financial resources. All the activities related to the national political, economic, military, cultural and diplomatic aspects are inseparable from money. Currency is not only a symbol of national power but also indicates the key to success or failure of a country. People cannot live a single day without money. In order to maintain the stability of the price, rulers may use currency to judge the value of items and to manage them. Money is the power of the sovereign and a magical thing that guarantees the rule of the emperor. Therefore, ordinary people can never be allowed to cast money on their own. Zhang strongly recommended that the emperor manage the currency himself. All the coins must be cast by the nominated institution. The ruler must strictly enforce law and order so as to maintain the mintage authority of the national government. People who cast coins by themselves had to be severely punished and executed. Those who provided assistance to cast coins, for example, by offering accommodation, providing funds and shielding the criminals had to all be punished. The officials who inspected ineffectively would also be punished by the court. Those who used nine kilograms of copper to make coins would be sentenced to death and a discipline inspection committee would be set up. All of these measures had proved Zhang Fangping's attention to currency rights.

However, Zhang and his predecessors had not realized that the rights of money and the power of the market could never be controlled by manpower, nor could they be controlled by administrative bans and severe penalties. The shortage of money had been a hot topic since the middle of the Tang Dynasty. The amount of coins was insufficient and the copper shortage was intensified at the same time. As long as the value of copper was higher than money and it was profitable to dissolve copper coins, the government could not prevent people from doing so. As long as the essential characteristics of commercial capital (including bureaucrat capital) remained unchanged, the money capital would increase its own value in the process of constant circulation. Long-distance trafficking and overseas trade were already well developed during that period of time. The exchange of local products between different regions and countries was very common. However, this kind of buying and selling required large amounts of money and it was not feasible without funds. Some countries used Chinese coins in circulation; therefore, the outflow of Chinese coins could not be banned, neither could the tens of millions of dollars circulating in trade and the fact that the merchants had already lent a large amount of money during the reign of Emperor Xianzong of Tang (an emperor in the Tang Dynasty, from 806 to 820).[10] In 817, Emperor Xianzong gave an order and asked all the officials (those with a higher social status, such as

---

[10]Emperor Xianzong of Tang, personal name Li Chun, was an emperor of the Chinese Tang Dynasty; he was the eldest son of Emperor Shunzong, who reigned for less than a year in 805 and who yielded the throne to him later that year.

princesses, infantas, county owners and envoys, as well as those with a lower status, such as soldiers, merchants, abbots in temples and officers managing the system of lanes and markets) to hold less than 5,000 *guan* privately. Those who held more than 5,000 *guan* were told to go shopping to meet the demand within one month or they would face harsh punishments. However, merchant princes used Imperial Guards as a pretext, making the orders hard to enforce. In 830, Emperor Wenzong of Tang reiterated the previous order but failed to enforce it. Since the Tang Dynasty, China's position in domestic and foreign trade had also created difficulty in the demand and supply of money. Based on the order of Emperor Zhezong of Song (an emperor in the Northern Song Dynasty), Chinese coins could legally flow into other nations. As Su Shi (a well-known poet of the Song Dynasty) stated, "as long as the benefits exist, this trend is unstoppable. Millions of coins are casted in Song Dynasty, however, it still cannot meet the demand of the market. The only reason is most of the coins have already flowed into other nations." The commercial and usury capitals further exacerbated the money shortage and the money shortage further promoted the vitality of usury. The law was unable to stop it.

The root cause of the money shortage was that copper coins could not meet the needs of the development of commodity currency relations. Copper was a base metal that was only suitable for small transactions of small production. Lenin once said, "money is the crystallization of social wealth, the crystallization of social labor and the basis for collecting tribute from all workers." Copper coin was an important means for feudal rulers to plunder and extract resources. The emperors in the Tang and Song Dynasties cast the copper coins and directly used them to trade with small producers in city. Sometimes the copper coins were distributed between royal aristocrats and bureaucrats as wages or rewards; they could use them to buy products from those small producers. Under the condition of the flourishing of bureaucratic, commercial and usury capitals, the conflict between the need to aggregate as well as transfer huge amounts of money and the objective reality of the low-priced copper coins circulating in the market was inevitable. If the status of copper circulation could not be changed, then people would never be able to emerge from the hardships of money shortage. In short, Zhang Fangping and most of his senior colleagues did not grasp the essence of the money shortage. Although they had made great efforts and explorations in this field, they could only understand and analyze these phenomena on the surface level. They endlessly played the same old tune with regard to the policy of banning copper and coins but found no measures to solve this problem.

4. The monetary theories of Li Gou, Ouyang Xiu and Su Zhe

4.1. *Li Gou's view on silver and gold as currency*

Li Gou was born in Nancheng County in the Northern Song Dynasty (today's Nancheng county of Jiangxi Province). His style name, also known as courtesy name, was Tai-bo. He had a good relationship with Fan Zhongyan. He was an enthusiastic supporter of The Qingli Reforms[11] and an enlightened thinker. He was often praised by Wang Anshi and his utilitarian view was the pioneering thought of Ye Shi. He failed the Imperial Examination twice, but was recommended by Fan Zhongyan as well as other officials and finally became a teaching assistant in the imperial college. He became a lecturer and taught all his life. He proposed the establishment of Xujiang College and was called Dr. Zhijiang and Dr. Xujiang at that time. His main works included the "Dr. Zhijiang set" and "Xujiang set." The latest version of the "Li Gou set" has also been published. Li Gou began to write articles at the age of 22. Since he basically lived in town, he could fully understand the financial problems and the hardships of the local people. His books centered on the prosperity of the nation and the well-being of the people. In his articles, he made political commentaries related to political problems and made cautionary statements for the whole society. His monetary views were reflected in the third and eighth chapters of *The Tactics of Enriching the Country*.

Guanzi Qingzhong[12] once noted the following on currency: "Therefore, the king first used it in accordance with its degree of dearness, stipulating that the jewels and jades are regarded as the first-class currency, the gold

---

[11]The Qingli Reforms, also called Minor Reforms, took place in China's Song Dynasty under the leadership of Fan Zhongyan and Ouyang Xiu. It was a short-lived attempt to introduce reforms into the traditional way of conducting governmental affairs in China.

[12]*Guanzi Qingzhong*: It is an agglomeration of the currency thought of ancient China.

as the medium currency and the knife and spade coins can be regarded as the third-class currency. The emperor restricted the role of the knife and spade money as well as the gold by increasing or decreasing the value of the gold." In order to meet the needs of the development of the times, Li Gou made timely adjustments to the lower-class currency in the Tang and Song Dynasties, where silver had already played a role in the historical currency stage. He stated, "at the very beginning, the jewels and jades were regarded as the first-class currency, the gold was the middle-class currency and the platinum was the last class currency. However, the price of the jewels, jades and gold was extremely high, thus the creation of the ancient coins is inevitable." He first affirmed the natures and statuses of the precious metals and less noble metals such as gold, silver, treasure, jewels and jades. Owing to their high values, they were not that convenient for daily transactions and sporadic transactions. He analyzed, "a long times ago, people once used gold, silver and Ancient Chinese coinage as currency. However, the use of gold and silver was controlled to a certain amount and not put to use widely." He certainly reversed the historical sequence of gold, silver and coins. But he expressed his expectation of silver as currency of the nation and saw silver instead of the knife and spade money as the development trend of the lower-class coins. This was not a momentary impulse or a clerical error, but a rational judgement, because he objectively stated that gold and silver were too valuable to be used as intermediaries in sporadic petty trade and found a reason to make an irrefutable claim.

Second, gold and silver were in short supply. The washing and eating utensils, knickknacks, jewelry and decorations were made using a large amount of platinum for the wealthy. Although all the gold was used, it still could not meet people's demand. Therefore, Li wondered how the government could make sufficient gold for people to use and cheap silks that are easy to obtain.

Li Gou finally came up with two conclusions. First, the status of copper was irreplaceable. Second, the use of gold and silver must be limited by the court. For the use of gold and silver, a clear hierarchy must be established and could not be arbitrarily changed, so as to ensure the normal use of gold. Only the use of ancient coins was the right way. This embodied his habitual dependence on copper coins. From the perspective of institutional economics, it is known as path dependence, which seems to be quite understandable. But the currency could not keep up with the requirements of the situation. Facing the shortage of money in circulation frequently, all countries and counties encountered such a situation from time to time. The amount of national statutory coins was insufficient, and coins of a low quality existed in the market and were received by the local people. This was a dilemma for Li Gou and reflected the characteristics of the Song Dynasty during the period of silver transition. The remedial measures he designed were as follows: "silver can only be used for state revenue and large-scale transactions." The future era of silver conformed to Li Gou's monetary policies.

He merely inherited the views of Lu Zhi (a well-known politician and litterateur in the Tang Dynasty) and others on the origin of money and price theory. Generally speaking, when more coins are issued, the price drops and inflation occurs. With fewer coins issued, prices rise and deflation happens. The rise and fall in prices is related to the national economy and people's livelihood. From a national perspective, it is better to issue more currency. What are the reasons? The market has a certain need for currency and it cannot be arbitrarily reduced. This is an argument based on the position of the ruling class, so there will be some deviation. After analysis, the reasons for the lack of circulation currency were found. The government advocated the elimination of low-quality coins, the melting of bronze statues and the discontinuation of their use by people. The government handled and used the bronze to make coins, which increased the number of coins.

4.2. Su Shi and Su Xun's views on paper currency and money shortage

Su Shi (1037–1101), also known as Su Dongpo, was a Chinese writer, poet, painter, calligrapher, pharmacologist, gastronome and a statesman of the Song Dynasty. His style name, also known as courtesy name, was Zizhan (known as Little Forward-Looking One) and he has also been known by his literary pseudonym Dongpo Jinshi (East Slope Householder). He was born in Meishan in Meizhou and was among "The Eight Great Men of Letters of the Tang and Song Dynasties." When the 1057 Jinshi examinations were given, Su Shi passed the civil service examinations to attain the degree of Jinshi. During the exam, Ouyang Xiu required — without prior notice — that candidates write in the ancient prose style when answering questions on the Confucian classics. The Su brothers gained high honors for what were deemed impeccable answers and achieved celebrity statuses, especially in the case of Su Shi's exceptional performance in the subsequent 1061 decree examinations. He was a major personality of the Song era and an important figure in the Song Dynasty, aligning himself with Sima Guang and others, against the New Policy party led by Wang Anshi. Su Shi was often at odds with a political faction headed by Wang Anshi. Su Shi once wrote a poem criticizing Wang Anshi's reforms, especially the government monopoly imposed on the salt industry. The dominance of the reformist faction at court allowed the New Policy Group greater ability to have Su Shi exiled for political crimes. The claim was that Su was critical of the emperor, when in fact Su Shi's poetry was aimed at criticizing Wang's reforms. Su Shi's first remote trip of exile was to Hangzhou. This post carried a nominal title, but no stipend, leaving Su impoverished. Then he was exiled to Mizhou, Xuzhou and Huzhou. In 1079, due to his strong attitude against the The New Policies, he was exiled to Huangzhou. During the Zhezong Dynasty, he served as a governor in Dengzhou. Then he served as a Longtu Academician in Hangzhou and did a good job. Beginning in 1060 and throughout the following 20 years, Su held a variety of government positions throughout China. After a long period of political exile, Su received a pardon in 1100. However, he died in Changzhou, Jiangsu Province, after his period of exile and while he was en route to his new assignment in the year 1101. Su Shi was 64 years old. After his death, he gained even greater popularity. His works included the well-known *Su Shi*.

Su Zhe (1039–1112) was a politician and essayist from Meishan, in modern Sichuan Province, China. As it was common for people in ancient China to have alternative names, he was also called "Zi You" or "Tong Shu." Su was highly honored as a politician and essayist in the Song Dynasty, as were his father Su Xun and his elder brother Su Shi. All of them were among "The Eight Great Men of Letters of the Tang and Song Dynasties." In 1070, Su Zhe wrote a letter to the emperor to point out that it was not wise to enact the reform. He also wrote to the chancellor Wang

Anshi to criticize the new laws. Then he was exiled to Henan Province. In 1079, his brother Su Shi wrote a poem just to criticize the chancellor Wang Anshi because he was often at odds with a political faction headed by Wang Anshi. However, his political opponents said that he was criticizing the emperor, so the government sent Su Shi to the prison and then had him exiled for political crimes. Su Zhe respected his brother very much and the brothers had a good relationship, so Su Zhe tried to save his brother from prison and he hoped to use his official position in exchange for his brother's safety. Unfortunately, he was also involved in that case and was exiled to Junzhou. Su Zhe's first remote trip of exile was to Junzhou, Shanxi Province. Then in the Song Zhezong Dynasty, he was asked to return to the court and act as the imperial minister. Later he was exiled to Leizhou. Finally, Su Zhe settled in Yinchuan in 1104 and he enjoyed a peaceful life there without the stir of society. He died in 1112. His main works included the *Luancheng* and others.

Su Shi was the earliest person to criticize paper currency with a metalist view in China. In one of his articles, he argued, "The reason why nongovernment people cast coins themselves was that the value of coins is low. If the price of the paper currency is the same as that of gold, people will never make coins without permission. In the district of Qin and Shu, people even use paper to make money, how can they stop people from doing the same thing?"

Su Zhe held a different view from that of Wang Anshi with regard to The New Policies. Before and after the reform, he issued personal opinions on the money shortage and currency circulation. He used the dual tax law in the Tang Dynasty to criticize the new law. Coins were cast by the government, and food and cloth were people's daily necessities. The ancient ruler cast coins for people to buy items, and at the same time produced food and cloth to make up for the lack in the market. So, the social order was peaceful and orderly. Later, the new law was enforced and people had no other choice but to pay for everything, and everything was cheap except money. Owing to that, people had no other choice but to get money. During the reign of Emperor Zhezong of the Song Dynasty, he wrote an article to analyze the reason for money shortage and brought forward solutions for the problems. The problems in the southeastern counties were mainly due to money. Coins were expensive and commodity prices were very low. Therefore, money shortage occurred. Since the period of Xining, people had to pay money for services and other taxes; the official money had all been taken by the local government, forcing local people to use the privately made coins. Farmers and weavers made great efforts but got almost nothing at all. The service-offering money accumulated; however, people still suffered from hunger and poverty. This problem existed for more than a decade. All the transport departments in the southeast regions would have taken out loans to buy food and clothes for the local armies for more than 3 years. Therefore, the prosperous vision of money circulation could have been formed. People would be enlightened and greatly encouraged. The turnover of the goods in the market would have been in a good condition and the resources in the warehouse sufficient. The armies could have been well supported owing to a change like that.

4.3. *Ouyang Xiu's view on the prohibition of the iron coins*

Ouyang Xiu (1007–22 September 1072), courtesy name Yongshu, art name Zuiweng (old man who is drunk) and Liuyi Jushi, was a Chinese statesman, historian, essayist, calligrapher and poet of the Song Dynasty. He was among "The Eight Great Men of Letters of the Tang and Song Dynasties." In 1031, he passed the civil service examinations to attain the degree of Jinshi, after which he was appointed to a judgeship in Luoyang. Politically, he was an early patron of the political reformer Wang Anshi, but later became one of his strongest opponents. In 1034, he was appointed to be a collator of texts at the Imperial Academy in Kaifeng, where he was associated with Fan Zhongyan, who was the prefect of Kaifeng. Fan was demoted, however, after criticizing the Chief Councilor and submitting reform proposals. Ouyang was later demoted as well for his defense of Fan, an action that brought him to the attention of other reform-minded people. The year 1043 was the high point in the first half of the 11th century for reformers. Ouyang and Fan spurred the development of the Qingli Reforms, a 10-point reform platform. In 1045, he was appointed as the official in Chuzhou, Yangzhou and Yingzhou. Then in the Shenzong Dynasty, he was an officer in Haozhou, Qingzhou and finally Caizhou. While a magistrate in Shandong, he opposed and refused to carry out reforms advocated by Wang Anshi, particularly a system of low-interest loans to farmers. He was finally permitted to retire in 1071. During his life, he praised and advocated for talented people and well-known personalities such as Zeng Gong, Wang Anshi, Su Xun, Su Zhe, Bao Zheng, Sima Guang and so on. He was in charge of creating *The New Book of Tang*[13] (1060) and his literary works included *The Ouyang Xiu Set*.

In 1044, he was appointed as the official in the Hedong region from April to August. He strongly opposed the use of iron coins of various sizes in this region. In his report to the throne, he used statistical numbers to clarify the currency issue. He spoke on good grounds and argued with certainty. Under the support of the statistical research, his views were quite persuasive and became important evidence in monetary history that could be learned from and demonstrated by later scholars. He said, "I went to Hedong District and made on-the-spot investigations to the amount of iron coins used by the local bureaus and army forces and I asked the local people and soldier's view on the convenience of the iron coins and concluded as follows. First of all, on the amount of the iron coins, more than 44,800 *guan* big iron coins and about 117,700 *guan* small coins were casted. The number of iron coins is less than the copper coins which was about 600,000 *guan* in total. The coins were all used by the government and local people." He also made numerous analyses on the profit of various sized coins in Jinzhou and Zezhou and calculated the income and expenditure of the Transporting Department.

After receiving this series of statistics, Ouyang Xiu appealed to abolish various iron coins for three reasons. First of all, according to the real income and expenses of the Transporting Department in the Qingli period, the bills broke even. There was a balance ("remainder") of more than 174,000 *guan*. This showed that there was no need to cast money to make up for the lack of financial resources. Second, the small coins were not profitable and they were unworthy of casting. Compared to the small coins, the big coins were so profitable that they were cast by an increasing number of people. If the use of big money was abandoned and only small

---

[13]*The New Book of Tang*, also named New Tang History, is a work of official history covering the Tang Dynasty in 10 volumes and 225 chapters. The work was compiled by a team of scholars of the Song Dynasty led by Ouyang Xiu and Song Qi.

money was circulated in the market, then the rules of copper coins would be undermined and more people would be sentenced to death. The profit of big coins was twenty times more than the small coins and even capital punishment could not prevent people from using them. Third, on the temptation of huge profit, implementation of the law in a fast or slow manner failed to achieve the purpose. The government could neither stop the people nor allow them to act without restrictions. Therefore, the local government could only forbid people from casting coins privately. Small coins had no profit and it was not worth casting. However, big coins were profitable and worth casting. In this case, if the government allowed people to do so without restrictions, an increasing number of people would commit crimes. Then, the use of iron coins would harm both the government and the local people. The coins were cheap and the commodities were expensive for a long time. Only those profit-making criminals could enjoy the profits; however, those disciplined people and officials had no other choice but to use high-priced goods. Therefore, both the officials and local people had experienced the low purchasing power of iron money and the high price of goods. It was the right time for them to relieve the pressure. Finally, local reserves were getting richer, but the number of military personnel was decreasing. Based on Ouyang Xiu's research, the military forces in the Hedong region obtained great profit from their own business in wine; at the same time, more soldiers were transferred to the capital. Generally speaking, the reserves were enormous.

Based on this, Ouyang Xiu concluded that "Today we can see that there are no more than 600,000 *guan* official and private money. The number is not that much, and it is easy to prevent people from using them. According to statistics, the army does not lack much resources and reserves." Obviously, Ouyang Xiu's mind was very clear and comprehensively analyzed and weighed everything from the perspectives of the state's financial status, border defense, military affairs, people's burdens, social order and iron casting. It is worth thinking about the unspoken rules that guided him to abandon the decision to make iron money, that is, the guiding principle. As far as we are concerned, the reasons are as follows: First, iron money was to be used to make up for the fiscal deficit, so once the financial situation improved, the iron money was to be abolished. In addition, the Hedong region was not as complicated as Shaanxi, and the deficit was quite serious. It could not be supported without casting iron money. Second, the value of iron coins was insufficient, and copper coins were full-value coins. Big iron coins depreciated even more than the small ones. As a result, it was a way to make profit for the government but a crime for the local people. The third reason was the drive of interests. It would be difficult to prevent people from casting money privately if the government did not make laws deliberately. The privately made coins were generally deficient which might have also led to the circulation of bad coins. To prevent the private casting phenomenon, it was necessary to abolish the deficient coins. Ouyang Xiu surely recognized these reasons, but did not express them directly.

5. Zhou Xingji's banknote issuance preparation theory

Zhou Xingji (1067–about 1125), courtesy name Gongshu and known as "Floating Mister," was a native of Yongjia (now Wenzhou City, Zhejiang Province). In the sixth year of Zhe Zong Yuanyou (1091), he was admitted as a doctor at the Imperial college. At the age of 17, he studied at Imperial College and accepted Wang Anshi's new school of thought. He was a disciple of Cheng Yi and retained what he had learned, and he was a pioneer of the Yongjia school of thought for utilitarianism in the Southern Song Dynasty. His works include *Float set*, and his writings of *Zhou Xingji* are still extant.

Before Huizong of the Song Dynasty, copper cash was used in most areas; Sichuan had access to iron money, and in Shaanxi and Hedong, copper and iron money were both used. In the first year of Qingzong (1041), Emperor Renzong cast iron money and when he became one of the top 10 richest people, iron money was circulated in Shaanxi. As prices rose, the coins were devalued and only the small iron money circulated in Hedong. In 8 years, the two irons were stopped and Dang 10 coins were changed to three. Tinned money was equal to two copper coins. Two years later, the 10 coins that were changed to five were changed to three. Later, when the 10 copper coins circulated only in the capital, and the Shaanxi, Hebei and Hedong roads were used, other coins were withdrawn from the banknotes. In the first year of Daguan (1107), the casting of 10 coins and tin coins was resumed. During a period of 3 years (1107–1110), Zhou

Xing wrote *The Book of Emperor Shang*. He proposed his own monetary theory in light of the chaotic situation of currency circulation at that time, designing a complete package to rectify the circulation of money. His monetary theories mainly included four aspects: the theory of virtual reality, the importance of everything, the expansion of coinage and the circulation of banknotes.

5.1. *The theory of currency deficiency*

Zhou Xingchi believed that "money is useless, things are useful, and things are real and money is virtual." It means that money ("money") can be used as an exchange medium ("use") because it had no use value ("useless"). The reason why a commodity ("item") could participate in exchange ("use") was because it had use value ("usefulness"), so the commodity was "real" and the currency was "virtual."

There are two sources of truth and weakness in the theory of virtual reality. One of them is the popular quotation from the Western Han Dynasty, which is still frequently used: "Pearl, jade, gold and silver are not edible in times of hunger, nor are they wearable in times of cold." Jia Shan said, "Those who use the money will die." The arguments that began to be propagated were that money is useless and has no use value. In fact, born out of *Guanzi State Storage*, it was stated that "The grip of the tri-currency is not warmed up, and food is not enough." Although there are differences in expression, they all agree that money has general social use value that ordinary labor production does not have, but it is the medium of exchange of goods, and the tool of the ruling class to carry out political rule and economic plunder. Therefore, if you think that you have money, you might still suffer from hunger and cold. Jia Shan believed that the currency "can be easy to use and lead to wealth." The *Guanzi State Storage* stated that "The first king took possession of property to defend the civil government, and the world was equal." It can be seen that they do not recognize that money, like other commodities, has its own special use value, which is useful. They make the common mistake of the nominalism, deny the commodity property of money and deny that currency is a kind of special commodity that must be separated from the commodity masses at a certain stage of the development of commodity production and commodity exchange. Therefore, Confucius in the Eastern Jin Dynasty summed up the following: "The sacred system makes useless goods to circulate useful wealth." After Zhang Fangping's modification and refinement, it became both "useless and useful," and Zhou Xingji's idea was that "money is useless." These are their interpretations of the statement made by Confucius.

The second source of truth is the concept of virtual reality. The correspondence between reality and virtual reality first appeared in the book *Laozi*. "Emptying the heart and filling the belly" belongs to the category of moral cultivation. The words of Sang Hongyang, the doctor of the royal house, as stated in *Salt and Iron on Tillage* which made him step into the economic category, are as follows: "in order to make the end of the book easier to use, use the money to regulate the supply and demand of market goods, and replace the agriculture with industry and commerce." With the purpose of fickleness, the false and true meanings are more abstract. It seems that money is false and goods are real. *Journal of Foods in the New Tang Dynasty* records the first year of the reign (758–759) when the government adopted an inflation policy and cast a *Qianyuan Zhongbao* as 10 *Kaiyuantongbao's* "Xuan Yuan Shi Dang." After that, the emperor cast a reel of money that was equivalent to 50 existent coins. In the first year of the period (760), "the public devaluation of the rerolling money was a one-for-one 30, and when the opening and the 10-dollar were all one-10th, the 'grinding' was accepted, the real money was obtained, and the virtual money transaction was all 10. When money is used, money is a real name." Real money refers to full-value coinage, and virtual money refers to depreciating bad money. Zhou Xingji's actual and practical meanings are not the same as this. His "material is real and money is virtual" refers to articles that have use value. Virtual refers to the currency that has no special use value as an exchange medium. Of course, he also refers to the devaluation of the virtual value of insufficient value; in fact, he refers to the full value of small money: cash can be cashed in, which "is a real payment," and the cash delivery that cannot be honored is false. The process of changing the meaning of reality and virtual reality is as follows: In the Han Dynasty, Sang Hongyang combined the light and heavy theory, falsely pointed out the price policy, actually referring to the goods; the Tang Dynasty began to refer to the depreciation value of the devaluation and the coinage; and the Zhou Dynasty and the Song Dynasty combined the two theories with the theory of severity.

5.2. Currency theory of lightness and heaviness

Zhou Xingji believed that "Money is not heavy and light essentially, but due to things that are heavy and light." It means that the currency was not as important as it seemed. Why did the currency have no importance? In the premise that money is virtual, things are real and "money is useless," he believed that there were two situations. The first was as follows: "it starts with a small amount of money and so on. And with more money, the big money is light and heavy." At that time, the situation was as follows: In the beginning, a small amount of money (*Kaiyuan Tongbao*) was circulated, and later on, a large amount of money (*Zhaoyuan Zhongbao*), which was not worth enough, appeared when the price of the big money was low and the price of the commodity was high. The second kind of situation was as follows: "Beginning with copper coins and so on, things are set. And with iron money, iron money is light and heavy." In the beginning, copper was used for pricing, and later in circulation, iron was used instead. Iron prices were low, and commodity prices were high. Taken together, the "price" of commodities in these two situations did not change, but the large sums of money or high-valued copper that originally served as the standard of value turned into insufficiency, or the iron prices could not be equalized. Furthermore, "copper money is valuably expensive, while iron money cannot be transported." That is to say, copper could perform the functions of circulation and storage, and was not subject to any conditions; on the contrary, iron money was limited in the implementation of the means of circulation, and it was even impossible to store. Therefore, the former was precious and the latter was of a low grade. Therefore, Zhou Xingji believed that the currency did not have much importance, but in comparison, the change in the proportion of the existing currency and the original two different currencies showed differences in light and heavy: "It is lighter than its weight, and its appearance is more important." When the quality, fineness, weight, size and nominal value of a currency are exactly the same as the actual value, there is no question at all. Any change in any of them will change the quality, and thus the consequence.

Therefore, the appearance of the phase will be more important. As regards the weight of goods, because they varied widely and they were priced using the same pricing system, the level of high and low was still very different, and it was still "a matter of priority." Therefore, the meaning of its severity refers to the difference between high and low prices and high purchasing power. "Priority" is achieved under the same price condition. It can be assigned that it originated from a comparison under the same conditions and that it was an indication of importance.

Zhou Xingji expressed the importance of commodity prices in terms of severity, and differences in the purchasing power of currencies were not novel. The repeated emphasis on multi-disciplinarity in the *Guanzi Weight* section was to use light and heavy policies to achieve the great cause of ruling the country. His emphasis was based on "the weight of money and everything is light, the currency is light and everything is heavy," which is based on the theory of supply and demand value, that is, the corresponding changes in the supply and demand of money and commodities that show the relationship with the severity. Moreover, the "Government Graduation" chapter advocated the use of light and heavy policies to achieve redistribution that was conducive. Therefore, he believed that the price leveling off was not fixed at all, and that the leveling off required that prices fluctuate frequently and could not be fixed. The fixed price or flat price also did not allow the price to be adjusted. If the price could not be adjusted, the price would have to be fixed. If the price was fixed, it would be uniform and it would not serve the interests of the ruler. However, Zhou Xingji was not the same. He was in a period of depreciation of currency, price volatility, lack of financial resources and floating population. In order to seek to get rid of financial difficulties, stabilize prices, stabilize finance and establish a new social and economic order, his theories naturally had to obey the requirements of the current situation. Therefore, he put forward the view that money and things were equal to one another and that they were equal in value. Obviously, he opposed the ruler's deviation from the theory of ignorance and actuality, arbitrarily adjusting the nominal value of money, changing its purchasing power and making it less important. Zhou Xingchi advocated that a balance between the purchasing power of money and the total price of commodities should be achieved, and that the price level should be stable. Therefore, it is quite different from the basic price policy of the article *Guanzi Weight*. So, people's views were different, and even the opposing.

5.3. *The devaluation theory of currency*

Faced with the reality of the devaluation of the coin, Zhou Xingji theoretically explored its causes and harms. In the absence of a theory of labor value, the harm caused by the circulation of money and its influence on the ruling class and the masses of the people could not be easily assessed. He believed that the light and heavy theory was the tool of the ruler and was the economic power of the country ("The art of the Holy Spirit, the goodness of the country"). The country's policy of currency depreciation and arbitrary increase in the nominal value of coinage could not be sustained. Value is equivalent to only three small money or big money, the government is forcibly stipulated as 10 small money, and circulation will eventually force it to devalue and return to the original starting point, "but when 10 must be three, then can be flat." This was tantamount to saying that the policy of depreciation of currency was not feasible. The rulers violated the false reality theory, and in particular violated the phase of comparison, in a trivial manner.

Zhou Xingji studied the severe and destructive harm caused by the currency depreciation policy in four aspects. The first was the prevalence of private casting and the country's financial resources being dispersed. The currency depreciation policy encouraged the popularity of private casting ("The caster of the country, the 10 casters of the people"). The amount of coinage in circulation greatly increased, and it exceeded the amount in objective requirements, resulting in inflation and dispersal of the country's financial resources. So, "The country weighs at one point and loses a lot of interest." It is worth noting that the loss of the country's food and currency was detrimental. The second aspect was rising prices. Zhou Xingji thought that "monetary profits are twice as expensive as objects," and price increases were much higher than the devaluation of the coin. The state "takes double the interest, when it doubles," and the country's double benefit from the devaluation of the coin must be guaranteed in order to pay twice as much money as the price rises, "the price is heavier, and the country is using more money." Moreover, the official government also cast tin money, "not a single point, and things have been three times more expensive." Private casting further boosted the price, and the prices rose. "Because of the self-imposed law (issued as 10 coins), the official cast geometry and the private cast geometry. Although the official cast strikes, private casting is not. If the private casting is endless, then the prices will be high." Official casting promoted private casting and private casting promoted price increases like fanning the flames, with the central government bringing harm to a country already at a disadvantage. The third aspect was that the country had self-destructed. These points had directly or indirectly exacerbated the government's financial difficulties as shown by the following statement: "the things are out of the people, the money is out of the government, and the world's ten-tenth tax is often ten, and the ten-tenth-of-ten-of-a-kind, and the Buddha's offerings, and the devices used by them, will be traded by money." "It is said that four-tenths of the food needed by the country comes from taxation, six-tenths of it comes from the market, and a large number of goods and equipment come from the market. In the devaluation of the coin, the purchasing power of the currency declined during the soaring price of goods, resulting in a situation where 'the weight of the people is often heavy (the price is angst) and the officials are often light (the purchasing power of the currency is low).'" The rate of increase of prices far exceeded the rate at which coins were issued. Relying on the grain supply provided by the market required a payment of coins that was several times more than the increase in the market price, which threatened the purchase. This naturally caused more difficulties for the state's finances. "The country can use its energy!" The fourth aspect was the creation of a disaster for the people. The laws on money had changed repeatedly and people had suffered because of it. During the Chongning years (1102–1106), the southeastern region reorganized the currency, and two changes were made with regard to the 10 coins: "From ten to five, all ten people go to their forty and a half; from five to three, the people of all ten go to it. Seven Miles." The rectification was actually plundering. Once more, half or even seven tenths of the people's property transformed into nothingness. This is how cruel it was. The government also issued small bills to recover 10 coins, which also endangered the people. "The method of small banknotes has always been consistent from one hundred." The people in the transaction could hardly distinguish the authentic money from the fake one. "The people in the southeast are not willing to use the 'three easy change banknotes' and sell them as the 'yellow money'." This was a protest against the ruler for the currency depreciation policy. Zhou Xingji analyzed and understood the depreciation of currency from the perspectives of price, private casting, people and the government a lot better than 16th century European scholastic academic Olesem.

The devaluation of the coin would cause much trouble for the government and the people. But how was one to eliminate the failing system? According to the theory of reality and severity, Zhou Xingji proposed three kinds of countermeasures. First of all, he was against the simple devaluation of big coins from being equivalent to ten small coins to being equivalent to three small coins. Instead, he advocated the practice of selling different official titles for the retrieving of these big coins, after which "they would be changed to be equivalent to three small coins and circulate in the country." He believed that the advantages of doing so were as follows: one, "the country does not have to spend, and to accept millions of dollars for the use"; two, "public and private without any damage and the price can be flat"; and three "thieves cannot cast, and leads to imprisonment." He advocated casting a full-value coin and maintaining the normal order of currency circulation. It undoubtedly helped to stabilize prices, quell stolen casts and greatly benefited market transactions and social order. It was not necessarily true that the country was free from fees, because selling a bureaucracy and devaluing a currency were not related to each other and could be promoted at the same time. Moreover, the seller could be undeniably self-serving. Greed had a long history in ancient China, and it was after all the cause for corruption of the regime. The sign of decline was by no means a perfect measure to judge the rectification of currency.

The second countermeasure was that iron money, tin money and copper coins were distributed and circulated. Iron money and clip tin money only passed through the Hebei, Shaanxi and Hedong regions, while other regions exclusively circulated copper coins. Zhou Xingji was of the opinion that the contrast lay in their lightness. As long as copper money was used in combination with iron money and tin money, it could not be affected by price fluctuations and could ensure the normality of currency

Financial Thought of the Northern and Southern Song Dynasties 281

circulation and trading activities. The government and the people were not immune to the devastation caused by currency depreciation. They could also receive the social and economic benefits if "coin money does not flow in the two countries" when "they are not misled by the people." As for whether iron or tinned money was more or less important, whether they had shortcomings and whether they had to be taken into consideration or omitted, it is not known. If the currency circulation operation between different regions was different, then if the same item circulated in different currency areas, there would have been different light and heavy trade-off standards. It was not conducive to the circulation of commodities in a wide range, which hindered the development and growth of a unified market. Whether or not the market's internal laws could accept Zhou's design and arrangements, and comply with people's subjective intentions, they also had to accept the test of objective real economic life, as in the unknown.

The final countermeasure was that the Hebei, Shaanxi and Hedong regions traded with other regions. Zhou Xingji advocated "setting a child to be like a Sichuan law," and a three-way issue would not deliver cash notes, that is, physical notes. In other areas, credits were issued that could be exchanged for copper coins. Because it would be honored, and was "credible to people, feasible in the world," natural circulation was not a problem. This kind of trade could be issued and circulated in the three districts, cashed in and out of the three districts. How could one ensure the stability of prices in the three regions and guarantee a reasonable issuance and normal circulation of iron money, clip tin money and the like, and maintain the prices in the three districts? How could one balance prices with other regions and ensure that the currency circulation and price of the three regions did not affect one another? Zhou did not know this. Of course, he should have known that iron and tin money were of inferior quality and could easily be stolen. Tin money could be used to impersonate copper as long as it was dyed. However, if paper money was not stipulated, a green light will be issued without restriction. He concentrated on the idea of iron money, tin money and money delivery on the three-way road. It was difficult to stabilize the three-way currency circulation and it was difficult to suppress prices. Moreover, the three-zone banknotes would flow to other areas, and the three-way instability would spread to other areas as well. Therefore, Zhou Xingji's rectification plan was not complete, reflecting that he not only protected the long-term interests of the ruler from threats but also found a solution to protect the ruler's immediate interests, thereby encountering a conflict between his own theory and the highest interests of the ruling class.

5.4. Banknote issuance preparation theory

Zhou Xingji expressed neither suspicion nor opposition to the notes. He started from the theory of light and practicality and pointed out in good faith that "the disadvantages of the method of making money by hand are not paid by the money. They are not collected by money, so they are not feasible." The result was certainly not optimistic. That is to say, the issuance of banknotes was not restricted by money. It was also not considered whether or not it could be honored, without which it would greatly reduce the credibility and affect normal circulation, because "the people's trade cannot understand its authenticity, and loses money and not get the money. The people in the southeast are not willing to use three money change and do a good job for the yellow money (sacrificial use (Paper money)), so the disadvantages of the previous day have also been made." The people in the southeast refused to use the three money to exchange small bills. Zhou Xingji thought that if the money can be exchanged for copper, then "paying the bills is true." In his view, copper coins were substantial and paper money was not and the banknotes are fake. Only by insisting on exchange can there "be credibility for people and work in the world." That is to say, the credibility of the banknote cannot be guaranteed, while the normal issuance and circulation of the banknote can be guaranteed. It can be seen that Zhou Hang has advocated the circulation of full-value currency, and that the notes should be used to redeem cash.

At the same time, Zhou Xingji also suggested that only two-thirds of the preparations for the issuance of banknotes together with the current money bills were required and it need not be 100%. "If the law is implemented, the iron money must wait, and the country often has a 31%

advantage. Loss, the thieves' ambiguity, and the accumulation of past and present, often occupy one of them. They are paid in 3 years by means of annual payment, public documents (that is, cash receipts, and drafts issued by grain). That is, the so-called 'three-points can be used in two points'." That is because one-third of the banknotes in circulation could be lost or damaged in fire or water disasters ("loss of water and fire"), or lost in robbery and theft ("the rogue"), or stranded in circulation, that is, banknotes in circulation that cannot be withdrawn from circulation but will not be honored ("The product of contacts"). The former belongs to natural consumption, which is a personal loss, and the latter is the lowest stock in the circulation. Although Zhou Xingji's understanding of the second situation was incorrect, his analysis of the two situations, especially the latter, was particularly commendable.

Therefore, as long as two-thirds of the cash was kept, the banknotes issued each year (compensation, together with the official receipts) would be enough to meet the needs of cashing ("every two-point, three-point"). Li Gang (1083–1140) wrote *The Matching of the Right Hand with the Right Hand* in Shaoxing, in the sixth year (1136) of Gaozong of the Southern Song Dynasty. He also mentioned the method of *Sichuan Jiaozi*. He said, "At that time, the managers were properly prepared and they often kept millions of dollars in capital. They used 3 million to pass through the sub-subsidiary. They shared public and private, and the circulation was unrestricted. As a good social effect, it was recognized by people." According to Peng Xinwei's *History of China's Monetary History*, the highest issuance limit of the Northern Song Dynasty *Guanzizi* was 1,256,340 baht, and cash (*Sichuan Tonghang Tiecian*) was 360,000 baht. Cash reserves only accounted for 28% of the issuance quota. In other words, the preparation rate proposed by Zhou Xingji was roughly close to the actual ratio. The theory of this set of banknote issuance reserve proposed by him was indeed the first in the world, and it is a theory of banknote issuance preparation that does not require full cash. Although the theory lacks scientific and systematic analysis, he was, after all, the first person to understand the rules of banknote circulation and to scientifically summarize it. He greatly enriched the treasure house of ancient Chinese currency thought.

6. Ye Shi's theory of paper notes

Ye Shi (1150–1223), known as Mr. Shui Xin, lived in Shuixin Village outside Yongjia City in his later years and Wenzhou Yongjia (now Wenzhou, Zhejiang Province) in the Southern Song Dynasty. In the fifth year (1178) of the scholarships of Emperor Xiaozong, he was known as the assistant minister of the state of Chuzhou, the authority minister, the *Jianjian Kangfu* and was part of the Jiangjiang system, the Baowen Court system and the Jianghuai system. A representative of the Yongjia School, in academic thinking he undertook Xue Jixuan, advocated utilitarianism and opposed empty talk. He believed that the rich were the pillars of the ancient national fiscal revenue, and the usury activities are the country's way of "supporting the people." He advocated that feudal countries should "protect the wealth" as their objective, opposing the weight and suppressing the end, opposing and restraining mergers and acquisitions, and that the rulers should be good at financial management; he advocated "to share the world's wealth and the world," opposed the state's implementation of the severity policy, accused the government of direct management and controlled business and industry by infringing on the interests of business people. He advocated "business support for workers, support for merchants and circulation of money." His works include *Ye Jiji* and *History Record Preface*.

Ye Shi's currency expositions include the following: "The Financial Planner" in the 12th year of Xiao Zong Chunxi (1182) and the 3 years of Guangzong Shaoxi. In Huaixi, he was promoted and transferred to the official title of legal advisor as well as iron and salt supervisor. The text of *Coins II* discusses the relationship between currency and commodities, the best currency theory of copper coins, the theory of banknote deportation and other disadvantages of currency circulation. This is described in the following section.

6.1. *On commodities and currency*

Ye Shi believed that money originated from the "quartiles of merchants and the system of handing over to the near and far. Things cannot be self-made, so they use money to do it." That is to say, money originated from the exchange of goods and was born in order to overcome the inconvenience of commodity exchange. It was born in three generations. This understanding is nearer to the truth than St. Regis's traditional preaching on currency creation. It can be said that Sima Qian's "agricultural industry and commerce transaction path and the currency of the turtle shell money and knife cloth" are not exactly described. The formulation of Sima Qian has metamorphosized the primary nature of commodities, the second nature of money and the inevitable outcome of the development of commodity exchange. Ye Shi admitted that although the currency originated from the exchange of commodities, he seemed to think that the motive power of commodity exchange was currency, and that commodity circulation was the result of money circulation. "Things cannot be made on their own, so they should be done in money." "If it does not pass through, it will be used to make money by casting money." If there is no currency, commodity trading cannot be concluded, and commodity circulation will become empty talk. This reverses the causal relationship between the circulation of money and the circulation of commodities, reverses the causal relationship between money and commodities, forms a conflict of views and exposes his theoretical immaturity.

Ye Shi believed that the history of the evolution of currency circulation had gone through three periods. First, there was very little money in the three generations. Second, the use of money by the Chinese during the Qin and Han Dynasties gradually increased. Third, in the Southern Song Dynasty, money was not used. The reason for this change was that in the three generations, "in households, since the rice, cloth, vegetables, and fish were of great importance due to their power," people "made an investment in safety, and money was useless, so they used it least." This, coupled with the opposition of various countries, closing the country, the need for self-sufficiency and multi-national trade not being carried out, was the main reason for the change, "not to bother with the camp." How could a lot of money help? Only "Traders of merchants and the court can rely on the use of money." After that, it was different. The production of all things was caused by money.

How much do high and low prices (currency capital) determine the production of a variety of things and to what extent ("everything is money, so money for things")? Under the simple commodity circulation condition, it reflects the use of profit as a means of production and management. Handicrafts and commerce are separated from the natural economy of self-sufficiency. "All of the world's food and beverage resources are from money, from two to one, and much more. All are made of money. From the use of the court, from the private transfer of *Gong*, the county party committee, merchant trade, all make use of money, so the future generations of money are a hundred times greater than the former. He believes that this is all due to the country's unification, regardless of east, west, south, or mainland borders. 'If there is one thing, the people in the world will not be transported to the Quartet. The merchants will come and go. North and south will be mutual, more than in the past. Money will not be secure.'" In ancient times, the Han Dynasty used gold and silver coins. After Xuanyuan, gold coins were all withdrawn from circulation. After the Eastern Han Dynasty, gold was the least used metal, and because of the prevalence of Buddhism, gold and silver were the ornaments of civil engineering. As for currency, "the money is only used for money," so the later generations used a lot of money. Of course, the national government played a crucial role in the country's economic development, but it was by no means the fundamental determinant and determined the key reason for currency development. It determined the level of development of commodity production and commodity exchange, and the production and exchange of commodities were determined by the level of development of the productive forces. The economy was the foundation, and the superstructure was the manifestation of the economic foundation. This relationship could not be reversed. Moreover, the period of formation of the Chinese currency economy was the Warring States Period rather than the Qin and Han Dynasties.

6.2. *On copper coins as the best currency*

Ye Shi advocated coinage of full value. He believed that copper was the best currency. That was a belief shared with him by Lv Zuqian, both of whom were metalists.

He maintained that if you use money, you will be able to use it to make more money. The king's use of money also meant that money was being spent. It was a waste of all things. Copper coins were just one of many, along with silver coins. This is different from Sima Qian's understanding. Ye Shi's analysis of the reasons for the withdrawal of gold and silver from the ranks of currencies only captured the superficial phenomenon and saw the "appropriateness" of copper coins. In the end, it was price (at the time not worth mentioning). The weight of both gold and silver was appropriate, or because of the relationship between religion and gold, the stock of gold and silver was reduced. Both were withdrawn from circulation, or as is said today, a low level of productivity was determined. The use of copper as a currency was enough to take gold and silver out of circulation. Nevertheless, no matter how he analyzed it, he had not grasped the real reason why copper was suitable as a currency.

Of all the different copper coins, Ye Shi ranked *kaiyuan* copper coins the first. He believed that the circulation of copper coins was based on the "*Kaiyuan* money" and it was to be given priority. The coins valued at five and a half money were very thin and not suitable for use. *Kaiyuan* money should have been used as the law to standardize prices. The quality of *Taiping Tongbao* and *Tianzhu Tongbao* at the beginning of the Song Dynasty exceeded *Kaiyuan* money, with *Taiping* money being the most important. "If Qian Wenyi is one, both the size and the importance should be equal, then the people will not doubt it, and they will not misunderstand it." In Huaixi, iron money was cast with the words "Four seasons are words." The new money weighed five pounds and eight pounds, and was a few rounds older than the previous one. It was too large as compared with old money, and was very difficult to identify. "In the same season, self-casting workers cannot remember it so how can the people identify it for themselves." This is how the currency-trading media function. The key to making coins appropriate in both the size and the shape is that the state must monopolize the right to coinage, and it must not remove the ban. Instead of using mint coins, it is a means for the government to increase its fiscal revenue. Ye Shi's understanding was consistent with Liu Zhi and Jia Yi. Taking history as an illustration, he pointed out that the Emperor of the Western Han Dynasty tried to "become prosperous through thrifty means, and mistakenly thought that when the world did not use money, why should the government recover the right to coinage, resulting in the coins of Wu and Deng's being spread out in the world and Wu Wang's use of it. The southeast was in chaos." Jia Yi thought that as long as the money is good, it will not devaluate the currency if the work cost is not included. Based on this, he believed that the reason why the Tang Dynasty had more evil money was that the imperial court could not help the people's self-infliction. After the Tang Dynasty of Emperor Xuanzong, especially the Kaiyuan and Tianbao eras, the financial expenditure increased dramatically.

"The court is eager to benefit." Since Emperors Suzong and Daizong of the Tang Dynasty "gradually resorted to the pursuit of the end of the world to seek money and the people," although individual households also needed to use currency, from then on, "the things in the world did not disappear," the market was depressed and production and life became sluggish. In the Song Dynasty, there was a time when drums were cast. Since Xining years had only thought of casting more, he cut corners drastically. "The money is slightly worse." The coins minted in the Qiandao and Shaoxing years were even worse than those minted in the Xining years. Ye Shi strongly opposed the Song government's implementation of currency devaluation and inflationary policies; he opposed the government's major casting of undervalued coins, which revealed its ruthless fiscal issuance aims to "always make a lot of money in a hurry," and "gain riches but reduce labor fee." Because the government did not recognize the masses as their biggest victims, they said that the currency was widely circulated. "If you use the end of the levy to conquer the world, you seek the money and the people, and you go up and down, you're in private homes and the product is not money." However, it was not so much a result of upward efficiency, but rather an inevitable product of the development of commodity economy.

Ye Shi attached great importance to the function of the means of circulation of money and neglected the functional role of the means of storage. It was believed that "the goods of money and goods to God do not have any way to save money, but they can only see their usefulness." "The wealthy people in this world are not only responsible for collecting money, but the imperial court is also making full use of the world's money to enter the palace .... I do not know how money has any benefit passing around the world, although the accumulation of a lot of money is something different." It meant that money could play a role only when it was in circulation. If it was stored in a house, stored in the treasury or hidden in a rich room, it would not be used as a mediator in exchange, causing the currency to degenerate and be stored more. What is the difference between money and ordinary items? In circulation, it had "weight on all things," from the court to the people. Everyone respected money because it "can pass through the uses of all things." Moreover, he believed that "those who know nothing about money cannot accumulate, but they do not know their obstacles and do not flow; the amount of disciplinary knowledge cannot be small, and they do not know that those who have gathered have survived, and they have been forced to use it on their behalf instead." "It's not wise to have money in the world." He criticized the Southern Song Dynasty, saying that the court knew that the copper money would be hindered from being circulated, and that it would not be allowed to circulate. It also knew how to accumulate numismatic coins, and thought that there should be a reasonable degree of concentration. The court emphasized the function of the storage of coins, while ignoring its circulation, that is to say, negating the meaning of the existence of money, "the reason why money is respected from top to bottom, and its power is as heavy as it is to people of all things, is so that it can be used for the use of all things; if it is not made, it will be tantamount to a thing." Ye Shi denied theoretically the function of currency storage. This is consistent with his denial of the role of banknotes. To "restore the money he has collected" meant to work hard to realize the normal circulation of copper coins from two different perspectives.

6.3. On the expelling of coins by paper money

With the circulation of banknotes, copper coins would retreat from public and private collections and from circulation, "there is less money, only when it is used. The line is ridiculous and the money is less. Therefore, it is not something that cannot be obtained but money will not be available." The phenomena of libel and money benefit were not only present but could also not be controlled. Because banknotes were "less than a 1,000 times lighter" than coins, they were convenient to carry. The conversion of coins to banknotes was profitable, and the temptation of "the winning of 11" could not be underestimated. "Respect for the money, and its potential is also solid." Since this trend was irresistible, as long as the banknotes were circulated, there was no way to reverse the poor usage tendency of copper coins. "Those who claim money today are anti-accepted and repentant. They have money and few benefits. Even those who suffer from this problem cannot save themselves. The so-called patient pointed out: 'The world is suffering from money and has been rampant for 20 years. All things are considered as goods, and the money is used to control its power. The money is light and heavy and its size is small, but it is self-contained and not worth the money. In parallel, the system will do its best; while it will not be enough, as for the attainment of power and right; all the so-called money is anti-obedient to the deceit, and the deed will be the benefit of money.' 'So the currency is an important part of it.'" Ye Shi believed there were three shortcomings in the circulation of banknotes: One was that the circulation in big cities was occupied by banknotes and copper coins were already withdrawn. The second was the devaluation of the banknotes, causing economic losses to the holders ("unexpected record, invincible"). The third was the lack of supplies and the shortage of goods ("the goods are also lacking"). Among these, the first one was of utmost importance. The market in big cities brought together merchants from all directions. There was no exchange of trade between them. "There is no more use of money. After 10 years, I will not be afraid of a big city. I'm afraid that the copper coins in the neighboring areas will also be used as collectors. People 'will hand over the empty coupons and the emperor will be unable to do anything. This is not a big worry in the world!'" When referring to "empty coupons to make money," he meant unusable cash. Ye Shi discovered that "holding empty money to make things is not something to do, but it is about holding short vouchers to make money!" The so-called "empty money" referred to money that could not be used without purchasing more money. In the Song Dynasty, more money was spent than previous generations. Although it was money that was driven out by banknotes, there were many places where money could be used in real social and economic life. "From the top to the bottom, there are soldiers and materials; the counties rely on the import of salt, wine and groceries, and the people's trade is transportation, which is mostly money. Therefore, even if the virtual vouchers are used to contain the money in the world, they are still not enough to make possession of the money." It was said that from the court down to the people everyone still needed to use copper coins, copper coins could not be completely withdrawn from circulation and a minimum amount of copper was needed to be kept in circulation. The so-called "virtual vouchers" referred to the irresistible inevitable trend of copper coins that could not be exchanged for paper money. This regular reminder was Ye Shi's contribution to the theory of currency circulation.

In this regard, Yuan Biao (1144–1224) later stated clearly, "After the pirates view the current state and counties, they must go for the same thing. The money is used to fill the committee and the money is often insufficient. There are pure copper coins that are not miscellaneous and the money is. There is more than enough to know that the only thing that can damage the copper is the incompetent copper" (*The Famous Officials of The Ages, Then the People Will Be Sparse*, vol. 273). These philosophers elaborated on the law of bad money expelling good money more than 600 years before the West did.

Of course, before them, people had already discussed the objective phenomenon of this rule in Chinese history. For example, Jia Yi said, "If the money is rampant, the money will die every day" (*Casting Money*). In the Northern and Southern Dynasties, Yan Yan said, "If something is fine, it's not cast …. In one year, we must do our best" (*Song Shu Yan Shuo Biography*). Unfortunately, this line of thinking was not discussed by the regular people.

"I don't know what the evil is doing. It's the money that drives the world." Ye Shi could not find the root cause of this phenomenon correctly, due to the currency metalist's prejudices about the circulation of paper money and the fear that the paper money will replace copper coins completely. It was said that the minister of Xingli was "empty and creative," and as the gainer from the coin suffering, he "has been evil since ancient times, and it has continued until today, with extreme changes and the material changes." The "disadvantage," "extreme" and "change" all refer to coins as children. As long as one is "discarding children," all problems will be solved. It can be seen that he does not understand the necessity and nature of the banknotes.

6.4. *Other drawbacks of currency circulation*

Ye Shi thought that there were drawbacks in the circulation of money at the time. In addition to the above, there were also a few problems. The first was the presence of a large amount of money and little risk. He thought that there was more money and less commodities than needed, leading to the tendency of devaluing money but treasuring commodities. In the past, the price of rice in the southeastern region had risen to four or 10 times more per 1,000 kilograms. At the southern tip of the border (now near Hanoi, Vietnam) and in the vast regions of the territory, the rice in the fields of Jing and Fu was "hundreds of dollars." Originally, medium-sized farmers could be self-sufficient without spending money. But later, they were as good as robbed and even bankrupted. The productivity of the countryside was destroyed and it was therefore stated, "the money and goods are in the market, and things cannot be out of the ground." The low purchasing power of money, the scarcity of supplies and the increase in prices meant that "all things were expensive and money," both in the public and private sense, was insufficient. This formed a vicious cycle of monetary phenomena where there was more money and less suffering in inflation. In fact, money was not in real shortage, but only a small amount of material was deficient. This is the reason why people said, "money has been bleaker and less prone to happen." Ye Shi put the issue of currency circulation at that time into the overall socio-economic environment. This idea is worth appreciating and the conclusion is correct.

The second was the countermeasures of the Southern Song Dynasty governments. Ye Shi believed that the use of administrative coercive measures to prevent the outflow of copper coins, the "money-forbidden prohibition" technique of destroying money and the "money-saving technique" of collecting copper and casting money were useless and had little effect. Because the former has cut off the north–south outflow and the domestic ban as a device, it cannot be said that it was not strict enough. What was the effect of the implementation of the ban? "This is a ban on suffering from incompatibility." It was said, "The prohibition of copper money cannot be stifled, but the ruler who manages Huaiyin is not afraid of stipulations. He is openly (moving) out of the world and cannot be banned." Copper money required mineral deposits for excavation and mining, but "the production of heaven and earth, the copper in the southeast, has not been restored yet." Even if there were financial managers in the era of Emperor Wu of the Han Dynasty, such as Qi Xian Shang Dong and Guo Xianyang, how could Nan Ye Daye Kong's clever arrangement of calculations be able to achieve anything? Based on this, out of prejudice, Ye Shi mistakenly believed that only "when it is discarded can the money he collected be returned, and restoring the only legal status of coins is the way out." His so-called thought of "everything is changed, things change" was a daydream.

The third issue was the issue of iron money being exchanged for copper. At that time, Song Jin confronted the government of the Southern Song Dynasty to prevent copper from flowing into the gold country, and Jiangbei adopted measures to disable copper coins and divert iron money. Jiangbei, Huai, Jingxi and Jingmen were dedicated to iron money. Northbound travelers exchanged copper coins for iron money. Jianghuai's iron money could not cross rivers, and people could not exchange money for copper in the south of the Yangtze River. "The gold and silver official associations are all noble and wealthy businessmen are hindered by financial resources," and the residents of both sides of the Huai River were in dire straits. Coupled with the crudity and evil of iron money, the phenomenon of stolen coins was rising, and the currency value had fallen. As Ye Shi said, "No merchants for Huai people to trap" and "public and private citizens suffer, people shake." As a result, "iron money is not divided between official and private, and the public does not distinguish between good and bad, and money can be used." Since illicit money was banned, the people were punished (vigilance), customs were traded and people had to choose between the law and the implementation. People resorted to the following to maintain normal social and economic life: people referred to official money as private money and refused to accept it; they accepted it as long as they got a sample of money and proof that Ru Shu (now in Anqing, Anhui Province) and Yi (now in Hunchun, Hubei Province) people only make the accepted amount; they accepted it as long as the new government cast official money; "While buying money and buying things, it was always withdrawn from three or four hundred"; or they even refused to use iron money and exchanged things directly instead. "They can claim to be self-reproducible, the city can still be worthwhile, and the village is even worse." The Southern Song Dynasty's policy of currency segregation hindered normal commodity circulation between the Lianghuai, Hubei and Beijing West Roads in the southeastern region, and affected the normality of social and economic life and the stability of people's lives. Ye Shi actively advocated amendments to relevant regulations to improve specific management methods. He believed that the South should have also allowed the iron money to cross into the river and become "copper"; that is, "If you want to mention (measures to prevent currency devaluation), you will get a fair share of justice. When you make iron money over the Jiangnan, you will also like the copper money crossing Jiangbei. There are places for exchange, and there are no two places for discarding." The specific approach was to "roughly half the copper money in Jiangnan County, or take one cent and two cents of copper, and exchange iron money directly." He believed that as long as the two Huai People understood that the iron money would cross the river, they would be converted into coins. To be valued, business travelers in Huainan would not dare scorn iron money. The exchange rate of the gold and silver official councils and other goods would be lowered. "As such, even if you use iron money, you can prolong the time without harm." Ye Shi's countermeasures were reasonable. They were conducive to the normalization of iron money by circulation and trade, and conducive to carrying out battle for copper money across the country and stabilizing the social order in the Jiangbei area. However, in addition to stopping the flow of copper coins, the purpose of the Southern Song government's implementation of iron money was to concentrate the private money and government treasures in the Jiangnan area. Like the production of banknotes, in order to "drive the world's money, the inner plots are stored in the warehouses, and are hidden away in the rich room." Therefore, Ye Shi's proposition was difficult to adopt in the imperial court and it could not become a realistic monetary policy.

7. Debates over the government-run lending

7.1. *Wang Anshi and Xining's new policies*

Wang Anshi (1021–1086), courtesy name Jiefu, also known by his literary name Banxian, was born in Linchuan District, Fuzhou City, Jiangxi Province in the Song Dynasty. Lenin hailed him as the reformer of 11th century China. In the second year of Qinli (1042), he became a successful scholar in the imperial exam and then took charge of Yin County. His achievements were as follows: He built dikes and dredged banks, thus facilitating water transportation; he loaned crops from the government to commoners who would repay with interest added, so that the old crops in the official granary could be exchanged for new ones; he set up schools and was strict with the household registration system, making it convenient for commoners. Then, he became aware of the benefits of reform and obtained the relevant information. After taking three important positions in Shuzhou, Changzhou and Kaifeng, he recognized that "the Song government were unable to deal with concerns for the state and barbarians," and realized the urgency for the reform of politics. In the third year of Jiayou, he submitted his suggestions to Emperor Renzhong of Song, including cultivating talents, reforming the legal system and rectifying institutes, which laid the foundation for the implementation of reforms in the future although they were not adopted. After Emperor Shenzhong ascended the throne, Wang Anshi took charge of Jiangning and became a Hanlin Academician, as well as Shijiang. He submitted his memorial to the emperor, in which he cited the current problems and expounded the essence of reform. In the second year of Xining (1069), he held the post of Deputy Chancellor, and in the following year, he served as Chancellor and presided over the reform. He successively enacted new laws and regulations on farmland water conservancy, green shoots, state finance and trade, the household registration system, market trade, horse breeding and land tax, which were known as Xining New Law, namely, Wang Anshi Reform. Recalled by the emperor in the seventh year, he regained the position in the following year but was recalled again in the ninth year. Afterward, he returned to Jiangning as an official under the county magistrate who administered lawsuits, and lived in Banshan Garden there. His writings included *Collected Works of Wang Anshi*.

The reform movement initiated by prominent politician Wang Anshi was a major event in the Song Dynasty and also a major event in the country. In history, he was referred to as the "New Party" because of his proposition and persistence in the reform while those opposed to the reform were called the "Old Party" headed by Sima Guang. The fierce struggle between these two factions lasted from preparations for the reform — when Wang Anshi came into power in the second year of Xining, to the death of Emperor Shenzong in the eighth year of Yuanfeng — to 10–30 years after Wang Anshi was recalled for the second time. It never stopped because of the successive deaths of Emperor Shenzong and Wang Anshi. Although the two factions were the representatives of the ruling cliques, Wang Anshi's ideas of "three fearless" spirit and "people didn't have to be afraid of social changes, follow ancestors and worry about rumors" stood in sharp contrast to the principle of "rules of the ancestors were not changeable" obeyed by Sima Guang. They had different understandings and interpretations of "the truth of righteousness, the joys and sufferings of the people, and the safety of the nation," which manifested as contradictions and struggles between reform and conservatism.

In terms of money management, Wang Anshi proposed to prevent despotic mergers and exploit nature for national prosperity. Besides, he negated the traditional concept of "advocating justice but depreciating benefit," being the first to openly declare war on orthodox ideas. Moreover, he put forth a new concept of justice and benefit, suggesting that government affairs were supposed to contribute to money management in the form of justice, making money management the priority of the administration. He advocated the principle that "based on developing production, the country could be prosperous and then people will be able to consume." He firmly believed that "as for social governance in the history, nothing but the means of money management had been able to become the public concern." He held that "financial management was the top priority." That is to say, increasing the state's fiscal revenue was the most urgent matter. In specific implementation, he "gave priority to farming issues." He thought that "as for agriculture, it was necessary to reduce burdens on farmers, prevent merger and arouse the enthusiasm of the farmers."[14] Taking Sang Hongyang as an example, he firmly believed that "those who could manage money well" could "obtain enough money for the country to spend" without adding taxes. Indeed, he fulfilled his own promise because after 10 years of reform, he expanded financial resources in terms of the state's finance. "If everything went well, money and grain from exemption of military service, official market, ferry and farmlands without owners would be no less than 10 million and could be used by the local officer (the Ministry of Revenue in feudal China) for 20 years. Then half of the revenue of *Sansi* (three departments of the state financial commis-

---

[14]Li Tao, *Continuation of History as a Mirror*, vol. 16, p. 5351.

sion) would be a surplus."[15] Besides, there would be a balance between fiscal revenue and expenditure with a surplus. Bianjing was extremely prosperous. Besides expenditures, "grain and money of the official departments from the years of Xining to Yuanfeng were also ample, and the amount of money collected by small counties was no less than 200,000."[16] The difficult situation of national finances had been reversed. From the aspect of price, the prices of rice and other silk had generally declined, and the achievements in building water conservancy projects of farmland had been remarkable. Besides, he achieved the goal of making the country richer and stronger and followed the ideals of reducing poverty and weakness that had accumulated in the Song Dynasty over the previous 100 years. The opposition party also had to recognize the actual effects in the country's financial management.

The ideology of the credit policy embodied in Wang Anshi's reforms focused on the Changping Law, namely, Green Shoots Law, enacted in September in the second year of Xining, and the Market Trade Law enacted in March in the fifth year in the capital city. The argument surrounding the government-run lending between the reform party and the conservative party, that is, the country's management of agricultural loans and commercial credits, started with different attitudes and different evaluations.

7.2. Government-run lending — Green Shoots Law[17] and Market Trade Law

In rural areas, rampant usury was not only an important cause of the bankruptcy of general farmers but also a reason that caused despots to annex customers. Due to the old system in the Song Dynasty, the Changping and Guanghui granaries were established. According to regulations, in a good

---

[15]Bi Zhongyou, *Suggestions Submitted to Menxia Officer Sima Wen.*
[16]*History of the Song Dynasty·Biography of An Tao,* vol. 30, p. 10568.
[17]Reform of the law of Changping granary turned the Changping Law into the Green Shoots Law and was also called the Pingxin Law. The cost of green shoots was different from those in July in the second year of Emperor Daizong in the Tang Dynasty when "the tax of green shoots was used as officers' salary." The cost of green shoots in *History as a Mirror Tang Dynasty Emperor Daizong* was tax which was accumulated in light of the number of *mu* (15 copper coins per *mu*), namely, the prior requisition of land tax rather than loan.

year, the county governments in each prefecture were to increase grain prices and purchase large quantities of grain to increase reserves, while in a famine year, they were to sell it at a lower price than that of the market to send a relief to the area suffering from famine. The governments were to employ people to cultivate farmlands with no owners, to provide relief to people who were old or young and could not be self-sufficient. As for the Changping Law itself, the hardships faced by farmers were not confined to the famine years alone. Every year when they faced food shortages between two harvests, they had no choice but to turn to usury. Even if relief was offered, the beneficiaries were often scoundrels of the marketplace who loafed around without a legitimate business. In addition, in the implementation process, it was inconvenient for people to buy grain which was adulterated at an extremely high price. Some officials bought grain for private use, some colluded with rich merchants and shared profits, some were "annoyed at buying and selling process" and "didn't use it for urgencies," while others diverted it for military use and "reserved it completely." In the 1130s, the government supplemented the military salary with the capital from the Changping granary, so the original function of the granary to adjust the grain price and provide relief for farmers gradually disappeared. Given its congenital deficiencies and shortcomings, the reform of Changping and Guanghui granaries became an urgent task.

Together with his practice of "loaning grain from the government to commoners who should repay with interest added" (Shao Bowen, *Record of Shao's Experience*, vol. 11), Wang drew lessons from the successful implementation of green shoots money by Li Can, an official of Shanxi, in the year of Emperor Renzong in the Song Dynasty (1425). Green shoots money referred to the means by which local people calculated the prospective output of the grain that year, borrowed it from the officials and paid the grain back after it was ripe. Therefore, he genuinely believed that the Green Shoots Law could help supply people's needs and advocated distribution instead of collection, so that people would have more savings, the price of the grain would be fair, farmers would always have farm work to do, mergers would be prevented and farmers would not lack grain when they were cultivating. Besides, the government was to select officials to instruct farmers, and build water and soil conservancy projects, so that farming would be governed well. In other words, first, it could help poor people not neglect their farm work and have crops to eat when last season's crops were almost completely consumed and the new ones were not yet ripe. Second, it could advocate distribution instead of collection, make the price of the grain fair, help people have more savings, circulate the old crops and the new ones, so that the old grain would not decay or be wasted, and it would offer convenience to both officials and commoners. Third, it could prevent usury lenders, despots and mergers from disrupting the agricultural production and promote the development of the production. On September 4, in the second year of Xining (1069), the three departments enacted the Green Shoots Law for the purpose of spreading benefits and initiating causes beneficial to people to subsidize cultivation and cut the excess to supplement the deficiency. With the crops and money of about 1,500,000 *guan* and *dan* from granaries of Changping and Guanghui, the government issued agricultural loans to help the farmers cope with famine or the shortage of grain. The specific approach was that, before the unripe season in summer and autumn, farmers who voluntarily requested loans would convert the loaned food into cash. The amount of loans would be determined according to the assets of the rural households and divided into five levels. The amount of the first level would not exceed 15 *guan*, the second would not exceed 10 *guan*, the third would not exceed 6 *guan*, the fourth would not exceed 3 *guan* and the fifth would not exceed 1.5 *guan*. If there was an excess, households at the third level could loan more. The interest was 3 or 2 points. Five households or 10 households could assemble as a group according to their wealth and those above the third level could be the leaders in charge of salt laborers. At the time of restitution, the tax was added to the amount to be paid back (in July in Summer and November in Autumn). If there was a famine, the restitution could be postponed to the next harvest. The Green Shoots Law was first introduced in Hebei, Jingdong and Huainan, each place with a special officer. Although there was no successful experience, it was implemented around the country.

At that time, someone commented on the new law that it was not bad, but its implementation "could not be as good as before, which disturbed people." People analyzed that the fast implementation speed of the new law was due to the urgent requirement of Emperor Shenzong, which violated Wang Anshi's initial intentions. Besides, the government employed people thoughtlessly so there was no suitable person available. Sima Guang and others did not cooperate with Wang Anshi and did not recommend anyone. In recent times, according to people's analysis, the key to the new law's failure was that Wang did not find a qualified candidate to implement it, and it was inevitable that it would deform and lose its original intentions during implementation. The fiercest opposition to Green Shoots Law rested in different understandings of the actual implementation process. As many prefectures and counties regarded the scattering of loans as a success, they forced people who were rich but unwilling to borrow money to borrow green shoots money in order to collect more interest, whereas they did not provide loans to impoverished commoners who were in desperate need of loans as they were afraid that those people would not be able to repay the principal and interest in the future. Some prefectures and counties handed over an integral amount of loans to several people regardless of whether they were willing or not, and instructed them to make mutual guarantees. After autumn, those people were to return both principal and interest. Even worse, they claimed principal and interest from those they did not lend to. These problems were not in the theory of green shoots money itself, but in the executors and the governance. Therefore, it was similar to the Two-Tax Law of Liu Yan in the Tang Dynasty. About 20 years later, in the sixth year of Yuanyou of Emperor Zhezong (1091), what Zhao Xijun, who was an imperial minister, said made an objective and clear judgment about the law: "In recent years, material resources were in destitution, even worse than the periods of Xining and Yuanfeng. Then we consider that the reason why the implemented Green Shoots Law failed might be that about tens of millions of *guan* of money and crops were manipulated by officers without being distributed. The old law, though not perfect, made millions upon millions in money and crops distributed among people. Despite the fact that the transaction law was perfect, without being implemented, people wouldn't obtain money and crops. Therefore, it's no surprise that the difficulties are even more severe than before. Besides, crops at a low price value buying, while crops at a high price depreciate selling and then farmers wouldn't be harmed in a good year and wouldn't have to worry about the food in a famine year. Publicly, it would enrich the granary, and individually, it would prevent mergers, which could be the best way to stabilize the country and enrich the people."[18] Although green shoots money could get interest, it focused on circulation; if the circulation of money was accelerating, it would be simple to ease the problem of valuing money and depreciating goods. The society was always stuck in the physical form of the natural economy, and it seemed like the rural areas and peasants had nothing to do with money, which was a disaster for them instead. This was incommensurable with Wang Anshi's theory of evolution. Moreover, Wang took corresponding measures, established the prohibition of money and increasing the freedom of circulation. Since the commodity currency economy had developed in the Song Dynasty, it should have been diverted and supported rather than being rejected theoretically. This relationship was of crucial importance and could have made the result completely different.

In cities, huge dealers with sufficient capitals resorted to various means in trading activities to exploit and extort ordinary residents and small- and medium-sized businessmen. On the contrary, they provided facilities for usury activities, which promoted the development of usury and the pawn industry. Based on granaries implemented by Sang Hongyang in the Western Han Dynasty, Qin Fenglu (including department of Shanxi, Gansu and Qinghai) and Wang Zhao from the Management and Strategy Department advised the government to establish a department of market affairs in the third year of Xining. According to them, "borrowing the official capital to benefit from merchants and then the income in a year wouldn't be less than 100,000–200,000 *dan*." Wei Jizong, who claimed to be "the center of the public," proposed the establishment of Market Trading Department to regain the "right to sell and buy crops" from huge dealers, suppress prices and make the government share some commercial profits to increase fiscal revenue. On March 26, in the fifth year of Xi Ning, a department of Market Transaction Officers was established in Bianjing with 1 million *guan* allocated from the inner warehouse and 0.87 million *guan* from Jingdong City, totaling 1.87 million *guan*. Later, the Jingshi Market Transaction Officer was changed to Metropolitan Market Transaction Department, which took charge of Market Transaction Officers around the country. Moreover, Market Transaction Officer

---

[18]Li Tao, *Continuation of History as a Mirror*, vol. 31, p. 11040.

departments were successively established in border areas and major cities around the country. The 12th clause in Market Transaction Law had some contents closely related to the government-run lending. First, it said, "deeds should be mortgaged with gold and silver" and "balance should be cleared." Second, businessmen could hold some posts of the supervising officer of market transaction and they could borrow official money with "real estate as the mortgage" and pay 20% interest annually. Third, people who wanted to be businessmen should declare their property, or borrow gold and silver from others as the mortgage, and five or more persons could be combined as a group. Fourth, street vendors could also borrow money from the office. The Market Transaction Officer determined "equal sharing and debt clearing" of the stores according to the amount of the property mortgaged. After the stores got the goods, they would sell them at the price with profits added within the limited selling period of 6 months or 1 year. When repaying the selling debt, the stores must pay 10% interest for half a year and 20% for 1 year, and overdue debt must be repaid with 2% penalty added every month. During the implementation process, the interest was not just from buying and selling products but also from items of emergency, burial and mortgages of silver tax, and wheat and rice, with the range of goods in operation greatly exceeding the prescribed limit. From the fifth year to the seventh year of Xining, the interest earned by Market Transaction Officer was more than 1,043,030 and the market's profits were nearly 98,000. For one thing, it restricted the speculative activities of huge dealers to a certain extent, controlled commodity prices and was conducive to commercial prosperity. For another, it not only made the official government obtain more interest but also greatly increased the income from commercial taxes, which greatly boosted the state finance. The first round of the debate between the reformists and the conservatives focused on the Green Shoots Law. There were three major issues: the first was whether government-run lending should levy interest or not, and if interest were to be levied, what the standard was. The second was about scattered distribution and forcible apportionment. The third was whether the Green Shoots Law could replace the Changping Law, that is, whether monetary credit could replace physical credit. The second round of arguments is omitted here.

7.3. The dispute over interest

The dispute over interest was whether green shoots money from government-run lending — it could be regarded as government-issued agricultural loans to assist farmers — should be levied with interest or not, and if the interest was to be levied, what was the standard. The reformists and the conservatives were greatly divided over green shoots money.

Han Qi, the main force of conservatives, criticized that the green seedling law as "the skill of the disabled people," and stated that the officials "jealous of the rich people took more (interest) and less." This was one step between 50 steps. As a result, two points of interest were abolished. Ouyang Xiu appeared to be more cunning and ingenious. He made a difficult suggestion: "cover two points of interest, think that we cannot take more from the people, not much of the money." The meaning of the words cannot be understood.

In the *Answer to Zeng Public Book*, Wang Anshi responded forcefully to all the censure, pointing out, "if two points are less than one point, one is less than the disadvantage and loan, and the loan is not the same. However, if he does not relate to it, he will be divided into two parts, and that is why he cannot have a good future. If we cannot succeed, we will not benefit from politics. However, there are officials' salaries, chariots, droughts, and the consumption of rat finches, but it is necessary to wait for the lack of famine and to be straight with it, but there are no two points; also in Changping, how can it be easy?" This refutation not only respects the reality of the economic life of the objective society but also meets the requirements of the objective law of the credit.

Of course, the interest rate of the green seedling money is only two points on the surface, that is, half a year's two-cent interest rate. The whole year is four points, which is a 40% interest rate. In this regard, Wang Anshi said, "we all think of the people, and the public does not benefit from it." This is a kind of decoration to conceal the real purpose of expanding financial resources and increasing revenue. In addition, some malpractices had also taken place in the implementation. For example, "as a result of the work, the people who do the job are able to borrow more, not to the people's wishes, but the people do not make the best of it, so they suffer, and don't benefit." There is no doubt about this. First, we can not only govern our country without giving favors and receiving favors but also the way for the state to save money can be only through official lending. It is the only possibility by which the state does not increase its burden and starts lending and neither giving any favors to the common people nor giving relief, nor free gifts or alms.

Second, in order to continue to carry out the official business, it was necessary to use interest income to compensate for the official expenses of the government, such as salaries, freight, transportation and other expenses, and to prevent the arrears or losses caused by disaster, without interest of less than two points. This understanding shows that Wang Anshi had grasped the essential characteristics of credit, not only to collect interest but also to repay principal and interest at maturity. Otherwise, it would have been difficult to continue, and it was impossible to run it over repeatedly.

Third, the sacred scriptures of green seedling money were not for public benefit, but to attack them by drawing profits and stripping them of wealth. Wang Anshi thought, "the officials of the Liquan government of the Zhou Dynasty, the people who borrow money from the government can earn twenty to five, while the 'wealth of state' should be used. The new law of Changping is pre-given to the green money. (Take interest) no more than three points .... It's only two points. That is, unlawfully for the engraving. It is not much more than that of Zhou Li and the loan people, and the price is too high for the pre-paid price to meet two points, which is less than that of Zhou Li. In the Yuan Dynasty, 'we need to save money and reduce the current price.' In addition, the 'Zhou Li' state affairs money is provided with the interest of the officials of the Quan Fu, and the present Changping does not lead to the three divisions." That is to say, the interest income of green seedling money was all used in the two aspects of administrative management expenses and relief for the people. The former reduced the state financial expenditure, realized the self-care of the funds and no longer increased the burden of the state; the latter improved the ability of disaster prevention and resistance, improved the living environment, increased the agricultural output and raised the income of the peasants. It was only necessary to earmark the funds, which was necessary for Wang Anshi. Therefore, in the "farmland water conservancy treaty," which was promulgated two months later by the law of

Qinghai Province, it was clearly stated that "reclaimed waste fields should be reclaimed, water conservancy, construction of water conservancy, construction of embankment, repairing polder, etc., should be done. Industrial service is great, civil power cannot be given, and households can borrow in Changping Guanghui barn." Since these two expenditures belonged to the normal expenditure items of green shoots and money, they were not to be included in the category of "state owned wealth." Therefore, in Wang Anshi's view, the thought that "the public does not benefit from their entry" is tenable.

Fourth, in the social and economic life of the Song Dynasty, the usual interest rate before the reform had been between 100% to 200%, so once the farmers fell into usury, they would lose their homes and scatter. During the reign of Emperor Zhen Zong (998–1022), Kou Zhun said in his play, "the people (Yong Xingjun) are rich, who have more money than the poor, and take the rest of their interests. Sun Fu, a rich man in Kaifeng, is a great master of Beijing. He pays special attention to money and interest, pays attention to his interests, and appraised their products and their women." The rampant usury activities, ranging from villages to cities, from remote counties to the best places, left their footprints everywhere. In this regard, the original pros and cons written by Ouyang Xiu in 1040 were also revealed: "the family of agriculture is not rich but has a livestock house, with enough for death and burial rites of the spring and autumn shrine and the marriage. Their income is divided into two categories: interest and income. As he works in the field at the end of the twilight, he feeds on it, and then he raises it again. Therefore, in winter and spring, it means that the wheat is compensated, while in summer, the wheat is in full use. In the 7 years of Xingguo (982), in June, Song Taizong, who had made money for the rich, could not double it. It can be seen that interest rate is 100% or even higher, which is a very common social phenomenon. Although the interest rate of the green money is not low, it is much lower than that of the private usury at that time. Therefore, the majority of the producers have greatly reduced the burden and pain of high profit exploitation. It ensures the smooth progress of simple reproduction. In a sense, it is sure that the workers' enthusiasm for birth and production is called, and the law of the green seedlings is rapidly popularized." As Wang Anshi said in *A Memorial on Five Things to Zhao Xu*,

Shenzong of the Song Dynasty, "the poor in the past raise interest to the rich and the poor today raise interest to the officials. When officials are thin and their interests are saved, they are saved. The law has been carried out rapidly with the support of the vast majority of the workers, and the opposition's accusations are not unjustifiable. They only lack theoretical basis and ignore the history and reality, but only seize the problems in the implementation process as their attacks on the law of the green seedlings. The law of the green seedlings stipulates that 'do not suppress people'. It seems that the execution has gone the same way, not only suppressing distribution, but also forcing interest." The officials, Bao Zheng and the chief of the guard were guilty of cheating and blackmail. In 1071, Sima Guang responded, "(Shaanxi) A *dou* of aged rice loaned to the poor would be paid back by 1.87 *dou* of wheat or 3 *dou* of millet, with the interest rate at roughly 100%." Chao said, "Yuan Shou three years (1100), Ying Zhao, also said, 'fame is two points of interest, and actually eight points of interest.'" What these two people said is not necessarily incompatible with the facts, and they are not exactly incorrect. As Su Zhe revealed, "the officials are always cheating. I am afraid that it is also a chronic disease which cannot be cured in ancient China. I am afraid Jae Hee is also to blame. Suppressing annexation is actually helping annexation. It is natural for the poor to be rich and secure."

7.4. *The dispute between the scattered and the suppressed*

According to the regulations of the green seedling law, the threat of annexation was a guarantee with the poor households. This policy had aroused strong reactions from the opposition. Bi Zhongyou criticized in the "green seedling debate" that "the family is self-sufficient, with no false official money, but strong and it makes interest." The badge of "foolish people" was actually peeling off; the name was Huimin, and it was really beneficial. In *On the Three Pests of the Green Miao*, Fan Zhen made a full statement in the interest of the family of the strong and powerful: "ten rich families are worth two or three. It is not open to the benefit of the family, but is responsible for holding down the household, while the next person escapes to the rich. It is the promotion of the rich to the poor." Similarly, in the memorials of the *Invitation to the Qing*

Dynasty, Han Qi explained the opinion of the opposition in a concise and systematic way. "There is a family in the country, but a family that has never been annexed." "Today, we have to borrow more money. For every 1,000 loans, 1,300 will be paid by the government. It is absolutely against the idea of annexation, which is not acceptable to the people. Also, the country must have materials for people to use, and although the cloud is not passing, the owner has the power of owning materials, but is not willing to please. The officials of the house cannot be sent to the family. Is it not a bad charge for the head in order to compensate for it?"

In their eyes, there were many problems in the collection and release of the official farm loans, which cannot be established. No matter whether the loan was of high value or not, whether it was needed or not, it would be distributed equally. The upper class and other big households were originally the families of the merger, but they had since been forced to borrow the green money and pay the interest, which was "suppressing mergers and wasting." Moreover, these rich households had to be the leaders of the customers. They were not willing to guarantee them, but they would not be able to pay the rest of the poor households. In this way, the rich would become poor. "I am afraid that there are no more than 10 years of rich people."

The purpose of Wang Anshi's implementation of the law of the green seedlings was to use the method of scattered table and restrain the potential of the merger, so as to realize the structural adjustment of the different interests within the ruling group, and to realize the inclination of the government representative of the state to redistribute it. Therefore, the loan object designed by Wang Anshi was not only for the poor but also for the rich. Moreover, three and more rich households were not equal to the family of strong and powerful. They "also have a lack of debt. Are they all the families of the annexation? Because in the year of the disaster, the farmer and the small and medium landlords were swallowed up by the annexed home, while the green money was in the 'bad year'." It played a role in easing land concentration and speeding up poverty and bankruptcy. Unfortunately, under fierce attack from the opposition, Song Shenzong, originally wavering, no longer supported the anti-distribution form, and Wang Anshi was unable to insist, and the purpose of restraining the merger could not be realized.

The official battalion loan was issued by the mortgage loan, which was made up of gold and silver goods, or the credit loan, which was guaranteed by the person who had the ability to repay the principal and interest. At that time, only three or more rich families had this kind of capacity, so the law made corresponding regulations to prevent government officials from eating down the accounts, so as to ensure that the blue and green money began to go around and develop continuously; otherwise, it would have been possible to abandon the money and destroy it. Therefore, it was in line with the requirements of the credit law that the rich and the poor mix together to form a guarantee.

7.5. The dispute between the green shoots and Changping

Wang Anshi replaced regular warehouses with green money, which was to take the place of money loans instead of physical loans, replaced private high-interest loan with low profit and credit of official camp, and replaced relief loan with productive loans. The use of money to replace grain relief was the key.

In Wang Anshi's view, relief was only a temporary expedient, not a long-term policy because "with limited food for millions of people, there is not a single hundred of them." Only by restoring and developing production, could they base themselves on the principle of self-rescue. In particular, "the people therefore support the country, and have not heard of the state's support for the people." In the agricultural society, the way out for the common people to feed the country was to develop the agricultural production, and the state was based on agriculture and the farmers relied on the agricultural production to find a fundamental way out. This was in line with the state's long-term policy and the basic requirements of the farmers. Based on the seasonality of agricultural production, Wang Anshi borrowed money from government management credit to solve the urgent need for production, so that the people were free from the plunder of usury, developed agricultural production and increased financial revenue. He aimed to implement the Changping Law to create more food, give out the chaff and provide numerous people a limited amount of food. "There are not one hundred of them who live, but the dead, with their white bones have been wild." "Fang Tian Tian San is home, especially when the money is not available."

The division of the three also pointed out that "the old law is in the present new law, but it is not possible to save extensively in the old law, and to suppress the annexation and relieve the poor." The new law was not a total negation of the old law, but a reform and improvement on the basis of the original law. Under the conditions of regular warehouse, famine and drought still could not save the people from fire and water, and could not guarantee safety to the poor. Under the old mode of production, people did not need money, and it was difficult to see money. Wang Anshi's reform changed this situation.

However, Wang Anshi maintained the landlord system and recognized the existence of the rich and poor. He was not generally opposed to making a family rich, but opposed "the annexer, the powerful man of the hero, his argument enough to move the scholar and doctor," and opposed the "Yuan traitor, the dancer to the people," "the school and the interests" and the "rich surname officials, and the field family." That is, he opposed the landlords who were strong and rich, who had the right to be powerful and unrestrained. They intervened in the government, shaking their decisions and positions, and threatening the stability of the government. They used government decrees, bullied, profited, exploited, seized the profits and infringed on the small landlords and the poor peasants. He advocated that through the decree system, economic means would be properly restrained and restricted for the powerful. In the category of commodity money economy, as a duty of the government, he encouraged, "win and I will take it, and let it go to the camp." Under the guidance of this kind of thought, the green seedling law was introduced, and its outstanding feature was borrowing money from things.

The law of Changping was metered out and measured with money. The implementation of the Changping Law had been going on for thousands of years, and the rule of the young people had been attacked by opposition representative Sima Guang. Especially on the issue of money lending, he yelled, "the husband and the force, the people are born; the grain and silk are being used; people can be ploughed and mulled. As for the money, the county magistrate is casting, and the people should not do it privately as well. Since the new law has not been adopted, the money of the people has been reduced. It is the people who use the ancient method. Each is taken by it. And the end of the Tang Dynasty is the beginning of the tax money." Therefore, Bai Juyi mocked, "private money buys free stove, flat land without Copper." "There is nothing for the people to blame. Today, there is no rule of law. No one asks the people of the marketplace, from the poor to the rich, from the old to the young. The goods are heavy and the profits are low. The year is hungry, but the valley is not very expensive, and the people are more tired."

It was the inevitable development of the form of credit to take the place of money borrowing and lending. It was a progress rather than a retrogression, which was unacceptable and not tolerated by Sima Guang. The green seedling law had changed the old way of physical loans between the rich and the poor, and the rich had no "self-spoiling" ideas, and Sima Guang could not tolerate it. "The rich often lend money to the poor, but the poor often resort to loans to enrich the people. Though they are unhappy, they still share with each other in order to protect their health. Now the county magistrate is paying his own money (in order to run the green seedling money). After 10 years of fear, the rich have no foundation. Under the condition of the development of commodity currency exchange, it is bound to impact the basic industry of natural economy — agriculture. In the long run, the natural economy will be eroded and disintegrated by commodity economy and currency exchange." In this regard, Sima Guang had a keen sense of vigilance, so he raised Bai Juyi as a talisman. In fact, commodity exchange by means of money, as well as money lending and taxation, did not begin until the end of Tang Dynasty. According to Sima Guang, the only way to return to the original form of barter was to take a completely closed, self-sufficient natural economic road. This could only be a dream of a "mountain forest wild man." The development of commodity currency exchange could not be stopped by any individual or group. It would never allow any force to maintain the stability of the natural economy by use of power, so that people were forced to change to maintain a "constant."

Green seedling money was conducive to speeding up the circulation of money to promote the acceleration of commodity circulation and logistics, and the phenomenon that the weight of money was lighter than before.

What Shen Kuo said was confirmed. In the rural areas where the natural economy was the main body, the new force of the commodity economy was tenacious, and the resistance to it stubbornly continued. It was also reflected in the ruling group. It was the trend of trends, or the force of the customary forces, and the opposition was formed. Sima Guang strongly opposed the key to the green shoots law. He opposed moneylending and stubbornly maintained physical loans. Zhu Xi once mentioned the true meaning of the new reforms: "green seedlings, their original intention of legislation is not bad. But it also gives it gold instead. The valley, which is located in the county rather than the township is also not for a gentleman who is a township official, and it is not a loyal heart to amass a disease. Wang Anshi's new law changes physical borrowing and lending to moneylending, and is not rooted in the country but in the county town, relying on the local gentry tyrants and officials, only looking at the rich and strong of the country, without taking into account the interests of the gentry, and naturally suffering the stubbornness and defamation of the representatives of the old and wild forces of the country and the country. I think Lu You has been behind Sima Guang for 120 years." He has refuted his argument that wealth does not exist in the people. In Lu's *Afterword of Historical Reflection*, he said, "Mr. Sima, the Prime Minister, said: 'heaven and earth are born, of wealth and goods, there is this number, not owned by the people but by the official.' 'It says the argument, the reason, is not good. Since ancient times, goods were not owned by the people but not by the officials either. Or by the power minister, or by those in close proximity, or by the strong general, or by mergers, or by the old release. When the time is up, then the Treasury is exhausted, and the people are poor.' 'Why do we not manage the world? Why do we not have it?' This is the same as what Wang Anshi did. Wang Anshi's 'restraining annexation and saving the poor and weak' is really for the wealth and strength of the country, the accumulation of financial resources for the Song court, the wealth of the Treasury, the great industry, as if it should not be reproached or exclaimed, but the interests of the powerful ministers, the family, the strong vassal, and the temple of the Lao Zi is violated, and naturally they will oppose and have a problem."

Liang Qichao wrote high praise for the Wang Jinggong book in 1908. He praised Wang Anshi, saying, "if he is seeking perfection in the three generations, he will be enough to do so." Fully affirming Wang Anshi's practice of administering the country according to law and attaching importance to talents, Liang thought that his financial thought was consistent with the principles of modern economics and finance. His "green seedling law" was quite similar to the government-run bank, the Jinggong Huimin administration. "However, the interest of a bank in its efforts to destroy the annexation is minimal, and the nature of banking is to be run by the private sector rather than the government. The Chinese know that financial institutions are the lifeblood of the national economy. This is the highest honor, unparalleled." When discussing the law of the city, Liang said, "the market is pragmatic, and the nature of a bank is as well." He said that the law was like an official agricultural bank, and the city was like a commercial bank. "Eight hundred years ago, Wang Anshi knew that the bank was the most important organ for the national economy. However, the city easy law is not feasible." Liang thought it was because, first, the bank should not be run by the government; second, "the government and officials are caging the world goods and no regular people dared compete with the competition principle; third, in the running of the country, the state is the only annexer and it is anti-Yan, and the people are haggard and unable to resist." Liang's opinions might as well be biased. But, if the market economy needed to be set up, it was not necessary for Wang Anshi to take a negative or skeptical view of the opposition of Sima Guang or to betray him on this issue. In fact, his methods were a deviation from the intended direction, and cost him the loss of self and censure in history.

8. Monetary theories during the early Southern Song Dynasty

The Southern Song Dynasty was an era of great change due to currency circulation. The circulation of banknotes was gradually pushed from Sichuan in the Northern Song Dynasty to the whole country. In terms of a money system, the Southern Song Dynasty was no longer mainly using copper coins, but mainly using iron money. The use of silver was more extensive, and it had been widely used in many aspects, such as currency tax, bulk trading, gift, payment, rewards and purchase of rice. The withdrawal of banknotes slowed down and accelerated price changes.

In terms of money thought, the heated extent of the debate was unprecedented. The focus of the debate was mainly on the currency problems in the economic life of the time, especially in the Southern Song Dynasty, and the devaluation of paper currency became the focus of attention. Few people expressed their opinions in basic theoretical research, and even if they expressed their opinions, there is very little lasting evidence of it. People's attention was focused on finding effective ways to cope with the expansion of paper money and the outflow of coins. So, the idea of management called for the emergence of the art.

8.1. *A discussion of Guanzi in the sixth year of Shaoxing*

In 1131, Zhao Gou, Emperor Song Gaozong, stationed troops in Wuzhou and raised military pay and provisions in the way of *ruzhong*. He ordered the merchants to use *jianqian guanzi*, which could be used for a reduction of the price in their purchasing. Later, it was deflated and the government lost much of its credit, which, in consequence, led to a debate on the issuing of *jiaozi*. In the end, the proposal on the issuing of *jiaozi* was abolished.

Li Xin's biography of "Jian Yan recorded in annual record" mentioned this debate. There were three anonymous speakers quoted in the biography, who might have been admonished officers.

One of the people, from the *jiaozi*, Sichuan, mentioned the exchange of money, thought to be public or private, not belonging the dissenters, but the non-officials, with there being no suspect. "So if you want to make a successful issue, you have to 'see money on the pile of the shilling, the day of exercise, to the person who asks money, not to be paid, to pay immediately, but for a long time.' On the contrary, 'it or pile money is not enough, it has been piled up instead of used, or run in the private sector, and it is not allowed to go to the official library, or to go all the way, but not to fill it up'." Nanguan library was a normal return channel for banknote circulation, and it was also a guarantee for the government to trust the people. If the government only put money into circulation and did not make withdrawals, it would naturally keep paper money in circulation, and the people would not dare to believe in paper money. "If the legislation is forbidden, we cannot win." In the face of market rules, executive power was dwarfed and weak.

The other two anonymous people also believed that if there was no cash preparation, it would have been impossible for them to make more contributions. For the time, people commented on their sons, with there being four advantages, one harmful reason and one bad reason. Because "the number of children is too many, people must know that there is no such thing in the government." Although there was a vast amount of money, it could not be given, but the method of the *Jiaozi* was bad. Although Li Xin cited Sichuan *jiaozi* as an example, he pointed out that he had loaned the reserve money to Shaanxi for purchase, or because the official had not accepted the bill. After 30 years of effort in sorting it out, it began to resume traffic. In later years, because of "dealing with army needs, the number of cases is more than before but the parties are worried about their bad law." It seemed that a little negligence was also considered unacceptable. In the discourse, we feel the anxiety of the people of that time. In issuing banknotes, it was difficult to control the amount of issuance, regardless of whether there were officials or not. This was only one aspect of the problem, and the worst one. Governments only issued, and did not consider recycling. There was the issue of misappropriation, with officials not receiving money and paper money not being cashed, causing credit loss, which was proved by history. Li Xin thought that "the operation of financial management" was not necessary. If he really issued the *jiaozi*, it made hundreds of things expensive and the military support was insufficient. So how would it be done? He still advocated limited circulation, with only hundreds of thousands of ways to facilitate the merchants, aid provincial transportation and ensure the intention of enacting Guan Zi. That is, to meet the financial deficit and cope with the supply issues of border, they gradually developed the necessary means.

There were three anonymous opponents against the use of *qianyin* in Zhejiang Province. They put up five reasons. He pointed out that money was available but not for the military and the people, and the road was still available, but not at the end of the evening. Although the *jiaozi* and money were used, there was not enough of it. The military and the people had to share the food and manage daily life in the city. "The thing is heavy, the money is light, and its time is long." This lesson is beneficial to us even today.

Zhao Pei said, "officials have no capital, fear that the people do not believe it, their inconveniences." "At the beginning of the law, people will have doubts, and if they fail to do so, they will have disputes. If there is a reduction, it is prohibited. It is necessary to pause. Trading in the market must be private, and the price will be straight if the money is paid. The price will be doubled if the price is paid. Today, we spend thousands of dollars on paper, but we are tired of it. A piece of paper cannot be split, thousands of money cannot be used. Day after day, materials have weight and are light. The money is hidden in private, is scarce in official life. Civil and private usage is universal. There is no falsehood in the public. If we strictly enforce the prohibition, we can punish the person who takes the law."

Everyone mentioned the five inconveniences of paper money. They did not speak in opposition to the exercise of paper money, but refused to use it. The attitude was clear. So, according to them, first, it was not convenient for the army and the people, or even illegal activities, and was also bad for merchants. The second was that it was inconvenient to find zero or an agreeable point of origin and this was purely technical. This did not interfere with the grand purpose, nor could it be solved naturally. In particular, when the state was able to meet the military needs and make up for the financial deficit, the civilian and military requirements were not considered. The third was the rise in prices, which led to speculation. Fourth, it was impossible to get money out of the bank. The fifth was the theft of money. These problems were not necessarily caused by the paper money itself, but rather the mishandling or mismanagement of it, and the lack of understanding, was what inevitably led to catastrophe, making it difficult to change and adding to the confusion.

Hu Jiaoxiu also went to Chen Li. He thought that he had a great deal of money. For a long time, he said, "the money is divided into two grades, and the city has two prices." *Jiaozi* was more expensive, and it required hundreds of papers on a single day. For a long time, when money was in the home, merchants could not do anything. There was no point repenting later. Li Gangyi objected to this.

Li Gang (1083–1140) was from Shaowu of Fujian Province. He was against peaceful agreement with the Jin tribe. As a result, he was demoted. His works include the *Complete Works of Li Gang*.

On Jiangxi, Li Gang appeased the system of "making friends with the right people," and thought that "the law of making friends is beneficial to

Sichuan, while doing harm to others is harmful." There were two reasons: One was that the natural environment of paper currency was different. The Sichuan mountain road was dangerous, and iron money was heavy, so it was difficult to make it easily. "Now the southeast road is convenient and the copper money is light. If you want to make it convenient for the people, you will not have to wait for your son to deliver the money." If the iron money was compared with the copper money, one could not deny what Li Gang was talking about; however, if it was unable to solve the long-term problems of money shortage and the increasing status of silver money, it could not be doubted that the resonance of copper money was the echo of "the difficult way of the hundred kings." The second was that the circulation of paper money was prepared for different means. In "Sichuan" at that time, "the people who managed to put it properly, often pre-piled a 100,000 dollars, and used the right of 3 million passes, both public and private, and the circulation was unimpeded. In recent years, no money has been piled up, its law has been harmful.... There must be millions of piles of money or an embarrassment of riches for the household, in the Bank of *Jiaozi*. The good people break through (the loss), and sell the *yuan* (the original price) 10 for two or three; the annexed house stops the price rise and enjoys the thick profits." Li Gang stressed the need for preparation for the issue, but confirmed that the reserve would only be 1/3. He did not mention the dangers of preparation, and the fact that no guarantee was issued, the amount of circulation was difficult to control and the management was strictly controlled. How could anyone not worry? And how could it be supported? This was the opinion of Li Gang and many others.

Against the opposition of most people, Shaoxing's 6 years of issue and delivery in Southeast China were shelved.

8.2. *Zhao Kai and Wang Zhiwang on the management of currency*

(1) *Zhao Kai's discussion on the use of money*
Zhao Kai (1066–1141), style name Ying Xiang, was a Puzhou resident (now Tongliang County of Sichuan Province). He was famous for his financial talents. Though in a disharmonious relationship with his

superior, he was later promoted and got his name recorded in the *History of Song Dynasty*.

He insisted that "the source of wealth should be unified" and held the opinion that the divided handling of financial affairs would lead to much trouble.

For banknotes, he advocated that "mulberry is more than light, and money must be used to collect it." "We should make a big fuss about the word 'collect,' that is to say, we should grasp the withdrawal of note money and ensure the smooth circulation of banknotes." The main measures he took were as follows: First, in Qinzhou (the present Gansu Tianshui), he set up money to attract business, casting copper money and expanding circulation of cash in the state. The second was the official selling or donation of silver, listening to the people with money or copper money, increasing the cage channel, reducing the circulation of paper money and increasing the government circulation preparation. The third was "the equal treatment of the expenditure of both common people and the official spending." The fourth was that there should be a firm control of the spending of common people in their daily activities. This method not only conformed to the circulation of paper currency but was also convenient to carry, and was convenient for large payments. It was convenient for the holder's interests. Therefore, his plan was put into action, the law was circulated and the people thought that it would be done as planned.

Zhao Kai had a clear understanding of the nature of banknotes, and was good at grasping and handling complex matters skillfully. One time, he seized 300,000 in counterfeit money, and fifty people were suspected of being thieves, and Zhang Jun was supposed to be executed by the Senate. Zhao Kai said, "The monarch is mistaken. It is true to make an imprint. His disciples make three hundred thousand *yuan* a day, and fifty people die." Indeed, as Zhao Kai said, as long as the counterfeit bill was stamped with an official seal, it would be considered a real note. The true and false lay in whether it was recognized by the government, whether it was a compulsory issuing by the government and whether or not there was no official seal. If people who make counterfeit money make use of their skills to create money for the government, they can also avoid death penalties and kill two birds with one stone. Zhang Jun adopted Zhao Kai's advice, and increased the circulation of *chuanyin* from a little over

2.5 million to more than 41.9 million. "People are not tired of the increase, the price is not reducing" indicated that the circulation was smooth and normal, with the issuance of enough money to meet the needs of circulation. Zhao Kai did not think that the money could be issued unrestrictedly and completely in accordance with the wishes of the provincial capital. The historical intercourse he made before his death was that "if we do not recover, Shu will be very sleepy, and I will be the evil leader." It meant that he had to increase the amount of money when he increased military spending, though it was out of nothing. He could only postpone the urgency of the matter and try to return to normal after that. Otherwise, Zhao Kai would be the chief culprit if a disaster unfolded. His brief entrustment indicated that the people had an understanding and deep grasp of the essential characteristics of paper money. The ancients were not ignorant of the wisdom of the present, but conducted bold practical activities and had a profound understanding of things.

(2) *The theory of Wang's view on using things as criterion*
Wang Zhi Wang (1103–1170), style name Zhan Shu, a native of Gucheng, Xiangyang, lived in Taizhou. In 1138, he was appointed as a young official and later promoted to different posts.

"In order to maintain the stability of the currency value and the normal circulation, we must pay attention to the circulation preparation. In addition to the iron money, there must be a large amount of materials, such as salt and wine, etc., as well as the expansion of the circulation and the circulation channel, and the relative increase in the demand for the currency." As was recorded in *Major Events since Jianyan*, in 1161, "there was more than 1.2 million *jiaozi* in Sichuan. Now there was more than 41.7 million *jiaozi*. There were also a couple of scattered *jiaozi* among common people. So there was not much disorder in the world."

In this regard, the material guarantee, the common needs of urban and rural people, and goods that can be preserved for a long time, such as salt and wine, warranted the realization of the purchasing power of banknotes. Along with the credibility of banknotes, the currency was stable. The key was material guarantee. Otherwise, it was unbelievable. This was a pioneering work, which had not been thought of by predecessors and had been put into practice. It shows that the preparation of materials for distribution was not carried out first by Sun Zhongshan or the Chinese Communists in modern times. It was already done in the early Southern Song Dynasty in China 800 years ago. It was also strange news at that time, leading to the evolution of world currency for centuries.

There was a demand for expanded circulation and increase of banknotes. The book also records, "The Qianyin of Sichuan are convenient to carry about and to circulate. In the future, it would also be used in Shaanxi. We would implore the king to permit the use of *qianyin* in Shaanxi in the event of conquering that area." Money had a good reputation. Wang's confidence would expand its circulation area and extend its circulation from Sichuan to Shaanxi. This was not a dream. The actual practice proved that as long as the currency value was guaranteed, it would have strong vitality, facilitate the army and the people, expand circulation and achieve the expected effect. From Wang's practical activities, we can get a sense of the pioneering ideas, not bound by the rules of the old, with careful observation and experience of life, in practice, and the courage to forge ahead. It shows that the ancients had a deep understanding of the relationship between commodity circulation and currency circulation. There was a lack of in-depth and systematic rise to complete rational knowledge, which was mostly scattered and intuitive cognition.

Because of his loyalty to the court, Wang was extremely helpless. Although he did not want to be completely passive, he hoped to be ready in advance, but also worried about the leakage of news, the roaming of the people and the credit crisis of the money. Therefore, he made a request, "the accumulation of the present official library should be dispersed, and if added, it must be carried out as news. Begging for a visit, I would like to give a brief account of the number of payments. In order to make it look at the discretionary matter, or 3.5 million, or hundreds of thousands of road, make the addition of the race, not to the number of people to know, enough to give it, and do not need to increase as the aim. When it comes to attracting more money, the price will be lost. If the army fears that it will be folded, it will invite more silver silo, which will temporarily obstruct the dispatch. And the money is not printed, but it cannot be repaid, and it is very light and harmful to the number of people in the world." He worried that the unprepared issue of arbitrary distribution would cause the people to be restless and would shake the field of money, leading to market unrest and great social problems even if the damage was small. We can understand his painstaking, astute sense of responsibility, and his understanding of banknotes was far beyond our imagination and the cognition of the ancients.

8.3. Theories on paper money during the reign of Emperor Xiaozong

(1) *Emperor Xiaozong on the stable money administration*
Zhao Shen (1127–1194), Xiaozong of the Song Dynasty, ascended the throne in 1162. As the second emperor of the Southern Song Dynasty, he paid much attention to "money and grain matters." He professed to "be quite restless for almost ten years in consideration of monetary matters." In order to implement a more stable currency policy, various measures were taken to ensure a relatively stable currency.

Emperor Xiaozong paid attention to financial management, and he held that "officials of present day have a Western Jin Dynasty style, looking down upon financial affairs. They are oblivious to the fact that ancient classics and sages all stressed financial management." He also thought that a king should not be greedy. This provided a rather sound theoretical basis for his currency management.

He did not advocate multiple prints. Chun Xi said, "if you use a child, you will have less and more weight." It was a very difficult lesson for the monarch to learn.

What is worth noting is that he put into practice what he knew. First, he did not deny that money was made to make up the shortage of currency. In the 10th year of Chun Xi, he said, "raising troops costs money, and the country uses tens of thousands of troops to raise troops." In the 12th year, he said, "the number of meetings is not enough. If he saves troops, he must receive the meeting." He realized, "if I want to spend all, I will end up killing the people." In his view, issuing banknotes was only an expedient measure and was by no means a policy of long-term stability. The second is his idea of preparing for a rainy day. In the 3 years (1167) of the emperor's pilgrimage, the chronicle of events was as follows: In the first year of the Long Xing (1163), there was much currency for circulation, and he had more than 2 years of gold and silver to receive it. Therefore, Zhao Xiong said, "Shen's concern is far-reaching, and no printing is added. It is hard for the people to be hard and valuable." Song Xiaozong's feared being flattered by his inherent courtiers, and his careful intentions also came to light. And Wu Yong recorded in *Collections of Helin* that "Emperor Xiaozong admonished his officials that 'too much currency in circulation would end in a devaluation of money'." The third is that he advocated the issuance of paper money. He said, "the paper money is feasible at the place, but it must be paid for." The fourth is the use of silver in the money recycling paper. Chen Liangyou mentioned the disadvantages of his meeting. He wanted to donate money to help the people. He said, "What is the use of my wealth?" If you send your gold in the Treasury, you will receive tens of thousands of dollars. According to the book, Chun Xi spent one million and two in silver in 2 years, and accepted two million and two in silver in 3 years.

Song Xiaozong's paper currency thought, countermeasures and actual effect became the norm of ancient Chinese rulers in discussing paper currency, managing currency and coping with currency depreciation. Because of its special position, it became a good phrase for later generations.

(2) *Yang Guanqing's discussion on the rescue of the paper money*
Yang Guanqing (1139–?) was from Jiangling (now Hubei).

He mentioned the issue of paper money in "the theory of heavy money." The theoretical basis for saving the paper money was in the fact that "the weight of things depends on me" and "the right of weight is not in my name." He thought, "things have no weight, and things and things can be light and heavy." "The owner of the object of the object is also the right holder. Therefore, the weight does not depend on the material, and the weight of the matter has to follow me. Qi Zhijun and the Lord of Han hold the right of things, so they want to be heavier and heavier, lighter and lighter. It is foolish to know what is wrong and what is right. In view of its meaning, I, in opposition to things, refer to emperors, monarchs, and monarch monarchs; things not only refer to the goods of the department stores, but also of the goods of money, the high price of prices, the size of the purchasing power of money, the idea of one of the emperors, a word, and a decision, depending on the size of power." This is the entire statement on the name of state. He thought that the money was not enough. "Iron is of quality and easy to be damaged. It cannot be hidden for a long time." "It is the copper people who are expensive; the iron people are cheap, so the iron and paper trees of Shu are parallel without any disadvantages. The bronze of this day is being hidden by the rich family of Jali, and they will not use their ears lightly. If it means that the book is empty, its disadvantages are also unspeakable. In the case of Kuang Fu, there are many kinds of books that are endless. The loss of the folk is only expensive for copper coins. Why do I suffer from the fact that I am so cheap? It is true that the relationship between the copper coins and the paper money is explained by the fact that the copper coins are real, and the money of the Broussonetia is empty. Copper coins are real, so there are no disadvantages. They will be collected by wealthy families. The Broussonetia is parallel, the broussonnet is empty, the iron money is similar, but Yang does not make a positive explanation. The writer pushes and derivates the iron, and can't compare with the expensive copper coin, and no one will collect it, so it won't be tired. In Sichuan, it is possible to achieve the parallel situation of iron and paper mills, but not the end result of copper shortage. Yang Guanqing's idea is not wrong."

Yang Guanqing agreed that there is no view to the southeast. However, it is thought that Sichuan is different from the Southeast China. It was not suitable for Southeast China. Because the method of saving the harm was implemented in Shu, there is no net exhausted income in the southeast, and two were incomplete. One was the income of tax, tea and wine, and the liang of the city. The second was that "cheap is the official who gives money to receive it instead of making it cheap." The result of this was that in Shu, "Chu and iron are often in power and the public and private constant, what's the harm!" It seemed to circulate relatively normally, not more than in the southeast; in the southeast, "this is otherwise, the world is not responsible for the tax, but must be responsible for money, the official business has no money, but the apprentice is easy to take. When the government sends a small amount of money to the people, it is not enough for the people to ask for it. In the southeast, the government does not collect paper money, but it is just the official price. Even the government does not take it seriously. The people will not take it seriously and believe in its true ability."

Yang Guanqing's strategy for saving the money was that he had no money from Fujian, Guang, Jing and Chu Chu. "If the husband wants to make the people look at the brass, it looks like copper. The problem seems to be happening below. Actually, the root causes are still in the top. In the imperial court and in the government, it is not common people." "It doesn't care to care about it. Today, the law says that I have no weight with copper, and I will do the same. From today's past, those who lose far and near to the public are half or half of the money. For example, those who are not close are heavy, and those far away are heavy. Far from being heavy, there is a leak in the vicinity. The price of paper money will not be reduced, but the weight of copper will also change. Although it is not supported by the official, its price is from the official with the official, the weight of the weight is not in me!" He noticed the abuse of the government's money. This policy proposal was a good thing. It helped to recover the money and helped restore the credit. As to whether it was proportional to the release of coins and whether it could form a virtuous circle or not, we cannot consider it first. Just as far as Yang's proposal is concerned, the following scenarios arose: (1) what should be done in the process of execution, if there is no completion or non-execution in the distance, and subsequently what should be done in the distance, or (2) if there is a policy and there is a countermeasure, how to supervise and check or not to reward and punish; not to mention, it seems to be just a paper talk — even if it is granted to the heaven, it may not really be put into practice. Because he was conducting a policy study, not purely theoretical research, pertinence and effectiveness were very strong. While this work is not well known, its practical value cannot be doubted.

(3) *Lv Zuqian's comment on money*
Lv Zuqian (1137–1181), called Mr. Dong Lai, and was born in Jinhua (now Zhejiang). He was a famous scholar of literature and history in the Southern Song Dynasty. He was erudite, and along with Zhu Xi and Zhang Shi, they were considered the three virtuous men in Southeast China. His main aims were to compile a line, oppose empty talk and open the eastern School of thought. The book includes the collection of the history of the East Lele and a detailed history of dynasties.

His *History of the Dynasties* is divided into 13 sections, and coins are one of them. The origin, function, money law and paper money are widely discussed in this article. He continued the doctrine of the traditional money, supported the theory of heavy capital and suppression of the end, affirmed the positive effect of money under this premise, affirmed the relative value theory of "salty gains, little money, little money, heavy money, heavy money, heavy money, mutual rights" under the established material wealth, affirmed the monetary theory of the metal school and objected to the theory of monetary theory. As to the cost reduction of the minted money, he held that the *wuzhu* coins of the Han Dynasty and the *tongbao* coins of the Tang Dynasty were the most appropriate in terms of their size and weight, which could serve as examples of excellent money. The big coins coined under the rule of Liu Bei and the *qianyuan* coins minted under Diwu Qi's instruction were only improvised or makeshift. The substitutes for money like deer skin or tortoise shells were the worst of all.

Lv's understanding of paper money, on the one hand, was that "it is the right way to save the corrupt." He thought that paper money was not authentic, and was only adapted to save the corrupt politicians, but could not make it useful in the whole country. On the other hand, he thought that the paper money was produced by the folk spontaneously and not as the masterpiece of the sage of Saint King, "the method of *Jiaozi* comes from the people and the official, so it is feasible." Although this is not entirely accurate, it is reasonable, reflecting some of the facts. Again, he thought "the iron money is inconvenient, the *jiaozi* even." This is not a matter of paper money alone.

Zhu Xi (1130–1200) of the Song Dynasty had an opinion on the regional issue of the circulation of paper money, thinking that the government should set up an exchange house, the rate of exchange and the "Zhu Ziyu class on money." He said, "two Huai iron and iron money exchange, try to make no place to make a choice, if not allowed to cross the river in the meeting, only to use the cross." This meant that if the Huai people wanted to cross the river to buy and sell, the south of the Yangtze River must have their own people to do so too, so that they could exchange money. It was not for the court to donate tens of thousands of dollars to buy *jiaozi* in the south of the Yangtze River, but it had been sent to Huainan to circulate. This attitude was positive and prudent. As for the theory of money origin, the leakage of copper coins and the destruction of money, Zhu Xi's theory was mediocre.

(4) *Xin Qiji's discussion on the real copper*

Xin Qiji (1140–1207), literary name Jiaxuan, courtesy name You'an, was born in Licheng (now in Jinan), Shandong Province. He was the number one scholar in theoretical elaboration of the support for the *chu* coins. Xin was a famous Chinese poet whose poems are considered by many critics to be the best of the Southern Song Dynasty. His writings were collected in *The Complete Works of Xin Qiji*.

In 2 years the Hui Zi had devalued and then stabilized the value of the currency, but the problem of stabilizing the whole currency was solemnly placed in front of the court, and Xin Qiji, the officer of the warehouse department, played the book "on the use of the meeting on the line." In order to find out the root causes of the abuse, the following suggestions were put forward for stabilizing the currency value.

Support the circulation of paper money: Xin emphasized the theoretical key points, and pointed out that "the common disciples see copper is valuable, but the paper money is cheap." Copper and paper notes cannot be resolved directly in order to solve the problem of food and clothing. This breakthrough in understanding, breaking the secular prejudices that persecute people for a long time, had certain practical significance and were affirmed. The idea of more expensive or less expensive is on the surface, the real quality could only be judged by a sample, in which there was no difference. This understanding was quite profound, especially the ideas of the epoch mint, paper money, the full value of the currency goods and the value of the negative. It is just that we cannot demand that the ancients' ideas work for modern people. So, Xin thought, "the money has the like (move) the work that carries the work, the goods and goods have the low disadvantage; as for the meeting son, the coiling and carrying, the hard work, the thousand is also not discounted, so it is more convenient for the people!" This meant that when there was nothing, the army and the people will not have disadvantages. When the time comes, there will be no shortage of profits. In peacetime, the military and the people have the convenience of paper money. When the military situation is urgent, the court will not be too short of funds. How can people not accept new things as frankly and enthusiastically as the forefathers in order to further the development of the monetary form and find theoretical reasons for it? In the great development of economy in the Song Dynasty, the development of money and finance was extraordinary.

The analysis of the reasons for the devaluation of the meeting: The disadvantage was that the pros and cons lay in the instability of the currency value. The first was "the light of the court." "In the past, people had been given more money and less money if they were sent to the public. As a result, the folklore has always been 602. The army and the people whining, the road grudges. This is not his, the light of the reason. In recent years, the military and the civil service, with the meeting son in the half of the money, compared to it, then the son from the expensive, cover change of 700 money is strange (740 Jiangyin army change money, Jian Kang Fu 710 feet). There is no him, a little heavier." That is to say, the court and the government themselves took the lead in making money, Thereby putting only their money in the market. They did not consider recycling. The second was that "the husband's sons are light, and the good ones are created by India. Now it is called the place of the exercise of the son, but the army is stationed in the county, and the number of counties within the city of the city (the suburbs of Beijing), as for the villages and towns, a little far away from the city, the other remote states are also known. The quantity of issuance is not based on market demand, but is to meet the needs of military expenditure, and the circulation area is narrow and the amount of absorption is limited. This phenomenon of contradictory asymmetry has been discovered for the conscientious people. It is not a theoretical breakthrough, but an intuitive analysis, which is enough to be recognized."

The way to stop the fraud: In view of the above problems, Xin said, "want to beg to live in printing, stop in order to see in the number of ways to reduce the command, since Chun Xi 2 years later, should be Fujian, river, lake and other roads, folk three, and other households to rent Fu, and use 7 minutes, three points to see the money (the remote state has not been a son, the shilling three families to lose, avoid the middle and lower households suffer the fraud). The price of private buying and selling of farmland is known to be in the deeds of money, money and money, or in violation of the rules. Two of the transactions are made, and the cases are reported by the teeth. The monk way is not the money, but also the money, the half of the meeting. In his courtiers, the number of the members of each path, though not knowing how much, was 100,000 for the rate, which had lost 100,000 of the officials, and was hidden at home for 100,000 of the losers in the coming year, and then the merchants exchanged with the peddler to the Road and 100,000. It is because of the number of 100,000 in the distance, and the number of more than 30 million people in the city will be released. The number of meetings is limited, and the meeting is endless, which is bound to buy the place where the troops are stationed. In this way, the price of the son is bound to be expensive, and the proceeds from the army are better than the money. One or 2 years, the people of all roads, although in the army, the market to buy, and do not give, and then many lines of printing, so that the road to sell, the price is straight, make sure to see the money, then the people will see A Kiya." The policy of saving and cheating was mainly from limiting the amount of circulation, increasing the recovery and expanding the circulation area.

Control the amount of paper currency issuance: The ancients recognized the importance of regulating the money supply, which is the law of the ancient paper currency circulation. However, the key is whether one can put this idea into practice and turn it into a consistent and unswerving action. Song Xiaozong also acknowledged that the paper currency was issued for military expenses. It was a means of expedience and would not harm the people. This reflected that Song Xiaozong was a metalist and reflected the facts of the time. In such a grim situation, it was useless to talk about paper money only as paper money, as it was difficult to control the issue amount. Similarly, it was very difficult for Xin to increase the proportion of paper money collected by households above three. Could the military frontier be accepted? Could the functional department agree? "The household department, the left Tibet West Bank not much money, all the monthly coupons will wait for money, and want to take the silver conference." The expenditure was as follows: the officers and men of the division six points silver, and the Army (team) five points silver. Such a standard of expenditure was not easy to adjust, as it was related to the fundamental interests of the officers and soldiers in front of them. The boycott of increasing the proportion of paper money and reducing the ratio of money to silver was expected to shake all resolutions and decisions. The law of circulation of paper money had not succumbed to any foreign strength. In the trend of derogatory currency, the paper money was like a hot potato; no one could hold it in their hand. This sped up the circulation of the paper money, which was equal to an increase of the amount of paper money. Since the government had put paper money into the market, there were transitional difficulties; but there was a repudiation plan. If the emperor took out money and silver in the circulation of paper money, but did not close the circulation gate, it would be of no help. The money and property that were put into the market were just like the stones that washed away. Therefore, even if the idea was not bad, it would be more difficult to implement. The Yuan Dynasty pushed the banknote to the whole country, but it could neither save itself from or slow down its progress toward its fate.

9. Monetary theories after the reign of Emperor Xiaozong of the Southern Song Dynasty

After the reign of Emperor Xiaozong, the issuance of paper money was repeatedly conducted, causing inflation to become increasingly serious, and the financial situation deteriorated, which had a bad effect on the whole society. The attention of the people was mainly focused on the stability of the currency value and on the increase in the issuance of paper currency, which were supposed to stabilize finance, the market and economy, but which caused more disagreements. The representative figures were mainly Wanli Yang, and Yuan's father and son, Wei Jing and Wu Qian, respectively.

9.1. *Yang Wanli's monetary theory*

Yang Wanli (1127–1206) was born in Jishui (now Jiangxi). In his youth, he studied with sincerity. Later, he grew tired of being a doctor in the Imperial College and became Secretary for supervision and deputy director of Jiangdong transport. Ningzong (1201–1224) was straight and upright, fair and honest. The poetry of the time was from Cheng Zhai, Yu Tai, Fan Chengda and Lu You, who were known as the four masters of the Southern Song Dynasty. Yang Wanli wrote *Cheng Zhai Ji*, which is now accepted by the Wanli Yang Ji Jian school.

The Song Dynasty's history was written in five volumes: "Two years (1166) in June," (Xiao Zong) stated, "the two Huai River crosses the south of the Yangtze River. The people of the south of the Yangtze River cross two Huai areas, and they also use money or meetings to carry out exchanges. It can be seen that in the south of the Yangtze River, the two Huai lines were different with the currency, and the two Huai issued 2 million intersections of the *jiaozi*." *The History of the Song Dynasty* stated, "at the end of Shaoxing (1162), there were no two Huai and Huguang Provinces. After that, there were too many children and insufficient capital. In the two years of the dry road, two hundred, three hundred, five hundred, and consistent Jiao Zi 3 million were used for two Huai. In the past three years, the imperial edict made 1 million and three hundred thousand new deliveries, and the Huainan Cao division was assigned to the State Army to make a new line of exchange, which was not limited to years." Three years (1192) of *shin szong* stated that the authorities should expand the scope of iron money, issue 3 million rounds of the two Huaihe iron money, and the circulation area should be expanded beyond the two Huai, including the Jiangnan marsh eight states. Wanli Yang opposed the iron money spreading to the south of the Yangtze River. In August, he begged that the military be sent to the south of the Yangtze River. In order to infuriate the prime minister Liu Zheng and Zhao Ruyu of the Ministry of Justice, he gave up his deputation with the Jiangdong transport company and bid farewell to officialdom. However, for a variety of reasons, the court failed to use the iron money in the south of the Yangtze River.

In order to lend weight to his opinion, Yang had borrowed the traditional Chinese mother theory and applied it to the new historical conditions of the parallel copper and iron in the Song Dynasty, thus creating the new theory of the "two mother and two child" with the principle of "the mother and son are not separated." He explained his thought in this way: "to see the meeting of the money is the legacy of the old and the mother." There were two types of coins: the copper money in the south of the Yangtze River and the iron money on the Huai River. "There are two of the children: the son of the meeting, the son of the copper money. This is the son of the new meeting, the son of iron money. Mother and son are not separated, and then money will be used." He believed that the relationship between the money and the paper money in circulation formed the relationship between the mother and the child in circulation, that is, the relationship between the first and the following, and the separation, the dislocation and the independence; the relationship between the mother and son could not be reversed and intersected. Because it was two mothers and two sons, and it was unavoidable to make some mistakes, but that was not allowed and could not happen. As to whether the mother and son were parallel in the market or not was a different issue. As long as they were freely convertible and kept within the established proportion, the mother would be present in person. Similarly, in different circulation areas, copper mother and child would be allowed to exchange proportions. This was Wanli Yang's new interpretation of the theory of mother and child rights, which constituted Yang's theory for observing and commenting on the iron coin in the eight states in the south of the Yangtze River. From the perspective of modern people, Yang seemed to have realized the nature of paper money. It was not a value entity, but a symbol and a substitute.

He also said, "the law of meeting children is to exercise money with money." Today, the law of Xinhui Zi has been used seven hundred and seventy times. The son is the circulation, and the money is exchanged. Later, Xinhui Zi had seven hundred and seventy feet of iron money, but it was clearly iron money, not copper coins. Huai Shang used iron money and used Xinhui Zi, while Hui Zi Si had money to pay. In the south of the Yangtze River, there was no money in circulation but huizi. "I do not know whether the army and the people will exchange the money with the city. If you want to exchange the money, there is no money. There is a son without money. It is the son of no mother. It is the handover and no money in parallel. One money and two money, 10 money and five money, trade and business travel, and how business travel through?" "The conclusion was that, in the region south of the Yangtze River, it was not all right to have copper money in circulation, which would interfere with the exchange of commodities. That region used to use iron money." So he was not against such practices.

In the case of non-convertibility, if the Commission in circulation could be received by the government, it would not become a problem, and there was a return. The normal circulation of the son would not be a problem. But if this was not the case, that is, if the left bank and the internal Treasury were not affected, then the people would lose their property and the state and county will not suffer. "State county is not accepted, it is Xinhui Zi is public and private, not up and down.... If there is any conflict between them, then the competition will start. In this way, if the eight states in the south of the Yangtze River are willing to run the iron coin club, the people in the south of the Yangtze River will be disturbed." Therefore, one would rather disobey, abandon the official, and leave behind one's employment, and never do anything contrary to reason, which injures people's affairs, if one wants to be respected by later generations.

Yang advocated the exchange of paper money, insisted that the mother and son follow, and not be separated. He also advocated that everything be adapted to the needs of the times, with continuous development, which is worth affirming. As to whether the exchange was a legal exchange or not, the difference between the exchange of coins and the exchange of notes was not the same. Because Yang did not give the theory, we cannot comment on it.

9.2. Father and Son of the Yuan family on currency

Yuan Xie (1144–1224) was from Yin county (present-day Ningbo). A disciple of Lu Jiuyuan, he served as an official for a number of years. His son Yuan Fu was also a distinguished scholar, served after him as an official, and did much innovation and reform.

Yuan Xie's currency theory was seen in terms of the "convenience of the people" and "the general outline of food consumption."

In terms of the relationship between paper money and coins, he put forward the viewpoint that money is not enough, the virtual and the real were the same. They can be scattered and can be collected. One should regard money as a representative of, instead of real money. This required real purchasing power of comparable conditions, that is, the so-called power, trade-off, regulation control should be analyzed. When the purchasing power of both parties was not quite equal, they could not be put into a transaction; but real money would play a role instead of using virtual currency. When Yuan Wen talked about paper money, he said, "today's paper money is lighter." When it came to copper coins, he said, "copper coins are few." Paper money was light, naturally speaking, and its purchasing power was low, and its value was depreciated. Copper coins were few and their purchasing power was strong. Yuan Wen did not discuss the value problem directly. He wanted to explain the purchasing power, otherwise it would be far-fetched and contrary to the original intention of the ancients.

After the celebration of Ningzong, the meetings became malignant and inflated. In the first year (1195), the issue amount of each meeting was limited to 3 years in the 4 years of the Xiao Zong Qian Road, and 3,000 million in 10 million circles. During the Kaixi period (1205–1207), because of the war against the Jin Dynasty, the government issued *huizi* in abundance, with the 11th, 12th and 13th issuing amounting to 140 million. In 1209 or 1211, the government issued the 14th currency in exchange for the 11th and 12th currencies. With a rate of 1 to 2, the old currency depreciated by 50%. In August of the same year, the government decided to carry out the iron money in the areas north and south of the Huai River.

The word *"chengti"* was used in the Northern Song Dynasty, and meant to improve the purchasing power of iron money. In the second year of Zongyuan (1199), Shang Shu Province proposed that it should be "closely related to the half of the month and how to deal with it, which can be called a little heavy money and a slight price." The derogation of iron money and high prices were recorded in the Song History of food and goods in the Southern Song Dynasty of Ningzong in the third year spring of Jiading. Gaozong praised Prime Minister Shen Gai's way of maintaining the circulation of paper currency by way of exchange. "The officials often have millions of money, if the price of the chancellor is reduced, the official uses money to buy it, so it has no disadvantages." Chen Qiqing, the chief of Qingtian, said, "the ministers thought that today's business is not only to mention coins, but also to mention copper coins." So, the object was also extended to copper money. Therefore, it can be said that, where the value of the currency was maintained, the value of the devalued currency was raised, and the purchasing power was also restored to the normal level, whether it was copper money, iron money or paper money, and the purchase and sale prices of various goods were also expanded in the same period, with no lack of denomination.

Yuan Xie began his criticism in the first paragraph of his *A Memorial for the Convenience of the People*: "the minister used to listen to the use of mulberry coins, as long as he was poor. This legislation is also considered poor." But on that day, the so-called "mulberry coins," as referred by the speaker, could be the fruit of the growing economy. Hong Mai "Rong Zhai made a note of three points in the official meeting," declaring the Yuan year of Ningzong as an "imperial edict." Jiang and Zhejiang Zhuo must have paid seven hundred and seventy coins to buy the money (consistent). Yuan Shi also said, "if a stranger entered the province, there must be no pardon." Only a few people heeded to his words. Within a short while, there were three points and seven points, and the change was repeated. It was apparent that in the near future, government will no longer make a rigid regulation on the exchange rate. But soon, the three cents, i.e., the 7%, of the money will be exchanged, and finally, the old method of returning half of the money would be followed. One way by which Yuan rebuked was by abolishing his own laws. "If the ruler reigns well, people who initially wanted to abandon it, will reconsider it." Subsequently, the people were anxious to accumulate wealth and did everything possible to stabilize the price fluctuations and remove the trade difficulties. In the past, there were many currencies made using paper and there were fewer currencies that were made using copper coins, and usage of iron money was much less. In the past, there were more coins, so the prices were expensive, but in that period the iron coins were not expensive. The reason why the paper money was valued so highly was because copper coins are too small to sell. If we look into the decline of the usage of copper coins, we see that sailors who travelled in sea vessels faced various problems such as the sale of money, the reuse of money and the damage of copper coins, which are just a few of the many reasons that existed (as the Yuan's formulation for paper money).

While being the administrator in Jiangxi, he summed up Xiaozong's measures of stabilizing paper currency, and thought that if he could not follow the experience of Xiao Zong, he could not guarantee the smooth circulation of banknotes. Ning Zong used "Kai Xi" (1205–1207) to employ troops, making a lot of coins, so the price was very low. He admitted to expanding the issue of banknotes in order to make up for the deficit and ensure military spending. In this regard, he stood with the government's position and had nothing to criticize. Only when facing reality and focusing on how to do it was he anxious and worried when taking remedial measures. So he said, "to change its law today, and not to be in circulation but not poor, it cannot be taken by the emperor," to follow the emperor, to work hard, to collect too much paper money in circulation and to ensure that work is unimpeded. His theoretical foundation was to "cover the books as many things, many are cheap, few are expensive, and the rest are few." His so-called "many are cheap and few are expensive" is synonymous with Xiaozong's saying that "less will be valued and many will be devalued." It was Yuan's understanding that changes in the circulation of banknotes were caused by changes in the absence of cash flow. In his view, "wealth is abundant, but when it comes to the price of paper money, it is cheap, so it is urgent to receive it. Why should it be expensive?" When the financial resources are abundant, we should examine the value of the currency. If the value of the currency is low, it will be recycled. This is not a conventional recovery, because the value of the currency is derogatory. After a period of time, the price will go up again, so that it will rise and fall repeatedly. This is the model of Xiao Zong which won. At that time, faced with the financial crisis of issuing banknotes, and trying to ensure the smooth circulation of paper money, he had to take certain measures. Otherwise, the financial crisis may have led to an economic crisis, resulting in a crisis of power. Yuan said, "What worries most is not paper money, but the problem of bureaucracy. As time goes by, we can fight for the benefit of the people, but we can do nothing for the rest of the world." He expressed the "pain, punishment and corruption, the praise of the public, the male and the Qing scholar, the book of the book, the sale of the defense, strict transaction tax agreement, the money will be half of the system, then the wealth is abundant." In the long-term interests of the rulers, from the maintenance of the normal order of the ruling class, the plan designed by the ruler would not be reproached and would stop the decline of the Song Dynasty and prevent the indiscriminately devaluation of the paper money.

His son Yuan Fu's thought of saving Chu was mainly manifested in two aspects, one against the collection of *mu* and the other on the four commandments of the meeting.

In 1245, Zheng Qingzhi, the prime minister, proposed the method of retrieving the paper notes in circulation by counting the *mu* of each household. The specific way was that every person who had one mu of land had that land divided into six limits. Yuan Fu, who was a storyteller of Chung Shu Shu and Chong Zheng hall, used to play for the emperor, thinking it was "the most unpleasant heart." However, the reasons for this were neither theoretical arguments nor different political views, but disagreement on some of the operational concepts or specific practices in the implementation, which were related to its success or failure: "this letter is to explain the question of the world, and to give up the small resentment of the world."

With regard to trustworthiness, when the acreage meeting was held, the envoy would be intercepted by the state forces in order to remove the imperial court after being abandoned. With loopholes in the lawsuits, nobody would have any faith in the legal practice. But with one authority making the decision, nobody would cast any doubt. At the moment, though there were difficulties in losing money, they will know less and increase in price, and they will benefit on other days.

Thinking of the subordinates: In the case of an acre, one should take a strong view of the situation, of the great temple, the big room and the strong officials. "Make the state county a powerful home, set the time limit, no extension, and the price of a meal is inevitable; the two is not the power of the family, hoping to survive; the three poor people see the county strictly, and the heart of the county." "Wait for everybody to be enough, then urge the middle door .... In the end, if we consider how much we should take, we should consider the matter, and urge the poor or the small number of households." Wei Leweng (1178–1237), a famous scholar at that time, also had a chapter, which was similar to Yuan Fu's views for the middle and lower families, while Wu Qian (1196–1262) argued for the officials and the monasteries. Later, the royal court really held a meeting with officials and temples, and with Yuan Fu, regarding manpower arguments.

The revelation of Yuan's plays was whether a good policy could be implemented to finally achieve the desired goal. The great knowledge could not be ignored. It was also related to the overall situation of success or failure. After deciding the major policy, how was one implement it in a careful manner.

In 1240, with the 16th and 17th printing of paper money amounting to 500 million, the government planned to substitute the old money with the 18th printing at a ratio of 1 to 5. Yuan Fu, then the Vice-Minister of National Defense, put forward his ten points on reform.

His criticism of the monetary policy at that time was "repeated change, without any effect." In such an environment, people were "afraid of uncertainty," so that "prices will increase sharply in the next 2 months, the price will be cut down, the city will be desolate and the mood will be depressed." Although there was no universal policy, it would have been better than the disadvantages. In the 18th sector, the plan of the new club was put forward. As per Yuan Fu's ideas, first was that "the eighteen circles come out, and the old and the new are parallel. The more something is used, the cheaper it is. The second was "new must be led by the old .... If the people do not accept, they will make disputes. It is used in the case of the people's letter A, but the lawsuit is strong enough to be an official street, but it will lead to a failure in business and shop." The third was a military voucher, "in case of a new meeting in group .... The court has no accumulation in the new meeting .... How will the issuing organ be?" The fourth was that the issuing organ saw "2 million yuan" money in a year. "If the court can make up to 1,000 million pieces of chisel, why do we have to eliminate these (40 million) old people? We fear that the old will be cheap and the prices will be more expensive." The fifth point was that "if the taxes should be collected in the newly printed money, how should the circulating agency respond to the needs of the Ministry of the Revenue and the common people? There would surely be a paradoxical situation indeed." The sixth was that the three general household departments wanted to see money each year, by "drawing up the deposit of money in the court." "Internal support .... The number is limited .... The imperial court is always obeying the strength of its strength and desires, so the military situation must be divergent in the imperial court." The seven was that the court expected the new meeting to be very meaningful, but how could one save the present? The eighth was, "if the cost is five, then the number of officials will be broken down. If each discipline is exercised consistently, it will be on its own." The ninth was that even when the people refused to give up money, they would not save it. The tenth referred to a piece of paper. "To destroy it is to be clear, and to call it darkness."

"1234 (Ping) has the name of cutting and chisel, and no doubt is true." To sum up, he wanted the emperor to have four "restraints": the first was to restrain from using the same money in three different areas; the second was to restrain from devaluing money; the third was to restrain from depositing too much; and the fourth was to restrain from setting up insufficient boundaries for the newly printed money. These four aspects "should never be violated."

In fact, the key to Yuan Fu's opposition was "the old and the new, the old and the three." Therefore, he advocated that "we should take urgent measures to deal with it, and strive to speed up our efforts. Then we will exchange for the best, and raise the old society of 50–60 million. The work is reliable, and the validity can be established." At that time, however, the ideal elements were too large to be effective.

9.3. Wei Jing's comment on the local conditions

Wei Jing (?–1226), a native of Huating, Jiating, moved to Kunshan of Pingjiang. In 1184, he was number one in the highest imperial examination. After serving several posts at the court, he was demoted because of the jealousy of the prime minister and became the ruler of Tanzhou, where he became close friends with Zhuxi. His writings were compiled into *Houle Collections*.

In 1215, when Wei Jing was the ruler of Fuzhou, he learned the idea of saving Chu in Jiading's "Shang Fuzhou Temple" on Wei Jing. Based on the knowledge of banknotes, he believed that as long as the government did not issue in excess and had the issue ready, it would probably be unimpeded. He used the notes for the first time to carry out Xi Shu as an example, and pointed out that the number of children in the southeast was different from that of the West.

Wei Jing reviewed the process of the devaluation of the paper currency in the Southern Song Dynasty. In 1208, the government issued new currency to replace the old ones. At first, the common people did not have much objections to this. But the rich were reluctant to have the new currency in circulation because they would suffer great losses. Consequently, the middle class also followed suit. "The officials will fear that they will not be used early, and that they will be scattered abroad, and that they will never be changed. A little light, the price also decreases, this is the human nature. If we endure hard, managers may not be able to renew their old habits. The border court claims that it is too urgent for the people to take the trouble to think that it will be more urgent and more suspect than ever. He pointed out that 'what we call' is still weighing on things. Right is equal to everything, and right and material are all equal. Today will be the right, the money is still. There will be more and less money, but the weight is lighter than the weight. So far, what has he said to make it smooth?"

In the view of Wei Jing, because of the fear of devaluation of the money of the rich family and the middle-class people, and the loss of their own interests, and to the laws regarding hoarding of paper money, paper money was treated like an outcast. As long as there was a way of coping with the ups and downs, with step by step governance, it was not necessary to make the paper money smooth, especially if the market was normal. However, the authorities made an urgent call, causing the people to doubt, along with the political uncertainties. He believed that this was a result of mishandling.

Wei Jing put forward his own opinions at that time. The first thing was the circulation of goods and materials. People wanted to hide, and not be strong. Administrative coercion, "at the same time, such as household registration and other Tibetan associations" will be absorbed at one time and then added again. So, he argued, "take the light of the weight, the urgency, the measure, the help of the maintenance and the comfort and comfort the people who do not know and wait for it for a long time." He advocated calm and an unhurried attitude in order to dispel doubts, "keep the middle and half system and hold it for a long time, and strictly prohibit the price reduction." He did not think that the method of exchanging the old was bad for the people's faith, and did not think that it was a violation of the interests of the people. "I do not believe that banknotes which do not have money to prepare can function normally." It is difficult to achieve the ideal state of "no money, silver, pure meeting, and how to set people together." Also, "if the husband raises the national plan, the expenditure is spent, the funds will be increased, and the surplus will accumulate, and there will be a slight surplus." It is the deepening and concretion of the first proposal. He objected to the idea of exchanging money for money with officials. He thought, "not thinking about official money is limited. A non-district exchange can be a sudden return. In ancient times, this rescue plan is contrary to the original intention of issuing paper money by the government. The government is hard to accept it, and it is not possible to put it into practice in the past."

9.4. Wu Qian's discussion on paper money as the lifeblood of the country

Wu Qian (1196–1262) was from Xuanzhou (now Anhui Province). In the 11th Jiading year of Ningzong, he was the number one scholar. He served twice as the prime minister during the Chunyou years of Lizong. In his later years, he was demoted. His writings were collected in *Lvzhai Yiji*.

Song Lizong Shaoxing issued a total of over 320 million *guan*. The following year, the president of the Qing Dynasty, Wu Qian, who led the Huaixi financial Fu, shouldered the responsibility of saving the paper money, and of the nine affairs of the state, the eighth one being "the new system of the money of the paper money." He attached great importance to the role of the paper money, and pointed it out as the height of the national lifeblood. In the event of floods and droughts, when brigades levied fees, it was inevitable that the paper notes would become the lifeblood of the country. That year, on the occasion of the Yuan's death, he seemed to say, "the death of the golden man, though Tartars, is also a light thing with a Broussonetia, or a Broussonetia, or a broussonchu three, or a five, and 10 for a hundred, but the man does not think heavy at the end of the day. At the end of the day, it is easy for us to make one side of the book." This view was similar to that of Xiu (1178–1235). He also said, "the government is not heavy, the people are not heavy, the officials are leaning on the law prohibition and people are not satisfied, the Broussonetia, the country is not our country." The expenditure on state military expenditure and the running of the regime depended entirely on the paper money. Wu Qian went on to say, "the disadvantages of the new books are already worse than before. In the case of the officials, the people do not pay much attention to the people. The people who rely on the officials are forbidden in law, and the people do not accept it. The country is not my country, but the country is not our country. Since the mulberry coins are related to the survival and death plans of the country, saving the paper money is equal to saving the nation." Therefore, he stated, "Jing Yue Shi's theory of saving Chu, the relationship between them is not more important than the purchase of public and private money," and put forward his ideas on "what is the source and how to save the paper money." In the "third notes on Yin Jing," he pointed out that "the lifeblood of Mi Naimin is the lifeblood of the three" and "the blood of the people is the blood of the people." The so-called "paper money" was both light and heavy, especially as the rice price surged. So, could the country manage it within the deadline?

Wu Qian's way to save the paper notes was to buy salt with salt bills in the time limit, and to use other methods to increase the strength of paper money. "If there is an operation to drive a merchant, make it eager to take it." He estimated that each generation of salt would take 30 points, and the 3 million generation of salt could recover 90 million dollars.

During the transfer of the power of Jiangxi to Wu Qian of Longxing mansion, it was thought that "the present price is gradually poor, the price is decreasing, the printing of the imperial court, the forgery of the forged people, the leakage of the copper money, and the end of the full Eve." Not even a year old, the disadvantages were expected to be apparent quickly. Therefore, "there are nine harms and only one benefit." It was thought best to gain a quick profit, without damaging the interests of the monastery and the people, as the country was in a mess and the people were not in a state of harmony.

9.5. *Chen Qiqing's theory of copper money*

Chen Qiqing (1180–1236) was born in Linhai (now Zhejiang). He passed the Jinshi, became a Qingyuan school professor, a national history compilation officer and also joined the Imperial Academy. Chen Qiqing made a special explanation after Wanli Yang's understanding of the relationship between the coins and the paper money.

He said, "the money is still the mother, and so is it." "Mother and son are so right, not baryons and light mother. When the husband has money, then there are many books. Now he is in opposition, and he talks about painting day and night, but he never speaks of money. There are more days in the paper money, but less money. The width of the fruit is not the same, but the width is bigger than the others. When the money is consumed daily, then its life is returned to the Broussonetia, and its disadvantages are in the Broussonetia." Chen's intention was to make it clear that the attention was focused on the metal coins in a normal manner.

"The minister's thought of today's business is not only to mention coins, but also to mention copper coins." He put emphasis on coins, and put forward that "today's law of copper coins, those who commit crimes are punished less and those who catch money are lighter. If the offenders are punished lightly, they will easily be traitors. The minister is foolish, the desire is good, and the strict leakage of the constitution is the best way to capture the Scriptures. It has been captured to a number of people, especially with the attached categories." He thought that the only way was to "call it the duty." According to Chen, to the situation required two aspects, banknotes and coins, which was not unique. But at that time, if one could not change the monetary policy of inflation, and fill the financial hole, the state could not enrich the country and utilize the army. It could only be treated as a rule, searching for a valid cause and rescuing people from difficulty.

9.6. *Xu Heng on the theory of money exchange*

Xu Heng (1209–1281) was born in Henei (now Qinyang of Henan Province). He learned from the works of Cheng Yi, Cheng Hao and Zhu Xi and considered it his duty to put what was right in practice. During his participation of government affairs, his viewpoints were quite extraordinary. He served in quite a few government posts. His writings were included in *The Posthumous Writings of Xu Heng and Collections of the Writings of Luzhai.*

"The general examination of the continued literature and the coin one" was carried out by Song Lizong, and 2 years later (1238) Xu Heng pointed out that "the discount of the money of the Broussonetia" is not to be referred to. "The ancient people are the city, with the grain and silk fabric, self-phase trade, the spring goods have not been cast, and the vouchers of the people are the real goods of the common people. With the money of paper and ink, it is easy to produce the goods of the people in the world." Put in today's words, Xu used metal money theory to look at paper money. Since ancient times, in addition to the exchange of objects, it was metal currency that acted as the medium of transaction. He was not clear about the circulation of deer skin currency and its comparison with paper money. Nor did he study the production of paper money, an inevitable outcome of the development of commodity economy. He stood on the opposite side of the banknote, easily negated it and mistakenly assumed that banknotes could be printed as needed without being restricted by any rules. "Later generations do not want to be extravagant, but they cannot afford to be extravagant. Though they are wise, they cannot avoid them. It is a curse that cannot be forged without forgery and cannot be forged without forgery. Paper money is a curse. It cannot be extravagant or forgery." This meant simply a reversal of cause and effect and a cover for all evil activities. Xu Heng believed that the circulation of paper money was extremely convenient for the rulers and based on their own needs, often leading to forgery by the traitors, but one could not draw the conclusion that paper money was the root of the evil, as the evil was caused by people's ulterior motives.

Xu Heng reviewed and revealed the history and consequences of paper money, as well as the predatory restrictions on the usage of notes in the new and old ways. He pointed out, "for the past 30 or 40 years, the inability to speak for the policy makers has helped the imperial court, but it is known that every effort has been made, and the common people have been losing everything. The practice in Jiading is to offer one in exchange for two, which means the common people would lose half of their goods. The practice in Duanping is to offer one in exchange for five, which means the common people would lose 80% of their goods. That was utterly unjust." The result was that people were suffering from hardships, and the value of the currency was increasingly worsening. First of all, during the reign of Emperor Ningzong in Jiading, half of the people's property was seized, and then during the reign of Emperor Lizong, 4/5th of the people's property was seized. "This is not much more than a word. We should know that benevolence, righteousness, courtesy, wisdom and faith are the roots of ancient governance. The meaning of words is not spoken, and the state is hard to maintain."

Where was the way out? Xu Heng put forward, "if we do not accept the real voucher, we will save the day before yesterday and be worthy of the people. What is the real cargo? Salt is the same." There were both advantages and disadvantages to the use of salt to recycle paper money. It did not cause losses to the people nor did it cause financial difficulties to the state. He thought that since ancient times, millet and silk, steel, gold and silver were enough to be used in the country. More than 4,000 years since the time of the Yellow Emperor, this truth had been talked about. How could it be possible to speak of it in his time alone! Then, when the early Southern Song Dynasty was built, "there are strong enemies, there are groups of thieves, looking for the gang, the stagnation of the river left, the inner 100 officers and the common mansion, outside for the pay of the year, not the official meeting, the state is also gradually rich and strong, so the state's wealth, also the ear." The Southern Song Dynasty had just crossed the river, and there were neither internal nor external troubles. Neither officials nor official money had been issued. Why was this so? Xu Heng was not deeply involved in society and was influenced by Cheng Zhu's theory of science. In the face of the problem of the circulation of real paper money and the attitude of broad and extensive corruption that had taken hold, the reality of the empty monetary policy was apparent.

10. The credit theory of Yuan Cai

Yuan Cai, styling himself as Junzai, was from Xin'an of Quzhou (now Zhejiang Province). He passed the imperial examination and became a Jinshi in the first year of Longxing of the Southern Song Dynasty (1163 AD). Then, he served as a county magistrate, monitoring the *Dengwen* Drum department (a drum outside the court for people to beat and file complaints in feudal China), and was known for integrity and honesty. In the fifth year of Chunxi (1178 AD), he was a county magistrate of Yueqing County, advocating "forging relationship and making custom better." He wrote *Xunsu* (which means civilizing people) on three aspects, namely, *Muqin* (harmony with neighborhoods), *Chuji* (the way one gets along with people) and *Zhijia* (family management). Secretary Liu Zhen wrote a preface to the book and thought that the book could "not only be applied to Yueqing County, but also could benefit later generations."

Therefore, the book was renamed *The Yuan Family Education*. Ji Xiaolai, an influential scholar of the Qing Dynasty, praised that the book as instructing people on "conducting oneself in society … and was second to *Yan Family Instructions*."

Yuan integrated Chinese Confucian ethics with economic thinking in the chapters *Chuji* and *Zhijia* of the book. He advocated "harmony" and concealing wealth, and did not claim to expose wealth. He believed in the sayings, "the rich should not save too much gold in case of stealing," "we must live in harmony with neighborhood to protect ourselves if in danger" and "peace is the most precious among neighbors." Chapter *Chuji* advocated the use of expenditures for the purposes of saving and spending. Hence, Yuan wrote such sentences as "there were some laws of prosperity and decline," "we should make ends meet," "it was a convention to live frugally," "we should make a long-term plan to make our own fortune," "we should live simply and pursue truth from our own life" and "thinking twice before acting, nevertheless, we would miss opportunities." In the chapter *Zhijia*, he also wrote about property lending, "interest must be proper in lending," "it was not a long-term plan to be tricky," "money and food could not be borrowed too much" and "we should not easily get into debt."

10.1. On ethical lending

In the section "interest must be proper in lending," Yuan first advocated the idea of "the rich and the poor should help each other" and said that "lending money and grain, and repaying the interest and principal was an indispensable way that the rich and the poor helped each other. In the Han Dynasty, 1,000 strings of money were lent out and 20 strings of interest would be earned in 1 year, but now was less than two strings." The viewpoint of aiding people financially was stated clearly by Sima Guang in *Opinion on Political Reform*. "The reason why there were rich and poor was due to their intelligence. The rich were proactive and would rather suffer from hardships, eat and wear poorly, and generally did not borrow money from others. Therefore, they were in surplus and not reduced to poverty. However, the poor were lazy and never thought about future. They always drunk and had no extra money left. In times of emergency, they often borrowed money from others. However, they could not repay it and finally, they would sell their children and wives. They would not feel regret even they died of freezing and starving. Hence, the rich became richer because they lent money to the poor, and the poor struggled to survive as they often borrowed money from the rich. Although the hardships and enjoyment the rich and the poor experienced were not equal, the two supported each other to ensure their survival." The view about the rich and the poor was built on the basis of fatalism, which stated that there was a difference in wisdom and diligence among people. Under the arrangement of God, the rich and the poor depended on each other, and their happiness and unhappiness were uneven. Therefore, it was considered normal that the rich exploited the poor and the poor lent their debts to the rich to protect their lives. The rich saved the poor from freezing. As the spokesman of the rich and a guardian of the Confucian ethics and morality, Yuan's thoughts and understanding were consistent.

Yuan Cai also said, "taking today's system as an example, the monthly interest rate of a pawnshop ranged from 2 to 4 *fen*, and the monthly interest rate on loans ranged from 3 to 5 *fen*. If the grain was harvested once a year, the loan on grain ranged from 3 to 5 *fen*. It was not excessive. The pawnshop charged the monthly interest rate of one *fen*. For example, a man from Jiangxi Province borrowed one string of money and agreed to repay it a year later, and he should repay about two strings of money. A person from Kaihua of Quzhi (now part of Zhejiang Province) borrowed one scale of millet and should repay two scales, and a person from Zhexi borrowed one stone of rice (about 100 *jin*) must repay extra eighty *jin*. Such actions were unkind. However, the father ancestors borrowed money or grain from others; his later generations must repay them. It can be seen the heaven's justice." On the criteria of loan interest, he advocated that one charge according to the moderate level, neither too high nor too low. He called it the way to gather money and guarded the moderate system strictly. The so-called up line was that the interest of loan on money or other actual materials be about twice that of the principle, which was roughly the meaning of *Hezi*, that is, the interest and the principle were equal. He probably thought this practice was too tyrannical and inhuman and not allowed by Confucian ethics and also harmed society. On the article of "the reason of stealing" in chapter *Zhijia*, he wrote that "even though robbers were mean persons, they also had insights. If the rich were not mean and benevolent, they would protect themselves in wartime. Robbers often stole from those who often did evil things. Hence, the rich should often introspect themselves." This way of life determined that he would not charge a high amount of interest. He believed that it was mutual funding and support. Of course, he was not willing to charge too low an interest amount, which meant that one would suffer a lot. Once he did that, he would charge neither too high nor too low and the borrower also would have no complains. Thus, he would feel at ease. That was the magic of the moderate system. According to Yuan, private lending could be divided into pawnshops and loans, and loans differed in money and grain. The interest rate of pawnshops was lower than that of loans on money and grain. The monthly interest rate of the former ranged from 2 to 4 *fen*, while the interest rate of the latter was 3–5 *fen*. The difference between them was 1 *fen*, that is, a difference of 20–30%. The interest rate ceiling varied from place to place. Whether it was 100% or 80%, and even *The Penal Complex of Song* stipulated that the monthly interest rate was 6 *fen*, all of which were not adopted by Yuan, or even tolerated by him. This marked the bottom line of Yuan's financial ethics. The core of Confucius's thought was benevolence, and the benevolent should love others. As *The Analects of Confucius-Tai Bo* recorded, Zengzi said that "Benevolence was your duty," which meant that benevolence was a gentleman's unshakable moral duty and responsibility. Hence, Yuan believed that one had to restrain oneself and strive to put it into practice. True Confucianism should not violate its own creed. Naturally, doubling the interest in lending should not be allowed. He believed that people should not do it, and people's family members and descendants were also not allowed to do so. However, the viewpoint that righteousness and benefit were not incompatible was questioned in the Song Dynasty. Li Gou, a famous educator of the Northern Song Dynasty, clearly stated that "pursuing benefit and desire was human nature," which was contrary to Confucius's traditional thinking of "why should we say benefit." Wang Anshi, the famous reformer of the Northern Song Dynasty, proposed that "financial management was righteousness" from the perspective of political reform. Ye Shi put forward the proposition of "pursuing righteousness and interest." Zhu Xi simply put forward "the theory of righteousness and benefit was of utmost importance for

Confucians."[19] "The principle of nature and human desire were not incompatible. If we want to pursue the principle of nature, we must eliminate our desires, and then the righteousness and benefit would be clear."[20] It emphasized the conscious awareness of the "spiritual" moral practice and inner spiritual world. Under the conditions of the struggle between justice and benefit, there emerged a Confucian utilitarianism ethics thought which advocated practical utility. On finance, Yuan Cai would not give up pursuing interest or seeking the minimum standard. Instead, he encouraged people to "earn interest to benefit the public." That constituted a new realm of financial ideology and ethics. The most radical utilitarian Chen Liang (1149–1194) in the Southern Song Dynasty held the same opinion as Yuan Cai on the issue of borrowing money and interest rates that low-interest loans which were "borrowed by the poor, and charged proper interest"[21] were a necessary way that the rich and the poor helped and supported each other.

10.2. On the operation of loans

On managing families and loans, Yuan Cai thought that people should put their family affairs in order first. He put forward that "we should not borrow money easily," as he held that "if an ordinary person dared to borrow money, he must be able to repay it one day. However, if he did not have money at hand, how could he repay it in the near future?" He made an analogy between loans and walking. "For 100 miles, you must walk in two days, which meant you had to walk 50 miles each day and you would reach the destination naturally. If you want to finish it today, you had to walk a whole day and even so hard, you also could not make it." Then, he drew a conclusion that "those who had no foresight, borrowing money in order to obtain the immediate wealth, would be indebted in the future. Such people were the black sheep in the family. We should learn from it." He claimed that people should not pursue immediate interests and should

---

[19] *Collected works of Zhu Xi*, vol. 24.
[20] *Quotations of Zhu Xi*, vol. 113.
[21] *Collected works of Chen Liang Records in Puming Temple*, vol. 2, pp. 279–280, Zhonghua Book Company, 1987.

make a long-term plan. He did not mean that people should not borrow money but that they should not borrow it easily. Therefore, he exhorted that people should be overcautious, do everything according to their financial capabilities and consider carefully before making a decision, which reflected the characteristics of the self-sufficient small-scale operation and the financial principle of not asking other people for help under this small-scale peasant economy. Then, he put forward that "money and grain should not lend out too much," "tenants and servants were not allowed to borrow money from their master's wives and children without notifying the master privately," "tenants should be treated kindly, and the master should not force the tenants to be in debit in order to seek high profits," "relatives should not be borrowed from frequently" and "you might as well lend money to your relatives, friends, and the poor based on your financial capability." To put it simply, money and grain should not be lent out easily. He gave the following reasons: "you might not lend money to people who borrowed money easily. Those people were definitely unreliable person and did not try to repay it. Money and grain lent out would be easily repaid if less, otherwise, would not be repaid. Therefore, those who lent to others 100 *dan* of grain (1 *dan* was nearly 100 *jin*), and one hundred strings of money, even had the ability to repay, but were unwilling to pay back and would rather use the money to file a suit." He also believed that people should not lend money to tenants and servants: "some tenants, servants, and women, were keeping their master in the dark and borrowed money from their master's wives and children, claiming that 'you should not let your parents know', and also promised to pay more interests. When they borrowed money and grain or other materials to cope up with emergency, they had already made a decision of not paying back. As money and grain were lent out secretly, they did not dare to ask for it. Unfortunately, it would be denied. As a family leader, you should always tell these things to your family members and remind them about it." Even so, to the tenants, people must give necessary care and monetary support. His reasons were that the country was agriculture-oriented, and the source of food and clothing all came from it. All that depended on the hard work of the tenants, so how could one not care about tenants? When people needed money for birth, marriage, constructions and death, the family leader had to give proper money support. "During cultivation periods, if tenants were in debt, the family leader should charge less interest.... We should not force them to borrow money or grain in order to seek high profits." In the long run, the enthusiasm of the tenants was maintained and the simple reproduction of agriculture was not affected. That was determined by the basic characteristics of ancient traditional production management methods and business concepts. Based on the concrete agricultural-oriented theories of Confucianism, the labor force was the most important factor in the labor process. Simple reproduction was the basic requirement for subsistence, and actively maintaining the bottom line of this standard was a wise move on the business front.

Yuan advised against lending money frequently to relatives as well. First, he believed that it was an annoying fact that families, relatives, and neighbors often borrowed something due to poverty, even rice, salt, wine and vinegar, which were not worth much money. Second, "if such things as clothes and utensils were lent out, they were easily damaged and easily exchanged for money. Once lent out, the master would always keep thinking about it and hope things would be returned as soon as possible. Sometimes, borrowers did not repay it and seemed to have nothing to worry about. Moreover, they also said to other people that 'I had never borrowed anything from him'. If these words were passed to the owner's ear, would not that arouse animosity?" That would affect the harmony with one's family members and neighbors. Therefore, he advised that if the poor or friends wanted to borrow money, you might as well "give them some based on your financial capability" and not expect them to repay it. In his opinion, "even if they wanted to repay it, how could they pay it back? Some borrowed money to do business, but most of them lost their business because they were destined to be poor. When he begged to borrow money ... we'd better to be sympathetic to his poor family, and support him based on our ability. I would never expect he could repay it. Then in his heart he would not have any thought to return and would blame me." It seemed to be that he wanted to make concessions to avoid trouble in handling the loan relationship with relatives and old friends. However, from his perspective, the poor were short-sighted and shameless. To avoid the poor returning ingratitude for kindness and incurring resentment because of money, he proposed to offer financial assistance to the poor, but in fact it was an action of driving them away. The so-called helping based on financial capability was only a method of abstaining from trouble and saving people's reputation, which was an inevitable reflection of rich and poor fatalism.

10.3. On the management of loans

Yuan Cai advocated supporting the management of family and opposed fixed deposits of gold and silver on the premise of maintaining the rights of the paternal family. He believed that "the rich should not store too much money to avoid being stolen." There was a sentence under one of the articles to explain, "we'd better store less silk and gold in the house and if stolen, we would not suffer a huge loss." That could be regarded as a reason for his beliefs, but not the main reason. He thought that we should use money to do business and make money from it. The principal would bring interest, and interest became principal. Money was inexhaustible. That was the most important. Under the article that "money should not be stored privately if cohabitating," he pointed out that "brothers and sisters lived together, and only if you had a lot of property in private. Considering the worries of splitting property, it is extremely stupid to buy things like gold and silver and collected them privately. If you used hundreds of gold and silver to buy estates, you could earn 10 thousands of gold and silver in 1 year. More than 10 years later, you could earn hundreds of property, which meant you had already gotten the principal back. The money given to your family members was the interest. What's more, interest was still earned from estates. If you used thousands of gold and silver to run the pawn industry, its profits would double 3 years later. It could be said that you had gotten thousands of property, and money shared by other family members was only interests. Moreover, another 3 years later, you could earn lots of profits. Why did you hide money in the suitcase? Why not took the opportunity to earn profits to benefit everyone? I once saw someone lending their personal belongings to other family members. They used the money to run a business, and they only spent the principal and stored the interest. Gradually, they became richer than ever and such fortune also extended to their brothers and sisters. That was the reward of the person who was good at dealing with affairs." Yuan Cai advocated selling property to get cash. He believed that storage was stupid behavior, as it was not only getting dead money but also incurring theft. If one used the money to do business, then the principal produced interest and in turn interest generated the principal. At the very least, one could lend money to help others run their businesses while only collecting the principal. This was also a way to accumulate virtue if one became rich. All this related to borrowing and pawning, namely, credit or mortgage lending; other aspects of business operations were not mentioned in the book. It seemed that his thoughts still remained on land, housing, lending, securities and other commercial activities. In addition to consumption, commercial activities were mainly in the circulation field in the Song Dynasty as it took 10 years to recover cost for agriculture, but only 3 years for circulation. Operating was always better than fixed deposit. Such a change in consciousness reflected the economic development and credit theory of the Song Dynasty, the unprecedented development of commercial economy, credit in paper form, the introduction of Chinese trading markets centered on *Jiaoyin* shops (like today's securities exchange company), reflections on the financial management ideology, the rejection of the traditional value storage concept and the advancement of utilitarian ethics.

Yuan Cai firmly opposed depositing wealth in friends' homes or setting up an estate in the name of one's wife. He said that "there someone stole possessions or deposited it to his wife's parents' home, or in-law relatives. At last, it was appropriated by others and dare not ask for it or even little money was returned. Some bought the real estate in the name of their wives or in-laws, and eventually, the real estate was forcibly occupied. Some also bought lands in the name of their wives, and if they died, their wives would cart away all possessions once remarried. A gentleman should learn from it and was wary of it to avoid similar things from happening. As ideology and society developed, one would become aware of family inheritance based on patriarchy, which was unshakable and unquestionable.

Traditional Chinese society was a patriarchal system and characterized by co-construction of home and country Therefore, the traditional Chinese family, as a cell of society, assumed a relatively complicated and arduous sociological and political role. The problem was that the focus of the family was not on financial management, but on governing family, that is, on how to maintain the stability and harmony of the clan order based on kinship ties. Family governance took filial piety as the basis, and country governance took ritual, music, benevolence, righteousness, wisdom and integrity as the bases for benevolent rule. It was the characteristic of Chinese traditional political ethics. However, ruling of life and governing the country which were of economic significance never vanished. The people-oriented principle that people should become rich first if countries wanted to be rich constituted the ethical ideology of traditional Chinese economy from the perspective of economy. After the Qin and Han Dynasties, utilitarianism penetrated and merged with Confucianism and constituted the characteristics of Chinese traditional financial ethics. This kind of feature was reflected in Yuan Cai's *The Yuan Family Education*. It can be seen that it not only advised the maintenance of the ties of patrilineal kinship but also encouraged entrepreneurship to enrich the future generations. It advocated helping one's relatives, friends and the poor based on one's financial ability, but did not advise one to frequently lend money to others. It not only advocated an interest-taking system but also advocated that grain should not be lent out more. This book was a wonderful combination of business and ethics, and also a statement on the betrayal of the traditional exploitative system by usury. Among the traditional books, *Family Instructions* can be described as an ethical education and also financial management manual, so it is actually a rare and time-honored book.

Chapter 6

Financial Thought of the Yuan and Ming Dynasties

1. Introduction

Paper money dominated the circulation of money in the Yuan Dynasty, and silver gained currency status in this period, with gold and copper coins occasionally found in circulation. Paper money of the Yuan Dynasty was the first nationwide circulated paper money in the world, and also the paper money with the most rigorous management system in the ancient world. It featured the oldest paper money management system, with policies, methods and agencies dedicated to the management thereof, namely, the Jiaochao Minting Agency in charge of paper money issuance, the Pingzhun Repository (stabilizing and benchmarking) in charge of exchange between gold, silver and paper money, and the Huiyi repository for the disposal of broken money.

There were different types of paper money including Zhongtong paper money (1260), Zhiyuan paper money (1287) and Zhizheng paper money (1350). The former had remained in circulation throughout the Yuan Dynasty, and had been the dominant currency throughout the Yuan Dynasty. In March of the 24th year of the Zhiyuan Period (1287), the government promulgated the *14 Rules Governing the Circulation of Zhiyuan Baochao Paper Money* drafted by Ye Li,[1] which enacted a

---

[1] Ye Li (1242–1292), courtesy name Taibai, another courtesy name Shunyu, was born in Hangzhou in the period between the Song Dynasty and the Yuan Dynasty.

complete set of organization and management principles for paper money circulation, including unit name, issuance reserve, legal tender capacity, and issuance replacement, which remained in effect until the demise of the Yuan Dynasty. These institutions marked the fact that the circulation of the Yuan Dynasty paper currency entered the phase of perfection, and was ranked as the earliest monetary system regulations in the world. However, due to the fact that the Yuan government engaged in constant warfare which brought about staggering military expenses, as well as astronomical expenses including awards to princes, conducting Buddhist activities and imperial expenditure, "which resulted in a situation where the annual revenue could not sustain the expenses for half a year, the remaining amount had to be borrowed from the principal which had been set aside as collateral for paper money issuance."[2] Additional Baochao was issued on the one hand and new modified paper money was introduced on the other hand, and an inflationary policy was implemented at an aggravating rate. Meanwhile, full circulation capacity had not been designated to paper money in regions south of the Yangtze River, where there was serious supply shortage of small denomination paper money; on the contrary, Zhizheng Tongbao copper coins were minted to be circulated alongside copper coins minted by the previous dynasties, which further accelerated and intensified paper money inflation and commodity price surge. The collapse of the monetary system resulted in a situation "where it was impossible to buy a *dou* (volumetric measure in ancient China, equal to 10 liters) of grain with a ten *ding* paper money, and thereafter barter trade was practiced in all counties and prefectures, all paper moneys, governmental and private, ceased circulation." Circulation of copper coins was restored in the localities.

Zhu Yuanzhang established the Baoquan Bureau in the 21st year of the Zhizheng Period of Emperor Huizong in the Yuan Dynasty (1361) to mint Dazhong Tongbao money, and established the Baoquan Bureau in Jiangxi and the various provinces to mint five types of Dazhong Tongbao after defeating Chen Youliang in the 24th year. In the Ming Dynasty, money was named Tongbao as there was the character "Yuan" in the name of Emperor Zhu Yuanzhang (to avoid directly mentioning the emperor's name) and money needed *Tong* (circulation; to be circulated); therefore,

---

[2]"Money" in *Comprehensive Survey Continued*.

the name settled on was Tongbao. In the 7th year of the Hongwu period in the Ming Dynasty, the paper money law was enacted and the Baochao Tiju Bureau (paper money promotion bureau) was established; a great amount of Baochao of the Ming Dynasty was used in the extended period of 130 years from the 8th year to the Hongzhi period. Paper money and coin had become the folk name of money. In the Hongwu period, copper coins, gold and silver were repeatedly banned from circulation, and paper money alone was circulated. In the two hundred strong years of the Ming Dynasty, only one paper money was issued and circulated, with one *guan* being the biggest face value; this was the point different from that of the Song, Jin and Yuan Dynasties.

However, in the Ming Dynasty, paper money circulation was in a situation where there was only issuance without a corresponding callback, or there was large issuance with small callback, which was actually a defect. The practice resulted in the increasing accumulation of paper money in circulation, and paper money devalued. A difference occurred between the new and the old money, "in the 13th year of the Hongwu Period, 'Paper Money Replacement Method', a method of replacing old money with new money was instituted, by the 30th year, all businessmen in the various prefectures of Hangzhou engaged in pricing commodities in gold, regardless of the value thereof."[3] The Ming government had instituted various administrative methods to safeguard the circulation of Baochao to little avail. In the Hongzhi period (1488–1505), paper money existed in name only. After the Chenghua period and Hongzhi period of Emperor Xianzong of the mid-Ming Dynasty, silver gradually gained the status of principal money, with taxes, rents, labor service and wages for employees being calculated in silver; big-value transactions were conducted in silver and small-value transactions were conducted in small bits of silver. The emperor, government officials and the nobles pursued and accumulated silver at an amazing speed and scale for the purpose of quenching their selfish desires, hunting for land, squandering and pursuing luxuries, and only a small amount of the silver accumulated was invested in production, most was retained in the realm of circulation, employed in speculative activities of buying low selling high. By the end of the Ming Dynasty,

---

[3]*Zhu Yuanzhang Chronicles*, vol. 251, March, 30th year of the Hongwu period.

foreign silver dollars were already entering China. Circulation of standard copper coins, namely, copper coins minted by the government, was restored from the mid-Ming Dynasty. The government employed silver and the people used copper coins in transactions, with silver and copper coins being used side by side.

Usury was rampant in the Yuan Dynasty. The rulers engaged in constant warfare, taxes and rents were exorbitant and frequent, and all participated in the usury business; capital contributions were made by the Khans, the princes, the princesses, the queens and the concubines. Usury became the order of the day, with far-reaching effects and the annual interest could be as high as 100%. If the borrower failed to repay the loan at maturity, the interest would be converted into capital. A *ding* of silver could be turned into 1,024 *dings* after ten years of accumulating, and the loan could not be paid even with land, houses and cattle taken away, and the person's wife and children being taken as servants. After the Yuan Dynasty unified China, the rulers had once decreed to ban the practice of usury; however, it was only a cover-up, which exactly indicated that usury had become a serious social issue. The pawn business was well developed in the Yuan Dynasty, with pawn shops, pawn stores, etc. The government established public pawns, called *Guanghuiku* (universal beneficiary store), and encouraged houses of solid means to engage in the pawn business, giving loan on mortgage or on credit. Usury was prevalent in the Ming Dynasty. Landlords, merchants and usurer operators were three entities in one, and the situation in the countryside was even worse, as pawn businesses were more prevalent, with a greater variety of names, such as pawn store, pawn shop, hypothecation shop, etc. Pawn shops became the universal name thereafter. The bigger shops had capital in excess of 10,000 taels of silver, and the smaller ones also had capital of 1,000 or 2,000 taels. In addition to providing loans, the pawn shops also engaged in buying and selling army provisions as well as the exchange business. The term for mortgage loan was generally two years, or ten months in some places (shorter term for smaller items and lower value). The wealthy and powerful houses opened "account chambers" engaging in credit loan business, targeting government officials. As the bud of capitalism sprung up, usury was impacted, and the interest rate trended lower. By the end of the Ming Dynasty, pawn rates dropped to 20%, and the phenomena of extra extortion and exacting redemption terms were less prevalent. By the end of the Ming Dynasty, private banks appeared, which engaged in issuing checks, making loans, providing exchange service and financing among individuals. The exchange business was handed over to the government, which was a mode of loan, and drafts gradually became an instrument of circulation. In cities with well-developed commerce, the people started issuing drafts, which was the harbinger of the banking business, the birth and starting point of capitalist production relations. Gold and silver exchange businesses were well developed in the Yuan Dynasty; silver shops and silversmith shops which manufactured silverware also engaged in buying and selling as well as exchange of silver and gold, and exchange of copper coins.

A lecture on *Chinese History on Hudson River by Huang Renyu* provided little help to our understanding of the social consequences due to the frequent replacement of able financial ministers as well as some specific financial notions in the Yuan Dynasty. He wrote, "Under the then despotic imperial authority, regulation of finances and taxes conducted by fawning ministers such as Ahmad, Lu Shirong, Sangge, etc., would certainly not end well."

At that time, an accounting system of exact verification could not be established; therefore, if the guiding principle was established as "benevolence," then everything would be done perfunctorily, whereas if the guiding principle was shifted to "practicality," then cruelty and mistreatment in the lower levels of the government could not be contained. It is hard to say it was a mistake of any individual.

In the realm of ideology, after Kublai Khan and the Mongolian rulers brought China under their rule, they accepted the argument that "the laws of the Han nationality should be instituted as the state learning" and were firmly convinced that "the laws of the Han nationality" should be established as the "model after which the empire shall be founded," and that Confucianism should be upheld and esteemed. Faced with the foreign rule of an alien nationality, some Confucian scholars tried to direct their code of conduct with the idea of "converting the barbarian tribe into Huaxia people"; in the ruling group, the powerful represented by Ahmad went all out to stop the cultural exchange between the Mongol and the Han nationalities, which manifested as strife and chaos, whereas in the domain of thought, there had been strife between following the established Mongolian customs and screening and adopting new laws of the Han nationality.[4] Having summarized the ruling experiences from the previous dynasties, Zhu Yuanzhang of the Ming Dynasty worked out and promulgated a set of mature tyrannical political practices, and set an unshakable rule for posterity: "Anyone who talks about reforming the ancestral system shall be deemed as a traitor." Therefore, this mentality of firm adherence to the ancestral system of the Ming Dynasty emperors not only dominated politics but also produced tremendous impact on other fields,[5] and of course, financial thought was no exception.

2. Wang Yun on Zhongtong paper money

Wang Yun (1227–1304), courtesy name Zhongmou, style Qiujian, was born in Jixian County of Weizhou (currently within Henan Province). He took up posts including reviewing official, composer in the Imperial Academy and compiler in the Academia Historica, and also assumed posts such as assistant to the executive secretariat, royal censor, circuit inspector for Henan, Hebei, Shandong, Fujian regions, etc., and scholar at the Imperial Academy. His works were compiled into the *Complete Works of Scholar Qiujian*.

In the period from September of the first year of the Zhongtong period to the following September, he accompanied the executive secretariat to the Kaiping (present-day Plain Blue Banner in Inner Mongolia) conference, and wrote *Zhongtong Chronicles*. In the 19th year (1282) of the Zhiyuan period, he wrote the *35 Conveniences for the People — On Monetary Law*[6] when he was in the post of deputy inspector for the east and the west regions of Shandong region, in which he summarized the experiences of success and failure in the preliminary issuing of Zhongtong paper money.

---

[4]Liu Fusheng, *China's History of Ancient Thoughts — Volume of Song, Liao, the Western Xia, Jin and Yuan*, pp. 86–94, Guangxi People's Publishing House, 2006.
[5]*Tian Peidong Study on Socio-Economic History of the Ming Dynasty*, pp. 1–4, Beijing Yanshan Publishing House, 2008.
[6]*The Complete Works of Scholar Qiujian*, vols. 80 and 90. No more citations shall be provided for further quotes hereinbelow.

2.1. On the experience of Zhongtong paper money issuance

In the 2nd year of the Zhongtong period (1261), when Zhongtong paper money had just been issued, officials from the executive secretariat and the promotion bureau in charge of the affair drew extensive opinions from various sources, weighed carefully the merits and demerits, and proceeded with great prudence, "for fear that it might be stagnant in circulation inconveniencing both the private and the government." In order to guarantee the smooth circulation of Zhongtong *Baochao* (hereafter referred to as "Zhongtong paper money") and maintain the stability of currency value, in addition to seriousness and prudence in attitude, a relatively complete paper money management system was implemented. Wang Yun summarized effective experiences into seven measures:

First, the silver reserve money system was implemented. With paper money as the son and silver the mother, "an equilibrium must be maintained" so that stability of currency value and commodity prices may be properly maintained.

As for "Leveling and stabilizing prices," as a representative and token of silver, paper money "circulates as though they are physical silver." The unit of account for financial expenditure and revenue in government documents was *"ding,"* with 50 taels of silver converting into one *ding*, equal to 10,000 *guan* of paper money. However, the unit of account for copper coins was set as the unit of account for Zhongtong paper money: "the denomination of *guan* is conspicuously printed on the paper money, the paper money and the coins stand in the relation of interdependence as the inside and outside of the same entity, the instrument serves as the fundamental evidence. Its value ranged from 10 *wen* to 10 *guan*, ten scales in between in total."

Second, a full silver reserve policy was implemented. "There is usually no shortage of silver reserve for the amount of paper money." Repositories for leveling, stabilizing and promoting the use of paper money were established in the *Lu* (ancient Chinese administrative division name, usually bigger than a province), paper money repository for short. "When a certain amount of paper money is issued, an equivalent amount of silver must be simultaneously set aside, as though physical silver is circulated." The various *Lus* should set aside silver for reserve in an amount which was equivalent to the amount of paper money issued, and immediate redemption must be guaranteed, so that the credit and stability of the paper money was safeguarded.

Third, a system of exchange between paper money and silver was practiced or trade-in service was provided. Paper money may be freely exchanged into silver, and the deposited silver reserve is set aside for redemption. Only the cost of production can be deducted from redemption: "when paper money is redeemed for silver and worn and broken paper money is replaced, no extra charge other than the cost for craftsman and ink be deducted therefrom." Production cost was set "at 30 *wen*. Reduced to 20 *wen* at the 3rd year. The cost was reverted to the original amount in the 22nd year. Value denomination is conspicuous and distinct, circulation is mandatory even with a little damage to the paper money, criminal charge shall be imposed on anyone refusing to accept such."[7] Stabilizing repositories were established in all *Lus* across the country. Paper money gained outstanding credit and reputation.

Fourth, all taxes and rental fees were to be collected in paper money. "The intermediate bodies may not set up any obstacle, all industry and commerce taxes, labor service of any amount, shall be denominated in paper money, the form may be not entirely intact and new, acceptance thereof is mandated."

The government could not refuse to accept broken and worn paper money. Only in this way could the smooth circulation of paper money be guaranteed.

Fifth, the amount of paper money issued was put under strict control. Paper money issuance could not be employed to make up for fiscal deficit. "Except for expenses related to production thereof by the relevant repositories and bureaus, no fund may be borrowed from the reserve, be the cause urgent or not." Therefore, the annual issuance of paper money did not exceed 100,000 *ding* before 1273, and the total paper money issuance did not exceed 1,600,000 *ding* by 1275.

Sixth, local officials were mandated to keep paper money circulation under strict control. They were required to acquire timely knowledge of

---

[7]*History of the Yuan Dynasty — Shi HuoZhi — Monetary Circulation*, vol. 8, Zhonghua Book Company, 1976, p. 2370.

and handle change in financial situations. "A three-day limit is set for *Xuanfusi* (promotion and pacification bureau, the chief officer in a *Dao*) in the seven *Daos* (administrative division name, another name for *Lu*) to report whether there is stagnation in paper money circulation or price fluctuation which hinders paper money circulation and harms the interests of the people, relevant measures shall be worked out to deal with such circumstances."

Seventh, in the meanwhile, stabilizing repositories would be set up to bring commodity prices under strict control and to stabilize paper money value. Once the price of corn, on which the national livelihood of the people and the national economy hinged, was stabilized, the stability of purchasing power could be forcefully upheld. The government set up stabilizing warehouses in the administration at various levels. They would buy corn at a relatively higher price when corn price was low in a good year, and sell corn at a relatively lower price when corn price was high in a lean year. "Production cost of paper money is to be factored into the paper money, such cost shall be separately designated for the various administrative bodies at different levels, and such shall be established as the reserve principal for stabilizing purpose." "When this scheme is employed for a couple of years continuously without interruption, then over a period of three years, a profit of a million *Dan* (Chinese volumetric unit, 100 liters) of corn could be obtained without costing any labor, hence a reserve for a year could be continuously maintained." "When the harvest is not so good in a year, the corn is to be released at a fair price; by so doing, the paper money reserve is maintained, and the people would be able to live on in peace."[8]

Wang Yun spoke highly of paper money circulation of this period, considered the monetary system at that time very convenient and summarized seven advantages from it. Paper money supply was kept under a certain amount; hence, acquiring paper money was difficult, and purchasing power thereof remained firm. The situation wherein commodities were much more valuable than paper money which harmed both the people and the government was avoided, and therefore he stated, "paper money was often hard to come by, this is one advantage."

---

[8]*The Complete Works of Scholar Qiujian — On Reinstalling Stabilizing Warehouses and Paper Money.*

Two, cost was saved. This meant that fiscal deficit was eliminated, currency value was held stable and the market remained stable. "Three, the silver reserve is maintained at full amount without being appropriated." This meant that people were not worried about paper money redemption, its creditworthiness stayed firm and its value stable. "Four, there were few forgers." This meant the necessary condition for the proper circulation of paper money. "Five, paper money is valued much more than gold and silver." On the condition that paper money value remained stable, paper money was more convenient to keep, carry and transport than metal money, and hence more conducive to commodity production as well as the extensive and in-depth development of exchange. "Six, monetary value is constantly kept firm"; "Seven, money value is maintained and commodity prices are stable." The market remained stable, which was an important guarantee for social reproduction and peaceful livelihood of the people.

2.2. On lessons learned from the failure of the Zhongtong paper money issuance

However, the prosperous situation did not last long, and stable paper money circulation was maintained for only about a score of years. After the 13th year of the Zhiyuan period (1276), Ahmad (?–1282) dominated the imperial power, engaging in excessive paper money issuance in order to grab wealth. Soon the collapse of the Southern Song and expansion of territory of the Yuan Dynasty made the demand for paper money surge, and Zhongtong paper money issuance rose to two or three hundred thousand *ding* before the 13th year from the original 73,352 *ding*, and further surged to 1,419,665 *ding* by the 13th year. Issuance reserve was appropriated, and Zhongtong paper money became irredeemable paper money in practice, losing 90% of its value. That is, "today's one *guan* is only equivalent to former 100 *wen*, the depreciation is so extensive and extreme." Wang Yun summarized the causes into four points:

1. The first one was that silver reserve for issuance had been appropriated, and there was no reserve left. "From the 13th year of the Zhiyuan period on, all gold and silver deposited in the various repositories

along with taxes and paper money reserve were removed to the capital, which was the very way to scrap the reserve system, thus was one reason leading to the depreciation of paper money." The powerful courtier Ahmad moved all gold and silver deposited in the stabilizing repositories from all *Lus* to Dadu (present-day Beijing). Wang Yun considered it the topmost cause for the depreciation of Zhongtong paper money. Wang Yun was born a hundred years after Zhou Xing; however, he still adhered firmly to the traditional concepts of full reserve in paper money issuance theory. Though he was not very definitive in advancing his proposals, he repeatedly emphasized the point that it was better to set aside as much paper money reserve as possible, and that was an unshakable foundation. Hence, it could be seen that the full reserve and incomplete reserve proposals were both ignored, which failed to draw the attention of the authorities.

2. The second was the runaway minting and issuing of Zhongtong paper money due to which the market was flooded with excessive paper money. When Zhongtong paper money was first minted, the situation was different: "minted paper money was exclusively issued to the governments at lower levels, and the repositories and pertinent bureaus shall conduct replacement for broken and worn paper money for further circulation. Such paper money was used for purposes including labor service and taxes, therefore, there was a quantity limit to issuance, the quantity limit was controlled sparingly and not being exceeded, hence the internal and external factors were balanced and checked by each other which was set as the basis for paper money circulation law. Therefore paper money was often hard to come by, commodity must wait for paper money before they could be transacted. Under these circumstances, how could paper money not be cherished? The situation was different when Zhongtong paper money was first issued. Minting and issuing paper money were placed under strict control, a portion of paper money stayed in the realm of circulation for a long period of time, except where new paper money was required to replace broken and worn paper money, the rest was retained in circulation for repeated employment, that was what was called the inherent quota on which issuance was based; and there was also an external quota on which paper money issuance was based, that is, the

amount of taxes and rents were set as the basis in determining the amount of paper money issuance." These two quotas constituted the objective restraining mechanism for paper money supply. If the rules were followed, then the paper money amount in circulation would not be excessive: "weighing the practical situation and balancing the internal and external restraining factors, for the essential purpose of circulating the money." If these rules were not followed, then "there would be no limit to minting of paper money, all expenses including those of tens of millions of dings were to be paid from the newly minted paper money, which was veritably all minting and no retiring. Those paper moneys not secured by reserve were easily available to the people in great quantity, hence commodity price surged and could not be purchased with such paper money, this was the second reason leading to the depreciation." If the rules were not followed, and "the government issued paper money without any restraint and without calculating the paper money supply, took no consideration of how to retire excessive paper money, then things will definitely go wrong."

3. The third was that Zhongtong paper money was used as advance payment in snapping up purchase of commodities. The government valued commodities more than paper money in the first place, considering paper money an object easily obtainable with little production effort: "for fear of commodities being purchased by others before them, therefore they held paper money light and were prone to purchase stuff with it without much restraint." Actually, implied in this statement was the theory that when the currency value of Zhongtong paper money decreases, in order to maximally reduce or avoid loss, the government would "purchase in advance before crops were harvested." More paper money was issued in order to snap up commodities, which resulted in the situation "commodities are more valuable than paper money." The situation fell into a vicious cycle, and was ever aggravating.

4. The fourth was that the managing staff engaged in malpractice and profiteering activities. The heads and employees of the paper money promotion repositories of the peripheral *Lus* charged extra production cost when recovering broken and worn paper money privately, making a profit therefrom. "When people carried broken and worn paper

money to the repository and could not get replacements within the specified time, the people had to continue using such broken and worn paper money. Hence such broken and worn paper money got more broken and worn, till it was difficult for such paper to be circulated; and a grade system was established for such paper money. Commodity purchase must be made with superior quality paper money, while other grades must be discounted when used in purchasing commodity." Replacement specified by the regulations was not conducted if no benefit was offered. According to historical records, paper money repository limited replacement to three or four hundred ding every day, and some even refused to handle replacement. Hence, what was circulated on the market was all broken and worn paper money. Sometimes officials engaged in blackmail, or even fabricated gold and silver buyers to rig prices; they would sell gold and silver purchased from the repository at a government-fixed price at an exorbitant price, which created gold and silver black markets.[9]

The first two points of understanding were very important. So long as there is paper money circulation, there will surely be a chain reaction of value diminishing, commodity price rising, credit destabilizing, financial market getting constrained due to runaway paper money issuance and insufficient issuance reserve.[10] These two principles stay unshakable to this day, which indicates that Wang Yun's understanding of paper money circulation was very insightful. However, his understanding of issuance reserve was still incomplete.

Regarding the depreciation of Zhongtong paper money, Wang Yun raised two remedies. The first was insistence on redemption of paper money, "recovering paper money with physical silver." Two thousand *ding* were to be appropriated to bigger *Lus*, and one or two hundred *ding* for

---

[9]See Peng Xinwei, *A History of Chinese Money*, p. 585.
[10]Contemporary scholar Liu Xuan (1233–1288, courtesy name Bo Xuan, minister of the ministry of rites, minister of the ministry of personnel), also analyzed and understood the matter from the two aspects when he engaged in discussing the reformation of paper money following the mandate of the executive secretariat in December of the 23rd year in Kublai Khan's Zhiyuan period (1286).

smaller areas: "when paper money becomes scarce, the people would surely bring their silver to the repository to exchange for paper money, hence the value of paper money increases and silver flows back to the government." Paper money value increases and silver concentrates in the government, killing two birds with one stone — what a wonderful thing! In September of the 19th year of the Zhiyuan period, the executive secretariat promulgated *Measures on Regulating Paper Money Circulation*, decreeing that the government shall be engaged in buying and selling gold and silver to maintain paper money price, private transaction of gold and silver was prohibited and officers engaging in malpractices were to be punished. It should be said that these measures were connected to the opinions advanced by Wang Yun. The second remedy was producing and issuing new silver-backed paper money: "one hundred new paper money shall be converted to two hundred old paper money, and the outstanding paper money would be gradually recovered." That is, he advocated that the government should compulsorily shrink the amount of paper money circulation by openly plundering paper money bearers. This measure was definitely beneficial to the fundamental interests of the top ruling group and class represented thereby; however, it would harm the interests of other classes and social strata. Hence, it was a scheme of extreme appeal to the government. Five years later, the first minister Ye Li recommended the issuance of Zhiyuan paper money, with one *guan* of Zhiyuan paper money converting to five *guan* of Zhongtong paper money, and the silver standard being restored: "modeled after the original setup of Zhongtong paper money, official repository was set up in the various *Lus*, in charge of selling and buying gold and silver, stabilizing paper money."[11] The connection of these measures to views of paper money theory held by Wang Yun cannot be denied.

The remedy advanced by Wang Yun for handling inflation failed to address the essence of the issue. Without reducing and limiting the amount of paper money issuance, placing a check on warring activities, bringing under control the expenses arising from awarding and Buddhist activities, and eliminating fiscal deficit, the solution for treating inflation would go

---

[11] *Institutions of Yuan Dynasty — Paper Money — Rules Governing the Circulation of Zhiyuan Baochao Paper Money.*

nowhere; all were but treating the symptoms without touching the root cause.

After Wang Yun, Zhang Zhihan (?–1296, courtesy name Zhouxiang, style West Rock Senior, practiced an old school style of conducting office, and wrote *West Rock Collection*), a scholar at the Imperial Academy, noted in *On Chubi (Paper Money)*, "no concern of the present day world is more acute than the worry for inadequacy of wealth; whereas no concern in the use of wealth is more acute than in the weakness of paper money .... From the Zhongtong period (1260–1263) to this day, over a period of more than 20 years, treacherous courtiers dominated the power, their sole purpose was to amass wealth, the amount so amassed was dozens of times of that in the beginning of the dynasty. Paper money was expanding by the day and its price diminishing by the day; gold, silk, pearl and jade were getting scarcer by the day and the value thereof rising by the day, all were attributed to the lack of temperance in issuing and retiring paper money." He put forward three strategies for issuing and retiring paper money: "for instance, offer gold for redemption, and make it widely accepted, this is strategy one. Mint metal money and set it into a relation of interdependence with paper money, and set a proper conversion rate, this is strategy two. Making new paper money to replace the outstanding one, make the people accept and use it, this is strategy three." His first and third strategies corresponded with the strategies proposed by Wang Yun, and Wang Yun did not mention the second one, neither could it work as a fundamental cure. Liu Xuan also advanced four "remedies." The first was "nothing but to stop producing *guan* denominated paper money, only producing small denomination paper money." That is, stop issuing big denomination paper money, only issue small denomination paper money, in order to facilitate people making changes in payment and replacing broken and worn paper money, and reducing the inflationary pressure. The second was "restoring the gold and silver reserve for paper money, returning them to their original places to pacify the people." This meant restoring the gold and silver reserve system for paper money, and the gold and silver was to be returned to the stabilizing repositories of the various places to safeguard the credit of paper money. The third was "strictly forbidding powerful officials and wealthy people from engaging in fraudulent transaction in the repository." Eliminating malpractices including speculating in gold and silver and embezzlement of the repository fund was essential. The fourth was "the state treasury must tailor its expenditure according to the revenue, for instance, if the annual taxes, revenue, etc. bring about a million ding, while annual expenditure is only five or seven hundred thousand ding, the surplus old paper money can be immediately destroyed." By implementing the foregoing measures, financial surplus would be guaranteed, and paper money issuance was not only not to be used to make up for fiscal deficit but the surplus paper money in circulation was to be gradually called back. He opposed issuing new paper money, considering it was nothing but "renaming the old stuff, without security by gold and silver, there is no restraint in drawing therefrom by the army and the country, after a few years it would fall into the same old rut as the old Zhongtong paper money had done" (*New Compilation of the History of Yuan Dynasty*, vol. 87). His understanding was pretty profound, and his ideas were also superior and to the point. However, Ghsang dominated the central government from 1281 onward, and advocated circulating Zhiyuan paper money; hence Liu Xuan's proposal was shelved and failed to make any impact.

2.3. On promotion of Zhongtong paper money

The Zhongtong Chronicles was written by Wang Yun in the first year of the Zhongtong period (1260) when the central government was first established and he was sent to the capital and promoted to the post of examiner in the executive secretariat. In the spring of the second year, he was transferred to the Imperial Academy as composer and compiler, and concurrent compiler for the national history museum. Many imperial edicts and decrees issued in the early phase of Kublai Khan's rule were mostly from him. He had accompanied officials of the executive secretariat to the Kaiping Conference, and kept a journal while performing his official duties ("daily journal on duty at the executive secretariat"). The data were highly creditable, providing us with relevant historical materials relating to the Zhongtong paper money rules and Wang Wentong.

Before the inception of the Zhongtong period of the Yuan Dynasty, the various Daos had made paper money to be used within their respective jurisdictions; there was no uniform paper money, and therefore no unified and sound paper money system took form. When Kublai Khan ascended the throne, he applied himself to forge a prosperous country; however, he faced mounting problems of tremendous military expenses arising from the previous war of the Khan succession, enormous expenditure for building palaces and homes, instituting military and administrative organizations, emoluments for the various staff and annual awards to the tribal clans and princes, while there was little reserve and inadequate savings in the state coffer, with the income falling short of national expenditure.

Wang Wentong (?–1262), courtesy name Yidao, was born in Dading prefecture of Beijing Lu in the Jin Dynasty (present-day Ningcheng of Inner Mongolia). Wang passed the imperial palace examination as a scripture scholar; he had widely read books of ingenious strategies and plots in his youth, was fond of persuading people in debate and was indeed a man of talent and intelligence. He was recommended to Kublai Khan and was rapidly promoted in the central government. Having been appointed as an officer supervising all government bodies in the executive secretariat, his initial post was director of government affairs, in charge of reforming general administrative affairs. He promoted Zhongtong paper money. A rigorous monetary law was one of the three major contents of his wealth management system (the other two being household rectification and allocation of salt franchise), together with facilitating commerce and life of the people, improving national financial revenue and expenditure; these became the most conspicuous wealth management achievements of Wang Wentong, which won Kublai Khan's approval and recognition from political dissenters. In the inception of the Zhongtong period, the imperial edict proclaimed the intent to have paper money circulated in the country without obstruction: "soon the imperial edict ordered the executive secretariat to produce Zhongtong paper money .... In winter of the year, Zhongtong paper money was first launched, value thereof ranging from ten *wen* to two thousand *wen*, ten scales in total, which was to be circulated in all *Lus* across China without time limit, taxes and rents were all to be accepted in such."[12]

In January of the 2nd year of the Zhongtong period, the executive secretariat posted announcements notifying the various *Lus*, saying,

---

[12] *History of the Yuan Dynasty — Biography of Wang Wentong*, vol. 15, p. 4594.

"governments at the various levels shall produce Zhongtong paper money according to the model print, and paper money so produced shall be circulated in the various *Lus* without time limit. Payments in paper money for the various taxes shall all be accepted by the government. If anyone brings paper money to the repository to exchange for silver, then silver shall be paid to such person according to the number stipulated by the regulations, no delay is allowed. Except for three percent production cost on paper money, no more extra charge is permitted to be imposed thereon. The following provisions shall be followed in the use and circulation of paper money. Where anyone impedes and subverts the implementation of monetary laws, legal liability thereof shall be investigated and punishment shall be imposed thereon in accordance with the law."

It is sufficient to see the determination and conviction of the government in unifying national paper money. No time limit was set for the circulation of the paper money. It was to be used in all *Lus*, acceptable to the government. It was not instituted as a provisional measure, nor was it a regional currency. It was meant to be a permanent system. This was the first feature. The second feature was that the paper money could be redeemed into silver at any time, except for the deduction of the necessary production cost, all handled in accordance with the stipulations, with no extra deduction allowed; meanwhile, specific provisions were made to ban procrastination and full payment was to be made. This not only indicated that the issuance of paper money was backed up with reserve and that there was no need to worry about its creditworthiness but also that it was designed to prevent the handling officials from engaging in malpractice and hindering the proper circulation and redemption of paper money. In order to guarantee smooth circulation, there were specific provisions regarding retiring paper money: all fiscal taxes could be paid in paper money; so long as the government accepted paper money, the people would use paper money; if the government only issued and refused to accept paper money, then excessive paper money would be retained in the hands of the people, and proper circulation of paper money would be impeded. The disastrous warning from the Song Dynasty still rang fresh. The third reason concerned the two relevant regulations implemented governing circulation. The first was that Zhongtong paper was to be used to purchase all commodities, including gold, silver, silk, cloth, satin and corn, on the market. A *guan* was equivalent to a tael of paper money, and two *guan* equivalent to a tael of silver; this rate was established as the permanent rate in circulation, with no further change ever to be made. Denominations included 10 *wen*, 20 *wen*, 30 *wen*, 50 *wen*, 100 *wen*, 200 *wen*, 300 *wen*, 500 *wen*, one *guan wen* and two *guan wen*. These regulations were obviously specific expositions of the internal and external working mechanisms of silver. The second was replacement of old paper money: "the formerly circulated old paper money and IOUs are to be recovered by the original issuing bodies gradually, shall be entirely recovered from market, retired from circulation (announcement shall be posted on the various government bodies to notify the people of the undertaking), the people shall be kept from harm." The original issuance agency was to be in charge of recovering and replacing old paper money, and a time limit was set for replacement and interest of the people was not to be harmed during the replacement. It should be acknowledged that these three rules were clear and accurate. In the replacement process, Wang Wentong accepted the advice of Liu Su (Promotion and Pacification Envoy of Zhending Lu), ordered that old paper money must be replaced with Zhongtong paper money in full and that the interest of the people must not be harmed.

As Zhongtong paper money was backed up by silver and commodities, all *Lus* were to transfer their formerly held gold and silver to the executive secretariat in exchange for paper money. However, the gold and silver originally held by Zhending had already been moved to the capital. Upon negotiation by officials dispatched by Buluhaiya, the Promotion and Pacification Envoy, an exception was made, and five thousand *ding* of Zhongtong paper money was allocated to Zhengding as a special treatment, which guaranteed the smooth implementation of old paper money replacement.[13]

When Zhongtong paper money was first circulated, for fear that the monetary law was too unwieldy and stagnant which might inconvenience both the government and the individual, Wang Wentong held discussions with officials from the secretariat and bureaus for days on end, deliberated the matters extensively, weighed the merits and demerits of paper money

---

[13] *History of the Yuan Dynasty — Biography of BuLuhaiYa*, vol. 10, p. 3071.

and worked out rigorous measures. In Wang Yun's description of seven points of experience in *On Experiences of Zhongtong Paper Money Issuance*, these had been embodied to varying degrees: "A paper money repository is to be established in the various *Lus*. When a certain amount of paper money is issued, an equivalent amount of silver must be simultaneously set aside, as though physical silver is circulated. According to the amount of tax silver received, regardless of the amount, such silver shall be stored in the various repositories as reserve, a relation of balance and check between silver and paper money shall be established for the purpose of stabilizing prices. There is usually no shortage of silver reserve for the amount of paper money issued. When paper money redemption for silver and worn and broken paper money replacement were conducted, no extra charge other than the cost for craftsman and ink is allowed to be deducted therefrom. The intermediate bodies may not set up any obstacle, all industry and commerce taxes, labor service of any amount, shall be denominated in paper money. Paper money paid thereby may be broken and worn, acceptance must be made. A three-day limit is set for the promotion and pacification bureau in the seven *Dao* to report whether there is stagnation in paper money circulation as well as price fluctuation which hinders paper money circulation and harms the interests of the people, relevant measures shall be worked out and such circumstances shall be addressed. Paper money is to be minted in the general repository in the capital, except for expenses related to production thereof arising from the relevant repositories and bureaus in the *Lus*, no fund may be appropriated from the reserve, be the cause urgent or not. The denomination of *guan* is to be conspicuously printed on the paper money, the paper money and the coins shall stand in the relation of interdependence as the inside and outside of the same entity, the instrument serves as the fundamental evidence. When an entire year had elapsed, tax package silver generated exceeded sixty thousand *ding*, and paper money issuance amounted to over five hundred thousand. It was said in the discussion that if paper money issuance reached a million, interest generated from such paper money would be enough to relieve the requirement for labor service package around the country. The reason was that there was tremendous damage, wear and tear to the paper money in the process of buying and selling commodity therewith over the period of a year, such constituted the yield for the government." He specifically emphasized that Zhongtong paper money could be used to pay the various taxes and rents. During the reign of Mongke Khan, the tax package for one household was four taels, which comprised two taels of silver and two taels of silk satin and dyestuff." When the people had no way to obtain silver for such taxes, and the local governments could not turn in taxes in time, they could only resort to usury, and got exploited, which resulted in a situation where "the taxes in arrears accumulated to more than a million in ten years, and the chief official absconded from office in dodging taxes, most left office the moment they were appointed to the post."[14] In the initial years of the Zhongtong period, an imperial edict was promulgated to relieve silver requirements for taxes in arrears; in the fourth year all taxes packaged were to be paid exclusively in Zhongtong paper money.

Zhong Tang Chronicles also noted that "Paper money has several very convenient features: for one, it is difficult to obtain; for two, the saving of cost; for three, the silver reserve is often maintained at full amount without being appropriated; for four, there are few forgers; for five, paper money is valued much more than gold and silver; for six, monetary value is constantly kept firm; for seven, commodities prices are held stable." There might be some exaggeration in these statements; however, they were not far from the fact, especially in the first 17 or 18 years after Zhongtong paper money was first issued, a great effect was attained. The price level at the time was roughly that a *guan* paper money could purchase a bolt of tough silk, 50 or 60 *wen* paper money could purchase a *liang* of silk, 60 or 70 *wen* for a *dan* of corn, 500 or 600 *wen* for a *dan* of wheat, and 400 or 500 *wen* for half a bolt of silk cloth. The situation was veritably what Hu Zhiyu had said in *Paper Money Circulation*, "In the first year of the Zhongtong period, paper money was first instituted, it was cherished by all walks of life, the government and the people, the high and the low, it circulated as though flowing water." Marco Polo also wrote about the novel and delicate paper money in his travelogue, noting that this nationally issued and circulated instrument was like the dream-like golden touch, it both facilitated the people and improved the state revenue and expenditure, "the finance and property management method excels all treasures of the world combined."[15]

---

[14] Yao Sui Mu, *An Collection — Tombstone on the Clan of Fuyang, Cizhou*.

[15] *History of the Yuan Dynasty — The Travels of Marco Polo*, translated by Feng Chengjun, Zhonghua Book Company, 2004, p. 284.

2.4. Discussions of monetary reform by Lu Shirong

Lu Shirong (?–1285), former name Mao, generally known by his courtesy name, was born in Daming of the Yuan Dynasty (in present-day Hebei). Initially he was a Jiangxi tea-selling envoy. In 1284, he took up the post of the first prime minister in the executive secretariat, and was in charge of finance. He "rectified monetary law of paper money." Zhiyuan copper coins were minted under his supervision. He allowed the people to trade gold and silver without government intervention, and instituted monopoly sale of iron, wine, horses and a portion of salt.

In February of the following year, a planning office was established to work out plans for monetary and corn affairs, and people good at commerce were made officials. In March, promotion and pacification envoys and transportation envoys were installed in the various *Lus* in charge of taxation. Lu Shirong was envied by the ministers, and impeached repeatedly less than six months after adopting the post for exorbitant fleecing of the people and depleting of national wealth as well as disparity between what he preached and what he conducted. In November he was imprisoned and put to death.

There were four key points in the reform program proposed by Lu Shirong.

First, the focus was placed on the situation of financial revenue and expenditure which determined the stability of the currency. He advocated "that the people should be allowed to engage in free trade," abolished the post of bamboo supervisors which opened up trade for bamboo products between the south and the north, reformed taxation on fishery, amended courier station management and made use of many such facilities available to the people: "Reduced and suppressed the encroachment of the powerful" (other than the 932,600 *ding* of annual taxes, no more was to be collected from the people; besides increasing income by suppressing the powerful, such measures could bring in an annual revenue of up to 3 million *ding*), "open ports for international trade" (setting up Quangzhou and Hangzhou as international trade ports, setting up transportation bureaus, building government ships to engage in sea-faring trade, with 70% of profit going to the government and 30% to the merchant), "regulate the market and reform taxes," "institute wine monopoly by the government" (prohibiting the powerful and the rich from operating wineries, the government monopolized wine sale, banned exorbitant salt prices in the selling of salt and wine by the rich merchants and the government and established a salt price stabilizing bureau to sell salt at a fair price). He also acquitted the people from 3-year taxation, exempted the local taxes for the capital area, relieved labor service tax for those who had resumed business after return from fleeing, did not impose a tax on those who produced vinegar and increased remunerations for government officials. He stated, "it is appropriate to order the various *Lus* to set up stabilizing repositories for emergency relief, reduce monthly interest and make loan to the people. If such is carried out, then there would be great multitudes requesting for loans, and the principal shall not be lost." It seemed that he advocated the idea of modifying the stabilizing repository into a stabilizing repository for emergency relief, which could work the effect of stabilizing the paper money while the remaining capital could be loaned to the poor at a lower interest, which would have multiple effects, including facilitating production, peaceful living, increasing financial revenue, promoting economic prosperity, relieving pressure on money issuance by finance and cracking down on the rampant activities of usury. These measures were indeed very insightful and brilliant.

The second point was promoting the use of Zhiyuan copper coin bonds, "following the established practices of Han and Tang Dynasties, collecting copper to mint Zhiyuan money, and producing thin silk money to be circulated alongside the paper money."[16] By so doing, pressure on paper money demand by the market might be relieved. Styles and forms of bonds had been submitted to Kublai Khan, and the emperor approved the proposal for implementation; however, pitifully, Lu Shirong was convicted before the measure was implemented.

The third point was to emphasize the function of the stabilizing repository, consolidating the position of the silver-backed paper money. He criticized that "though the state has established stabilizing repository, few know the operation thereof, which leads to the depreciation of paper money and surging prices of commodities. It is better to order the various Lus to set up stabilizing repositories for emergency relief."

---

[16]*History of the Yuan Dynasty — Biography of Lu Shirong*, vol. 15, pp. 4564–4570. No more citations shall be provided for further quotes from this book hereinbelow.

The fourth point was to allow the people to engage in free trade of gold and silver. "Gold and silver have been items of circulation among the people; since stabilizing repositories were established, private transactions between the people had been banned, from now on, private transactions among the people shall not be regulated." The amount of precious metals circulated on the market would be increased and excessive pressure on paper money in circulation would be reduced; hence, the reputation of paper money would be enhanced, the market force would be employed to automatically regulate the conversion rate between gold and silver and paper money, the value of paper money and the market would be stabilized and the proper circulation of paper money would be maintained.

In addition to the foregoing measures, he also proposed to close the paper money replacement repository. He had been attacked by some as trying to be different for wanting to close the replacement repository on the grounds that Zhongtong paper money was depreciating. According to the impeachments, "Closing the replacement repository on the ground that the paper money depreciates, then the broken and worn paper money held by the people would not be able to be circulated." However, now that broken and worn paper money was not allowed to be circulated, and no replacement was offered, the measure was contradictory to his real intent of "salvaging the monetary law, increasing taxes, promoting the country to prosperity and doing no harm to the people." As more detailed written records are not available, we make no comment and evaluation as to the accusations targeting him of "profiteering," "being harsh and oppressive to the people, incurring complaint to the state, leading to depletion of the wealth of the people and the state," the creditability and truthfulness of which remain an issue to be further investigated.

The Monetary Reform by Lu Shirong survived less than a hundred days because his policies of bringing the country to prosperity by way of regulating the finances, "not taking from the people," but "suppressing the powerful," directly harmed the economic rights and interests of the ruling landed class, and merchants (including Somaciuns) of Mongolian and Han nationalities. Besides, he rode roughshod over matters on backing imperial rule, retaliated against the disciplinary officials who had opposed him by removing them from office and abolishing the pertinent agencies involved, and had clashes of interests with powerful ministers. Both he and his financial regulating programs were strangled before his economic measures showed any effect.

The monetary system reform of Lu Shirong was two years after the treatise *On Monetary Law* written by Wang Yun. Lu Shirong did not elaborate on paper money in isolation, but proceeded from the perspective of improving the circumstances of financial revenue and expenditure, and took into consideration finances, money, commodity price and consolidating silver standards. His measures followed the same train of thought as that of Wang Yun. Even if he did not get inspired by the theory of Wang Yun, his measures proved that Wang's theory was representative of the time, especially the concept of concurrent circulation of metal coins and paper money, which had considerable impact on later generations.

3. Zheng Jiefu's theory of coins supplementing paper money

Zheng Jiefu, courtesy name Yiju, style Tieke, was born in Kaihua of Quzhou in the Yuan Dynasty (in present-day Zhejiang). In 1303, he submitted the *Strategy for National Peace and Prosperity*, in which he elaborated in one plot and twenty categories and forcefully proposed reform. His proposals were mostly to the point; however, he failed to draw any attention. One of the key points he discussed was monetary law. Later he took up the post of a teacher in the Leizhou Lu Academy and was also deputy chief of Jinxi county. Regarding the concurrent circulation of Zhiyuan paper money issued by Kublai Khan in 1287 which soon failed in a manner similar to Zhongtong paper money, resulting in paper money depreciation, in the reign of Temür (1295–1307), the problem of inflation was aggravated. "Scrapped coins are getting melted by the day, and counterfeit paper money is being spread ever widely, national liveliness dwindled, the great ruling power gets encroached, how profound the damage is!" Based on the checks and balance theory of the reserve and paper money, he held that paper money was beneficial to national finance and coins conducive to people's transactions; that is, "paper money is more convenient for national transportation, whereas coins are more portable and convenient for the transactions among the people." "Paper money is an expediency whereas coins are the ever-lasting solution." He advocated for "regulations of minting copper coins, making it a supplement to paper money" and "appealed for minting copper coins to supplement paper money circulation."[17] He strove to establish a stable monetary system with coins and paper money in concurrent circulation. A separate exposition is provided herein.

3.1. *Analysis and comparison of coins and paper money*

In Zheng Jiefu's opinion, there were four defects in paper money circulation. The first was that it made the price of commodities rise and the price of paper money drop. "Nowadays commodity price rises by the day, paper money price drops by the day"; "commodities are getting more valuable while paper money valueless, when this situation continues, paper money circulation will become more stagnant and unwieldy." He demonstrated empirically that the government had decreed "one *guan* Zhiyuan paper money converts to five *guan* Zhongtong paper money"; however, stuff worth one qian (a 100 qians) of Zhongtong paper money in previous years was at that time worth one *guan* of Zhongtong paper money. For instance, neither five *li* (five *qians*) nor one *fen* (10 *qians*) of Zhiyuan paper money could buy anything on the market, the people would not accept them. As time elapsed, "one *guan* of Zhiyuan paper money was worth only a *qian* of Zhongtong paper money." As the price of paper money dropped by the day, commodity price surged, credit thereof was shaken, circulation thereof was impeded, and promotion and circulation were getting more difficult.

The second defect was that broken and worn paper money needed to be destroyed. "Products made from paper could not last long; over a period of five years, they will become completely worn." A production cost of 3% would be withheld when broken and worn paper money was replaced; that is to say, when a small note of one *guan* was replaced, there would be 3% less new paper money in circulation, and the people would lose 30 *qians* for no cause. Moreover, such measures only benefited the city dwellers, "whereas the people of the various counties living in remote villages and places hundreds of miles away from the cities, their paper

---

[17]*Memorials of Famous Ministers of Past Dynasties*, pp. 9–15. No more citations shall be provided for further quotes from this book hereinbelow.

money seldom gets replaced." Besides, the government could only obtain a profit of 30 *qians* therefrom, while the denominations and edges are still distinct for some broken and worn paper money. Therefore, he argued that "it is really a pity to commit these to the flame in accordance with government regulations that broken and worn paper money must be destroyed. Government officials nowadays know only the profit of 30 *qians* obtained from production to the neglect of the loss of 970 *qians*, which is detrimental to both the state and the people." He proposed to abolish the replacement of broken and worn paper money, extend the circulation period of paper money, leave it to be phased out naturally, and opposed the charging of any production cost, the positive significance of which could not be denied. However, if broken and worn paper money was not recovered from circulation, ultimately someone would have to assume the economic loss; failing to answer or shunning the problem would be acquiescing to the practice of shifting the loss to the people. However, it would be a gross mistake to impute the diminishment of paper money in circulation to the destruction of broken and worn paper money and conclude that paper money in circulation would be "diminishing by the day, and the people would have no paper money to use."

The third defect was that there was too much forged paper money in circulation. "Production cost for paper money is so little, therefore forgers flock." "With the production cost of a *ding* a hundred *ding* could be produced, so huge is the profit, how could people stay put and not risk everything to do it." An exorbitant profit could be obtained from forgery, and many outlaws considered it a shortcut to make a fortune; even with draconian laws, such practices could not be stemmed out. In Zheng Jiefu's view, the forgers of the time were mostly powerful local people who pulled the strings of high-ranking officials in secrecy as backing. Forged paper money reached a staggering amount. "Nowadays, nine out of ten of paper money circulated on market is counterfeit money. Counterfeit money is circulated around the country." The order of the market was disturbed when the counterfeit could not be told from the genuine: "counterfeit from those skillful hands is not different from the genuine, even the knowledgeable could not tell the difference." When paper money was taken out from the repository and handed to merchants, "after repeated examination they would say, 'This is counterfeit money'. While counterfeit money was presented thereto, they would readily accept." When circumstance reached such an extent where fake was mistaken for the real, it was a pitiable situation: "Paper money, being the state taxes and a powerful instrument of the government, the use of which is now being shared with the people, what a situation to be cried over, to be wailed over!" The financial power was by no means to pass into hands of others, or encroached by the people, or shared by the people with the government.

Zheng Jiefu definitively pointed out that paper money was the tax of the state, which was equivalent to stating that increasing issuance was increasing tax in disguise, which could only be monopolized by the state, and no individual could encroach upon it. This understanding was very profound, and it was really a remarkable thing that he stated it in such frank and clear terms.

The fourth defect was that it led to polarization of the rich and the poor. Zheng Jiefu remarked, "In ancient times, people go out with ten wen copper coins and could drink wine to capacity and return; how could the people not live in peace and be rich? While today's people go out with ten *wen* paper money, it would not quench the thirst even though the money is used to buy ice; how could the people not be poor?" The people in ancient times were rich and the people in Zheng Jiefu's time were poor. The polarization of the rich and the poor resulted in a situation where at one time people could drink wine to capacity, while at another time they could barely quench their thirst with water for the same amount of money. These are all attributable to the fall of copper coins and depreciation of paper money. He believed that the denomination of paper money was too large, which would not conveniently satisfy people's transaction needs, daily production and every life; plus, the exploitation by intermediating merchants, who profited from them, made the life of the people even harder. The people "may acquire a piece of ten *guan* paper money but could not break it up, on the one hand, if they buy stuff with the paper money they would not get the change back, on the other hand, if they use up the paper money to buy stuff, they would not be able to put to use so much stuff, they have to suffer in many inconceivable ways." "They have to sell their hoarded items at low prices, they could not obtain fair prices for their products, while all profits go to the likes of merchants, how could the people not be poor?" He correctly reflected the fact that while commodity economy recorded substantial progress in the later period of the ancient society, the peasantry could no longer get rid of the disturbance and invasion of market and money; merchants and the government colluded in stepping up exploitation of the peasant, which resulted in the ever-deteriorating living standards and miserable situation of the peasant. However, his attribution of the cause of the situation to the extremely large denomination of paper money and the peasant being forced to accept the exchange mode of unequal values would hardly be tenable. His conclusion that paper money was the root of the people's poverty was a misguided accusation. Paper money of large denomination was not beneficial to commodity transaction and not conducive to the expansion and development of commodity economy. It could become a tool for exploitation and plundering; however, it was by no means the origin of exploitation and plundering.

His argument that paper money led to the poverty of the people was made to prepare the public opinion for reinstating copper coins. He not only revealed the defects in paper money but also expounded on the benefits of circulating copper coins as well the drawbacks in banning the use of copper coins, further demonstrating that copper coins should not be scrapped. First, he believed that there were three conveniences in using coin. One, it could make up for the deficit in financial revenue. Collecting old coins scattered among the people which was of no small amount filled the government coffer of the Jiangzhe (Jiangsu and Zhejiang) area to capacity: "when such is transformed to finance the national economy, it would be as much as the taxation amount for an entire year of the country, it would definitely not be of small benefit." Two, it would make trade fair and free from fraudulent activities, regardless of age and knowledge, which would be conducive to the expansion and development of commodity economy. "In market transaction, when change is no longer an issue, even a small child could go shopping without the concern that he might mistake a broken and worn paper money or counterfeit for a good one." Three, there were benefits to both the people and the state, by increasing national reserve and enabling the people with physical money. When there was paper money of ten thousand denomination, not only could small-amount transactions not be realized but "the state could not get the products of the people ... and the people could not have the use of the national paper money." However, "if the odd products could be transacted via copper coin, then paper money denominated in ten thousand would naturally get circulated, which would benefit both the state and the people."

Second, he further pointed out that there were three inconveniences in banning coins. One, it would turn useless copper into valuable treasure. When copper coins were banned from circulation, they were traded without restriction, got destroyed, melted and cast into vessels, which was really a pity. Two, it was detrimental to the promotion of paper money. When the denomination of paper money was too large and there was no change available for such an amount, "stores would offer change in salt parcel and paper marks, and wineries would offer paint, wooden plates, it was the custom practiced everywhere." Three, it was detrimental to the exchange of equal values and detrimental to the proper conduct of commodity exchange. When merchants stayed for accommodation on the road, if they did not have paper money in small denominations, "they would have to leave something as collateral or sell stuff at a loss. When civilians from villages go to the market to buy something, they would carry corn, or local produce, their products worth ten *qian* would not be able to bring about five *qian*, or they would have to engage in barter trade when they want to buy stuff worth one *qian*. Hence it would impede the exchange between agriculture, commerce, industry and merchants"; that is, it would be detrimental to the economic exchange between the industry and agriculture, the urban and the rural areas.

Following from the demonstration, did it mean that Zheng Jiefu opposed the use of paper money and prepared to abolish paper money circulation? The answer was negative. He only proposed that paper money should be employed for big denomination transactions, whereas copper coin should be employed for small-sum payments, and that paper money should be mainly employed by the government and copper coin by the people.

3.2. On paper money circulation law and metal coin circulation law

Zheng Jiefu believed that the issuance principle of money should be "benefiting the country and the people"; that is, when the government mints money, it should not only benefit the country but also the people, and no negligence or overemphasis on any side was permitted. He accused those who "could not move the government without making claim of exorbitant profit, tried to induce the state into implementing their theories." For instance, he thought that Ye Li was one such person. In his view, if their proposals were implemented, a situation where the state did not see any benefit but the people were severely harmed would occur; these were actually strategies jeopardizing the state, the defects of which continued till long after, such as the price of paper money dropping by the day and forgery being more prevalent. Ye Li advocated issuing Zhiyuan paper money, one piece for five pieces of Zhongtong paper money, and claimed that the profit would be five times greater in a year without adding any paper money production cost. However, the fact was that, after a few years, "one piece of Zhiyuan paper money was only equivalent to one Zhongtong paper money." Some advocated issuing Dade paper money at a rate of one piece of Dade paper money for ten pieces of Zhiyuan paper money. The argument was the same as that of Ye Li. Zheng Jiefu strongly opposed such a proposition, noting that adopting such a measure would "make the defect of Zhiyuan paper money exceed that of the Zhongtong paper money." He warned that the demise of the Song Dynasty could serve as a lesson for them to learn from. He opposed issuance of new paper money of higher denominations, especially large denomination of new paper money in the guise of it being equivalent to several old ones; in essence, he opposed the practice of inflationary policy. However, he advocated "producing new Dade paper money to be circulated concurrently with Zhiyuan paper money, five guan or two guan of Dade paper money equivalent to one guan of Zhiyuan paper money, on the surface it was replacing Zhongtong paper money with Dade paper money, in essence it was to remedy the depreciation of Zhiyuan paper money and ultimately to remedy the ill of the time." Actually it was but a name-changing game, without touching the essence of the policy, and little practical significance could be generated from it. Zheng Jiefu proposed concurrent circulation of coin and paper money, setting coin supplementing paper money as the basis of the theory, producing new paper money to brace the depreciated Zhiyuan paper money, replacing such money to safeguard the national interest and minting copper coins to get through the obstacle of paper money circulation. He even believed that there was no better way than this in bringing the country to a road of national prosperity and benefiting the people; that is, the ultimate broad way to benefit the country and the people lay in establishing metal money and paper money laws.

His understanding of paper money law included setting up a reasonable conversion rate between the new and old paper moneys, normal channels for paper money release and withdrawal as well as reserve for paper money. He believed that a reasonable conversion rate between the new and old paper moneys was "the strategy to remedy the ill of the time, new Dade paper money shall be produced, to be circulated concurrently with Zhiyuan paper money, making five *guan* or two *guan* Dade paper money equal to one *guan* Zhiyuan paper money." Paper money release channels included awards meted out by the central government, emoluments to the officials in the capital, payments to the officials and government staff at the various local administrative bodies, and purchasing silk and materials. The retiring channel for paper money was such a practice wherein "reserves for paper money are all items of practical use, while the paper money is spread all over the country, and the people shall sustain no loss." Therefore, it was sufficient to see that his purpose was to "make the people thrive more"; the topmost issue was not to harm them. Reserves for paper money had to be physical. Necessities such as corn, silk and linen for living and production could also be made into reserve for paper money; it was not necessarily metal moneys such as silver or copper coin. The understanding of Zheng Jiefu echoed the idea of taking physical silver as issuance guarantee as advanced by Wang Yitong; it was really brilliant.

Zheng Jiefu was opposed to abolishing copper coins. He emphasized that "minting copper into metal money is an unshakable law handed down from the ancient times, it is difficult for robbers and thieves to carry, fire and water could not destroy them, they are passed down as currency from generation to generation." He fiercely criticized opinions opposing the circulation of copper coins as short-sighted thinking, claiming that it was "in the name of benefiting the country and neglecting the interests of the people, ultimately jeopardizing the state." He frankly pointed out that accusations that the country did not benefit from minting as it costs a *wen* to mint a *wen* failed to understand that the entire country actually benefited from minting despite the production costs.

Zheng Jiefu also proclaimed that "the country and the people are actually one entity, if the people are rich then the country is rich, if the country is rich, then peace prevails. Though copper coin brings no immediate benefit and the priority is to enrich the people." That is, in the long run from the perspective of national interest, minting metal money was beneficial, which was the first advantage. The second advantage was that full-value minted coin could eliminate counterfeit minting. He expressed the idea by invoking words of the sages, "minting brings no profit, therefore it could last, just because the cost is so high therefore there is little counterfeit minting. As there is ready copper in the tax warehouses, calculated from copper prices, the cost would not be too high." Zheng Jiefu's design for the monetary system touched upon the relation between copper coin and paper money. He advocated, "I petition the government for minting copper coins to supplement paper money circulation." Copper coin is the supplemental money but with full value; that is, "the current copper price stands at one *guan* and five hundred *qian* (for) half a kilogram, and half a kilogram can be minted into one hundred and sixty coins, then the copper price equals the minted copper coin price, hence there would be no such defect as counterfeit minting." Paper money was the primary money, but it was not redeemable. Though he proposed to institute a non-redeemable paper money system, supplemented with minted copper coins as fractional money, setting physical materials of the state as issuance reserve, paper money was to be used in payments of large sums, whereas copper coin was to be used in small-sum transactions; the thought was commendable and should not be underestimated. Besides, he opposed depreciation of paper money, opposed inflation and tried to set up a stable non-redeemable paper money system. If such design was to be realized, the issuance amount of paper money should have been brought under strict control and in turn the amount of paper money in circulation would have been placed under control, otherwise his design was but empty talk.

3.3. The checks and balance theory of the reserve and paper money

Zheng Jiefu was very thorough in his exposition on the checks and balance theory of the reserve and paper money. He defined the connotation of the concept as follows: "Regarding things in the world, the heavier the parent, the lighter the offspring; the earlier comer is the parent, the later comer the offspring; if the relationships between the earlier comer and later comer as well as the heavier and the lighter are reversed, the law would not work." He distinguished several categories such as copper coin, silver versus paper money, and paper money versus other paper money according to historical records, and demonstrated them in the sequence of evolutionary process. He believed that in the Han Dynasty, copper coin was balanced against animal hide currency, animal hide currency being the parent and copper coin the offspring; in the Song Dynasty, copper coin was balanced against Jiaohui, Jiaohui being the parent, and copper coin the offspring; in the initial period of the Yuan Dynasty, 50 taels of Zhongtong paper money were established as one *ding* and silver bullion was the benchmark, silver being the parent and Zhongtong paper money the offspring. Not long thereafter, silver was disused, only paper money was circulated and gradually paper money in large denominations was established as the parent and paper money in small denominations the offspring. In Zheng Jiefu's time it developed into a situation where one *guan* of Zhiyuan paper money equaled five *guan* of Zhongtong paper money, which was a circumstance where the offspring outweighed the parent, the light outweighed the heavy, the later comer overtook the earlier comer. Following from the aforesaid principles, it could be seen that silver was the parent and Zhongtong paper money the offspring, which was a redeemable paper money system under silver standard. When this system was scrapped, Zhongtong paper money became an irredeemable paper money, and the system of irredeemable Zhongtong paper money in circulation came into being. Paper money in big denominations was the parent and paper money in small denominations the offspring. Until 1287, Zhiyuan new paper money was issued, and the rate of one for five was fixed, to be circulated concurrently with Zhongtong paper money, which was a very abnormal situation in violation of the checks and balance theory of the reserve and paper money, wherein the offspring outweighed the parent, the light outweighed the heavy and the later overtook the earlier; that is to say, depreciation of paper money took place ("commodity price rose by the day and paper money price dropped by the day"). Hence, he criticized that "though the state produced huge amount of paper money in Yuan Dynasty, little was scattered among the people, and it was very difficult for the grassroots people to gain." In the final analysis, he claimed that the imbalance was because of "the loss of checks and balance between the light and the heavy." On the other hand, he spoke extremely highly of the monetary circulation system of the Song Dynasty, and thought that it was an incredibly perfect system, stating, "Previously in Song Dynasty, copper coin was circulated concurrently with Jiaohui, the offspring was balanced against the parent, and the parent was more valuable. At that time, even the extremely poor had some savings of copper coin and government Huizi, the reason was simple, the parent and the offspring supplemented and balanced each other." Following the reasoning, he said, "in Han Dynasty, copper coin was balanced against animal hide currency" and "in Song Dynasty, copper coin was balanced against Jiaohui." Truly as stated by him, "in Song Dynasty, copper coin was circulated concurrently with Jiaohui, the offspring was balanced against the parent, and the parent was more valuable." If the theory that "silver is established as the parent, and Zhongtong paper money the offspring" was followed through, then copper coin should have been established as the parent and animal hide currency and Jiaohui the offspring. Yang Wanli and Chen Qiqing of the Song Dynasty both held that "coin was still the parent and paper money the offspring." According to the distinction he established, the heavier, the earlier-comer, was the parent and the lighter, the later-comer, the offspring. Obviously, copper coin was the heavier and earlier-comer and paper money the lighter and later-comer. What he said, "paper money is the form of copper," should have been right; however, he balanced paper money against paper money, betraying his own theory. Faced with the grim reality facing irredeemable paper money circulation, Zheng made unprincipled compromises and concessions which rendered his theory a sacrifice and a decorative article of realism, and also highly pragmatic in nature.

Cheng Jufu (1249–1318), before Zheng Jiefu was a minister of outstanding repute, wrote *Xuelou Collection* and more. In the era of Kublai Khan, he had advocated the concurrent circulation of coin and paper money. In *Extant Memorials — Copper Coin in Volume 10 of Xuelou Collection*, he proposed, "Though the state mandated paper money as currency, it is still counted by the units such as *guan* and hundred *qians* of copper coin, therefore we can see that paper money is the offspring of coin, and coin is the parent of paper money. Only when the checks and balance of the parent and the offspring are established could it last, whereas in practice the parent is scrapped, only the offspring remains in use in a void, therefore the amount of paper money is increasing and commodity prices are ever rising." He believed that paper money was placed in a paradox of scrapping the parent and placing the offspring in a void, which resulted in commodity price surge and paper money depreciation. Based on this theory, faced further with the issue that overseas trade still required copper coin and there was no lack of private minting of copper coin among the people, he pointed out that "venders and sea-faring merchant vessels as well as houses of smelting business destroyed and smelted various bronze vessels, which made coins of the various times end up in the hands of the people ... the government should recover and collect copper coins scattered in private hands, fix prices appropriately and buy in such bronze vessels, make the current coin circulate concurrently with paper money, so that the interest and right may be concentrated in one source and no chance is taken, which is also beneficial to the circulation of paper money. And besides, in these days promotion and circulation repositories all fixed price by comparing gold and silver in the government warehouses and paper money in the name of stabilizing the paper money, hence came the situation." In 1287, he made a more straightforward and specific representation of the concept of concurrent circulation of coin and paper money in a memorial titled *Advantages and Disadvantages to the People — The Use of Copper Coin Should Be Permitted, or More Small Paper Money Change Should Be Made Available as Jiangnan People Engaging in Small Sum Trade*. Zhao Mengfu (1254–1322, courtesy name Zi'ang, style Songxue Daoren, descendent of the Song imperial clan, famous painter and calligrapher, and author of Songxue Residence Collection) was promoted to the central government in the 23rd year of the Zhiyuan period, and Zhiyuan paper money was instituted the following year. The ministers were convened in the ministry of punishment to discuss measures dealing with graft, and the consensus was that anyone taking bribes reaching the level of two hundred *guan* of Zhiyuan paper money should be put to death. Zhao advanced the theory of balancing the virtual and the real, arguing that "in the ancient times, corn and cloth were the living necessities, called two real items. Silver and coin were balanced against these two physicals, called two virtuals. The four were valuable things, even though there was fluctuation in the values of them, such fluctuation would not be substantial, therefore calculating bribery in cloth would be most appropriate." This referred to the fact that corn and cloth were the physical and silver and coin were the virtual. Later, "when paper money was first produced, silver was established as the reserve, the virtual and the physical were balanced against each other; now, over a period of twenty years, the ratio between the light and the heavy has surged dozens of times. Therefore, Zhongtong paper money was replaced by Zhiyuan paper money. When another twenty years elapses, the Zhiyuan paper money would surely follow the same route of failure as that of Zhongtong paper money; it seems to be too exacting on the people to calculate punishment in terms of the amount of paper money." Over this period of time, silver was the physical and paper money the virtual; it was an inevitable trend for paper money to fall in a spiraling depreciation cycle. Paper money was established by the Song Dynasty, implemented in the frontier areas and the practice adopted by the Jin Dynasty, all out of necessity. When people's lives hinged on it, it seemed to be an unadvisable practice. He further noted, "now that the Zhongtong paper money depreciated, and Zhiyuan paper money was employed to replace it, how could it be reasonable to think that the Zhiyuan paper money would never go soft!" The "soft" herein seemed to refer to a decrease in currency value and credit, that is, monetary inflation. Zhao was a descendant of the imperial clan of the former dynasty, and a scholar of repute; however, he was not necessarily an expert in wealth management. But his criticism of his contemporaries as "not verifying with reason and trying to force other into submission" made people ashamed of themselves and convinced them that he was right. His arguments were prone to draw the attention of the people. However, why should people have been so particular about the real theoretical significance of his theory?

Zheng Jiefu held reservations regarding paper money, stating that "it would definitely not last to make paper into money." "Paper money was reserved for the use of ghosts and gods, not appropriate for human use. It was established by the Song Dynasty, and the life of Song was shortened; the government followed the established practice of failing Song, it was really a pity!" His understanding was tinted with superstition, and he imputed the demise of the Song Dynasty to the establishment and implementation of paper money, really a ridiculous conclusion. He proposed to replace paper money with silk money, with the state setting up a bureau and recruiting craftsmen to produce silk money in accordance with the paper money model, in the five colors of blue, red, white, black and yellow modeled after the five cardinal directions of east, south, west, north and the center in Wu Xing theory, and with seals of the five cardinal directions affixed thereon. He held that the advantages of such a practice lay in the following: "(a) it would last dozens of years, (b) forgers have no way to forge, (c) free from troubles of replacement and destruction, when this practice is in place for a few years, the silk money in circulation would be more than enough for use over the time of a few years." Actually, the positive significance of the proposal was no more than making forgery more difficult. Besides being a token of money and a symbol of value, paper money and silk money also faced the problem of issuance amount, and there was definitely no such thing as "there is more than enough for use." This was a continuation and development of the silk money theory advanced by Lu Shirong, and expounded theoretically; however, his theory did not hold water as he had to bow down to reality. His exuberance of praise in descriptions such as "enriching the people," "bringing strength to the country," "relieving the annual famine," "eliminating foreign troubles" and "a strategy opening up real and everlasting peace and order" was obviously exaggerated and his ideas impractical, which diminished the theoretical value and practical significance of his theory.

Zheng Jiefu's proposal to mint copper coins was not accepted. However, in October of 1309, when reformation of the "silver and paper money" system was instituted, Yao Sui (1238–1313) stated in the *Edict of Minting and Circulating Copper Coin* that "the law of coin can be traced back to ancient times, after the three generations, it was no longer followed. When the Kublai Khan first ascended the throne, and promulgated the issuance of paper money to facilitate the use of the people, there was already the intent to have concurrent circulation of coin and paper money, that is, coin was balanced against stuff and paper money against coin, the parent and the offspring depended on and balanced each other, the practice was trustworthy and well grounded. Nowadays the paper money law has been started afresh, expected to benefit both the people and the government, a lasting measure may be made therefrom, and the law of minting may be restored."[18] That is, big denomination paper money was to be produced, and *Dayuan Tongbao* and *Zhida Tongbao* were minted based on the concept and theory advanced by Zheng Jiefu. In 1350, Zhizheng paper money was produced and *Zhizheng Tongbao* was minted, all these measures following the same source.

4. Hu Zhiyu on paper money circulation

Hu Zhiyu (1227–1295), courtesy name Shaowen, style Zishan, born in Wu'an of Cizhou (in present-day Hebei) in the Yuan Dynasty, was an able minister in the initial period of the Yuan Dynasty, and a famous scholar. At the beginning of the Zhongtong period of Kublai Khan, he was recommended by Zhang Wenqian to take up the post of assistant department director. Wang Yun praised him as "really a man capable of steering economic matters and conversant in current affairs." He later resigned on account of illness. He was well versed in poetry, prose and various tunes, authoring *Complete Works of Zishan*. There is an annotated version of the Hu Collection currently available, with 22 volumes in total (*Miscellaneous Works — On the Law of Paper Money Circulation*[19]) (no further source will be provided in later citations), elaborating on specific issues including paper money circulation and paper money salvation.

4.1. *On the checks and balance between the parent and offspring of paper money and coins*

In *On the Law of Paper Money Circulation*, Hu elaborated on his objections to concurrent circulation of paper money and coin and to the

---

[18] *Mu'an Collection*, vol. 1.

[19] The article must have been written in the period from 1282 to 1287, after Ahmad was killed and before Ye Li promulgated the Measures Governing Circulation of Zhiyuan Paper Money, that is, about the 22nd year of the Zhiyuan period. We arrived at this conclusion because the treacherous minister referred herein must be Ahmad, and the Measures Governing Circulation of Zhiyuan Paper Money were not mentioned in the in the Measures Governing Circulation of Zhiyuan Paper Money.

proposal arguing for the replacement of old paper money with new paper money. He believed that it was the general trend for paper money to replace coin, a trend beyond human intervention. The foundation for his theory was the checks and balance between the parent and the offspring; however, his checks and balance theory was unlike that of the past. Regarding the relationships between different types of moneys, first there was the differences between the big and the small, the light and the heavy, and the earlier- and the later-comers of the same currency material rather than relationships between different currency materials, still less a relationship between the coin and the paper money. Here, Hu broke away from the restrictions of traditional concepts. He rejected the idea that the heavier should be the parent and the lighter the offspring, or the earlier-comer the parent and the later-comer the offspring, or metal coin the parent and the paper money the offspring. He said, "in the law of paper money circulation, the paper money should be the offspring and the commodities the parent, the parent and the offspring cover each other's back, and echo each other. When prices of commodities rise and paper money depreciates, the amount of paper money should be shrunk, whereas if prices of commodities drop and paper money appreciates, the amount of paper money should be increased; in this shrinking and expansion process, the mean is attained. Now that the parent and the offspring echo each other in creditworthiness, the paper money remains strong and commodity price stable, then even though after ten thousand generations, it will remain in circulation without a glitch. Anything other than that, once there is the intent for profit, the law will be corrupted. Nowadays, the paper money is priced too high and commodities priced too low, compared with the beginning of the year, one appreciates and the other depreciates, one gains value by fifty percent, the other halves in value. Those who are in charge of the affair benefit from the high value of paper money, from the frequent issuance and facility in circulation, they pay no heed to the harm brought to peasants, know no balancing of paper money. What the people have are only cloth and silk, what the government recovers is paper money; when cloth and silk are brought to the repository to exchange for paper money, the ones in charge of paper money are afraid of the trouble arising from conversion, refuse to deliver paper money thereto on account of lack of paper money, hence the prices of cloth and silk dwindle by the day."

Hu argued that there were differences between the paper money circulation law and the law of metal coin circulation, "though paper money is virtual, commodities physical." Paper money being the offspring and commodities the parent, so long as paper money was accompanied by commodities without parting of the two, there would be paper money circulation externally and security of commodities internally, and the corresponding relationship between the internal and the external could be maintained. Only through mutual protection, care and correspondence by the parent and the offspring could paper money circulation be kept away from developing into a problem. Because once paper money gained value, that is, the purchasing power of paper money increased, and commodity prices dropped, then such commodity should be purchased by the government or the supply thereof be diminished, and commodity price would be restored to its normal level. Once its purchasing power weakened, or the paper money depreciated, then commodity price would rise, or once commodity gained value, then paper money should be recalled from circulation. Only through such expansion and contraction in regulating the supply and demand relation of paper money and commodity could an appropriate relation between currency value and commodity price be maintained, the production, circulation and life of the people be maintained in a normal situation, and transactions be kept free from obstruction and stagnation. Only in this way could the people feel secure and live in peace, and therefore the statement "paper money may be virtual, and commodity physical, however, the people do not suffer." Then the people would have faith in paper money and in holding, using and keeping paper money. Otherwise, once there is a credit crisis in paper money, such paper money would be shunned by everyone like a hot potato; once anyone acquired any paper money they would try to spend it as quickly as possible, and therefore the statement, "now that the parent and the offspring should correspond in credit, the paper money remains strong and commodity price stable, then even though after ten thousand generations, it will remain in circulation without a glitch." This was the first point.

The second one was the principle of issuing paper money. "Once there is the intent for profit, the law will be corrupted." Stabilizing currency value, stabilizing the market, the people, production and life of the people should be the topmost purpose in issuing paper money; profit should never be the purpose. Once this principle is violated, the law will naturally be corrupted. Hu admonished the people in power as they may handle paper money problems solely based on their personal likes and dislikes by mechanically following bureaucratic solutions without regard for the circumstances of the people, the national livelihood and the need of the people, the fact and the law; even under the conditions of monetary circulation of paper money, balance and checks between the light and the heavy still must not be slackened. He examined the different requirements and mentalities from three layers of the ordinary people, the government, and the specific officials in charge. The ordinary people had cloth and silk in their hands, the government controlled paper money and the decision-making power, and the officials who were actually in charge were conducting conversion procedures and assumed responsibility therefor. The petty official refused to purchase cloth and silk on the pretext of paper money shortage due to a trivial reason, which resulted in the dwindling prices of cloth and silk. "In recent years, silk is sold at nine *qian* of paper money a *jin* (roughly equivalent to half a kilogram), whereas the government stipulated that a *jin* of silk should be sold at the price of one *guan* and five hundred paper money, when paper money gains value by the day, and silk loses value by the day, plus the fact that silk could not be sold, the people suffer greatly." There were quite a few crafty people in the market in addition to merchants, and there was no lack of collusion between the government and the merchants, plus some villains availed themselves of the situation to profiteer therefrom. These wily people constituted a network, which engaged in exploiting the people; "they also instituted a grading system for paper money including selective paper money, firm paper money to further increase the price of paper money. These practices transformed paper money from a treasure of circulation and a vehicle to even out the irregular prices of myriad items into an evil scheme harming the peasant and fleecing the market, blocking the circulation of commodities." The interest of those who were in charge of issuing paper money lay in "the high price of paper money, in frequent issuance and facility of issuance, they paid no heed to the harm brought to peasants, knew no balancing of paper money." These practices led to a situation where "the paper money is priced too high and commodities priced too low, compared with the beginning of the year, one appreciated and the other depreciated, one gained value by 50%, the other halved in value." It should be acknowledged that Hu's understanding was fair and profound.

We could perceive that there were at least two breakthroughs in Hu's understanding therefrom. First was the checks and balance theory between the parent and the offspring, evolved from the checks and balance between different types of money to that between money (substitution) and commodity, that is, the checks and balance theory between money and commodity. The reason was nothing but the diminishing price of paper money and the rising price of commodity because all metal coins, be it copper coin or iron coin, were physical entities, whereas paper money was not, it was only a virtual item. Money used to be embodied by physical metal money and in Hu's time it was embodied by virtual paper money. Hu did not express objection to this change; rather, he welcomed it and aired support thereto, arguing that "its only purpose is to facilitate transaction and circulate corn and silk, even out the prices of myriad commodities, no profit is sought therefrom." It seemed that Hu had realized the performance features of paper money which was only a medium of exchange instead of the real purpose of exchange. Though he did not conduct further in-depth analysis, such understanding was already a really profound insight which was rarely attainable. Such understanding was the result of in-depth examination and analysis of the change of money by closely following the evolution and development of money and grasping the direction of progress. Compared with his forerunners, such as Zheng Jiefu, Hu had made qualitative improvement or qualitative distinction; he took paper money as the offspring and commodity as the parent, and elaborated on the checks and balance theory between the parent and the offspring, which truthfully represented the relation between commodity and money. Such findings would be further conducive to regulating commodity price and stabilizing finance, pacifying society; at that time, the understanding was very advanced and ahead of its time.

Second, Hu specifically stated that paper money should not be issued for profit as, "once there is the intent for profit, the law would naturally get corrupted," the law would then become abusive and harm the people, making commodity circulation stagnant. The reason was simple; only when currency value remained stable could market prices be truthfully reflected and commodity be properly circulated, and the people would have faith in paper money in their hands and the creditability of paper money could remain stably high. Only in this way could production be properly developed, the normal social order be guaranteed and the maximum national interest be safeguarded. Otherwise, the relation between the parent and the offspring would not be appropriate, be it high commodity price and low paper money price, or low commodity price and high paper money price when commodity price and paper money price were imbalanced. "In recent years, prices for items including corn and cloth shot up, there is shortage of materials. When paper money depreciates by the day, it is due to oversupply of paper money. When there is oversupply, then this measure should be introduced to contract it." "The peasant and the craftsman both suffer from this situation, and the state is ultimately harmed. No strategy is superior to farming ...." That is, effort should be made and measures be taken in expanding revenue, reducing expenditure, and increasing production; by doing so, production is increased, consumption is reduced, commodity supply is guaranteed while at the same time issuance of paper money is reduced. The idea of considering the matter from both aspects was correct and commendable. However, neither aspect was acceptable to the rulers, let alone implementation of such a measure.

However, theoretically, Hu's proposal that paper money be "free from the intent for profit" required further investigation. He wrote, "Those who are in charge of the state should weigh the amount of the myriad items and paper money, and expand or shrink paper money accordingly. When there is a commodity price surge, then measures should be taken to shrink the amount of paper money. When there is price plunge, then measures should be taken to expand the amount of paper money. The point is that both commodity price and paper money are properly maintained, neither the peasant nor the craftsman is harmed, the offspring and the parent rely and depend on each other, the benefit for the state would be great when the state pursues no benefit." There are historical records attesting this fact; in 1260, when the paper money was first issued, both the people and the government cherished it as though it were a great treasure. Therefore, Zhongtong paper money circulated as smoothly as flowing water; a *guan* of paper money could purchase a bolt of tough silk, 50 or 60 *wens* of paper money could purchase a *liang* (about 50 gram) of silk, 600 or 700 *wens* a *dan* of corn, 500 or 600 *wens* a *dan* of wheat, and 400 or 500 *wens* half a bolt of cloth. "In recent years, prices surged six or seven times, even ten times, it was the same case with myriad items and hired laborers." Hu deliberated on the situation repeatedly; since there was no natural disaster, nor lack of corn or any lack of cloth and silk, the time was peaceful and harvest bountiful, "the people and commerce prospered, and surplus of commodities accumulated, however, commodity price rose by the day, the reason lay in the depreciation of paper money." The principle that profit-seeking should never be set as the purpose of issuing paper money is true of all times and all countries. Nowadays, issuing institutions have undergone radical changes and the central banks of the various countries are in charge of issuance obligations; the difference between an issuing bank and commercial bank lies in the fact that the central bank does not take profit-making as its purpose. Only in this way can it be worthy of the name of the bank of banks and the mission of the issuing bank. Over seven hundred years ago, Hu Zhiyu understood and put forward this principle unequivocally in the world, a fact that should not go unnoticed. To date, the statement regarding regulating the market, that is, of maintaining an appropriate balance between commodity price and currency value by the state under the condition of paper money circulation, is one of great significance. This was an exposition made by Hu following the traditional Chinese money regulating theory under new historical conditions; this finding shall not be disregarded either.

4.2. *On incompatibility of paper money and coin*

Earlier proposals mostly leaned toward the view that it was necessary to concurrently circulate paper money and coin; even proposals for paper money of a big amount and coin of a small amount were put forward, as well as proposals that coin should be used for the capital and the peripheral areas thereof and paper money for remote areas. Such proposals found no lack of followers. Only Hu Zhiyu proposed a theory on the basis of checks and balance between the parent and the offspring, reversing the tradition and stating, "firming of physical money will not only bring about multiple benefits, the entire world would benefit boundlessly from the single move."

His opinion was as follows:

> "Neither copper coin nor paper money could be put to use in time of coldness and hunger, none of the two is article of practical use. The sages held that silk and cloth could not be divided, while corn could not be carried afar, hence they facilitated transaction by employing the creditability of these two items. If these two are compared, then, paper money is superior to copper coin. Take the present situation for instance, Yuanbao paper money had been in circulation for over ten years, paper money value firms, and circulation thereof is as smooth as flowing water, this is due to the existence of the parent and the lone circulation of paper money without interference from other items. Once there is interference from other items, there comes into existence the distinction between the light and the heavy, the superior and the inferior. The concurrent circulation of copper coin and paper money is actually bringing in interference of other items. Now that the old paper money from previous imperial periods has been virtually destroyed and worn out of existence, even if there is still old paper money, new law shall be enacted to prohibit its use."

He pointed out that "the cost of minting copper coin was not insignificant, and that carrying coin to go afar for transaction was not as convenient as paper money" and that "it would be insufficient for circulation if coin mintage is small, and it would be pointless cost if mintage is too large, which will be piled up and of no use, such would only serve the purpose of disturbing paper money circulation." He further cited the fact that in the Tianbao period of the Tang Dynasty, minting was "an activity wasting the principal and working the laborer without bringing about any benefit." It was a thankless task. In Hu Zhiyu's time, eighty thousand *ding* of paper money was produced and circulated smoothly without the least hindrance. Since newly minted coins were spread among the people, one effect would be that "paper money gets diminished without official diminishment, gets stagnated without obstruction introduced." The second effect was "now that there are a great amount of coins, whenever there is need for great expenditure," "it not only wastes laborers in transportation, but also delays activities which require instant support." If a military activity is involved, proper measures might not be taken and an opportunity for a victory may be lost.

What is more important is that "inconvenience arises when there are two prices." Learning from the lesson from the Jin Dynasty, the custom thereof was "hoarding coins instead of paper money, therefore paper money circulation underwent multiple changes and deteriorated." Because coins and paper money got intermingled, when coins gained value and paper money lost value, it was natural that paper money would not be able to maintain its creditability. However, if coins were to be used only in the capital and the peripheral areas around it, "even if the value of coins and paper money remain unchanged, there would still be irregularities, when unevenness occurs, defect arises." When paper money was first issued, the trust of the people was yet to be obtained, and the practice of minting separately in different places was seldom not followed by corner-cutting activities in coin minting.

If a separate price was set for coin on account of its high minting cost, then paper money circulation would be corrupted immediately. When paper money lost value and coins were unfit for use, then both lost their medium function, which is a situation absolutely not to be tolerated. However, if shoddy work is conducted in minting, "coins which feature enormous labor in minting and difficulty in use would disturb paper money which features easy production and facility in circulation, and the proposal for minting coins seemed not appropriate as it hinders both state employment and upsets the mind of the people." Regardless of the price Hu discussed, the fact that he proposed that there was no tolerance for double prices on the market to avoid market chaos meant that he had some understanding in the exclusivity of the measure of value. His adamant upholding of the principle indicated his profound and unique understanding, which was extraordinary. This indicates that our ancestors had insightful understanding of the functions of money, which was no small matter.

In order to improve understanding, Hu also proceeded from the people-oriented Confucian ideas that food was the first necessity of the people, the people were the foundation of the state and without the people there was no monarch. He cited classics such as the *Book of*

History — Hong Fan to demonstrate the point that "money is used to weigh and circulate the commodities, it is the article employed to even out the myriad items and gain the trust of the people. If it deviates from this and the trust would be lost, then there would be no benchmark for the myriad items, some stagnate as though dirt, some soar and be valued higher than gold, or commodity price drops and coin price rises, or vice versa. The peasant and the craftsman will both sustain harm therefrom. When trust wanes, the myriad items have nothing to base on." Illustrating the events of his time with ancient events, he emphasized that "the ancients dared not forget balancing and checking money for a single moment." Proceeding from the remote to the approximate, he then emphasized the purpose and function of paper money circulation; the purpose of paper money was to "even out the imbalance of prices among the myriad items, facilitate transaction for the people to relieve them of the difficulty of transaction, therefore the mechanism of paper money or silk money is instituted, both the rulers and the ruled have faith in it, and it works when there is faith in it, the purpose is not to trade for the products of cream and labor of the people with useless paper which could neither feed nor clothe the people." The purpose of instituting paper money was to stabilize currency value and regulate commodity price, facilitate the proper conduct of transaction and prosperity of businesses. The function lay in the mutual trust between the rulers and the ruled. Only in this way could production prosper, then the rulers would have no lack of use, the ruled have sufficient subsistence and the medium of exchange then yield its utmost benefit. Hence, it could be seen that the inherent properties of paper money were not something that could be fixed by man.

4.3. *On paper money*

In Hu Zhiyu's opinion, paper money was the inevitable result of monetary development. It was not the product of the subjective will of the people, and naturally, it did not come from the intention of someone. If somebody stated, "Paper money is in the realm of the supreme power and supreme law of a country, the lightness or heaviness thereof rests on a word, there is nothing wrong with this." He would definitively rebuff, "No." He would take the white deer skin money of the Wudi emperor of the Han Dynasty as evidence and ask if it would really work if someone said that it was worth 400,000 *wens*. This was the same as replacing the old money with new money — was it not going back on its words? Besides, "the ancients used to use coins, and the later generations changed to paper money, the sole purpose thereof was to facilitate transaction and circulate corn and silk, even out the prices of the myriad articles, instead of seeking profit. Not that they would not like to, but that the circumstance deterred them from doing so." During transactions, once faith was lost, "when faith is not available in transactions, even articles of use would be discarded, let alone item of no use." He took a deed title (inscribed on wood and bamboo slips) as an example to illustrate that the key lay in trust.

If trust was not available, deed titles were nothing but scrap wood plates; when there was trust, transactions could be conducted repeatedly, and the people would not be afraid and would conduct transactions willingly. Otherwise, once trust was lost, "would an inscribed wood be reliable," let alone IOU words written on a piece of paper? Therefore, he believed that the way of issuing paper money lay in having the parent and the offspring watch out for each other, the internal and the external echoing each other.

Somebody said, "if new paper money is produced, one new for five old, within a year, the old would be scrapped naturally, and the paper money would be naturally adjusted to the myriad articles." He said, "when the new and the old are both called paper money, what are the differences between them, they are unlike the purities in metals, and there is no difference in difficulty of smelting." As mentioned above, the outcome of practicing abusive paper money law would be inevitable. Indeed, "In the first year of Zhongtong period, paper money was first instituted, it was cherished by all walks of life, the government and the people, the high and the low, it circulated as though flowing water ... however in recent years, prices surged six or seven times, even ten times, it was the same case with myriad items and hired laborers." Reflecting on the causes thereof, there was little change in external environment, nor occurrence of natural calamity or human induced disaster; "however commodity price rises by the day, the cause lies in depreciation of paper money. When there is a surplus of paper money, then the price of commodity rises, the rulers should be aware of the defect and salvage the situation."

Hu warned the rulers that if the amount of paper money issuance was not brought under control or no prudence was exercised there would be a structural imbalance in the ratio between paper moneys of different denominations, especially when small denomination paper money which was closely related to everyday life of the people was undersupplied and the replacement was difficult. Then monetary law and paper money circulation would go wrong. These were measures adopted by the powerful courtier Ahmad for the purpose of amassing money and wealth; he fattened his coffers on public expenditure, used the power entrusted in him to set up a private paper money repository and produced paper money, sold public offices and power, sought and accepted bribery, practiced rampant lending activities and shored up the price of gold to enrich his personal repository, which depleted the national treasury and depreciated the value of paper money. Though Ahmad was put to death, there was still the need to rectify the circulation of paper money and build up trust; the basis required reinforcing and the proper way required upholding.

Hu Zhiyu put forward seven "measures of remedying the vicious situation," of which the second and the third were consolidated into one. The following are the six itemized elaborations.

The first point was determining the supply of paper money in accordance with demand. That is, the demand under the principal of tailoring expenditure to revenue was to be calculated by taking into consideration the fiscal expenditure in accordance with the statistical number such as households, businessmen, government officials, the demand for issuing commercial money and requirements for scrapping broken and worn paper money, namely, the amount arrived at by calculating the statistical fundamental data instead of subjective conjecture or fiscal need. "There are such amount of households, such amount of taxes on commerce, such amount of taxes on tea and salt, such amount of package taxes and taxes on silk and cloth, such amount of paper money required for purchasing and employing, such amount of government official emoluments, the sum of the foregoing items and those money and property that should be included but not enumerated, the annual revenue and disbursement of the public repository, use by the individual families, such amount of paper money capable of continued use, and such amount of broken and worn paper money to be disused, total the number and produce paper money in accordance with the amount of revenue and expenditure." An issuance amount based on such statistical numbers, so long as there was no major omission in major items affecting the issuance and withdrawal of paper money, and no error in numbers, should be generally pretty solid and realistic; hence, he believed "so long as there is established law, balance and checks can be made discretionarily, there would be no excessive production leading to unreasonable waste, which results in paper money depreciation and commodity price rises; nor should there be underproduction which would lead to paper money appreciation and commodity price plummets. However, nowadays there is little accounting conducted, and there is unchecked excessive production to facilitate expenditure and supply, therefore paper money depreciates by the day." Prior to May 1282, Ahmad, the minister in charge of the finances, only saw mass producing paper money as the best way to solve the heavy fiscal burden. On the contrary, Hu advocated to proceed from reality, from statistics, follow established practices, base policies on figures obtained from study and calculations, refused to follow subjective conjecture, opposed the excessive production of paper money and instead proposed to limit the amount of issuance and apply controlled regulation thereon. This idea was greatly valuable.

The second point was the confiscation of private paper money. One of the causes was a treacherous courtier. This must have referred to Ahmad who had captured power and lined his pockets for nearly 20 years on the backing of the emperor. He had "privately produced paper money, engaged in malpractices and insatiable graft, raked in carts and boats fully loaded with bribes, such malpractices were rampant across all *Lus*, articles were purchased thereby ... which resulted in prevalent baseless paper money spreading across the country. If a mechanism is not devised to shrink it, the commodity price may not be brought down ultimately and paper money circulation would ultimately fail. There are not many ways to shrink paper money ... examine the current amount, recover into the government repository wherever such paper money is found, and measures for expenditure, issuance and circulation shall be separately worked out." All was to be confiscated into the public repository and all channels of paper money outflow were to be eliminated in order to reduce pressure on circulation expansion and disturbance, so that better rectification could be effected. The second cause concerned privately produced paper money which had not been released into circulation. "Treacherous courtier set up a general repository and made profit by lending out such .... Ever since the treacherous courtier got debunked, and the general repository thereof dissolved, however recovery has not been done immediately, principal and interest thereof shall also be entirely confiscated after verification, separate differentiation shall be discussed and worked out." In *Circumstances of Hardship of the People*, Hu enumerated the sources of paper money depreciation. The first one was "private forgery by the treacherous courtier, which was used in purchasing articles at increased price." The second was "setting up a general repository, general bureau, making loans for interest, such paper money was lent in the amount of thousands of *dings* to villains, corrupt and treacherous officials as well as to those title purchasing people." This one echoed the previous one, and both were the origin of financial market disturbance and paper money depreciation. That is, the powerful and treacherous minister corrupted paper money circulation and disturbed the market by abusing his power.

The third point was the status of provision which "prohibits people from approaching the government repository to exchange for gold and silver." The paper money law provided that "Every two *guans* of paper money is worth a tael of silver, every fourteen *guans* and eight hundred *wens* of paper money is worth a tael of gold." However, the treacherous minister Ahmad corrupted the paper money law himself, collected gold for taxes and one tael of gold was converted into a hundred taels of paper money. In southern provinces, only gold was accepted for buying official titles and commutation of sentence, and a tael of gold was charged for a 150 or 160 *guans* of paper money; when one tried to buy gold from the government repository, there was no gold for sale, which urged people to engage in private transactions of gold. Hence, the price of gold rose by the day and paper money circulation weakened by the day. Since the fall of the treacherous courtier Ahmad, "though the prices of gold and silver dropped naturally, the defect of prohibiting people from approaching the government repository to exchange for gold and silver remains; it is best to rectify the situation." The paper money law provided that paper money could be redeemed and there was also a government fixed official price for the gold and silver conversion rate, which was conducive for the government in stabilizing currency value on the market, regulating the amount of paper money in circulation and maintaining market order; these were key means of market regulations for the government, and were not to be turned into means of enrichment by any individual. When the prices of gold and silver rose, the prices of other items followed, which led to a situation where "in recent years, prices surged by six or seven times, and gradually rose up to ten times, which was true of all articles as well as prices for hired laborers." Of course, if the paper money law was not thoroughly followed through and redemption was prohibited from the government repository, which were equally corrupting the paper money law, these situations would not only disturb the mind of the people but also destabilize the market and tarnish the image and authority of the government, which would require urgent measures to be turned around so that the dilemma might be shaken off.

The fourth point was the proposition to "spend sparingly and encouraging farming, abstain from luxury, rid of redundancy and superfluity, suppress game and laziness." Hu believed that "firming physical money will not only bring about multiple benefits, but the entire world would benefit boundlessly from the single move." The treacherous courtier Ahmad had a passionate liking for profit and bribery carried the day; what he sought were fine gold, large pearls, beauties, fine steeds and exotic rarities. Those who aspired to acquire government positions and bend the law would not have had their wish fulfilled if they could not obtain such items; therefore, they trashed paper money. "In recent years, when officials in the capital banqueted, the simpler ones would cost over ten *ding* of paper money, and those more lavish doubled the cost, this trend should not go unchecked. Heavy punishment shall be meted out on those who engaged in bribery. Past faults may not be followed in banqueting and luxurious spending. Simplicity must be followed in clothing and travelling, this is also one law for the circulation of paper money." It is really not something easily achievable to advocate and practice industriousness and frugality in maintaining home and managing a state in a peaceful environment, though it is a traditional virtue of China. The extravagance may not be encouraged, but would increase the pressure on expanding fiscal expenditure and forming the mentality of extravagance emulation; if fiscal expenditure was not brought under control, paper money would have become a convenient way to make up for the gap, and the result would be self-evident. Hu tried to nip the vicious self-destructive bud of paper money; however, his painstaking effort would hardly work. Even in the present society, such a thing would be easier said than done.

The fifth point was to put paper money replacement efforts in place. Paper money circulation should neither be stopped nor stagnate, which were the fundamental conditions for normal circulation, and must be continued perseveringly. If such conditions were to be maintained, the effort of replacing paper money was a must. Any inconvenience or discontinuance in exchange of big and small denomination paper money, replacement for broken and worn paper money, and redemption for gold and silver would impede the normal functioning of paper money. At the time, "the government paper money repositories in the various *Lus* ignored the orders of their superiors, held back from releasing and distributing paper money, claiming that there was no official in charge of replacement, and petty functionaries sat idly behind closed doors, taking out wages without doing anything, loans were mostly made at great losses. Since there was no official exchange, people engaged in private exchange; the rich took the opportunity to profiteer, and the poor was resigned to discounted value and loss. Paper money power is of extreme importance, who upholds these phenomena?"

In *Circumstances of Hardship of the People*, Hu wrote, "the treacherous courtier had the power to engage in private production of paper money, while the government repositories in the various *Lus* refused to release and distribute paper money, the people had no way to exchange or replace it." Based thereon, he proposed, "the paper money repositories in the various *Lus* should count and examine the current paper money held in the respective repository, the current official in charge shall go to the ministry of revenue to report withdrawal and expenditure in the *Lu* where no loss is incurred; a new official shall be appointed for report where loss is incurred. Exchange and replacement shall be conducted to prevent paper money circulation being stagnated."

The sixth point was that supply for small denomination paper money would be guaranteed to facilitate small-sum transactions and change making among the people, maintain equal value exchange and ensure that the people did suffer therefrom, preventing commodity prices being propped up across the board unfoundedly due to price fluctuation of some commodities in exchange. He considered that the problem was "that in recent years small paper money change nearly went extinct due to wear and tear over the years, to the extent that there was barely any presence of paper money of a hundred wens. Therefore prices for article originally worth of five or ten wen now sold at prices several times of its original prices. Delivery could not be taken on spot when transactions were conducted, commodities got retained, hence fraud and stagnation ensued. For instance, if the amount of paper money repositories in the various *Lus* requested were taken as 100%, then small denomination paper money shall constitute seventy or eighty percent thereof in order to deliver the market from the dire situation and facilitate market transactions." Compared with silk cloth, linen cloth, gold, silver and satin, the advantages of paper money as a medium for exchange lay in the fact that it "is divisible." Moreover, "if there is no small denomination paper money, how could the people live by and how could a market be still called a market?" Therefore, "if things are not senselessly wasted, then there will be a surplus of the myriad articles, if there is a surplus of the myriad articles then prices thereof will drop by the day, if prices of the myriad articles drop then the paper money will gets firmer by the day." As stated previously, officials disdained to busy themselves for ordinary people; they disliked the trouble of issuing small denomination paper money and they would claim that there was no small denomination paper money even if there was. Such trivial matters of small denomination paper money remain a troublesome issue even in today's society, let alone in the ancient times, when such measures indeed sounded like empty talk. However, in practice, it was extremely necessary to keep the proportion of small denomination paper money in the overall paper money at an appropriate level, and an extra amount be produced to attain the proportion. In *Circumstances of Hardship of the People*, Hu wrote, "In recent years, small denomination paper money has almost gone extinct due to wear and tear, while the superior did not produce and issue such, when there is little small denomination paper money available, commodity price will naturally rise." This indicated that the production of small denomination paper money in the Yuan Dynasty was indeed insufficient, especially the two *wen*, three *wen*, five *wen* and the Li paper money; later, production of Li paper money was suspended, which made circulation more difficult and brought much trouble to the transaction process. The key to the problem lay in whether the rulers would take the trouble or make such an effort.

Hu Zhiyu considered that, if the defects in paper money circulation were eliminated, the value of paper money would naturally get firmer instead of weakening. However, if such defects were to be eliminated, the problem relating to the paper money would be relatively easier to fix, but the official governance and social problem would be more difficult to solve. Therefore, the significance of Hu's ideas in the history of financial thought and monetary thought far excelled those of his in current politics.

Annex: Paper money circulation regulations authored by Ye Li

Ye Li (1242–1292), courtesy name Taibai, or Shunyu, was born in Hangzhou. Being a scholar at the imperial academy at the end of the Southern Song Dynasty, he was exiled to Zhangzhou for his memorial opposing the Public Cropland Reform implemented by the Prime Minister Jia Sidao. When Jia was out of power, Ye returned to his hometown, retiring to Mount Fuchun. Upon repeated invitations by Kublai Khan, at the beginning of the 14th year of the Zhiyuan period (1277), he took up the position of director of Confucianism Promotion of Zhexi Dao, and in the 23rd year he went to the capital and served as imperial censor and second prime minister successively. As Ghsang was the prime minister at the time, when he failed in the power struggle, Ye Li was exonerated from punishment because Kublai Khan protected him; thereafter he resigned from office and returned to his hometown. He was against Cheng and Zhu's Neo-Confucianism, and was an advocate of mercantilism. He lived a simple and righteous life, was honest and upright in his post, and was high in Kublai Khan's favor. He petitioned to lift labor service constraints on Confucian scholar households, establish an imperial academy, dissuade relocating the Southern Song imperial clan and aristocratic families from south of the Yangtze River and a lot more, most of which were adopted. *The Rules Governing the Circulation of Zhiyuan Baochao Paper Money* worked out by him were the earliest, relatively perfect irredeemable paper money regulations in the world, which embodied the theory of monetary management, and were one of the contributions made by ancient Chinese to the theories of financial management in the world.

It was said that at the end of the Southern Song Dynasty, Ye Li submitted the *Rules on Paper Money* to the government and petitioned to replace Huizi with paper money; however, his proposal was not accepted. In the beginning of the Yuan Dynasty, Zhongtong paper money was redeemable; the mechanism had been in practice for about 17 or 18 years, and proper issuance had been maintained which safeguarded the stability of currency value and commodity price.

In the 18th year of the Zhongtong period (1281), Zhongtong paper money issuance surged to over a million (up to 1,904,800 *ding*), and currency value was undermined in the following year. The government conducted a discussion on "the defect of paper money depreciation"; paper money circulation was rectified in the 21st year, and a further discussion was conducted on "replacing paper money and minting coins" in the 23rd year, with neither move seeing any result. In the 24th year, regulations worked out by Ye Li who had just arrived at the capital were adopted, which became the relatively perfect irredeemable paper money regulations, that is, the *Rules Governing the Circulation of Zhiyuan Baochao Paper Money*. The *Rules* were promulgated for implementation by the Department of State Affairs, which launched a key reform on the paper money system in the Yuan Dynasty. The fundamental principles and relevant main provisions established this time remained valid throughout the Yuan Dynasty, and it left an indelible imprint on China and the world, the ancient and the contemporary times.

The full text according to the *Ministry of Revenue Six — Paper Money Law, Volume 20 of Yuan Dynasty Statutes* is given below, with titles bracketed for reference and retrieval:

"Fourteen articles of Zhiyuan paper money circulation law, the Department of State Affairs promulgated the *Rules Governing the Circulation of Zhiyuan Baochao Paper Money* decreed by the emperor in March of the 24th year of the Zhiyuan period. The text of the rules is appended herein.

1. (New and old paper money to be circulated concurrently) One *guan* Zhongtong paper money shall be worth five *guan* Zhongtong paper money, the new and old paper moneys shall be in circulation concurrently, for the use of the government and the people.

2. (Private transaction of gold and silver to be prohibited) The rules established in the beginning of Zhongtong period shall be followed, government repositories shall be set up in the various *Lus*, which shall be in charge of buying and selling gold and silver, regulating and stabilizing paper money circulation, private transaction thereof shall be strictly prohibited. Every one tael of high purity silver shall be purchased by the repository at an official price of Zhiyuan paper money two *guans*, sold at two *guan* and 50 *wens*, silver shall be traded in accordance with the foregoing prices. One *ding* of tax silver is officially fixed at two *dings* of paper money, and to be sold at one hundred and two *guans* and 500 *wens* of paper money. Pure gold price is fixed at 20 *guans* of paper money a tael, sold at 20 *guans* and 500 *wens*. The people may denounce anyone engaging in private transaction of gold and silver, the gold and silver involved shall be confiscated, half of which shall be awarded to the denouncing person, and a fine of two *dings* of paper money shall be imposed on the wrongdoer, payment shall be made immediately.
3. (Replacement of broken and worn paper money) When the people bring broken and worn paper money to the benchmarking and stabilizing repository in exchange for Zhiyuan paper money, the conversion rate is fixed at five to one, no production cost shall be charged thereon, the fixed practice of thirty *wen* per *guan* shall be charged.
4. (Payment of taxes) When the people under silver tax package plan intend to pay in Zhongtong paper money, only four *guan* shall be accepted therefrom according to the established practice. The various governments shall accept such payments, no refusal is allowed. When conversion is exercised in payment of other labor services and taxes, the foregoing rules shall apply.
5. (Salt taxes payment and acceptance) The price of each certificate of salt is officially fixed at 20 *guans* of paper money, and any salt certificate to be sold hereafter shall be fixed at Zhiyuan paper money two *guan* and Zhongtong paper money ten *guan*; old and new paper money each constitute a half of the price for salt certificate purchase, such paper money shall be accepted in accordance with regulations. If any buyer is willing to pay four *guans* of Zhiyuan paper money, such payment shall be accepted.

Financial Thought of the Yuan and Ming Dynasties 411

6. (Tax payment and acceptance) Tax payment for the various items in the various *Daos* including tea, wine, where Zhiyuan paper money is received, a conversion rate of one for five shall be practiced; where anyone would like pay such in Zhongtong paper money, acceptance thereof shall be made.
7. (Payment and acceptance of loan) If Zhiyuan paper money is to be paid for any public or private debt made in Zhongtong paper money, a conversion rate of one for five shall be practiced; if the borrower would like to make repayment in Zhongtong paper money, such repayment shall be made in guan unit. Anyone making such loan shall accept such payment arrangement immediately without delay and obstruction.
8. (Government official shall provide facility) The various government officials from the benchmarking and stabilizing repository in the various *Lus* shall provide facility to the people when transactions concerning payment and withdrawal are involved; no delay or obstruction is allowed. Where anyone seeks profit or creates any impedance in violation of these rules, and deliberately impedes paper money circulation, the actual situation shall be investigated thereof and punishment shall be imposed thereon.
9. (Market prices as usual) Where businesses, shoppers and travelers purchase articles with Zhongtong paper money, sale shall be made thereto at the original price, such may not be questioned, nor price hike is allowed; however, those who would cut prices in accordance with the season, let them be. If any deep-pocket vendor jacks up commodity price, actual situation shall be investigated thereof and punishment be imposed thereon.
10. (Small denomination to be issued to bring convenience to the people) A survey shall be made regarding whether there is shortage of small denomination paper money among the people, and facility of change-making in transactions. Now that Zhiyuan paper money is issued, denominations ranging from two *guans* to five *wens*, decimal scale, shall be employed to bring convenience to the people.
11. (Punishing forgery) Anyone who forges paper money shall be put to death. Anyone who first exposes a forger shall be awarded with five

dings of silver, and the private property of the criminal shall be awarded to the exposer.

12. (Supervision and inspection) The supervisors of the various *Lus* and the chief officers at the various levels of government are assigned the task of calculating the outstanding gold and silver, paper money in the stabilizing repository, where any appropriation and private lending, private transaction or any profit-making activity is discovered, the actual situation shall be investigated and a report shall be submitted to the central government for conviction and punishment. When the first officer was out on business trip, the second officer shall be in charge.
13. (No barter trade is allowed) When land or houses are pawned, such pawn shall be denominated in paper money, items such as corn or silk may not be used in pricing, which suppresses paper money circulation, criminal liability shall be investigated of anyone violating the provision.
14. (No appropriation is allowed) Officials promoted from the various *Lus* may not purchase gold and silver from the benchmarking and stabilizing repository or replace an excessive amount of broken and worn paper money, criminal liability shall be investigated of anyone violating the provision."

We can make a few brief summaries herein. The first was that the old and the new paper money circulated concurrently at a certain conversion ratio (1:5) in order to facilitate the use by the people and prevent loss from being incurred by the people; no time limit was set on replacement for new against old one. At the same time, stipulations were provided for relations between the new paper money and public as well as private debts and contracts, the relation between the new paper money and financial payment and acceptance, the relation between the new paper money and commodity price in market transactions, etc. There would surely be fluctuation in the officially fixed conversion rate, which would lead to financial fluctuation on the market. The issuance situation of the new paper money would also influence the stability of the new paper money, a vicious consequence of further depreciation of currency value which was most likely to occur. This situation was most vehemently attacked by contemporaries such as Zheng Jiefu, Wang Wei and others.

The second point was the prohibition of private transaction of gold and silver. The difference between Zhiyuan paper money and Zhongtong paper money was that one could not be redeemed for gold and silver. Gold and silver were concentrated in the benchmarking and stabilizing repository, and the government could regulate the market by buying and selling gold and silver on according to market changes; however, private transaction and circulation of gold and silver were prohibited. The people may buy or sell gold and silver from or to the stabilizing repository in name. However, private transaction was prohibited; even those promoted officials were not allowed to buy from or sell to the benchmarking and stabilizing repository, let alone the ordinary people. That is to say, the relation between paper money and gold and silver was cut off; buying or selling, storing and using of gold and silver were concentrated in the hands of the government. Just as Wang Yun said in the closing remarks in *On Paper Money*, "In this way, over a period of a few years, the status of paper money circulation may be restored, and the power of finances was forever held in the central government, and the power will not be relegated to the lower levels of government." In this way, the position and function of primary money for Zhiyuan paper money would be kept unharmed, while small denomination paper money was issued to be used by the people. Preventive provisions were made against official malpractice and forgery. These were the ideas of Ye Li on financial management, which constituted his outstanding innovative viewpoints.

The third point was that, though the Zhiyuan paper money was not redeemable, it was issued on the security of gold and silver; benchmarking and stabilizing repositories were set up accordingly, provisions were made such that officials from the pertinent departments could conduct a bimonthly inspection. Anyone practicing graft, embezzlement or appropriation to make loans, buying and selling without authorization and profit-making activities was to be investigated, and the circumstances would be submitted to the central government for conviction and punishment so that the creditability of Zhiyuan paper money may be kept from being tarnished. These provisions implied that issuance was to be controlled, or at special moment when the market ran unstably, the central government may regulate currency value and commodity price by buying and selling gold and silver. From the perspective of management theory, this was an improvement over the practices of the previous generation.

The fourth point was regarding the regulatory system. The relevant provisions were nothing short of rigorous and meticulous; the point was how it would be implemented and who would be in charge of inspecting the implementation thereof. In the macro environment where officials practiced graft and official governance slackened, laws were not abided by and provisions were but a piece of empty paper, a dose of bitter medicine for fooling the people; when such was exposed by the people, it would only be transformed into a catalyst arousing the people to riot.

From the *Rules Governing Zhiyuan Paper Money Circulation*, we can see that the monetary management theories of Ye Li, which included the unit of paper money, legal tender capacity of paper money, issuance reserve, replacement of old paper money with new ones, and principles of paper money withdrawal, supervision and inspection, bore a striking resemblance to the contents of modern paper money management. It was unprecedented in both China and the world at that time. He won the favor of Kublai Khan, who admonished the powerful courtier Ghsang that paper money may not be considered as simply a piece of mulberry paper, "I replaced the old paper money with Zhiyuan paper money on the recommendation of Ye Li, the use thereof lies in the law, the value lies in creditability; you may not consider it as a piece of paper, the principal may not be lost, you should acquaint yourself with this reason."[20] In our view, Kublai Khan admonished his able financial manager so that he would not plunder money and not consider paper money as the instrument that rakes money in, neither extort endless cream and wealth from the people, nor impose unrestrained taxes, nor stake out the imperial power and the reputation of the empire, thereby bringing the entire empire to ruin.

5. Wang Yi's theory of firm coin and weak paper money

Wang Yi (1322–1373), courtesy name Zichong, born in Yiwu (in present-day Zhejiang), lived at the end of the Yuan Dynasty and beginning of the Ming Dynasty. He was precocious at an early age, and his writings gained fame when he reached adulthood. At the end of the Yuan Dynasty, he lived and wrote in seclusion on Mount Qingyan, and his fame ascended by the

---

[20]*History of the Yuan Dynasty — Biography of Ghsang*, vol. 15, p. 4574.

day. In the 20th year of Emperor Huizong in the Zhizheng period in the Yuan Dynasty (1360), Zhu Yuanzhang, the founding emperor of the Ming Dynasty, took Wuzhou, summoned and appointed Wang Yi as a historian in the executive secretariat to supervise the composition of the History of Yuan Dynasty together with Song Lian. When composition of the history was completed, he was promoted to the position of Shizhi (scholar in waiting) in the Imperial Academy and authored the Collection of Wang Zhongwen Gong and many more.

His work *On Money*[21] was a piece composed after he returned to the south at the end of the Yuan Dynasty, which discussed the nature and position of money, theory of firmness and weakness of money, and a two-step design of monetary systems. He noted that the top priority of the time was to "promote coin law, shelve paper money law," and advocated minting gold and silver coins, circulating them with copper coin, standing them in the relation of the parent and the offspring.

5.1. *On the nature of the concept of money*

Wang Yi believed that "Quan refers to its flowing form" and "Huo refers to its function." (Quan Huo literally mean "fountain" and "commodity"). Quan (fountain) refers to its liquidity, as noted by Ban Bu, "flows in a fountain." Huo might refer to property, as noted by *Shuo Wen* (a Chinese philology classic), "Huo, property." It might refer to the function of weighing or comparison, as stated in "in the system, first came copper coin first and then paper money." Weighing refers to its function. If this theory stands, then it summarized the features of money as a universal equivalent, the nature of it being a general representative of social wealth, and also reflected the form of movement and basic functions of money.

Wang Yi also followed the established theory of the forerunners, disclosed the nature of money and believed that "the so-called money is to weigh the most valued items with the least valued item." That is to say, the least-valued item in the world was used to weigh and measure the most-valued items in the world, this was money. The reason to say that it was

---

[21] *Collected Essays on Statecraft of Ming Dynasty — Collection of Wang Zhongwen Gong.* No more citations shall be provided for further quotes from this book hereinbelow.

the least-valued item was that copper coin and paper money, both functioned as money, and as Chao Cuo said, "were neither helpful to keep people warm nor helpful to allay hunger."

This view remained fresh over a period of fifteen hundred years; however, the economic environments thereof had undergone substantial change, and commodity money has permeated into every aspect of social life, from the city to the countryside, from the central area to the remote regions, from domestic areas to abroad, from the handicraftsman to the peasant, from theory to practice; in short, money played an indispensably important position in the entire social, economic, political, military and cultural life of the society: "it is something whereto the great livelihood of the people forever hinges, therefore the state cannot go without it for a single day. A day without it would approximately have extinguished the entire livelihood of the state." In Wang Yi's view, the working mechanism of the entire society could not go without money for a minute, as without money the society would fall into stagnation and suffocation. That is to say, on the success of the monetary system hinged the survival of the state. Money was elevated to such a height, not in fictional works but in a monograph on money, that it was arguably the very first time in the entire history of ancient society that such a statement was made. At least it was the understanding by the people after the Yuan Dynasty was founded, and it truthfully reflected the growth of monetary economy.

Of course, in the separation of the social function from the special function of monetary material, the smaller the special function, the higher the possibility that such an item assumes the role of monetary material, and the less it is required in social production and life, the firmer its position as monetary material. From this point, "the most useless" aspect could be balanced by usefulness; he did not deny the existence of money as a value entity. What he said about the most useless and the most useful could be understood as the relative use value thereof. Monetary material evolved along this trajectory of what corn and silk are to copper, and what copper is to gold and silver.

5.2. *On firmness of money*

Wang Yi noted definitively, "paper money is a virtual item, whereas coin physical. When coin and paper money are used in combination, then the people would surely drop the virtual and take the physical." This was the clearest, most accurate statement on the relation between coin and paper money. "Paper money is a virtual item, whereas coin is a physical one." The statement referred to the deviation of the face value from the actual value of paper money. The face value of paper money represented the amount of copper coins; therefore, it was "virtual," and hence, paper money was only a representative and symbol for copper coin of equal amount. On the contrary, the situation for copper coin was different; it should be a physical entity of value, minted according to specified size, weight, purity and form. From the perspective of value, the nominal value and the real value may agree or disagree; from the perspective of use value, as an entity in the world, moneys of all forms were the most useless items.

The contrastive concepts of the virtual and the physical advanced by Wang Yi radically shifted from the relatively indefinite connotations assigned to them by foregoing theorists. He developed the contrastive terms from the immature stage where there was no established concepts for them, to the mature stage where there were definite and established concepts. Hence, he eliminated the confusion arising from the need for constant readjustment to changing time and environment. For instance, when money is compared with commodity, commodity was the physical and money the virtual, whereas when copper coin was compared with paper money, copper coin was physical and paper money the virtual. Still when par value paper money was compared with depreciated paper money, the par value paper money was the physical and the depreciated the virtual. Wang Yi took the physical entity of value as the physical and the value token as the virtual. Though he did not clearly state the value concept, he did proceed from examination of the physical entity of value and determined the criteria for distinguishing the virtual and the physical according to whether there was value. Following therefrom, Wang Yi's understanding had gained substantially over the progress of the forerunners.

Based thereon, he concluded that if coin and paper money were concurrently circulated, the people would discard paper money and pursue copper coin. In this way, two defects in money circulation in the Yuan Dynasty were discovered in the analysis. The first was that the issuance right was relegated downward, and the fate of the state was placed in the hands of the people. The state compulsorily implemented paper money; however, the people regarded it as a useless item and refused to use it.

On the contrary, the old coins were not recognized by the state as a statutory currency, and the people strove to use it. Wang Yi criticized the new monetary system implemented in 1350, saying, "Zhongtong money was of smaller value and Zhiyuan of bigger value, when the two paper moneys were circulated concurrently, the people would surely keep the one of bigger value and discard the one of smaller value." The past rule was that five *guan* Zhongtong paper money should be converted into one *guan* of Zhiyuan paper money, and Zhongtong paper money was later replaced by Zhizheng paper money, with one *guan* being converted into two *guans* of Zhiyuan paper money. Such changes drew suspicion from the people. "Therefore since the reform," the people would either scramble to use Zhongtong paper money or use Zhiyuan paper money alone; there was no constancy or normalcy among the people. Ultimately neither paper money was used, and only copper coin was accepted. "The central government engaged in coin minting but soon dropped the undertaking, and the minted coins failed to get accepted widely, therefore the coins the people used were all from previous times." Hence, the situation was reversed; the people held the power of the state and the livelihood of the state was in the hands of the people, "no defect of money is worse than such situation." The second defect was that "even if admonished with repeated edicts and bans," the people would not take it seriously; such orders aroused no awe, and officials in charge could do nothing but watch such defects develop. The popular opinion trended down in an inexorable manner as though water rushed down from a height. Wang Yi considered that an able ruler should do in a big way anything that benefits the people, he should follow readily whatever is right so long as it is a measure endearing the people. Monetary right moved downward. The defect of circulating coin and paper money concurrently was nothing more than what Wang Yi had projected. Paper money depreciation spiraled and the people chose to use coin instead of paper money, with normal social and economic life being impeded.

5.3. *On monetary reform*

The monetary system reform that Wang Yi designed for the monetary system of the Yuan Dynasty on its last leg could be divided into two objectives, the long-term and the short-term objectives, that is, a two-step process was to be involved. The short-term objective was of an urgent need, which needed to be dealt with immediately, that is, to rectify the circulation of minted coins and abolish paper money circulation. "The present circumstance makes it appropriate to temporarily shelve the paper money law, whereas coin law must be immediately addressed." In actual implementation, methods were to be grounded on "two measures, the first is to commence minting in a grand scale, and the second is to stop minting big denomination coin." That is to say, in order to meet the demand for means of payment and purchase of the market, additional minting of copper coin was required. However, no minting of over-valued big denomination coin was allowed, that is, Wang Yi was against inflationary policy; only full-value small denomination coins of high purity and superior quality were to be minted.

The advancement of the monetary system rectification plan for short-term reform was not only based on the theory of the virtual and the physical but also upon learning from the lessons of coin circulation in history. Wang Yi thought that all governments minted coins at places close to mines in consideration of the inconvenience of copper shipment, and set up special agencies in charge of it. In the Tang Dynasty, "regulatory bodies were set up close to places where copper was discovered, there were altogether ninety nine furnaces." In the Song Dynasty, "there were altogether twenty six regulatory bodies, and coins minted in the various Lus were of varying amounts, and the law could never be discarded." In 1308–1311 of the Yuan Dynasty, "six regulatory bodies were set up in Jianghuai area." He believed that Jia Yi was only against private minting instead of opposing government minting on a grand scale, "furnace minting shall be conducted on a grand scale," which was the first thing. The second thing was that the government engaging in minting big denomination coin was but an expedient move; it could only be viewed as a temporary measure and had never been meant as a measure for permanent peace and order. Since the times of King Jing of the East Zhou Dynasty and King Zhuang of Kingdom Chu, minting big denomination coins met with opposition. "The Chice coin of Han Dynasty was fixed at a conversion rate of one for five, the conversion rate of big denomination coin minted by Wang Mang was fixed at one for fifty, one for a hundred in Shu, one for a thousand in Later Zhou, and one for ten of Qianyuan in Tang, Yongtong in Later Tang and Xining in Song." Because "big denomination coin is of lighter weight and the profit is great, great profit draws many pirate forgers, and few cherish it due to its light weight." On the contrary, "small denomination coin cost a lot and the profit was evenly spread out, high cost attracts few forgers, evenly spread profit makes it an exchange of equal values." This statement remarked that overvalued big denomination coins were of lighter weight and highly profitable, leading people to forge even against the threat of stringent punishment, and these were cherished by few; this phenomenon originated in sloppy work. Hence, "these minted coins were soon scrapped, which led to the situation where few big denomination coins remain to this day." The situation was different for small denomination coins, "the Wuzhu (five-*zhu*) of Han, Kaiyuan of Tang, Dading of Jin, Daguang of Song and small denomination Zhizheng coins of the present day must be set up as a standard." That is, the standard coin must be a finely minted full-value coin, so that the principle of exchange of equal values is implemented — "exchange of equal values." Otherwise, it would be inconceivable. Actually, circulation of full-value coin was also relative, and it was different from small denomination coin circulation; even if it was not a full-value coin, so long as the amount of coins in circulation was kept under control, no unchecked issuance was conducted, and it would be equally capable of performing the functions of purchase and payment in place of money. The fact that Wang Yi insisted on the concept that only full-value coins were to be circulated indicated that he was a follower of metal money theory. The third thing was that the state must control sufficient quantity of copper in order to guarantee full value and fine workmanship of minted coins. He advocated that trade of copper must be banned, the government should have monopoly on copper trade, concentrated processing and minting should be accompanied by stringent official seals and outflow should be prevented. Besides minting coins, copper can only be used to make daily necessities such as mirror, musical instruments, nails, rings, buttons, etc., which cannot be substituted by other materials. Only lead, tin, earth and wood were allowed to be used in Buddhist activities, no copper material was permitted. "All bronze held by the people was to be sold to the government, and the government shall forge such into coins, besides the cost of mintage, only thirty percent of the profit is to be withheld, and the remaining seventy percent to the people." In minting, "a rule of weight must be fixed, and a balance between cost and price be struck." Only if the state practiced strict control and regulation, from monopoly sale to production, would supervision of the entire process of issuance be realized. "When coins of today circulate freely, coins of other dynasties will drop out of circulation without intervention." However, the problem lay in the state itself. Indeed as Wu Qian (1196–1262) said, "Nowadays, the state fiscal strength is depleted, corn is purchased with paper money, military expenses are disbursed with paper money, all are disbursed with paper money ... paper money will be inevitably used, hence paper money is truly where the national livelihood lies."[22] The state would absolutely not give up this last straw in times of financial straits, especially in critical moments of political and military crises; how would the state be willing to follow the preaching of Wang Yi, restraining itself in chains of his own making, blocking its financial source and resigning itself to fate?

In the long run, Wang Yi believed that gold and silver coins should be minted and issued. "In ancient times, pearl and jade were held as the superior, gold the intermediate, and silver the inferior. In later times, two types of money might have been circulated, Yi was the name of gold in the Qin system, and there was also copper coin. Nowadays indeed the case that both the government and the people have the right to mint gold, silver coins." In history, the Jin Dynasty did once use silver to mint Cheng'an silver coins, and there were some advocating minting of silver money; that is to say, along with the development of commodity monetary economy, social life had raised the requirement that general means of circulation shall be assumed by high-value precious metals, and this situation was recognized by the authorities. For this, Wang Yi made some theoretical exposition, remarking, "Nowadays it is indeed the case that both the government and the people have the right to mint gold and silver into money, the prices thereof shall be fixed in accordance with their quality and weight; such money shall be stood in a relation of balance and checks with copper coin as the parent and the offspring, there is nothing

---

[22] *Xu Guogong Memorial — Nine Key Matters of State Governance Submitted on Imperial Edict.*

wrong with this arrangement. And that in public and private transactions, if copper coin is employed, the weight thereof makes it inconvenient to be carried afar, therefore most people would carry both gold and silver, even though the pertinent department does not stipulate its use specifically, the government and the people would still use them without the least concern. This is the situation where gold and silver were used as money, to be concurrently circulated with copper coin, this is the situation of benefiting them with what benefits them." Gold and silver were the parents and copper coin the offspring, the parents and the offspring standing in a relation of balance and checks; it was no longer the original copper coin system, but a system where gold, silver and copper were employed concurrently, gold and silver coins being fixed as the price standard according to their quality and weight. Regardless of distance, public or private nature of transaction, gold and silver coins could play the functions of means of payment and purchase unconditionally. Admittedly, this was not Wang Yi's invention; he only rationalized the reasonable phenomena long in existence in practical economic life, which embodied the inevitable trend of the monetary development history. He captured the historical trend in time, advocated forcefully the minting of gold and silver coins and circulating gold and silver coins; this novel, positive recommendation must be recognized.

Regarding the monetary system reform plan of Wang Yi, his contemporaries had had similar ideas. Kong Qi from Qufu authored *Blunt Words* on the Zhizheng Period at the end of the Yuan Dynasty, in which there was an article titled *Perils of Paper Money* which enumerated the evils of excessive issuance of paper money at the end of the Yuan Dynasty. He put forward the following:

"I had privately proposed to classify these into three categories, gold and silver are both to be smelt into small ingots of two grades; such ingots must be made with the finest materials, and such shall be inscribed with the weight as well as the name of the supervising officer, names of worker, place of minting. Weight of ingot ranges from one tael to fifty taels. The third grade is minted copper coin.... In transaction, gold is to be used for high price article, silver for lower price article, and copper coin for the lowest price article. Copper coin is to be used for price not exceeding two *ding*, that is, one hundred *guan*, silver for price less than fifty taels, and gold for price less than ten taels. Each gold ingot shall weigh one tael, to be converted to ten taels of silver. A tael of silver shall be converted to several hundred *wen*, in this process, copper price and production cost must be publicly discussed and then such may be established as a rule." However, Wang Yi proposed that the people may freely mint gold and silver coins, which would make it difficult to have uniform weight and purity and would bring trouble into transactions; if minting was concentrated in the government, and the people conducted free exchange, the plan would be more sound. However, some people rejected the plan on the pretext that the established practices handed down from the ancestors were not to be changed and cited some books of prophecy, claiming that there was neither basis in the classics nor authentication by the deities in proposing the rejection of paper money and implementing coins. Wang Yi thought otherwise, and stated, "The law of the world, even the sage would not be able to make it last long and without defect, how could we confine ourselves rigidly to such opinionated views, to such platitude. Expansion or contraction shall be made fit for the time and the circumstance, only in this way good results may then be attained." Only by following the tides, grasping the opportunity and implementing monetary system reform without reserve can the defect be eliminated and the grand way of the people may be attained; the view of Wang Yi was indeed marvelous and admirable! We should follow his views and uphold them.

6. Pool and ditch theory of paper money by Ye Ziqi

Ye Ziqi, courtesy name Shijie, style Jingzhai, another style Caomuzi, was born in Longquan of Zhejiang. He was among the renowned scholars together with Liu Ji of Qingtian and Song Lian of Pujiang at the end of the Yuan Dynasty; he took up the position of a master of the rolls in Baling county after the Ming Dynasty was founded. In 1378, he was implicated in a case and sent to prison; during his imprisonment, he wrote *Cao Mu Zi* with improvised writing materials by grinding tiles, and finished writing it the following year when he was released from imprisonment. His other works include the *Jingzhai Collection*. In *Cao Mu Zi* — *Miscellaneous*

Systems,[23] he examined causes for the failure of the paper money law of the Yuan Dynasty, the paper money law reform and the law of paper money circulation to be followed.

6.1. On the scrapping of Yuan Dynasty paper money

He believed that the causes of the failure of the Yuan Dynasty paper money system lay not in the paper money itself, but in the cluelessness of the promoters and the improper method employed in issuance. "I had made investigation into the matter, it was not that the method was not good, but that the posterity failed to grasp the way of change."

This understanding was very important as it was the starting point for Ye Ziqi to comment on the success, achievements and merit of paper money. What attitude shall we have when such issues including depreciation, inflation occur? Shall we continue our support enthusiastically and summarize lessons learned therefrom, or shall we simply reject the cause entirely by overgeneration? In the development of commodity monetary economy, the choice of attitude determines whether we can adapt to the historical trend, keep up with the pace of the times and ideas that drive progress, and also determines the big issue of financial and monetary system development strategy. Ye Ziqi chose the former, the attitude of adaptation, which showed his farsightedness.

From the Song Dynasty to the end of the Yuan Dynasty, paper money had been employed to satisfy fiscal expenditure requirements including maintaining an enormous army, palace expenditure and military awards, plus the expansion of frontier areas and the surge of population, which ultimately led to inevitable swelling and depreciation, and the collapse of the paper money system. This collapse of the paper money system further quickened the pace of regime change. However, many ancient scholars refused to look squarely into this reality. Zheng Jiefu once proclaimed that the demise of the Song Dynasty was the consequence of "making paper into money," attacking paper money as "stuff fit for the use of deities and ghosts, improper for use in this world, judging from the fact that items for

---

[23]Cao Mu Zi, vol. 3, Second Part. No more citations shall be provided for further quotes from this book hereinbelow.

the ghosts were employed, we surely know that the regime of Song would not last." When such was the prediction of the future, after half a century, the Ming Dynasty indeed replaced the Yuan Dynasty, and he was unfortunately accurate in his prediction.

On the contrary, Ye Ziqi argued that paper money had a long history and by demonstrating its history, which cannot be affirmed or denied as one would like. "The paper money law of the Yuan Dynasty was the same as the Zhiji in Zhou and Han Dynasties, Qianyin of Tang Dynasty, Jiaohui of Song Dynasty, Jiaochao of Jin Dynasty. At its heyday, paper money was employed to balance and check coins." There was indeed great room for debate in his argument. The prevailing modern view holds that "Zhiji" was originally a deeds for transaction and "Qianyin of Tang" was indeed a mistake for "Feiqian" (flying money), which was originally a type of draft; none of these was paper money. However, we will confine ourselves to understanding his real intent, which is that paper money originated and took form inevitably in the development of the commodity monetary economy. We should not casually affirm or deny paper money as the cause for the regime change; it had its inherent reason for origination, formation and development. Paper money was absolutely neither a parasitic entity on a certain social formation, nor the other way around, becoming the grounds for the development of such a social formation.

Ye Ziqi considered that, in the development process of paper money system, if "adaptation" was poorly devised and an improper method was adopted, paper money circulation would be blocked and inflation would ensue, causing paper money to fail. In analyzing specific causes of the situation, he pinpointed the main cause and revealed it in a relatively accurate and thorough manner, which reflected his profound understanding of this issue. He condemned the prime minister for being impractical, aspiring exclusively for fame when he adopted the advice of the wily courtier Jia Lu: "on separately issued Zhizheng paper money, materials whereof it was made were inferior and easy to wear and deteriorate, and it was difficult to replace such, therefore the circulation of paper money stagnated and it ultimately fell into disuse. And when there is military agitation, national financial strength gets drained, more paper money is produced to fund the military operation, and there will be inflation, when there is no means available to stem up the situation, hence paper money circulation will be scrapped." Therefore, it could be deduced that the causes for the paper money system being discarded in wartime and in peacetime were different. In the former, the cause was sloppy work and excessive production out of eagerness for instant results and achievements, which jeopardized the reputation of paper money, leading to its stagnated circulation and disuse. Whereas in the latter case, paper money flooded the market due to excessive issuance by the government in order to satisfy fiscal requirements. Therefore, he further noted that "at the closing period of a dynasty, there was general shortage of both property and commodity, the government solely engaged in producing paper money to satisfy its expenditure requirements, and when paper money failed to be properly balanced, flow of the myriad articles is thus stopped. These are the main causes of the situation." This statement, together with the latter cause listed in the foregoing text, explains the measures adopted by the state to tide over the difficulties and get rid of the financial straits by issuing paper money in order to make up for the shortfall in fiscal revenue and situations where the revenue failed to meet the expenditure. However, things went athwart. As paper money was already excessively issued, commodity circulation was obstructed, which led to the collapse of the paper money system and the social economic order being dealt a severe blow. The aggregate results could not but expedite the demise of the dynasty itself.

6.2. On change of paper money

Ye Ziqi believed that if the passive situation of paper money circulation was to be turned around, "paper money law must be established, coins and commodity be established as reserve thereof"; a local government reserve repository and a private paper money issuance system were to be established. Commodity prices were to be regulated by issuing and retiring paper money.

Issuance Reserve Repository System at Governments of Various Levels: The prefectures and counties were to set up a coin repository "to deposit a certain amount of coins, establish paper money reserve and Qianyin (money certificate) system, modeling after the practice of *Jiaozi* in Sichuan implemented by Zhang." As for the *Jiaozi* instituted in Sichuan by Zhang, in volume one of *Xiangshan Anecdotes*, the following was recorded: "Zhang (self-styled Guaiya) established the rule of Zhiji (deeds) on iron, copper coin and other supplies in Sichuan, one Jiaozi was established to be worth one string of copper coins and such was to be renewed every three years. Sixty-six years elapsed from 1011 and the mechanism was commenced to 1076; there have been twenty two sessions rotated, even the most wise could not alter it."

It could be seen that Ye Ziqi was not actually intent on implementing a 3-year session renewal issuance system; he was just trying to elaborate on his own subject and sought a historical basis for controlling the amount of paper money issuance. Therefore, the various local governments should have set up issuance reserve repositories, the purpose of which was to stabilize currency value, commodity price and the market under the conditions of a redeemable paper money system. The amount of paper money issuance could be controlled by the size of the issuance reserve fund. The purpose was equally to stabilize currency value, commodity price and the market, and to attain the social effect of a guarantee and restraining mechanism.

Distributed System for Paper Money Private Issuance: That meant, "wealthy houses shall be in charge of the issuance, paper money is redeemed against coins, paper money is released on the back of coin deposit, the coins shall be set as the parent and the paper money the offspring, a relation of checks and balance shall be established between the parent and the offspring." Wealthy houses raised funds to issue paper money, a motion which originated in lessons drawn from the failures of government-dominated paper money issuance by the governments in the Song, Jin and Yuan Dynasties, which strove to restore the practice of "having wealthy houses dominate issuance of paper money" for a "just about perfect" situation; however, the prospect for the design was far from miraculous. The creditworthiness of private issuance was limited, which was far from that of government issuance, since the government might employ paper money issuance to make up for financial deficit and appropriate issuance reserve to plug fiscal shortfall and make redemption impossible. The same situation equally existed in private issuance such as appropriation and embezzlement of issuance reserve, issuer fleeing with the reserve fund and unchecked excessive issuance, which would ultimately lead to a situation where redemption was made impossible.

Exactly for this reason, the earliest *Jiaozi* established in Sichuan was taken over by the government, and modified into a government issue. There was no way for Ye Ziqi to not know the inevitable trend in the history of paper money development; he might have mistaken that so long as there were coins in the coffers of governments at all levels, there was no need to worry about instability in paper money circulation as long as the system of paper money reserve and money certificate was established. The reason was simple; he believed that paper money law must make coin and commodity the "basis" of paper money, instead of making coin alone the basis of it or commodity alone the basis of it. Undoubtedly, this understanding was correct and very insightful too; it was a scientific understanding distilled from the lessons of paper money system collapses. In times of political turmoil, there was a general shortage of both property and commodity, and the government knew that only "excessively producing paper money satisfied its expenditure requirements, and when paper money failed to be properly balanced, flow of the myriad articles is thus stopped." Paper money may not have been as adaptive as copper coin which could drop out of circulation and reenter circulation at any time. Therefore, he proposed to make coin and commodity the reserve for paper money, and demonstrated the reason with instances of salt certificate and tea certificate: "salt and tea are immediately delivered against presentation of respective certificate, if paper money law is made in a similar way, there would be no worry about whether the mechanism works or not." We know that tea and salt had certificates of exclusive right for their transporting and selling, and their issuances had to be based on the production and stock of tea and salt, with no unrestrained issuance allowed. The situation for paper money was different as paper money was not a certificate of exclusive right, but a token or substitute for universal equivalent, and its production may exceed issuance reserve; Zhou Xing had already revealed this feature. Issuance reserve and paper money issuance stood in a mutually restraining relation and coexisted in the same system; the relation between them was not only that of guarantee and restraining but also that of the guarantee function being brought out on condition that the restraint was acknowledged. If they were split into two and paper money issuance and issuance reserve worked their separate ways, then neither the restraining function nor the guarantee function would work. Controlling the amount of issuance and stabilizing finance would turn out to be ineffectual. Commodity price was to be regulated by releasing and withdrawing paper money. "Paper money is released on the back of coin deposit, the coins shall be set as the parent and the paper money the offspring, a relation of checks and balance shall be established between the parent and the offspring so that the myriad articles may be weighed. The paper money should be released when commodity price rose and withdrawn when commodity price dropped; the release and withdrawal should be weighed and regulated according to the situation, there is no reason why this would not work!" The so-called commodity price drop referred to the situation where, under the condition of single paper money circulation, market price drop reflected the fact that there was less paper money in circulation than was needed and currency gained value; on the contrary, commodity price rise referred to the situation where market price rise reflected that there was an excessive amount of paper money in circulation and currency lost value. Hence, Ye Ziqi proposed that paper money should be released when market price dropped and withdrawn when market price rose. However, the paper money Ye Ziqi described referred to the paper money reserve, wherein certificates were the offspring of paper money and copper coins (possibly also including silver) parents. On the condition of redeemable paper money circulation, redeeming paper money was as good as releasing copper coins; hence, releasing copper coin equaled withdrawing paper money.

On the contrary, if issuance reserve was increased, paper money may be released; if issuance reserve was reduced, paper money should be withdrawn. The amount of paper money issuance was to be limited by the amount of issuance reserve, and no unrestrained increase or decrease in the amount of paper money issuance was allowed; therefore, the purchasing power of paper money would remain stable, unless abrupt changes took place as the result of catastrophe or warring activities, and market price generally also would not undergo substantial change. In consideration of the calamity of long-term inflation, the people suffered in this abyss of misery and the regime clung onto power in a precarious way. Ye Ziqi strongly proposed the restoration of the redeemable paper money system; however, he could not surpass the limitations of his time. A distinction was made between redeemable paper money and irredeemable paper money, between paper money and copper coin. However, due to the fact that an additional link was introduced into the circulation of redeemable paper money, the situation was not as simple as he claimed. It seemed that he made no theoretical breakthrough in this aspect.

6.3. *On the law of paper money circulation*

Paper money that entered circulation would not automatically drop out of circulation; however, it must be maintained at an appropriate amount. When this amount was exceeded, it would turn into a disastrous flood and became the source of calamity. Ye Ziqi vividly described the phenomenon as a pond of flowing water. He wrote, "it was like water from a pond entering a ditch, if the amount of water entering the ditch equals that exiting the ditch, then water in the pond will stay flowing and circulating, hence it will be a pond alive. However, if the inflow ditch is open but the outflow ditch is closed, then water in the pond will be stagnant and still; hence the pond will be overflown with water, and the peril of flood ensues." The ditch mentioned in the statement obviously was the aqueduct and drainage in currency circulation in the words of Marx. The so-called unobstructed aqueduct should be referring to paper money release functioning properly, whereas the obstructed drainage should be referring to the channel for paper money withdrawal not being obstructed, and paper money redemption being obstructed, discontinued or stagnating. He specifically emphasized that disastrous flooding of overflowing pond water should be prevented and the drainage must be kept unobstructed; that is to say, redemption may not be forced out of operation due to the reserve fund being withdrawn or appropriated by the government, or malpractices or obstacles created by officials. He believed that these views were unlike those of his predecessors. Past governments knew only to compel and coerce the people into using paper money by employing administrative, legislative methods and exacting punishment, without knowing that these measures would work only at cross-purposes: They "knew only compelling the people into using it, therefore the more exacting the punishment the less likely the paper money is circulated, this was exactly why the Yuan Dynasty died without remedy."

Moreover, Daming paper money was issued in 1375, composed of six denominations, from one hundred *wen*, 500 *wen* and one *guan*, or one *guan* of paper money converting to 1,000 *wen* of copper coins, or a tael of silver, or four *guan* of paper money converting to one tael of gold. A paper money promotion agency was established to legislate on paper money circulation, a paper money standard was established, gold and silver transaction was prohibited, and gold and silver could only be sold to the government in exchange for paper money. Gold and silver could only be sold to the government, no redemption was allowed, tax payment could be composed of 30% coins and 70% paper money, and payment for the amount under 100 *wen* was to be made in coin. In 1376, an imperial edict mandated that silver, paper money, coin and corn should be used concurrently in payment; a tael of silver, a 1,000 coins and a *guan* of paper money should all be converted into a *dan* of corn as tax payment. When paper money was issued without restraint on amount, reserve, time and circulation area, and there was neither redemption nor paper money replacement, the release outnumbered the withdrawal and not long thereafter, the financial situation of the government got increasingly constrained. Paper money issuance was conducted to address the pressing situation, and the value of paper money dropped on a daily basis, with the laws promulgated being ignored by local officials; there was a great jumble of government-produced paper money, fake paper money and privately produced paper money. The remarks of Ye Ziqi were of special significance; on the surface it was a summary of the lessons from the failure of paper money issuance in the Yuan Dynasty, in essence addressed to the new rulers in power, warning them against taking the old road to failure. Though he overgeneralized the failure of paper money issuance as the cause for the demise of the Yuan Dynasty, he was the first one who had likened paper money circulation to "aqueduct and drainage" aside from the statement that appeared in *Guan Zi — Qing Zhong*; no other scholar had conducted so intensive an analysis and it should be acknowledged that his understanding was solid and profound.

He treated the law of paper money circulation as the object, or an objective entity outside the realm of subjective consciousness of human beings. He believed that what the rulers could do was only to understand it, follow it and master it, but not alter it with the mandatory power of the regime, otherwise it would only work at cross-purposes, and slip away further to the reverse end of the subjective wishes of the people. The supreme rulers finished their historical processes in exactly the same manner.

Though Ye Ziqi failed to elaborate on the specific content of the objective law in entirety, unlike the explanation made by Shen Kuo who specifically analyzed the functional relations between certain factors in currency circulation, Ye Ziqi may after all be regarded as the one who had definitively revealed that the objective law of currency circulation must be followed after Shen Kuo; he was the first to have discussed the law of paper money circulation, and warned the authorities that paper money circulation should not be organized and managed in violation of objective law, which was exceptional in the history of monetary thought in China. His thought was also ahead of its time in the world.

7. Monetary theory of Liu Dingzhi

Liu Dingzhi (1409–1469), courtesy name Zhujing, style Baozhai or Daizhai, was born in Yiongxin of Jiangxi. He was a scholar of profound learning, and made his name in the literary circles, posting many proposals. In 1434, in preparation for the imperial examinations, he wrote *Strategies for Ten Subjects*, which was circulated widely among the examination-taking scholars with quite some influence. He was enrolled in the following year. In 1436, he passed the palace examinations and ranked third in the final results, and he later authored the *Daizhai Collection*.

In 1375, Daming Tongxing paper money was issued, and the value thereof plummeted over a period of a few years. In the period of 1403–1424, commodity price surged multiple times, and in the Xuande period of Emperor Xuanzong (1426–1435), paper money failed. In the 3rd year of the Xuande period, issuance of new paper money was suspended, broken and worn paper money was recalled and anyone violating the edict was punished with planks. By the 9th year, the price of rice had risen to a thousand times that of the Hongwu period.

Imperial censors Chen Ying (1366–1430) and Xia Yuanjiin during the reign of the Chenzu Emperor proposed measures for recalling paper money, including household salt tax and introducing a store and stand taxes, to little effect. In the *Strategy for Revenue and Strategy for Works of the Strategies for Ten Subjects*, there were essays on *Merits and Demerits of Coin Law and Paper Money Law in the Various Dynasties, and Similarities and Differences of Coin Law and Paper Money Law*,[24] in which the main monetary issues Liu Dingzhi discussed included monetary consciousness, defects in monetary circulation and strategies dealing therewith. These reflected the development of commodity economy in the Ming Dynasty and problems present in the monetary circulation. There was novelty in them, and very insightful views as well.

7.1. On monetary consciousness

Commodity economy originated early in ancient China; however, it failed to mature ultimately. As early as the Western Han Dynasty, Chao Cuo, a scholar of great vision from the landed class, advanced the famous nominal theory of money which stated that money (including pearl, jade, gold and silver) "could neither fend the cold nor allay the hunger, however it is valued by many, the reason lies in that the ruler employs it purposefully." For over 1,000 years, this statement had gone unnoticed and unchallenged. However, Liu Dingzhi struck a different tune; he boldly struck out the "no" from the statement, broke with the established rules and laws of natural economy which worked for thousands of years and turned them upside down. He poignantly raised the point, "Pearl, jade, gold, treasures could be put to use but are scarce. Corn, cloth, silk could also be put to use but could not go afar. With ten thousand *guan* on the waist, paper money the size of inches in hand, cold could be fended off, hunger could be allayed, one can be rich without hoarding pearl and jade, sufficient without amassing gold and treasure, which probably is also a fine rule of the ancients pacifying the world and facilitating the people." His remarks that money "could both fend the cold and allay the hunger" were truly farsighted. This was not a play on words, but an objective reflection on the fundament change in fermentation of the then social and economic life,

---

[24]*Strategies of Master Daizhai*, vols. 6 and 10. No more citations shall be provided for further quotes from this book hereinbelow.

and an evident proof of the keen insight of the progressive scholar on the development of the then commodity economy and a dauntless, bold proposal thereof.

The basic feature of natural economy production was the production of physical products satisfying the living needs of the self, with most items traded on the market being surplus products. While land was the most important means of production in the period, the purpose of pursuing and storing money was to purchase land and transform money to a physical form. So long as people had land, requirements for clothes, food, living and traveling, and everything required for the consumption of corn, cloth and silk could be made available. The emperor himself was the biggest land owner of the country. Therefore, money was of limited purpose in this period, and was subjugated under physical items. It was really "neither capable of fending off the cold nor allaying the hunger."

The middle and later periods of the Ming Dynasty were a stage where commodity economy and especially commodity production gained universal development and attained prosperity. Agricultural production was to satisfy market requirements; corn production and growing and cultivating handicraft materials were to acquire money or produce commodity which may bring about more money. The means of production and means of livelihood people required were no longer produced by themselves; such requirements could be satisfied on the market, and dependence on the market was increasingly deepened. Social division of labor moved to the direction of specialization, with many specialized production industries or a certain degree of regional division of labor tailored to the local situation being brought into existence in this process. Examples were the cotton cloth industry in the Songjiang area south of the Yangtze River, the coal and iron industry of Guangdong, the pottery and porcelain industry of Jiangxi, and the papermaking and sugar industry along the borders of Fujian, Zhejiang and Jiangxi. Workshop handicraft industries began to appear, with laborers living on wages freely selling their labor service and receiving payment according to the degree of proficiency of skill. Commercialization deepened further and silver began to function as the basic statutory money. Money had gradually transformed from a servant submissive to commodity economy to a dignified and distinguished master.

As Lenin remarked in analyzing Russian villages, "Formerly, land used to be the ruling power — that was the case under the serf-owning system: whoever possessed land possessed power and authority. Today, however, money, capital, has become the ruling power. With money you can buy as much land as you like. Without money you will not be able to do much even if you have land: you must have money to buy a plough or other implements, to buy livestock, to buy clothes and other town-made goods, not to speak of paying taxes."[25] Although the bud of the advanced, modern commodity monetary economy had freshly sprouted in the Ming Dynasty, it was impossible for it to be as powerful and widespread as the monetary force stated by Lenin; however, such a phenomenon was indeed starting to grow in the city and the countryside of China. The natural economy started to disintegrate, traditional ideas sustained impact and monetary consciousness was reflected in theory. The following concepts were formed: pearl, jade, gold and treasure were scarce though they were considered social wealth, while corn, cloth, silk were inconvenient for long-distance carrying though they were also considered social wealth; moreover, in society people could be rich without having pearls, jade, gold and treasure and could get anything to their liking, the medium working in this process being money. So long as there was money, one would be rich, go afar, fend off the cold and allay hunger, and this would hardly be surprising at all.

Liu Dingzhi treated coin and paper money equally, and even considered paper money as conducive to the development of industrial and commercial activity as well as the growth of commodity economy. Hence, he by no means stressed that money in circulation must be metal money, nor stressed that paper money in circulation must be redeemable; he held that irredeemable paper money could totally replace coin in circulation. In his view, both had their defects, and if not dealt with properly, both may upset the people; on the contrary, if dealt with properly, both may be eliminated of their respective defect, benefit the people and facilitate commodity exchange. Therefore, he said, "the world may not go a day without paper money. What the people depend on for their lives are corn and silk, what is the use of the coin? However, coin may be employed in purchasing corn

---

[25]*Lenin: Selected Works*, vol. 1, p. 399.

and silk, therefore coin may be put to use. What the people depend on for use are coin and commodity, then what is the use of paper money the size of a feet, paper money may be used to replace coin and commodity, hence paper money may be put to use." Only with the backdrop of great development of commodity monetary economy could this monetary consciousness come into being. This monetary consciousness boded well with the bud of developed modern commodity economy that was rising on the horizon of ancient China. The one-word difference between Liu Dingzhi and Chao Cuo reflected the undertone of a nascent social formation, reflecting a world of difference with ancient social formation which featured self-sufficiency. It also made clear to the world that, in the traditions of China, there was neither inherent slavish adherence to established practices nor holding back from progress, still less a lack of admiration and pursuit of nascent things, which deserved great appreciation; however, it died prematurely under mounting pressure from the two fronts of conservative forces and foreign colonial forces.

7.2. On circulation of coins

Liu Dingzhi believed that coins had a long history of circulation: "coins had been continuously used since the Zhou Dynasty." The defect of coin circulation lay in the irregular weight thereof; the so-called irregular weight referred to the amount of metal content contained in the coin, instead of the purchasing power of such coins. He analyzed the weights of the coins from the various dynasties and concluded that "a coin weighing five *zhu* would be a fine rule." He specifically noted that coin weight shall be employed in determining which coin was appropriate for assuming the role as a measure of value and an instrument of circulation. For instance, the disadvantage of the three *zhu*, four *zhu* and Yujia coins in the Han Dynasty lay in the fact that they were too light, and so were the Eryan coins of the Wei Dynasty, Huanqian, Laizi and Xingye coins of the Northern and Southern Dynasties, Sifen Shenlang coins of the Eastern Jin Dynasty, and four Zhu coins of the Tang Dynasty; on the contrary, the disadvantage of the half tael and Chice coins was that they were too heavy, and so were the 150 Zhu coins of the Han Dynasty, Wuxing Dabu and Yongtong Wanguo coins of the Northern Zhou Dynasty, and Qianyuan

Zhongbao and Chonglun Qianyuan coins. He hence arrived at the conclusion, "when coin value drops and commodity price rises, then there is the problem of unwieldiness which hinders the exchange of commodity; when coin value rises and commodity price drops, and there is the problem of forgery. Only the likes of the five Zhu of the Han Dynasty, Kaiyuan of the Tang Dynasty attained the proper weight." This indicated that if the coin was of smaller weight, then commodity price would surely be higher, normal commodity exchange would be hindered, and commodity circulation would stagnate and be obstructed. However, if the nominal weight of the coin was bigger, then commodity price would be low and the coveting of forgery would be induced, which would lead to large-scale forgery. Liu Dingzhi traced the inverse ratio relation between the weight of coins and price of commodity to find the answer to maintaining the normalcy of monetary circulation. Though he had yet to understand the underlying cause for the inverse ratio relationship, he had shifted from the traditional concepts of "more coins lower the value of coins, less coins increase the value thereof," and stopped following the quantity theory of money and the train of thought of scarcity of commodity leading to higher price in explaining the relation between the change of money and commodity price. Compared with the quantity theory of money, this understanding was closer to revealing the nature of the phenomenon; there was more reasonableness in it and it was possibly more similar to the labor theory of value. However, his observation of monetary circulation was limited to the realm of phenomenon. It was inevitable that he would eventually misjudge and analyze it incorrectly.

In discussing the ratio relation between coin weight and commodity price, Liu Dingzhi only analyzed the relation on the surface between the purchasing power of money and commodity price, failing to understand the inherent cause of such a relation and failing to explore deeper the distinction between the nominal weight of coin and the real weight, between the nominal value and the real value, which led to a depreciation policy by rulers who deliberately lowered the metal weight and purity in coin or arbitrarily raised the nominal value thereof and minted overvalued big denomination coin to grab exorbitant minting profit and achieve the real purpose of effecting fiscal exploitation. There were other factors he failed to understand and employ, such as the change in commodity money and the various labor productivities; therefore, many of the overweight coins he enumerated were actually overvalued big denomination coins, the weights of which were actually lighter instead of heavier, for instance, one Zhongguan Chice five *zhu* was worth five five-*zhu* coins minted by the princedoms. Hence, it could be seen that these "overweighed coins" were actually priced higher, and there was great difference between the name and the real thing. Therefore, the tremendous profit from minting induced rampant forgery despite repeated prohibitions, and ultimately led to the endless trouble of "unchecked forgery." The consequence for the so-called "commodity price will necessarily rise" should have actually been that commodity price would necessarily drop, the other way around, which exposed the defects of the incomplete and unscientific characteristics of Liu Dingzhi's monetary theory.

As regards regulating coin circulation, he made little progress, just reiterating the theory of "neither copper nor labor should be spared in minting."

7.3. *On paper money circulation*

Liu Dingzhi held that there were different defects between paper money circulation and coin circulation. However, he did not address the issue regarding what led to the difference between the two.

The questions were what makes paper money circulation around the country difficult, what hindered its circulation and how it could circulate without hindrance. Liu Dingzhi's predecessors had paid attention to the issue and discussed it. In Emperor Chengzu's reign, Chen Ying, an imperial censor once remarked, "The reason for paper money failure this year was due to oversupply by the government without measures of withdrawing, which made commodity price rise and paper money price drop."[26] In Emperor Renzong's reign, Yu Qian (1366–1427) of Dalisi (the supreme court) remarked, "paper money failed, the origin of the defect thereof lay in release exceeding withdrawal, nowadays, so long as paper money is recalled through multiple channels and released sparingly, it would then be difficult for the people to obtain paper money, circulation thereof will

---

[26]*History of Ming Dynasty — Shi Huo Zhi Five.*

hence be restored."[27] Criticism focused on uncontrolled and arbitrary release, and inadequate withdrawal which led to excessive paper money staying in circulation. Liu Dingzhi believed that the defects of paper money circulation lay in the fact that "paper money has been in use since the foundation of Song, however, the defect in paper money is that there were irregularities between the expensive and the cheap." The so-called "the expensive and the cheap" must refer to the high and low monetary value of paper money, namely, whether the purchasing power was appropriate or whether it was too high or too low. The issue seemed to have a direct relation to paper money quantity; hence, he concluded, "small amount production makes paper money price rise, and too small amount would make it insufficient for use; big amount production makes paper money price drop, however too big is equally not workable. Paper money must be made like the Tiansheng of Song and Zhongtong of Yuan, then the denomination would be almost appropriate." It should be acknowledged that his analysis of the defect was to the point and very insightful. In today's words, when paper money is minted and released in insufficient amounts, the unit value of paper money will rise, the purchasing power thereof will rise in turn, and the commodity prices will drop accordingly.

However, if paper money is insufficiently produced and issued, it would not be able to satisfy the requirement of commodity exchange and ultimately hinder commodity circulation and hinder commodity production in turn. On the contrary, if paper money is oversupplied, unit price thereof will drop, purchasing power will drop in turn and commodity price will rise; if paper money is oversupplied, then paper money will not be accepted and will not play the role of a circulating instrument. This understanding differed from the quantity theory of money. When the monetary token is circulated, the value represented thereby, namely, the purchasing power, stands in inverse ratio relation to the amount of issuance, which is distinguished from the "weight" of coins; this understanding was unimpeachable and very insightful at that. Credit money is different from paper money which takes silk, silver or coin as the standard money. The Ming Dynasty neither established standard money for paper money issuance nor specified the total issuance amount and

---

[27]Yang Shiqi, *Dongli Collection — Tomb Inscription for the Late Scholar Yu*, vol. 14.

duration of circulation. In his view, "one *Jiao* worth one thousand *wen* makes a fine rule." The amount of production and release of paper money in the first year of the Tiansheng period of Emperor Renzong in the Song Dynasty was 1.25 million strings, which was the same as the amount there was in full reserve and redemption guarantee in the issuance of Zhongtong paper money in the Zhongtong period of Kublai Khan. Such measures maintained the stability of paper money value and appropriate purchasing power of paper money.

Liu Dingzhi summarized the lessons from paper money circulation from previous dynasties. In his opinion, their successes lay not in "regulating with draconian law, exploiting the people with excessive extortion," but in the contraction and release of paper money. Stringent law could only work a maintenance effect. When a choice was to be made between interest and breach of the law, the point lay in which weighed more between the return and risk; there had been too many instead of too few cases of staking everything out for profit. Contraction is to be ready to replace broken and worn paper money with new ones, "allowing the people to bring broken and worn paper money for replacement, and charge thereon the production cost thereof." Therefore, there would neither be excessive paper money in circulation nor paper money too worn out to be used in circulation, this was the first thing. The second thing was that the government should not only issue paper money, it should also try to retire paper money from circulation, that is, "allowing the people to pay taxes as well as pay for the likes of labor service to the government in paper money." Only when there is both issuance and withdrawal of paper money could it be circulated unobstructed, whereas "its price will surely surge if it is withdrawn without restraint." "Such as the practices of the Song Dynasty, the remote *Lus* may make payments to the central government in half coin and half *Huizi* (paper money), the people may pay taxes in half coin and half *Huizi*." He admired the practice of concurrent use of coin and paper money in the ratio of 50:50. Similarly, "the price of paper money will plummet if such is issued without restraint." "The practice of Song was that, a limit of three years was established for a session to rotate, the issuance for each session may not exceed one million, and it worked." On contrary, "if money denomination was as small as one *wen* and three *wen* in the Zhongtong paper money, or as big as one *guan* Zhiyuan paper money worth five *guan* of Zhongtong paper money, none of which worked."

Having analyzed the successful experiences and unsuccessful lessons from paper money circulation in previous dynasties, and examined the present society, Liu Dingzhi concluded that there existed three problems. The first was that paper money would not be able to be circulated repeatedly if it was issued without withdrawal: "paper money produced and issued from the central government, there is issuance without withdrawal." The second was that broken and worn paper money could not be replaced with new ones: "paper money is circulated around the country, there is no replacement even when they are worn and torn." The third was villainous petty officials who burdened the people with tax payment by demanding paper money, which drove the people into bankruptcy by extorting excessive taxes and levies to enrich the state treasury. That is, "when they demanded tax payment in paper money, wealthy merchants would hoard huge amount of paper money without being taxed, whereas the poor had to sell their properties and pawn their wives and children to obtain some paper money to deliver to the government. High ranking officials covetous of the state power would harass the people and be ruthless to the people, then collect paper money to stash away such in repository. Alas, who would have expected that a measure devised by the ancients for the benefit of the people turned out to be a source of evil which harried the people." This situation ran contrary to the original intent of paper money issuance, and was tyrannical toward the people. Paper money was originally devised to facilitate the people, to promote realization and development of production and exchange; however, it turned out to be a source which hampered the people. Though there was an undertone of debasing the present and glorifying the past, and an intent to exaggerate the function of paper money, there was not much glossing over the criticism lashed against the evils of the day. The defect of paper money circulation of the time was indeed as noted: the Daming paper money had depreciated, issuance was out of control and was increasing. Though measures of recalling paper money including collecting household salt tax and increasing tax in the Yongle and Xuande periods were implemented, depreciation of paper money was out of control like an unrestrained kite. The statutory price for Daming paper money was one *guan* for one tael of silver; however, in

1432, a tael of silver was converted to a hundred *guan* of paper money in tax collection in Huguang, Guangxi and Zhejiang. In 1435, the Emperor Yingzong ascended the throne. In 1436, Huang Fu, assistant imperial tutor and minister of the household department, remarked that "paper money was originally used concurrently with silver and coins, a tael of silver was converted to three or five *guan* of paper money, whereas the rate is one tael to over a thousand *guan* of paper money, nothing is worse than this situation."[28] Hence, it could be seen that the remarks of Liu Dingzhi were not groundless; however, he failed to grasp the true source of paper money depreciation.

Liu Dingzhi's strategies for dealing with paper money depreciation and paper money circulation failure were well targeted, that is, promoting methodical issuing of new paper money or recalling old paper money. The former may be realized by "producing new paper money and releasing such; the emperor awards those who receive emoluments and paper money could trickle down into the market, whereas paper money may be recalled from the people when payment for taxes or labor services are made." The central government might have released new paper money via channels including awards, emoluments and supply to the market, and the people may have the paper money they previously held thereby flown back to the government by way of paying taxes and the like. There would be normal channels for the release and withdrawal of paper money, and the circulation of paper money would be brought under orderly control and kept under the appropriate quantity; then "why should people still worry about that paper money might not work?" Regarding the latter, if the government planned to recall old paper money, there were four methods available. The first one was "collecting it from the merchants," that is, by adopting the policy of consolidating the fundamental and inhibiting the incidental, paper money could be collected by way of taxes. The second was "collecting via commutation of sentence and labor service," that is, recalling paper money by adopting the policy of commuting sentence and relieving labor service via paying paper money; in this way, two ends were attained in one move, imperial grace was demonstrated and each got his due. The third was "purchasing paper money with state treasury reserve,"

---

[28]*Records of Yingzong Emperor of Ming Dynasty*, vol. 15.

such as Emperor Xiaozong redeeming paper money with treasury silver; in 1166, a million tael of silver had been employed in purchasing *Huizi*. In 1176, "the ministry of revenue had revenue of twelve million taels, of which half were Huizi, and the state treasury purchased four million with gold and silver."[29] The fourth was "to purchase with public fund," as Zhao Kai (1064–1141, courtesy name Yingxiang, born in Anju of Sichuan in the Southern Song Dynasty) had done. These four methods all worked; he objected to the practice that the government was forever engaged in extorting the people. In his opinion, exploiting the people with excessive taxes and excises was an inferior strategy, which was contrary to the original intent of "benefiting the people by the ancients."

However, Liu Dingzhi also said, "to plan for the current situation, if the government does not intend to recall the old paper money, then it can simply produce and employ it." He did not prepare to recall the old paper money, only planned to produce and issue new paper money. Then did that mean that old paper money was to be discarded? If such was the case, then the old paper money held in the hands of the people would be discarded. How many would go bankrupt, sustain loss, be displaced and incur sufferance? Wouldn't that conflict the foregoing statement and also be an inferior strategy? Otherwise, wouldn't there be an increasing amount of paper money in circulation? Hence, it could be adequately seen that his thought was not mature and rigorous.

Exactly as remarked by Fan Ji in his memorial on eight issues, the law of paper money was the most important matter. He wrote, "Zhu Yuanzhang, the founding emperor of Ming Dynasty, decreed that the ministers should weigh the amount of property in the country and produce Daming paper money, one *guan* of paper money should be worth one tael of silver, the people scrambled for it, and no dominion of Huaxia did not follow the practice. To this day, fifty years have passed, the practice becomes a little defective, which was attributable to the situation of high commodity price and low paper money price ... paper money shall be reformed and reissued, the new shall not be stagnant and the old shall be circulated concurrently, appropriate adjustment be made to the original amount, and management thereof shall be made tailored to the use of the country." Chen Zilong of Ming

---

[29]*History of Song Dynasty — Shi Huo Section II*, vol. 3 — Huizi.

Dynasty commented, "paper money was employed to facilitate wealth flow, the practice of making paper money the wealth will never last."[30] He emphasized that paper money issuance should be kept under control and that no paper money issuance was allowed to satisfy fiscal requirements or plug fiscal deficit, unlike measures proposed by Chen Ying and Xia Yuanji. Chen Ying proposed the household and salt method and Xia Yuanji proposed to introduce store and stand taxes. In stepping up the paper money withdrawing effort, they had set vicious precedents in introducing more taxes; nothing was safe from being taxed thereafter, and a fivefold surge of taxes were made later. Such measures were initially introduced in the name of a temporary measure, but few impugned that paper money duty tax should have been permanently fixed, though there were some exemptions and reductions later. Such practices were rampant in the Xuande period, which really harried the people.[31] Huang Fu (1363–1440), minister of the ministry of revenue, proposed that "it is appropriate to measure out government silver … in both the south and north capitals … replacing old paper money, and shipping these to the capital at the end of the year, when the quantity of old paper money diminishes, releasing new paper money in exchange for silver and transport such silver back to the capital."[32] The government sold silver to recover paper money in circulation and increased withdrawal of paper money to reduce inflationary pressure; however, such efforts were but next to nothing in addressing the situation. If effort was not made to check the source, reduce expenditure and control issuance, recalling paper money by selling silver alone would ultimately exhaust all means available, which had been proved by historical records.

In short, Liu Dingzhi often engaged in tactics of criticizing the current evils by glorifying the ancients. His starting point and ending point were to admonish the government that the stability of currency value and paper money circulation should be ensured by controlling the amount of paper money being circulated. This advice was sound in theory; however, it was hardly workable in practice. Unlike Chen Ying, Xia Yuanji and Huang Fu who tried to fix the problem and defend the government from the

---

[30] *Collection of Statecraft of Ming*, vol. 29, *Memorials — Paper Money of Ming Dynasty*.
[31] *Comprehensive Literature Survey Continued — Money Four*, vol. 10.
[32] *Records of Ming Dynasty Emperors — Yingzong Emperor*.

perspective of high-ranking officials, as a scholar participating in the imperial examinations, Liu Dingzhi personally felt the impact of the development of the commodity economy from the grassroots standpoint and had firsthand experience of the monetary system; hence, his recommendation ran contrary to the true intent of the supreme ruler in mandatory issuing of excessive paper money, in contradiction with the immediate interests of the top rulers.

8. Qiu Jun's theory of monetary metal

Qiu Jun (1420–1495), courtesy name Zhongshen, style Shen'an, known as Scholar Qiongtai, was born in Qiongshan of Guangong. A thinker, politician and historian of the Ming Dynasty, he was an outstanding representative of economic thought in the 15th century of China, a Confucianism forerunner with economic mindset. He authored *Da Xue Yan Yi Bu* (*Appendage to Meaning Extension of the Great Learning*) (which was an appendage to the work authored by Zhen Dexiu of the Southern Song Dynasty, *Da Xue Yan Yi*), which was divided into twelve sections including ways of rectifying the government and officials; he dwelled on topics such as politics, economy and culture for the purpose of lasting peace and order.

In *Appendage to Meaning Extension of the Great Learning*, extensive space had been devoted to the discussion of economic issues, of which *Copper and Paper Moneys*[33] (two volumes) were devoted to the discussion of monetary issues. His labor theory of value, monetary origin theory, state monopoly of money issuance right, monetary system reform and other new monetary views shall be introduced in this section. An annotated *Appendage to Meaning Extension of the Great Learning* is also available.

8.1. *Labor theory of value*

The most outstanding achievement of Qiu Jun in monetary theory lay in his simple exposition of labor theory of value. In discussing paper money

---

[33]*Appendage to Meaning Extension of the Great Learning — Copper and Paper Moneys*, vols. 26 and 27. No more citations shall be provided for further quotes from this book hereinbelow.

circulation, he argued that the situation where the nominal value of paper money deviated from its real value was very unreasonable; a piece of paper money denominated 1,000 *qian* with actual production cost not exceeding three or five *qian* could be exchanged with commodity worth a 1,000 *qian*. It concerned the labor theory of value, that is, "though things come into being in this world, they would remain useless without human labor. The sizes thereof differ, efforts invested therein and prices thereof vary. Articles worth up to a thousand *qian* will definitely be of substantial size or of fine quality, which is definitely not attainable with a day's effort." It seemed that he had realized that whatever is traded must be a product of human labor. Articles coming into being in this world must be invested with "human effort" to be useful. It could also be understood the other way around, "though things come into being in this world, they remain useless without human labor." That is to say, natural objects without human labor invested therein did not count as useful articles. What he meant by useful articles must have referred to commodities; the so-called human effort referred to human labor, or the value of commodity in today's terms and the so-called usefulness referred to the use value of commodity. Hence, it seemed that his words might be understood to mean that a commodity must have value and use value, whereas articles had use value but not value when there was neither human labor nor human effort attached therein.

Once this theory had been advanced, it marked brilliant progress of human understanding. Qiu Jun revealed an insight undisclosed by the forerunners, and his idea marked the fact that the understanding of the theory of labor value in China had progressed to a brand-new stage in terms of the history of it since the mid-Ming Dynasty. This was the first point. The second point was that the price of commodity was determined by the amount of human labor contained therein, the amount of human labor being entirely dependent on the duration of labor and sophistication thereof. There were differences of size and quality, and also intensity of labor invested therein; hence, there would be a difference in price. If an article was worth a thousand *qian*, it must be either of substantial size or of fine quality, definitely not something which could have been made in a day. It could be seen that he had realized that commodity price was determined by the intensity and duration of labor invested in the product. It follows that it could be considered that money and commodity could be compared, as both were useful articles, and both had human labor invested therein, though the amount of human labor entirely depended on the duration and intensity of such human labor. This was strikingly different from the explanation of market price since ancient times, which expounded on the market price by way of the change of supply and demand and quantity of money, or it could have been said fundamentally in opposition to the preceding theories. Meng Ke had touched on a similar issue, however, failing to specifically address the question. When debating the issue with his disciple Chen Xiang, Meng Ke noted, "it is natural for things to be irregular in nature; the difference sometimes is as much as five times, or ten, a hundred times, or even thousands of times."[34] That is to say, the price of a commodity was not determined by the commodity itself. The price difference of five times, 10 times, a 100 times, a 1,000 times or tens of thousands of times was obviously a quantitative one on the basis of similar quality instead of a qualitative difference; it could only be a difference of exchange value or exchange price between different use values, and definitely not a difference of use value. Meng Ke regarded commodity price as a kind of "token," which was determined by the inherent "essence" of a commodity; this seemed to have touched on the issue of commodity value. However, he had by no means solved the puzzle of "essence," by no means revealed the inherent entity contained therein. Nevertheless, Qiu Jun made a breakthrough when he explained the phenomenon in terms of duration and intensity of human labor, that is, weighing human labor by comparing the amount of human labor. He made material achievement in understanding the scientific theory of value, as compared with foreign counterparts; this finding was by no means to be eclipsed.

Of course, this understanding was still very primitive; it was impossible for Qiu Jun to distinguish what kind of human labor it was, and there was no way to distinguish between concrete labor and abstract labor, simple labor and sophisticated labor, social labor and private labor. It was impossible for him to come to the conclusion that concrete labor determined the intuitively observable use value, or that abstract labor was what determined the value of commodities. It was impossible for him to understand that what

---

[34] *Mencius — Teng Wen Gong Zhang Ju*, First volume.

determined the duration of labor was socially necessary labor time, that is, the labor time necessary for producing use value on current social conditions and the socially average skillfulness and labor intensity. It was still impossible for him to distinguish the duality of labor, the relevant concepts of price, value, exchange value, etc., let alone make scientific generalizations and employ this brand-new theory in analyzing and understanding other economic propositions.

However, Qiu Jun's groundbreaking contribution to the history of China's monetary theory shone brilliantly, and his theory was far ahead of its time as compared to counterparts in the realm of history of global economic theory and 170 years earlier than the ideas of William Petty.

8.2. Theory of the origin of money

According to the labor theory of value, Qiu Jun held that the birth of money was to overcome the difficulty of barter trade, "market formed during the day, the people traded therein to help satisfy each other's needs. However, in barter trade, desired articles are not always readily available, hence money was invented." He also believed that the principle of exchange of equal values in exchange must be adhered to. All must abide by this principle, "the commodity and money must be of equal values without a great difference, then it may work for long without defect." Otherwise, "it will not work." This understanding was doubtlessly correct. There were but a few scholars holding this view in the ancient society of China, one of whom was Li Jin of the Northern Song Dynasty. In terms of specific understanding, there were still some difference between the two; Li Jin held that in barter trade, "there is nothing that determines prices of articles," whereas Qiu Jun thought "desired articles are not always readily available." The latter expounded the creation of money from the aspect of the realization of primitive exchange in barter trade, that is, the discrepancy between the needs of the two parties in exchange, which brought about unnecessary troubles and endless difficulties; however, "as exchange value had not achieved independent form, it was still bonded with use value."[35] The former expounded that the invention of money brought about the disintegration of barter trade from the perspective of the realization of exchange value.

---

[35] *Karl Marx and Frederick Engels*, vol. 13, p. 39.

Through comparison of barter trade and monetary circulation, Qiu Jun noted that there were many defects in barter trade: "probably all commodities of the world depend on money for circulation. The heavy would not be carried afar without the mediation of money; the stagnant would not be exchanged without the office of money; the indivisible big could not be employed for small use without the help of money. The reason lies in that commodities are heavy whereas money is light, commodities are stagnant while money could be carried everywhere."

The so-called heavy in his words referred to articles which were heavy and difficult to move; the stagnant referred to failure to strike deals when there was discrepancy in commodity needs; the big referred to a commodity which was best left intact, and it was difficult to have small-sum trade. These difficulties absolutely could not be overcome in barter trade; however, they posed no problem in money circulation. Therefore, money circulation displayed unparalleled superiority.

Qiu Jun also noted that the invention of money was closely related to commercial activity. "Money is produced to weigh the myriad articles, and the ones who circulate money are merchants. Hence, when there are a great amount of merchants and commodities, then money circulates." Hence, it could be seen that commodity production and the exchange of commodity determined money circulation, the invention of money was the inevitable result of the development of currency exchange and the development of monetary relation was the inevitable outcome of commodity economy. This finding was recognized, however, when confronted with the conventional statement of "the origin of minting gold into money was entirely due to flood and drought, it was invented to relieve the hungry and the needy"; he gave in, and considered it was nonetheless a reason for "minting gold into money."

This was similar to Li Jin, which indicated that they were not yet thoroughly scientific in theory.

8.3. *On monopoly issuance by the state*

Qiu Jun proposed to examine the necessity for the state to monopolize money issuance right from three aspects. The first was that it was favorable to maintain peace and order in the society. He learned from the historical lessons of Liu Bi (prince of the Princedom of Wu in the Western Han

Dynasty), who had minted money on the back of readily available metal extracted from the mountain in his territory and became extremely rich which led to his ultimate rebellion. Qiu Jun approved the viewpoint of Jia Shan: "money brings profit, it can make the pariah noble and the poor rich. None of the ignorant people does not shun poverty and abjectness and covets wealth and power! Only that they have no way of attaining it."

Money changed people's patriarchal ideas; ideas of hierarchy, social station and wealth of people depended on money possessed thereby. That is, the amount of money owned should constitute a standard for evaluating moral ideas, and such a standard should be deepened along with the development of commodity monetary economy, which was particularly embodied in the formation of consciousness of "the so-called money is an instrument whereon profit dwells." And, "money is where the economic right lies, if the ban is lifted, the people would be able to monopolize the economic right thereof. Profit, a source of contention." However, mintage and the right to issue money were the concentrated expression of rights, something the people pined for. "If the right is relegated, and the people are allowed to access it, then all those who disdain downtrodden life and aspire for the power, detesting poverty and dying for wealth would scramble for it. It is not only the source of pillaging and robbing, but the fountain of disaster and riot." Therefore, "those from the high having the peace of the country in mind would manage and keep it in hand, never have it fallen aside." The state must firmly grip the money-issuing right, "those from the high controls the right to issue money," and must not create the soil for the generation of inordinate expectations, and maintain a sound environment for law-abiding conduct, "the people have no reason to access it, therefore they would content themselves with their lots." Hence, "those from the high shall not have their entire family wiped out as what happened to Liu Bi, and those from the low shall not have their person put to death as what happened to Zheng Tong." The social order would be well kept; hence, the statement of "the ruler exercises the power of benefit, complementing such with righteous conduct, benefiting the people across the kingdom without putting them in peril." It should be acknowledged that this understanding was insightful. Gu Yanwu, a thinker of the period at the closing of the Ming Dynasty and the beginning of the Qing Dynasty, also criticized the monetary system of the Ming Dynasty: "it was a monetary law beneficial to the government, however it was detrimental to the maintenance of the regime ... to date, commodity price rose by the day, money price dropped by the day, illegal minting ran rampant, the right to be held in the hand of the ruler was rendered inaccessible thereto. Why? The reason was probably that money circulation was not only issued from above but also was withdrawn to the above."[36] There were quite some similarities, though they were from different angles.

The second aspect was that it was favorable for the state to have market price regulation. Qiu Jun drew from the historical lessons of Jingwang of the Zhou Dynasty minting big denomination coins, confirmed that the checks and balance theory of the parent and the offspring originated from King Mugong of the Kingdom of Shan, and explained that the central government "holds the regulatory power, practices balances and checks." The key was "to mint heavier coins if there was concern of it being too light, and to mint lighter ones if too heavy, while the heavier ones shall be retained." The reason was that "the offspring may be dispensed with, while the parent may not." The so-called offspring is the lighter, and the parent the heavier. "The heavier functions for its expensiveness, and the lighter functions for its inexpensiveness, the expensive and the inexpensive balance and check each other in circulation." We can see that the parent as he understood it should be the primary money working as the price standard, and the offspring the fractional money. The monetary system of a country may not go without standard money, while a price standard may go without fractional money; hence, the offspring could be discarded but the parent could absolutely not. (The reader is reminded that the so-called monetary system, primary monetary and fractional money are temporarily employed for convenience of narration; they may not be understood, weighed or examined in the modern sense.)

If the central government does not monopolize the mintage and issuance right, then it would be impossible for it to control the market price, and still less possible to make a corresponding adjustment according to changing supply and demand relation.

---

[36] *Collection of Poetry and Prose of Gu Tinglin*, vol. 6, *On Paper Money*.

The third aspect was that the monopolization was an important means to guarantee the growth of fiscal revenue. Qiu Jun eulogized the situation that the central government concentrated fiscal power out of "the intent to benefit the entire domain"; in his view, there were at least two benefits from the situation where "the rights of money were forever concentrated in the rulers," i.e. mintage or issuing right and the yields generated from regulating market price. For one thing, with reduction of taxes and labor services, "the surplus can be employed to reduce land rent and labor service"; for another thing, it could be employed to relieve people in disaster and misery, "to relieve the poor, benefit the widow and widower, free the people across the world of all cares of life." In short, the purpose was to make "the ruler regulate the power of profit and execute the righteousness conducts, keep the people across the world from peril and benefiting them." What a grandiose cause it was.

However, Qiu Jun's criticism had already exposed the real image of the monetary policy or fiscal policy of the central government. "The ruler and ministers thereof devised policies to stop the gap in expenditure and deceive the people across the world, rake in wealth of the world for their exclusive private use." How helpless and melancholy he was.

8.4. *On monetary system reform*

There were two important points in Qiu Jun's theory of monetary system reform. The first was to conscientiously control the supply of money and tailor it to the amount required for social commodity circulation. He wrote, "the article and money must be of equivalent values without discrepancy, then such money may circulate for long without evil." That is to say, the total amount of commodity price would equal that of the money (amount of value) and there would not be much deviation from the sum, then monetary circulation would operate properly without going wrong. "The great Being established the king to foster the subjects, the king should grasp the power of profits firmly in hand, and make thorough adjustment thereon to suit the great variety of needs of the society, instead of serving one family and one man." He paid special emphasis to bringing out the function as a means of circulation of money, believing that it should "connect the myriad articles and spread them across the four directions"; hence, he stressed the importance of issuing full-value metal coins, and opposed sloppy production and excessive issuance.

Qiu Jun carefully examined the issue of equilibrium between purchasing power of money and the quantity of commodity available. He held that "money shall be constantly kept from surplus, the corn be kept from undersupplied, the price be kept from fluctuating too much, and the people would not suffer from hunger anymore." Taking corn as the token for commodity naturally reflected the fact that the commodity economy was still underdeveloped, and there was a limited variety of commodity. However, he realized that the purchasing power generated by money supply must be guaranteed by a corresponding amount of commodity, so that an equilibrium was struck, commodity price was stabilized and the stability of corn price was especially emphasized, which was not only favorable to the peace and order of people's lives but could also "fix taxes, labor service" and thereon. That is, the realization of these functions helps both the proper working of monetary functions and realization of state fiscal revenue. As to other wealth, they were "but dispensable, and not to be worried about" in terms of the people; these were to be regulated by the market automatically, and prices determined thereby. This thought reflected the active aspect of enlightened minds of the ruling class in the middle of the Ming Dynasty. Though Qiu Jun was also a faithful defender of Confucianism and even inherited views from the Taoist school of the Song Dynasty, these did not hinder him from laying out a theoretical condition for the development of a commodity monetary economy, which was not only the budding of such an economy but also the answer to the question of why the ancient society lasted for so long a period in China. In ancient China, the ruling class tolerated the existence of factors such as commodity economy and exchange through money. This was exactly the reason why the commodity monetary economy in ancient China was more developed than that of Western Europe over the same period. It also indicated that Qiu Jun had kept the sufferings and hardships of the people in mind and watched out for the least remissness. Xu Guangqi (1562–1633) (courtesy name Zixian, style Xuanhu, born in Shanghai, and an outstanding scientist at the closing period of the Ming Dynasty) of later times expressed similar ideas: "gold, silver and coins are stuff employed for weighing wealth, they may not be made wealth themselves. The peril of today is that people seek money to the exclusion of tending crops, it serves them well to get poorer. These are caused by their ignorance of the distinction between the foundation and the dependent." Their differences were only in where they had set their footing.

The second point was refuting paper money in theory. His tentative exposition of labor theory of value stated above was made regarding paper money. He continued, "is it appropriate to sell a piece of paper money the size of a foot at three or five *qian*?" Paper money circulation did not follow the labor theory of value, was a violation of the principle of exchange of equivalent values and was unreasonable; he frankly pointed out that paper money was an instrument devised by the "kings to satisfy their personal desires by trading useful articles with useless items, an object worked out to satisfy their personal ends. This is by no means a providence." He condemned the situation where the ordinary people racked their brains to fleece others of their wealth; it was already a dereliction of duties for the authorities not to lift a finger to rectify the situation, let alone doing the same thing themselves. "At first, the people were defrauded by them, then awed by their power, had no other way but surrender. However, in due course, the providence ultimately prevails, and the scheme falls apart." In the end, not only was the profit of a thousand *qian* not obtained but the production cost of three or five *qian* was also not recovered. Hence, "support from the people was lost, and national livelihood was wasted, which were sources of upheaval and demise. The regime of the Yuan Dynasty was an example for people to learn from." The problems he revealed did exist; however, his conclusion was one-sided. It should be acknowledged that it was the inexorable trend for irredeemable paper money to replace metal money in circulation; there would be no problem so long as issuance did not exceed the quantity actually required. However, he neither believed that paper money could stand for metal money which had real value, nor believed that there was both a relation and distinction between the circulation of paper money and inflation; hence, he erroneously imputed the cause of inflation to paper money circulation. In practice, he believed that it would work so long as a middle road was taken between the workable and unworkable. However, he considered that later generations had employed copper and paper money exclusively, "instead of using gold and silver, hence there is no checks and balance for users, it is impossible for it to go without defect for long employment. Therefore, at the beginning when law was enacted, it might not be imperfect; however, none ends well. This is a law universally applicable in both the ancient times and the present day." This adequately proved that he was a staunch metal money theorist.

Summarized in today's words, the method of monetary system reform he proposed was one employing silver as the standard money, with silver working as the standard of price. He proposed a monetary system with three moneys in circulation concurrently. Specifically, he said, "I hereby petition your majesty to institute the ancient law of three categories of coin for the implementation of paper money circulation, silver shall be the upper money, paper money the middle and coin the lower, the middle and lower moneys shall be an instrument of circulation for both the government and individuals, and the upper money shall be the reserve for the purpose of balance and checks.... No other way is superior to implementing the mechanism of balancing and checking coin and paper money against silver." One *fen* of silver was to be converted to ten *wen* coins and a *guan* of new paper money was to be converted to ten *wen* coins or two *guan* of old paper money in circulation; old paper money with four corners intact was to be converted to five *fen* coin, old paper money broken in the middle to be converted to three *wen* coins and those blurred and broken ones with "one *guan*" character remaining legible to be converted to one *wen* coin. This monetary system was to be promulgated as the "established mechanism"; no unauthorized modification was allowed, "though there are bumper years and lean years, and fluctuation in commodity prices, the amount of silver, coin and paper money for circulation shall remain unchanged, and the system shall last for hundreds of generations and be spread to all corners of the world." We could tentatively state that in the eyes of Qiu Jun, silver was the primary money instead of other items.

In order to guarantee the position of silver as the primary money, he proposed that "silver may not be used for trade the value of which is less than ten taels," and that the method for authenticating silver purity "shall be subject to the rule of whitening under fire test." Qiu Jun considered that "the likes of gold and silver will be subject to wastage when divided into small pieces; the likes of money will be reduced to garbage when divided; only when copper is truly versatile, which could be minted into coins, more coins for more commodities, less coins for less." Unlike copper coins which could be minted into small denomination coins and were fit for payment of any amount, gold and silver could not be minted into small denomination coins and could be used for big denomination payment only; if they were used to make payments for small amounts, it would incur great waste and loss. The undertone was that gold and silver were precious metals and were rare, whereas copper was a base metal and the stock thereof was great; these two categories were not comparable. In specific analysis, Qiu Jun only talked about silver; he did not mention gold. Whether we are justified to view it this way or not, the economic life Qiu Jun faced was the early stage of the Ming Dynasty, and silver had started to play the role of money; it had become factual statutory money by the middle and end of the Ming Dynasty, which is an irrefutable fact. In China's history, gold had played the role of the primary money in certain periods or in certain areas. It had been used as a monetary material for a long period of time; however, it held a position different from that of silver, and hence Qiu Jun focused his discussion on silver. Such an understanding was reasonable and tenable. The pragmatism of Qiu Jun indicated that he was by no means opinionated and sticking to rigid rules; he could adjust himself to face the reality and the future. Great scholars in the ancient times were not all synonymous with bigotry and slavish adherence to the past.

As regards the proportional combination of the other two moneys, he suggested to adopt the method of "recalling coins with paper money when there are excessive coins, and recalling paper money with coins when there is excessive paper money." In short, "paper money and copper coin shall be circulated universally for all purposes, and be balanced and checked with silver." This design broke away from the train of thought held by Wang Wei and Kong Qi who regarded gold and silver as monetary materials, and emphasized the dominating, fundamental position of silver in the monetary system. Unequivocally proposing a price standard based on silver from the choices of gold and silver obviously was in line with the need of development of commodity monetary economy. The design was highly workable and satisfied the historical trend of development for monetary materials evolving from base metal to precious metal, from silver to gold; he also tried to stabilize the purchasing power of copper coin and paper money in order to solve the problem of paper money inflation. It was a well-thought-out measure incorporating the then monetary circulation circumstances, really "a measure satisfying the state and facilitating the people"; it should be acknowledged that the measure was favorable for economic development and production, a surefire measure to stabilize social order. Qiu Jun was worthy of being called the first man of vision.

However, Qiu Jun's design did not feature the contents and characteristics of modern monetary systems. Since he confirmed that "all is balanced and checked with silver," he should not have restrained the range of circulation for silver; otherwise, if silver was only limited to large-amount payments, such restriction would have conflicted with its position as the primary money. The nature of the monetary system reform he conceived was built on bimetallism of silver and copper instead of the monometallism of silver, as the conversion rate between silver and paper money was pegged on a fixed rate wherein the copper coin was set as the price standard for paper money. However, "duality of the measure of value conflicts with the function of the measure of value;"[37] the outcome going against the original intentions was not what Qiu Jun could have imagined.

9. Anti-usury theories of Lv Kun and Song Yingxing

9.1. *Lv Kun on usury killing people*

Lv Kun (1536–1617), initial courtesy name Shunshu, later modified to Shujian, styles included Xinwu, Baodu Jushi and Liaoxing Jushi, born in Ningling of Henan, was a famous thinker and politician of the Ming Dynasty. His work that is currently available includes *Complete Works of Lv Kun*.

The foundation of Lv Kun's thought was valuing the people and was people-oriented; in the field of economic thought, he promoted the people-enriching effect, and proposed that "benefit" should dwell on the ordinary people, "power" be vested in the ruler, and "emperors and kings are the prominent places where power dwells." He was aware that the

---

[37] *Karl Marx and Frederick Engels*, vol. 23, p. 114.

social and economic crisis might break out any time, and with unstoppable momentum.

Usury was exactly the kind of powerful weapon the rich employed in strangling the poor. From the middle of the Ming Dynasty, the usury market was very brisk. In Suzhou, loans were made to peasants on the terms of "ten percent interest accrual on the spot."[38] In Qinzhou, usury was made on the terms that "within some three or more months, the principal would be redoubled, the poor have no way to repay such amounts, interest would snowbal, and within the period of only one year, a principal of one tael would snowbal into seven or eight taels; such must be repaid with children or corn, persons or cattle, or even with the death of the debtor."[39]

The most typical usurer was none but the grand bureaucrat Yan Song (1480–1569) from Jiangxi. Much of his silver was consigned to handicraft shops or merchant stores, or pawn shops for interest, and "when the consignment is recovered, even over a period over twenty years the interest still could not be cleared off."[40] A Mr. Wu, a merchant from Huizhou, took five hundred gold and engaged in the loan business for profit, "operated for a period of several years, obtained a total of one thousand and eight hundred taels, principal and yield counted."[41] Once the peasant and the handicraftsman fell into the mesh of usury, what was in wait for them was nothing but bankruptcy, starvation and death. Exactly as Lv Kun said, usurers were both vicious and exorbitant; making loans was like grazing lamb. Though the law stipulated a monthly rate cap of 3%, the reality was that "private loans of corn were made in spring and were scheduled to be returned in autumn, some at a rate of fifty percent, some with interest equaling the principal."[42] Ruthless creditors often exploited debtors by means such as debasing the purity, diminishing the amount of the principal in making loans and forcing repayment on the back of powerful forces; the poor person was unable to get any respite, with no room for maneuvering.

---

[38] *Taiyou Collection*, vol. 35.
[39] *Collection of Lin Ciya*, vol. 11.
[40] *History of Ming Dynasty — Biography of Wily Ministers — Yan Song*.
[41] Yao Shiling, *Jian Zhi Compilation*, vol. 1.
[42] *Shi Zheng Lu (Records of Politics)*, vols. 5 and 2.

Though Lv Kun did not make any exposition or discussion on usury credit in theory, as a bureaucrat and a member of the landed class, he accurately revealed the law of getting rich by the rich, the cruelty of usury and its main exploitative methods, high interest rate, debasing purity, diminishing weight and forced repayment. These findings covered the three organic steps of usury activities, one running throughout the entire loan process, one at the time of loan making and one at the time of loan repayment. Having been plundered through the three steps, all fruits of labor (chattels, property and land) of the poor were completely pocketed by the rich. Such an understanding was insightful and deserved recognition.

Of course, as a member of the ruling and landed class, Lv Kun remonstrated with the creditor to show some leniency. He attempted to reform the evils of usury by resorting to the authority of the government, by way of upholding the virtuous and punishing the wicked through enforcing the law; however, while such a practice might be attainable in a certain place over a certain matter, there was little possibility for its implementation.

9.2. Song Yingxing on usury brooding upheaval

Song Yingxing (1587–1666), courtesy name Changgeng, born in Fengxin of Jiangxi, was a renowned scientist in the Ming Dynasty. In 1644, he abandoned office and returned home, and later served in the South Ming Dynasty, dying in the year around the reign of the Shunzhi emperor or the Kangxi emperor. He was an erudite and versatile scholar. He attached great importance to practical studies, especially in the field of agricultural and handicraft technology. His works mainly included *Tian Gong Kai Wu* (*Heavenly Creations*) and *Opinions of a Country Fellow*. His economic thought was most distinctive, deserving a place in the history of global economic thought, which figured prominently. His views on wealth could be summarized as follows: labor created wealth, wealth referred to the myriad articles, that is, handicrafts and agricultural products instead of money; money was only a means of material wealth and a medium of circulation. In *Opinions of a Country Fellow — On Wealth of the People*, a work he finished at the age of 50, he wrote, "The so-called wealth refers generally to the myriad articles, not specifically money. Not that silver is insufficient in the world, but that the corn, the lumber, the mulberry and fishes are wealth. If anywhere abounds in these stuff, silver, gold would rush here, those with tremendous amount of money would scramble to come there for trade." His conceptual understanding was more advanced than mercantilists of the same period in the West and the 18th century physiocrat Quesnay. The statement was more scientific and more accurate, coming into being 139 years before the concept of wealth by Adam Smith (1776).

Song Yingxing's views on credit were also found in the *Opinions of a Country Fellow — On Wealth of the People*, in which he expounded the argument that usury was the source of upheaval. He condemned the traditional exploiting class view that if the rich refused to make a loan then the poor would not be able to feed themselves. He was among the few who had aired vehement condemnation on usury in both China's history and the Ming Dynasty.

Usury had a riot-inducing effect. *The Opinions of a Country Fellow* was written in an era where a slew of peasant uprisings such as Li Zicheng and Zhang Xianzhong occurred which then swept across the entire country, when the Ming Dynasty was on its last legs. Having investigated its causes, Song Yingxing found that usury was the source of such uprisings. Under the back-breaking and marrow-sucking extortion and plundering of usury, the peasant and handicraftsman ended up only finding all the fruits of their labor looted by the usurer, going hungry and being reduced to a state of destitution. All their initiative of production vanished. When there was no possible way of making a living, they had no other choice but to turn to banditry.

Of course, in imputing riots to usury of the individual, Song Yingxing did not view it as the sole cause. He considered that the ordinary people were "the ignorant multitudes" (he was not as brilliant as Wang Anshi in this point), and there had to be standards for them to model after, the government had to provide stringent decrees for them to abide by, and the nobles and the families of great wealth had to uphold something for them to follow. When exploited and extorted under such exacting administration and vicious usury, the people were driven beyond the limits of their endurance; it was a natural development for them to rise up. However, Song Yingxing failed to mention the viper that extorted the poor together with usury — land rent.

Now that usury activity was of such ferocity and extreme destructiveness, why was it left untouched? It had been described in such miraculous terms over hundreds of years. As Song Yingxing saw it, the reason lay in the fact that "none of those who was capable of having their voices heard was free from engaging in the business!" This remark nailed it; there were few powerful families not engaging in usury business and few not enriching themselves by exploiting the poor. With the sharp sight of a scientist, Song Yingxing displayed equally keen insight, with a profound and accurate judgment of economics; the understanding of Song Yingxing, as well as that of Shen Kuo, was relatively deep and scientific.

In expounding the second function among the two functions of usury, Marx wrote, "Usury is a powerful lever in developing the preconditions for industrial capital in so far as it plays the following double role, first, building up, in general, an independent money wealth alongside that of the merchant, and, secondly, appropriating the conditions of labour, that is, ruining the owners of the old conditions of labour."[43] At the turn of the late Ming Dynasty and early Qing Dynasty, the bud of modern commodity monetary economy had already sprouted up: hired laborers living on their labor existed in both the city and the countryside, and traditional financial institutions such as pawn shops and money stores had already commenced the loan business. However, all these were still in the budding stage; a sharp conflict had not come into being between them and the old force of the traditional society. It had yet to develop into an irreconcilable situation. Therefore, Song Yingxing simply did not recognize the cupidity and danger of usury. It not only seized the surplus labor of laborers but also seized their necessary labor, reducing them into a situation where they lost both production and living conditions. "They would not be spared from starving and exposure to the elements, if they did not fancy such employment, their being particular would leave them nothing to live on." Hence, they completely lost the initiative for work and production as well as the possibility of maintaining their current livelihood. They had no choice but "turn to banditry." It should be acknowledged that his disclosing of the ferocity and destructiveness of usury exploitation was deeper and more

---

[43] *Karl Marx and Frederick Engels*, vol. 25, p. 690.

scientific than the ideas of Huan Tan of the East Han Dynasty and the Tai Ping Jing.

The hostile attitudes of Lv Kun and Song Yingxing toward usury were a manifestation of social progress and the reflection of the interests of the emerging burghers class in the intellectual sphere after the appearance of the new economic relation in China.

9.3. Ai Nanying on usury — pawn shops

Ai Nanying (1583–1646), courtesy name Qianzi, was born in Dongxiang of Jiangxi. He passed the imperial examinations in 1624. His works mainly included the *Complete Works of Tian Yong Zi* and *Complete Works of Ai Qianzi*.

His criticism and introduction of usury and pawn shops were laid out in the *Third Submission to Cai Taizun on Matters Concerning Offensive and Defense in Volume 6 of the Complete Works of Tian Yong Zi*. The article held that Anhui merchants followed the general practice in making loans in areas with a facility of transportation; however, Anhui merchants in Fuzhou of Jiangxi engaged in all sorts of irregularities, and caused worse harm than "roving bandits." The stealthy plundering of the pawn was much worse than those robberies in broad daylight, and the ferocity of their exploitation was outrageous.

When a loan was made, it would be counted as an entire month even though such a loan was made on the last day of the month, whereas in repayment, interest had to be paid for the entire month even though repayment was made on the first day of the month.

When interest was calculated, "a monthly interest rate of 30% was applied on those who redeemed as scheduled." Such a rate was many times higher than the conventional rate of "20% annually."

The practices of "light out heavy in" and "inferior out superior in" in weighing silver were employed in making loans and repayment, respectively, to exploit the borrower. Silver purity and weight were mostly tampered with. The pawn shops in Fuzhou of Jiangxi "withhold three or four *fen* from the silver for each tael at loan-making; and charge three or four *fen* more on the silver for each tael at repayment." During borrowing and repaying, through processes of paying out and taking in alone the borrower would sustain a loss of 7% or 8%. The borrower sustained more serious loss when purity swindling was counted in. The ferocity of exploitation could thus be seen.

Upon disclosure by Ai Nanying, the tricks employed by the pawn shops in Fuzhou were noted to be nothing short of unscrupulous pillaging. "Over the period of a year, four or five pawnshops would fleece the people of silver in excess of three or four thousand taels, hence the strength of the people got sipped away, the trend started five or six years ago"; the government turned a deaf ear to the situation and "does not ban the practice." These words were incisively descriptive and highly typical of the situation. One could not help but shudder on reading the article and could not dispel the gloom. Who knows how many instances like that of Fuzhou were occurring across the country?

Chapter 7

Financial Thought Around the Period of the Sino-British Opium War

1. Introduction

Around the period of the Sino-British Opium War, the main moneys in circulation were silver and standard copper coins.[1] During the Sino-British Opium War, there appeared the issue of silver appreciation against standard copper coin depreciation; that is, the purchasing power of standard copper coin dropped and the purchasing power of silver rose. The situation deteriorated rapidly after the war, with direct plunder by the British invaders, war reparations and international trade deficit after the war being the direct causes leading to silver appreciation and coin depreciation. It in turn escalated social conflict, and was one of the key reasons leading to the Taiping rebellion. In order to quell the peasant uprisings and step up fleecing of the people, and overcome the monetary crisis, the Qing government issued paper money (silver note, treasure note, capital money note and bureau note) and coins (eight categories of big denomination copper coins

---

[1] The Qing Government had issued paper money in 1651; however, it stopped paper money issuance in 1661 due to its understanding of defects arising from fixing fiscal deficit by issuing paper money, and it reached the conclusion that the demise of the Southern Song, Jin and Yuan Dynasties was connected with paper money issuance.

and three categories of iron coins) during the period from 1853 to 1868. Newly issued currency during the period from 1858 to 1861 amounted to a quantity equivalent to 79,250 silver dollars, taking up 69.5% fiscal revenue over the same period, of which silver note and paper money took up 84.82%, while iron coin and big denomination copper coin took up 15.18%. The circulation of the new currencies was enforced, and it was stipulated that the new currencies should be circulated in "complementation" to the original silver tael and standard copper coins, and be used in parallel; tax payments, government payments, official salaries and expenditures for various projects were to be made by combining the foregoing currencies. Great chaos was thereby induced. The people vehemently opposed such an arrangement; the conversion rate between the newly issued currencies and silver could not be maintained and monetary circulation stagnated gradually. "With the appearance of big denomination coins, old coins gradually withdrew from circulation, and with the appearance of iron coin, copper coins gradually disappeared." Inflation was uncontrollable; the fact that the government reduced the amount to be received or refused to accept any new currency violated the provision regarding combined use of currencies, and profiting therefrom made it more difficult for big denomination paper money to be circulated. The practices of "replacing coins with paper money," "replacing silver with notes" and "replacing copper coin with iron coin" further reduced the purchasing power and payment capacity of big denomination paper money, and the newly issued currencies completely collapsed by the end of 1868.

Financial institutions in China during this period included pawn shops, Zhang Ju (account shops), draft banks and private banks. Zhang Ju, also known as Zhang Zhuang (account bank), engaged in deposit and loan businesses, mainly commercial loans. Draft banks, also known as exchange banks, engaged in businesses including exchange and remittance, deposit and loan, commercial investment and commodity transactions. They gradually established relations with the Qing Government, and undertook the businesses of remittance, handling donations, provincial contributions to the central government, loans made to the Qing Government and official title purchases. Private banks, also known as money desks, money shops, exchange banks, silver stores, or money and corn shops, evolved from gold and silver shops and money shops, originally engaged in businesses including money exchange and proceeded to businesses of deposits and loans, remittance, issuing money notes, minting private copper coin and manipulating coin prices. The Xianfeng Emperor established five government banks with a Tian (heaven) in their names, four silver shops with a Qian (also heaven) in their names and five government money shops with a Yu (universe) in their names in order to effect the purpose of exchanging notes with paper money, coin with paper money, and money notes with notes and paper money when he engaged in abusive issuance of new currency.

These government-run financial institutions were the very beginning of bureaucratic capital, though of transient nature. Foreign banks came into being gradually. They mainly engaged in exchange; in addition to regular exchange business, they also engaged in speculative exchange activities. They attained great business volume and obtained substantial profits; however, the entire banking industry had yet to develop.

The social thought of the period was predominantly a new learning preaching pragmatism. Scholars represented by Gong Zizhen, Wei Yuan, Lin Zexu and Bao Shichen vehemently criticized the situation of the corruption of the bureaucratic group, touched on the tyranny of the ruler, the debasement of morality, disregard for the hardship of the people and the degeneracy of the scholars. They advanced specific reform plans in the realm of economy; Lin Zexu, Bao Shichen, Wei Yuan and others all deliberated on monetary systems. They also argued for actively withstanding the invasion of Western capital. As early as in the twenties or thirties of the 19th century, Bao Shichen, Huang Juezi and others had proposed to take defensive measures. After the Sino-British Opium War, an air of grief and indignation shrouded the world of thinkers, and scholars with shattered dreams of the heavenly kingdom started to examine the causes of the defeat. They were more eager to understand the West. In 1842, Wei Yuan expanded the *Encyclopedia of Geography* into the 50-volume *Records and Maps of the World*, and further expanded it into a 60-volume edition in 1847 and into a 100-volume edition in 1852, which marked the beginning of modern Western learning in China.

2. Debate on silver shortage before and after the Sino-British Opium War

2.1. Wei Yuan and Lin Zexu on imitation minting of silver coins

Wei Yuan (1794–1857), former name Yuanda, courtesy name Moshen, dharma name Chengguan, was born in Shaoyang of Hunan. He was a distinguished enlightenment thinker in the academic movement of the late Qing Dynasty and an outstanding patriotic thinker of the modern times. In 1844 during the reign of Emperor Xuanzong, he passed the palace examination, befriended Gong Zizhen and Lin Zexu, and discussed current affairs and learning with them. He had served under He Changling (civil administrator of Jiangsu), Tao Peng (viceroy of Jiangnan and Jiangxi) and Yu Qian as an aide. He inherited the progressive elements of traditional culture and advocated pragmatic theories of valuing the contemporary and slighting the ancient as well as reform. Proceeding from the interests of commercial capital, he opposed excessive exploitation of the traditional economy and opposed foreign aggression, but he was one of the forerunners who approved of commercial dealings with foreign countries and learning the production technology of the West to save China. As a representative of a group of Chinese supporting the ban on opium smoking and the opium trade, he advanced the concept of "checking the Western powers with strength learned therefrom," and became a scholar with far-sight appealing for learning from the West in modern China, and also a forerunner for the Reform Movement of 1898. He compiled the *Compilation of Essays on Statecraft* on behalf of He Changling, and his main works included *Sheng Wu Records and Records and Maps of the World*. His monetary views were mainly reflected in the *Sheng Wu Records — Military Reserve* written in 1842.

Lin Zexu (1785–1850), courtesy name Yuan Fu, another courtesy name Shaomu, Shilin, was born in Shenghuan of Fujian (present-day Fuzhou). Lin Zexu was the first in modern China to open his eyes to the world outside China in the ruling group, and was also the first to propose minting silver dollars in China. In 1811, he passed the imperial examination, and was promoted to the position of viceroy of Hunan and Hubei in 1837. Faced with rampant smuggling of opium, he propelled the Daoguang

Emperor to ban opium trade. As an imperial envoy and minister of the military ministry, he initiated a vigorous opium ban movement in modern China. He was removed from office in the following year and relegated to Yili as an aggravated punishment, "rendering his service and atoning for his crime"; he then engaged in reclamation and water conservancy, and promoted vigilance against Russian invasion. In the 25th year of the Daoguang Emperor, he was pardoned and reinstated as viceroy of Shan'gan and Yungui Provinces. His memorials, journals, official documents, books, letters, poems and essays were compiled into *Collection of Works* by Lin Zexu. His monetary views were found among the memorials, which were important works of literature reflecting the economic and monetary leaning of Lin Zexu; *Memorial Four* ("On Investigation and Discussion of Matters Concerning Silver Appreciation and Coin Depreciation for the Purpose of Eradicating Defects and Facilitating the People") and *Memorial Eight* ("On There Being No Great Concern over Coin and Paper Money, the Point Being on Eradicating Opium-Smoking and Stopping Opium Source") were submitted in the 18th year, and *Memorial 12* and *Memorial 13* written in the 26th and 29th year of the Daoguang Emperor, respectively.[2]

Wei Yuan's understanding of the relation between the fundamental and the incidental was different from the traditional concept. The theory of upholding the fundamental and suppressing the incidental which came into being at the closing period of the Warring States dominated the realm of economic thought in China for over 2,000 years. According to this theory, agriculture under the natural economy was the fundamental and the government had to render support thereto with policies, whereas industry and commerce were the incidental, which required the government to crack down on it or issue suppressive policies thereon. As the one occupying the last place in the social strata of scholar, peasant, handicraftsman and merchant, the merchant was similarly regarded as one of vile character who chased the superficies to the disregard of the fundamental, pursued profit without consideration of the righteousness, and deserved suppression and condemnation. Faced with such a situation and

---

[2]*Collected Works of Lin Zexu* — Memorials, vols. 1–3. Zhonghua Book Company, 1965, pp. 133–137, 598–601, 1145–1151. V. Article Number alone will be provided, neither page nor title shall be listed hereunder.

theory, Wei Yuan put forward a question, holding that the incidental was of equal importance as the fundamental. He wrote, "What is the benefit of expanding resources? Nothing brings more foods than land reclamation, and nothing brings more commodities than mining and reforming money.

The statement that gold and coins cannot both stand, it leaned to suppressing the incidental and upholding the fundamental, and food prevails over commodity; whereas the talk of suspending the fundamental and expediting the incidental preaches the idea that commodity prevails over foods." The difference between taking wealth as the fundament and taking it as the incidental lay exclusively in "whether there is land or not," instead of emphasizing one and suppressing the other. He did not follow old practices slavishly; instead, he adapted himself to the changing requirements of the times, which reflected the requirements for money and monetary fund of the development of industry and commerce, and reflected the importance of circulation which had become the source of wealth and competed with agriculture for the fundamental place. He proposed in a timely manner, "please allow me to state the urgent one first, all know that China's silver is being leaked to foreign countries." Silver outflow was a very serious issue then, and unprecedented silver depletion appeared; a situation of silver appreciation against coin depreciation and serious fiscal crisis came into being. Hence, the most urgent issue to be fixed in expanding financial resources was a monetary problem, "commodity prevailing over food," the advancement of the slogan "suspending the fundamental and expediting the incidental," which indicated that he was more outstanding in stance and attitude than earlier enlightenment thinkers. At the turn from the Ming Dynasty to the Qing Dynasty, the bud of capitalism in regions south of the Yangtze River came into being, with some progressive thinkers pinpointing their criticism to the idea of suppressing the incidental and upholding the fundamental. Huang Zongxi lashed out at the situation "where the industry and commerce are held as the incidental, and unjustified suppression thereof is proposed; the handicraft was naturally what the sage desired, and the merchant then makes it circulate around, both are the fundamental" (*Records of Thought of a Sage Under Distress Waiting to Be Discovered — Finance Planning Three*). A contemporary of Wei Yuan, Bao Shichen proposed in

Miscellaneous Essays of the Gengchen Year that "though silver coins are the incidental wealth, it balances and checks the coins. When both the fundamental and the incidental are plentiful, the people would be well provided." Wei Yuan inherited and learned from their progressive views, and advocated stressing both foods and commodity before the Sino-British Opium War, and he further developed his theory into "suspending the fundamental and expediting the incidental" after the Sino-British Opium War. He also proposed that China should learn foreign production technology, transplant new industries and trade from foreign countries and implement them. This was in bold defiance of the millennial thought of "upholding agriculture and suppressing commerce" that "gold and coin could not both stand."

The urgent need for expanding resources was so that the cause of silver depletion could be looked into. Wei Yuan considered that people only knew that "China's silver flowed to foreign countries, but did not know that most silver of China came from abroad, and that foreign countries using silver coin also predated China." In the monetary system of the Qing Dynasty, silver and coin were said to be used concurrently; however, from the perspective of financial revenue and expenditure, silver alone was employed for calculation, and actual payment was also predominantly made in silver. At the beginning of the Qing Dynasty, the Ming Dynasty monetary system was carried forward and silver flowed into China from abroad. The main issues at the time were the appreciation of silver and depreciation of coin as well as private minting and selling of standard copper coins. Starting from the Jiaqing and Daoguang Emperors, when benefits were expanded, perils had to be stopped, and there was no peril more serious than "opium consuming the cream of China, amounting to hundreds of billions annually; if such peril is not stopped, even if all turned to gold, such gold would still be insufficient to cover the expense for such peril." "While banning the people from practicing a certain business is actually a great power of the ruler in finance management, when the edict does not go far and the ban is ineffective, would not that make opium the only way to amass wealth?" "Even if foreigners engaging in opium trade could not be prohibited today, how difficult would it be to prohibit the people? If exacting penal code could not be implemented, why not start from the most lenient code?"[3] Only by eradicating opium import could silver outflow be stopped, and the grand peril to the finance be stopped. Foreign countries used silver before China, the first evidence of which was that "in the Western Regions silver coin was employed in ancient times, thousands of years earlier than China." The second evidence was "that Fujian and Guangdong had international trade in earlier times, hence silver was used there earlier than the rest of China," and the third evidence was that "there was no record of prohibition on silver export in earlier times, as though there is no talk of prohibition on exporting copper coin today." Previously, it used to be foreign ships carrying silver to trade for China's copper coin, causing copper coin to flow out and silver to flow in. Therefore, "the Song Dynasty prohibited shipping copper coin overseas, which was no different from today's prohibition of shipping silver overseas." In his opinion, "In China silver coin has been in circulation for hundreds of years, which must also be reformed in accordance with the change of times." The circulation and use of primary currency had its inherent objective necessity which was not to be altered by subjective will; it was to evolve further in the future and was not be stuck to the monetary material alone. This conclusion was correct. The objective necessity was a trend accommodating the needs for the development of commodity production and exchange, which had not yet been revealed. However, from the time of the Jiaqing and Daoguang Emperors onward, the situation of silver appreciation and coin depreciation was a vicious consequence arising from opium smuggling. "Over the last ten odd years, silver rate has risen from a thousand *qian* to fifteen or sixteen hundred *qian* per tael, while foreign silver dollar rose from eight hundred *qian* to thirteen hundred *qian*, the people began to awaken to the cause that it resulted from opium being smuggled in and silver being exported."[4] Only through eradicating opium could silver outflow be stopped, the fiscal gap be plugged and the latent peril to society in China be solved. This had already been a fact keenly understood and felt at the time.

---

[3] *Collected Works of Wei Yuan* — Article One of Military Reserve, vol. 2. Zhonghua Book Company, 1976, pp. 469–489. No more citations shall be provided for further quotes from this book hereinbelow.

[4] *Collected Works of Wei Yuan* — Article Three of Military Reserve, vol. 2, p. 483.

As early as in 1833 and 1838, in refuting Sun Lanzhi and Bao Xin, Lin Zexu pointed out that the origin to the situation of silver depletion did not lie in the existence of foreign silver dollar, but in saving and convenience, not in coin note, but in opium smuggling. "The situation of the people is that they would pursue saving and convenience, in everyday transaction, where payment of a tael of silver is to be made, they would use one foreign silver dollar instead for the sake of convenience; such practice would be more convenient, and would relieve people the trouble of conversion and change, plus that it is more portable, hence the use spread far and wide, even though there is a little shortage in silver weight, people would gladly employ such, this is the fact." On the contrary, "when opium is employed to trade for silver, it is really a murderous act." "Since opium came into the vogue, foreign countries do not necessarily trade silver with foreign silver dollar, they hold this stuff as a hard to come by rarity, the consequence thereof is far worse for livelihood of the people and the national economy, which was outrageous (*Memorial Four*)." He appealed in deafening cries, "if the situation is taken lightly, then after a few decades, there would hardly be any solider capable of fending the enemy, hardly any silver to finance the military expenses. When such thought occurred to me, how could I stay unconcerned" (*Memorial Eight*). Though without the background of modern monetary theory, Lin Zexu proceeded from facts and sought the truth, went deep among the people to conduct research, and hence he could freely speak his mind: "We have spoken to many old merchants, they all said that the price of foreign silver dollar could be depressed when it was not popularized. Strict prohibition might work then. However since its circulation expanded among the merchants in Guangdong, foreign silver dollar was more popular than silver among the people, this trend could not be abruptly stopped (*Memorial Four*)." There was little possibility for the trend of monetary system change to be stopped by sheer administrative order.

Proceeding from facts and not confined by his personal interests, Lin Zexu took the interests of the merchant and the people into account, and arrived at conclusions in conformity with the law of development from the forefront of the trend of historical development.

The profoundness of his forecast has already been proved by the modern history of China.

In order to expand financial resources, the monetary system must be reformed; only by monetary system reform could the requirement for currency circulation by commodity circulation be met. The sage always "weighs everything" by adopting different monetary systems according to the requirements of different times. "Two points must be followed. The first is to "model after the Western silver dollars" and the second is to "concurrently circulate jade money, shell money which had been circulated in ancient times" (*Article Three of Military Reserve*). Regarding Western silver money, he thought that Western countries used silver coin before China. Circulation of foreign silver dollar became one major social ill after opium and silver outflow; the Qing government had already realized the gravity of the issue and circulation of foreign silver dollar was prohibited at the beginning of the Daoguang Emperor's reign. However, the practice was long established, and repeated prohibitions failed to stop it. The practice of private minting of silver dollar in imitation of the foreign silver dollar was not a new occurrence among the people, and not confined to one province; such practices were found in Guangdong, Fujian, Jiangsu, Hangzhou and Jiangxi. Lin Zexu proposed imitation minting and made no secret of it, citing the precedence that Pu'er coin was minted for circulation in both the south and the north sides of Mt. Tianshan after Xinjiang and Xizang were pacified, when minting bureaus were established in various cities around Mt. Tianshan with the responsibility of "minting currency of the heavenly kingdom after the form of foreign countries." Silver coins of various sizes with the characters for "Qian Long Bao Zang" inscribed were minted in Xizang. These facts were adequate to prove that imitation minting was an old practice, and hence monetary reform was practical. "If one foreign silver dollar is melted, only six *qian* and six *fen* are obtained, however such foreign silver dollar is worth eight odd *qian* of silver," so when it was circulated at a premium, state interests were harmed. "However the people scrambled to use it, why shouldn't the government mint silver dollar to facilitate use by the people, checking the use of foreign pie (foreign silver dollars) with silver dollars imitated therefrom?" This was the extension of his thought of "checking foreign powers with techniques learned therefrom" in the field of monetary systems. Evolving from money by weight to money of account was a progressive, correct and bold conception which was in compliance with the objective requirements of the development of a commodity monetary economy. If transactions between the merchant and the people were made convenient, commodity production and circulation would be expanded and developed, which were conducive to withstand the silver outflow resulting from the price difference between silver and foreign silver dollar. Previously, in 1833, Lin Zexu opposed the measure of mandatory suppression of the price of foreign silver dollar proposed by Sun Lanzhi in a memorial jointly submitted with Tao Peng. He held that foreign silver dollar was convenient to use and welcomed by the people: "the situation of the people is that they would pursue saving and convenience, in everyday transaction, where payment of a tael of silver is to be made, they would use one foreign silver dollar instead for the sake of convenience; such practice would be more convenient, relieved people of the trouble of conversion and change, plus that it is more portable, hence the use spread far and wide, even though there is a little shortage in silver weight, people would gladly employ such."

This matter concerned the livelihood of thousands of families, was of great significance, decided the way of the popular will, was important for the peace and serenity of social and economic life and was not to be taken lightly. On the contrary, Lin was the first to put forward the idea that China should mint its own silver coin to check the circulation of foreign silver dollar: "if the foreign silver dollar is to be suppressed, nothing works more than the government minting its own silver coin, each coin shall weigh five qian of silver, the form and indentation shall all follow that of the standard copper coins.... Such new silver coin shall be first used in paying military expenses and be circulated among the people. The specific method of handling shall be: exchange rate with silver be made in accordance with the current rate, whereas the miscellaneous surcharges of the local repositories may be imposed thereon per this formula. That is, two silver coins shall be converted to a tael of silver, there would be of little difference when such is melted into small bullions together with silver wastage, and there would be nothing inappropriate to receive and make payment therewith by the repositories." Lin Zexu was very affirmative in stating silver coin minting as an item in monetary system reform. He considered that such practice was "nothing inappropriate" nor "exclusively for the purpose of imitating foreign silver dollar." His purpose for implementing the form of standard copper coin into silver coin was nothing more than "facilitating the use by people," as it was "more economical than foreign silver dollar"; therefore, Lin held that there was no need to prohibit the use of foreign silver dollar at the initial stage. After a few months of trial circulation, "evaluate whether the people like to use such coins, then weigh and adjust further plans. If gradual measures are implemented, no sudden unexpected loss shall be incurred by the people." It seemed that Lin planned to employ economic means to phase out foreign silver dollar from the field of circulation in China. Such a monetary system reform was of historical progressive significance and should deserve full recognition. Comparing the blind expulsion of foreign objects by the Qing government which adhered to ungrounded ancestral practices to refusing to mint silver coin and transforming from the system of silver by weight to a system of silver of account, there was a world of difference. Lin's foresight stood out unparalleled. However, the final authority over coin minting policy rested in the hands of the emperor alone; as a subject, what Lin Zexu could do was only counting on "his Majesty to decide on critical matter concerning monetary law." Proceeding from the interests of the merchant and the people, Lin put forward proposals conducive to the development of commodity production and circulation, customized to the national situation and the popular will; however, he did not hold such concepts as "the basis on which to proceed with discussion." However, the Daoguang Emperor considered it "changing the established law too radically, and would be inappropriate." This absurd practice continued for some seventy or eighty years, and the situation did not change until the midterm of the reign of the Guangxu Emperor. In 1836, Lin pointed out in his memorial, "In the beginning, the price of foreign silver dollar was converted to seven *qian* and one, two or three *fen* of silver, the price held steady among the government and the merchant; however, in the long run, the price thereof got gradually raised, the momentum was almost unstoppable. Recently, in the areas of Suzhou and Songjiang, one foreign silver dollar could be traded at a price up to eight *qian* and one or two *fen* of silver; compared to three or four years ago, the price has risen by one *qian* actually, it would bring about more than one hundred *wen* than silver in exchange for standard copper coins." "Custom would settle on practices that are convenient and easy, the momentum could not be abruptly stopped. Even if strict prohibition is administered, the people would pretend to comply." These statements were sufficient to indicate the limitations and powerlessness of administrative intervention. Previously, Ding Lvhuan (1770–1832), magistrate of Shandong Feicheng County, had proposed to mint gold and silver coins.[5] After Lin, Gong Zizhen (1792–1841), having understood the portability of foreign silver dollars, had also proposed to the government the minting of silver coin to be circulated in China: "who needs foreign ships to bring in silver dollars, why not model after the pie gold minted by Qi and Liang."[6] Their thought constituted the first cries for monetary system reform in modern China.

Even when discussing the issue of privately minted small denomination coins, Lin Zexu would not approve of stopping the practice by exclusively relying on administrative means and decrees. Given the fact that "private mints run by wicked people harm the monetary law the most, even with strict investigation and prohibition, it is still difficult to eradicate private peddling thereof."

Lin proposed that the government should purchase small denomination coin at a fixed price, and so long as it was reasonably priced, private minters would not find it lucrative. "If small denomination coin was purchased at the price of sixty *wen*, about two small denomination coins are converted to one *wen* of big denomination coin ... three *wen* of lead coins are converted to one *wen* of big denomination coin ... the people are allowed to buy such all the time, when their purchase has amounted to a certain volume, they may smash such and submit to the government, the government shall make payment thereto per the established price." Then, "even the most obtuse would not commit such crime against the law. Plus with extensive hunting, such evil will gradually die out in due course."

---

[5]His plan was as follows: Gold coins were classified into two categories, the one tael and five qian, the former worth 20,000 standard copper coins and the latter 10,000 standard copper coins. Silver coins were also classified into two categories, the eight *qian* and the four *qian*, the former being worth 1,000 standard copper coins and the latter 500. The government purchased gold and silver from the people with gold and silver coins; when such coins were circulated, non-coin gold and silver would be banned from circulation as a means of payment, and anyone violating the provision would be investigated for crime.
[6]Gong Zizhen, *Annotations on Poems Composed in the Yi Hai Year*, vol. 118. Zhonghua Book Company, 1980, p. 167.

Exactly as expected by Lin, on January 29, 1835, a memorial titled *No Private Minting and Small Denomination Coin Use after Seizure and Hunting in the Various Areas of Jiangsu* stated, "After years of purchase and seizure, all outstanding small denomination coins in the various areas have been completely collected and destroyed, coins currently in circulation in the market are all standard copper coins, without small denomination coin found mixed therein. This indicated that purchase and hunting have attained substantial effect." Therefore, it could be deduced that the expected results and practical effect would be obtained when the principle of interest and the popular will were followed.

Wei Yuan held that gold coin, shell and cloth moneys were used in ancient times, but in this time jade and shell moneys were employed to "make up for the inadequacy of silver coin"; so long as "the emperor brings out his repository collection, products from state-controlled mines are placed under monopolized sale," then "equal value may be inscribed thereon." Because such articles were the quintessence of nature, the treasure of the world, cherished by the people, felicity and auspice of the state, "there is neither the trouble of melting and minting nor perils of rotting and counterfeiting." Wei Yuan confused the boundary between the natural property and the social property of money, which exactly revealed the fact that his view of metal money theory was inconsistent with the requirements of economic and social progress and development; it was a retrogression, a return to the ancient ways, and was absolutely not workable. He wrote, "The so-called money is an institution the sage made to weigh all things to accommodate the time." Here, he emphasized the function of money as a measure of value, upholding the view that monetary systems should evolve according to development and changing times. There were gold, shell, knife, cloth and silver moneys in history; however, "these are all the quintessence of nature, minted with the concerted effort of the world" (*Article Three of Military Reserve*), and they were by no means to be driven out by corruptible paper money from circulation. The thing that serves as monetary material may not be ordinary commodity. He specifically stressed the function of money as a measure of value, understanding it from the perspective of a measure of value. He even demonstrated his view by alluding to *Guan Zi*: "Guan Zi said ... pearl and jade are superior moneys, gold the intermediate, and knife and cloth inferior ones. These are employed to weigh the myriad items, hence to administer the human affairs thereby, this is the origin of money" (*Article Two of Military Reserve*). Such was indeed a far-fetched allusion. What Guan Zi emphasized was that money was employed to protect property, maneuver civil affairs, and was a function of the means of circulation and store of value, which seemed to be a distinctive characteristic of the nominal theory of money. On the contrary, the theory Wei Yuan proposed by alluding to "weighing the myriad items" was the functioning of money as a measure of value, exactly the same as the statement, "The so-called money is an institution the sage made to weigh all things to accommodate the time"; this was the manifestation of the distinctive characteristic of metal money theory. He seemed to hold that shell, jade and precious metal were naturally money; however, he failed to understand that "money was naturally neither gold nor silver," and hence he confused the boundary of social property and natural property of money. There was a tinge of money fetishism in his theory.

Another way of expanding financial resources was to mine gold and silver. Wei Yuan asked, "What is the benefit of expanding resources? Nothing brings more foods than land reclamation, and nothing brings more commodities than mining and reforming money." Reforming the money system was what had been stated above, and mining gold referred to mining silver mines. He also said that "since ancient times, there has been more copper mined than silver." "Nowadays, about thirty or forty percent of silver has been mined from silver mines, however the portion not mined stays at about sixty or seventy percent" (*Article One of Military Reserve*). In *Article Two of Military Reserve*, he was diametrically opposed to the deeply entrenched conventional view which was against mining. He energetically supported mining silver and specifically supported the practice of allowing the people to mine on their own, lest the government engaged in mining and "the proceeds would be barely enough to cover the expenses and the fund was insufficient to go around." Lin Zexu was also of the same opinion when he was the governor of Yunnan and Guizhou. He believed that "land begets materials, and materials inherently loathe being left in ground, the ruler should make the best use of such a favorable situation, and stash wealth away among the people" and "if such is properly managed, it could surely be implemented without evil accompanying it." He was opposed to government-run businesses. The reason was that although it would be very effective for government-run businesses to follow government directives, the defect lay in there being no constancy in manager appointment and removal. "If succession was tangled with myriad issues, or if such incurs loss, then the management would have excuse for the poor performance thereof, and if the loss is made up for, then such practices would be modeled after by more. And that the local magistrates are busy with handling the various affairs, how could they find time for business management personally, they would have to resort to staff members who are petty officials, hence more loopholes and evils would arise therefrom." These were exactly the evils of government-run businesses in the Self-strengthening Movement. He predicted the unfortunate situation. He proposed to convene merchants and people, allowing them to raise funds and engage in partnership. If their businesses prospered, awards would be made thereto, and no punishment would be administered thereto if they were to disband their businesses. The advantage of such a practice lay in the fact that "the government has the power to supervise without the burden of incurring any loss, such mechanism seems that it could last without defect." He refuted the so-called views that "it is difficult to disperse the throng," emphasizing that Yunnan was mountainous all around: "there was neither ban nor prohibition, however the ordinary people flocked in the pursuit of profits. If the mine prospers, people would throng in; and when the mine is depleted, the people would leave without the need to be dispelled. There is absolutely no reason for them to stay in deserted mine caves and be content with maintaining a losing business." However, if a "mining application is submitted, even if richness of such a mine may not be determined immediately, it would be sufficient to subsidize the fiscal revenue and eliminate private strife" (*Memorial* 13). Lin considered that the government would have been said to have conducted its due diligence simply by strengthening the management of silver mines from the four aspects of promulgating rules, relaxing restrictions on lead, cutting surcharges and cracking down on frauds and counterfeit.

Wei Yuan did not oppose the circulation of irredeemable paper money. In *Article Three of Military Reserve*, he criticized the proposal on issuing paper money by Wang Liu who authored *Humble Remarks on Money*; this might be an earlier writing publicly criticizing Wang Liu. He restated the "ten conveniences of issuing paper money" of officials from the ministry of revenue at the closing period of the Ming Dynasty cited by Wang Liu ("saving in production, wide range of use, ease of storing, lightness of carrying, no difference of purity, saving in minting, elimination of wiles of silversmith and coveting by robbers, all discarded copper coins being forged into weapons and all depreciated silver going to the government repositories") and then diametrically pointed out that there were "ten inconveniences and not a single convenience" ("laborious to make, stagnant to use, easy to wear, multitudes of counterfeits, easy to be stolen, difficult to ban, multitudes of violators, bitterness of extortion, if metal coin is to be suppressed then metal coin would be stuck in commodities, if silver is to be suppressed then silver would flow abroad"). This understanding was strongly emotional and with some partiality. He classified paper money into redeemable and irredeemable, and considered that the irredeemable could not work, whereas the redeemable may work. He was being partial in negating the theoretical reasonableness of paper money. He approved redeemable paper money. He held that "the *Feiqian* of the Tang Dynasty, *Jiaohui* of the Song Dynasty were all based on government minted coins, rendering it possible for the merchant and the people to exchange the note for commodity … they worked on the ground that there was some basis whereto they attached," and "the practices specifically focused on exchanging the heavy for the light, balancing the offspring against the parent." The purpose thereof was to bring convenience to the people instead of netting profit. With government money established as the principal, and being redeemable, such paper money would circulate without obstruction. However, since the time of Cai Jing of the Northern Song Dynasty and "reformed paper money law, there was no more government money reserve," and thereafter "a piece of paper money produced at the cost of a hundred or ten *qian* exchange for items worth thousands of *qian*, this was like deed without corresponding land, note without owner, salt note without salt, bank note without money," and such was employed for profiteering purposes. Therefore, "wiles and counterfeits, endless imitations rose up in throngs, soon all fell to disuse in a matter of short period." As for the special paper money issued in the Jin, Yuan and Ming Dynasties, "even with the supreme authority of the emperor, it was still impossible to bend people's will to accept it," and hence such schemes failed successively. Though the characteristics of money functioning as a means of circulation determined the production of paper money, mandatory issuance and circulation thereof by the government on the authority the emperor made it irredeemable and did not set aside sufficient issuance reserve; such an arrangement should not have been problematic so long as the amount of paper money issuance was kept under an amount appropriate for the objective need of commodity circulation. This was a point Wei Yuan, as a proponent of metal money theory, failed to understand. However, he stringently pointed out the nature of paper money, the circulation whereof depended on the enforcement of the state power, and he further noted that neither the will of the multitudes nor the objective law of monetary circulation tolerated defiance. Having criticized the irredeemable paper money, the paper money circulation conspiracy preached by Wang Liu discussed both the ancient and contemporary situation, starting from the three categories of metal in the Han Dynasty, white deer hide money, the *Feiqian* of the Tang Dynasty, the *Jiaohui* of the Song Dynasty, and the paper money of the Jin, Yuan and Ming Dynasties, "by first laying out the causes of the rise and fall of the monies." He concluded that there were six aspects of impracticality in "replacing coin with paper money." By such a discussion he exposed the nature of paper money circulation employed by the rulers as a means of extorting wealth from the people and relieving fiscal crisis, which deserved recognition and approval.

Regarding circulation among the people of redeemable paper money, that is, money note, in response to the accusation of Bao Xing, Lin Zexu said, "Nowadays, silver price is rising by the day, a tael of sliver trades at the price up to sixteen or seventeen wen of standard copper coins, as the money notes issued by wily merchants, though annotated with redeemable, they did not have ready coins and dodged redemption requirements. Please strictly prohibit the private banks dodging redemption, the various private banks must conduct business in ready cash, so that the prevalent defect may be stopped." Lin recognized the defect of money note as a fact: "it lies in issuing blank note without the backup of ready cash … when such notes issued reach the thousand and there is no physical cash available for redemption, the banking merchant would abscond by the night, while those note bearers meet with little success in retrieving their silver."[7] However, Lin was not very concerned about the defect in money note, as in his opinion, on the one hand, such a "prevalent defect is not difficult to cure."

So long as a chain security system is established and an exacting penalty imposed, it would not be difficult to check the momentum. On the other hand, Lin held that the prevalent defect of money note concerned only "fleecing and harming the people," while "it does not concern the state revenue and expenditure much." Money note had been in circulation for decades, and it does not start from today, why the silver was not as expensive as it is today! Even though "wicked merchants were wily" "and engaged in fleecing people by charging exorbitant prices, they could add a few wen or about ten wen of standard copper coins for a tael. How could they raise the price of silver from one thousand *wen* to sixteen or seventeen hundred *wen*? I'm afraid there is absolutely no such reason." In addition to that, Lin believed that the circulation of money note was not only faultless but also merited commendation.

He noted that "it has been found that recently silver was in great deficit, it was already very strenuous to make payment for coin, corn, salt tax, tariff, circulation was rendered possible only with the complement by private money note which could slightly make up for the inadequacy. If money note is banned, then the financial situation would immediately fall into straitened circumstance."[8] He fully recognized the positive function of money note, and did not follow blindly established rules handed down from the ancient times, nor did he listen to the platitudes. On the contrary, he was at the forefront of the times, adapted himself to the development momentum and loudly proclaimed his support for money note and paper money circulation.

Such an understanding by Lin was not acquired at the spur of the moment, let alone taking advantage of the moment; it was his mature findings after he had conducted in-depth research in social economy, along with careful analysis and deliberation.

Not confined to the established traditional practices, Lin tailored his arrangement to the times, advocating the practice of issuing paper money

---

[7] *Collected Works of Lin Zexu*, pp. 598–599.
[8] *Ibid.*, p. 599.

to purchase silver for the purpose of both solving the issue of silver appreciation against coin depreciation and withstanding opium smuggling; such a proposal was conducive to both the development of commodity economy and withstanding foreign economic aggression.

Annex: Wei Yuan on foreign financial theory

In *Records and Maps of the World — Foreign Situations — Records of International Intercourse*, Wei Yuan compared the Chinese and Western economies. He specifically pointed out that "China is founded on agriculture, whereas the Western countries are founded on commerce."

The rules established by such countries to benefit the ruling and the ruled included silver notes, silver houses, silver checks and security society.

Wei Yuan compared the silver houses in the Western countries and the silver shops of China. There were similarities as well as differences in the comparison, and functions and purposes of silver houses as well as the position thereof in the country could be understood.

However, his introduction was still preliminary and superficial, far from accurate and comprehensive if examined seriously. He briefly introduced the banks of the Netherlands, France, England and the United States. Due to the complexity of the source of materials, and lack of first-hand materials due to time constraints, there were errors, inaccuracies and some diametric falsehoods. However, his introduction was the first time the Chinese had opened their eyes to the world, and was a glaring ray of light cast on the general outline of international financial circle; no blemish could eclipse its brilliance. It was only recently that we were able to uncover the dust-sealed records with great reverence and high spirits. He introduced that "Holland silver house started in 1609," which was the year Spain officially recognized the independence of the Netherlands instead of the year wherein the Netherland Bank was incorporated. He remarked that the "articles of association of the Bank were equitable and trusted by the various countries." This is a revelation. The French "Bank with capital contribution of twenty million silver dollars failed due to excessive withdrawing for military expenses in the reign of Jiaqing Emperor." This history was sufficient to warn the people and the government of China that banks would invariably fail if employed improperly when the capital thereof was employed to make up for the gap of military expenses, however substantial the capital was.

Wei Yuan concluded that of the four items listed above, only security society was not found in China. He posited that there were three categories of security society: ship security, property security and life security. This was what was called an insurance company.

Wei Yuan's breadth of mind, perseverance and passion, keen perspective and modesty in learning, absence of arrogance, open mind and practical spirit in introducing modern financial industry to the Chinese deserve our respect and protection.

2.2. Theory of focusing on the fundamental and suppressing the incidental by Xu Zi and Zun Dingchen

Xu Zi (1810–1862), courtesy name Yizhou, style Yicai, was born in Liuhe of Jiangsu. He passed the palace examinations in 1845. His works include *Collection of Weihui Chamber*. The article titled Memorial on Mining Issue Planned written in 1841 from the Collection and *On Consolidating the Fundamental* reflected his monetary views.

Sun Dingchen (1819–1859), courtesy name Ziyu, style Zhifang, was born in Shanhua (present-day Changsha) of Hu'nan. He passed the palace examinations in the same batch as Xu Zi. His works include *Collected Works of Cang Lang*, of which *On Governance Five*, *On Money One and Two* and *On Silver Coins from Tang Dynasty and Preliminary Discussion of Ben Tang* represented his monetary views.

In order to solve the monetary crisis resulting from silver appreciation and coin depreciation, Xu Zi and Sun Dingchen vigorously advocated attaching more importance to coin and slighting silver or discarding silver. Faced with silver outflow due to the opium trade, one remained reticent (Xu Zi) and the other took the matter lightly (Sun Dingchen), ridiculously imputing indiscriminately to the practice of "making silver the money" the following issues: monetary crisis, fiscal crisis, as well as all social crises of the time such as depleted warehouses, wealth inequality, exorbitant taxation, shortage of military provision, official graft, manipulation of monetary right by wily merchants and powerful businessmen, vagabond and fraudulent activities, luxurious and lustful customs, land annexation by the powerful, and the rich throwing their money to form factions which developed into a situation where "foreign countries become the place wherein silver ends up, nothing could stop the situation," and claimed it "the grand peril to the country to date" (*On Governance Five*). They cursed that it "led to the displacement of the fundamental and the incidental, blurred the measure of propriety, the infeasibility of kingly governance, the customs failed to turn mellower, all resulted therefrom" (*On Money One*). These statements indicated that they represented the diehard landed ruling class and were intolerant to the development of the commodity and money relation; they spared no effort in imputing all unreasonable, negative, decadent, backward and dark aspects to the practice of making silver the money, attempting to pull the wheel of history of Chinese society back to the beaten path of a natural economy dominated society.

Around the time of the Sino-British Opium War, the depletion of silver induced a monetary crisis; the deepening social conflict had become a topic hotly debated in society, with fierce clashes between different social forces and thoughts. Wei Yuan and Lin Zexu were diametrically opposed to the views of Xu Zi and Sun Dingchen. Wang Liu's views were substantially different from the views of Bao Shichen. Each aired his views on the institution of making silver the money in an irreconcilable situation. As representatives of the most reactionary and the most conservative force, they availed themselves of the moment to put forward their proposal of consolidating the fundamental and suppressing the incidental.

Xu Zi and Sun Dingchen believed that so long as the fundamental was given great importance, the world would stay peaceful. Of course, they realized that the circulation of silver was conducive to the collection and employment of wealth by the ruling class, which expedited the disintegration of natural economy.

Xu Zi and Sun Dingchen believed that silver was the grand evil of the world, "an item on which great evil is attached." No one would not desire it, all would rack their brains to engage in unscrupulous and desperate pursuit of it, it was corrosive, soul-severing soup, life-claiming ghost, the root cause of all evils. Sun Dingchen enumerated the 10 evils of silver in *On Governance Five*. Using silver was conducive to escalating extortion and exploitation by the government and officials, and more conducive to the fleecing and expropriation of petty producers and the various social strata by usury capital and commercial capital. Hence, two diametrically different conclusions were arrived at with respect to silver, negation, debasement or recognition, eulogization, which manifested two different stances and attitudes. Veritably as Marx once said, "The ancients therefore denounced money as subversive of the economic and moral order of things. Modern society, which, soon after its birth, pulled Plutus by the hair of his head from the bowels of the earth, greets gold as its Holy Grail, as the glittering incarnation of the very principle of its own life."[9] In the great historical upheaval when the ancient Chinese society was about to collapse, the clash of the two views stimulated tremendous repercussions.

On strategies dealing with monetary crisis Xu Zi claimed that silver, coin, corn and cloth could all be employed as monetary material, except that silver should be established as a means of payment or pricing standard, and a fixed rate should be established for coin, corn and cloth conversion, with all commodity transactions being "conducted subject to the standard of coin, corn is fixed at the price of a certain amount of coins, cloth a certain amount of coins, and silver a certain amount of coins. The actual price shall fluctuate as the people see fit, the government shall not interfere therewith" (*On Consolidating the Fundamental — Rules Ten*). Then in market circulation of money, "corn and cloth shall act on behalf of silver, that is, corn and cloth shall share the function of silver." "Corn and cloth shall be the primary money and silver the complementary (*On Consolidating the Fundamental — Rules One*)." That is to say, it was a return to the times where physical money such as corn and cloth dominated, practically amounting to retrogression to the times of natural economy where barter trade dominated. In their view, "laying emphasis on agriculture entails placing corn and cloth in the first place, while placing corn and cloth in the first place further entails banning luxury; when luxury is banned then there leaves little profit for commerce and merchants, when there is little profit for commerce and merchants then more would engage in agriculture, spinning and weaving, when more engage in agriculture, spinning and weaving, then there would be more corn and cloth produced, when there are more corn and cloth produced then the

---

[9] *Karl Marx and Frederick Engels*, vol. 23, pp. 152–153.

prices of gold and silver would drop, when the prices of gold and silver drop then sale of private hoards would be slow, when sale of private hoards is slow then the source of money is opened" (*Memorial on Mining Issue Planned to be Submitted*). Therefore, he attempted to turn back the wheel of history as he liked it and according to his personal subjective conjecture. Xu stated that in 1391 in the Ming Dynasty when articles were converted into silver and deposited into the government repository, the government repository held silver up to the amount of many millions; however, the straitened state situation was getting more aggravated. When the North Song Dynasty gave way to the South Song Dynasty, the mechanism of conversion was introduced, and the state fell to great plight. Such preposterous remarks are not worth refuting; they simply attempted to demonstrate that if the profit and function of silver were reduced then the price thereof would naturally fall. When corn and cloth were employed, it would be natural not to be concerned about silver shortage, and therefore no need to suffer the exorbitant price of silver.

In *On Governance Five*, Sun Dingchen emphasized that "silver must be repudiated before corn to be placed in the first place"; in Sun's opinion, "if silver is not repudiated, it would compete with corn for importance, and hence corn could not be placed in the first place." "If agriculture is to be given emphasis, the first place must be placed on corn, silver must be repudiated before silver is to be placed in the first place." Hence, he proposed "that corn and cloth shall be employed for agriculture, goods and wealth be employed for commerce, coin shall assume the role of goods to iron out the shortcoming of corn and cloth." In *On Coin Two*, he further proposed that "when the military and state uses are involved, silver and coin shall each constitute half thereof, if such arrangement is employed in expenditure and revenue, then political ideal is attained." Hence, he treated the government and the people, the military and the commerce, and even international trade and domestic transactions with some difference and dared not to promote his "repudiating silver and employing coin" in a comprehensive manner. Regarding silver circulation, Xu Zi and Sun Dingchen failed to attain correct understanding. For one, Sun believed that "the so-called silver is neither something obtained from plowing nor from weaving." "The higher the price of silver, the more straitened agriculture would be," and "if the use of silver is counted on, it is necessarily dwindling by the day, which is carried on by the momentum."

Indeed, silver was not obtainable from plowing or weaving; however, mining and smelting could produce silver, and foreign trade could also import silver. These were the two important sources of silver monetary material since the Song Dynasty; similarly, by the end of the Ming Dynasty, foreign silver dollars were already entering China. Hence, the following was a groundless statement: "silver is employed and there is concern that the amount of silver would dwindle, if corn and cloth are employed there is no concern that the amount thereof would dwindle, as corn and cloth could be produced by the labor of the people, whereas silver could not be obtained by the labor of the people" (Memorial on Mining Issue Planned to be Submitted). However, with some terminological difference, the gist of *On Money One* by Sun Dingchen was to negate the position and function of silver as the primary money.

Xu Zi and Sun Dingchen cursed that it "led to the displacement of the fundamental and the incidental, blurred the measure of propriety, the infeasibility of kingly governance, the customs failed to turn mellower, all resulted therefrom" (*On Money One*).

While the fluctuation of silver price was determined by the unit value amount contained therein, that is, determined by the change of average amount of socially necessary labor and the change of labor productivity, the change of market supply and demand was only an influence factor, by no means the determining factor. Hence, it could not be determined if the amount of silver would dwindle when it was employed as a monetary material and if silver price rise was an irreversible trend. If this statement stands, then it follows that copper coin was equally not obtained from plowing or weaving, "could not be obtained from the labor of the people," and equally the amount of copper would necessarily dwindle by the day. The higher the price of the copper, the more straitened agriculture would be, which was an irreversible trend. The fact was, the decrease of silver price along with increase of market supply of silver was the inevitable trend of development. The issue of silver outflow which was an irrefutable fact was shunned by so doing. Regarding foreign aggressors, they poisoned the Chinese with smuggled opium, transformed their deficit situation in trade with China and turned it into a surplus, hence leading to the plight of China's financial situation, which further caused China's social and national crises. The situation exposed the banality and outdatedness of socio-political, economic, military, humanistic and national concepts and thought in China. Objectively, these theories had the effect of assisting the activities of colonialists, which was extremely pernicious and required heightened vigilance. In a society where the means of production is privately owned, money is the instrument the ruling exploitative class employed for exploitation and plunder, and silver as a precious metal was more conducive to effect this function than copper which is a base metal. In the situation where commodity–money relationship developed a little, the appearance of money, especially when precious metal silver assumed the role as monetary material, and the social relation were increasingly embodied as a relationship of gold and silver. Failing to understand this point, on the contrary, Xu Zi and Sun Dingchen made many an accusation, the first of which was that "never had there been a country counting on silver not getting impoverished, the more silver there was, the poorer it would be." The second was, "why is the state counting on silver never failing to get impoverished? The so-called silver is neither something obtained from plowing nor from weaving." The third accusation was, "if the use of silver is counted on, it is necessarily dwindling by the day, which is carried on by the necessary momentum." In their minds, "all come with advantages and disadvantages, however hoarding silver brings about advantages alone without accompanying disadvantages. Hence there would be more people engaging in commerce and less in plowing and weaving ... corn and cloth shortage would be more acute, and silver price higher, while silver hoarders would be more reluctant to part with their hoards." The fourth was, the ills of mining had deep and far-reaching repercussions: "the ill of silver shortage is less serious, while the ill of silver mining was more profound. The less the amount of the silver the later ill attacks, whereas mining would expedite the attack of the ill." "One man mines, ten families hoard, one prefecture smelts, the entire world hoards, the production of silver is limited, while hoarding by the people is unlimited; how can the amount of silver remain undiminished (*Xu Zi Memorial on Mining Issue Planned to be Submitted*)?" Finally, the source of coin and commodity would stay unobstructed when focus is placed on agriculture. Xu believed that "the most important thing for treating an ill person is to get to know the source thereof, and the rulers should know the fundament of the state. The key to governing the country for today's rulers lies in agriculture." In reality, they failed to understand the law of nature. First, society evolves. Sun Dingchen remarked in On Money One, "The way of things tends to change gradually, knowing such change and prevent it, is that an act achievable by the sage alone?" Afraid of change and taking preventive measures at every step, such was indeed the act of a mediocre talent instead of a wise minister. Monetary material evolves from the inferior to the superior, from base metal to precious, not subject to "three generations," let alone setting the three generations as the perfect state or highest standard. Otherwise, social progress would stall and even retrogress to the state where agriculture was the fundamental and all people engaged in the fundamental.

Second, while the other conditions remained unchanged, silver price and corn price displayed a reverse ratio relation; that is, on the one hand, when silver price rose corn price dropped; on the other hand, when silver price dropped corn price rose. Of course, this was only a move to resolve the contradictions by attempting to deny the historical status and the role of the silver as the primary money against the circumstance of rising silver price. Such a helpless move could only be described as a cowardly and lazy strategy, which was both clumsy and stupid. They could not negate the positive effect of money. Otherwise, even such monetary materials as corn, cloth and copper coin would have to be negated, and the society would have to retrogress to the primitive and backward state where barter trade held sway. They had pushed their theories to the situation of self-contradiction which they had not expected. Third, the exclusiveness and monopoly of money determined that it was impossible to have a primary money in circulation made of several different monetary materials. As for which article should be chosen as the monetary material, it was to be a result determined by historical development, not something determinable by human effort. It had to accommodate the need of development for commodity production and exchange, a law emperors or sages could not alter. Besides, the employment of corn and cloth as money was a sort of waste; this law had already been recognized by the ancients. Sun Dingchen pinned his hope of implementing his retrogressive plan of debasing silver and valuing corn on the judicious rulers who held the final administrative authority. In *On Silver Coins from Tang Dynasty*, he noted, "the use of silver was employed by kings covetous of goods and ministers craving profits." "When silver is valued, the state fundamental is weakened."

He attributed the adoption of silver entirely to the subjective wishes of kings and emperors. It was no wonder he arrived at a conclusion in diametrical violation of the law of social development; it followed from his conclusion that the status and function of silver as the primary money could equally be revoked with the authority of kings and emperors. His specific strategies were introduced in *On Money Two*, "by way of big denomination coins"; that is, he suggested a "proposal of adopting big denomination coin from silver shortage, if coin is well circulated then silver shortage is nothing to be worried about, the benefit is colossal. If the momentum of silver is to be defeated and the ancient state financial system, big denomination coin is the necessary way to be availed of." Neither copper nor labor should be stinted on in minting denomination coin. In order to defeat the rising momentum of silver, they went so far as to preach retrogression and return to the ancient form of society; once such thought gained traction, how could the state or the nation remain safe? This was exactly the sign of a dangerous situation. Fourth, Xu Zi specifically pointed out that fiscal revenue and expenditure should be based on silver as the pricing standard, whereas market circulation should be based on coin as the pricing standard. This arrangement rang resoundingly like bimetallism; however, he then tried to keep them strictly within their respective area, the former for the area of distribution and the latter for the area of circulation. However, if government revenue and expenditure were to be conducted on the basis of silver as the pricing standard, how could it require market transactions to be made on the basis of coin as the pricing standard? Fifth, Xu Zi made a grand scene of himself on the issue of price, claiming that "when more corn and cloth are produced, the price of gold and silver will drop"; "when supply of corn and cloth diminishes, silver price rises." This statement exposed his ignorance in the relation between commodity and money. He held profound prejudice against silver, claiming that "no silver conversion method of taxes and rents had ever been employed in any prosperous times, and the people did not use silver for market transaction, hence prices of corn and cloth were high"; this was purely groundless fabrication.

In order to find a fundamental way out of the silver shortage crisis, the only way in their minds was to retrogress entirely to the self-sufficient natural economy. The impracticalities raised by Xu Zi against mining silver had either been downplayed by free mining and commercial mining under the supervision of the government proposed by Wei Yuan and Lin Zexu or were nothing but platitudes repeating the words of the ancients; among the intellectuals, while there were already some people opening their eyes and casting their sight beyond the national boundaries, disseminating new technologies and knowledge from the Western countries, there were also some dwelling on the ideas of the ancients, parroting banal thought.[10] They stubbornly refused to conduct independent thinking and courageous exploration. This not only reflected their conservatism and reactionary nature regarding commodity money but also reflected their stiffness and decadence in method of thinking and ideas.

2.3. Theory of valuing coin over silver by Bao Shichen

Bao Shichen (1775–1855), courtesy name Shenbo, style Juan in later years, was born in Jingxian county of Anhui.

In his administrative practice as an aide and assistant to the various governors, he studied agricultural administration, canal transportation, salt administration, silver shortage, money, the opium issue and historical anecdotes intensively. He excelled in the administration of rivers, salt and canal transportation. He took the following statement as philosophy: "when a gentleman puts forward his words, he must have expected such being put through without obstruction." His reformation proposals were also to point out the ills of the then-current affairs. As his proposals hurt the interests of officials in power, he was rejected all his life and his proposals were not adopted. He exposed the evil of opium, argued strongly for fighting Great Britain and opposed surrendering. His works were compiled into *Four Categories in Anwu* in his later years.

---

[10]Some went so far as to have proposed employing shells to replace silver as the primary form of money.

In the area of economic thought, he represented the interests of the landed class which had also engaged in industry and commerce businesses of the regions south of the Yangtze River. He claimed that he "was fond of talking about interests" and proposed to confiscate the profits of wily people, with 30% going to the state and the remaining 70% to the people. He laid great stress on the function of commerce and money. His monetary views were mainly reflected in Volume 6 of *Four Categories of Anwu* written in 1820.

Bao Shichen's first view was the theory of valuing coin over silver.

The basis for the problem was excessively high silver price. Bao Shichen believed that this was the "urgent matter for today" and "the most serious and the most urgent matter" (*Letter to Xu Caichang the Former Grand Minister of War*). In his opinion, "though silver coins belong to the incidental wealth, it can balance and check the coins. When both the fundamental and the incidental are plentiful, the people would be well provided for. Even the sudden occurrence of flood and drought could not cause calamity. This is the source of law for all times, and the plan for all posterity." Excessive silver price resulted from a shortage of silver; the situation of silver shortage was very serious. It was feared that a silver shortage would develop into a silver depletion. Therefore, there were two ills. The first ill was "the ordinary people would be gravely straitened" under the circumstances. "Nowadays money only includes silver and coin, the ordinary people received their payment in coin, whereas merchants sell their commodities against payment of silver. When they sell such on market, they convert their silver priced commodities into coins, hence silver shortage leads to higher price, and higher silver price further leads to higher commodity prices. And still that taxes and rents are converted into coins, higher silver price leads to more coins in conversion" (*Miscellaneous Articles Composed in the Year of Gengchen Two*). In *Complementary Exposition on Silver Shortage*, Bao demonstrated that the shortage of silver led to social insecurity, with the government facing increased burden and decreased revenue and the people facing increased burden and increased expense, the fundamental cause of which was that the price of coin fell along with the rise of the price of silver and wastage increased. "The world suffers from silver shortage for long. In May 1839, silver price rose to one thousand standard copper coins converting to six *qian* and one *fen* of silver, which meant a tael of silver is converted to more than one thousand six hundred and thirty *wen*. In remote countries where commerce is under developed, the people pay corn taxes in coin; taking the current practice, for instance, the receiving counter would charge one thousand eight hundred and eighty-five *wen* for corn tax of a tael of silver, and the government actually receives one thousand eight hundred and twenty seven *wen* after deducting handling charge of fifty eight *wen*. It is universally known as the established rule that one tael of silver is converted into one thousand standard copper coins. Now the tenants have to pay one thousand eight hundred and eighty five *wen* for a tael of silver tax, handling charge included, which is really exorbitant. Besides, in a period of two or three years, when harvest is good, a *dan* of corn could only bring about five hundred *wen*, and at the time of temporary corn shortage, corn could bring about no more than seven hundred and a few scores *wen*." Under the grave circumstance of excessive silver price and plummeting coin prices, the burden of the people got increasingly heavier. Along with graft and irregularities of officials, how could the people still shoulder such a burden? He believed that the situation could equally overburden the government. The second ill was that "foreign countries fatten on the depleting of China, which is of substantial significance"; such a situation could not be taken lightly, as it was the reason for the state financial crisis. "So long as opium is available on market, then all silver will go to foreigners."

According to Bao's calculation, the number of opium smokers in Suzhou alone amounted to several hundred thousand. Assuming a person per day spends one *qian* on opium, then the daily cost for opium would amount to10,000 taels, and the number rocketed to 3 or 4 million taels per year: "the cost would amount to a hundred million tael per year when the key metropolises are included" (*Miscellaneous Articles Composed in the Year of Gengchen*).

In order to overcome the silver shortage, in the aspect of the monetary system, Bao proposed the following: "employ coin as the exclusive money, all governmental affairs are to be conducted in metal coin, and paper money shall be the instrument governing all monetary use, complementing the inadequacy of metal coin." That is to say, the central government would designate the standard copper coins as the statutory money, all financial revenue and expenditure would take copper coin as the pricing standard and paper money would be the currency, serving as the means of purchase and payment in circulation. It resembles the situation in the past, "the *Book of Han* stated, 'a *jin* of gold is worth ten thousand coins', it was still coin-based pricing system and circulated coins were like knife money, cloth money, etc." However, in his time, "all are silver priced on the basis of silver, not only pearl, jade, gold are not considered money, but coin is also excluded from the category of money." "However calculation of labor services, taxes, official remunerations, donations and redemption are all silver based, even property transaction pricing among the people are eight or nine out of ten silver based." Silver is superior to coin, and silver has wider use: "houses of fortune strive to hoard silver, hence silver supply dwindles. The merchant purchases salt, corn, and daily necessities with silver and sells for coin, hence commodity price rockets" (*Second Reply to Wang Liangsheng*). The fine method salvaging the money lies in establishing standard copper coin as the statutory money, that is, "only by designating coin as the money could this ill be cured." After the monetary system reform, "all price calculations, governmental and non-governmental, shall be silver based, and silver price shall fluctuate as the market moves." Copper coin was to be established as the pricing standard. It was to be employed for determining the amount of rents, taxes, remunerations, donations and redemption, transactions among the people, deed titles, etc. Then, did it mean to expel silver from the field of circulation? The answer was negative. It just meant to retire silver from the position as the statutory money of account, till it no longer played the function as the measure of value; however, it would still have continued playing the role as a means of circulation. That is, "the key is to manifest that coin shall be established as the money, and subject silver to coin, deprive the function of silver and assign it to coin" (*Letter to Xu Caichang the Former Grand Minister of War*).

However, he was also aware of the fact that the circulation of silver was not affected by human wishes, it was an inevitable trend "not something human effort could affect." There was a force beyond human effort moving the evolution of monetary materials. Meanwhile, he opposed setting silver as the statutory money of account and assuming the function of the measure of value; he believed that such an arrangement would "amount to jeopardizing oneself," as though "designating silver as the money" which ailed both the government and the people was something arising out of human effort, a result attained through nationwide promotion and universal acceptance by the people. Out of special preference for copper coin, he praised it as "national treasure." Regarding the practice that "all is calculated on the basis of silver, while coin is subject to silver," he thought otherwise. He believed that setting copper coin instead of silver as the statutory pricing standard was the logical result and there were more adequate reasons. There were two main reasons for this. The first was that "today's law provides that anyone guilty of using fake silver shall be exiled, whereas private minting is punishable with the death penalty, this is absolutely valuing coin over silver." The second was that "the people call those wealthy houses 'rich in coins', lowlifes such as gamblers would call their activities in gambling stands or halls 'gambling coin'; no talk about gambling silver has ever been heard, this obviously demonstrated that coin is the money" (*Second Reply to Wang Liangshen*). He took customs and the state penal code as the objective standard for judging the reasonableness of an economic category; such a method was not only far-fetched but also very childish. He believed that his goal could be attained by resorting to the coercive power of the regime, "subjecting silver to coin, depriving the authority of silver and assign it to the coin." He also concluded, after summarizing the historical experience, "the ill of the former Ming Dynasty, all arose from powerful and treacherous ministers urging for reformation ... the key lay in manifesting coin as money, subjecting silver to coin, depriving the authority of silver and assign it to the coin, popularizing the use of coin via the circulation of paper money, and there are already established means for handling paper money. It would be appropriate for the government to stipulate in definitive terms that all payments, government and non-government, shall be made in coin; and silver price shall fluctuate as market moves, and be subjected to the coin. And now that coin is weighty and cumbersome, such shall be placed under the domination of the light and portable paper money" (*Letter to Xu Caichang the Former Grand Minister of War*). These statements were not only self-contradictory, but exposed his shallow understanding of money. Since the midterm of the Ming Dynasty, silver had already acquired the status of the primary money, which was a necessary development for accommodating commodity economy. It had real value; since it performed the function of the means of circulation, it could equally perform the function of the measure of value. The two basic functions were inseparable from each other, and one could not stand without the other. Nowadays people attempt to relegate it to the state of fractional money with human effort, but it was also "nothing that could be altered by human effort."

Bao Shichen conceived a gradual classified implementation of staged program for the retrogressive process from silver standard to copper coin standard, and planned differential treatment thereto. In his opinion, "silver price has been high for too long, there are specific provisions regarding payment in silver, once payment is changed from silver to coin, it would be unavoidable for people to hold grudge, and it would be particularly difficult to reconcile." If military pay is disturbed, then military stability would definitely be disturbed, and that would amount to undermining oneself. Therefore, he proposed, "it seemed appropriate to change the monthly military pay of one tael of silver to thirteen hundred standard copper coins, other remunerations to officials shall also be changed from the former arrangement of silver to standard copper coins at the rate one tael of silver converting to twelve hundred standard copper coins." As stated thereby, the people "are universally aware of the provision that one tael of silver is priced at one thousand *qian*, they are already complaining when they are made to pay one thousand eight hundred *qian* for the tax of one tael of silver. Even the people pay at such an exorbitant rate, the government still incurs a loss of twenty or thirty *wen* qian for every tael it receives." If coin is established as the money, the balance of one income and one expense is, "only a thousand three hundred and twenty *wen*. Besides, officials could make it a basis for government business, even though there are corrupt officials, cost would still be less than the former times." Hence, the people would make payment without being urged and it was unlikely for stagnation to occur. Bao Shichen proposed to establish standard copper coins as the standard money; in the meanwhile, he was opposed to minting big denomination coin. In refuting Wang Liu's views that "big denomination coin to be used as ten or a hundred qian shall be minted to remedy the cash shortage and the copper ban shall be strengthened to promote the monetary law," he noted that first "once monetary law of paper money is implemented, then existing cash would be sufficient for use, and private minting would naturally disappear." The second was that a strict copper ban was difficult to implement: "no copper ban was more strict than in the reign of the Yongzheng Emperor, during whose reign all decrees were carried out to the letter, however copper ban could not work, let alone in today's situation. The third was that big coin denominations harmed the people, which was a time-honored law. "Though it was a practice seen in history to establish one coin to be worth ten or a hundred wen, the Tang Dynasty had implemented such practice due to the riot in Hebei, which gravely harmed the people. In a few years such big denomination coins were used as worth no more than one *qian*, while in these years, it incurred huge loss to the government, in addition to the harm done to the people" (*Second Reply to Wang Liangshen*).

Bao Shichen's second view was the proposal to subject all to paper money.

Bao Shichen was acutely aware of the ills of "importability of coin (copper coin)"; he believed that issuing paper money was "a fine measure to cure the ill" (*Letter to Xu Caichang the Former Grand Minister of War*); however, such was not "a great path (law) for finance management." This principle was theoretically grounded and with precedence in history. According to the tangible and intangible theory of check and balances, he believed that "it is the ultimate truth valid for the ancient times as well today that the light and the heavy balance and check each other without fail. Issuing paper money would be establishing a balance and check relation between the intangible and the tangible. Silver is the tangible whereas paper money the intangible." According to this theory, paper money issuance must be guaranteed by silver, as circulation of intangible paper money without the backup of tangible coin would be doomed to failure. He refuted Wang Liu's argument that "silver and paper money are the same," and specified the connotation of the theory of the tangible and the intangible proposed by Zhao Mengfu of the Yuan Dynasty as "silver being the tangible and paper money the intangible"; that is to say, metal money had real value, silver and copper coin were both tangible, whereas monetary token was without real value, paper money being the intangible. Therefore, the circulation of paper money had to stand in the "relation of 'balance and check between the tangible and the intangible', otherwise paper money might fail once there is emergency, whereas silver would never fail." This embodied the reason that "it is the ultimate truth valid for the ancient times as well today that the light and the heavy balance and check each other without fail." Hence, Wang Liu's proposal of "issuing paper money and discarding silver" was actually a move to "discard the tangible in order to boost the intangible," which was totally impractical. He also pointedly reminded people of the most profound lesson in the history of paper money that nothing was more dangerous than regarding issuing paper money as an inexhaustible source. He specifically pointed out that the ridiculousness of Wang Liu's beliefs lay in his thinking that "a million produced is a million obtained, ten million produced is ten million obtained, it is an inexhaustible source of revenue," which was exactly the root cause of the fact that "paper money issuance is difficult to implement and easy to fail." He specifically pointed out that the key to Wang Liu's paper money issuance theory was "benefiting the people in name but ramifying into further harm" (*Second Reply to Wang Liangshen*). Therefrom, he proceeded to expose the evil nature and sinister objective of issuing paper money by the rulers of the various dynasties, and touched upon the real cause for the failure of paper money issuance.

The other paper money issuance principle raised by Bao Shichen was "benefiting the people at the expense of the government," which was put forward in opposition to Wang Liu's principle of "the topmost goal being satisfaction of the government's needs." The so-called benefit at the expense of the government referred to the fact that the government "must redeem silver with paper money at prevailing market rate; the county and prefecture shall redeem such at the rate of 94% the face value and transfer it to the pertinent bureau, and the pertinent bureau transfer such at 97% of the face value to the ministry." Hence, "the wealthy people witness the convenience of paper money, they would be aware that silver price would drop by the day, therefore they would definitely part with their silver hoard; the more such silver hoard is redeemed, the less the use of silver would be, silver price would necessarily plummet," until silver price dropped to the rate of "one tael of silver converting into one thousand standard copper coins, which was the baseline thereof." Bao Shichen estimated that in the first year of paper money issuance, the government would incur a loss of about 10 million *qian*, of which half would benefit the people and half the officials. Loss incurred by the government would facilitate the circulation of paper money, and "the more the loss incurred to the government, the quicker circulation thereof is promoted. With circulation quickened, the government may see no loss in the following year, and it would be net benefit to the government thereafter, such benefit would exceed imagination." The loss to the government would be limited to the first year, but the government would benefit substantially from the circulation of paper money and a fall in the price of silver, and the benefit would go through the roof in the second year. For the sake of the long-term and fundamental interests of the rulers, he warned, "the final purpose of benefiting the government is to benefit the people." Only in this way can the arrangement stay without ills.

Therefore, Bao Shichen proposed to limit the amount of issuance of paper money: "when paper money is initially produced, a limit which covers half of the amount for a year's taxes and rents would suffice" (*ibid.*), and the amount would be increased annually, "till it equals the amount for a year's taxes and rents; and thereafter the issuance and withdrawal of paper money shall be conducted in a cycle, issuance shall be stopped when there is enough paper money for the people to use." That is to say, a maximum quota shall be established for paper money issuance, or in other words, issuance shall be limited to the amount equivalent to the annual fiscal revenue of the government. So long as circulation and cycling are guaranteed, it would not be an issue to meet the need for commodity circulation. The understanding of controlling paper money issuance touched upon the key point of the issue, which deserved appreciation. However, the arrangement that he established of fiscal revenue as the standard rang suspiciously of satisfying fiscal requirements, instead of satisfying the objective requirements of commodity circulation. Not only were they two different concepts but they were also not comparable in total amount. Though fiscal revenue could be established as the security for issuing paper money, how could it guarantee that there was no fiscal deficit and still be balanced? Hence, such a devise would be neither scientific nor correct.

The monetary theory of Bao Shichen discussed a controlled and procedural issuance of paper money, guaranteeing the smooth turnover of money circulation; such a theory was raised to safeguard the interests of the ruling class by way of benefiting the use thereof by the people while keeping the people from the harm of inflation. However, his theory could not be implemented and could not be adopted by the rulers. Before the Sino-British Opium War broke out, the Qing government faced the tremendous pressure of financial crisis; it naturally would not pay the interests to the people, nor would it share with the people.

3. Nominal theory of money of Wang Liu

Wang Liu (1786–1843), former name Zhongliu, courtesy name Zijian and Liangsheng, later style Hepan Shanren, was born in Wuxian county of Jiangsu.

He failed the imperial examinations repeatedly, and made a living by teaching and serving as an assistant and aide to government officials. His works include *Manuscripts from Hezhou Garden* and *Humble Remarks on Money and Coin*. *Humble Remarks on Money and Coin* was his most favored work. He followed the instructions of his father and wrote *Humble Remarks on Money and Coin* in 1828 and printed it in 1831. In 1837, he amended the work and printed it again. Then he printed the second edition, third edition, etc. He claimed that he "had researched the subject for over thirty years" by extensive gathering of information and investigation. After printing, he had presented it to a "minister in power," expecting to "attach himself to the lofty to attain immortality"; hence, he regarded it as the stepping-stone to joining the ruling group. Though some individual members from the ruling group supported and spread his proposal, in the end the proposals failed to get adopted by the government, and he failed to gain access to the ruling group. *Humble Remarks on Money and Coin* was composed of four sections: there were 10 essays in *On Coin and Paper Money* which demonstrated the monetary proposals theoretically, 20 articles in *My Drafted Measures for Coin and Paper Money* which concerned specific proposals regarding paper money issuance and minting of big denomination coins, *Judicious Remarks from Virtuous Ministers of Former Times* which collected remarks on paper money issuance from the Song Dynasty to the Qing Dynasty with annotations annexed, and *Replies to Friends* which included correspondence with Bao Shichen and Gu Chun. The second edition included 32 articles on paper money debated with Bao Shichen, which were highly theoretically oriented. Wang Liu's monetary theory was mainly reflected in the book.

3.1. On monetary reform

Wang Liu came to understand that opium import was the root cause for the situation of silver appreciation and coin depreciation; so he proposed to issue paper money to solve the issue of silver outflow. In *A Letter to Zhang Hengpu on Eradicating Opium*, he wrote, "the only measure to make foreigners profitless was to issue paper money. If paper money is issued, then all silver of the people would be traded for paper money, though foreigners bring in opium and exchange it for our paper money; such paper money would not be able to be used in their countries, then opium trade would stop without being banned." Such wishful thinking and ungrounded planning were shattered by historical facts, which proved that such assumptions would not stand and were impractical. Judged from the starting point, the assumption was highly subjective and metaphysical, which dictated that even if his proposal was adopted for implementation, it would be doomed to failure.

The monetary system reform of Wang Liu could be summarized in the following six articles:

The first article classified paper money into seven categories — big denomination paper money worth 1,000 *guan* and 500 *guan*, intermediate denomination paper money worth 100 *guan* and 50 *guan*, and small denomination paper money worth 10 *guan*, three *guan* and one *guan*. Superior-quality paper would be chosen for producing paper money, and the people would be prohibited from trading such paper. Ten fine calligraphers would be selected from across the entire country for writings on big denomination paper money, five or six for intermediate denomination paper money and copperplate-etched aphorisms would be inscribed on small denomination paper money. Paper money would then be decorated into a hand scroll. The largest will be one foot in width and 20 or 30 feet in length, and the smallest about the size of one foot by one foot.

Paper money verifiers would be installed across the country and strict prohibition would be established on counterfeiting.

The second article stated that coin would be classified into three categories — worth 100, 10 and one *qian*. The big denomination coin would be made of argentan, with production and material cost about 90-odd *wen*; intermediate and small denomination coins would be made of brass or pure copper, with production and material cost about nine *wen* for a 10 *wen* denomination coin, and the production and material cost for a one *wen* denomination coin about equal to its denomination. Such were to be employed for small-sum payments under one *guan*. Bronze instruments, private trade and setting up bronzeware shops were to be banned. Government bronzeware shops would be established to engage in manufacturing musical instruments, locks and buttons for the convenience of the people; bronze collection offices would be set up, and private copperware would be purchased at redoubled price with paper money. The third article stated that paper money and big denomination coins would be distributed to private banks, and the private endorsement of banknotes and money notes would be prohibited. When private banks redeemed silver, they would obtain a 10% profit and the people obtained a 10% profit.

The fourth article stated that official remuneration would be redoubled at the beginning of paper money issuance; the base remuneration would be paid in silver, and the amount in excess of the base remuneration would be paid in paper money. After paper money circulation was established, all payments would be made in paper money, and official remuneration would be raised several times.

The fifth article stated that silver would not be used as money.

The sixth article stated that barter trade alone was allowed in foreign trade, and no silver was allowed; however, if a foreign country would trade paper money with silver, they would be allowed to purchase Chinese goods with the paper money so obtained.

It could be seen from the foregoing text that the monetary system reform program proposed by Wang Liu centered on paper money issuance, promoting the established theory of banning silver from being used as money and banning copper from being manufactured into instruments as raised by his forerunners. Starting from the interests of the supreme ruler, he was convinced that issuing paper money was the sole way to rid of the fiscal straits of the government and in keeping with the interests of the Qing Dynasty. Regarding the financial and economic situation and social conflict, in his view, there was no choice but to issue paper money in order to expand financial expenditure, raise remuneration to keep the officials free from graft and ease social conflict. He also publicly criticized the ill-curing measures suggested by Lin Zexu, Wei Yuan,

Bao Shichen, etc., including mining silver, starting marine transportation, cutting surplus charges and banning opium, as difficult to implement for there were defects therein.

In his view, issuing paper money was nothing short of an "undisclosed treasure" which could bring back the dead and save the day, and once his plan was adopted, all social ills such as depletion of financial resources and economic rights being encroached would naturally disappear without human intervention. He dwelled at great length on the great variety of benefits that would be brought to the people and the state in issuing paper money, such as increase in official remuneration, reduction in taxes and rents, lowering of tariff and destitute people such as widows, widowers and orphans having living subsistence. Proceeding therefrom, water conservancy would be increased and waste land reclaimed. Not a single man in the entire country would not benefit from this policy. It would not only benefit the country but could also ease social conflict, ridding the country of the harassment of economic aggression by the Western countries.

Once the lofty-sounding slogan was put forth, no one would still dare doubt its miraculous effect. According to his wording, the benefits of issuing paper money were wishfully exaggerated beyond imagination; he went to great lengths by piecing together far-fetched materials and even distorted, avoided or reversed previous conclusions to the disregard of historical facts and basic conclusions. Hence, the praises of issuing paper money were sung, and it became a panacea for all financial and economic problems as well as other social ills, working wonders and defying description.

Actually, the miraculous method of issuing paper money, the high praises of which were sung by Wang Liu, was nothing but a naked, thorough and entirely inflationary policy, a theoretical weapon for unscrupulous, unrestrained and excessive paper money issuance prepared for the rulers. In addition to swindling wealth from the pockets of the people into the depleted national treasury with fancy paper, there was also resistance to various progressive reform programs in his proposal. The theoretical basis thereof was the extremely well-developed nominal theory of money in traditional society as well as economic thought in opposition to the traditional Confucian concept.

3.2. Precondition for nominal theory of money

Wang Liu's purpose in preaching about issuing paper money was to implement an inflationary policy. He cleared the way in basic theory, opposed the traditional Confucian concept and put forward an economic view of "top priority being the satisfaction of the needs of the ruler." He targeted You Ruo's remarks in *The Confucian Analects — Yan Yuan*, "If the people have plenty, their prince will not be left to want alone. If the people are in want, their prince cannot enjoy plenty alone." That is, if the people had plenty, there was no reason why the prince should be left to want, and vice versa, if the people were in want, how could the prince have plenty! He claimed that the situation was because "at the times of the three sovereigns, the people and the rulers were living in common, hence there was only the issue of ensuring that the people have plenty, there was no such thing as ensuring that the ruler was not left in want.

So long as the people have plenty, the ruler would naturally not be left to want; it was like the parents would not be in want so long as the offspring have plenty." After the three sovereigns, the people had already deserted the ancient maxims; however, nobody would reveal this point, "after the times of the three sovereigns, the people and the rulers were no longer living in common, there came into being the issue of both ensuring that neither the rulers nor the people be left in want; and so long as the rulers have plenty the people would necessarily not be left in want, which is like that so long as the parent have plenty the offspring would not be left in want." Hence, "if the people are to be left in no want, nothing works better than farming, if the ruler is to be left in no want, nothing works more effectively than exercising the right to manipulating the money." The phrases "So long as rulers have plenty, the people would necessarily not be left in want" and "the top priority being to satisfy the needs of the rulers"[11] became the starting point for his entire paper money issuance program, and the precondition for his nominal theory of money. The view of satisfying the needs of the rulers by Wang Liu was in opposition to the traditional view of satisfying the needs of the people held by the reformist of the landed class.

---

[11] *On Coin and Paper Money One.*

The traditional view of satisfying the needs of the people was put forward considering the long-term interests of the ruling class, aimed at reconciling the immediate interests and the long-term interests of the ruling class, and settling the conflict of interest between the ruling and the ruled, and between the reformist of the landed class, who represented the townspeople's interests tinged with some capitalistic factors, and the diehard conservatives of the ruling class.

Wang Liu stood for the interests of the die-hard conservatives from the ruling class. He proceeded from the characteristics of the times wherein he lived. In order to solve pressing needs, he stopped upholding the time-honored tune of "if the people have plenty, their prince will not be left to want alone," and could not help but put forward an economic theory to help the government to get rid of the straitened situation and replenish government finance. He openly proclaimed that the traditional theory was outdated, and replaced it with a new theory of "the top priority being to satisfy the needs of the rulers" and "if the ruler is left in no want, the people will enjoy plenty." He promised in an imposing manner that issuing paper money would bring benefits to the state, and that once the state had nothing to want, such benefits would go to the people. Benefits included an increase in official remuneration, reduction in taxes and rents, lowering of tariff, and destitute people such as widows, widowers and orphans having living subsistence. Not a single man will be left without benefiting therefrom. It would not only benefit the state but also benefit the people! The optimal way to attain this miraculous world would be to collect silver via paper money issuance. He was convinced that if the ruler was to be left in no want, nothing works more effectively than exercising the right to manipulate the money, that is, issuing paper money. According to him, the causes leading to the right to issue paper money being encroached were as follows: destroying coin to make instruments, popular acceptance of foreign silver dollars, merchants manipulating silver prices, private minting by wily people, wealthy houses issuing money note, drafts, etc. Therefore, in order to control the right to issue money, silver had to be collected by issuing paper money, and silver would be rendered too base to be capable of being used as money. Copper had to be collected with paper money issued as well, with sufficient copper needed to mint coins extensively. Moreover, Wang considered that when other materials were employed as money, there was a time for such material to be used up; however, paper money issuance alone could produce a million or a billion if a million or a billion were required, with the state able to obtain "financial resource which is inexhaustible." In the eyes of Wang Liu, in order to bring benefit to and improve the financial strength of the state, no aspiring minister would take the shortcut which would inevitably harm the interests of the people. Only issuing paper money could attain the objective of benefiting both the state and the people with inexhaustible resources. It was wishful thinking that "the top strategy" could "enrich both the state and the people"!

The enriching of the state talked about by Wang Liu was real, whereas enriching the people was not real; benefiting the state was real and benefiting the people not real; satisfying the needs of the ruler was real and satisfying the needs of the people not real.

On the one hand, Wang Liu put on an air of fairness by criticizing the Green Sprout Law (*Qing Miao Fa*) introduced by Wang Anshi as being a measure of benefiting the people at the expense of the rulers and making loans for profit as being a preposterous and unreasonable move, while praising his own proposals, "assigning the right to manipulating the money to the state while assigning all actual benefits to the people, such proposals were made out of fair and grand grounds, and it will absolutely be workable by reason."[12] On the other hand, he bared his fangs and proclaimed that the real intent of issuing paper money was to tighten the plundering and exploitation of the people. He was elated with his skillful tricks. In plain language, his plan was for the state to offer a small benefit to the people and completely grab their wealth; only a fool would not do it. This plan was nothing short of tremendous benefit for the supreme ruler. According to him, the people meant not just the ordinary people but also the officials, merchants and usurers. This was what Wang Liu had expected.

In *Six Essays on Paper Money Issuance*, he further clarified his position.

He attempted to contain the "rampant wild gossips" by raising official remunerations, or even redoubling such remunerations, in order to "bring the unbounded benefit to both the state and the people"; however, this was nothing but a renewed ruse of self-deception. It was extortion on the

---

[12]*On Coin and Paper Money Nine.*

pretense of remuneration raise; hence, Wang Liu's proposals met with opposition from most officials. Similarly, Wang Liu targeted merchants for plundering; the private banks and silver stores they ran would lose the benefits of issuing money note, silver note and draft. They would lose the opportunity to manipulate the conversion rate between silver and coin and profit therefrom, and they would also be deprived of the privilege of hoarding silver as the coercive collecting of silver by the government progressed. The only thing they would obtain was a huge pile of paper money of an equivalent amount plus interests of one-tenth of their conversion and exchange businesses; the 20% profit they would be offered was no different from bait. For the sake of the supreme ruler's interests, he would not scruple to sacrifice the interests of the people, including the average members of the ruling class, and net all wealth for the use of the emperor.

Though Wang Liu exerted all his effort to devise plans for the supreme ruler and sang high praises of his attention-grabbing paper money issuance program, he failed in the end to disarm the vigilance of the emperor to paper money. From the Song Dynasty to the Ming Dynasty, there had been a history of 500 years of paper money circulation, and extremely rich theory and historical experience had accumulated over time. The lessons of failure in issuing paper money from the previous dynasties were too profound, and the emperor would definitely not resort to it without much deliberation unless absolutely desperate. Besides, Wang Liu replaced practical research with subjective conjecture, esteemed the power of the ruler as too important, disregarded the inevitable trend of money development and evolution, the evolution from base metal coin to precious metal coin, and attempted to stop the progress of the wheel of history. Measures including banning silver from being employed as coin, producing fine paper money and issuing big denomination coin were all vaunted as perfect, which was absurd. He treated issuing paper money as the most important wealth management technique along with land management and operation, and attempted to eliminate the irreconcilable social conflict of land occupation relation, which was thrown into sharp contrast with the past and present of paper money circulation. People could not but doubt his reliability and chance of success, and he ultimately failed to win the appreciation and appointment of the supreme ruler. He failed even to land an office like the months-long appointment of Jiang Chen. This was a great irony to the ambitious Wang Liu.

3.3. The complete form of China's traditional nominal theory of money

The nominal theory of money is a basic theory of money in opposition to the metal theory of money in bourgeois political economics.

It refuses to recognize the commodity nature of money, holding that money is only a unit or token of calculation adopted for the convenience of commodity circulation. The theory fundamentally denies the value of money, equates the nature of money with the means of circulation of money, distorts the function of money as a means of circulation, denies the relation between the token of money and precious metal money, and claims that it suffices to have nominal value.

Regarding the nature of money, Wang Liu denied that there was any value in money, falsely alleging that the ideas raised by metal money theorists were incorrect: "paper money being the intangible and silver the tangible is not much the case. When people talk about the fact that silver has tangible properties such as form and substance, paper money also has properties of form and substance; when it is claimed that paper money could neither feed the hungry nor fend the cold, then silver is the same" (*ibid.*). There were already universally accepted views on the connotations of intangible paper money and tangible silver, though they were not quite clear about the connotation of value; the intangible and tangible obviously meant the fruits of labor. Wang Liu employed the tactic of stealthy replacement of concept, demonstrating that there was no difference between paper money and silver by stating that both had certain natural properties (form and substance), neither was of use value, and the use value alluded thereby was limited to feeding the hungry and clothing the cold; thereby, he further denied the existence of difference between their real values ("the intangible and the tangible"). Hence, he equaled silver to and paper money, and metal money to paper money.

This was untenable in theory; it should be known that for gold and silver to become money was the inevitable outcome of the development of the form of value. It was the unique choice of the natural property of gold and silver, which could not be matched by paper money. Wang Liu obliterated the distinction between the special use value of ordinary commodity and ordinary use value of commodity money, and obliterated the distinction between metal money which had real value and the representative and token thereof, that is, the distinction between the physical entity of value and token of value. He denied the commodity nature of money, and paved the way for unlimited issuance of paper money. He had inherited and carried forward the theory of "similarity between copper coin and paper money" proposed by Xin Qiji. He was the typical proponent of China's traditional nominal theory of money.

Therefore, it would be natural for him to put forward arguments for "tricks of designating debris as gold" and turning paper into gold. Chen Zilong (1608–1647, courtesy names Renzhong Wozi) of the closing period of the Ming Dynasty had the opinion that "prior to the deterioration of the imperial repository, paper money was viciously turned into gold." Wang Liu gave full play to it and claimed repeatedly that "if paper money is employed, then paper could be transformed into money in hundreds or thousands of millions."[13] He speculated that he had found a life-saving straw for the dying ancient society in China and the Qing Dynasty which faced internal extravagance, corruption and grave capitalistic challenges.

Wang Liu believed that paper money was the ideal money: "money made of anything other than paper money has an end, whereas paper money has not, a million produced is a million obtained, ten million produced is ten million obtained."[14] Compared to the statement of "designating a hundred and a hundred is obtained, designating a thousand and a thousand is obtained" raised by Qian Bingchen (1612–1693) of the closing period of the Ming Dynasty, his was 10,000 times expanded. This sufficiently demonstrates his confidence as a thorough theorist of the nominal theory of money as well as his eagerness to please the supreme ruler for reward.

If paper money could be issued in such great amounts, it would literally mean inexhaustible resources, and the rulers would die for it. The problem was how to maintain the stability of the purchasing power of

---

[13] Letter submitted to He Xiancuo.
[14] *On Coin and Paper Money.*

paper money and ensure the stability of paper money circulation; otherwise, the ruler would constantly be reminded of the bitter lessons from history, and no such desperate move would be adopted unless absolutely necessary.

However, it was very difficult to justify his theory and make monetary circulation stable and smooth. The first reason for the difficulty was that the state would establish the value of paper money through the exercise of coercive power.

The state may establish the value of paper money and enforce the circulation thereof through the coercive power of the regime. Wang Liu did not bother to disguise the fact that the state may issue paper money on the back of state power, whereas money note issued by private banks could not be done coercively. Private banks could only count on their own creditworthiness and through redemption guarantee and their established reputation in society ensure the issuance and circulation of the money note. Hence, there was a difference between money note and paper money; the circulation of paper money was based on the precondition of full confidence placed in the state power by the people, instead of issuance reserve and redemption. Hence, it could be deduced that the state power could dictate the value of paper money and amount to be issued as it saw fit; this was the argument of state determinism upheld by proponents of the nominal theory of money.

The history of money circulation demonstrated that "the state could naturally launch into circulation of paper with any name or any amount printed thereon; however, its control vanishes together with the end of the mechanical movement. Once the token of value or paper money enters the realm of circulation, it will be regulated by the inherent law of circulation."[15] The inherent law requires that the amount of paper money issuance not exceed the amount of objective need; once such an amount is exceeded, paper money will depreciate and commodity price will rise, causing inflation.

This had been demonstrated by the history of paper money circulation in China, a common sense, universally known understanding. Wang Liu disregarded the fact and exaggerated the force of state power without jus-

---

[15] *Karl Marx and Frederick Engels*, vol. 13, pp. 109–110.

tification, averring, "a fixed amount is specified on the paper money, therefore it could not be tampered by anybody, hence encroachment and embezzlement by petty officials.... There is a fixed value in paper money, the merchant may not raise or lower it, therefore the intent to fraud by the people may be eliminated."[16] He further wrote, "When there is a fixed value in paper money, then even a scholar, a farmer, a child, an old man, a woman, a lady can all employ such paper money according to the characters printed thereon, there would be no room left for trickery."[17] When confronted with Bao Shichen's accusation that "it was exactly the cause for paper money issuance to fail easily and difficult to implement," he reasoned in a far-fetched manner, "the reason that paper money issuance was quick to fail and difficult to implement lay in such defects as inferior production, susceptibility to mold and wear, and surcharge over replacement, it has nothing to do with the inexhaustibleness thereof." He either imputed the issuance mistake of the ruling class to the lower officials or glossed over it technically. In China's history, Wang Liu was the first to avow that state power may determine the value of paper money and guaranteed that it would not depreciate in circulation. Even Qian Bingchen and Chen Zilong had not dared to exaggerate the coercive power of the state regime. Blind faith in the supreme authority made him unreasonable and speak preposterously.

Actually, Wang Liu also had qualms about people's abhorrence toward inflation; therefore, he concealed his real intent. He also mentioned the limit of paper money issuance; however, he did not elaborate and was inconsistent, which exposed his perfunctoriness and insincerity. For instance, he wrote, "though paper money is an inexhaustible resource, when the state produces paper money, the only purpose is to satisfy its need, hence it would limit the amount."[18] There were two definitions of quantity in order to "satisfy its need": one was "to collect silver from the people across the country," which was a restatement of Jiang Chen's "placing all money in the imperial repository."[19] The other was a quote

---

[16] *On Coin and Paper Money One.*
[17] *The First Planned Strategy to Enrich the State and the People.*
[18] Debate with Bao Shichen on *Paper Money and Coin.*
[19] *Records of Huaizong Emperor of Ming Dynasty*, the 16th year of Chongzhen Emperor.

from *The book of Rites — Wang Zhi*, "constantly prepare the state with thirty years' reserve."

It was not difficult to see that the true nature of Wang Liu's limit was tailored to the fiscal requirement of the state, instead of determining the amount of issuance in accordance with the amount objectively required in circulation. This revealed his true purpose of satisfying the unfathomable desire of the Qing Dynasty by plundering the people, in line with his guiding principle of paper money issuance.

The second reason for the difficulty in making monetary circulation stable and smooth was that the state may secure the stability of monetary circulation by way of retiring paper money. Targeting the famous remark of Emperor Xiaozong of the Song Dynasty that "Huizi appreciates when insufficiently supplied, and depreciates when oversupplied," Wang Liu ranted, "however big the amount of issuance is not an issue of concern, whereas the amount to be retired is." That is, there was no need to worry about the amount of issuance, the only concern was that too little was retired. His concern was that "issuance and retirement are properly managed" or "revenue is put into brilliant use," that is, the government retires paper money by collecting taxes and rents in paper money from the people. The other measure was for the government to issue coin and retire paper money. "The various government repositories shall accumulate coins, paper money shall be purchased with coin when there is surplus paper money, so that no stagnation occurs."[20] With the state issuing paper money according to financial requirement, it would definitely make the amount of paper money issuance elastic. If the state taxes could be imposed arbitrarily according to financial requirement, why would it need paper money issuance to make up for the difference between revenue and expenditure? Obviously, state taxes were of an inflexible nature. Under such circumstance, wouldn't it be a monstrous absurdity to attempt to maintain paper money value by fiscal retirement thereof? Implementation of the fiscal retirement of paper money is more difficult than the elasticity of state revenue. Minting coin to supplement paper money and limiting it under the narrow scope of small-amount payment under one *guan* were

---

[20] Forty measures on *Paper Money and Coin*.

far from adequate and were futile measures. Wang Liu was doing nothing other than engaging in self-deception.

It was of vital importance to keep the paper money issuance amount under the reasonable limit; otherwise, it would be difficult to guarantee redemption. This was already known by the ancients. On the contrary, Wang Liu was convinced that the failures of paper money issuance in history were mainly due to constant change in paper money law, inferior paper money production, susceptibility to mold and wear, surcharge on paper money replacement, etc. It should be acknowledged that the constant change of paper money law was the result of the inevitable failure thereof, instead of the cause of the failure for paper money circulation. Wang Liu was wrong in reversing the cause and effect. The remaining causes he raised were technical factors. The fundamental purpose of doing so was to defend the state for issuing paper money to collect silver and deny the necessity for the state to establish a limit on paper money issuance, establish issuance reserve and guarantee redemption, so as to ignore the real responsibility for safeguarding the stability of the value of paper money and proper circulation thereof.

The third reason for the difficulty in making monetary circulation stable and smooth was that the people would store away paper money instead of silver, which would reduce the amount of paper money in circulation. Wang Liu believed that paper money may perform the function as a store of value: "the wealthy houses store silver for silver being the money, now that silver is no longer the money, wealthy houses would cease storing silver and shift to storing paper money. It is a natural law, storing paper money for contingent use."[21] Under the condition of metal money circulation, the performance of the function as a store of value must be assumed by metal money with real value; otherwise, the function cannot be performed. However, Wang Liu was convinced that there was no difference between paper money and metal money; he erroneously held that paper money could equally exit from circulation and enter the realm of storage. They both have values designated by the state; once the state issues a surplus of money, such surplus would naturally be stored away and serve as a reservoir. This was the typical viewpoint of the nominal

---

[21]Debate with Bao Shichen on *Paper Money and Coin*.

theory of money. He even equaled the store of value function of money with cultural relics and treasure. "Ten fine calligraphers shall be selected from across the entire country for writings on big denomination paper money, and five or six for intermediate denomination paper money, and copperplate etched aphorisms be inscribed on small denomination paper money. And paper money shall then be decorated into a hand scroll and encased in a gold container."[22] It was a pity that he confused the physical entity of value with token of value, money with paper money, and the boundary between paper money growing out of function as a means of circulation and cultural relics having historical artistic value. These statements were really unprecedented and inaccurate.

According to the measures specified hereinbefore, Wang Liu flatly denied any relation between inflation and commodity price rise, denied the slew of facts demonstrating that vicious inflation of paper money led to commodity price rise, claimed in a far-fetched manner that "if commodity price rises, it has nothing to do with paper money issuance,"[23] and treated history as though a doll in his hand, to be manipulated, glossed over and distorted to his favor, trying to confuse public opinion.

In conclusion, Wang Liu was the epitome of the nominal theory of money in the feudal society of China. He aired the main traditional doctrines of the nominal theory of money, and wantonly distorted and refuted any views other than those that agreed with his. A hint of his basic theory could be found in the state determinism of modern nominal theory of money; for instance, according to the modern nominal theory of money, German economist Georg Friedrich Knapp (1842–1926) stated that the so-called paper money was the optimal money and equated paper money with metal money, which was once considered a major finding. Knapp averred that "money is a product of the rule of law," which was exactly the same as the view of Wang Liu, the only difference being that Knapp approved neither unlimited paper money issuance nor entirely discarding precious metal standard (gold). He was the epitome of advocating the implementation of inflation policy by the ruling class in China's feudal society. Wang Liu preached the theory of paper money issuance far and

---

[22]*My Drafted Measures for Coin and Paper Money.*
[23]*On Coin and Paper Money Four.*

wide as "the inexhaustible source of wealth for the state." Even Kang Youwei, the bourgeois reformist, and Sun Yat-sen, the great forerunner of the democratic revolution, both had firm faith in it, and aspired to find a way to bring China out of financial straits therefrom.

4. Theory of metal money by the Xu brothers

Xu Mei (1797–1870), courtesy name Jinmen, style Xinmu, was born in Haining of Zhejiang. He passed the palace examination in 1833, and had served as the director of the Guizhou bureau under the ministry of revenue. He returned home on sick leave after three years of service, and then taught and wrote, opposing retrogression. In order to refute the *Humble Remarks on Money* by Wang Liu, he wrote *On Paper Money and Coin* and published it in 1846, which brought him popular approval. Chen Qitai remarked that it was "trustworthy and justified" and "not arbitrary." Cheng Wan noted that his itemized rebuttals of Wang Liu's *Humble Remarks on Money* were "straight to the point, bared the ins and outs as though observing under a magnifying glass. After a few years, implementation of paper money fell into stagnation, all was as predicted thereby." His works had been compiled into some collections on economics and money. In 1860, he taught in Dunshan Academy Tongzhou.

His elder brother Xu Lian (1787–1862), courtesy name Shuyan, style Shanlin, passed palace examination in the same term, and served as prefecture chief of Pingdu of Shandong, Xuzhou and Zhenjiang. He wrote a prologue for *On Paper Money and Coin*, appended with multiple annotations of some creative views.

4.1. "On Paper Money and Coin" by Xu Mei

Xu Mei's *On Paper Money and Coin* was the first monograph on monetary issues by a metal theorist in China. He criticized the arguments of the nominal theory of money held by Wang Liu in a comprehensive and systematic manner, and analyzed the various vicious consequences resulting from the paper money issuance proposed by Wang Liu. Although the theory of metal money came with inevitable limitations, it reflected the common interests and appeals of the merchant, small and intermediate landlords as well as the ordinary people in opposing inflation, reflected the wishes of the city dwellers in establishing a stable monetary system of silver standard, and criticized rulers of the various dynasties for plundering the people through paper money issuance inducing vicious inflation. He developed the theory of metal money in the feudal society of China to its zenith.

Initially, Xu Mei focused his criticism on the imperial power which mandatorily issued paper money, accusing the feudal state of interfering with monetary circulation which led to vicious inflation. He denounced the situation whereby paper money issuance had been employed as an important vehicle of the state in the extremely vicious exploitation of the people. He stated that the last emperors of the Song, Jin and Yuan Dynasties "were not very incompetent, however, faced with great consumptive expenses such as floods and droughts, military riots and uprisings, imperial clan sacrificial and festival events and unexpected events, fiscal revenues thereof were a little constrained. They were forced to resort to exorbitant measures on the people beyond the regular taxes and rents. While in a time of paper money circulation, in addition to exorbitant measures on the people, increasing paper money supply was the only means available. However if paper money supply is not increased, revenue would be insufficient to go around for state expenditure; whereas if paper money supply is increased, paper money would certainly be sufficient for use by the country, however such increase in excess of the amount required for circulation then would depreciate the paper money and the state is still left in want. The closing periods of Song, Jin and Yuan Dynasties all fell to this ill."[24] Xu Mei put forward the concept of "satisfying the use by the country while still inadequate for the use by the state"; the former referred to the requirement of paper money in circulation, that is, in today's terms what we mean by the connotation of money issued for economic purposes, while the latter referred to the need for paper money by the central government, that is, the connotation of money issued for fiscal purposes. The closing periods of the Song, Jin and Yuan Dynasties all incurred fiscal deficit due to natural calamities (floods and droughts), war and riots (military riots and uprisings), and unrestrained luxuries (imperial clan's

---

[24]Itemized discussion of *Paper Money Production Seven*.

sacrificial and festival events and unexpected events). Hence, extensive money issued for fiscal purposes became the optimal solution to plugging fiscal deficit. However, money issued for fiscal purposes would further lead to paper money depreciation and commodity price rise, and in the end the state fiscal need was still not met. Therefore, the implied meaning was that fiscal deficit and inflation would drive each other into a vicious cycle, and paper money circulation would entirely collapse in the end. This was the problem of paper money circulation. This analysis was straight to the point and more insightful and scientific than the accusation made by Qiu Jun that "support from the people was lost, national livelihood was wasted, which were sources of upheaval and demise."

Proceeding from the stance of city dwellers including private bank owners, merchants, and small and intermediate landlords, Xu Mei accused that paper money issue by the feudal state would not only harm the interests of the people but also drive private banks into the red. "The state takes silver from the people in the amount of hundreds of millions, and starts to transform it into paper, was not that a loss? And nowadays the private banks were not all run in the red. However after paper money issue, a slew of private banks incurred loss.

'When the people hear that paper money would be launched, they would scramble to withdraw their money for fear that the money note might turn into scrap of paper. Over a period of a few days, people from far and wide would gather and withdraw their money, bigger private banks might be able to tide over such situation, while the smaller ones would not be able to survive, what other result but loss could they face?'

'However, what drives the private banks into the red is paper money.'"[25] The government issued paper money to fleece the people and the merchant, force handicraftsmen and merchants into bankruptcy, reduce the people into destitution and the drive the economy into recession. "The implementation of paper money was forced through payments made to officials, soldiers and the functionaries and laborers, when they carry such paper money for purchase, a multitudes of merchants closed businesses."[26] The purpose of replacing money with paper was to trade in

---

[25]Itemized Exposition of the Benefit of *Paper Money* — Issue 5.
[26]Itemized Exposition of *Paper Money* — Issue 3.

the wealth of the entire country at little cost. Xu Lian held that "when private banks went out of business, they could still have something to count on, when the poverty-stricken held valueless paper money and could buy nothing therewith, the children and wife thereof grieved beyond endurance."[27] During inflation, the ordinary people were hurt the most, with the handicraftsmen and merchants coming next; this was literally satisfying the exclusive desire of the central government at the expense of the public interests of the multitudes. On the contrary, proceeding from the position of the state and the emperor, from the views "when the need of the emperor is satisfied the need of the people is satisfied" and "the first priority is to satisfy the need of the emperor," Wang Liu attempted to gain fame by fooling the world with statements like "issuing paper money would eliminate the loss of private banks." Xu Mei harshly denounced the absurd theory put forward and spread by Wang Liu's statements: "Regarding the absurd theory put forward and spread by Wang Liu that "the supreme ruler is invested with the economic right to everything, and the supreme ruler sells such to the ruled, then the dignity of the state is manifested," Xu Mei harshly denounced "exhaust the source of interests of the people and place such in the hand of the supreme ruler exclusively, what dignity is there in such arrangement![28] That is to say, in order to monopolize the source of economic interests, the central government would be unscrupulous and stop at nothing, let alone preserve the government's dignity! In response to Wang Liu's absurd theory of "the economic benefit is boundless and the emperor should hold the right to manipulate it," Xu Mei categorically criticized it, saying, "if the emperor holds the right, the people would suffer."[29] Targeting the wishful thinking of "the state may obtain nine times of profit with the issue of small denomination paper money; and in issuing big denomination paper money, a huge profit of nineteen times may be obtained," he hit the nail on the head, stating, "taking away nine times or nineteen times of silver from the people, and paying with paper the size of ten feet or one foot, the state indeed benefits therefrom, what about the loss the people sustain! Now that the people

---

[27] Itemized Exposition of the Benefit of *Paper Money* — Issue 5: Comment.
[28] Itemized Exposition of the Benefit of *Paper Money* — Issue 2.
[29] Itemized Exposition of *Paper Money* — Issue 18.

sustain a loss, paper money would definitely not work, then the nine times or nineteen times of profit would absolutely not be obtained."[30] When the failure of paper money circulation loomed ahead, what was the point of conjecturing how many times greater profit could be obtained? What benefit would it bring to the state? Targeting the childish measures that "if paper money is to be issued, rules and regulations thereof shall be promulgated to acquaint the people the benefit of paper money issuance, and an oath is taken before the god that the law of paper money shall never be changed," he righteously exposed, "Never change the law, easier said than done. The reforms in late Song, Jin and Yuan Dynasties were necessitated by the circumstances that paper money failed, not that they would love to. Failures compelled them to resort to reform in order to make it work. When such reforms failed again, they were compelled to make further reforms. The failures thereof were attributable to their harmfulness, not that they were harmful to the supreme rulers, but that they were harmful to the ordinary people, hence they all failed."[31] Monetary crisis caused by inflation compelled the repeated reforms of paper money law, with which billions in silver and the money of the people "turned to scraps of paper overnight"; private banks incurred huge losses and went bankrupt, markets were rendered into chaos, commodity prices shot up, silver prices rocketed, circulation got blocked, businesses closed and the people were pushed into an abyss of misery; where was the benefit of issuing paper money?

In opposing imperial power, Xu Mei was more aggressive than Wei Yuan. Wei Yuan only targeted his attack on the reform of paper money law by Cai Jing, denouncing that he "totally lost the real intent of *Jiaohui* (paper money)" and "setting aside no reserve and producing paper money without limit, which depreciated paper money to one min worth some ten qians, and he kept his mouth shut on the issue of setting aside special reserve."[32] However, Xu Mei directed his attack straight to the emperor; Wei Yuan pinned his hope on wise rulers, whereas Xu Mei did not have any hope of the government eradicating the monetary issue. Xu

---

[30] Itemized Exposition of *Paper Money* — Issue 6.

[31] Itemized Exposition of *Paper Money* — Issue 11.

[32] *Collected Works of Wei Yuan* — Article Three of Military Reserve, vol. 3.

Mei did not put forward any strategy on eliminating monetary crisis; his view was that "the circulation of silver around the country is already enough for the use thereby ... had there not been such silver outflow, it will work without fail for long."[33] He heaved a deep sigh, "Alas! Who conjectured up such an ill harming the people to this day, one cannot but grieve at the beginning of such silver outflow."[34] His friend Wei Yuan remarked, "someone said if paper money law does not work, then what law could be implemented? I said it has already been discussed in the works. There is something exhaustible by reform. When there is ill in a law, then the law must be reformed; however if the ill does not lie in the law, what reform could have been done on the law? This has been the issue both Xu Mei and I are deeply concerned about."[35] It reflected the consensus that some intellectuals from the landed class lost faith in the feudal society which had started to collapse, and ceased placing hope therein after the Sino-British Opium War. In their minds, if there was no outflow of silver, the monetary system of the Qing Dynasty could still "work effectively without ill thereafter"; however, their view that the outdated monetary system of the Qing Dynasty required no major overhaul was wrong.

With respect to monetary theory, Xu Mei was opposed to Wang Liu and represented the culmination of the theory of metal money in the feudal society of China. Although when he published *On Paper Money and Coin*, 6 years after the Sino-British Opium War and 3 years after Wang Liu's death, due to the lagging effect of thought, the issue of commodity money still centered on the understanding and theory level preceding the Sino-British Opium War, which basically fell into the category of rational understanding of traditional Chinese commodity money. Meanwhile, it represented the interests of the city dwellers with thought of some capitalistic leaning and implied defiance and attack on the imperial authority. Of course, Wang Liu had made an extensive effort to study the paper money history of China, but Xu Mei was not as well read in this field, so it was

---

[33] General Survey Seven.
[34] General Survey Eight.
[35] Chen Qitai, Epilogue to *On Paper Money and Coin*.

somewhat beyond his reach to criticize Wang Liu's distortion of history and only some of his criticism was quite appropriate.

4.2. Theory of metal money by Xu Mei

Xu Mei was convinced that the monetary position of silver was the inevitable outcome of historical developments; the state power could not affect it in the least, nor reverse the trend. He examined the history of silver as a monetary material and occupying the position of primary money, and came to understand that monetary material evolves from base metal to precious metal. Silver has a long history as a form of money; however, it was not as prevalent as it is today. The government and the people of the various dynasties had long been using silver; however, it was not employed as a means of payment for taxes. Silver as a form of money met the requirements of the expansion and development of commodity circulation, as it was of superior quality and high value, boasting unparalleled superiority to copper coin. Along with the expansion of silver production, it could satisfy the objective need for commodity circulation, which allowed it to approximate the objective circumstance and the law of social development. In Xu Mei's opinion, this was perfectly natural and beyond doubt. "When the quantity of silver increases, while copper coin is heavy and unfit for long distance travel, the circumstance makes it move to silver." Therefore, employing silver as money and silver assuming the role of primary money were two distinctly different things occurring in different stages of the history of money evolution, and silver assuming the role of primary money was a more recent matter: "the phenomenon of silver being collected as taxes started from the Ming Dynasty, and it gained popularity with the government and the people. It peaked in the Ming Dynasty instead of starting in the Ming Dynasty, nor did it start from Jin Dynasty."

Xu Mei further noted that "if silver is to be discarded from circulation, the only means lies in elimination of silver"; otherwise, "even if the government discarded it, it sticks with the people."[36]

---

[36] General Survey Six.

What a wonderful remark! What was implied thereby was that the trend must be followed, otherwise any effort to reverse the trend would surely be met with failure. This statement was categorically opposed to the view preached by Wang Liu. Xu was convinced that only silver was the primary money. Even if the central government promulgated discarding silver, the people would still use silver; the thing that played the role of money could only be silver. This trend could not be altered by any subjective will, as any design intending to discard silver would be doomed to failure, even if started by the emperor! This was the unswerving view of the theory of metal money, which was really extraordinary in the history of China.

Along with other metal money theorists, Xu considered money as a commodity. In *Itemized Exposition of the Benefit of Paper Money Fourteen* he noted, "The customs of the world hold that there are things superior to silver, foreign silver dollar. Though there are differences between silver and foreign silver dollar, they both fall under the category of silver."

There was further argument that if "there is an article worth a tael of silver, and there is a silver cup here which weighs a tael, the article is traded with the cup. Such practice could be equally applied to a situation at an expanded scale of ten, a hundred taels. Would people refuse to accept it for its vessel form? Or should it be accepted as money?"[37] In short, be it a silver bullion, silver coin or silver vessel, they may differ substantially in form, and while they are not mutually substitutable in function, but they all have a common natural property, and they all could be reduced to a certain amount of silver.

Xu further argued that the principle of exchange of equal values had to be implemented between silver and commodity in commodity exchange; the exchange value of money had to be the same as the commodity value, as exchange of unequal values was not allowed. For example, he wrote that a certain amount of silver must be exchanged with other commodity with equivalent amount of value; otherwise, the act of exchange would not be conducted. He described a universally known and time-honored law, that is, the principle of exchange of equal values.

---

[37]Itemized Exposition of *Paper Money* — Issue 9.

Then, what determines the value of gold and silver as well as all other commodities? Xu Mei inherited the view of Wei Yuan that "if there is more gold than soil, then the price of gold would be different," believed that "rarity makes an item expensive, plenty makes an item cheap." He specifically put forward "abundance brings down the price, scarcity brings up the price,"[38] which was a traditional view held by quantity theory of money in China. If such a view was employed in the explanation of the value represented by paper money, it would absolutely work; that is, "the ill of paper money lies not in its limitedness but exactly in the fact that there is no limit to paper money production while coins are limited."[39] However, the object he theorized had already exceed the scope of paper money; therefore, it was not theoretically tenable. The value of commodity, including the value of money commodity, is determined by the socially necessary time of labor, not by the quantity thereof in its natural form. Paper money could only be a representative of money, but it was by no means the money itself; these must not be confused.

Xu Lian explained that commodity price could not be swayed by the subjective will of people from the perspective of the objective nature of commodity value; he held that "if a million paper money is issued, then the price shall be held low by the people; whereas if a million gold or silver is sent out across the country, it will definitely not be slighted by the people. Therefore it could be seen that the value of an item is determined by its inherent property which could not be tampered by people."[40] He criticized the nominal theory of money while pointing out the difference of the determining factor between the value of metal money and paper money as well as the difference between their purchasing powers: "when other items are designated as money, there are always the issues of weight and alteration, with the exception of gold and silver." "Time elapses; however, the values of the two items remain constant across all ages.

A tiny amount is deemed inadequate, a million is not considered too much. When it comes to paper money, its price will drop if a million thereof is suddenly introduced, and will plummet when ten million is

---

[38] Itemized Exposition of *Paper Money* — Issue 10.
[39] Itemized Exposition of the Benefit of *Paper Money* — Issue 1.
[40] Itemized Discussion of *Paper Money* — Issue 7.

introduced."[41] He was right to affirm the stability of the value of gold and silver; this was one of the advantages of precious monetary materials. However, he absolutely affirmed the stability, overstating it; the statement "remaining constant across all ages" was equally unbelievable. Since the value of commodity money was no longer determined by its quantity, nor by its natural property, what determined it? Xu did not answer this question. In China, as money, silver had never evolved from money by weight to money of account. Nor had it been minted into standard copper coins, making the nominal value equal to the actual value thereof, and making it an entity of value with fixed form, weight and purity.

As for the fact that paper money issued by the various dynasties all failed in the end, the exposition made by Xu Mei in the earlier-cited *General Review One* had already implied the difference between the entity of value and the token of value, that is, silver as money by weight and paper money. Proceeding from the perspective of affirming the commodity nature of money, the Xu brothers totally negated paper money; they only recognized the reasonableness of the existence of draft and money note. They referred to the former as "substituting money with money" and the latter as "withdrawing money with paper," holding that one could redeem paper money, "making payment here and withdrawing money there"[42] and "a thousand gold will be drawn if the bearer of the note denominated a thousand gold so desires."[43] As for the redeemable paper money issued by the government, they recognized these in a conditional manner, such as "the *Feiqian* (draft in nature, not paper money) of the Tang Dynasty, modeled after the *Jiaozi* of Song Dynasty, which were all withdrawing money with a piece of paper, these were all good practice."[44] Because they all "had some conditions to conform to for their implementation, and were not paper, it was nothing like that money was employed to trade for the silver from the people and the paper money would retire from circulation."[45] Credit money issued by a private entity usually

---

[41]Itemized Exposition of the Benefit of *Paper Money* — Issue 1.
[42]General Survey One and Two.
[43]Itemized Discussion of *Paper Money* — Issue 3.
[44]General Survey Three.
[45]General Survey Four.

required capability of being redeemed, and then did not tend to depreciate. However, when it came to paper money issued by the government, so long as the capability of being redeemed was maintained, depreciation was likewise not an issue. The problem was that paper money issued by past dynasties collapsed due to inflation; this feature figured prominently in the monetary circulation in the Song, Jin and Yuan Dynasties, which facilitated the formation of the theory of metal money in China. Of course, paper money backed up by adequate issuance reserve would not depreciate; otherwise, paper money would be reduced to "useless paper." This could hardly hold water in theory, and the current situation of paper money circulation in various countries demonstrates its falsehood.

The focus of the debate between the Xus and Wang Liu was whether "paper could be employed to substitute money." The Xus proceeded from the position of the theory of metal money, holding that "the various categories of item are heavenly fixed, even silver could not substitute gold, how pointless to say that paper may substitute money. That is inconceivable."[46] In their mind, silver was silver and paper was paper; the two may never be confused. Comparing paper money and silver, there was a world of difference between the two. Therefore, people's love for silver and paper was also substantially different; they were two distinctively different items.

All commodity exchange, exchange between paper money and money, even the exchange between different metal moneys, had to be based on the entity of value. Different moneys could not substitute each other, let alone substitute money with paper money which was way too different. Some thought that paper would necessarily replace silver, and saw everything as a benefit, and some thought that paper may never replace silver and saw everything as a problem; these were all the product of deception and fatuity, and were "policies of swindling the people" employed by the government! Under the historical conditions of the times, the understanding of the Xu brothers was conducive to stabilizing the value of money, conducive to opposing the practices of plundering the people with paper money by the imperial government, and was of progressive social significance.

---

[46] Itemized Discussion of *Paper Money* — Issue 1.

The Xu brothers also negated paper money circulation by way of analyzing money as a store of value. Xu Lian demonstrated that paper money would not work by invoking the historical account of Lv Dongbin turning to Zhong Liyun for the art of turning stone into gold. Having learnt that the gold so turned would transform back into stone after three thousand years, Lv Dongbin remarked, "pitifully it would harm the one who bears the gold three thousand years later," and rejected it. Similarly, the purpose of those who preached the practice of replacing silver with paper money was to turn all silver held by the people into paper; it was an unwise act of malevolence. Regarding Wang Liu's proposal of replacing silver with paper money that "such practice would suddenly bring about profit of twenty percent, who would refuse replacing silver with paper money," Xu Mei refuted, "Nowadays a wealthy house with tens of thousands of taels of silver assumes taxes in kind converted to silver amounting to less than a hundred taels," "if such thousands of taels of silver is to be turned into paper money, who would like to replace silver with paper money?"[47] He criticized the arrangement of replacing silver with paper money saying that it transformed valuable social wealth into a pile of valueless paper. Hence, the proposal of issuing paper money by Wang Liu would not only be unable to attract people to trade silver for paper money and therefore stem silver outflow but would also further stimulate the tendency of silver hoarding among the people or further drive silver overseas.

Xu Mei also proceeded from the theory of metal money and analyzed the cause of silver appreciation and coin depreciation, pointing out that the cause did not lie in silver proper but in the situation of opium inflow and silver outflow. He correctly pointed out, "the use of silver expanded to an ever grand scale till the Ming Dynasty, and reached its peak around the time of the Qianlong Emperor and Jiaqing Emperor. Silver distributed and circulated around the country was already sufficient for use by the country, while payment for taxes and labor services was collected in copper coin, and the government would exchange such payment collected with silver and transfer silver to the government repositories, there was no such ill of the use of silver as pointed by Gu Yanwu. Had there not

---

[47] Itemized Exposition of *Paper Money* — Issue 4.

been such silver outflow, it will work without fail for long. And to date, half of silver accumulated over thousands of years in the country got leaked out through silver outflow, and the trend shows no sign of subsiding."[48] He further remarked, "silver outflow was beyond measure, amounting to hundreds of millions, while the quantity of copper coins remained unchanged, therefore a situation of silver appreciation and coin depreciation occurs." He distinguished between the two phenomena of "silver appreciation and coin depreciation" and "coin depreciation and silver appreciation," noting that the two differed in the form of expression: "if there is a surplus of coins in the repositories while the amount of silver remains unchanged, this is called coin depreciation and silver appreciation." That is, if the amount of coin increased while silver remained unchanged, then a situation of coin depreciation and silver appreciation would ensue. On the contrary, "if silver outflow was beyond measure, amounting to hundreds of millions, while the quantity of copper coins remained unchanged, therefore a situation of silver appreciation and coin depreciation occurs." That is, if silver in circulation decreased sharply, while the amount of copper coin remained unchanged, a situation of silver appreciation and coin depreciation would ensue, such a situation was caused by decreased amount of silver compared to copper coin. However, if the situation of coin depreciation and silver appreciation resulted from an increase in the amount of copper coin, such a difficult situation could be cured by reducing the amount of copper coin in circulation.

However, if a situation of silver appreciation and coin depreciation was caused by silver outflow, the normal conversion rate between silver and copper coin attained by reducing the amount of copper coin in circulation would soon be upset, and a new situation of silver appreciation and coin depreciation would come into existence.

Was the paper money issue plan proposed by Wang Liu feasible? It was equally infeasible because "if paper money is employed to replace silver, then not only would silver not be discarded but the paper money would be turned into an instrument for brutally treating the people." Hence, if the issue of copper coin circulation was to be solved, the plan

---

[48]General Survey Seven.

of discarding silver and issuing paper money would be equally infeasible without first solving the prevalent monetary issue. Silver outflow was like filling water into two vats; if one was filled to the brim and the other had a small amount of water, there was the possibility to even out the two, drawing water from the full one to fill the half-empty one. On the contrary, if the difference was that one was leaking and the other watertight, then evening out the two was impossible. This understanding was far superior to that of his predecessors, very insightful. However, it could hardly hold water theoretically to demonstrate the change of conversion rate between silver and copper coin from the perspective of supply and demand of silver and copper coin alone, because it is the factor of inherent amount of value of silver and copper coin which determines such change; the change in supply and demand relation would only work on the condition that their inherent amounts of value are established beforehand.

4.3. *Criticism on Wang Liu's monetary theory*

The Xu brothers employed the metal theory of money as a weapon to oppose the so-called benefits of issuing paper money, as advanced in *Humble Remarks on Money* by Wang Liu, and especially to criticize the twenty-two benefits enumerated therein which have been elaborated in the preceding section; a few key arguments are specifically introduced as follows.

The first argument was that money must be theoretically based on inherent value, and Xu Mei unfolded criticism on the argument that "the value of paper money is fixed, and merchants may not raise or lower it at will" based on the nominal theory of money as held by Wang Liu. Xu Mei wrote, "the value of paper money in previous dynasties was not necessarily unfixed, and merchants of those times were no different from today's merchants; however, there was never a blank period on the history of article price rise and paper money depreciation; what else could these be but rise and drop of paper money value?" He analyzed, in a specific and in-depth manner, the inconsistency and the many ridiculous mistakes of arbitrarily fixing the "nominal price" and "floating price" of the face value of paper money and the preferential measures thereof by the government.

Under such an arrangement, a *guan* of paper money could only be traded for nine hundred *wen* of copper coins from the government; this had already "discounted paper money by one hundred *wen*"; when paper money was paid to the government, an additional hundred *wen* was required per *guan*, that is, "up-floating a hundred *wen*." The government had already raised or lowered the price of paper money before merchants could do anything about it.

He further noted, "if a million produced is a million got, ten million produced ten million got, then all taxes of the country could be rid of, why could this not be done?"[49] In the comment, Xu Lian also remarked specifically that the state had the power to fix the face value of paper money; however, it was powerless in fixing the actual value in circulation represented by paper money. "Nowadays a tael of silver is employed simply as a tael of silver and a thousand qian is simply as a thousand when the merchant employs such. When silver and coin are exchanged, price differences are immediately seen; whereas a *guan* of paper money is only a *guan* of paper money, how can it be ordered to be taken as a thousand qian by the merchant?"[50]

Regarding the confusing proposal advanced by Wang Liu that if all state taxes were to be collected in paper money and it was not difficult for the people to trade silver for paper money, then the people would be aware that paper money could be the substitution for silver, and they would value paper money more and it would not be difficult to have the people trade silver for paper money, Xu Mei refuted this, saying that other than payments made to the government in paper money, all paper money was valueless paper: "Suppose at the beginning of *Jiaohui* issue, an abundance of valueless paper is produced to trade the coin of the people, and it is decreed that thirty or forty percent of such paper is to be paid to the government as taxes; then the people would know that such paper other than tax payment is valueless paper, who would then be willing to trade for such valueless paper with ready coin?"[51] This rebuttal was very powerful but was slightly lopsided. The view that irredeemable paper money is all

---

[49]Itemized Exposition of the Benefit of *Paper Money* — Issue 8.
[50]Itemized Exposition of the Benefit of *Paper Money* — Issue 10: Comments.
[51]General Survey Two.

valueless paper, refuting the reasonableness of irredeemable paper money in theory, showed the limitation of his argument.

Wang Liu denied that excessive issue of paper money would lead to rocketing commodity price and resorted to sophistry: "nonsensical talks that paper money issue would necessarily lead to commodity price rocketing are due to ignorance that rocketing commodity price has nothing to do with paper money issue." Xu Mei refuted, "the fault of the statement of paper money issue leading to commodity price rise lies in the poor demonstration of the theorist. When a pie is sold at ten thousand *guan* old paper money, it is not that the pie is expensive, but that the old paper money is cheap. In the tumults of Dong Zhuo, Shi Jilong, it was indeed the case that corn price shot up, not that the price of coin and gold dropped."[52] He pointed out that Wang Liu blurred the boundary between paper money and metal money, which deserved recognition. However, Xu Mei confused the boundary between coin and metal money; coin could be either of full value or not full value, and coin may evolve to paper money, that is, transformation from an entity of value to a token of value, which was determined by the functional feature of money as a means of circulation. In this respect, Xu Mei's understanding was one-sided, which indicated his limitation.

Wang Liu believed that paper money was wealth: "when all state taxes are collected in paper money, then the surcharge of minting cost would be eliminated." Xu Mei refuted, "if paper money is decreed as coin, it would only rid of the minting cost, and if a million produced is a million got, ten million produced is ten million got, then all taxes of the country could be rid of, why this could not be done!"[53] Of course this was impossible as it was an unrestrained additional tax imposed on the people, and was another chain of economic exploitation yoked on the people. This was a criticism straight to the point on the nominal theory of money, laying bare its defects.

The second argument was a rebuttal of various arguments put forward by Wang Liu in defense of unlimited paper money issue. With respect to the ridiculous statement of Wang Liu that "all silver held by the people is

---

[52]Miscellany Three.
[53]Itemized Exposition of the Benefit of *Paper Money* — Issue 8.

the basis for state issue of paper money, why should the state set aside silver reserve in advance," he hit the bull's-eye in remarking that it was a pretext under which the central government plundered silver held by the people in the name of issuing paper money: "the people have hundreds of millions of taels of silver, and the state produces paper money to trade for it; it is setting paper money as the basis on which silver is traded; where does it set silver as the basis for issuing paper money? Even the Song Dynasty could not have traded for the coin of the people with Jiaozi not based on coin, how can the present government trade for the silver of the people with paper money not based on silver?"[54] The mask of Wang Liu that all silver held by the people was the basis whereon the state issues paper money was torn down by Xu Mei, and Xu Mei was convinced that since such a fraudulent artifice had not worked in former times, it would be absolutely impossible for it to work in his times! With respect to the promotion effort of Wang Liu that "if all state taxes are collected in paper money, why would the people refuse to trade silver for paper money," Xu Mei exposed the nature of his employing state taxes as an instrument for plunder and deception. Collecting taxes in paper money was no different from showing the people that paper money could circulate, luring the people to trade paper money with silver and familiarizing them with paper money; hence, "nowadays the proponent of issuing paper money is attempting to trade all the silver of the entire country with valueless paper money."[55]

With regard to Wang Liu's view that wealthy houses would unearth their hoarded silver and exchange for paper money "once they hear the news of reform" and therefore the situation of stagnant currency as well as the pernicious practice of hoarding silver would be reformed, Xu Lian pointed out that this was preposterous talk, and the people would not only refuse to exchange but would also bury silver at hand which they had not planned to stash away deep in the ground. People were concerned that "if they deposit silver in private banks they would worry about their silver being confiscated and getting paper money in return; if they buy goods with it, then they would worry about officials coercively buying goods

---

[54] Miscellany One.
[55] General Survey Two.

with paper money."[56] Hence, neither depositing it in private banks nor employing it in business would be as safe as stashing it away underground. On the condition of inflation, it was a universal practice to "stash away the stable and reject the unstable." However, if this was applied too mechanically, then it would be inevitably liable to one-sidedness. However, under the then historical condition, the important social significance could not be denied.

The third argument was a rebuttal to the paper money issuing technology proposed by Wang Liu. Carrying an idea divorced from reality, Wang Liu devised a monetary system reform program out of his subjective imagination which was contradictory to the actual situation of monetary circulation and could not be implemented. For instance, he claimed that the "Xiaozong Emperor of the Song Dynasty traded gold and silk for paper money" and "paper money was treated as more valuable than gold"; he proposed to store paper money in cases, with gold being employed for case-making by the government repositories and wealthy houses, and stone for poor families, so that fire would not be able to harm it. Xu Mei refuted the proposal as ridiculous, childish, and preposterous delirium which perverted reality. When paper money did not work, people traded it with gold and silk to make it work; as we see it, this indicated that gold was more valuable than paper money. Never had there been such a strange phenomenon of paper money being more valuable than gold.

If paper money was more valuable than gold, why would people hold gold and silk rather than paper money, and what was the point of all this preaching, aside from being ridiculous? Besides, one-thousand-*guan* grand paper money measures twenty or thirty feet long, a handful when folded, and the case measures longer than the folded paper money, around 1.8 cm thick; the production cost for the case would amount to thirty or forty tael of gold. Converted to the gold price of the time, it was worth a thousand guan. Hence, "a case worth a thousand guan holds paper money of a thousand guan. If the paper money could be used, it could be said that the case and the paper money are of equal price. However if the paper

---

[56]Itemized Exposition of the Benefit of *Paper Money* — Issue 15.

money could not be used, it could be said that scrap paper money is stored in gold."[57]

What a monstrous absurdity it was! Wang Liu further engaged in meaningless talk: "engaging good calligraphers for the production of big denomination paper money, the handwriting thereof could be verified, the names of supervising ministers shall be affixed thereon, and counterfeiters may never imitate characters from so many hands." Xu Mei equally exposed this lie, pointing out that, if not a great connoisseur, the genuine and the imitation of the works of great calligraphers were often indistinguishable in the eyes of the common people. Refusing to leave the matter at that, Xu Lian further broke down the details of the claim: even with great industry, it would hardly be possible for one to finish writing three thousand characters a day, amounting to about one million characters a year; with combined effort of thirty persons for a year-long toil, the output of paper money would only be about ten million *guan*, while the need for paper money would easily exceed ten million *guan*. Therefore, "it is already difficult for supervising ministers to stay in post, still more difficult to write their names thereon."[58] Propagation of such impossible things was nothing but gaining notoriety by deceptive means. Wang Liu also believed in "installing paper money verifiers everywhere" to curb the ill of counterfeit money. Xu Mei stated that it was nothing but pointless talk because if you install one person then one person is installed, install ten persons and ten persons are installed, it would by necessity be impossible to install persons everywhere; and a person installed in one place could supervise one place only, though it is claimed that such persons may be installed everywhere, it is actually a mission impossible. These ideas were overstatements and irresponsible.

As for a rebuttal to the separate issuance of paper money in the various provinces as proposed by Wang Liu, Xu Mei further noted that issuing paper money separately in the various provinces would make it necessary to trade paper money with paper money within the different provinces, and then such trade centers would need to be set up in metropolises and thoroughfares. This would hamper businessmen's travels greatly as they

---

[57] Itemized Exposition of *Paper Money* — Issue 12.
[58] Itemized Discussion of *Paper Money* — Issue 4.

would neither be able to take other routes or detours, nor be able to take a shortcut; especially if they are held by rough weather or if they have an urgent need for paper money to be exchanged and there is a great distance to the government bureau, how should they deal with such situations? Many inconveniences would be caused thereby.

Xu Lian analyzed the defects from the perspective of the government, believing that setting up one government bureau at a metropolis or thoroughfare would necessarily lead to "terrible plight."

Take Jiangsu for instance. Merchants visiting the region would number thousands, and if all required paper money verification and exchange, the burden would destroy the government bureau. "Whereas the appetite of pertinent supervisors is more appalling, nobody can get away without serious loss induced thereby."[59] Inconvenience to exchange, in addition to the rogue style of the government bureau, and the extortion and exploitation from the exchange process would harm the smooth operation of business activities.

In conclusion, the metal theory of money held by the Xu brothers was somewhat one-sided in their understanding, and theoretically not scientific and complete enough. However, their ideas were socially progressive in criticizing the nominal theory of money of Wang Liu, especially in exposing Wang Liu for trying to justify and create a theoretical basis for the ruler to engage in unrestrained plunder of the wealth of the people, which would lead to commodity price rise, money depreciating, market depression and difficulty in the livelihood of the people. The Xu brothers stood for the interests of the city residents, and this theory was favorable to the development of commodity monetary economy, acclimated to the requirements of the capitalist elements under development, reflected the interests and demand of the great multitudes of the working class, made it a weapon of thought against the ruling class and inflation policy in theories of traditional culture in China. With respect to traditional monetary and financial theory, the Xu brothers were the last and most brilliant monetary theorists in modern China.

---

[59] Itemized Exposition of *Paper Money* — Issue 8.

5. Theory of "maneuvering the intangible by mobilizing the tangible" of Wang Maoyin

Wang Maoyin (1798–1865), courtesy name Chunnian and Zihuai, was born in Xixian county of Anhui. He was the most brilliant representative figure in the final stage of traditional monetary theory in China, and the only Chinese theorist mentioned in full name by Marx in *Das Kapital*. He drew the attention of Chinese scholars due to the annotation attached in Marx's *Das Kapital*, and his monetary theory loomed on the horizon of research. He passed the imperial examinations in 1832 during the reign of the Daoguang Emperor, serving under three emperors, namely the Daoguang, Xianfeng and Tongzhi Emperors, in posts including supervisor, assistant department director in the ministry of revenue and deputy minister of the ministry of revenue. His memorials after 1851 were compiled into *Memorials of Wang Shilang*, and annotated as *Collection of Wang Maoyin* in print.

Before assuming a government position in the tenth year of the Daoguang Emperor's reign, he took over his father's business, and spent one year managing the Luhe Sensheng Tea House, acquainting himself with commerce, related financial institutions and business activities related thereto. While safeguarding the supreme rights and interests of the rulers, he also tried to keep the interests of the merchant and the people from harm; in opposing inflationary policies, he proposed to issue redeemable paper money, even disregarding any loss to his personal career; as a key official in charge of government finance and money, he maintained his integrity and self-discipline. He was of a temperate disposition, with few hobbies and desires. He stayed in the capital for thirty years during his service in the government, and usually stayed alone in his mansion. He practiced simplicity and economy, lived a serene life after stepping down from office, entertained himself with reading and was widely respected by the people of that time.

5.1. *On monetary system reform*

After the movement of the Taiping Heavenly Kingdom broke out from 1851 to 1864, the military expenses of the Qing Dynasty surged, fiscal revenue plummeted, sources of monetary material (copper and lead) were obstructed, government treasury depleted, official emoluments suspended and the government finance was in a dire situation. In order to redress the fiscal crisis, on September 19th, 1851, in the post of the Shaanxi supervisory censor, Wang Maoyin submitted the *Memorial of Itemized Proposal on Monetary Rules*,[60] advocating the issuance of silk-woven Da Qing Tong Xing Paper Money, denominated in silver tael, in two face values of 50 taels and 10 taels, with a maximum quota of 10 million taels of treasury standard silver. 100,000 taels per year was to be issued at the beginning; "if it is accepted in circulation," then it was to be redoubled every year in an ascending manner. Issuers should be financially solid silver stores in the various localities, and salt stores or pawn shops were to be entrusted with issuance business where there were no silver stores in a place. After silver stores collected paper money, they were required to pay silver to the government according to the face value thereof; "they are allowed to have a small margin therefrom," for each 50 taels of treasury standard silver (50 taels of Beijing treasury standard were converted to 1,862 *fen*), they were allowed to pay in 50 taels of municipal standard silver (50 taels of Beijing municipal standard were converted to 1,780 *fen*; 74 *fen* may be withheld for every 50 taels of silver). Such paper money could be put to use after silver stores had affixed their logos and seals. After issuance, silver stores were to be responsible for redemption and assumed risks related thereto. That is, it did not specify the responsibility of the state, but mandatorily transferred the obligation for redemption to private financial institutions, silver stores; though there was a stipulation specifying the amount of issuance, as the paper money issuing entity was the state which assumed no responsibility while the redemption entity was the private silver store, the arrangement was practically saying that the state may issue paper money without being limited by the quota, and would not "assume responsibility" over issue of paper money, while those who "assumed responsibility" were private silver stores which had no power in the arrangement. That is to say, the state transferred the

---

[60]*Memorials of Wang Maoyin*, vol. 1. No more citations shall be provided for further quotes from this book hereinbelow.

fiscal crisis to silver stores and further transferred it to the people through issuing paper money. Such paper money was redeemable in name; however, as the government assumed no responsibility of redemption, it was actually irredeemable paper money. The government fixed several secret marks on the paper money to prevent forgery. Donations made by persons who purchased government positions in the capital were allowed to be paid half in paper money and half in silver. Taxes in the form of money and corn were allowed to be paid half in paper money and half in silver to the repositories. This was Wang Maoyin's first monetary system reform plan, and he was also the first to propose issuing paper money during in the Xianfeng reign; though his plan was rejected at the ministerial deliberation, he became a prominent figure of the time because of it.

As early as during the reign of the Jiaqing emperor, some people (scholar-in-waiting Cai Zhiding) proposed to issue paper money, and more raised the proposal in the reign of the Daoguang Emperor (imperial censor Li Enqing and others); however, none was adopted by the central government. In 1852, the Qing government's finances were on the verge of collapse, as additional fiscal expenditure, military expenses and water conservancy expenses "amounted to twenty strong million taels,"[61] taking up two thirds of fixed annual expenditure. The rampant development of Taiping troops posed tremendous threat to the Qing Dynasty. Faced with such extreme urgency, the Qing Dynasty had no option but to take the desperate move and adopt the plan proposed by Hua Shana (1806–1859) of minting and issuing big denomination coins. Wang Maoyin was promoted to the position of deputy minister of the ministry of revenue and director in charge of monetary law the following year; he became one of the powerful officials exercising the power over finance and monetary law in the Qing government.

On February 27, 1853, the Qing government issued silver notes (official note) based on silver tael, minted big denomination coins worth 10 and 50 *wen* in May and August, respectively, minted big denomination coins worth 100, 500 and 1,000 *wen* on November 20, and the following

---

[61]*History of Qing Dynasty — Economy Five.*

year (1854) minted big denomination coins worth 10 *wen* in March, and minted lead coin in June.

These moves resulted exclusively from proposals of Hua Shana and the ministry of revenue; not only did they have nothing to do with Wang Maoyin but they were also fiercely opposed by him. Though his paper money issuance proposal was exactly what the Qing government hoped for, he adamantly opposed issuing depreciated big denomination coin and insisted on issuing redeemable paper money. After big denomination coins worth 10 and 50 *wen* were issued, the powerful minister further petitioned for minting big denomination coin worth 100, 500 and 1,000 *wen*. On November 21, Wang Maoyin submitted *Memorial on Issuing Big Denomination Paper Money*, energetically objecting to the arrangements. However, his memorial was ignored by the government. On January 12, 1854, he submitted *Memorial of Further Deliberation on Increased Minting Big Denomination Coin*, and laid out in plain language the three difficulties and two ills of big denomination coin in incurring loss to the state and harming the people. Previously, in order to check the momentum of expanding paper money issuance, stem inflation which had already been underway and control paper money depreciation, he submitted *Memorial of Itemized Ministerial Deliberation on the Difficulty of Silver Note and Silver Store and Petition for Further Deliberation of the Previous Memorial on Monetary Law* on January 8, 1853; he also submitted *Memorial of Petition for Planning Commerce to Pacify the People* on March 25, and he submitted *Memorial of Further Deliberation of Monetary Law* on March 5, 1854. In trying to stop the serious inflation which had already been underway,[62] he was acutely aware of the pressing circumstances of the time: "financial resources are depleted, the various needs and expenses could not be satisfied, issuing paper money is an

---

[62] According to the textual investigation reported in the article *Wang Maoyin and the Monetary System Reform under the Xianfeng Reign* conducted by Wu Han, within two years of the promulgation of the paper money law, the purchasing power of paper money dwindled, while coin price rose; a tael of silver or Baochao paper money notes was worth about 400 or 500 standard copper coins. Five years later, the prevailing price in the capital for a tael of silver notes was only 200 *wen*, while physical silver was worth more than 6,000 *wen*, and 20 taels of silver notes converted to one tael of physical silver; copper coin note also plummeted to the low of every 1,000 *qian* worth 100-odd *wen*.

inevitable means." However, Wang held fast to his belief, "the value of monetary law lies in progressiveness and fidelity in execution." "People naturally understand that it would be inappropriate to issue too much paper money over a short period." Having summarized the merits and demerits of issuing paper money in the various dynasties, he concluded that "they were all tangible for maneuvering," "till the Ming Dynasty, the intangible was applied to the people while the tangible collected to the government, hence the monetary law failed." At the time, "when previous arrangements failed, debaters focused their efforts exclusively in devising methods to collect the tangible from the people ... however there are more issues than recall in the capital, there is release without recall in the armies, and recall without release in the provinces, prefectures and counties."

When recall and release were imbalanced, circulation was obstructed; such circumstances were the natural outcome. Only in smooth turnover and circulation could paper money law operate without a hitch. Therefore, Wang Maoyin proposed, "no scheme works without the office of merchants therein, no scheme will ever work without workable method and obtainable profit offered to the merchant."

The plan would not work without counting on the merchant, and it still would not work without a proper method worked out; even if merchants were counted on, there had to be an appropriate method in the execution of the plan. Anything detached from such a requisite would still not avail. Wang Maoyin also energetically proposed the following: "paper money could be used to withdraw copper coins," "silver note can be used to withdraw silver," "paper money could be used to withdraw silver at the various stores," "proportional combination of paper money is allowed in payment for inbound and outbound articles at pawn shops." He also planned to reform irredeemable paper money to redeemable paper money. This was his second monetary system reform plan.

The two monetary system reform plans both proceeded from the long-term fundamental interests of the state for the purpose of relieving the Qing Government from the financial crisis arising from the Taiping Heavenly Kingdom movement, restoring and perfecting normal social and economic order, and establishing a relatively normal and sound financial order. He was opposed to inflationary policy, proposed to strictly control the overall quantity of paper money being issued, and sought to avoid phenomena including paper money depreciation, commodity price rise, market chaos, industry and commerce stagnation and economic recession.

However, the social and economic foundations of the government at the time were already in a decadent and dilapidated state; under the heavy blow of the peasant uprisings, the edifice of feudal society teetered on the edge of collapse. His hope of "first to not burden the people and then to benefit the state, then legislation may be deliberated" was nothing but wishful thinking detached from reality. To the Qing Dynasty which was suffering from desperate financial straits, Wang Maoyin's issue principle became an obstacle. When the central government rejected the proposal of Wang Maoyin and adopted and implemented the plan of Hua Shana and the ministry of revenue, he complained and showed his displeasure, claiming that "the current government note, Baochao paper money" were not what "he had originally drafted," and that he himself "incurred hatred and complaint," was "considered vicious," and all vicious consequences were "imputed to me," "I should be blamed for all." "I petition the emperor to place me under pertinent ministry for strict investigation of my fault to appease the entire country and soothe the sentiment of the people so that rampant gossip may abate slightly. Even if I am removed from office or relegated, I dare not harbor the slightest grudge." Though it seemed like he stubbornly adhered to his idea on paper money issue and minting big denomination coin out of consideration for the central government, it obviously appeared as if he were shifting responsibilities. What made him especially intolerable was that he pointed his complaint to his direct superior. Such a complaint irritated the Xianfeng Emperor who rebutted him as "being directed by merchants and conducting matter detrimental to the state and benefiting merchants," stating, "having examined your intent, it was really attempting to fail the paper money."[63] Princes and ministers followed suit in condemning him. In *Das Kapital*, vol. 1, p. 146, Marx alluded to this matter in one of the footnotes: "The mandarin Wan-mao-in, the Chinese Chancellor of the Exchequer, took it into his head one day to lay before the Son of Heaven a proposal that secretly aimed at converting the *assignats* of the empire into convertible bank-notes. The assignats

---

[63]*Materials of Modern Chinese Monetary History*, vol. 1, Book 2, pp. 393–395.

Committee, in its report of April, 1854, gave him a severe snubbing. Whether he also received the traditional drubbing with bamboos is not stated." Actually, it was quite like a punishment that Wang Maoyin was transferred from the ministry of revenue, which held real power over finance and monetary policy making, to the ministry of war, which existed in name only.

5.2. On the tangible and the intangible

(1) Theory of "mobilizing the tangible to maneuvering the intangible"

As the last follower of the theory of the intangible and the tangible in China, Wang Maoyin inherited the theory of "silver being the tangible and paper money the intangible," and believed that there remained fundamental differences between metal money (silver) and paper money. He presented a new exposition of the theory of the tangible and the intangible by incorporating the actual situation in the reign of the Xianfeng Emperor, and put forward a fresh understanding. Compared to traditional points of view, his theory reflected features of the times where merchant capital and traditional financial strength played an increasingly important role.

Unlike the average metal theorists of money in the past and of his time who contrasted the intangible and the tangible, paper money and metal money, and proceeded therefrom to negate paper money simplistically, especially negating the irredeemable paper money therein, Wang Maoyin followed the relation and change between the intangible and the tangible to conduct his analysis and explained that paper money may be circulated in complementarity to metal money; however, it was not to be issued excessively and redemption thereof must be conducted. Proceeded therefrom, he proposed a standard based on silver tael, a monetary system where silver tael and paper money as "the tangible and the intangible run parallel," emphasizing the monetary law where "paper money is employed to complement silver, instead of silver employed to complement paper money."

Hence, the function of paper money was only to complement metal money, instead of replacing metal money. He raised the theory of "maneuvering the intangible by mobilizing the tangible." On the one hand, he demonstrated paper money circulation by the statement, "employing several tangibles to complement one intangible"; on the other hand, he demonstrated the difference between paper money and big denomination coin by the statement, "designating tangibility to the intangible." The theory of "maneuvering the intangible by mobilizing the tangible" was the foundation of Wang Maoyin's monetary theory, the theoretical weapon for his monetary system reform and a new development in the theory of the tangible and the intangible in the field of China's monetary circulation.

Wang Maoyin proposed a theory of "employing several tangibles to complement one intangible." In *Memorial of Itemized Proposal on Monetary Rules*, his first monetary system reform plan, he proposed the following: "model after the practice implemented at the beginning of the empire, initially a hundred thousand tael should be produced every year, that is, five thousand pieces of ten tael note and a thousand pieces of fifty tael note. Having tried the practice for one or two years, if such is found workable, then the amount may be redoubled annually; if such is still found workable, then further redouble it annually. The maximum amount of paper money shall be kept under the limit of ten million taels. Revenue and expenditure of the state are only a few scores of million taels, when several tangibles are employed to complement one intangible, and such arrangements are introduced gradually, and a limit imposed thereon, there will be no such ill as stagnation when paper money is employed to complement silver instead of silver complementing paper money." Since paper money was intangible and metal money tangible, it would not pose any problem for the arrangement of paper money circulation complementing metal money. Paper money was an institution out of necessity; it could not replace the dominant position of metal money in circulation. "Financial resources are depleted, the various needs and expenses could not be satisfied, issuing paper money is but an inevitable means." The financial revenue and expenditure of the Qing Dynasty were no more than a few scores of millions of taels (about 40 million taels). It would have been impractical to immediately implement the arrangement of "employing several tangibles to complement one intangible," and paper money issuance had to balance the issue of both avoiding disturbing the dominant position of silver in circulation and maintaining the stability of paper money circulation; hence, the key was that "the value of monetary law lies in progressiveness and fidelity in execution as well as placing limit thereon." Paper money would be "firm when undersupplied and sluggish when oversupplied," and "too much paper money would surely lead to stagnation and commodity price rise." A strict limit had to be set for paper money issue: "when there is no limit set for paper money issue, it seems like a great benefit to produce without limit; however, few know that the more paper money is issued, the less it is valued." Therefore, the key lay in strictly restricting the amount of paper money issue, keeping the maximum issue amount under one fourth of the fiscal revenue, that is, under 10 million taels. In the structure of financial revenue and expenditure, metal money had to constitute a majority and paper money a minority. In monetary circulation, silver played not only the monetary function but also had to be circulated concurrently with paper money at an amount several times that of paper money.

The first reform plan adequately demonstrated Wang Maoyin's theoretical viewpoints as a metal theorist of money. He failed to correctly interpret the relation between paper money and metal money and failed to correctly understand that paper money performed the circulation function in place of money; so long as the amount of paper money circulation did not exceed the actual need of commodity circulation for money, it may completely substitute metal money circulation and induce no paper money depreciation. Of course, the arrangement of "employing several tangibles to complement one intangible" proposed by Wang Maoyin could have functioned as a restrictive and preventive measure against excessive issue of paper money by the Qing government, and it could also have checked the amount of paper money to be issued, stabilizing currency circulation and the financial market. These were doubtlessly in line with the long-term fundamental interests of the state; however, it hindered the Qing Government which was bogged down in dire fiscal straits from trying to relieve itself therefrom, as well as from engaging in unscrupulous plundering of the people, including industry and commerce. Hence, his proposal held up the original intent of the Qing Government in issuing paper money. The purpose of paper money issue, "first to not burden the people and then to benefit the state, then legislation may be deliberated," was nothing but an empty statement. Under the financial plight at the time, if the people and the merchants were to benefit, it would certainly be detrimental to the interests of the ruling group.

The theory of "employing several tangibles to complement one intangible" was untenable and therefore wrong. The mistake lay in the so-called "several tangibles," which referred to the quotas of annual fiscal revenue and expenditures of the state instead of the actual needs for currency circulation of commodity circulation. Under the circumstance of metal money circulation, maintaining the stability of the currency circulation of paper money depended on whether the amount of paper money in circulation exceeded the amount of metal money necessary for circulation; if the amount was exceeded, "even if we ignore the risk of bankrupting creditability, it after all only stands for the amount of gold determined by the inherent law of commodities, that is, the amount of gold it is capable of representing."[64] Financial revenue and expenditure were not the objective conditions for determining the necessary amount of currency circulation for a contemporary period.

Wang Maoyin not only proposed "employing several tangibles to complement one intangible" but also required that paper money be made redeemable. Proposing the determination of a maximum quota on paper money issue in theory was progress over the foundational law of the paper money system of the Song, Yuan and Ming Dynasties. However, he mobilized the tangible to complement the intangible, and held that there was not necessarily a full reserve set aside therefor; he noted, "when silver can be readily withdrawn everywhere, then it can be used everywhere, hence no silver withdrawal is necessary." "When the silver can be withdrawn, the people will not scramble for it, when had private drafts of private banks been entirely withdrawn?" Moreover, the one that assumed redemption responsibility was not the government but the private silver stores and money shops which dealt paper money issue on behalf of the government. "The various taxes and rents are already silver ... when silver can be readily withdrawn everywhere, then it can be used everywhere, hence no silver withdrawal is necessary." The local financial revenue was established as the redemption reserve for paper money, and paper money was further retrieved via payment for government position

---

[64]*Karl Marx and Frederick Engels*, vol. 23, p. 147.

purchase and silver stores responsible for making and receiving taxes and rents; the state assumed no direct responsibility for redemption, only assumed responsibility for a final symbolic guarantee for paper money issue. In phenomenological terms, it seemed to be plausible to call it redeemable paper money; however, in reality, it was redeemable paper money issued by the state and redemption responsibility was mandatorily imposed on private silver stores. In devising the plan, Wang Maoyin probably proceeded from two considerations, one of which was that wealth management "tolerated no delay. The military affair in west Guangdong had yet to abate, and water conservancy was in great urgent need of expenses. However the state revenue was fixed; how could it provide such extraordinary expenses?" The optimal way to relieve the urgent need of the state was issuing paper money. By virtue of its characteristics, "paper money circulation is imposed from the top, originally it was not enforced upon the people. However, with the advantages of portability for distant travel, free from the disadvantages of purity and weight issues, it is superior to gold and silver, and brings convenience to the people." Wang Maoyin only affirmed one aspect and concealed the other aspect; that is, if paper money did not depreciate, it would naturally be more convenient to the people than gold and silver. However, once it depreciated, it would not be as convenient to the people as gold and silver. His aim was to "increase the benefit of paper money." He drew lessons from the history of paper money issue, and was well aware that it was impossible to issue paper money without defect and that paper money could work only if the defects were removed: "the first aim is to not burden the people and then to benefit the state, then legislation may be deliberated." He established the foregoing as the main purpose of paper money issue, or set it as the starting point and destination for issuing paper money. He emphasized that paper money should neither "hamper the people" nor "hold the people in doubt," and "if paper money gets stagnant, commodity price would necessarily rise." However, the original purpose of issuing paper money by the Qing government was to make up for the fiscal deficit and get out of financial straits; such a purpose was only attainable by implementing inflationary policy. How could it set up an issuance reserve fund and establish a redemption system? This was nothing but nonsensical talk and there was not the least plausible ground therefor. Entangled in this contradiction, he attempted to guarantee redemption by employing mandatory stipulation of state power; that is, silver stores had to assume the responsibilities for promoting paper money, guaranteeing redemption of paper money and maintaining the currency value thereof. If the amount of paper money issue was kept within an appropriate limit, there was possibility for his conception to be realized; however, if paper money issue was out of control, and substantially exceeded the need of money in circulation, there would be bank run, and it would be definitely impossible for silver stores to maintain redemption on their own and perform the responsibility of stabilizing the finance. If so, his conception would collapse. The motivation of paper money issue and follow-up development thereof both determined that the outcome for silver stores' redemption arrangement could only be the latter instead of the former. Therefore, it was nothing but a doomed cause. Hence, Wang's theory of "maneuvering the intangible by mobilizing the tangible" was a justification for a new means of extra-economic plunder by the country through mandatory power, coercing others to make up for the depletion of the state financial strength with finances of their own. Such paper money, from the perspective of the state, was paper money rather than a coupon, "a receipt of collecting tributaries from all laborers" (Lenin), and a receipt for withdrawing silver from proxy silver stores. Therefore, the conception and nature of Wang's paper money were actually at cross-purposes.

On March 5, 1854, inflation deteriorated by the day, as "paper money was first issued in last December, and now the total amount has exceeded over a million and hundreds of thousands. Hence, soldiers who collected their payments in paper money found it difficult to buy any commodity therewith; and merchants could not purchase any stock with said paper money. Such a situation brought about much inconvenience and burden to the people." The original proposal of Wang that paper money shall comprise only a small fraction of the fiscal revenue had been shattered to pieces by the harsh reality. He said, "Though the current government notes, paper money, did not originate with the plan worked out by me, paper money issue actually started with me." If the principle of "maneuvering the intangible by mobilizing the tangible" had been further adhered to, the purpose of issuing paper money would have been lost. In *Memorial*

Revisiting Paper Money Law,[65] he amended this principle out of his own accord, and advanced the principles of "maneuvering the paper money by employing the tangible and ridding of the need to raise paper money reserve separately" and "maneuvering the paper money by employing the intangible and without burdening the people too much" to replace the earlier one. "The memorial I submitted in the first year of your reign was exclusively a law of maneuvering the intangible by mobilizing the tangible. Now that compelled by social circumstances, the previous law failed, proposers then tried exclusively to find a way to cure the situation by retiring paper money, truly virtuous such intent is." While he emphasized the redemption of paper money, he also emphasized retiring paper money in order to cure the prevailing ills in an attempt to check runaway inflation.

Proceeding from theoretical analysis, he believed that if paper money "is allowed to be exchanged for copper coin in addition to being able to make various payments to the government, it would inevitably be more valued." The reason was that "the top priority lies in pacifying the mind of the people." This can be viewed from two perspectives: "the first is that people would not strive to withdraw their money when there is abundant ready coin for withdrawal"; "the second is that when there is ready cash available for withdrawal, the people would be of peace of mind and wait for their turn. However, if copper coin stock is approximating depletion and paper money still floods in for redemption, resulting in failure to make a redemption, then notice specifying suspension of redemption may as well be posted and exhorting the people to come again for withdrawal after six months, and the people would be glad to comply." This arrangement would be greatly beneficial to the state. "It may seem that an extra cost of several hundred thousand *qian* is incurred; in reality, more than a million more paper money could be placed in circulation." On the contrary, that which required redemption was only a small fraction of the total amount of paper money issued. Although Wang Maoyin's understanding was very shallow, compared with the exposition on government title purchase by his predecessor (Bao Shichen), he made a great leap in progress, touching on the cause for paper money not necessarily being redeemable

---

[65]*Memorials of Wang Maoyin*, vol. 6. No more citations shall be provided for further quotes from this book hereinbelow.

while still being able to alleviate the craving for paper money by the state. Likewise, a "decree that silver could be withdrawn with silver note is to be worked out." In the view of Wang Maoyin, the then current silver note and paper money were all universally circulated. However, when it came to traveling afar, the silver note would be most appropriate. "If the purpose is to travel afar, availability of commerce is a prerequisite, and if commerce is to be made available, ready silver available for withdrawal is a prerequisite." All taxes and duties were collected in silver: "now that silver note is allowed as a payment to the government, shouldn't silver so converted in payment go to the merchant? And since they are allowed to make payment therewith, what harm would it make if they are allowed to make redemption!" Hence, "the merchant has the convenience of using paper money, they may carry paper money directly home without having to melt and forge silver themselves, and silver stores will have the convenience as well." When the trouble of collecting taxes and rents from the prefectures and counties was cleared, there had to be some silver stores to exchange coin into silver, melting such silver and forging into silver bullion so that there was no duplication of effort in transportation to the imperial capital. That is to say, "in addition to being used as a means of payment to the government, facility of being capable of redemption is superimposed thereon, paper money would be more valued by the people. When silver can be readily withdrawn everywhere, then it can be used everywhere, hence no silver withdrawal is necessary." On the contrary, "if redemption is permitted, then it will be valued for its capability of withdrawal, even if it could not be withdrawn immediately." The then situation was that the silver note "was neither universally accepted nor universally rejected. If it is accepted in one place, then the monetary circulation is unobstructed in one place … when bearers of silver note could redeem their silver note everywhere, then the amount of silver moved out of the capital may be reduced, and the silver of the various provinces may find its way into the capital; special attention should be paid to this aspect when decision-maker makes plan for the overall situation." In terms of specific measures, in addition to permission for redemption, two more measures were introduced: one was that "the various stores may trade paper money for silver" and the other was that "the various pawn shops are required to use a proportion of paper money in their receiving and making of payments."

This is to say, Wang still wanted to make paper money and metal money convertible so as to enhance the credibility of paper money, guarantee the normal circulation thereof, effect the real purpose of paper money issuance, and ultimately safeguard the fundamental long-term interests of the Qing Dynasty.

The second monetary system reform plan was modified to shift the responsibility for redemption to the government. He proposed that the copper coin required for redemption should be set aside by the ministry of revenue and the bureau of money transfer in a monthly manner and that a redemption reserve of three hundred thousand strings should be set aside over a time span of three months. The redemption of silver note was different from that of paper money; the silver collected by the various local governments as payments of taxes and duties was to be melted and minted into silver bullions by the government mint and then transferred to the central government. If the central government allows these certificate bearers to redeem physical silver from the silver stores, then "the existing silver note, paper money, could be circulated around the country, while silver note is more fit for distant travelers. If the purpose is to facilitate travailing afar, unobstructed commerce is a prerequisite, and if commerce is to be made available, ready silver available for withdrawal is a prerequisite." "If the facility of redemption is imposed thereon in addition to being accepted as a means of payment to the government, then paper money would be more valued. When silver can be readily withdrawn everywhere, then it can be used everywhere, hence no silver withdrawal is necessary." If the government permitted redemption, then it would not be necessary to effect redemption, and circulation would be smooth, currency value stable and credit firm; otherwise, if the government did not permit redemption, then exactly the opposite effect would occur, bank run, paper money stagnation and currency value instability, all of which were of a very dialectical understanding. That was as much as saying that the old notion of dealing exclusively with issuing and retiring paper money without regard to circulation was being replaced by the new idea of "throughness" which endorsed unobstructed circulation; therefore, a new concept which may unclog paper money circulation, cure stagnation and alleviate the pressure of need for silver in the capital was fermenting. Wang Maoyin had yet to advance the concept of reserve here; however, he was already aware of the possibility that the issuance reserve could be substantially smaller than the amount of paper money issued. This was exactly the case of "when there is cash ready for withdrawal, and the people would not strive to withdraw. When have these private banks been entirely drawn down in their business operation?" "When bearers of silver note could redeem their silver note anywhere, then the amount of silver moved out of the capital may be reduced; while the silver of the various provinces may find their way into the capital. Special attention should be paid to this aspect when decision-makers make plan for the overall situation."

Motivations for the earlier and later monetary system reform plans of Wang Maoyin were different: the former was intent on preventing inflation, which at that time existed only in theory and in history, while when the latter was advanced, inflation was already a harsh reality and was showing signs of aggravating. Therefore, the focus of the first plan was to place a limit on paper money issue, and the purpose of decreeing silver stores to handle redemption was to facilitate promotion of paper money.

The focus of the second plan shifted to redemption, the purpose of which was to cure the ills and effectively curb the development of paper money depreciation. However, in the eyes of Wang Maoyin, the first plan alone was his ideal and a superior one, while the second was nothing but a move out of convenience, an inferior one at the best.

Wang Maoyin emphasized the function of merchants in designing the monetary system reform plan. He was honest and upright in conducting his office, and he had quite some thoughts on those officials who preyed on the people and lost credibility with the people. He remarked, "all ordinary people are afraid of dealing with officials, however they are not afraid of dealing with silver stores." He attempted to promote monetary system reform by enlisting the power of the merchant, so that "the intangible and the tangible are both operating, which are circulated among the merchant and the people, so that there would be no stagnation in circulation."

Therefore, he stated, "no scheme works without the office of merchants therein, no scheme will ever work without a workable method and obtainable profit offered to the merchant." Only merchants would perform the function of mediation between the government and the people, alleviating stagnation in circulation. He specifically analyzed the three key players in silver circulation of the time: "those who trade silver for copper coin are the officials and the people; those who trade coin for silver are the myriad stores; and those both trade silver for coin and trade coin for silver are the private banks which are actually the hubs in the process." The stores could redeem silver against the notes received from business transactions on the day, while government paper money could not be redeemed in the same way, which hindered the circulation of paper money.

If it was decreed that the stores had to accept a proportion of paper money when accepting payment, then the stores would be glad to accept paper money. While the government and the people traded silver for coin, they did nothing more than purchase stuff from stores; if the stores were accepting paper money, the government and the people would naturally not refuse to use paper money. Therefore, anyone requesting private banks to issue money notes against silver payment for the benefits of use and portability would allow the private banks to issue proportional paper money thereto, and when private banks could issue proportional paper money, then there would be no issue for payment with proportional paper money at the various stores. "For anyone focusing on unclogging obstructions in the three key areas and endeavoring to make silver and coin support the circulation of paper money, this is the rule for interconnected circulation of the various trades; though it seems like a coerced cause on the people, the initial purpose is not to harm the people, it looks like not a big peril."

Against the backdrop of escalating inflation, credit collapse, financial crisis and market chaos, it would be virtually impossible to tie in substantial paper money in proportional payment. Wang Maoyin's understanding of the function of merchants, commercial capital and financial institutions in regulating currency circulation was unheard of among his forerunners. He did not believe that the government could transcend the inherent law of currency circulation, behave in an unrestrained manner and engage in wanton practices. His demand won the understanding and approval of merchants; this understanding far exceeded that of the sages and predecessors, reflecting the position and function of commercial capital in the then social life which could not be overlooked. This inclination offended the authority of the supreme ruler and incurred condemnation.

However, Wang Maoyin confused the boundary between redeemable paper money and irredeemable paper money in his monetary system reform plans. He failed to understand that redeemable purchasing power could control and regulate the amount of purchasing power in circulation due to its redemption capability, therefore stabilizing currency value and in turn stabilizing purchasing power. When there was excessive issue of irredeemable paper money and no regular channel for its exit from circulation, it was impossible for it to exit the circulation; hence, it had to be absorbed entirely in circulation, which led to the situation "the more issue, the less value," "too much paper money issue and stagnation thereof would inevitably lead to the tragedy of commodity price rise." He demonstrated the relation between paper money issue and commodity price from the viewpoint of paper money flooding circulation and in excess of circulation need; this was far more superior than the views of past metal theorists of money. The conclusion would naturally apply to irredeemable paper money; however, it was a mistake to apply it to redeemable paper money. Nevertheless, he employed the mechanism to explain paper money circulation, and was hence grossly wrong.

(2) Theories of big denomination coin "employed as the tangible while in essence being the intangible" and "appearing tangible while in reality being the intangible"

In *Memorial of On Issuing Big Denomination Coin*,[66] Wang Maoyin said, "Paper money law may be employed as mobilizing the tangible to maneuver the intangible and it could be made tangible even though it is intangible; big denomination coin could be employed as the tangible while in essence remaining intangible, and appearing tangible while in reality remaining intangible." The tangible here must refer to metal money of silver and copper coin, whereas the intangible refers to the paper money or overvalued coin, that is, overvalued big denomination coin. Paper money law herein should have referred to the law governing redeemable paper money, as it was the token of metal money (silver); therefore, it could "be employed as the tangible to maneuver the intangible, and the intangible could be made tangible." Be it of copper, iron or any other

---

[66]*Memorials of Wang Maoyin*, vol. 6.

material, all big denomination coins were depreciated coin; it was overvalued coin where there was a great gap between its actual value and nominal value. Big denomination coins of the Qing Dynasty were overvalued ones; it "is employed as the tangible while in essence remaining intangible, and appearing tangible while in reality intangible." When the nominal value far exceeded that of its actual value, its purchasing power in practice would inevitably fall back to its actual value; that is, "while the government may fix the price of the coin, it may not fix the value of commodity," "when private minting is rampant, commodity price shoots up, sometimes a *dou* of corn is sold at the price of seven thousand *qian*, this is another conspicuous sign of it." Therefore, it seemed that the seemingly "tangible" overvalued big denomination coin was not as feasible as the irredeemable paper money which was "intangible"; "paper money may stay in circulation for scores of years, while big denomination coin could only last for a couple of years." What a miserable fate for the big denomination coins! This situation deserved vigilance. His demonstration touched on some of the substantive issues of paper money and big denomination coins, revolved around the relational change between the nominal value and actual value of paper money and big denomination coins, and injected new content into the ideas of the tangible and the intangible. Wang broke through the confines of the traditional theory of the tangible and the intangible which set metal money such as silver and copper as the tangible, paper money and big denomination coins as the intangible, assigned new connotation thereto, and made a brilliant exposition thereof: "how come paper money stayed and big denomination coin was gone? Why wasn't it known that paper money law employs the tangible to maneuver the intangible, the intangible could be made tangible; big denomination coin could be employed as the tangible while in essence remaining intangible, and appearing tangible while in reality remaining intangible."

Wang Maoyin's analysis of big denomination coin and his distinction between big denomination coin and paper money were correct. However, his conclusion drawn therefrom merited study as paper money could be employed "as the tangible to maneuver the intangible and it could be made tangible though it is intangible." Because it was redeemable, so long as there was adequate issuance reserve, the purchasing power of paper money could be maintained stably and it could stay in circulation for long periods of time; while the nominal value of big denomination coin made of metal was far deviated from its actual value, its nominal value would sooner or later revert to its actual value, that is, via depreciation, discount, etc., and financial instability and social turmoil would ensue.

This insight of Wang far excelled that of his contemporaries including Bao Shichen and Xu Mei; its insightfulness and accuracy attained the peak of the traditional monetary thought in China. Hence, he was diametrically opposed to minting big denomination coin. Actually, big denomination coins and paper money were of the same nature; that is, they both were "tokens of value — be it paper or gold and silver with debased purity — the proportion representing the weight of gold and silver per the price fixed by the minting bureau was not determined by the substance underlying these tokens, but by the quantity thereof in circulation."[67] When the amount of paper money issued did not exceed the objective demand of commodity circulation, the nominal value it stood for would definitely not be affected; that is, the currency value and purchasing power thereof would remain stable. This law applied to both purchasing power and big denomination coin. On the contrary, if the objective demand of commodity circulation was exceeded by paper money, the nominal value it stood for would be reduced; that is, the currency value and purchasing power thereof would be undermined. This was also true of both big denomination coins and purchasing power. If this aspect was disregarded, it was one-sided to believe that "the profit of issuing paper money would be tenfold that of minting big denomination coin, whereas the ill thereof would be no more than failure due to forgery." Hence, he was flatly opposed to minting big denomination coin and advocated issuing paper money in his memorial petition. The redeemable paper money issue he advocated required an issue limit, and an adequate issuance reserve would need to be set aside to ensure ready redemption. If such conditions were not available, then the currency value thereof would not be held stable and the circulation thereof would not last for long. He was reproved by the Xianfeng Emperor due to his failure to adapt to the

---

[67] *Karl Marx and Frederick Engels*, vol. 13, p. 110.

prevailing political atmosphere of the time and adhering firmly to his principles.

He refuted the viewpoints of the nominal theory of money defending minting big denomination coin. In deliberating on the implementation of the paper money law in 1852, Sha Huana remarked after the manner of Wang Liu, "All benefits have their points of depletion, gold could be used as a gold, while the benefit of paper money is boundless, a hundred thousand produced is a hundred thousand obtained, a million produced is a million obtained"; "the economic right goes to the emperor, and to be meted out to the people, the propriety of the central government would be honored."[68] Hence, in *Memorial on Issuing Big Denomination Coin*, Wang pointed out, "proponents further noted that 'if the state designates it a hundred then it is a hundred, designates it a thousand then it is a thousand', who dares to defy such stipulation? It is indeed the case. However, the government may fix the price of coin, it has no way to fix the value of stuff. If the coin is designated as a thousand, the people dare not to take it as a hundred; however, if an article is worth a hundred, it would not be difficult for the people to sell it at a thousand." He distinguished the two concepts confused by the nominal theorists of money — the nominal value and actual value of money — and specifically noted that the state had the power to fix the nominal value of minted coin; that is, "the government may fix the price of coins," "if a coin is designated by the government as a thousand, the people dare not to take it as a hundred." However, the government has no power to fix its actual value and actual purchasing power; that is, "it has no way to fix the value of stuff," "if an article is worth a hundred, it would not be difficult for the people to sell it at a thousand." Hence, he debunked the theory enshrined by the nominal theorists of money which held that state power created monetary value, forcefully refuted the depreciation policy of money or inflation policy instituted by the state, and exposed its nature, that is to say, state power may not have everything its way and conduct affairs unchecked before the law of monetary circulation. What it was capable of was nothing but the rampant minting of a huge amount of overvalued big denomination coins, and it could also arbitrarily raise the nominal value of big denomination coins;

---

[68]*Collected Biographies of Qing Dynasty*, vol. 41.

however, it could not keep the value of big denomination coins from depreciating with coercive state power. It could neither peg down the monetary purchasing power and commodity price on the market, nor could it avoid or eliminate the various grave social consequences resulting from violating this law. This was a brilliant and concise argument.

However, on the precondition of controlling the amount of paper money issue, the state power could ensure the stability of the currency value and purchasing power of paper money; this was something Wang Maoyin failed to recognize.

Based on the foregoing analysis, in order to safeguard the circulation of full-value copper coin, Wang Maoyin was flatly opposed to minting overvalued big denomination coins. He repeatedly emphasized that "having examined the monetary laws of the past dynasties, there were an excessive variety, and the shops and stores would inevitably be hampered and burdened; when big denomination coins are denominated too much above its value, they will soon be scrapped ... when there is too much discount (ratio between big denomination coin and small denomination coin), and too much disparity in their weight." "Therefore, paper money may stay in circulation for scores of years, while big denomination coin could only last for a couple of years, this is a conspicuous sign." "Scrapping of big denomination coin is mostly attributable to rampant private minting and commodity price rocketing incurred thereby."[69] Small denomination coin led the way and big denomination coin followed; when big denomination coin led the way, private minting followed; this was the rule which had always been in place in the monetary history of China. In the end, the law of value would force the nominal value of big denomination coin to revert to the level of actual value; hence, it would not only be unable to solve the issue of money depletion but would also introduce the trouble of monetary system chaos. This discovery of Wang Maoyin's was indeed extraordinary. Based on such insight, he conducted comprehensive theorization of the big denomination coins worth 10, 50, 100, 500 and 1,000 *qian* issued after the 10th year of the Xianfeng period; he concluded that there were three difficulties and two ills inherent in overvalued big denomination coin. The first

---

[69]*Memorials of Wang Maoyin — On Issuing Big Denomination Coin,* vol. 6.

difficulty was that coins were of like sizes, and distinction thereof was based on characters inscribed thereon, which easily led to chaos in thought and transaction. The second was that the original purpose of copper coin was to facilitate small-sum payment; since standard copper coins were in short supply, and big denomination coins were of very big face value, "it is difficult to break big money when it is used for purchase on the market; there is no change to break big money when it is to be exchanged into standard copper coins."

Circulation and use were made extremely inconvenient. The third was that the provision stipulated that big denomination coin was allowed to comprise 50% of payments to the government; however, the 50% payment allowable to be made to the government included government note, paper money, and big denomination coin. "How could these all concurrently comprise such payments?" However, compared with the two ills, these three difficulties would matter little. "No trouble is bigger than private minting." If wily people minted two big denomination coins with four taels of copper, it would be equivalent to one tael of silver in making payment to the government, and the state would suffer incalculable loss. Every one thousand old standard copper coins weighed 120 taels, 60 taels of copper could be obtained therefrom when such old standard copper coins were melted; when these copper so obtained were minted into big denomination coin of a thousand *qian*, such big denomination coins could be worth thirty thousand *qian*. "If such wily people melt standard copper coins to mint big denomination coins on a daily basis, the people would no longer be able to have standard copper coins for use, and it would further harm the people beyond description. It would be impossible to stop these two ills alone,"[70] let alone the others. This understanding was very anticipatory; however, the Qing government ignored the proposal and implemented its own plan single-mindedly. The big denomination coins designated as worth 1,000 *qian* or 500 *qian* "got stagnated soon after they were issued" "due to too much discount and rampant private minting." The scheme lasted for only 5 months, and big denomination coin minting was terminated by July of the fourth year of the Xianfeng period. While big denomination coin designated as worth under a hundred could barely

---

[70]*Memorials of Wang Maoyin — On Additional Issuing Big Denomination Coin*, vol. 6.

be circulated in and around the imperial capital, it would cease to be accepted in areas beyond the circumference of a hundred li, and its value dwindled by the day. The development was exactly as predicted by Wang Maoyin: "when a myriad of big denomination coins appear on a daily basis, the people would be inevitably deeply concerned, the market would be inevitably disturbed, and there is nothing they could trust. Money is a daily necessity for all, it is an item of critical importance on which the enrichment of the country and the people is hinged. If the situation really develops as I have feared, then it will bring about great regret."[71]

Besides, Wang Maoyin paid special attention to foreign businessmen manipulating the conversion rate between silver and coin and the speculative activities conducted thereby, exposing them in a timely manner and putting forward strategies to deal with them. In 1857, he submitted a memorial titled *Urgent Memorial Petitioning to Increase Minting Standard Copper Coin and Temporarily Relieving Hardship of the People in Peripheral Provinces*, in which he noted bluntly, "silver price used to stand at about two thousand odd standard copper coins per tael in Jiangsu and Zhejiang area, however the price of standard copper coin shot up since British businessmen started to hoard standard copper coins; and the rate between silver and standard copper coins gradually being halved, the current rate is that a tael of silver could only bring in eleven hundred standard copper coins; this situation hampered both the military and the people, while foreigners hold it as a source of profit."[72]

In the following year, in the *Memorial on Petitioning to Discretionarily Reform Monetary Law*, Wang Maoyin further noted that the southern provinces were ailed by depletion of money, while the capital was ailed by a surplus of money. "For instance, corn is sold at six thousand *wen* a *dan*, which required payment of five tael of silver, how could the soldier and the people not be hampered thereby; while these foreigners could unhurriedly trade coin for silver, bought low and sold high, in this issue alone, they had monopolized all economic rights therein." British businessmen conducted unrestrained purchase of standard copper coins, availing the opportunity of money shortage in Shanghai, which resulted in

---

[71]*Ibid.*, *Memorial On Issuing Big Denomination Coin*.
[72]Donghua Records of Xianfeng Period.

copper price surge and silver price drop; they then took the opportunity to buy in silver at a lower price, and sold silver at a higher price when silver price rose, thereby obtaining a huge profit from these dealings. Then, what strategy was the Qing Dynasty to adopt? He believed that the government should have already placed strict restrictions on prohibiting copper and silver export; if the circulation of big denomination coins was to be promoted, even though the reality was that it was already clogged in the imperial capital and was difficult to promote, then it would be more difficult to promote it in the peripheral provinces. In fighting foreign businessmen, he proposed to mint standard copper coins in great quantity on the basis of calculatedly reforming monetary law in order to temporarily relieve the financial straits of the people and check the purchase by foreign businessmen. The monetary law reform he proposed was nothing less than reducing the weight of standard copper coins and debasing purity thereof so that minting profit may be increased and the need for circulation was satisfied, while the people would have money for circulation. This move might not look brilliant, but his keen insight, activeness in providing a fighting strategy and safeguarding national spirit in fighting colonists on the financial front deserve commendation.

All in all, like the other predecessors following the metal theory of money, Wang Maoyin was not influenced by Western monetary theory; the concepts he employed and the viewpoints he held all displayed traditional Chinese characteristics, and the monetary system reform plan he proposed was also of Chinese style. His thought took form spontaneously from among China's traditional monetary thought system, and his understanding of the law of currency circulation was deeper than that of Wei Yuan and Xu Mei. He employed the viewpoint of "mobilizing the tangible to maneuver the intangible" to demonstrate the relation between paper money and metal money; though it was not perfect and scientific enough, he had nevertheless raised the issue and commenced research thereon. He was the most brilliant, most important monetary theorist in China's traditional monetary thought system. He was extremely familiar with commercial credit and business activities of silver stores and private banks; he even had some sort of profound connection with merchants and commercial capital of that time. He set special store by the functions of the merchant, silver stores, money shops and even pawn shops in socio-economic life; meanwhile, he paid attention to the issue of integrity in connection with commodity economy, which far surpassed common sense awareness, especially as a high-ranking government official. He gave consideration to the interests of the merchant, opposed excessive paper money issue and flatly opposed the idea of minting big denomination coin, which were conducive to the development of monetary economy and the growth of capitalist factors in China.

5.3. On credit

(1) "Credit is a national treasure"

In memorials on paper money law, Wang Maoyin repeatedly emphasized credit, that is, honesty without fraud, vouchers, notes and credit. He believed that "the value of paper money law lies in incremental expansion and maintenance with integrity."[73]

"The present big denomination coin, paper money are all expedient measures, the key thereof lies in maintaining such with integrity and holding it steady without abrupt change."[74] Paper money issue was forced upon the people because it was "mobilizing the intangible to maneuver the tangible, it could be made tangible though it remains intangible"; hence, it could win the faith of the commerce, and "get circulated among the merchant and the people almost without obstruction."[75] "Therefore at the beginning of paper money issue, though it was forced upon the people, there was no intent to harm the people, the interests of the people would not be harmed in the use of paper money." Under the circumstances of metal money circulation, "if there is no fixed amount in paper money issue, then paper money would be issued without limit; it seems to be a great profit, however, who knows that the more it is issued the lower the price it will be."[76] The rulers may not, according to the need of the state finances, engage in unlimited paper money issue as they like. Wang Maoyin had already realized that the ancestors of the Chinese had gained

---

[73] *Memorials of Wang Maoyin — Revisiting Paper Money*, vol. 6.
[74] *Ibid.*
[75] *Ibid.*
[76] *Memorials of Wang Maoyin — Revisiting Paper Money*, vol. 1.

some understanding in this field. "Xiaozong Emperor of Song Dynasty said, 'Huizi appreciates when it is insufficiently supplied, and depreciates when it is oversupplied.' This was the key to the success of paper money circulation." In *Memorial of Itemized Deliberation of Paper Money Law*, Wang proposed that paper money would be modeled after the practice implemented at the beginning of the dynasty. A hundred thousand tael of paper money circulation would be issued per year, that is, five thousand pieces of 10 tael silver notes and one thousand pieces of fifty tael notes per year. The program would be a trial run for one or two years. If circulation would turn out well, then the issue amount thereof would be redoubled every year, and if such redoubled issue would turn out well in circulation, then the issue would be further redoubled, and the maximum paper money issue would be limited to 10 million taels. Because "the annual national fiscal revenue and expenditure are but a few scores of millions of taels, if the principle of employing multiple tangibles to support one intangible is implemented, and issue of paper money is conducted with restraint and limit, paper money shall be employed to supplement silver instead of eliminating silver to use paper money alone, then there would be little defect of stagnation." In 1651, when Fulin took over the reins of the government upon coming of age, he took after the established arrangement of the Ming Dynasty, producing and issuing paper money to be circulated concurrently with coin due to uncertainty of fiscal revenue, extensive expenditure and an unfilled state treasury. 128.172 *guans* were issued in the year and the paper money remained in circulation for 10 years till 1661. The issue amount was not large, prudence was practiced throughout the process and no major adjustment in policy was made; therefore, no obvious ill was found in the process. Wang believed that "miraculous employment of such measures in relieving the financial straits of the time as an expedient measure could be modeled after by hundreds of generations." Wang proposed 10 articles of paper money law to avoid: The first was an enumeration of more than 10 counts of the "ills of paper money," banning the use of silver and setting up multiple rules which hampered the people before bringing any convenience to them. The second was repeated changes of law in order to make profit which raised suspicion of the people before gaining their trust. The third was that the pertinent bureau was glad to issue paper money but loathe to call it back which exactly showed that they did not value paper money. The fourth was that the arrangement of replacing old paper money with a new one introduced additional cost to the people. The fifth was that the paper material used was too light to be durable. The sixth was that it was too confusing to distinguish the genuine from the fake. The seventh was excessive paper money issue leading to stagnation and commodity price rocketing. The eighth was that unreasonable elaboration in paper money production led to rampant fraud and fake money. The ninth was that paper money handled by government officials was intimidating to the people and led to doubts and hostility by the people. The 10th was sloppy production and cutting corners in material and production of paper money.[77] Silver was the foundation of the monetary system in the Qing Dynasty, with large-sum payments being conducted in silver. However, a slew of stipulations were introduced which banned the use of silver and promoted the use of paper money; before bringing any benefit to the people, it had already hampered them.

In order to obtain exclusive profit from paper money issue, the government changed the law repeatedly; the people had already cast doubt thereon before faith was established in paper money. The pertinent officers were fond of issuing paper money but loath to recall it, which undermined the credit foundation of paper money. The people loathed the sizable cost attached to replacing broken and worn paper money, which made broken and worn paper money continue in circulation. The paper quality for paper money production was too inferior and easily damaged, which made it turn into broken and worn paper money very quickly. Sloppy anti-forgery measures made it difficult to tell the genuine from the counterfeit and made the people distrustful of it, which increased difficulty in paper money circulation. Excessive issue led to commodity price increase, and circulation of paper money became more difficult. Unreasonable elaboration made the paper money production process too trifling and led to rampant frauds and forgeries. Officers at the various levels of government were installed in charge of issuing and receiving paper money, which intimidated people and kept them from using it. Sloppy production, cutting corners and lack of uniformity made it still

---

[77]*Ibid.*

more difficult for people to place faith in using paper money. In conclusion, laws and decrees must be strictly enforced, and such should not be changed too frequently, nor should they be implemented without thoroughness and consistency. Exquisiteness in producing paper money must be maintained, and a limit be placed thereon: "the top priority in issuing paper money lies in management of issuing, retiring and circulation thereof, if retiring of paper money could be expanded, then issuing thereof would not be stagnant."[78] Under government monopoly, the government cared exclusively about issuing to the disregard of circulation, and no retiring was taken into consideration. The key issue was lack of integrity, that is, lack of integrity on the side of the government, and lack of integrity on the side of officials. It seemed that the Xianfeng Emperor was also aware of this situation. In the imperial edict delivered on February 16, 1853, he remarked, "it was originally employed to make up for the lack of state revenue, the arrangement was neither to scrap silver and replace it with paper money nor to pressure the merchant for turning in silver. The repositories may not lean too much on either issuing or retiring paper money in the handling thereof, then paper money may be promoted far and wide, so that the entire country gets to know it as a national treasure, and it may be held as valuable as silver and coin. The treasury and repositories should equally treat the issuing and retiring of paper money, which would demonstrate faith and dispel doubt, and the people would gradually take to it, then paper money could be properly circulated, such would further facilitate distant travel."[79]

It could be seen that the Xianfeng Emperor understood the two-in-one and one-in-two interdependent relation between paper money issue and integrity. Therefore, he claimed that paper money was a national treasure, and demanded that the treasury and repositories treat issuing and recalling paper money equally, and circulate silver, coin and paper money concurrently to "display faith and dispel doubt." When the people were in doubt and the merchant had scruples, improper conduct from the government and functioning officers would lead to silver and coin vanishing and paper

---

[78]*Memorials of Wang Maoyin — Petition for Further Deliberation of Prior Memorial on Paper Money Law*, vol. 3.
[79]*Records of Xianfeng Emperor*, vol. 19.

money stagnating. The people would awaken to the reality and paper money would pick up pace of depreciation and the people would further lose faith therein. Hence, the purposes of plugging the financial gap and filling up the tremendous military requirement would fail. The problem was these were inherently insincere remarks. How could these be implemented consistently by the pertinent officers at different levels? However, Wang Maoyin was faithful in his conduct to his statement and had been unswerving in his faith until he was transferred from his position when reproved by the Xianfeng Emperor. In *Memorial on Issuing Big Denomination Coin*, he specifically emphasized that "credit is a national treasure, the present big denomination coin, paper money are all expedient measures, the key thereof lies in maintaining such with integrity and holding it steady without abrupt change."

In the eyes of Wang, big denomination coin and paper money were connected in nature. In general, "copper coin is a daily necessity for everybody, it is of critical importance whereon the wealth and convenience of the people are hinged."[80] Since the monetary law concerned a multitude of families, and was indispensable in the life and production of the people, "the law is best left unchanged without proper cause."[81] If a radical change was introduced within a few months of its issue, the situation would necessarily lead to "myriads of big denomination coins being brought to market every day, the people would inevitably be deeply concerned, the market would be surely disturbed, and there is nothing they would trust."[82] The situation disturbed the people and the market, jeopardizing the stability of the financial market and social tranquility. "Though paper money seems like a forced cause on the people, the original purpose is not to harm the people, it looks like not a big peril."[83]

"The program is implemented from the top, the original purpose is not to force the hands of the people."[84] In the process of issuing such a token

---

[80] *Memorials of Wang Maoyin — Memorial on Issuing Big Denomination Paper Money*, vol. 6.
[81] *Memorials of Wang Maoyin — On Additional Issuing Big Denomination Coin*, vol. 6.
[82] *Memorials of Wang Maoyin — Memorial on Issuing Big Denomination Paper Money*, vol. 6.
[83] *Memorials of Wang Maoyin — On Revising Paper Money Law*, vol. 6.
[84] *Memorials of Wang Maoyin — Memorial of Itemized Proposal on Monetary Rules*, vol. 1.

of value, the government was establishing and safeguarding state credit; only through upholding state credit could the state guarantee benefiting the people and bringing profit to the people, and at least "not harming the people." How could the state guarantee the normal circulation of the token of value? In addition to deciding on a proper monetary policy, the state was required to resolutely implement the established policy and guidelines, institute a complete set of measures and plans and have a reliable mainstay to organize and implement policies and plans; otherwise, all was but pointless talk.

(2) Establishing Private Banks as a Hub

While proposing to establish state credit, Wang Maoyin also proposed to establish commercial credit, and tried to guarantee the credit of paper money via commercial credit institutions — silver stores and money shops. He noted that "it is forever the case that ill follows enactment of laws, such ill originates not with the law but the people. Examination found that the ones that bring about ills are more government officers than merchants and people."[85] Because "the ills of the merchant and the people could be cured by government officials; while the merchant and the people have no way to defy the ills of government officials ... if a government official is determined to profiteer therefrom, and hence engages in soliciting bribe, extortion and giving short measures, what could hinder him therefrom?"[86]

Lack of supervision or incompetent supervision would "render paper money a name only, and make it unfavorable to circulate among the government and the people."[87] Therefore, "if the prefectures and counties have competent officials installed, then the merchant and the people would abide by the law; if the governors are competent, then officials would be law-abiding people."[88] He believed that if paper money could not work out, it seemed that not only the paper money was unworkable but the law

---

[85]*Memorials of Wang Maoyin — Memorial of Itemized Proposal on Monetary Rules*, vol. 1.
[86]*Ibid.*
[87]*Ibid.*
[88]*Ibid.*

was at fault too. Just as remarked by Qiu Jun of the Ming Dynasty, "paper money failing to work is due to the fact that the user has no right." The right is not the exercise of authority, but the exercise of balance, "therefore the most important issue in issuing paper money lies in well-measured method," that is, the most valuable thing therein was to regulate paper money supply and maintain the stability of currency value according to prevailing market prices. Hence, "when the law of balance is properly administered by the financial minister according to the gravity of circumstances of the times, it may last for a long time." Actually, not only should the financial minister be conscientiously in charge, weighing the opportunity, thoroughly acquainting himself with and having under his complete control the entire situation of issuance reserve, market prices and purchasing power of money but also the trust and support of the emperor, the supreme decision maker, must be obtained, otherwise all would be but pointless talk. The greed and coercion of government officials coupled with the absolute helplessness of the people made it impossible for the people to escape the extortion and exploitation of paper money.

Wang criticized the shameful conduct from the standpoint of the merchant and the people, and arrived at the conclusion that only silver stores and money shops could unclog the layer after layer of "key juncture points and make silver and coin support the circulation of paper money, this is the rule for interconnected circulation of the various trades."[89] Wang had a sober and definite understanding of the exchange nature and function of money shops; he pointed out, "The circulation of silver and coin is like a circle without end. The so-called hubs must refer to the exchange agency for silver and coin, centers for that. Further, "now that the various stores and shops receive commercial notes every day, the people would go to the money market to buy silver, while money shops sell them silver."[90] Since money shops became the hub of exchange for silver and coin, naturally they could receive and redeem commercial notes; hence, the question arose of why paper money could not be included in the receiving and redeeming cycle! According to Wang's design, paper money must be redeemable; hence, he proposed, "I hereby request your

---

[89] *Memorials of Wang Maoyin — Revisiting Paper Money*, vol. 6.
[90] *Ibid.*

Majesty to decree that money shops must make a proportional payment in paper money whenever any person buys silver note, then the various shops and stores may trade paper money for silver, hence they would not be afraid of using paper money any more."[91] This kind of paper money supply via money shops, silver stores and pawn shops was the channel for commodity circulation; it was more easily accepted by the merchant and the people, and did "not constitute a huge burden on the people." However, the precondition thereof was that paper money issue should be limited, plus redeemable, which would necessarily tie down the hands of the state finances, and the government would not be able to issue paper money as it saw fit to plug financial deficit. Hence, it was difficult for the central government to accept such a design, and the Xianfeng Emperor furiously rejected it.

As silver and coin stores conducted businesses in exchanging silver and coin as well as handling business of receiving and redeeming commercial notes, "these functions could be conducted by the merchant but could not be performed by the state."[92] There was "more supply than recall of paper money in the imperial capital, there was supply without recall in the military, and there was recall without supply in the provinces, prefectures and counties; it would be impossible for it to work without the office of merchants, and it would not work without feasible methods and benefits obtainable therefrom offered to the merchant."[93] The so-called "feasible methods and benefits obtainable therefrom" referred to the situation that money shops, silver stores and pawn shops must be guaranteed a certain realizable benefit before they could operate therein. Feasible methods referred to "making paper money capable of withdrawing coin," "making silver note capable of withdrawing silver," "making the paper money held by the various shops and stores capable of exchanging for silver," and "paper money shall make a portion of all payments in pawn shops."[94] In short, the government must guarantee the

---

[91] *Ibid.*
[92] *Memorials of Wang Maoyin — Itemized Memorial on Ministerial Deliberation of Difficulties in Implementing Silver Note and Silver Store*, vol. 3.
[93] *Memorials of Wang Maoyin — On Revising Paper Money Law*, vol. 6.
[94] *Ibid.*

redemption of paper money in a definitive manner; otherwise, it would be difficult to maintain the circulation of paper money. Of course, the silver stores were not prohibited from affixing their own seals and emblems on the back of paper money after they had withdrawn such, and they were allowed to use such paper money anywhere they saw fit: "and such paper money is also allowed to make payment for government title purchase, and shall be in the ratio of fifty to fifty with silver in making payment."[95] The benefits of operation were exactly "allowing them a marginal profit at the time when silver stores were withdrawing paper money."[96] In Wang's conception, the government may establish the present silver stores and money shops as agencies for paper money supply and recall, and a certain fee must be offered thereto. That is, the difference between the treasury standard and municipal standard shall be established as their fees in handling paper money, roughly 1–2 grams per tael.

That is to say, both the fee for handling paper money issue and the fee for assuming risk were included to ensure that silver stores may act on behalf of the central government in issuing paper money. In Wang's opinion, it was as much as saying that he believed the merchant rather than the government, and he proposed to share profit with the merchant. This very assumption enraged the Xianfeng Emperor, as demonstrated in the reprimand decree, "the institution of paper money is to enrich the state and bring convenience to the people." Bringing convenience to the people may not be established as the dominant cause; enriching the state was the real and the most important goal.

The emperor reproved Wang for not able to "work harmoniously with the central government through the vicissitudes, who engaged in conducts exclusively benefiting the merchant to the disregard of the general situation in memorials submitted thereby, which was a gross negligent of propriety; and he further petitioned to place himself under stringent examination, which was extraordinarily defiant." Wang was single-mindedly making plans in the interests of the central government. Out of consideration for long-term interests, he was trying to help the financially straitened and tottering corrupt and incompetent government

---

[95] *Memorials of Wang Maoyin — Itemized Deliberation of Paper Money Law*, vol. 1.
[96] *Ibid.*

to tide over and also maintain the stability of currency value, while attempting to ensure financial security and safeguard the normalcy of socio-economic order. His thoughtfulness and benign motivation reflected exactly the response of the commercial capital and traditional financial industry which had attained some sort of development. However, before the supreme ruler of a highly centralized regime, Wang repeatedly aired his complaints and sometimes defended himself in an enfeebled manner, and acknowledged that he "demanded with some threat that his requests in memorial submitted be satisfied,"[97] which offended the supreme ruler who reproved him for his stubbornness, pique and failure to observe the propriety of being a subject, failing to be grateful for being promoted to an influential government position and render services in helping the state relieve urgent requirements of the military.

5.4. On loan shops

As the imperial capital, Beijing, was the seat of politics and economy of the empire, that is, "the fundamental place in the Qing Dynasty, the people's livelihood may not be settled unless circulation conducted by the merchant and the myriad articles flock thereto."[98] Among the various shops and stores, in addition to money shops, silver stores and pawn shops, there was also a type of financial institution called silver and coin loan shop.

In *Memorial of Petition for Planning Commerce to Pacify the People* written on March 25, the third year of the Xianfeng Emperor's reign, Wang Maoyin noted, "Loan shops used to make loans, mostly in one-year terms. Around May and June, commodities from the various provinces arrived at the capital, and great amounts of loans were taken out. When loan term expired, the capital and interest shall be collectively brought to

---

[97] *Compilation of Modern Chinese Monetary History — Reign of the Qing Dynasty (1840–1910)*, vol. 1, Book 1. Zhonghua Book Company, 1964, p. 393.
[98] *Memorials of Wang Maoyin — On Issuing Memorial of Petition for Planning Commerce to Pacify the People*, vol. 3. No more citations shall be provided for further quotes from this book hereinbelow.

the loan shop for review, this practice was called the meeting of the capital and the interest. Having inspected such, the loan shop would take in the interest and substitute the old loan certificate with a new one, then ask the borrower to take the principal home; it was an annual practice."

Therefore, it could be seen that loan shops specialized in loan making and the maximum loan term was one year. At the expiration of the term, both the principal and the interest were to be brought to the loan shop for inspection; when the principal and interest were examined and no fault was found, both would be repaid, and the loan hence closed. If extension was required, then interest would be retained and a loan certificate renewed. Though the loan-making procedure was like that, the relation between the shops, stores and loan shops was quite close. The shops and stores operated on the basis of loans; after years of business operation on loans, they would not be able to operate without loan shops. Therefore, Wang remarked, "shops and stores of various trades with capital fully contributed by owners were less than ten or twenty percent of the total; the rest relied heavily on loan for circulation." Hence, it could be deduced that shops and stores mostly relied on loan shops for working capital and relied on loans for continual operation; otherwise, they could not carry on their businesses. Around May and June, commodities from the various provinces arrived at the capital, and great amounts of loans were taken out, and it was the busiest time for the loan shops. The expansion or contraction by loan shops would absolutely control the bloom or doom of the market in the imperial capital.

As Wang mentioned, there were only two types of participants in loan shops, the shareholder and the employee. Shareholders were the investors; when market went into depression with dwindling transactions and increasingly tight credit, "the shareholders of ... were determined to call back their principals, no loan renewal would be allowed when borrowers made repayments, which led to market stagnation." Shareholders must have been the investors, but it remains unclear whether they got involved directly in business operation and management or they entrusted others with such activities. While the number of employees was determined according to the scale of a loan shop, "the employees of the various loan shops totaled in excess of ten thousand people ... small ones have several employees, and bigger ones several dozen."

When the political situation was more intensified, and the market stagnated, loan shops wanted to call back their principals and interest and became more prudent in making loans; loan shops should not be blamed for the issues.

Faced with the grave market situation of the time, Wang remarked, "I plan to petition the emperor for an edict to notify the various silver and coin loan shops that they should conduct business as usual." He further put forward five specific measures: The first was that "when a loan expires, it is better not to have the principal entirely taken back." The second was that "interest on renewed loan is better not to be increased." The third was, "where anyone fails to repay interest, rigorous investigation and severe punishment shall be permitted." The fourth was that "no immediate collection of principal from the existing shops and stores is permitted." The fifth was that "discretionary increase in punishment of the current provisions regarding debt shall be considered, where anyone who fails to repay the principal from the loan shop shall be investigated for liability and severe punishment be administered thereon in accordance with the law; repayment of debt must be pressed thereupon." The interests of shareholders were safeguarded with such measures, and the shops and stores of various industries were offered the convenience and use of funds, which helped them tide over working capital shortage and gained them a reprieve via government intervention: "and shareholders of the loan shops may be emboldened in slowing down capital callback." The government intervened and notified the various loan shops that they may not mandatorily recall their loans or raise interest rates; the government also warned the shops and stores that they may not expand business on loans or postpone repayment of interest. The government also amended laws to step up punishment for those who failed to repay the principal and interest of their loans.

The essay also mentioned pawn shops, which were a channel for those financially straitened to tide over their difficulties.

We could infer from the essays of Wang Maoyin that the traditional Chinese financial institutions had already assumed the functions of economic bellwether and hub for social capital; at least the rise and fall of money shops, silver stores, pawn shops and even loan shops had a great bearing on the socio-economic order as the commodity transaction centers of cities and towns, never failing to draw the attention of the authorities and the people. They ceased being an irrelevant part of society. However, due to their small scale and limited capital, they stayed in the field of circulation and failed to enter the field of production, and hence regulate the entire economic life of the society therefrom and became the general accounting entity for the whole of society, the all-purpose elaborate institution and exquisite body in economic life.